Secured Transactions

Secured Transactions

By Linda J. Rusch
Professor of Law
Gonzaga University School of Law

SECOND EDITION

WEST.
A Thomson Reuters business

© West, a Thomson business, 2006
© 2012 Thomson Reuters
  610 Opperman Drive
  St. Paul, MN 55123
  1–800–313–9378

ISBN: 978–0–314–27575–2

Preface

This "Black Letter" is designed to help a law student recognize and understand the basic principles and issues of law covered in a law school course. It can be used both as a study aid when preparing for classes and as a review of the subject matter when studying for an examination.

This "Black Letter" is divided into two major sections. The **Capsule Summary** is an abbreviated review of the subject matter which can be used both before and after studying the main body of the text. The main **Text** explains the rules and exceptions, and provides many **Examples** for study. Studying the main text does not substitute for reading the statutory text and comments. The **Table of Contents** is in outline form to help you organize the details of the subject. At the end of each Chapter are **Review Questions**, with answers given in Appendix A. Appendix B contains a comprehensive **Practice Examination** question and answer. Appendix C contains a **Table of Statutes** cited to facilitate quick isolation of the parts of the main text and capsule summary that cite or discuss statutory sections. In addition, in **Perspective**, the author discusses how to approach the topic and use these materials in learning and understanding the legal rules and their application to typical factual scenarios.

The materials in this "Black Letter" will facilitate your study of the law of Secured Transactions and assist you in learning how to analyze situations in which this law is applied. We wish you success.

THE PUBLISHER

Summary of Contents

■ I. INTRODUCTION TO SECURED TRANSACTIONS

■ II. THE SCOPE OF UCC ARTICLE 9

■ III. ATTACHMENT OF A SECURITY INTEREST OR AGRICULTURAL LIEN

■ V. PRIORITY OF SECURITY INTERESTS AND AGRICULTURAL LIENS

■ VI.   ENFORCEMENT OF A SECURITY INTEREST OR AGRICULTURAL LIEN

■ VII. LIABILITY FOR VIOLATION OF ARTICLE 9

■ APPENDICES

Table of Contents

■ I. INTRODUCTION TO SECURED TRANSACTIONS

■ II. THE SCOPE OF UCC ARTICLE 9

■ III.   ATTACHMENT OF A SECURITY INTEREST OR AGRICULTURAL LIEN

■ V. PRIORITY OF SECURITY INTERESTS AND AGRICULTURAL LIENS

■ VI. ENFORCEMENT OF A SECURITY INTEREST OR AGRICULTURAL LIEN

■ VII. LIABILITY FOR VIOLATION OF ARTICLE 9

■ APPENDICES

Capsule Summary

■ I. INTRODUCTION TO SECURED TRANSACTIONS

A. DEBT DEFINED

Debt is an obligation a person owes another. A debt may be contingent or fixed, liquidated or unliquidated, mature or unmatured, disputed or undisputed, and secured or unsecured.

B. HOW DEBT IS CREATED

Debts may be created by contract, through principles of law such as tort, and by statutes.

C. REGULATION OF DEBT CREATION

When debt is created by contract, there are various types of regulation of the debt creation. Some examples are usury laws which determine the allowable rate of interest on an obligation, consumer protection laws which may prohibit or regulate certain terms of the contract, consumer protection laws which require disclosure of information in connection with the transaction, and laws prohibiting certain types of discrimination in making lending decisions.

D. COLLECTING DEBT THROUGH INFORMAL METHODS

A creditor owed a debt has several options for collecting that debt without resorting to judicial process. The creditor may request payment, withhold goods or services that the debtor needs, or exercise a right of setoff if there are mature and mutual debts between the creditor and debtor. If the creditor does not have a lien in specific assets of the debtor, the creditor has no right (other than the right of setoff) to take the debtor's property in payment of the debt without the debtor's consent.

E. COLLECTING DEBT THROUGH JUDICIAL PROCESS

To collect a debt through judicial process, the creditor must obtain a judgment providing that the debtor owes the creditor a certain sum of money. The process for collecting on that judgment is prescribed by statute in each state and thus the following summary only states general principles that are usually part of the state statutory scheme.

1. Finding the Debtor's Assets, Execution, Levy and Sale

Once judgment is entered, the creditor may execute on the judgment by obtaining a writ of execution from the court clerk and giving that writ to the local law enforcement officer. The officer will levy on the debtor's property pursuant to the writ. Generally that levy will create a lien (an execution lien) on the seized property, which will then be sold at a public auction. The proceeds of the sale will first satisfy the officer's expenses and then be paid over to the creditor to apply to the judgment amount. In order to find out what property a debtor has, most states allow for a post-judgment discovery process in which the judgment creditor may make inquiries from the debtor or others regarding the debtor's assets.

2. Purchasing at the Sale and Redemption From the Sale

The judgment creditor is often the only bidder at the sale and bids in an amount that will be credited against the judgment amount. The purchaser at the sale obtains title to the sold property subject to any liens that are superior to the execution lien and free of the execution lien and any liens subordinate to the execution lien. In some states, a post-sale redemption period is allowed. If allowed, the debtor may redeem the property from the sale by tendering the sale price, plus interest, to the purchaser.

3. Time Limits on Obtaining Writs of Execution and Enforcing Judgments

Most states have a time limit in which the judgment creditor must obtain the writ of execution following the judgment. If the judgment creditor wants to obtain a writ of execution after that time, the creditor must ask for court permission to do so. Most states also have a statute of limitations for enforcing a judgment. In order to extend the life of a judgment beyond the period of the statute of limitations, the creditor must start an action on the judgment within the limitations period and obtain a "judgment on the judgment." The new judgment would have a new full time period under the statute of limitations.

4. Garnishment of Obligations

If a third party owes the debtor an obligation, that obligation is an asset of the debtor. Most states provide for a process, often called garnishment, in which the judgment creditor serves process on the third party instructing the third party to pay the judgment creditor (or law enforcement officer) instead of the debtor. The third party (called the garnishee) must pay the obligation to the designated party or risk liability to the judgment creditor.

5. Exemptions From Execution and Garnishment Process

In many states, individual debtors are allowed to exempt designated property from being levied on or garnished, that is, the designated property may not be seized and its value applied to the judgment debt. The type of property and the value of the property that may be exempted varies widely from state to state. Under most state laws, debtors that are not individuals are not allowed to exempt property from execution or garnishment. Exemptions do not generally effect the debtor's ability to grant a consensual lien in the exempt property.

6. Enforcement of Judgments Across State Lines

If the judgment creditor obtains a judgment against the debtor in one state and the debtor has assets in another state, the judgment creditor has two options for reaching those assets in the second state. The judgment creditor may start an action in the second state on the judgment rendered by the first state, get a judgment in the second state and use the execution and sale or garnishment process of the second state to obtain the value of the assets. Alternatively, the judgment creditor may use the Uniform Enforcement of Foreign Judgments Act (assuming the second state has enacted it) and register its judgment in the second state and then use the execution and sale process or garnishment process of the second state to obtain the value of the assets. Under the Full Faith and Credit Clause of the United States Constitution, the courts of the second state must give full faith and credit to a valid judgment entered in another state.

7. Pre-Judgment Remedies

On occasion, a creditor may qualify to have a law enforcement officer seize and hold the debtor's assets, including obligations owed to the debtor, prior to entry of judgment against the debtor. To obtain a pre-judgment remedy, the creditor must generally show a severe risk to the creditor's ability to eventually collect on the judgment that the creditor is asking for. Because the debtor's asset will be tied up before there is even an adjudication of the debtor's liability to the creditor, the statutes providing for pre-judgment remedies will require a pre-seizure hearing in front of a judicial officer, after notice to the debtor, and posting of a bond to protect against harm to the debtor if a judgment is not eventually issued. In extremely exigent circumstances, a court may order the debtor's property seized before giving notice to the debtor. If that happens, a prompt post-seizure hearing is generally required.

F. CONSTITUTIONAL ISSUES

Whenever state actors (such as judges and law enforcement officers) are involved in seizing a person's property, there are constitutional issues.

1. Violation of Procedural Due Process

The United States Supreme Court has considered whether pre-judgment remedies violate the rights of a debtor to procedural due process under the 5th and 14th amendments to the United States Constitution. The Court balances the private interest affected by the prejudgment remedy, the risk of erroneous deprivation and the value of additional or alternative safeguards, the creditor's interest in obtaining the remedy, and the government's interest in providing the procedure and its attendant burdens.

2. Improper Search and Seizure

The 4th and 14th amendments to the United States Constitution prohibit unreasonable searches and seizures. In both the pre-judgment and post-judgment context, entry upon the debtor's property and a seizure of property might be determined to run afoul of this constitutional right. The litmus test is one of reasonableness.

3. Private Creditor's Liability for Violation of Constitutional Rights

A private actor (such as a creditor) may be civilly liable for damages for violation of a debtor's constitutional rights if the creditor acts in concert with government actors in violating the debtor's rights.

G. REGULATION OF THE DEBT COLLECTION PROCESS

A variety of state and federal statutes regulate the debt collection process in addition to the statutes mentioned above.

1. Prohibited Collection Terms or Practices

Some consumer protection statutes prohibit certain terms in contracts, such as confessions of judgments, or taking a negotiable note for an obligation.

2. Fair Debt Collection Practices Act

This federal law, 15 U.S.C. §§ 1692–1692p, regulates "debt collectors" in collection of "consumer debts." This may include attorneys acting on behalf of clients in collecting debt. The Act regulates the manner in which the debt collector may communicate with the debtor and others regarding the consumer debt. The Act prohibits harassment or abusive behavior, false or misleading representations, and unfair practices. A debt collector that violates the Act is liable for actual damages, statutory damages, and reasonable attorneys' fees and costs.

3. Fair Credit Reporting Act

In the debt collection process, a creditor may threaten an adverse credit report in order to leverage payment from a reluctant debtor. The Fair Credit Reporting Act, 15 U.S.C. §§ 1681–1681x, regulates consumer credit reporting agencies in the collection and dissemination of information in consumer credit reports. Persons that violate the Act are liable for actual damages and attorneys' fees and costs, and in the case of a wilful violation, punitive damages.

4. Tort Law

Creditors are subject to tort law and thus will be liable if they commit a tort during the process of debt collection.

5. Lender Liability Issues in Debt Collection

In addition to the potential liability of a creditor under federal or state statutes, or tort law, a creditor may be liable for breach of contract if it violates its contract with the debtor, including acting with a lack of good faith, or engages in impermissible methods of control of the debtor to the detriment of other creditors.

H. FRAUDULENT TRANSFERS

Under the Uniform Fraudulent Transfer Act as enacted in the majority of states, or other similar enactments, a creditor may recover property that the debtor has transferred to a transferee or obtain a judgment against the transferee for the value of the asset, if the debtor transferred the property (i) with actual intent to hinder, delay or defraud creditors or (ii) for lack of reasonably equivalent value and one of the following situations exist: the debtor's enterprise was undercapitalized; the debtor's debts were beyond the ability of the debtor to pay when due; or the debtor was insolvent or rendered insolvent.

I. EFFECT OF DEBTOR'S BANKRUPTCY ON DEBT COLLECTION

If the debtor files bankruptcy, the creditor's ability to collect the debt is affected. Filing a bankruptcy creates a bankruptcy estate consisting of all property of the debtor. The creditor's efforts to collect a debt against the debtor, the debtor's property, and the property of the bankruptcy estate is automatically stayed upon the filing of a bankruptcy petition regardless of whether the creditor knows of the bankruptcy filing. An individual debtor may obtain a discharge of its obligation to pay the debt owed to the creditor, even if the creditor's lien on the debtor's asset remains intact. The creditor is liable for violations of the automatic stay or actions taken to collect a discharged debt.

J. REDUCTION OF RISK IN DEBT COLLECTION

A creditor may attempt to reduce the risk that the debtor will not pay the creditor by obtaining a guarantee of the debt obligation from a person other than the debtor or by obtaining a lien in specified property of the debtor or another person pursuant to a contractual agreement. A guarantee reduces the risk of nonpayment by obtaining the right to pursue another person for the obligation to pay the debt. A lien reduces the risk of nonpayment by giving the creditor advantages in the collection of the debt, a priority for its lien in the specified asset, and better treatment if the debtor files bankruptcy.

K. OVERVIEW OF THE UNIFORM COMMERCIAL CODE

The Uniform Commercial Code (UCC) is enacted by the states and contains 11 substantive articles governing various types of transactions such as sales and leases of goods, negotiable instruments, bank deposits and collections, commercial funds transfers, letters of credit, bulk transfers, documents of title, investment securities, and secured transactions.

L. OVERVIEW OF UCC ARTICLE 9

UCC Article 9 governs attaching, perfecting, and enforcing security interests and agricultural liens in personal property. It also contains an extensive priority scheme for determining the priority of security interests and agricultural liens as against other lien claims to the personal property.

■ II. THE SCOPE OF UCC ARTICLE 9

A. CONSENSUAL SECURITY INTERESTS

1. Security Interest

Article 9 applies to consensual interests in personal property or fixtures created by contract to secure payment or performance of an obligation. This consensual lien interest is denominated a "security interest." UCC §§ 9–109(a)(1), 1–201(b)(35). The asset must be determined to be "personal property" for Article 9 to apply. Certain items, such as licenses to engage in activity, may not be "property" under other law. Article 9 does not govern the question of whether the item is "property." Other law must be consulted. The creditor with the security interest is the "secured party," the person whose property is subject to the security interest is the "debtor," the person who owes the obligation to pay the creditor is the "obligor," and the property subject to the security interest is the collateral." UCC § 9–102.

2. Created by Contract

Article 9 applies primarily to liens created by contract.

3. Form of the Transaction

Article 9 will apply to contractually created interests in personal property or fixtures to secure payment or performance of an obligation regardless of the form of the transaction. Thus, the parties may not by agreement dictate that Article 9 does not apply to a transaction. The court will examine the substance of the transaction to make that determination.

a. Sale or Lease of Goods

A transaction that the parties label as a "lease" of goods may in fact be a disguised security interest. UCC § 1–203 details factors that will help determine whether the transaction is a "true lease" or a disguised security interest. The key inquiry is whether the buyer/lessee is obtaining more than the right to possess or use the goods for a period of time and whether the seller/lessor is retaining a meaningful residual interest in the goods.

b. Consignments for Sale

A transaction that the parties label a "consignment" may in fact be a disguised security interest. A consignment at common law is typically a bailment to a merchant giving the merchant authority to sell the goods on behalf of the bailor with the obligation of the merchant to return the goods if they remain unsold. Article 9 does not contain any test for determining whether a transaction is a "true consignment" or a disguised security interest. If a transaction is labeled a "consignment" but is actually a disguised security interest, Article 9 will apply to the transaction.

c. Other Transactions

The rule of UCC § 9–109(a)(1) is very broad. This provision allows the court to examine the substance of the transaction to determine whether the transaction in fact creates an interest in personal property to secure payment or performance of an obligation.

B. TRUE CONSIGNMENTS

Even if the transaction is a "true consignment" based upon common law principles, Article 9 will apply to the transaction if it meets the definition of consignment given in Article 9. UCC §§ 9–109(a)(4), 9–102(a)(20).

1. Consignment Defined

A "true consignment" governed by Article 9 must meet the following criteria: (i) a delivery of goods to a merchant for sale, (ii) the merchant must deal in goods of the kind under a name other than the name of the person that delivered the goods, (iii) the merchant must not be an auctioneer, (iv) the merchant must not be generally known by its creditors to be substantially engaged in selling goods for others, (v) the value of the goods delivered must be more than $1,000, and (vi) the goods must not be consumer goods immediately prior to delivery.

2. Effect of Inclusion

If the transaction is a true consignment within the definition of "consignment, the person delivering the goods to the merchant is the consignor and secured party. The merchant is the consignee and debtor. The property delivered is the collateral. UCC § 9–102. The interest of the consignor is denominated a "security interest." UCC § 1–201(b)(35).

3. Effect of Exclusion

If the transaction is in substance a true consignment but is not within the definition of consignment, the transaction is not governed by Article 9 and is in effect a bailment. UCC § 9–109, cmt. 6.

C. SALES OF CERTAIN TYPES OF ASSETS

Article 9 applies to sales of accounts, chattel paper, payment intangibles and promissory notes. UCC § 9–109(a)(3). The buyer is the "secured party." The seller is the "debtor." The subject matter of the sale is the "collateral." UCC § 9–102. The buyer is treated as having a "security interest" for Article 9 purposes even if the transaction is a sale. UCC § 1–201(b)(35). Sales of these types of assets are included within the scope of Article 9 because it is difficult to distinguish a sale of these types of assets and transactions that create a lien interest to secure an obligation. Article 9 does not give any criteria for determining whether the transaction is a sale of the asset or the creation of a contractual lien interest in the asset.

D. SECURITY INTEREST ARISING UNDER OTHER ARTICLES OF THE UCC

Article 9 applies to security interests that arise by operation of law under another article of the UCC. Those security interests are provided for in Articles 2 (sales of goods), 2A (leases of goods), 4 (bank collections), and 5 (letters of credit). UCC § 9–109(a)(5), (6).

1. Articles 2 and 2A

These four security interests arising under Articles 2 and 2A are governed by Article 9. UCC § 9–110. A seller that "retains title" to goods delivered to the buyer is limited in effect to a security interest in the goods. UCC § 2–401. If the seller ships the goods under reservation, the seller has retained a security interest in the goods to secure the amount due for the price of the goods as long as the goods are in the possession of the carrier. UCC § 2–505. If a buyer rightfully and effectively rejects goods or justifiably revokes acceptance as to goods delivered under a contract for sale, the buyer has a security interest in the goods to secure any prepayment of the price and certain expenses related to the care, custody, and transportation of the goods, as long as the buyer has possession or control of the goods. UCC § 2–711(3). If a lessee rightfully and effectively rejects goods or justifiably revokes acceptance as to the goods delivered under a lease, the lessee will have a security interest in the goods to secure the amount of rent already paid, any security deposit, and expenses in the transportation, care and custody of the goods, as long as the lessee has possession or control of the goods. UCC § 2A–508.

2. Collecting Bank's Security Interest in Items and Documents

A collecting bank has a security interest in items and accompanying documents in its possession and submitted for collection until it receives a final settlement for those items or releases possession of the items for a purpose other than collection of the items. The security interest secures amounts given as withdrawable credit against the item. UCC § 4–210.

3. Security Interest of Letter of Credit Issuer or Nominated Person

The issuer or nominated person has a security interest in documents presented under a letter of credit and in its possession to the extent it has given value for the presentation or honored the presentation by paying under the terms of the credit and has not been reimbursed for its payment. UCC § 5–118.

E. AGRICULTURAL LIENS

Article 9 applies to agricultural liens. UCC § 9–109(a)(2). An agricultural lien is a lien, created under a statute other than Article 9, in farm products which are goods with respect to which the debtor is engaged in farming operations. The goods which are considered to be farm products are livestock, crops (other than standing timber), products of crops or livestock in their unmanufactured state, and supplies used or produced in a farming operation. The agricultural lien in farm products secures obligations for goods or services furnished to the farmer in the ordinary course of the farmer's farming operation or for rent of real property leased as part of the farming operation. The statute creating the lien must provide for the lien in favor of a person that either supplies goods or services in the ordinary course of the supplier's business or leases real estate that the farmer uses in the farming operation. UCC § 9–102(a)(5), (34). The effectiveness of the lien cannot depend upon the lienor's possession of the farm products. The agricultural lienholder is a "secured party," the farmer with the property interest in the farm products is the "debtor," and the farm product is the "collateral." UCC § 9–102. The agricultural lien is *not* denominated as a "security interest." UCC § 1–201(b)(35).

F. EXCLUSIONS FROM ARTICLE 9

Various transactions that would fall within the scope of Article 9 are excluded from Article 9 by UCC § 9–109(c) and (d). The effect of excluding the transaction from the scope of Article 9 is to have other law apply to whether an interest in that property may arise to secure payment or performance of an obligation.

1. Federal Law Preemption

If federal law preempts the application of Article 9 to a particular transaction, federal law will govern to the extent of the preemption. UCC § 9–109(c)(1).

2. State Governmental Units and Foreign Countries as Debtors

If the state or foreign government has a statute that expressly governs creation, perfection, priority, or enforcement of security interests that are granted by that governmental entity, Article 9 does not apply to the extent the issue is governed by that other statute. UCC § 9–109(c)(2) and (3).

3. Transferee Beneficiary of a Letter of Credit

Article 9 excludes from its scope the right of a transferee beneficiary of a letter of credit to the extent its rights are superior to the rights of an assignee of a letter of credit. UCC § 9–109(c)(4).

4. Nonconsensual Liens Other Than Agricultural Liens

Article 9 does not apply to nonconsensual liens created by statute or common law other than agricultural liens (as defined in Article 9), except for priority of that nonconsensual lien as against a security interest or agricultural lien. UCC § 9–109(d)(1), (2).

5. Wage Assignment

Article 9 does not apply to any transaction that is an assignment of wages, salary, or employee compensation. UCC § 9–109(d)(3).

6. Assignment of Certain Rights to Payment

Article 9 does not apply to: (i) a transaction that is a sale of accounts, chattel paper, payment intangibles, or promissory notes as part of the sale of the business that generated those rights to payment, UCC § 9–109(d)(4); (ii) an assignment of accounts, chattel paper, payment intangibles, or promissory notes to another for the purpose of collection only, UCC § 9–109(d)(5); (iii) an assignment of a right to payment (in whatever form it is held) if the assignee is also required to perform under the contract, UCC § 9–109(d)(6); and (iv) the assignment of a single account, payment intangible, or promissory note to an assignee in full or partial satisfaction of a preexisting debt, UCC § 9–109(d)(7).

7. Assignment of Rights Under Insurance Policies

Article 9 does not apply to an assignment of a right under an insurance policy except if the right under the insurance policy is proceeds of another type of collateral or if a person assigns rights under a health care insurance policy to a health care provider for services rendered or a health care provider assigns its rights under a health care insurance policy to another. UCC §§ 9–109(d)(8), 9–102(a)(46).

8. Assignment of a Judgment

Article 9 does not apply to an assignment of a right under a judgment unless the judgment was on a right to payment that was already subject to a security interest. UCC § 9–109(d)(9).

9. Recoupment or Setoff

Article 9 does not apply to the right of recoupment or setoff unless the issue is priority of those rights as against a security interest when the asset is a deposit account or if someone is obligated on a right to payment where that right to payment is the collateral subject to a security interest. UCC § 9–109(d)(10).

10. Real Estate Interests

Article 9 does not apply to the creation or transfer of interests in real property, including a lease and rents under a lease, except for fixtures and certain enforcement rights when the secured party has lien interests in both real and personal property. UCC § 9–109(d)(11).

11. Assignment of Tort Claims

Article 9 does not apply to transactions that are assignments of tort claims except commercial tort claims or tort claims that are proceeds of other collateral in which there is a security interest. UCC § 9–109(d)(12).

12. Assignment of Deposit Accounts in Consumer Transactions

Article 9 does not apply to an assignment of an interest in a deposit account in a consumer transaction unless that deposit account is proceeds of other collateral in which there is a security interest. UCC § 9–109(d)(13).

13. Security Interests in Secured Obligations

Article 9 applies to security interests in obligations that are secured by collateral in a transaction even if that underlying transaction is not within the scope of Article 9. UCC § 9–109(b).

G. IMPORTANCE OF DEFINITIONS

The application of Article 9's provisions depend upon a thorough understanding of the definitions. The first and most important category of definitions is the various collateral types. The second category is the transaction types. The third category is actor types.

1. Collateral Types

a. Goods

A "good" is a thing that is movable at the time the security interest attaches. Fixtures, standing timber to be cut and removed under a sales contract, unborn young of animals, crops growing or to be grown and manufactured homes are all included within the definition of a "good." UCC § 9–102(a)(44).

b. Subcategories of Goods

Defined subcategories of goods are "fixtures," UCC § 9–102(a)(41), "manufactured home," UCC § 9–102(a)(53), "accession," UCC § 9–102(a)(1), "as-extracted collateral," UCC § 9–102(a)(6)(A), "consumer goods, UCC § 9–102(a)(23), "inventory," UCC § 9–102(a)(48), "farm products," UCC § 9–102(a)(34), and "equipment," UCC § 9–102(a)(33).

c. Money

Money is a "medium of exchange" adopted or authorized by a domestic or foreign government. UCC § 1–201(b)(24).

d. Obligations Owed

Obligations owed to the debtor are personal property assets of the debtor. These obligations may be embodied in a particular piece of paper or may merely be memorialized on the paper. For some types of obligations that are traditionally embodied in a particular piece of paper, Article 9 recognizes an electronic record instead of the paper record. The defined terms are: electronic or tangible "chattel paper" UCC § 9–102(a)(11), (79), (31); electronic or tangible, negotiable or nonnegotiable "document of title," UCC §§ 1–201(b)(16), 9–102(a)(30); negotiable and nonnegotiable instruments (in tangible form only), UCC § 9–102(a)(47); a type of "instrument" called a "promissory note," UCC § 9–102(a)(65); an "account," UCC § 9–102(a)(2); a type of account that qualifies as "as-extracted collateral," UCC § 9–102(a)(6)(B); a type of account called a "health-care-insurance receivable," UCC § 9–102(a)(46); "commercial tort claim," UCC § 9–102(a)(13); "deposit account," UCC § 9–102(a)(29); a "letter-of-credit right," UCC § 9–102(a)(51);

a "mortgage," UCC § 9–102(a)(55); a "supporting obligation," UCC § 9–102(a)(78); a "general intangible," UCC § 9–102(a)(42); a type of general intangible that is a "payment intangible," UCC § 9–102(a)(61); and a type of general intangible that is "software," UCC § 9–102(a)(76).

e. Investment Property

"Investment property" is a broad category that includes a certificated or uncertificated security, securities entitlement, securities account, commodity contract, and commodity account. UCC §§ 9–102(a)(14), (15), (49), 8–102(a)(4), (14), (15), (16), (17), (18), 8–501(b).

f. Proceeds

Proceeds falls into the following categories: (i) whatever rights are acquired upon disposition of the collateral including disposition by sale, lease, or license of the collateral; (ii) whatever is collected or distributed on account of collateral; (iii) rights arising out of collateral; (iv) claims arising out of loss, defects, infringement, or other impairment of the value of collateral; and (v) insurance payable by reason of claims arising out of loss, defects, infringement or other impairment of the value of the collateral. UCC § 9–102(a)(64). Proceeds may be either "cash proceeds" or "noncash proceeds." UCC § 9–102(a)(9), (58).

2. Transaction Types

Article 9 also defines the following transaction types: "consumer transaction," UCC § 9–102(a)(26); "consumer-goods transaction," UCC § 9–102(a)(24); "manufactured-home transaction," UCC § 9–102(a)(54); and "public-finance transaction, " UCC § 9–102(a)(67).

3. Actor Types

Article 9 also defines the following actors: "debtor," UCC § 9–102(a)(28); "consumer debtor," UCC § 9–102(a)(22); "secured party," UCC § 9–102(a)(73); "obligor," UCC § 9–102(a)(59); "consumer obligor," UCC § 9–102(a)(25); "secondary obligor," UCC § 9–102(a)(72); "consignee," UCC § 9–102(a)(19); "consignor," UCC § 9–102(a)(21); and "account debtor," UCC § 9–102(a)(3).

■ III. ATTACHMENT OF A SECURITY INTEREST OR AGRICULTURAL LIEN

A. ATTACHMENT AND ENFORCEABILITY

Attachment of a security interest or agricultural lien to an item of collateral is a necessary prerequisite to the secured party's ability to enforce the security interest or agricultural lien. Enforcement refers to the process of obtaining value from collection of the obligation owed to the debtor by a third party or seizing and selling tangible collateral through the Article 9 enforcement process. UCC § 9–601. Attachment of a security interest and agricultural lien is also a required step in the process of perfection of the security interest or agricultural lien. A security interest or agricultural lien is considered perfected when it has attached and the prescribed perfection step has been taken. UCC § 9–308(a), (b). Attachment of a security interest or agricultural lien, however, does not make the secured party liable in contract or tort for the debtor's acts or omissions. UCC § 9–402. An agricultural lien attaches to farm products according to the terms of the statute that allows the agricultural lien to arise. See UCC § 9–102(a)(5)(B). To attach a security interest by contract, subject to some limited exceptions, the debtor must agree to grant the security interest to the creditor, value must be given, and the debtor must have the right, as a matter of property law, to grant a security interest in the collateral. UCC § 9–203(b). The security interest attaches when all three of the requirements for attachment of the security interest are fulfilled.

B. THREE REQUIREMENTS FOR ATTACHMENT OF A SECURITY INTEREST

To attach a security interest by agreement of the parties, subject to some limited exceptions, three basic requirements must be met. The debtor must agree to grant the security interest to the creditor, value must be given, and the debtor must have the right, as a matter of property law, to grant a security interest in the collateral. UCC § 9–203(b). The agreement between the secured party and the debtor may postpone the time of attachment to a time later then when all three of the requirements are met. UCC § 9–203(a).

1. Debtor's Agreement to Grant a Security Interest, Generally

The debtor, by an agreement with the creditor, will grant the creditor an interest in personal property to secure payment or performance of an obligation owed to that creditor or will sell accounts, chattel paper, payment intangibles or promissory notes to a buyer (denominated a "secured party"). The parties' bargain in fact (the "agreement," UCC § 1–201(b)(3)) thus creates a "security interest" (UCC § 1–201(b)(35)) and is denominated the "security agreement." (UCC § 9–102(a)(74)).

a. Evidencing the Security Agreement

The security agreement must be evidenced by one of the following three methods: an authenticated record with an adequate collateral description, possession of specified types of collateral, or control of specified types of collateral.

b. Security Agreement as a Contract

The security agreement is a contract subject to all of the usual doctrines of the common law concerning contracts except as those doctrines are altered by a provision of Article 9 or other statute. The grant of a security interest is not only effective as between the secured party and the debtor, but is also effective as to third parties, except as otherwise provided in Article 9. UCC § 9–201(a). The exceptions are explored in Chapter V on priority. A transaction subject to Article 9 may also be subject to other law that regulates certain classes of transactions, such as with consumer debtors. Article 9 does not displace that other regulatory law or change the effect of that other law on the transaction it regulates. UCC § 9–201(b), (c), (d).

c. Debtor's Use, Possession, and Control of Collateral

The mere grant of a security interest in the debtor's property does not prevent the debtor from using, possessing, controlling, collecting, or disposing of the collateral nor make such actions fraudulent as to the debtor's other creditors. UCC § 9–205(a).

2. Debtor's Security Agreement Memorialized in a Record

Unless the creditor has possession or control of certain types of collateral pursuant to a security agreement with the debtor, the debtor must authenticate a record that memorializes the security agreement and that contains an adequate collateral description.

a. Record and Debtor Authentication

The memorialization of the security agreement must be in a record which is either tangible or electronic. UCC § 9–102(a)(70). A security agreement in a record is authenticated when the debtor adopts or executes a symbol or process with the present intent to identify itself and adopt or accept the record. UCC § 9–102(a)(7).

b. Collateral Description

The authenticated security agreement must contain an adequate description of the collateral and, if the collateral is timber to be cut, a description of the land that contains the timber. UCC § 9–203(b)(3)(A).

(1) General Rule
An adequate collateral description or the described real estate must "reasonably identify what it describes." UCC § 9–108(a).

(2) Reasonably Identifying What it Describes
A collateral description is deemed to meet the test of reasonably identifying what it describes if it falls into one of the following types of description: a specific listing, a category, a type of collateral defined in the UCC, a quantity, a formula or procedure, or any other method where the "identity of the collateral is objectively determinable." UCC § 9–108(b). A description of the collateral in the security agreement using "all assets" or "all personal property" of the debtor is deemed to be an inadequate description of the collateral for purposes of attachment of the security interest to the collateral. UCC § 9–108(c).

(3) Description of Investment Property

In a nonconsumer transaction, to describe collateral that constitutes a securities account, a securities entitlement, or a commodity account, the security agreement may use those terms, may describe the collateral as "investment property" or may describe the underlying asset that is held in the securities account or commodity account or is the basis of the securities entitlement. UCC § 9–108(d).

(4) More Specific Descriptions Required in Some Circumstances

Describing the collateral as a "commercial tort claim" is an inadequate description of the collateral in the security agreement. More specific information about the commercial tort claim must be included in order to have an adequate description. UCC § 9–108(e)(1). In a consumer transaction, a description by type alone of "consumer goods," "security entitlements," "securities accounts," and "commodity accounts" is not an adequate description of the collateral. UCC § 9–108(e)(2).

c. Composite Document Doctrine

If the three critical components, debtor authentication, the provision for the security interest, and the description of the collateral, are not all contained in one record, the courts may construe a number of records together to find that this requirement is met. This court construction is called the "composite document doctrine." The essence of the court's inquiry in this situation is whether, based upon the composition of the records in evidence before the court, the records evidence an intent of the debtor and secured party to grant a security interest in the described collateral. A secured party should not count on a court applying the doctrine to rescue the secured party's attempt to attach a security interest to collateral.

3. Secured Party's Possession Pursuant to a Security Agreement

As an alternative to a debtor-authenticated security agreement with an adequate collateral description, the secured party may take possession of certain types of collateral pursuant to an *agreement* with the debtor (either oral or memorialized in a record) that the collateral is subject to a security interest. UCC § 9–203(b)(3)(B).

a. Types of Collateral That May be Possessed

The types of collateral that may be possessed, and thus subject to attachment of a security interest through an oral agreement with the debtor, are tangible negotiable documents of title, goods, instruments, money, and tangible chattel paper. UCC § 9–313(a).

b. Possession Defined

Possession is not specifically defined. The concept of possession is that the secured party or its agent has dominion over the collateral and the debtor is excluded from access to the collateral. UCC § 9–313, cmt. 3. Generally, debtor access to the collateral will destroy the secured party's attempt to attach the security interest through possession. See UCC § 9–205(b).

4. Secured Party Taking Delivery of a Certificated Security Pursuant to a Security Agreement

The secured party may take delivery of a certificated security pursuant to the debtor's agreement to grant a security interest in the certificated security. UCC § 9–203(b)(3)(C). Delivery of a certificated security means acquiring possession of the certificate or obtaining the acknowledgment of the possessor, other than a securities intermediary, that the possessor holds the certificate for the benefit of the secured party. Delivery of a certificated security to a secured party also takes place if a securities intermediary has possession of the certificate in registered form and the certificate is registered, payable to, or indorsed to the secured party. UCC § 8–301.

5. Secured Party Control Pursuant to Security Agreement

The secured party may "control" certain types of collateral pursuant to the debtor's agreement to grant a security interest in that type of collateral. UCC § 9–203(b)(3)(D). The types of collateral that may be "controlled" by a secured party in order to attach a security interest, in the absence of a security agreement memorialized in an adequate record, are deposit accounts, electronic chattel paper, investment property, letter-of-credit rights, and electronic documents of title.

a. Control

Unlike the concept of possession, however, control does not mean that the debtor must be excluded from access to the collateral. Rather, control is defined for each type of collateral for which a secured party can obtain control.

b. Control of Deposit Accounts

A secured party may obtain control of a deposit account in one of three ways. None of these three methods require that the debtor be excluded from access to the funds maintained in the deposit account. UCC § 9–104(b). The secured party will have control of a deposit account of the debtor if the secured party is also the depositary bank where the account is maintained. UCC § 9–104(a)(1). A secured party that is not the depositary bank may obtain control of the deposit account by obtaining a record authenticated by the debtor, the secured party, and the depositary bank that the depositary bank will agree to the secured party's directions regarding disposition of funds from the deposit account without any further consent of the debtor. UCC § 9–104(a)(2). A secured party that is not the depositary bank may obtain control of the deposit account by becoming a customer of the bank on the deposit account. UCC § 9–104(a)(3).

c. Control of Electronic Chattel Paper

To obtain control of electronic chattel paper, the records comprising that chattel paper must be created and stored in a database or other electronic medium in a manner that reliably establishes that the secured party is the person to whom the chattel paper was assigned. UCC § 9–105(a). A safe harbor consisting of six criteria, if met, will be deemed to be control of the electronic chattel paper. The records constituting the chattel paper must be designated in some manner as the "authoritative copy" which is "unique, identifiable, and [subject to certain exceptions] unalterable." Any copy of the authoritative copy must be readily identifiable as a copy that is not authoritative. The authoritative copy must identify the secured party as the assignee of the records. The authoritative copy must be maintained by the secured party or a designated custodian. Copies or revisions to the authoritative copy that add or change the assignee must be made with the consent of the secured party. Any revisions to the authoritative copy must be readily identifiable as authorized or unauthorized. UCC § 9–105(b).

d. Control of Investment Property

(1) Control of a Certificated Security in Bearer Form

A secured party will have control of a certificated security in bearer form if the secured party has taken delivery of the certificate. UCC §§ 9–106(a), 8–106(a). Taking delivery of the certificate in bearer form means either the secured party taking possession of the certificate or a person, other than a securities intermediary, holding possession of the certificate and acknowledging to the secured party that it holds possession on behalf of the secured party. UCC § 8–301(a).

(2) Control of a Certificated Security in Registered Form

A secured party will have control of a certificated security in registered form if the secured party takes delivery of the certificate and the certificate is indorsed to the secured party or in blank or the certificate is registered in the name of the secured party. UCC §§ 9–106(a), 8–106(b). A secured party takes delivery of a certificated security in registered form if it obtains possession of the certificate or obtains an acknowledgment from a person, other than a securities intermediary, that it holds possession on behalf of the secured party. If a securities intermediary has possession of the certificate and the certificate is registered to, payable to, or indorsed to the secured party, it has been delivered to the secured party. UCC § 8–301(a).

(3) Control of an Uncertificated Security

A secured party has control of an uncertificated security if the security is delivered to the secured party or the issuer of the security has agreed to comply with the secured party's instructions without the further consent of the registered owner of the security. UCC §§ 9–106(a), 8–106(c). An uncertificated security is delivered to a secured party if the issuer registers the secured party as the owner of the security or a person, other than a securities intermediary or the debtor, is the registered owner and acknowledges that it holds the security for the benefit of the secured party. UCC § 8–301(b). The secured party has control even if the debtor has a right to deal with the uncertificated security. UCC § 8–106(f).

(4) Control of a Security Entitlement

A secured party has control of a securities entitlement if it is the entitlement holder, the securities intermediary has agreed to comply with the instructions of the secured party without further agreement of the entitlement holder, or if another person has control of the security entitlement on behalf of the secured party or acknowledges that it holds the securities entitlement on behalf of the secured party. UCC §§ 9–106(a), 8–106(d). If the secured party is the securities intermediary that is holding the securities entitlement, the securities intermediary automatically has control. UCC §§ 9–106(a), 8–106(e). The secured party has control even if the debtor retains the right to deal with the securities entitlement. UCC § 8–106(f).

(5) Control of a Securities Account

If a secured party has control over all of the securities entitlements in a securities account, the secured party has control of the securities account. UCC § 9–106(c).

(6) Control of a Commodity Contract

A secured party has control of a commodity contract if it is the commodity intermediary that holds the commodity contract. UCC § 9–106(b)(1). If the secured party is not the commodity intermediary that is holding the commodity contract, the secured party has control of the commodity contract if the commodity customer, the secured party, and the commodity intermediary have agreed that the commodity intermediary will apply any value derived from the commodity contract as directed by the secured party without any further consent of the commodity customer. UCC § 9–106(b)(2).

(7) Control of a Commodity Account

If a secured party has control over all commodity contracts in a commodity account, the secured party has control of the commodity account. UCC § 9–106(c).

e. Control of Letter-of-Credit Rights

A secured party will have control of letter-of-credit rights if the secured party obtains the consent of the issuer or any nominated person to the assignment of the proceeds of the letter of credit. UCC § 9–107. Consent to the assignment of proceeds of the letter of credit is an agreement of the issuer or nominated person to recognize the secured party's claim to the proceeds. Consent to the assignment is not the same as recognizing the right of a transferee beneficiary to make a demand for payment under the letter of credit. UCC § 9–107, cmts. 1, 4.

f. Control of Electronic Documents of Title

A secured party will have control of an electronic document of title when the secured party is designated by the system used to evidence interests in the electronic document of title as *the* person entitled to the goods under the electronic document of title. UCC § 7–106(a). The system is deemed to satisfy that standard if the following six criteria are met. The records constituting the electronic document of title must be designated in some manner as the "authoritative copy" which is "unique, identifiable, and [subject to certain exceptions] unalterable." Any copy of the authoritative copy must be readily identifiable as a copy that is not authoritative. The authoritative copy must identify the secured party as the assignee of the records. The authoritative copy must be maintained by the secured party or a designated custodian. Copies or revisions to the authoritative copy that add or change the assignee must be made with the participation of the secured party. Any revisions to the authoritative copy must be readily identifiable as authorized or unauthorized. UCC § 7–106(b).

6. Value Has Been Given

The second requirement for attachment of a consensual security interest in the debtor's personal property is that value must be given. UCC § 9–203(b)(1). Value must consist of one of four things. First, value may be any consideration that is sufficient to support a contract. Second, value may be a binding commitment to extend credit. Third, value may be security for or total or partial satisfaction of a preexisting claim. Fourth, value may be accepting delivery under a preexisting purchase contract. UCC § 1–204. The debtor need not receive the value and the secured party need not be the one who gives the value.

7. Rights in the Collateral or Power to Transfer Rights in Collateral

The third requirement for attaching a consensual security interest in collateral is that the debtor must actually have rights in the collateral or power to transfer rights in the collateral to the secured party. UCC § 9–203(b)(2). A security interest attaches to whatever property rights the debtor actually has in the collateral. UCC § 9–203, cmt. 6. A debtor need not have full title to the collateral in order to grant a security interest in the collateral to a secured party. UCC § 9–202. If a provision of law allows the debtor to grant more rights than it has in the collateral to another person and the secured party is a person that may take advantage of that other law, the debtor may grant those greater rights to the secured party. UCC § 9–203(b)(2), cmt. 6. A good faith purchaser of goods (including a secured party) from a person with voidable title, or who is a buyer (including a secured party) of accounts, chattel paper, promissory notes, or payment intangibles may be able to obtain greater rights than its transferor had. UCC §§ 2–403(1), 9–318, 9–330, 9–331. In addition, a consignee of goods in an Article 9 consignment may transfer greater rights than it has to its secured party. UCC § 9–319.

C. AFTER-ACQUIRED PROPERTY AND FUTURE ADVANCES CLAUSES IN THE SECURITY AGREEMENT

1. After-Acquired Property Clause

Article 9 allows the security agreement to contain an after-acquired property clause to attach a security interest to items that the debtor acquires rights in after the execution of the security agreement as long as those items fall within the collateral description. UCC § 9–204(a). A typical after-acquired property clause provides that "the security interest attaches to all of the debtor's (insert collateral description here such as "goods, chattel paper, accounts") in which the debtor currently has rights or acquires rights hereafter." An after-acquired property clause does not effect an attachment of the security interest to a commercial tort claim that arises after the authentication of the security agreement and does not effect an attachment of the security interest to consumer goods, other than an accession, unless the debtor acquires rights in the consumer goods within 10 days after the secured party gives value. UCC § 9–204(b).

2. Future Advances Clause

Article 9 gives effect to a future advances clause in the security agreement. UCC § 9–204(c). A typical future advances clause provides that the security interest in the described collateral secures "all obligations that the debtor owes the creditor now or hereafter."

3. Cross Collateralization

The effect of a well-drafted after-acquired property clause and a well-drafted future advances clause in the same security agreement is to provide for cross collateralization of all of the debtor's obligations owed to the same secured party.

D. EXCEPTIONS TO THE RULE REGARDING COLLATERAL DESCRIPTION

In six circumstances defined in Article 9, attachment of a security interest in one type of collateral results in automatic attachment of the security interest in another type of collateral.

1. Attachment of a Security Interest to Proceeds of Collateral

When a secured party obtains an attached security interest in any type of collateral, the security interest automatically attaches to any identifiable proceeds of that collateral. UCC §§ 9–203(f), 9–315(a)(2). The security agreement need not state that the collateral for the obligation secured includes "proceeds" of collateral types that are described in the security agreement.

a. Proceeds Defined

"Proceeds" fall into the following categories: (i) whatever rights are acquired upon disposition of the collateral including disposition by sale, lease, or license of the collateral; (ii) whatever is collected or distributed on account of collateral; (iii) rights arising out of collateral; (iv) claims arising out of loss, defects, infringement, or other impairment of the value of collateral; and (v) insurance payable by reason of claims arising out of loss, defects, infringement or other impairment of the value of the collateral. UCC § 9–102(a)(64). In order to be "identifiable," the proceeds must fall into one of the categories of proceeds set forth in the definition and result, in a factual sense, from the original collateral. UCC § 9–102(a)(64).

b. Commingled Property

Article 9 provides that if proceeds are commingled with other property, the proceeds are still "identifiable" in some circumstances. If the proceeds are goods that are commingled with other goods, then the rules on commingled goods set forth below apply to determine the continued attachment of the security interest in the commingled goods. UCC § 9–315(b)(1). If the proceeds are not goods, then the secured party may use equitable methods of tracing the proceeds to identify what portion of the commingled property is considered to be proceeds. UCC § 9–315(b)(2). The most commonly applied tracing method is called the "lowest intermediate balance" rule.

2. Attachment of a Security Interest to the Product or Mass of Commingled Goods

If a security interest is attached to goods and then those goods are commingled with other goods, a security interest will attach to the product or mass of commingled goods. UCC § 9–336(c). Goods are considered "commingled goods" when the goods are united in such a way that the individual identity of the goods is subsumed within the product or mass that results from the commingling. UCC § 9–336(a).

3. Attachment of a Security Interest to Supporting Obligations of Other Collateral

When a secured party obtains an attached security interest in any right to payment which is supported by another obligation that qualifies as a "supporting obligation," the security interest automatically attaches to the supporting obligation. UCC § 9–203(f).

4. Attachment of a Security Interest to a Security Interest, Mortgage, or Lien Interest

When a secured party obtains an attached security interest in any right to payment that is secured by a security interest, mortgage, or any other type of lien interest, the secured party also obtains an attached security interest in the security interest, mortgage, or lien interest. UCC § 9–203(g).

5. Attachment of a Security Interest to Securities Entitlements in a Securities Account

If a secured party attaches a security interest to a securities account, the security interest attaches to all securities entitlements carried in the securities account. UCC § 9–203(h).

6. Attachment of a Security Interest to Commodity Contracts in a Commodity Account

If a secured party attaches a security interest to a commodity account, the security interest attaches to all commodity contracts carried in the commodity account. UCC § 9–203(i).

E. ATTACHMENT OF A SECURITY INTEREST WITHOUT THE DEBTOR'S SECURITY AGREEMENT

1. Security Interests Arising Under UCC Articles 2 and 2A

A seller's security interest that arises through retention of title, UCC § 2–401, and shipment under reservation, UCC § 2–505, and a buyer's or lessee's security interest in rightfully rejected goods or goods as to which acceptance has been justifiably revoked, UCC §§ 2–711(3), 2A–508, are attached as long as the debtor does not have possession of the goods. The secured party does not have to have a debtor-authenticated security agreement that describes the collateral or have possession of the goods pursuant to the debtor's security agreement. UCC § 9–110(1). The security interest attaches as specified in UCC §§ 2–401, 2–505, 2–711(3) and 2A–508.

2. Security Interest of a Collecting Bank Under Article 4

The security interest of a collecting bank in items in its possession attaches when withdrawable credits are given against the item. UCC § 4–210(a). No security agreement is necessary to make the security interest enforceable as long as the collecting bank does not receive final settlement for the item or give up possession or control of the item for purposes other than collection of the item through the banking system. UCC § 4–210(c)(1).

3. Security Interest of Bank Issuing Letter of Credit

The letter of credit issuer's security interest in documents in its possession presented under a letter of credit attaches when the issuer gives value for the presentation or honors the presentation. UCC § 5–118(a). A security agreement is not necessary to attach the security interest to these documents as long as the issuer has not been reimbursed or otherwise recovered the value given under the letter of credit. UCC § 5–118(b)(1).

4. Attachment of a Security Interest in Cases of Successor Liability

If an original debtor enters into a security agreement with a creditor and the original debtor transfers substantially all of its assets to a new debtor and the new debtor becomes generally obligated for the obligations of the original debtor, that new debtor, UCC § 9–102(a)(56), is bound by the security agreement entered into by the original debtor, UCC § 9–102(a)(60). UCC § 9–203(d)(2). The original security agreement between the original secured party and original debtor is sufficient to create a security interest in the new debtor's assets that are within the description contained in that security agreement. UCC § 9–203(e).

5. Security Interest of Securities Intermediary in Securities Entitlement

If a securities intermediary allows a person to buy a financial asset through the securities intermediary under an agreement to pay for the asset at the time of purchase, and the securities intermediary credits the asset to the person's securities account before the person actually makes the payment (thereby creating a securities entitlement), the securities intermediary has a security interest in the securities entitlement to secure the person's obligation to pay the purchase price. UCC § 9–206(a), (b).

6. Security Interest of Person Delivering Certificated Security or Financial Asset Represented by a Writing

If a person in the business of dealing with securities or financial assets delivers a certificated security or other financial asset that is represented by a writing to another person also in the business of dealing with securities or financial assets under an agreement in which the transferee is to pay for the delivery, the transferor has a security interest in the certificates or financial asset represented by a writing to secure the transferee's obligation to pay for the certificated security or financial asset. UCC § 9–206(c), (d).

F. EFFECT OF DISPOSITIONS OF COLLATERAL ON ATTACHMENT OF A SECURITY INTEREST OR AGRICULTURAL LIEN

The disposition of the collateral to another person does not strip off a security interest or agricultural lien that has attached to the item of collateral unless the secured party authorizes the disposition of the collateral free of the security interest or agricultural lien or a priority rule in Article 9 specifies otherwise. UCC § 9–315(a)(1). The secured party's authorization to dispose of the collateral free of the security interest or agricultural lien may be express or implied. The fact that the secured party has a right to the proceeds obtained upon disposition of the collateral, UCC § 9–315(a)(2), is not an express or implied authorization to dispose of the collateral free of the security interest. UCC § 9–315, cmt. 2.

G. ABILITY TO STOP ATTACHMENT OF A SECURITY INTEREST

The debtor may grant a security interest in the debtor's assets even if the debtor by contract or the legal rules governing that type of asset provide that the debtor cannot transfer its rights in the asset.

1. Contractual Agreements Not to Create a Security Interest or Transfer Rights in the Property

a. Agreements Between the Debtor and Secured Party

An agreement between the debtor and secured party that prohibits the debtor from transferring its rights in the collateral or makes such a transfer a default under the agreement is not effective to prevent the transfer from being effective. One type of transfer is the creation of another security interest in the collateral. UCC § 9–401(b).

b. Agreements Between the Debtor and an Account Debtor or an Obligor on a Promissory Note

A term in an account, chattel paper (other than a lease), a general intangible or a promissory note that requires that the obligor on that right to payment consent to the debtor granting a security interest in the right to payment or performance or that purports to prevent the creation of a security interest in that right to payment or performance is not effective to prevent the attachment of the security interest that the debtor grants to the secured party. UCC § 9–406(d), 9–408(a). This rule may be subject to other law to the extent that the other law establishes a different rule for an obligor on an account, chattel paper, or payment intangible who incurred that obligation primarily for family, personal or household purposes. UCC § 9–406(h).

c. Term in a Lease Agreement

A term in a lease that prohibits the creation of a security interest in either party's rights under the lease or requires the consent of one party to the lease contract to the creation of the security interest in the other party's rights under the lease is not effective to prevent attachment of the security interest to the debtor's rights under the lease or the debtor's residual rights in the leased property. UCC § 9–407(a).

d. Term in a Letter of Credit

A term in the letter of credit that purports to prohibit or to require the consent of the issuer, applicant, or nominated person to the creation of a security interest in a letter-of-credit right is ineffective to prevent attachment of a security interest to the letter-of-credit right. UCC § 9–409(a).

2. Legal Rules Prohibiting Assignment of Personal Property

If a legal rule prohibits or conditions assignment of the debtor's rights in accounts, chattel paper (including a lease), promissory notes, or general intangibles, that legal rule is not effective to prevent attachment of a security interest in the debtor's rights in those obligations. UCC §§ 9–406(f), 9–408(c). This rule may be subject to other law to the extent that the other law establishes a different rule for an obligor on an account chattel paper, or payment intangible who incurred that obligation primarily for family, personal or household purposes. UCC § 9–406(h). If legal rules, customs, or practices concerning letters of credit prohibit or condition the assignment of a letter-of-credit right on the consent of the issuer, applicant, or nominated person, those rules, customs and practices are ineffective to prevent attachment of a security interest in those letter-of-credit rights. UCC § 9–409(a).

H. OBLIGATIONS OF SECURED PARTY REGARDING COLLATERAL

1. Secured Party in Possession of Collateral

The secured party has the obligation to take reasonable care of the collateral in its possession. UCC § 9–207(a). A secured party in possession of collateral (i) may charge reasonable expenses of taking care of the collateral to the debtor and secure those expenses with the collateral, (ii) has the obligation to keep the collateral identified, but may commingle fungible collateral, (iii) may use or operate the collateral in order to preserve the collateral and its value or as permitted by court order (or in a nonconsumer transaction, as agreed with the debtor), (iv) may hold any proceeds, other than money or funds, received from the collateral as additional security, (v) must apply any proceeds that are money or funds to reduce the secured obligation or remit those proceeds to the debtor, and (vii) may create a security interest in the collateral. If the insurance coverage for the collateral is inadequate, the debtor has the risk of loss from accidental loss or damage to the collateral. UCC § 9–207(b), (c). If the secured party is a buyer of accounts, chattel paper, payment intangibles, or promissory notes or if the secured party is a consignor, these obligations do not apply with one exception. If the secured party is entitled to recourse against the debtor or a secondary obligor on account of uncollected collateral, the secured party must take reasonable care of collateral in its possession. UCC § 9–207(d).

2. Secured Party in Control of Collateral

A secured party that is in control of an electronic document of title, a deposit account, electronic chattel paper, investment property, or a letter-of-credit right has several rights and obligations. A secured party (i) may hold any proceeds, other than money or funds, received from the collateral as additional security, (ii) shall apply any proceeds that are money or funds to reduce the secured obligation or remit those proceeds to the debtor, and (iii) may create a security interest in the collateral. UCC § 9–207. These provisions do not apply if the secured party is a buyer of accounts, chattel paper, payment intangibles, or promissory notes or if the secured party is a consignor. UCC § 9–207(d). If there is no obligation outstanding or any commitment to give value, the secured party must take a action within ten days of receiving an authenticated demand from the debtor to release the rights the secured party has obtained by virtue of control of the debtor's asset. UCC § 9–208.

3. Secured Party That Has Notified Account Debtor of Its Interest in Accounts, Chattel Paper, or Payment Intangibles

If a transaction is not a sale of an account, chattel paper or payment intangible, there is no outstanding secured obligation or any commitment to give value and the secured party has notified an account debtor of the assignment of the account, chattel paper, or payment intangible to the secured party, the secured party has an obligation to send an authenticated notice to the account debtor that it has no obligation to the secured party. That notice must be sent within 10 days after the debtor makes an authenticated demand on the secured party to release the account debtor. UCC § 9–209.

4. Debtor's Request for Statements of Collateral and for an Accounting of the Secured Obligation

In transactions other than consignments, and sales of accounts, chattel paper, payment intangibles, or promissory notes, the secured party has an obligation to respond to the debtor's requests for an accounting of the obligations remaining unpaid and a list of collateral subject to the security interest. The secured party must respond within 14 days after receiving the debtor's authenticated request. UCC § 9–210(a), (b).

I. EFFECT OF DEBTOR'S BANKRUPTCY ON ATTACHMENT OF SECURITY INTEREST AND AGRICULTURAL LIEN

1. Automatic Stay

The automatic stay prevents the secured party from taking any action to create a security interest or agricultural lien in the property of the estate or in the debtor's property. 11 U.S.C. § 362.

2. Collateral Part of Bankruptcy Estate

If the security interest or agricultural lien has attached prior to the filing of the bankruptcy petition, that attachment does not prevent the collateral itself from becoming part of the bankruptcy estate. 11 U.S.C. § 541.

3. Effect on Security Interest in After-Acquired Property Including Proceeds

If the debtor acquires property after the filing of the bankruptcy petition to which the secured party's security interest would attach under an after-acquired property clause or the rule allowing for automatic attachment of the security interest in proceeds, the security interest will not attach to the after-acquired property that is not proceeds of collateral that was subject to the security interest. 11 U.S.C. § 552.

4. Debtor Use, Sale, or Lease of Collateral

The debtor in possession or the trustee may use, sell, or lease collateral that is part of the bankruptcy estate in the ordinary course of the debtor's business without the need for court approval. Court approval is required for the use, sale or lease of collateral that is part of the bankruptcy estate if that use, sale, or lease is not in the ordinary course of the debtor's business or the collateral is cash collateral. 11 U.S.C. § 363(b), (c). Cash collateral refers to collateral such as cash, negotiable instruments, documents of title, deposit accounts, or cash equivalents. 11 U.S.C. § 363(a).

5. Adequate Protection

A secured party with a security interest or agricultural lien in the collateral may request that the court order the debtor to adequately protect the value of the secured party's interest in the collateral. 11 U.S.C. § 363(e), 362(d). The value of the security interest or agricultural lien is a secured claim in the debtor's bankruptcy. 11 U.S.C. § 506. Measures employed to protect against decreases in value of the secured claim include granting replacement liens on other collateral, requiring periodic payments to the secured party, obtaining insurance on the collateral, or prohibiting use of the collateral. 11 U.S.C. § 361.

6. Right to Post-Petition Interest as Part of a Secured Claim

If the value of the collateral that is subject to the secured party's security interest or agricultural lien is more than the amount of the obligation owed, the post-petition interest that accrues on the obligation is added to the amount of the secured claim until the value of the collateral is exhausted. 11 U.S.C. § 506.

7. Future Advances

Even if the security agreement contains a future advances clause, if the secured party advances value to the debtor after the debtor files bankruptcy, that new value will be unsecured unless the bankruptcy court approves the advance on a secured basis. 11 U.S.C. § 364.

■ IV.   PERFECTION OF A SECURITY INTEREST OR AGRICULTURAL LIEN

A. PERFECTION OVERVIEW

Perfection of a security interest or agricultural lien requires that the security interest or agricultural lien has attached (as discussed in Chapter III) and that a required perfection method has been completed. UCC § 9–308(a), (b).

1. Types of Perfection Methods

Article 9 provides for five different perfection methods: filing a financing statement, taking possession of collateral, taking control of collateral, merely attaching a security interest to the collateral (automatic perfection), or complying with other law.

2. Perfection Methods and Collateral Types

Whether one or more of the five types of perfection methods is effective to perfect a security interest depends upon the type of collateral that is the subject of the security interest.

3. Continuous Perfection

If the security interest or agricultural lien in the collateral is perfected by one method allowed under Article 9 and subsequently perfected by another allowed method, and there is no time in which the security interest or agricultural lien was unperfected, the security interest or agricultural lien is continuously perfected. UCC § 9–308(c).

4. Choice of Law Issues in Determining Compliance With a Perfection Method

Because Article 9 is a matter of state law, to the extent action, such as filing a financing statement, must be accomplished in a particular state in order to perfect the security interest or agricultural lien, the choice of law issue is critical.

5. Post-Initial Perfection Events that May "Unperfect" a Security Interest or Agricultural Lien

Even though a secured party has properly perfected its security interest or agricultural lien in the collateral, events that take place subsequent to that initial perfection may have the effect of "unperfecting" the security interest or agricultural lien.

B. FILING A FINANCING STATEMENT AS A PERFECTION METHOD

Unless there is an exception provided in Article 9, filing a financing statement is the only acceptable method for perfecting a security interest.

1. Agricultural Liens

As to an agricultural lien, filing a financing statement is the only method of perfection. UCC § 9–310(a).

2. Timing of Filing a Financing Statement

A financing statement may be filed before the security interest attaches and will be effective if the filing is authorized. A financing statement to perfect an agricultural lien is not authorized to be filed until the agricultural lien actually exists. UCC §§ 9–510, 9–509.

3. Collateral Types Where Filing a Financing Statement Is Not an Allowed Perfection Step

A filed financing statement is not sufficient to perfect a security interest in deposit accounts, money, or letter-of-credit rights unless the deposit accounts, money, or letter-of-credit rights are identifiable proceeds of other collateral and a security interest in the original collateral was perfected. In addition, if a letter-of-credit right is a supporting obligation to a right to payment as to which an effective financing statement has been filed to perfect a security interest in the original right to payment, the security interest will be perfected in the letter-of-credit right as a supporting obligation based upon the filing as to the original right to payment. UCC §§ 9–312, 9–315, 9–308(d). A filed financing statement under Article 9 is not sufficient to perfect a security interest in collateral if (i) a federal statute, treaty, or regulation provides a method for a secured party to obtain priority over the rights of a lien creditor and that method preempts Article 9, (ii) a certificate of title law of a state provides that security interests are to be noted on the certificate of title as a condition to or result of perfection, or (iii) state law provides for a central filing system other than Article 9 for a particular type of collateral. UCC §§ 9–311(a), 9–102(a)(10). Even if a motorized vehicle is subject to a certificate of title law, however, during any period where that motorized vehicle is held as inventory for sale or lease, compliance with the certificate of title law is not the applicable perfection step for perfecting a security interest in that vehicle. UCC § 9–311(d).

4. The Requirements of the Financing Statement

The financing statement is a record, in either electronic or paper form, filed in the filing office designated in UCC § 9–501.

a. Sufficiency to Perfect as Opposed to Requirement of Additional Information to Prevent Rejection of the Record

That record must contain certain information in order to be sufficient as the perfection method. UCC § 9–502. Other information is included in the record, some of which, if not included, provides a basis for the filing office to reject the record. UCC § 9–516.

b. Philosophy of Notice Filing

The Article 9 filing system is a system for providing notice of possible interests in the debtor's personal property but does not provide all of the information that a searcher will need to determine the state of interests in the debtor's personal property.

c. Requirements for Sufficiency of the Financing Statement as a Method Of Perfection

To be sufficient to perfect a security interest or agricultural lien, the financing statement must not only be appropriate for the type of collateral at stake, the financing statement must also provide for three items of information: (i) the debtor's name; (ii) the secured party's name or the name of the secured party's representative; and (iii) an indication of the collateral. UCC § 9–502(a).

(1) Real Estate Related Collateral

If the collateral is as-extracted collateral, timber to be cut, or fixtures where a fixture financing statement is to be filed, the financing statement must also provide (i) an indication that the type of collateral is as-extracted collateral, timber to be cut, or fixtures, (ii) an indication that the statement is to be filed in the real estate records, (iii) a real property description for the real estate that is related to the as-extracted collateral, timber to be cut, or fixtures, and (iv) the name of the record owner of the real estate if the debtor does not have an interest in the real estate. UCC § 9–502(b). A mortgage may satisfy these requirements as to as-extracted collateral, timber to be cut, and fixtures related to the real estate that is subject to the mortgage as long as the mortgage indicates the goods or accounts it covers and the mortgage is properly recorded in the real estate records. UCC § 9–502(c).

(2) The Debtor's Name

The financing statement must provide the debtor's name. Whether the debtor's name is correct on the financing statement depends upon whether the name meets the standard set forth in UCC § 9–503. The entity listed on the financing statement as the debtor must be the person that has a property interest in the collateral covered in the financing statement. UCC § 9–102(a)(28) (definition of debtor). The correct name of the debtor depends upon what type of entity the debtor is: a registered organization, a nonregistered organization, a decedent, a trust, or an individual.

(a) Registered Organization

For a registered organization, UCC § 9–102(a)(71), the financing statement must show the debtor's name as the name is stated in the debtor's most recently filed, issued, or enacted public organic record which purports to state, amend or restate the debtor's name. UCC § 9–503(a)(1).

(b) Nonregistered Organization

If the debtor is an organization, UCC § 9–102(a)(25), (27), but is not a registered organization, the correct name of the debtor is the "organizational name" of the debtor. UCC §§ 9–503(a)(6) (Alt. A), 9–503(a)(5) (Alt. B). If the debtor does not have an "organizational name," the financing statement must provide the names of the partners, members, associates or persons that comprise the debtor. UCC §§ 9–503(a)(6) (Alt. A), 9–503(a)(5) (Alt. B). These names must meet the standard for names of that type as set forth in UCC § 9–503.

(c) Decedent's Estate

If collateral is being administered by a decedent's personal representative, the correct name of the debtor on the financing statement is the name of the decedent. UCC § 9–503(a)(2). The name of the decedent is the name indicated on the order appointing the personal representative. UCC § 9–503(f). The financing statement must also indicate that a personal representative is administering the decedent's assets. UCC § 9–503(a)(2).

(d) Trust

If collateral is held in a trust that is a registered organization, then the rules regarding the name of a registered organization as discussed *supra* will control. UCC § 9–503(a)(1). If the trust is not a registered organization, the correct name of the debtor on the financing statement is the name of the trust in its organic record. If the trust does not have a name specified in the organic record, the name of the settlor or testator of the trust is the debtor's name. If the debtor's name is the name of the settler or testator, the financing statement must also provide any information necessary to distinguish the debtor from other trusts of the same settlor or testator. In any case in which the trust is not a registered organization, the financing statement must also indicate that the collateral is held in a trust. UCC § 9–503(a)(3).

(e) Individual

If the debtor is an individual, the individual's name must be provided on the financing statement. Article 9 provides the states two alternatives (Alternative A or Alternative B) for enactment regarding what constitutes an individual debtor's name for purpose of the financing statement. UCC § 9–503(a)(4).

(i) Alternative A

If the state in which the financing statement must be filed to perfect as to the collateral (see *infra* Section G regarding choice of law) chose Alternative A, has issued a driver's license to the debtor, and that license is unexpired, the debtor's name is the name on the license. If the state has not issued a driver's license to the debtor, or the issued license is expired, the debtor's name is either the debtor's "individual name" or the debtor's surname and first personal name.

(ii) Alternative B

If the state in which the financing statement must be filed to perfect as to the collateral (see *infra* Section G regarding choice of law) choose Alternative B, a secured party may use any one of three alternatives as the debtor's name: the "individual name"; the surname and first personal name; or the name indicated on the driver's license issued by that state and that is not expired.

(iii) Either Alternative A or B

If the state has issued more than one license, then the most recently issued license is the one to use. UCC § 9–503(g). For a mortgage that is filed for fixtures, as-extracted collateral, or timber to be cut, the name of a debtor that is an individual must be either the "individual name" of the debtor, or the surname and first personal name of the debtor. This is an exception to the requirements stated in UCC § 9–503(a)(4) in either an Alternative A or B state. UCC § 9–502(c)(3)(B).

(f) Trade Names

Trade names are not part of the debtor's correct name. UCC § 9–503(b)(1). A financing statement that lists only the debtor's trade name as the name of the debtor has not sufficiently provided the name of the debtor. UCC § 9–503(c).

(g) Multiple Debtors

A financing statement may provide more than one debtor on the financing statement. UCC § 9–503(e).

(h) Seriously Misleading Financing Statements Due to Errors in the Debtor's Name

If a financing statement contains errors in the debtor's name so that it is seriously misleading, the financing statement is insufficient to perfect the security interest or agricultural lien. UCC § 9–506(a). A financing statement that does not provide the debtor's correct name as provided in UCC § 9–503(a) is per se seriously misleading. UCC § 9–506(b). That per se rule is subject to one exception. If a search of the records using the filing office's standard search logic under the debtor's correct name turns up the financing statement with the incorrect name on it, that financing statement with the incorrect name is deemed to not be seriously misleading and thus deemed to be sufficient to perfect, providing the secured party's name and the collateral indication is sufficient under UCC § 9–503. UCC § 9–506(c). The seriously misleading test also applies to the additional information that is required in UCC § 9–503(a)(2) regarding collateral being administered by a personal representative and in UCC § 9–503(a)(3) regarding collateral held in a trust that is not a registered organization. UCC § 9–506, cmt. 2.

(3) The Secured Party's Name

The financing statement must also provide the name of the secured party or a representative of the secured party. UCC § 9–502(a)(2). If the financing statement names a representative of the secured party, failure to indicate the representative status of that person does not render the financing statement insufficient to perfect. UCC § 9–503(d). The financing statement may provide more than one secured party's name. UCC § 9–503(e). Comment 2 to UCC § 9–506 indicates that "an error in the name of the secured party or its representative will not be seriously misleading."

(4) The Indication of Collateral

The financing statement must also contain an indication of the collateral. UCC § 9–502(a)(3). To properly indicate the collateral, the financing statement must meet one of two tests. Either it must follow the rules for collateral description in UCC § 9–108 discussed in Chapter III, or it must indicate that the financing statement covers "all assets" or "all personal property." UCC § 9–504. A financing statement may be seriously misleading if there are errors in the collateral indication. UCC § 9–506(a).

(5) Future Advances and After-Acquired Property Clauses

A financing statement is sufficient to perfect even if it does not indicate that the collateral secures future advances or that the financing statement covers after-acquired collateral. UCC § 9–502, cmt. 2.

d. Other Information Required in the Financing Statement

A filing office must refuse to accept a financing statement if it does not have certain types of information or for other listed reasons specified in UCC § 9–516(b) but only for those specified reasons. UCC §§ 9–516(b), 9–520(a). Accurate information of the type listed in UCC § 9–516(b) is not required in order for a financing statement to be sufficient to perfect. If the filing office accepts the financing statement, even if the filing office should have refused the financing statement, the sufficiency of the financing statement for purposes of perfection is tested under UCC § 9–502 as described above, not UCC § 9–516(b). UCC § 9–520(c). A filing office may refuse to accept a filing if any of the following occurs: (i) the method or manner of communication of the filing is not allowed; (ii) the applicable fee is not tendered; (iii) the filing office is not able to index the record because the debtor's name is not provided on an initial financing statement, the filing of an amendment or correction statement does not reference the initial financing statement or the initial financing statement has lapsed, an individual debtor's surname is not provided, or a real estate related filing does not provide an adequate real estate description; (iv) the record does not provide a secured party's mailing address; (v) the record does not provide the debtor's mailing address; (vi) the record does not indicate that the debtor is an individual or organization; (vii) the record is an assignment of an initial financing statement and does not indicate the name and mailing address of the assignee; and (viii) the record is a continuation statement that is not filed during the time period permitted for continuation statements. If the filing office cannot read or decipher the information, the information is considered not provided. UCC § 9–516(c)(1). If the filing office refuses to accept a financing statement for a reason other than as allowed under UCC § 9–516(b), the filing is still considered effective except as to a purchaser of the collateral that gives value in reasonable reliance upon the absence of the financing statement from the filing office records. UCC § 9–516(d).

5. Authority to File

In order for a financing statement to be effective to perfect a security interest or agricultural lien, the secured party must have authority to file the financing statement. UCC §§ 9–510(a), 9–509.

a. To Perfect a Security Interest

In order to file an effective initial financing statement regarding a security interest, the debtor must authorize the filing in an authenticated record. UCC § 9–509(a)(1). The debtor's authentication of the security agreement automatically authorizes the secured party to file a financing statement covering the collateral described in the security agreement and any collateral that is identifiable proceeds of that original collateral. UCC § 9–509(b). The debtor also automatically authorizes the filing of a financing statement as to collateral the debtor acquires that is subject to a security interest. UCC § 9–509(c).

b. To Perfect an Agricultural Lien

In order to file an effective initial financing statement covering farm products subject to an agricultural lien, the secured party must actually have an agricultural lien in the farm products at the time of the filing and the financing statement may cover only those farm products that are subject to the agricultural lien. UCC § 9–509(a)(2).

c. Ratification

If the secured party does not have authority to file a financing statement at the time it filed the statement, subsequent acts of the debtor may ratify the secured party's act of filing the financing statement, rendering it an authorized filing.

6. The Process of Filing

Each filing office will determine whether it takes electronic filings and the form of those filings. If the filing office takes paper financing statements, it must accept the standard form set forth in UCC § 9–521.

a. Determining the Correct Filing Office

Once it is determined which state to file in (Section G, *infra*), most filings will be within one office within a state as designated in that state's UCC § 9–501. A secured party will file a financing statement in that central designated state office for all collateral except for three types of real estate related collateral. UCC § 9–501(a)(2). When the collateral is fixtures and the secured party files a fixture financing statement as set forth in UCC § 9–502(b), as-extracted collateral, or timber to be cut, the correct office in which to file the financing statement is the office where a real estate mortgage would be recorded for the real estate that is described in the financing statement. UCC § 9–501(a)(1). If a secured party wants to perfect in fixtures as goods and not file a fixture financing statement in the real estate recording office, the correct office in which to file the financing statement is the central filing office in that state. UCC § 9–501(a)(2). To perfect a security interest in the collateral of a transmitting utility, the financing statement will be filed in the state's central filing office. UCC §§ 9–501, 9–102(a)(81).

b. What Constitutes Filing

Tender of the financing statement and applicable fee to the filing office constitutes filing of the financing statement. UCC § 9–516(a). The financing statement is filed unless the filing office rightfully rejects the financing statement for the reasons stated in UCC § 9–516(b). UCC § 9–516(d).

c. Rejection of a Financing Statement

The filing office may rightfully reject a financing statement only for the reasons stated in UCC § 9–516(b). If the filing office rejects the financing statement, the filing office must notify the secured party that the financing statement has been rejected, the reasons for the rejection, and the date and time the financing statement would have been filed if not rejected. UCC § 9–520(b). Whether a financing statement fulfills the requirements of UCC § 9–516(b) is evaluated for each debtor. If the information required by UCC § 9–516(b) is given for one debtor but not another, the filing office must accept the financing statement for the debtor whose information is complete and reject it for the debtor whose information is not complete. UCC § 9–520(d).

7. Time Period That a Filed Financing Statement is Effective

A filed financing statement that is sufficient under UCC § 9–502 as to the type of collateral as to which a filed financing statement is a sufficient perfection method is generally effective for five years from the date of filing. UCC § 9–515(a). If an initial financing statement is filed with respect to a public-finance transaction, the financing statement is effective for a period of 30 years from the date of filing if the financing statement indicates it is filed in connection with a public-finance transaction. UCC § 9–515(b). If an initial financing statement is filed with respect to a manufactured-home transaction, the financing statement is effective for a period of 30 years from the date of filing if the financing statement indicates it is filed in connection with a manufactured-home transaction. UCC § 9–515(b). If the debtor is a transmitting utility, an initial filed financing statement that indicates that the debtor is a transmitting utility is effective until the financing statement is terminated through another filing. UCC § 9–515(f). If a creditor files a mortgage that qualifies as a fixture financing statement, the mortgage is effective as a fixture financing statement until the mortgage is released or terminated as to the real property it covers. UCC § 9–515(g).

8. Lapse and Continuation of Period of Effectiveness of a Financing Statement

A financing statement lapses at the end of the 5-year or 30-year term, as applicable. UCC § 9–515(c). Upon lapse, the financing statement is ineffective to perfect a security interest or agricultural lien rendering the security interest or agricultural lien unperfected. The lapsed financing statement is also deemed ineffective to perfect a security interest or agricultural lien as against a person that purchased the collateral for value prior to its lapse. UCC § 9–515(c). In order to continue the effectiveness of the financing statement beyond the 5-year or 30-year term, as applicable, a secured party must file a continuation statement within the last six months of either the 5-year or 30-year time period, as applicable. UCC § 9–515(d). A continuation statement filed outside that six-month window is ineffective to continue the effectiveness of the financing statement. UCC § 9–510(c). A secured party has authority to file a continuation statement in the same circumstances in which the secured party has authority to file the initial financing statement. UCC § 9–509(a) and (b). If the continuation statement is timely filed, it continues the effectiveness of the financing statement for 5 years from the date the initial financing statement that was continued would have otherwise lapsed. UCC § 9–515(e). A secured party may file successive continuation statements to continue the effectiveness of a financing statement indefinitely as long as the secured party has the authority to file the continuation statements.

9. Duties of Filing Officers

The filing officer has an obligation to accept a financing statement that complies with the requirements of UCC § 9–516(b). UCC § 9–520(a). The filing office also has the duty to accept the standard form if the filing office accepts paper forms. UCC § 9–521.

a. Acknowledge Filings

The filing office must provide an acknowledgment of the filing that contains the unique filing number and the date and time of the filing. UCC § 9–523.

b. Assign a Unique Number to the Initial Financing Statement

The filing office must assign a unique number to the initial financing statement, and that unique number is used for all subsequent filings. UCC § 9–519.

c. Maintain a Public Record of Financing Statements Filed

The filing office must maintain a record showing the financing statements filed, the number assigned to the financing statements, and the date and time the financing statements were filed. The financing statements must be available for public inspection, UCC § 9–519(a), and must be offered for sale or license to the public on a regular basis, UCC § 9–523(f). The filing office must maintain a record of the information in a financing statement for at least one year after the lapse of the effectiveness of the financing statement. UCC § 9–522(a).

d. Index the Financing Statements by the Debtor's Name

The filing office must index all financing statements and related records by the debtor's name. UCC § 9–519(c). The filing office may not remove the debtor's name from the index until after one year after the financing statement lapses. UCC § 9–519(g). If the collateral is as-extracted collateral, timber to be cut, or the secured party has filed a fixture financing statement, the filing must also be indexed under the name of the record owner of the real estate. If the real estate record system allows for it, the real estate related filing must also be indexed under the secured party's name as if the secured party was the mortgagee, and under the description of the real estate. UCC § 9–519(d), (e). The filing office's failure to correctly index a financing statement does not render the financing statement insufficient to perfect the security interest or agricultural lien. UCC § 9–517.

e. Allow for Search and Retrieval of Financing Statements

The filing office must maintain the capability of retrieving the financing statement and all associated records by the debtor's name and by the unique filing number. UCC § 9–519(f). The filing office must respond to a search request for all financing statements filed as to a specific debtor within two business days of the filing office receiving the request. UCC § 9–523(e). The filing office search response must consist of the information from all of the financing statements that identify the specific debtor as a debtor on the financing statement and the date and time that each financing statement was filed. The filing office must indicate a date and time at which the records were on file, but not more than 3 days before the search request. UCC § 9–523(c).

f. Time for Filing and Indexing

The filing office has to file and index all financing statements no later than two business days after it receives the financing statements. UCC § 9–519(h).

e. Delay

The filing office will be excused from compliance with the time deadlines set forth in the statute if it encounters circumstances beyond its control, such as computer failure or war, if the filing office exercises reasonable diligence under the circumstances. UCC § 9–524.

10. Amendments of an Initial Financing Statement

A financing statement may be amended. Amendments include continuation statements and filings that add or delete collateral, add or delete a debtor, or add or delete a secured party. An amendment may also terminate the effectiveness of a financing statement. The amendment must identify the initial financing statement by its file number in order to relate the two filings together. UCC § 9–512(a). If the amendment does not do so, the amendment is treated as an initial financing statement. UCC § 9–516(c)(2).

a. Additions of Collateral or Debtor

To be effective, amendments that add collateral or debtors must be authorized by the applicable debtor. UCC §§ 9–510(a), 9–509.

b. Authority of Secured Party

As to all amendments, other than the ones that add collateral or a debtor, or a termination statement in a particular circumstance discussed *infra*, the secured party of record must authorize the filing. UCC § 9–509(d).

c. Assignments to a New Secured Party of Record

An amendment of an initial financing statement may reflect an assignment of the secured party's authority to amend an initial financing statement by identifying an assignee and providing the mailing address of the assignee. UCC § 9–514.

d. Time of Effectiveness of Amendments

Authorized amendments that add a debtor or collateral are effective as to that added debtor or collateral only from the time the amendment is filed. UCC § 9–512(c), (d). Amendments, other than continuation statements that are appropriately filed, do not extend the time period of effectiveness of the initial financing statement. UCC § 9–512(b). Amendments filed by one secured party of record do not affect the rights of another secured party of record. UCC § 9–510(b).

e. Deletion of All Debtors and Secured Parties

Amendments that purport to delete all debtors or all secured parties of record without providing for at least one remaining debtor and one remaining secured party of record are ineffective. UCC § 9–512(e).

f. Termination Statements

A termination statement is an amendment of an initial financing statement that identifies the initial financing statement and indicates that the effectiveness of the initial financing statement is terminated. UCC § 9–102(a)(79).

(1) Requirement to File Termination Statement if Collateral is Consumer Goods

If the financing statement covers consumer goods as collateral and there is no obligation owed or any commitment to give value or if the debtor did not authorize the filing of the initial financing statement, the secured party of record must file a termination statement within the earlier of one month after there is no outstanding obligation or any commitment to give value or within 20 days after the secured party receives an authenticated demand for a termination statement from the debtor. UCC § 9–513(a) and (b). If the secured party of record has assigned its right to payment of the obligation to another secured party, the secured party that is not of record has the obligation to cause the secured party of record to file the termination statement. UCC § 9–513(a).

(2) Requirement to File Termination Statement if Collateral Other Than Consumer Goods

If the collateral indicated in the financing statement is not consumer goods, the secured party of record must file a termination statement within 20 days after the debtor makes an authenticated demand for termination if there is no outstanding obligation or commitment to give value or if the debtor did not authorize the filing of the initial financing statement. This requirement to file a termination statement does not apply if the collateral is accounts or chattel paper that have been sold (unless the account debtor has discharged its obligation on the collateral) or goods that are subject to a consignment. UCC § 9–513(c).

(3) Authority to File

Generally, a secured party of record must authorize an amendment that is a termination statement. If the secured party of record does not file a termination statement when required as described above, the debtor may authorize the filing of a termination statement as long as that statement indicates that the debtor has authorized the filing. UCC § 9–509(d)(2).

(4) Effect of Termination Statement

A termination statement that is appropriately filed terminates the effectiveness of the initial financing statement. UCC § 9–513(d).

11. Information Statements

Article 9 allows a filing called an information statement that identifies the initial financing statement and states the basis for the person's belief that the record is inaccurate or wrongfully filed. The information statement does not affect the effectiveness of the initial financing statement or any amendments to that initial financing statement. UCC § 9–518.

C. POSSESSION OF COLLATERAL AS A PERFECTION METHOD

For some types of collateral, a security interest may be perfected by possession of the collateral. UCC § 9–310(b)(6).

1. Collateral Types

To perfect a security interest by possession, the collateral must be tangible negotiable documents of title, goods, instruments, money, or tangible chattel paper. UCC § 9–313(a). If the collateral is money, possession is the only method of perfecting a security interest in that collateral unless the money is identifiable proceeds of original collateral in which the secured party had a perfected security interest. UCC § 9–312(b)(3). If the collateral is a good that is covered by a certificate of title law, the secured party ordinarily cannot perfect its security interest in that good by taking possession of the good, except in one circumstance. UCC § 9–313(b).

2. Possession Defined

The concept of possession for perfection is the same as the concept of possession for purposes of attachment as discussed in Chapter III, Section B.3. An agent of the secured party, other than the debtor, may have possession of the collateral on behalf of the secured party. If the collateral is the type of collateral in which a security interest may be perfected by possession and is not a certificated security and not goods covered by a document of title, the secured party may obtain an authenticated record from the third party (other than the debtor, the secured party, an agent of the secured party, or a lessee of goods from the debtor) that has possession of the collateral that the third party holds the collateral for the benefit of the secured party. UCC § 9–313(c). A secured party is also deemed to have possession if it delivers the collateral to a third party in the ordinary course of the secured party's business with a notice to the third party that the third party is holding possession of the collateral for the secured party's benefit or the third party has to redeliver the collateral to the secured party. UCC § 9–313(h).

3. Effectiveness of Possession as a Perfection Method

As to the collateral types where possession is a potentially effective perfection method, possession is effective as a perfection method only as long as the secured party, its agent, or the third party has possession of the collateral. UCC § 9–313(d).

4. Delivery of a Certificated Security

A secured party may perfect its security interest in a certificated security by taking delivery of the certificated security. UCC §§ 9–310(b)(7), 9–313(a). Delivery is defined in UCC 8–301. See Chapter III, Section B.4.

5. Possession by a Third Party of Goods Covered by a Document of Title

If the goods are covered by a negotiable document of title, the secured party should perfect its security interest in the goods by perfecting a security interest in the negotiable document of title. UCC § 9–312(c). Negotiable documents of title may be either tangible (paper) or electronic. UCC § 1–201(b)(16). That perfection in the negotiable tangible document of title may be by taking possession of the document of title. UCC § 9–313(a). If the goods are in possession of a bailee and covered by nonnegotiable documents of title, the secured party may perfect its security interest in the goods in one of three ways. The secured party may (i) obtain a document of title issued to the secured party, (ii) send a notice to the bailee of the secured party's interest which the bailee receives, or (iii) file a financing statement as to the goods. If the secured party sends a notice to the bailee, the bailee does not need to acknowledge the secured party's interest in order for the secured party's security interest in the goods covered by the nonnegotiable document to be perfected. UCC § 9–312(d).

6. Secured Party's Obligations While in Possession

While a secured party has possession of collateral in which it has a security interest in order to perfect its security interest, the secured party has the same obligations as to the collateral that it has if it has possession of the collateral in order to attach the security interest. See Chapter III, Section H.

D. CONTROL OF COLLATERAL AS A PERFECTION METHOD

A secured party may perfect its security interest in deposit accounts, electronic chattel paper, electronic documents of title, investment property, and letter-of-credit rights through control of the collateral. UCC §§ 9–310(b)(8), 9–314(a).

1. Relationship to Other Perfection Methods

As to electronic chattel paper, electronic documents of title, and investment property, the secured party may also perfect its security interest by filing an effective financing statement. As to deposit accounts, control is the exclusive method of perfection unless the deposit accounts are identifiable proceeds of other collateral in which the secured party had a perfected security interest. UCC § 9–312(b)(1). As to letter-of-credit rights, control is the exclusive method of perfection unless the letter-of-credit rights are identifiable proceeds of other collateral in which the secured party has a perfected security interest or the letter-of-credit rights are a supporting obligation of a right to payment that the secured party has a perfected security interest in. UCC § 9–312(b)(2).

2. Control Defined

Control for these types of collateral for perfection purposes is the same as control for the purpose of establishing attachment of a security interest as discussed in Chapter III, Section B.5.

3. Effect of Control on Perfection

As to deposit accounts, electronic chattel paper, electronic documents of title, and letter-of-credit rights, a secured party is perfected in that type of collateral by control from the time the secured party obtains control until the secured party no longer has control. UCC § 9–314(b). As to investment property, a secured party is perfected by control from the time the secured party obtains control until the secured party does not have control and one of three things is true: (i) if the collateral is a certificated security, the debtor acquires possession of the certificate; (ii) if the collateral is an uncertificated security, the debtor becomes the registered owner; or (iii) if the collateral is a securities entitlement, the debtor becomes the entitlement holder. UCC § 9–314(c).

4. Obligations While in Control

While a secured party has control of collateral in which it has a security interest for perfection purposes, the secured party has the same obligations as to the collateral that it has if it has control of the collateral in order to attach the security interest as discussed in Chapter III, Section H.

E. COMPLIANCE WITH OTHER LAW AS A METHOD OF PERFECTION

Article 9 defers to other law to control perfection of a security interest in three situations: when a federal law preempts the Article 9 filing system, when a state certificate of title law provides for security interests to be noted on the certificate of title as a condition or result of perfection, and when a state law provides for a central filing statute regarding particular types of collateral. UCC §§ 9–310(b)(3), 9–311. Compliance with the non-Article 9 law is treated as the equivalent of filing the Article 9 financing statement. When goods covered by a certificate of title law are held for sale or lease by someone in the business of selling goods of that kind, thus the collateral is the debtor's inventory, the proper method of perfection in that inventory is not through notation of the security interest on the certificates of title, but rather through using one of the other methods of perfection permitted for goods that are inventory, such as filing an effective financing statement. UCC § 9–311(d).

F. AUTOMATIC PERFECTION

In some circumstances, the security interest is automatically perfected upon attachment of the security interest to the collateral.

1. Purchase Money Security Interest in Consumer Goods Not Covered by a Certificate of Title

A purchase money security interest in consumer goods is automatically perfected upon attachment as long as the consumer goods are not subject to a certificate of title law that requires perfection of a security interest to be accomplished through notation of the security interest on the certificate of title. UCC §§ 9–310(b)(2), 9–309(1).

2. Insignificant Assignments of Accounts and Payment Intangibles

The security interest created by an assignment of accounts or payment intangibles that does not effect a transfer to the same assignee of a significant part of the assignor's outstanding accounts or payment intangibles, either standing alone or in conjunction with other assignments, is automatically perfected upon attachment without the need to file a financing statement. UCC §§ 9–310(b)(2), 9–309(2).

3. Sales of Payment Intangibles and Promissory Notes

A security interest created by a sale of a payment intangible or a sale of a promissory note, UCC § 9–109(a)(3), is automatically perfected upon attachment of the security interest. UCC§§ 9–310(b)(2), 9–309(3), (4).

4. Assignment of Health-Care-Insurance Receivable to the Health Care Provider

The security interest created by the assignment of the insured's rights under the health care insurance policy to the health care provider is automatically perfected. UCC §§ 9–310(b)(2), 9–309(5).

5. Security Interests Arising Under Other UCC Articles

Article 9 governs the manner of perfection of those security interests created under the other UCC articles.

a. Security Interests Arising Under Articles 2 and 2A

A seller's security interest that arises through retention of title, UCC § 2–401, and shipment under reservation, UCC § 2–505, and a buyer's or lessee's security interest in rightfully rejected goods or goods as to which acceptance has been justifiably revoked, UCC §§ 2–711(3), 2A–508, are automatically perfected upon attachment until the debtor obtains possession of the goods. UCC §§ 9–310(b)(2), 9–309(6), 9–110.

b. Security Interest of a Collecting Bank Under Article 4

A collecting bank's security interest in items taken for collection through the banking system is automatically perfected when it is attached. UCC §§ 9–310(b)(2), 9–309(7).

c. Security Interest of Issuer or Nominated Person on a Letter of Credit Under Article 5

The letter of credit issuer's or nominated person's security interest in documents in its possession that were presented under a letter of credit is automatically perfected when it is attached if the documents are not in tangible form. If the documents are in tangible form and *are not* certificated securities, chattel paper, documents of title, instruments, or a letter of credit, the security interest of the issuer or nominated person is perfected when attached as long as the debtor does not obtain possession of the documents. UCC §§ 5–118, 9–310(b)(2), 9–309(8).

6. Security Interest Created When Delivery of a Financial Asset

If a person in the business of dealing with securities or financial assets delivers a certificated security or other financial asset that is represented by a writing to another person that is also in the business of dealing with securities or financial assets and the transferee is to pay for the delivery, the transferor has a security interest in the securities or financial assets delivered to secure the purchase price. UCC § 9–206(c), (d). That security interest is automatically perfected upon attachment. UCC §§ 9–310(b)(2), 9–309(9).

7. Security Interest in Investment Property Created by Broker or Securities Intermediary

If a broker or securities intermediary grants a security interest in investment property it holds, the security interest is automatically perfected upon attachment. UCC §§ 9–310(b)(2), 9–309(10).

8. Security Interest in Commodity Contracts or Commodity Account Created By Commodity Intermediary

If a commodity intermediary grants a security interest in commodity contracts or commodity accounts it holds, the security interest created is automatically perfected upon attachment. UCC §§ 9–310(b)(2), 9–309(11).

9. Assignments for Benefit of Creditors

An assignment for the benefit of creditors is automatically perfected when it takes place and all subsequent transfers by the assignee are also automatically perfected. UCC §§ 9–310(b)(2), 9–309(12).

10. Assignment of Beneficial Interest in Decedent's Estate

A security interest created by an assignment of a beneficial interest in a decedent's estate is automatically perfected when it is attached. UCC §§ 9–310(b)(2), 9–309(13).

11. Sale of Right to Payment From Game of Chance

An individual's sale of a right to payment arising from a game of chance authorized or run by a state by creates a security interest that is automatically perfected when it has attached. UCC §§ 9–310(b)(2), 9–309(14).

12. Perfection in One Type of Collateral Results in Perfection in Related Type of Collateral

A secured party that has perfected a security interest, using any permitted method of perfection, in a right to payment has also automatically perfected a security interest in a supporting obligation for that right to payment. UCC§ 9–308(d). A secured party that has perfected a security interest, using any permitted method of perfection, in a right to payment that is secured by a security interest, mortgage, or other lien in property that secures that right to payment has also automatically perfected its security interest in the security interest, mortgage, or other lien in property. UCC § 9–308(e). A secured party that has perfected a security interest, using any permitted method of perfection, in a securities account has automatically perfected a security interest in all security entitlements carried in the securities account. UCC § 9–308(f). A secured party that has perfected a security interest, using any permitted method of perfection, in a commodity account has automatically perfected a security interest in all commodity contracts carried in the commodity account. UCC § 9–308(g).

13. Periods of Temporary Perfection

Article 9 also allows automatic perfection of security interests for short periods of time as to certain types of collateral in defined circumstances. UCC § 9–310(b)(5). If a security interest attaches to certificated securities, negotiable documents of title, or instruments in exchange for new value under an authenticated security agreement, the security interest is automatically perfected for a period of 20 days from the time it attaches. UCC § 9–312(e). If the secured party has already perfected its security interest in either a negotiable document of title or goods that are in the possession of a bailee that has not issued a negotiable document of title covering those goods and in a manner other than filing an effective financing statement concerning the collateral, the security interest remains perfected for 20 days even if the secured party makes the document of title or goods available to the debtor for the purpose of ultimate sale or exchange or dealing with the goods in a manner preliminary to sale or exchange. UCC § 9–312(f). If the secured party has already perfected its security interest in a certificated security or an instrument through a manner other than the filing of an effective financing statement concerning that collateral, the security interest remains perfected for 20 days even if the secured party delivers the security certificate or the instrument to the debtor for the purpose of ultimate sale or exchange or for presentment, collection, enforcement, renewal or registration or transfer. UCC § 9–312(g).

G. CHOICE OF LAW RULES

1. Choice of Law Regarding Which State's Article 9 Applies

The first choice of law question is to determine which state's Article 9 controls. This question is not determined by Article 9 but rather by other choice of law principles that govern in the state where any litigation concerning the parties' transaction may be commenced. An example of a choice of law statute that a court may consult is found in UCC § 1–301.

2. Choice of Law Regarding Perfection of the Security Interest or Agricultural Lien

After the court determines which state's Article 9 controls, that state's Article 9 is consulted to determine the question of which state's law governs perfection of the security interest or agricultural lien. That state's Article 9 will contain several sections that set forth choice of law rules concerning the perfection method. UCC § 9–301 through § 9–307.

a. Perfection of an Agricultural Lien

The law of the location of the farm products will govern perfection of an agricultural lien in those farm products. UCC § 9–302.

b. Dominate Rule: Law of the Debtor's Location Governs Perfection of a Security Interest

For most types of collateral and transactions, the law of the debtor's location will govern the perfection of a security interest. UCC § 9–301(1), (2).

c. Determining the Debtor's Location

(1) Location of Registered Organization
A registered organization organized under state law is located in the state in which it is organized. UCC § 9–307(e). A registered organization organized under the law of the United States is located in the state the federal law designates as the location or in the state the registered organization designates, if the law allows the registered organization to make a designation. If these circumstances do not apply, the registered organization is located in the District of Columbia. UCC § 9–307(f).

(2) Foreign Banks
If a branch of a bank is not organized under the law of a state or the law of the United States (and thus is not a registered organization) and it has a license to do business in only one state, the branch bank is located in that state in which it is licensed. UCC § 9–307(i). When the bank is licensed to do business in more than one state, a bank that is not organized under the laws of the United States or a state (and thus not a

registered organization) is located in the state a federal law designates as the location or in the state the bank designates, if the law allows the bank to make a designation. If none of these circumstances apply, the bank is located in the District of Columbia. UCC § 9–307(f).

(3) Foreign Air Carrier

A foreign air carrier is located at the place at which it has designated its agent for purposes of service of process. UCC § 9–307(j).

(4) United States

The United States is located in the District of Columbia. UCC § 9–307(h).

(5) Location of Individual Debtors and Organizations Other Than Those Specifically Provided For

An individual debtor's location is the location of the individual's principal residence. UCC 9–307(b)(1). An organization that is the debtor, that is not a registered organization, a foreign bank, a foreign air carrier, or the United States, and that has only one place of business is located at the place of business. If such an organization has more than one place of business, it is located at its chief executive office. UCC § 9–307(b)(2), (3). The debtor's place of business is where the debtor conducts its affairs. UCC § 9–307(a). For individual debtors or organization that are not registered organizations, foreign banks, foreign air carriers, or the United States, if the law of the debtor's location does not have a filing or public notice system in place for giving notice of nonpossessory security interests in order to obtain priority over lien creditors with respect to the collateral, the debtor is deemed to be located in the District of Columbia. UCC § 9–307(c).

d. Exceptions to the Debtor-Location Rule

(1) Possessory Security Interests

If the security interest is perfected through possession of collateral (and possession of collateral is an effective method of perfection as to that type of collateral), the law of the jurisdiction where the collateral is located will govern perfection of the security interest. UCC § 9–301(2).

(2) Fixture Filing

If the security interest is in goods that are fixtures and perfection is through filing a fixture financing statement, then the law of the jurisdiction where the fixtures is located governs perfection. UCC § 9–301(3)(A).

(3) Timber to Be Cut

If the security interest is in timber to be cut, the law of the jurisdiction where the timber to be cut is located governs perfection. UCC § 9–301(3)(B).

(4) As-Extracted Collateral

If the security interest is in as-extracted collateral, the law of the jurisdiction where the minehead or wellhead is located governs perfection. UCC § 9–301(4).

(5) Goods Covered by Certificate of Title

If the security interest is in goods that are covered by a certificate of title and the goods are not inventory held for sale or lease by the debtor, then the law of the jurisdiction that issued the certificate of title governs perfection until the goods cease to be covered by the certificate of title. UCC § 9–303(c), cmt. 5.

(6) Deposit Accounts

If the security interest is in a deposit account, the law of the jurisdiction where the depositary bank is located governs the perfection of the security interest. UCC § 9–304(a). Section 9–304 contains specific rules regarding where a bank is deemed to be located.

(7) Investment Property

If a security interest in investment property is perfected by filing, the law of the debtor's location will govern perfection of the security interest. The law of the debtor's location will also govern perfection of a security interest when the security interest is created by the broker or securities intermediary in investment property or by a commodity intermediary in a commodity contract or commodity account. UCC § 9–305(c). In other cases, the law governing perfection depends upon the type of investment property. The law of the location of the certificated security will govern perfection of a security interest in the certificated security. UCC § 9–305(a)(1). The law of the location of the issuer will govern perfection of a security interest in an uncertificated security. UCC § 9–305(a)(2). The law of the location of the securities intermediary will govern perfection of a security interest in a securities account or securities entitlement. UCC § 9–305(a)(3). The law of the location of the commodity intermediary will govern perfection of a security interest in a commodity account or commodity contract. UCC § 9–305(a)(4). Sections 9–305 and 8–110 contain specific rules for determining the location of the issuer, the securities intermediary, and the commodities intermediary, as applicable.

(8) Letter-of-Credit Rights

Unless the security interest in the letter-of-credit right is automatically perfected because it is a supporting obligation to a right to payment in which a security interest has been perfected, the law of the location of the issuer of the letter of credit or the law of the location of the nominated person as to the letter-of-credit will govern perfection of a security interest in a letter of credit right as long as the issuer or nominated person is located in a state in the United States. UCC § 9–306(a). If the issuer or nominated person is not located in a state of the United States, the general rule that the law of the debtor's location governs perfection will apply. UCC § 9–306, cmt. 2. Section 5–116 contains provisions to determine where an issuer and nominated person are located.

3. Choice of Law Regarding Priority and the Effect of Perfection and Nonperfection

The choice of law rules also contain provisions for the choice of law concerning application of priority rules and the effect of taking or not taking a perfection step. In some circumstances, the law of one jurisdiction will govern the acts necessary to perfect the security interest and the law of a different jurisdiction will govern the priority of the security interest. See Chapter V, Section G.

H. POST-CLOSING ISSUES AND EFFECT ON PERFECTION

Once a security interest or agricultural lien attaches and is properly perfected, the secured party must think about and take appropriate action to maintain perfection of its security interest or agricultural lien as events unfold.

1. Passage of Time

The secured party will need to file a continuation statement in a timely manner in order to continue the effectiveness of the financing statement beyond its initial term. UCC § 9–515.

2. Loss of Possession or Control

If perfection is accomplished through possession of collateral and the secured party loses possession of the collateral or if perfection is accomplished through control and the secured party loses control of the collateral, the perfection of the security interest is ended. UCC §§ 9–313(d), 9–314(b), (c).

3. Change in Use or Characterization of Goods

Changes in use of the collateral after perfection does not matter to maintaining perfection unless the effect of the change in use is to require a different manner of perfection or a different place of perfection be used to perfect the security interest.

4. Loss of Purchase Money Status

A purchase money security interest in consumer goods that are not covered by a certificate of title is automatically perfected. Refinancing the loan, obtaining additional nonpurchase money collateral to secure the original purchase money debt, or securing additional nonpurchase money obligations with the purchase money collateral may destroy the purchase money status of the original security interest in the consumer goods, rendering the original automatic perfection no longer effective. In a nonconsumer goods transaction, Article 9 provides that these types of events do not destroy purchase money status of the original security interest. UCC § 9–103(f).

5. Sale or Disposition of Collateral

A financing statement remains effective as to collateral disposed of even if after a disposition the original debtor is no longer the debtor with respect to that collateral. UCC § 9–507(a). This general rule is subject to an exception if the collateral is transferred to another debtor that is located in another jurisdiction thereby changing the law governing perfection of the security interest. UCC § 9–316. By acquiring collateral subject to a security interest or agricultural lien, the acquiring debtor authorizes the secured party to file a financing statement against the acquiring debtor covering that collateral and its proceeds. UCC § 9–509(c).

6. Perfection in Proceeds

If the security interest in the original collateral was perfected, the security interest in the identifiable proceeds is automatically perfected for a period of 20 days. UCC § 9–315(c). To maintain perfection of the security interest in identifiable proceeds beyond the 20-day time period, one of three circumstances must be true. Article 9 does not address perfection in proceeds of an agricultural lien.

a. Security Interest in Original Collateral Perfected by a Filed Financing Statement

If a filed financing statement covers the original collateral and is effective to perfect a security interest in the original collateral, the identifiable proceeds are not acquired with cash proceeds, and the proceeds are the type of collateral that could be perfected by filing a financing statement in the same office as the filed financing statement that already exists, the security interest in the identifiable proceeds is perfected. UCC § 9–315(d)(1). The security interest in identifiable proceeds that is perfected due to the effectiveness of the financing statement as to the original collateral is perfected until the financing statement lapses or is terminated. UCC § 9–315(e).

b. Security Interest in Identifiable Cash Proceeds

If the security interest in the original collateral is perfected by any method and the proceeds are identifiable cash proceeds, the security interest in the identifiable cash proceeds are perfected as long as the proceeds remain identifiable cash proceeds. UCC § 9–315(d)(2).

c. Security Interest in Proceeds Perfected as if Proceeds Were Original Collateral

If neither of the above two provisions apply, the secured party has to take the appropriate perfection step as to the identifiable proceeds of the type involved in order to perfect its security interest in the identifiable proceeds beyond the 20-day time period of temporary perfection. UCC § 9–315(d)(3).

7. Debtor Name Change: Security Interest

If a security interest is perfected by a filed financing statement, UCC § 9–503 provides what name is sufficient on that financing statement. If a debtor's name does not meet the requirements of UCC § 9–503, and that noncompliance makes the financing statement seriously misleading, the filed financing statement will not be effective to perfect a security interest in collateral acquired after four months after the financing statement became seriously misleading unless within the four-month period the financing statement is amended to reflect the debtor's name as required under UCC § 9–503. The debtor's name on the financing statement will be considered seriously misleading if a search of the filing records under the debtor's correct name does not turn up the filing under the debtor's old name. UCC § 9–506(c). As to collateral acquired by the debtor within that four-month period, the financing statement with the debtor's seriously misleading name is still effective to perfect the security interest. UCC § 9–507(c). The debtor's authentication of the security agreement provides the authority for the secured party to file an amendment to reflect the debtor's correct name. UCC § 9–509(b).

8. Debtor Name Change: Agricultural Lien

A debtor's name change does not affect the effectiveness of a financing statement filed to perfect an agricultural lien. UCC § 9–507(b).

9. Debtor Structural Changes

When a new debtor becomes bound by an old debtor's security agreement, the effectiveness of the filed financing statement against the collateral depends upon when the new debtor acquired the collateral. For purposes of this discussion, assume that the old and new debtor are both located in the same jurisdiction so that a change in the governing law is not implicated.

a. Collateral Acquired From the Old Debtor

The financing statement filed against the old debtor remains effective as to the collateral the new debtor acquires from the old debtor. UCC § 9–507(a).

b. Collateral Acquired by the New Debtor After Becoming the New Debtor

The financing statement filed against the old debtor is effective as to collateral the new debtor acquires subsequent to becoming the new debtor. UCC § 9–508(a). That rule is subject to an exception if the difference between the name of the new debtor and the old debtor is such that the filed financing statement as to the old debtor becomes seriously misleading. In that circumstance, the financing statement filed against the old debtor continues to be effective as to collateral acquired by the new debtor within four months after becoming the new debtor. As to collateral acquired after the four-month time period, the financing statement against the old debtor is not effective unless within the four-month time period a new initial financing statement is filed against the new debtor. UCC § 9–508(b). A financing statement against the old debtor will be seriously misleading if a search of the system under the new debtor's name does not reveal the filing under the old debtor's name. UCC § 9–506(c), (d).

c. Authority to File New Financing Statement

By becoming bound as a new debtor, the new debtor authorizes the filing of a financing statement covering the collateral. UCC § 9–509(b).

10. Secured Party Name Change, Structural Change, or Change in Location

Even though the secured party's name must be on a financing statement to make it effective to perfect, UCC § 9–502(a), and an address must be given as required in UCC § 9–516(b), a change in the secured party's name, business structure, or location does not affect the effectiveness of a filed financing statement. UCC § 9–507(b).

11. Assignment of Security Interest or Agricultural Lien

A secured party may assign its rights to another person. While the secured party may file an amendment to a financing statement in order to reflect the assignment, UCC § 9–514, the secured party is not required to do so in order to maintain the effectiveness of the perfection of the security interest or agricultural lien. UCC § 9–310(c).

12. Change in Governing Law

Because the debtor's location, the collateral's location, or a third party's location, determines the law that governs perfection of a security interest or agricultural lien, a change in the location of the debtor, collateral, or third party, as applicable, may have the effect of undoing the perfection of the security interest or agricultural lien.

a. Relocation of Debtor

If the location of the debtor determines the law governing perfection, the change in location of the debtor to another jurisdiction will require that the secured party take action to keep its security interest perfected.

(1) Collateral in Which the Security Interest Has Attached at the Time of Relocation

The law of the debtor's old jurisdiction will continue to govern questions regarding the perfection of the security interest in collateral to which the security interest has attached at the time the debtor relocates until the earlier of the following three events: (i) the expiration of the old financing statement by its own terms; (ii) four months after the debtor's location changed to the new jurisdiction; or (iii) one year after the collateral has been transferred to a person that is located in another jurisdiction and that is a debtor with respect to that collateral. UCC § 9–316(a). If the secured party takes the necessary perfection step in the jurisdiction of the debtor's new location within the applicable time period, the security interest is perfected by that new step. If the secured party does not take the necessary perfection step in the jurisdiction of the debtor's new location within that time period, the security interest becomes unperfected and is deemed to be retroactively unperfected as against a purchaser of the collateral for value. UCC § 9–316(b). The debtor's authentication of the security agreement is authority for the secured party to file an initial financing statement in the new jurisdiction to perfect a security interest in collateral covered by the security agreement and its proceeds. UCC § 9–509(b).

(2) After-Acquired Collateral

Assume the security interest attaches to collateral acquired by the debtor after relocation to a new jurisdiction under a properly constructed after-acquired property clause. As to collateral acquired within four months after the debtor's relocation, the financing statement filed in the first jurisdiction continues to control for the shorter of the time of four months or when the statement would have lapsed. If the secured party files a proper financing statement as to the collateral in the second jurisdiction during that time period, the security interest will remain continuously perfected. If the secured party does not file in the new jurisdiction within the time period, the security interest as to that after-acquired collateral becomes unperfected and is deemed retroactively unperfected against a purchaser for value. UCC § 9–316(h).

b. New Debtor

When a new debtor becomes bound to the old debtor's security agreement, the filed financing statement against the old debtor continues to be effective to perfect a security interest in the assets of both the old and new debtor for a period of time. UCC § 9–508. If the new debtor is located in a jurisdiction that is different than the jurisdiction of the old debtor, additional rules apply.

(1) Assets Transferred from Old Debtor to New Debtor

As to the assets transferred from the old debtor to the new debtor in the new jurisdiction, the secured party must perfect its security interest in the new jurisdiction within the time period of effectiveness of the financing statement against the old debtor or one year after the assets were transferred to the new debtor in the new jurisdiction (whichever is shorter). UCC § 9–316(a).

(2) All Other Assets of New Debtor

As to the assets of the new debtor that were not the assets of the old debtor and the assets that the new debtor acquires within four months after becoming the new debtor, the law of the old jurisdiction will provide the governing law for perfection purposes for four months or the period of effectiveness of the old jurisdiction financing statement. If the secured party files an effective financing statement against the new debtor in the new jurisdiction within that time period, the security interest in the new debtor's collateral that did not come from the original debtor will remain continuously perfected. If the secured party does not file in the new jurisdiction against the new debtor within that time period, the security interest in the new debtor's collateral that did not come from the original debtor is deemed retroactively unperfected against a purchaser for value. UCC § 9–316(i).

c. Relocation of Collateral

If the location of the collateral controls the perfection step, and the collateral moves to a new jurisdiction, the law of that new jurisdiction will control perfection. For an agricultural lien, if the farm products move from one jurisdiction where the secured party has filed a financing statement to another jurisdiction where the secured party has not filed a financing statement, the agricultural lien immediately becomes unperfected as there has been no perfection step in the new jurisdiction. If a security interest is perfected by possession and the collateral moves from one jurisdiction to another, as long as the security interest in the collateral is perfected in the old jurisdiction and, under the law of the new jurisdiction, the security interest is perfected in the collateral when it enters the new jurisdiction, the security interest is continuously perfected. UCC § 9–316(c).

d. Certificate of Title Goods

If a security interest in a good is perfected in any manner in one jurisdiction and the good becomes covered by a certificate of title issued by another jurisdiction, the security interest remains perfected based upon the law of the first jurisdiction as if the certificate of title was not issued by the second jurisdiction. UCC § 9–316(d). The security interest that was perfected by the appropriate action in the first jurisdiction when the good becomes covered by a certificate of title in the second jurisdiction is deemed unperfected as to a purchaser for value unless the secured party takes the appropriate action in the second jurisdiction within the earlier of four months after the goods become covered by the certificate of title issued by the second jurisdiction or the time perfection would have expired of its own force in the first jurisdiction. UCC § 9–316(e). If the goods are subject to a security interest that is perfected in any manner and the goods become covered by a certificate of title issued by another jurisdiction, the secured party may perfect its security interest in the goods by possession even though the goods are now covered by the new certificate of title. UCC § 9–313(b).

e. Relocation of Third Party

The law governing perfection of a security interest in deposit accounts, letter-of-credit rights, and investment property when perfection is by a non filing method is determined by the law where the bank, issuer, nominated person, securities intermediary, or commodity intermediary (as the case may be) are located. If those entities move jurisdictions so as to implicate a different governing law, the security interest remains perfected until the earlier of the time the security interest would be unperfected under the law of the first jurisdiction or four months after the relevant entity moves to the second jurisdiction. UCC § 9–316(f). If the security interest becomes perfected in the new jurisdiction within that time period, the security interest is perfected thereafter. If the security interest is not perfected within that time period, the security interest is unperfected and deemed retroactively unperfected against a purchaser for value of the collateral. UCC § 9–316(g).

13. Effect of Bankruptcy on Perfection of Security Interest or Agricultural Lien

Generally, if the security interest or agricultural lien is perfected when the debtor files bankruptcy, the Bankruptcy Code does not effect the perfection of the security interest or agricultural lien. Collateral that is subject to a perfected security interest or agricultural lien becomes property of the debtor's bankruptcy estate, 11 U.S.C. § 541, and the secured party is subject to the automatic stay preventing the secured party from taking any further action with respect to the collateral and its security interest, 11 U.S.C. § 362. Persons with possession or control of property of the estate (which the collateral would be) are under an obligation to turn the collateral over to the bankruptcy trustee, 11 U.S.C. §§ 542, 543, and may be subject to liability for contempt of court for failing to do so. Relinquishing possession or control of collateral may result in a loss of perfection for the security interest. An exception to the automatic stay allows the secured party to file a continuation statement during the pendency of the bankruptcy case to continue the effectiveness of a filed financing statement. 11 U.S.C. § 362(b)(3).

■ V. PRIORITY OF SECURITY INTERESTS AND AGRICULTURAL LIENS

A. BASIC CONCEPT OF PRIORITY

The concept of priority of security interests and agricultural liens in the debtor's assets is the concept of the hierarchy of property claims as against specific assets of the debtor. Generally, a creditor will want as high a priority as possible for its property claim against the debtor's asset as that high priority will increase the likelihood of the creditor being able to realize value out of the asset.

1. Fundamental Priority Principle

Many priority rules are based upon a fundamental property principle that the priority of interests in property will be based upon the time the interest is sufficiently attached to the property. This basic "first-in-time" principle is subject to much further definition and refinement.

2. Security Agreement Effective Against Third Parties

Article 9 provides that a security agreement is effective against purchasers of the collateral and creditors of the parties. UCC § 9–201(a). This general rule is subject to numerous exceptions.

3. Priority Is Determined by Asset

The priority hierarchy requires that the analysis concerning priority be considered on an asset-by-asset basis. The precise question that must be answered is what is this creditor's priority position for its property claim in this particular asset of the debtor.

4. Priority Is Determined by Type of Creditor

The priority positions of the creditor's property claims to the debtor's asset will also be determined by what type of creditor is involved in the priority contest as against the security interest or agricultural lien.

5. Priority May Be Determined by the Method of Perfection

If a secured party has alternative methods of perfection of its security interest, such as by filing a financing statement covering the collateral or by taking possession of the collateral, the priority of the security interest as against other claims to the same asset may be different depending upon the method the secured party used to perfect its security interest.

6. Methodology

To determine the hierarchy of property claims against a particular asset, determine the asset and its type, determine what creditors have property claims to the asset, determine the type of property claim, and then determine the relative priority of that creditor's type of property claim as against each of the other creditor's property claims to the asset by selecting and applying the appropriate priority rule.

7. Subordination

Even though application of the priority rules results in a determination of the priority of a creditor's property claim, the creditor may agree with another creditor that its property claim will be subordinated in priority to the other creditor's property claim. UCC § 9–339.

B. SECURITY INTEREST AND AGRICULTURAL LIEN AS AGAINST LIEN CREDITORS

A lien creditor is a creditor that has obtained a lien on the debtor's personal property by execution, attachment or levy. A lien creditor also includes an assignee for the benefit of creditors, an equity receiver, and the trustee in bankruptcy. UCC § 9–102(a)(52).

1. Basic Priority Rule

Subject to two exceptions, a security interest or agricultural lien that is attached but unperfected at the time the lien creditor becomes a lien creditor is subordinate in priority to the lien created by the lien creditor. UCC § 9–317(a)(2)(A).

2. Exception to the Basic Priority Rule: No Value as the Only Missing Step to Perfection of a Security Interest

If the secured party has filed an effective financing statement against the debtor and has obtained the debtor's authenticated security agreement with an adequate collateral description but has not yet given value at the time the lien creditor's lien arises, the secured party's security interest created subsequently, through the giving of value after the lien creditor's lien arises, will be superior to the lien creditor's lien. UCC § 9–317(a)(2)(B).

3. Exception to the Basic Priority Rule: Purchase Money Security Interests

If a purchase money security interest has attached but is not perfected prior to the lien creditor's obtaining of its lien and the purchase money secured party filed a financing statement covering the collateral within 20 days after the debtor received delivery of the good subject to the purchase money security interest, the security interest is not subordinate to a lien creditor's lien that arises between the time the security interest is attached and the time the secured party files the financing statement. The same result should obtain if the secured party complies with an applicable certificate of title law during that time period instead of filing a financing statement. UCC § 9–317(e).

4. Treatment of Future Advances

If the secured party makes future advances and the secured party's security interest is otherwise superior to the lien creditor's lien, the lien creditor's lien will be subordinate to the security interest that secures those advances unless the advance is made more than 45 days after the date of the lien creditor's obtaining of the lien. Even if the advance is made more than 45 days after the lien creditor's lien arose, the security interest securing the advance may still have priority over the lien creditor's lien if the advance is made without knowledge of the lien creditor's lien or made pursuant to a commitment entered into without knowledge of the lien creditor's lien. UCC § 9–323(b). This rule subordinating security interests securing future advances to the lien creditor's lien does not apply to secured parties that are buyers of accounts, chattel paper, payment intangibles, or promissory notes or a secured party that is a consignor of goods. UCC § 9–323(c).

C. SECURITY INTEREST AS AGAINST POSSESSORY STATUTORY OR COMMON LAW LIEN

If a possessory nonconsensual lien is created under other law and there is also a security interest on that property, the lien created under other law is superior in priority to a perfected security interest if (i) the other lien is a possessory lien in goods that secures payment or performance of an obligation for services and materials that the lienholder furnished with respect to the goods in the ordinary course of the lienholder's business, (ii) the possessory lien was created by a statute or rule of law other than Article 9, (iii) the effectiveness of the lienholder's lien depends upon possession of the goods, and (iv) the statute creating the possessory lien does not expressly provide otherwise. UCC § 9–333.

D. SECURITY INTEREST OR AGRICULTURAL LIEN AS AGAINST OTHER AGRICULTURAL LIENS OR SECURITY INTERESTS

1. General Rules

a. First to File or Perfect

The general priority rule for determining the priority of perfected security interests or perfected agricultural liens as against other perfected security interests or perfected agricultural liens in the same asset is that priority dates from the time an effective financing statement covering the collateral is first filed against the collateral or the security interest or agricultural lien is first perfected as long as there is no time thereafter when there is neither an effective financing statement filed as to the collateral nor perfection of the security interest or agricultural lien. UCC § 9–322(a)(1). Because compliance with a federal preemptive filing system or a certificate of title system is deemed to be the filing of a financing statement, this rule also applies to situations in which the secured party complies with those systems. UCC § 9–311(b). For purposes of applying the first to file or perfect rule, the time of filing or perfection as to the original collateral is deemed to be the time of filing or perfection as to proceeds of the original collateral and supporting obligations to the original collateral. UCC § 9–322(b).

b. Perfected Has Priority Over Unperfected

If the security interest or agricultural lien is unperfected, it will be subordinate to a perfected security interest or agricultural lien. UCC § 9–322(a)(2).

c. When Both Unperfected, First to Attach

If conflicting security interests and agricultural liens are unperfected, the first security interest or agricultural lien to attach will have priority. UCC § 9–322(a)(3).

2. Exceptions to Three General Priority Rules: Methodology

To analyze the priority of a security interest or agricultural lien as against other security interests or agricultural liens, first determine who would have priority in the asset based upon the three general rules given above. Then determine if any of the following exceptions to the general rules apply. If the exception applies, the exception will control the priority of the security interest or agricultural lien as against another security interest or agricultural lien.

3. Exception: Subordination Due to Error in Financing Statement

In the event the financing statement is sufficient to perfect under UCC § 9–502 but has errors in the information required by UCC § 9–516(b)(5), the security interest or agricultural lien perfected by that inaccurate financing statement is subordinated to a conflicting perfected security interest if the holder of that conflicting perfected security interest gave value in reasonable reliance on the incorrect information. UCC §§ 9–322(f)(1), 9–338(1).

4. Exception: A Different Priority Rule Stated in an Agricultural Lien Statute

If the statute creating an agricultural lien expressly provides, a perfected agricultural lien has priority over a conflicting security interest or agricultural lien even if the perfected agricultural lien would otherwise be subordinate under the first to file or perfect rule. UCC § 9–322(g).

5. Exception: Purchase Money Security Interests

a. In Goods or Software Only

Purchase money security interests must either be in goods or software.

(1) Purchase Money Security Interest in Goods Defined
A security interest in goods is a purchase money security interest if one or more of three situations is present: (i) the security interest in goods secures the value given to enable the debtor to acquire rights in the goods; (ii) the security interest in goods secures value given to enable the debtor to acquire rights in software in the same transaction in which it acquired rights in the goods and for software that is for use in the goods; or (iii) the security interest is in inventory and secures value given to enable the debtor to acquire other items of inventory that the secured party also has a purchase money security interest in. UCC § 9–103(b). In each situation, the value given must actually be used by the debtor to acquire rights in the goods or software that is for use in the goods.

(2) Purchase Money Security Interest in Software Defined
A security interest in software is a purchase money security interest if the secured party has given value to enable the debtor to acquire goods, the secured party has a purchase money security interest in those goods, the software was acquired in the same transaction in which the debtor acquired the goods, and the software was acquired for the principal purpose of using it in the goods. UCC § 9–103(c).

(3) Consignor's Interest
The consignor's security interest in the goods in a consignment is deemed to be a purchase money security interest in inventory. UCC § 9–103(d).

(4) Effect of Subsequent Events on Purchase Money Security Interest Status
In a transaction other than a consumer-goods transaction, the secured party has the burden to demonstrate the extent of the purchase money status of the security interest. UCC § 9–103(g). In such a transaction, a purchase money security interest remains a purchase money security interest even though it is refinanced, the goods or software secures nonpurchase money debt, or the purchase money debt is secured by collateral other than what was purchased. UCC § 9–103(f). In such a transaction, if payments are made on the debt, the payments are applied in accordance with the following hierarchy of preference: (i) any reasonable method to which the parties have agreed; (ii) in accord with the payor's direction at the time of payment; (iii) to obligations that are not secured; or (iv) to obligations secured by purchase money security interests in the order those obligations were secured. UCC § 9–103(e). In a consumer-goods transaction, courts are directed to apply their own established approaches to these issues. UCC § 9–103(h).

b. Priority in Goods Other Than Inventory and Livestock

If the collateral is goods other than inventory and livestock, a purchase money security interest has priority over a conflicting security interest in the same goods as long as the purchase money security interest is perfected when the debtor receives possession of the collateral or within 20 days thereafter. UCC §§ 9–322(f)(1), 9–324(a).

c. Priority in Inventory

If the collateral is inventory, a purchase money security interest has priority over a conflicting security interest in the same inventory if (i) the purchase money security interest is perfected when the debtor receives possession of the inventory, (ii) the purchase money secured party has sent an authenticated notice to the holder of the conflicting security interest, and (iii) that holder has received that notice within five years before the debtor receives possession of the inventory. UCC §§ 9–322(f)(1), 9–324(b). The notice must state that the purchase money secured party has or will have a purchase money security interest in the inventory and describe the inventory that will be subject to the purchase money security interest. UCC § 9–324(b)(4). The holders of conflicting security interests in the same inventory that must receive the notice are those that have filed a financing statement against the debtor covering inventory before the date the purchase money secured party filed its financing statement or the date that starts the temporary 20-day perfection period described in UCC § 9–312(f). UCC § 9–324(c).

d. Priority in Software

If the collateral is software, a perfected purchase money security interest in the software has priority over a conflicting security interest in the same software if the perfected purchase money security interest in the goods in which the software is used has priority over conflicting perfected security interests in those goods. UCC §§ 9–322(f)(1), 9–324(f).

e. Priority in Livestock

If the collateral is livestock that are farm products, a perfected purchase money security interest in the livestock has priority over a conflicting perfected security interest in the livestock if (i) the purchase money security interest is perfected when the debtor receives possession of the livestock, (ii) the purchase money secured party has sent an authenticated notice to the holder of the conflicting security interest, and (iii) that holder has received that notice within six months before the debtor receives possession of the livestock. UCC §§ 9–322(f)(1), 9–324(d). The notice must state that the purchase money secured party has or will have a purchase money security interest in the livestock and describe the livestock that will be subject to the purchase money security interest. UCC § 9–324(d)(4). The holders of conflicting security interests in the same livestock that must receive the notice are those that have filed a financing statement against the debtor covering livestock before the date the purchase money secured party filed its financing statement or the date that starts the temporary 20-day perfection period described in UCC § 9–312(f). UCC § 9–324(e).

f. Conflicting Purchase Money Security Interests

If both purchase money security interests would qualify for priority over other security interests under the rules stated above, the seller's purchase money security interest will have priority over the non-seller secured party's purchase money security interest. UCC § 9–322(g)(1). If neither of the conflicting purchase money security interests are held by the seller, the general rules of UCC § 9–322(a) apply. UCC § 9–322(g)(2).

6. Exception: Priority in an Accession

An accession is a good that is physically united with another good in such a manner that the identity of the two goods is not lost after the unification. UCC § 9–102(a)(1). The good that is added to another good is the accession. The good that the accession is added to is called the "other goods." The good with the accession added is called the "whole." A secured party with a security interest in the accession will have its security interest continue in the accession even after the accession is united with the "other goods." UCC § 9–335(a). If the security interest is perfected in the accession before the accession is united with the other good, the uniting of the accession with the other good does not affect the perfection of the security interest in the accession. UCC § 9–335(b). With one exception for certificate of title goods, the other rules in Article 9 that govern priority will determine priority of a security interest in the accession. UCC § 9–335(c). If the goods are covered by a certificate of title, any security interest in an accession is subordinate to a security interest in the whole (the other good and the accession) if the security interest in the whole is perfected by compliance with a certificate of title statute. UCC § 9–335(d).

7. Exception: Priority in Commingled Goods

Commingled goods are goods that are united with other goods in such a manner that the identity of the original goods is lost in the united product or mass. UCC § 9–336(a). If a secured party has attached and perfected a security interest to goods before they become commingled, the security interest will be attached and perfected in the product or mass after commingling. UCC § 9–336(c), (d). The priority rules for security interests in commingled goods are governed by the other Article 9 rules for priority, with the following exception. UCC § 9–336(e). If more than one security interest attaches to the product or mass because the security interests were in the goods before the goods were commingled, the following two rules apply: (i) a perfected security interest in the product or mass has priority over an unperfected security interest in the product or mass; and (ii) if both security interests are perfected in the product or mass, the security interests rank equal in priority according to the proportion of value of the collateral at the time it was commingled up to the amount of the secured party's debt. UCC § 9–336(f), cmt. 4.

8. Exception: Priority of Security Interests Noted First on a Clean Certificate of Title

If a secured party has perfected a security interest in goods by any method and a state issues a certificate of title for those goods, the security interest remains perfected even though the law governing perfection of the security interest is changed to the law of the jurisdiction issuing the certificate. UCC §§ 9–303, 9–316(d). The secured party has the lesser of four months or the time perfection would lapse in the first jurisdiction to obtain perfection of its security interest by notation on the certificate of title or the security interest is deemed unperfected as against a preexisting purchaser of the good. UCC § 9–316(e). If that new certificate of title does not show the goods are subject to the existing security interest or contain a notation that the goods may be subject to security interests not shown on the certificate of title, the secured party's unnoted security interest is subordinated to a security interest that is perfected on the clean certificate by a secured party that did not have knowledge of the first security interest. UCC § 9–337(2).

9. Exception: Priority in Goods Covered by a Negotiable Document of Title

If a secured party perfects a security interest directly in goods while the goods are covered by a negotiable document of title, that security interest perfected directly in the goods is subordinate to a security interest in the goods that is perfected by perfection of a security interest in the negotiable document of title. UCC §§ 9–322(f), 9–312(c). The priority of security interests in the negotiable document of title, and thus in the goods covered by the document of title, will be determined by the three general rules of UCC § 9–322(a), as it applies to filing or perfection in the negotiable document of title, subject to the following two rules. If a secured party becomes a holder of a negotiable document of title by "due negotiation," that secured party will take the negotiable document of title and the goods covered by the document of title free of a security interest perfected in the document of title by a different method, such as by filing a financing statement. UCC §§ 7–502, 9–322(f), 9–331. However, if a secured party has a perfected security interest in goods prior to the goods being covered by a document of title and the goods subsequently become covered by a negotiable document of title, the rights of a holder of that negotiable document of title are not superior to the first secured party's rights in the goods unless the first secured party entrusted the goods or the document of title to the debtor with actual or apparent authority to ship, store, sell, or otherwise dispose of the goods or the first secured party acquiesced in the debtor's procurement of the document of title. UCC § 7–503.

10. Exception: Priority in Chattel Paper

If a purchaser (including a secured party) in good faith takes possession of tangible chattel paper or control of electronic chattel paper in the ordinary course of the purchaser's business and gives new value for the chattel paper, the purchaser will have priority over a security interest in the chattel paper that is claimed merely as proceeds of inventory subject to a security interest as long as the chattel paper does not indicate that it has been assigned to an identified assignee other than the purchaser. UCC § 9–330(a). If a purchaser in good faith takes possession of tangible chattel paper or control of electronic chattel paper in the ordinary course of the purchaser's business and gives new value for the chattel paper, the purchaser will have priority over a security interest in the chattel paper that is claimed other than as merely proceeds of inventory subject to a security interest as long as the purchaser is without knowledge that the purchase violates the rights of the secured party with the conflicting security interest. UCC § 9–330(b).

11. Exception: Priority in Instruments

If a person purchases an instrument for value, takes possession of the instrument (either negotiable or nonnegotiable) in good faith, and does not have knowledge that the purchase violates the rights of the secured party, the purchaser (including a secured party) will take priority over a conflicting security interest perfected by a method other than possession. UCC §§ 9–322(f), 9–330(d). A holder (including a secured party) in due course of a negotiable instrument takes the instrument with priority over a security interest in the instrument even if the conflicting security interest is perfected. UCC §§ 3–306, 9–322(f), 9–331(a).

12. Exception: Priority in Deposit Accounts

A security interest in a deposit account perfected by control will have priority over a security interest in the deposit account that is not perfected by control.

UCC §§ 9–322(f), 9–327(1). If more than one secured party has perfected its security interest in the deposit account by control, the security interests rank in priority based upon the time control was obtained unless one of the two following rules apply. UCC §§ 9–322(f), 9–327(2). The security interest of the depository bank in the deposit account (which is automatically perfected by control, UCC § 9–104(a)(1)) has priority over a conflicting security interest held by another secured party except as provided by the rule below. UCC § 9–327(3). If the secured party perfects its security interest in the deposit account by becoming the depository bank's customer on the account (UCC § 9–104(a)(3)), that security interest will have priority over the depository bank's security interest in the deposit account. UCC § 9–327(4). If the depositary bank has a right of setoff against the deposit account, that right of setoff will have priority over a secured party with a perfected security interest in the deposit account unless the secured party is a customer on the deposit account and the bank's setoff is exercised based upon the bank's claim against the debtor, not as against the secured party. UCC § 9–340. A transferee of funds from a deposit account will take those funds free of any security interest in the deposit account even if the security interest is perfected unless the transferee acted in collusion with the debtor in violating the rights of the secured party with a security interest in the deposit account. UCC § 9–332(b).

13.   Exception: Priority in Money

A transferee of money takes the money free of a security interest in the money even if the security interest is perfected unless the transferee acts in collusion with the debtor in violating the rights of the secured party. UCC §§ 9–322(f), 9–332(a).

14.   Exception: Priority in a Letter-of-Credit Right

A security interest perfected by control of a letter-of-credit right will have priority over a security interest in the letter-of-credit right which is not perfected by control. UCC §§ 9–322(f), 9–329(1). If the conflicting security interests in a letter-of-credit right are all perfected by control, the priority is based upon the time that control is obtained. UCC §§ 9–322(f), 9–329(2). The right of a secured party that is a transferee beneficiary under a letter of credit has priority over the rights of a secured party that has merely obtained a security interest in the letter-of-credit rights. UCC §§ 9–109(c)(4), 5–114.

15.   Exception: Priority in Investment Property

a.   Security Interests Perfected by Control Have Priority Over Security Interests Perfected by Means Other Than Control

A security interest in investment property that is perfected by control has priority over a security interest in investment property perfected by a method other than control. UCC § 9–328(1).

b.   Priority of Security Interests That Are All Perfected by Control

A securities intermediary's security interest in securities entitlements or securities accounts maintained by the intermediary (and thus perfected by control, UCC §§ 9–106, 8–106) has priority over any conflicting security interest held by a secured party even if that secured party has obtained control of the securities account or securities entitlement. UCC § 9–328(3). A commodity intermediary's security interest in commodity contracts or commodity accounts maintained by the intermediary (and thus perfected by control, UCC § 9–106) has priority over any conflicting security interest held by a secured party even if that secured party has obtained control of the commodity account or commodity contracts. UCC § 9–328(4). When the conflicting security interests in a security, a securities entitlement, or a commodity contract are each perfected by control but neither secured party is a securities intermediary or a commodity intermediary (as the case may be), the priority of the conflicting security interests is determined by the order in which the secured parties obtained control. UCC § 9–328(2).

c.   Priority of Security Interests in Certificated Security in Registered Form

If the secured party takes delivery of a certificated security in registered form but does not have control of the certificated security (because it is lacking the necessary indorsement or registration), the secured party will have priority over a conflicting security interest in the certificated security that is perfected by a method other than control, such as by filing a financing statement. UCC § 9–328(5).

d. Priority of Security Interests Created by Broker, Securities Intermediary, or Commodity Intermediary

If there are conflicting security interests in investment property created by a broker, securities intermediary, or commodity intermediary and those interests are not perfected by control (that is, they are automatically perfected), the security interests will have co-equal rank. UCC § 9–328(6). If the conflicting security interests are both perfected by control, then the time of obtaining control will determine priority. UCC § 9–328(2). If one of the conflicting security interests is perfected by control and the other security interest is perfected in a manner other than control, then the security interest perfected by control will have priority. UCC § 9–328(1). When the securities intermediary grants to a creditor a security interest in the securities entitlements it holds, and the securities intermediary does not have enough securities entitlements to satisfy the claim of the secured party and the claims of the entitlement holders, the priority rule as between the security interest of the secured party of the securities intermediary and the claims of the entitlement holders depends upon whether the secured party has obtained control. UCC § 9–309(10). If the secured party has perfected its security interest in the securities entitlements held by the securities intermediary by control, the secured party's security interest will have priority over the claims of the entitlement holders. UCC §§ 9–331(b), 8–511(b). If the secured party has not perfected its security interest in the securities entitlements by control, the entitlement holders claims will have priority over the secured party's claims.

16.   Exception: Priority of Security Interests Created Under Other Articles

a. Security Interest of Collecting Bank in Items Sent for Collection

A collecting bank has a security interest in items sent for collection and accompanying documents and proceeds of the item for credit given against the item until the bank receives final settlement for the item or the bank gives up possession of the item and documents for a purpose other than collection. The collecting bank's security interest has priority over conflicting perfected security interests in the item, accompanying documents, and proceeds. UCC § 4–210.

b. Security Interest of Issuer of a Letter of Credit or Nominated Person

An issuer or nominated person under a letter of credit has a security interest in the documents presented if the person gives value or honors the presentation and that security interest continues as long as the issuer or nominated person is not reimbursed for the value given. If the documents are in tangible form and *are not* a certificated security, chattel paper, a document of title, an instrument, or a letter of credit, the security interest of the issuer or nominated person will have priority over a conflicting security interest as long as the debtor does not obtain possession of the documents. UCC § 5–118. If the documents are in intangible form or are tangible documents that *are* a certificated security, chattel paper, a document of title, an instrument or a letter of credit, then the priority rules of Article 9 are applicable.

c. Security Interests Created Under Articles 2 and 2A

A seller has a security interest arising under Article 2 for the price if the seller retains title to delivered goods or ships the goods under reservation. UCC §§ 2–401, 2–505. A buyer has a security interest arising under Article 2 for a refund of the price paid and certain incidental damages if the buyer has possession of goods it has rightfully and effectively rejected or as to which it has effectively and justifiably revoked acceptance. UCC § 2–711(3). A lessee has a similar security interest arising under Article 2A for a refund of rent already paid, security deposits and certain incidental damages if the lessee has possession of goods it has rightfully and effectively rejected or as to which it has effectively and justifiably revoked acceptance. UCC § 2A–508. These security interests will have priority over conflicting security interests in the goods created by the debtor as long as the debtor does not obtain possession of the goods. UCC § 9–110.

17. Exception: Priority in Proceeds

For purposes of the first to file or perfect priority rule, the filing or perfection as to the original collateral is the time of filing or perfection as to the identifiable proceeds of that original collateral. UCC § 9–322(b). Because part of the first to file or perfect rule is that in order to use that time to establish the priority of the security interest that there be no time thereafter when there is neither an effective filing or perfection as to that collateral, continuous perfection or filing as to the collateral, including proceeds is critical. The first to file or perfect rule for priority in proceeds is only applied if none of the following three exceptions apply.

a. Qualified for Priority in Collateral Under any of the Exceptions to the Three General Rules in UCC § 9–322(a)

If a security interest in the type of proceeds qualifies for priority against a conflicting security interest in that same type of proceeds under any of the priority rules that are exceptions to three general rules in UCC § 9–322(a) as outlined *supra*, then the security interest that has priority under the exception has priority in that type of proceeds. If this rule applies, then it governs priority in the proceeds and the other two exceptions to the first to file or perfect rule as applied to proceeds, explored *infra*, do not apply. UCC § 9–322(a), (f).

(1) Subordination Due to Error in Financing Statement Information
In the event the financing statement is sufficient to perfect but has errors in the debtor's mailing address or does not indicate whether the debtor is an individual or organization, the security interest or agricultural lien perfected by that financing statement with the errors is subordinated to a conflicting perfected security interest if the holder of that conflicting perfected security interest gave value in reasonable reliance on the incorrect information. The subordination rule is not limited in terms of the type of collateral to which it applies. UCC §§ 9–322(f)(1), 9–338(1).

(2) Proceeds of Perfected Purchase Money Security Interests in Goods Other Than Inventory and Livestock
If a secured party has a perfected purchase money security interest in goods, other than inventory and livestock, with priority over a conflicting security interest in those goods and the purchase money security interest in identifiable proceeds is perfected, the perfected purchase money security interest in the proceeds will also have priority over a conflicting security interest in those same proceeds as long as the purchase money security interest in the proceeds remains perfected. UCC § 9–324(a). That priority rule is subject to an exception if the identifiable proceeds of the goods is a deposit account. In that situation, the priority in the deposit account will be determined by the special rules for deposit accounts in UCC § 9–327.

(3) Proceeds of Perfected Purchase Money Security Interests in Inventory

If a perfected purchase money security interest in inventory has priority in the inventory, the security interest in certain types of identifiable proceeds of that inventory will have the same priority as the purchase money security interest in the inventory. UCC § 9–324(b). If the identifiable proceeds of inventory are chattel paper or instruments, the purchase money security interest in the chattel paper or instruments will have priority over a conflicting security interest in the chattel paper or instruments only if the secured party qualifies for priority in the chattel paper and instruments under the special priority rules for purchasers of chattel paper and instruments in UCC § 9–330 as discussed *supra*. UCC § 9–324(b). A secured party with a perfected purchase money security interest in inventory is deemed to give new value for chattel paper that is identifiable proceeds of the inventory. UCC § 9–330(e). If the proceeds are identifiable cash proceeds that are received by the debtor on or before the inventory is delivered to a buyer, the secured party with a perfected purchase money priority security interest in the inventory will have priority over conflicting security interests in those cash proceeds unless the cash proceeds are a deposit account and the conflicting secured party's security interest qualifies for priority in the deposit account under the rules of UCC § 9–327. As to any proceeds of inventory, the other priority rules in Article 9 apply, including the three general rules of UCC § 9–322(a) and the exceptions to those three general rules, if applicable.

(4) Proceeds of Perfected Purchase Money Security Interests in Livestock

If a perfected purchase money security interest in livestock has priority over a conflicting security interest in the livestock, the purchase money secured party's security interest will also have priority in a perfected security interest in identifiable proceeds of all types and identifiable products in their unmanufactured state. If the identifiable proceeds are a deposit account, the priority of conflicting security interests in the deposit account is determined under UCC § 9–327. UCC § 9–324(d).

(5) Proceeds of Perfected Purchase Money Security Interests in Software

If the secured party's purchase money security interest in software has priority over a conflicting security interest in the software, the secured party's perfected security interest in any type of identifiable proceeds of the software will have priority over a conflicting security interest in the same proceeds if the perfected purchase money security interest in the goods in which the software is used and proceeds of the goods has priority over conflicting security interests in the goods and the proceeds of the goods. If the proceeds are a deposit account, the rules on priority of a security interest in a deposit account control, UCC § 9–327. UCC § 9–324(f).

(6) **Conflicting Purchase Money Security Interests and Proceeds**
If two or more secured parties qualify for purchase money priority in goods, software, or proceeds, a seller's perfected purchase money security interest in goods or software and the proceeds in which it has priority above will have priority over a non-seller's perfected purchase money security interest in the same proceeds. UCC § 9–324(g).

(7) **Priority in Proceeds That are Negotiable Documents of Title**
If the proceeds of collateral consist of negotiable documents of title, a secured party that becomes a holder of the negotiable document of title by due negotiation will take the document free of a conflicting security interest in that document of title. UCC §§ 9–331, 7–502.

(8) **Priority in Proceeds That are Chattel Paper**
If the proceeds of collateral consist of chattel paper and a secured party obtains possession or control of the chattel paper as set forth in UCC § 9–330 as outlined earlier, the secured party will have priority over a conflicting security interest in the chattel paper.

(9) **Priority in the Specific Goods Covered by the Chattel Paper**
If a secured party has priority in chattel paper under the rule of UCC § 9–330, then the secured party has priority in the proceeds of the chattel paper that consist of the specific goods covered by the chattel paper if those goods are returned to the debtor in a transaction in which the debtor acquires rights in the goods even if the secured party's security interest in those returned goods is unperfected. UCC § 9–330(c).

(10) **Priority in Proceeds That are Instruments**
If the proceeds of collateral are instruments, a secured party that qualifies for priority over conflicting security interests in instruments under UCC § 9–330(d) or as a holder in due course of a negotiable instrument under

UCC § 9–331 will have priority over conflicting security interests in the instrument.

(11)   Priority in Proceeds That are Deposit Accounts

If the proceeds of collateral are a deposit account, and a secured party has control of the deposit account, UCC § 9–104, the rules on priority of conflicting security interests in deposit accounts controls. UCC § 9–327.

(12)   Priority in Proceeds That Are Money or Funds From a Deposit Account

If the proceeds are money or a transfer of funds from a deposit account, a transferee (other than the debtor) takes those proceeds free of a security interest unless the transferee acts in collusion with the debtor to violate the rights of the secured party. UCC § 9–332.

(13)   Priority in Proceeds That are a Letter-of-Credit Right

If the proceeds of collateral consist of a letter-of-credit right, the special priority rules for letters of credit will control priority in the letter-of-credit right. UCC §§ 5–114, 9–109(c)(4), 9–329.

(14)   Priority in Proceeds That are Investment Property

If the proceeds of collateral are investment property, then the special priority rules for investment property will determine priority in the investment property. UCC § 9–328.

(15)   Collecting Bank's Priority in Proceeds of Items and Accompanying Documents

A collecting bank has priority in the proceeds of an item and accompanying documents in which it has a security interest as against other secured parties with security interests in those proceeds. UCC §§ 4–210, 9–322(f).

b. **If the Collateral is Deposit Accounts, Investment Property, Letter-of-Credit Rights, Chattel Paper, Instruments, Negotiable Documents of Title and the Proceeds are Cash Proceeds or Proceeds of Same Type as the Original Collateral**

If a security interest in deposit accounts, investment property, letter-of-credit rights, chattel paper, instruments or negotiable documents of title qualifies for priority over a conflicting security interest in the same collateral under UCC § 9–327 through UCC § 9–331, then the security interest with priority in that collateral also has priority in proceeds of that collateral if the following criteria are met. First the security interest in the proceeds of the collateral must be perfected. Second, the proceeds must either be cash proceeds or proceeds of the same type as the original collateral. Third, if the proceeds are proceeds of proceeds, all intervening proceeds are either cash proceeds, proceeds of the same type as the original collateral, or an account relating to the collateral. UCC § 9–322(c). This rule is subject to being trumped by the first exception, that is, if a particular rule provides for priority of a security interest in the type of collateral that is proceeds. UCC § 9–322(f).

c. **If the Collateral is Chattel Paper, Deposit Accounts, Negotiable Documents of Title, Instruments, Investment Property, or Letter-of-Credit Rights in Which a Security Interest is Perfected by a Non-Filing Method and the Proceeds are Not Cash Proceeds, Chattel Paper, Negotiable Documents of Title, Instruments, Investment Property, or Letter-of-Credit Rights**

If a security interest in certain types of collateral is perfected by a non-filing method and the proceeds of that collateral are of a particular type, the priority of conflicting perfected security interests in the proceeds is determined by the order of filing a financing statement covering the type of collateral that is the proceeds. The original collateral must be chattel paper, deposit accounts, negotiable documents of title, instruments, investment property, or letter-of-credit rights. The proceeds must *not* be cash proceeds, chattel paper, negotiable documents of title, instruments, investment property, or letter-of-credit rights. UCC § 9–322(d), (e). This rule is subject to being trumped by the first exception, that is, if a particular rule provides for priority of a security interest in the type of collateral that is proceeds. UCC § 9–322(f).

d. **Exceptions to the First to File or Perfect Rule That Do Not Address Proceeds of These Types of Collateral**

Some of the exceptions to the first to file or perfect rule do not address the priority of the secured party's security interest in proceeds of that item.

(1) **Priority in Proceeds of an Accession When the Whole Is Covered by a Certificate of Title**

If goods are covered by a certificate of title and there is an accession to those goods, a secured party that has perfected its security interest in the goods as a whole (including the accession) through notation of its security interest on the certificate of title will have priority over a secured party that has perfected its security interest in the accession. UCC § 9–335(d). If the goods covered by the certificate of title are sold, the priority rule does not state that the secured party that has perfected by notation on the certificate of title will have priority in the proceeds of the goods as a whole over the security interest perfected in the accession as to the proceeds attributable to the accession.

(2) **Priority in Proceeds of Commingled Goods When Security Interests Have Co-Equal Priority**

If conflicting perfected security interests in a product or mass both attached to the product or mass because they were attached to goods before they were commingled, the conflicting perfected security interests in the product or mass have co-equal priority based upon the value of the goods commingled at the time of commingling. UCC § 9–336(f). The section does not state that the co-equal priority extends to the proceeds.

(3) **Priority in Proceeds of Goods Covered by Clean Certificate of Title**

A secured party's security interest that was perfected in goods and as to which a clean certificate of title is issued is subordinated to a secured party's security interest that is subsequently perfected on that clean certificate of title without knowledge of the previously perfected security interest. UCC § 9–337(2). The priority rule does not state that the priority for the second secured party extends to proceeds of the good covered by the certificate of title.

(4) **Priority in Proceeds of Goods Covered by a Negotiable Document of Title When Conflicting Security Interest Perfected Directly in Goods**

If goods are covered by a negotiable document of title and a security interest is perfected in the document of title, that security interest will have priority in the goods over a security interest perfected directly in the goods while the goods are covered by that negotiable document of title. UCC § 9–312(c). The rule does not specify that the priority carries over to the proceeds of the goods.

(5) Priority in Proceeds of Documents Presented Under a Letter of Credit
The priority for an issuer or nominated person in certain documents presented under a letter of credit does not specify that it applies to proceeds. UCC § 5–118.

(6) Priority in Proceeds of Goods Subject to a Security Interest Created Under Articles 2 and 2A
The priority for a seller, buyer or lessee that is provided under UCC § 9–110 does not specify that it applies to proceeds of the goods subject to the security interest.

18. Exception: Priority in Proceeds of Collateral Subject to Agricultural Liens

Article 9 leaves to other law the priority rules for proceeds of collateral that are subject to agricultural liens. Whether the agricultural lien attaches to proceeds of farm products subject to the agricultural lien (assuming the proceeds are not farm products), how to perfect the agricultural lien in proceeds of the farm products, and the priority of the agricultural lien in the proceeds of the farm products, assuming it does attach, are all left to other law. UCC § 9–315, cmt. 9.

19. Exception: Priority in Supporting Obligations

If a security interest in deposit accounts, investment property, letter-of-credit rights, chattel paper, instruments or negotiable documents of title qualifies for priority over a conflicting security interest in the same collateral under UCC § 9–327 through UCC § 9–331, then the security interest with priority in that collateral also has priority in supporting obligations of that collateral. UCC § 9–322(c). This rule is subject to being trumped by a particular rule that provides for priority in that type of collateral, such as UCC § 9–329 which provides for priority in letter-of-credit rights. UCC § 9–322(f).

20. Exception: Future Advances

The priority of the security interest that secures the future advance has the same priority as the first advance unless the security interest secures an advance that is made when the security is perfected automatically under UCC § 9–309 or UCC § 9–312(e), (f), and (g) and while the secured party has taken no other perfection step as against the collateral. In that case, the security interest that secures the future advance has priority from the date the future advance was made. UCC § 9–323(a). This exception does not apply if the secured party has made a binding commitment to give value while the security interest is perfected by a method other than temporary perfection under UCC § 9–309 or § 9–312(e), (f), or (g). UCC § 9–323(a). In the case of a sale of accounts, chattel paper, payment intangibles, or a promissory notes or in a consignment subject to Article 9, only the general rule applies, that is, the priority of a security interest for subsequent advances is the same as the priority for the security interest securing the first advance. UCC § 9–323(c).

21. Exception: Double Debtor

If a transferee acquires collateral that is subject to a security interest, UCC § 9–315(a)(1), that existing security interest is perfected when the transferee acquires the collateral, and that existing security interest remains perfected thereafter, any security interest created by the transferee is subordinate to the security interest created by the transferor. UCC § 9–325(a). This subordination rule operates whenever the security interest created by the transferee would have priority over the preexisting security interest under the three general rules in UCC § 9–322(a) or under the purchase money priority rules in UCC § 9–324. The security interest of a buyer or lessee created under Articles 2 or 2A is also subordinated to the preexisting security interest under this rule. UCC § 9–325(b).

22. Exception: New Debtor

a. Both Old and New Debtor Located in Same Jurisdiction

Assume the old and new debtor are located in the same jurisdiction so as to not implicate a change in governing law for perfection purposes. UCC §§ 9–203(d), 9–316. As to existing collateral that is transferred to the new debtor, the secured party's financing statement against the old debtor remains effective to perfect its security interest in that collateral. UCC § 9–507. As to collateral that the new debtor acquires within four months after new debtor became bound to the security agreement that the old debtor had entered into with the secured party, the financing statement filed against the old debtor is effective to perfect the secured party's security interest in that newly-acquired collateral. UCC § 9–508. A secured party of the old debtor may need to take action to obtain perfection of a security interest in collateral that the new debtor acquires more than four months after the new debtor becomes the new debtor if the difference between the name of the old and new debtor is seriously misleading. In that case, the secured party of the old debtor must file a new initial financing statement against the new debtor. UCC § 9–508. If there are conflicting security interests in the collateral in the hands of the new debtor, the following priority rules apply.

(1) **Financing Statements Effective Solely Under UCC § 9–508**
   If the filed financing statements against the new debtor are effective solely because of the rule of UCC § 9–508 that allows the financing statement against the old debtor to be effective to perfect a security interest against the new debtor's collateral that the new debtor has or acquires after becoming the new debtor, the priority rules that are detailed above control the priority of the conflicting security interests unless the security agreements were entered into by different original debtors. UCC § 9–326(b).

(2) **Financing Statements Not Effective Solely Under UCC § 9–508**
   If the filed financing statement of a secured party against the new debtor is effective solely because of the rule of UCC § 9–508 that allows the financing statement against the old debtor to be effective to perfect a security interest against the new debtor's collateral that the new debtor has or acquires after becoming the new debtor, that secured party's security interest is subordinate to a security interest that is perfected against the new debtor by a method other than under UCC § 9–508. UCC § 9–326(a).

(3) **Different Original Old Debtors**
   If the conflicting security interests are perfected solely by a filing that is effective under UCC § 9–508 and the security agreements that the new debtor is bound to were entered into by different old debtors, then the conflicting security interests have priority in the order in which the new debtor became bound to the security agreements. UCC § 9–326(b).

b. New Debtor Located in Different Jurisdiction Than Old Debtor

Assume a new debtor becomes bound to the old debtor's security agreement. UCC § 9–203(d), (e). If a new debtor is located in a jurisdiction that is different than the old debtor, a secured party's financing statement filed against the old debtor in the old jurisdiction will be effective for one year to perfect a security interest in collateral that the old debtor transferred to the new debtor. UCC § 9–316(a). As to collateral that the new debtor has and acquires within four months after it becomes the new debtor, the financing statement filed against the old debtor in the old jurisdiction will remain effective to perfect the security interest of the old debtor's secured party in those assets. UCC § 9–316(i). If there are conflicting security interests in the collateral in the hands of the new debtor, the following priority rules apply.

(1) Financing Statements Effective Solely Under UCC § 9–316(i)(1)

If the filed financing statements against the new debtor are effective solely because of the rule of UCC 9–316(i)(1) that allows the financing statement against the old debtor to be effective to perfect a security interest against the new debtor's collateral that the new debtor has or acquires within four months after becoming the new debtor, the priority rules that are detailed above, control the priority of the conflicting security interests unless the security agreements were entered into by different original debtors. UCC § 9–326(b).

(2) Financing Statements Not Effective Solely Under UCC § 9–316(i)(1)

If the filed financing statement of a secured party against the new debtor is effective solely because of the rule of UCC § 9–316(i)(1) that allows the financing statement against the old debtor to be effective to perfect a security interest against the new debtor's collateral that the new debtor has or acquires after becoming the new debtor, that secured party's security interest is subordinate to a security interest that is perfected against the new debtor by a method other than under UCC § 9–316(i)(1). UCC § 9–326(a).

(3) Different Original Old Debtors

If the conflicting security interests are perfected solely by filed financing statements that are effective under UCC § 9–316(i)(1) and the security agreements that the new debtor is bound to were entered into by different old debtors, then the conflicting security interests have priority in the order in which the new debtor became bound to the security agreements. UCC § 9–326(b).

E. PRIORITY OF SECURITY INTERESTS AGAINST REAL ESTATE CLAIMANTS REGARDING FIXTURES

The priority dispute between a security interest in a fixture and a person whose claim in the fixtures arises under real estate law is determined by the priority rule of UCC § 9–334.

1. Real Estate Interests

The interests arising under real estate law are those of the owner of the real estate (as long as the owner is not the debtor), the person with a property interest in the fixture, and an encumbrancer of the real estate. An encumbrancer is a person with a property interest, but not an ownership interest, in real property. UCC § 9–102(a)(32).

2. Fixtures

A fixture is a good that is considered to be related to the real estate in such a way that an interest in the good can be granted under real estate law as well as personal property law. UCC § 9–102(a)(41). Building materials that are incorporated into an improvement on real estate are not considered to be fixtures (i.e. personal property) but rather are part of the real estate. UCC § 9–334(a).

3. Perfection of a Security Interest in Fixtures

To perfect a security interest in fixtures, the secured party may perfect either by filing a financing statement against the goods in the central filing office of the debtor's location or by filing a fixture financing statement in the real estate recording office for the real estate where the fixture is located. UCC §§ 9–301, 9–501. The fixture financing statement has additional requirements in order to file it in the real estate records, including a description of the real estate on which the fixtures are located. UCC § 9–502.

4. General Priority Rule

A security interest in fixtures is subordinate to the conflicting claim of an encumbrancer or owner of the real estate (other than the debtor). UCC § 9–334(c). This rule is subject to several exceptions.

5. Exception for Purchase Money Security Interests in Fixtures

If the secured party has a purchase money security interest in the fixture and perfected its security interest in fixtures by filing an effective fixture financing statement in the real estate records before the goods become fixtures or within 20 days thereafter, the security interest will have priority over the conflicting interest of the real estate owner (that is not the debtor) and an encumbrancer if the interests of the owner and encumbrancer are in the real estate prior to the goods becoming fixtures and the debtor has an interest of record or is in possession of the real estate. UCC § 9–334(d). The secured party with a purchase money security interest in fixtures is not entitled to priority in the fixture over the interests of a construction mortgage holder if the construction mortgage holder recorded its mortgage prior to the filing of the fixture financing statement and the goods become fixtures before the construction project is complete. UCC § 9–334(h).

6. Exception for First-Filed Interest

The security interest in the fixture will have priority over the interests of the owner of the real estate or the encumbrancer in the fixture if (i) the secured party has perfected its security interest in the fixture by a filed fixture financing statement prior to the recording in the real estate records of the interest of the encumbrancer or owner of the real property, (ii) the security interest has priority over the interest of the predecessor in title to the owner or encumbrancer, and (iii) the debtor has an interest in the real estate or is in possession of the real estate. UCC § 9–334(e)(1).

7. Exception for Security Interests in Particular Types of Fixtures

A perfected security interest in the fixtures will have priority over the conflicting interest of the owner of the real estate or encumbrancer in those fixtures if (i) the goods that become fixtures are readily removable factory or office machines, equipment that is not primarily used or leased for operation of the real estate, or replacements of domestic appliances that are consumer goods and (ii) the secured party perfects its security interest in those goods in any manner (including filing a financing statement that is not a fixture financing statement or automatic perfection, if applicable) before the goods become fixtures. UCC § 9–334(e)(2).

8. Exception for Legal or Equitable Liens

If the security interest is perfected through any method permitted under Article 9 (including the filing of a non-fixture financing statement or automatic perfection) and the holder of the conflicting interest obtained its lien in the fixture through equitable or legal proceedings as against the real estate, the security interest will have priority over the legal or equitable lien. UCC § 9–334(e)(3).

9. Exception for Manufactured-Home Transactions Governed by Certificate of Title Law

If a manufactured home is a fixture, a security interest that is perfected in the manufactured home under an applicable certificate of title law has priority over the interests of the real estate owner or encumbrancer in the manufactured home. UCC § 9–334(e)(4).

10. Exception Based Upon Consent of Real Estate Claimant

A security interest will have priority over the conflicting interest of the encumbrancer or owner of the real estate if the encumbrancer or owner has consented, in an authenticated record, to the security interest or disclaimed an interest in the fixture. UCC § 9–334(f)(1). The security interest in the fixture need not be perfected for this rule to apply.

11. Exception Based Upon Debtor's Right to Remove the Goods

If as against the owner of the real estate or the encumbrancer, the debtor has a right to remove the fixture from the real estate, a security interest in that fixture will have priority over the rights in the fixture of the encumbrancer or real estate owner. UCC § 9–334(f)(2). The security interest in the fixture need not be perfected for this rule to apply. This priority for the security interest will continue for a reasonable time to allow removal of the fixture if the debtor's right to remove the fixture as against the owner or encumbrancer expires. UCC § 9–334(g).

12. Exception for Crops

A security interest in crops has priority over the interest of the encumbrancer or owner of the real estate if (i) under real estate law the interests of an encumbrancer or owner of real estate extends to the crops growing on the land, (ii) the debtor has an interest of record or possession of the real estate where the crops are grown, and (iii) the security interest in the crops is perfected in any manner permitted under Article 9. UCC § 9–334(i).

F. PRIORITY OF A SECURITY INTEREST OR AGRICULTURAL LIEN AS AGAINST TRANSFEREES

Mere attachment of a security interest does not prevent the debtor from transferring its rights in the collateral to other parties. If the transferee is another secured party (that is the transfer creates a security interest), the rights of parties with conflicting security interests or an agricultural lien are generally governed by the rules set forth previously in this Chapter regarding priority. In some circumstances, however, the transferee that is a secured party may be able to use the rules that follow to establish its priority position in the transferred collateral.

1. General Rule

The general rule is that collateral that is subject to a security interest or agricultural lien remains subject to that security interest or agricultural lien even after the collateral is transferred to another person. UCC § 9–315(a)(1). That general rule is subject to several exceptions as set forth below.

2. Exception Based Upon Secured Party's Consent

If the secured party that holds the security interest or agricultural lien consents to the disposition of the collateral free from the security interest or agricultural lien, then the transferee will take the collateral free of the security interest or agricultural lien. UCC § 9–315(a)(1).

3. Exception for Transferees in Ordinary Course of Business

a. Buyer of Goods in Ordinary Course of Business

A buyer in ordinary course of business of goods (other than farm products) from a seller that has created the security interest in the goods (that is, the seller is the debtor) takes the goods free of a perfected security interest in the goods even if the buyer knows that the security interest exists. UCC § 9–320(a). The buyer in ordinary course of business also takes the goods free of an unperfected security interest. UCC § 9–320, cmt. 2. A buyer in ordinary course of farm products will take the farm products free of a security interest even if it is perfected and even if the buyer knows the security interest exists unless the buyer and secured party have complied with a federal notification scheme. For the buyer to take the farm products free of the security interest, the buyer must buy the farm products in the ordinary course of business, the seller must be a person engaged in farming operations, the seller must sell the farm products in the ordinary course of the seller's business, and the seller must be the person that created the security interest. This protection for the buyer will not exist if the notification scheme prescribed in the Food Security Act is followed. 7 U.S.C. § 1631(d).

b. Lessee in Ordinary Course of Business

A lessee in ordinary course of business of goods will take its leasehold interest in the goods free of a security interest created by the lessor. This protection applies even if the security interest is perfected and the lessee knows that the security interest exists. UCC § 9–321(c).

c. Licensees in Ordinary Course of Business

A licensee in ordinary course of business under a nonexclusive license takes its rights free of a security interest in the general intangible that is being licensed if that security interest was created by the licensor. This protection applies even if the security interest is perfected and the licensee knows that the security interest exists. UCC § 9–321(b).

d. Security Interest that Secures Future Advances

A buyer in ordinary course of business or lessee in ordinary course of business that take the goods free of a security interest created by the seller or lessor under Article 9 also take the goods free of a security interest that secures an advance made after the sale or lease. UCC § 9–323, cmt. 6. Presumably the licensee in ordinary course of business has the same protection but the comment does not explicitly state that rule.

4. Exception for Transferees When the Security Interest or Agricultural Lien Is Unperfected

a. Buyers of Certain Tangible Collateral

A buyer (other than a secured party) of tangible chattel paper, tangible documents of title, goods, instruments, or a certificated security takes those items free of a security interest if the buyer gives value for the item and takes delivery of the item without knowledge of the security interest or agricultural lien and at a time when the security interest or agricultural lien is unperfected. UCC § 9–317(b). Even if a buyer takes possession of goods at the time the security interest in the collateral is unperfected, if the security interest is a purchase money security interest and the secured party perfects its security interest by filing a financing statement within 20 days after the debtor received delivery of the goods, the buyer will take the goods subject to that purchase money security interest. UCC § 9–317(e). If a buyer not in ordinary course of business takes the goods subject to a security interest because the buyer does not qualify to take free of the security interest under UCC § 9–317(b) and the secured party subsequently makes an advance, the buyer will take the goods free of the security interest that secures that future advance if the secured party made the advance with knowledge of the buyer's purchase or made the advance 45 days or more after the purchase. UCC § 9–323(d). The buyer not in ordinary course of business will not take the goods free of the security interest that secures the advance if the secured party made the advance or a commitment to make an advance without knowledge of the purchase and before the end of the 45-day time period. UCC § 9–323(e).

b. Lessees of Goods

A lessee of goods that gives value and takes delivery of the goods without knowledge of the security interest or agricultural lien while the security interest or agricultural lien is unperfected takes the goods free of the security interest or agricultural lien. UCC § 9–317(c). Even if a lessee takes possession of goods at the time the security interest in the collateral is unperfected, if the security interest is a purchase money security interest and the secured party perfects its security interest by filing a financing statement within 20 days after the debtor received delivery of the goods, the lessee will take the goods subject to that purchase money security interest. UCC § 9–317(e). If a lessee not in ordinary course of business takes the goods subject to a security interest and the secured party subsequently makes an advance, the lessee will take the goods free of the security interest that secures that future advance if the secured party made the advance with knowledge of the lease or made the advance 45 days or more after the lease contract becomes enforceable. UCC § 9–323(f). The lessee not in ordinary course of business will not take the goods free of the security interest that secures the advance if the secured party made the advance or a commitment to do so without knowledge of the lease and before the end of the 45-day time period. UCC § 9–323(g).

c. Licensees of General Intangibles

A licensee of a general intangible takes the general intangible free of a security interest in the general intangible if the licensee gives value without knowledge of the security interest and while it is unperfected. UCC § 9–317(d). Unlike a buyer or lessee of goods, a licensee of software does not take subject to later perfected purchase money security interest in the software. UCC § 9–317(e). Unlike a buyer or lessee of goods, a licensee of general intangibles not in ordinary course of business that takes subject to the security interest does not have any protection against future advances that are secured by the security interest in the licensed general intangibles. *See* UCC § 9–323.

d. Buyers of Certain Intangible Collateral

A buyer (other than a secured party) of collateral, other than tangible chattel paper, tangible documents, goods, instruments, or a certificated security, takes the collateral free of a security interest in the collateral if the buyer gives value without knowledge of the security interest and while it is unperfected. UCC § 9–317(d). Presumably if a buyer of this type of collateral takes free of a security interest under this priority rule, it would also take free of any security interest in that collateral that might otherwise secure a future advance. See UCC § 9–323, cmt. 6. Unlike a buyer or lessee of goods, buyers of these types of intangible collateral that take subject to the security interest do not have any protection against future advances that are secured by a security interest in the sold collateral. See UCC § 9–323.

5. Exception for Consumer Buyers of Consumer Goods

If a consumer sells its consumer goods to another consumer who buys the goods primarily for personal, family, or household purposes, the buyer takes free of a perfected security interest in the goods if (i) the consumer buyer does not have knowledge of the security interest at the time it bought the goods, (ii) the consumer buyer gave value, and (iii) the buy takes place before an effective financing statement is filed against the goods. UCC § 9–320(b). Compliance with a certificate of title statute to perfect the security interest is the equivalent of filing an effective financing statement. UCC § 9–320, cmt. 5.

6. Exception for Buyer of Certificate of Title Goods When Certificate Does Not Note Security Interest

If a state issues a certificate of title when a security interest in the goods covered by that certificate has been previously perfected by any allowed method and that new certificate does not show that security interest or indicate that security interests that are not noted may exist, a buyer of that good covered by a "clean" certificate of title will take the good free of the unnoted security interest if the buyer meets certain criteria. First, the buyer must not be a secured party and must not be in the business of selling goods of the kind. Second, the buyer must give value and receive delivery of the goods after the clean certificate of title was issued. Third, the buyer must give value and receive delivery of the goods without knowledge of the security interest. UCC § 9–337(1).

7. Exception for Purchasers of Collateral in Reliance on Certain Incorrect Information on a Financing Statement

In the event the financing statement is sufficient to perfect under UCC § 9–502 but contains errors in the information required by UCC § 9–516(b)(5), a purchaser of collateral in reasonable reliance on that incorrect information takes the collateral free of the security interest or agricultural lien that is perfected by that inaccurate financing statement. The purchaser must not be a secured party and must give value in reasonable reliance on the incorrect information. If the collateral is tangible chattel paper, tangible documents of title, goods, instruments, or a certificated security, the purchaser must also take delivery of that collateral in reasonable reliance on the incorrect information. UCC § 9–338(2).

8. Exception for Certain Transferees of Investment Property

A transferee of investment property that qualifies as a protected transferee under the rules of Article 8 will take the investment property free of a perfected security interest in the investment property. UCC § 9–331. A secured party or a person other than a secured party may qualify for this protection of transferees.

a. Protected Purchaser of a Security

A protected purchaser of a security (whether certificated or uncertificated) that gives value, does not have notice of any adverse claim to the security, and takes control of the security will have priority over a previously perfected security interest in the security. UCC §§ 9–331(a), 8–303(a).

b. Priority of a Person That Becomes an Entitlement Holder of a Securities Entitlement

A person that acquires a securities entitlement for value and without notice of an adverse claim is protected from any assertion of an adverse claim, including a claim of a security interest, in the securities entitlement. UCC §§ 8–502, 9–331(a).

c. Priority of a Purchaser From a Securities Intermediary of a Securities Entitlement

A purchaser of a securities entitlement from a securities intermediary takes free of the entitlement holder's property claims to the securities entitlement if the purchaser gives value, obtains control of the securities entitlement, and does not act in collusion with the securities intermediary in violating the securities intermediary's obligations to the entitlement holder. UCC §§ 8–503(e), 9–331(a).

d. Priority of a Purchaser From an Entitlement Holder of a Securities Entitlement

A purchaser of a securities entitlement from an entitlement holder takes free of adverse claims, including security interests, to the securities entitlement if the purchaser gives value, does not have notice of an adverse claim, and obtains control of the securities entitlement. UCC §§ 8–510, 9–331(a).

9. Exception for Transferee of Funds From Deposit Account

A transferee (including a secured party) of funds from a deposit account will take those funds free of a security interest in the deposit account even if the security interest is perfected unless the transferee acted in collusion with the debtor in violating the rights of the secured party with the security interest in the deposit account. UCC § 9–332(b).

10. Exception for Transferees of Money

A transferee (including a secured party) of money takes the money free of a security interest in the money even if the security interest is perfected unless the transferee acts in collusion with the debtor in violating the rights of the secured party with a security interest in the money. UCC § 9–332(a).

11. Exception for Purchasers of Instruments

If a person (including a secured party) purchases an instrument for value, takes possession of the instrument in good faith, and does not have knowledge at the time it takes possession that the purchase violates the rights of the secured party, the purchaser's rights in the instrument will have priority over the security interest if that security interest is perfected by a method other than possession. UCC § 9–330(d). If the instrument is a negotiable instrument and the holder (including a secured party) of the instrument qualifies as a holder in due course of the instrument, the holder in due course will take the instrument free of the claims of the secured party with a security interest in the instrument even if the security interest is perfected. UCC § 9–331.

12. Exception for Holders of Negotiable Documents of Title

If a person (including a secured party) becomes a holder of a negotiable document of title by due negotiation, the holder will take the document of title and the goods covered by the document free of a security interest in the document and the goods even if that security interest is perfected. UCC § 9–331. This rule is subject to an exception if the security interest is perfected in the goods prior to the issuance of the negotiable document of title and the secured party did not entrust the goods or the document to the debtor with apparent or actual authority to dispose of the goods nor acquiesce in the debtor's procurement of the document of title. In that case, the secured party's security interest in the goods is not defeated by the interest of the holder of the negotiable document of title. UCC § 7–503.

13. Exception for Purchasers of Chattel Paper

If a purchaser (including a secured party) in good faith takes possession of tangible chattel paper or control of electronic chattel paper in the ordinary course of the purchaser's business and gives new value for the chattel paper, the purchaser will have priority over a security interest in the chattel paper that is claimed merely as proceeds of inventory subject to a security interest as long as the chattel paper does not indicate that it has been assigned to an identified assignee other than the purchaser. UCC § 9–330(a). If a purchaser (including a secured party) in good faith takes possession of tangible chattel paper or control of electronic chattel paper in the ordinary course of the purchaser's business and gives new value for the chattel paper, the purchaser will have priority over a security interest in the chattel paper that is claimed other than as merely proceeds of inventory subject to a security interest as long as the purchaser is without knowledge that the purchase violates the rights of the secured party with the conflicting security interest. UCC § 9–330(b).

G. CHOICE OF LAW FOR PRIORITY AND THE EFFECT OF PERFECTION OR NONPERFECTION

1. General Rule for Agricultural Liens

The law of the jurisdiction in which the farm products are located will govern the effect of perfection or nonperfection and priority of agricultural liens in the farm products. UCC § 9–302.

2. General Rule for Security Interests

The general rule is that the law of the debtor's location governs the priority and the effect of perfection and non perfection of a security interest in the collateral. UCC § 9–301(1). That rule is subject to the following exceptions.

a. Exception for Possessory Security Interests

If the security interest is a possessory security interest, the priority and effect of perfection or nonperfection of the security interest will be determined by the law of the state where the collateral is located. UCC § 9–301(2).

b. Exception for Tangible Collateral

If the collateral is tangible negotiable documents of title, goods, instruments, money, or tangible chattel paper, the effect of perfection or nonperfection and priority of the security interest will be determined by the law of the jurisdiction where the collateral is located if the security interest is a nonpossessory security interest. UCC § 9–301(3).

c. Exception for As-Extracted Collateral

If the collateral is as-extracted collateral, the effect of perfection or nonperfection and priority of a security interest will be determined by the location of the wellhead or minehead. UCC § 9–301(4).

d. Exception for Goods Covered by a Certificate of Title

If the collateral is goods covered by a certificate of title, the effect of perfection or nonperfection and priority of a security interest in those goods will be determined by the law of the jurisdiction issuing the certificate of title until the goods cease to be covered by that certificate of title. UCC § 9–303.

e. Exception for Deposit Accounts

If the collateral is a deposit account, the effect of perfection or nonperfection and priority of a security interest in the deposit account will be determined by the law of the depositary bank's jurisdiction. UCC § 9–304(a).

f. Exception for Certificated Security

If the security interest in a certificated security is perfected by a method other than filing a financing statement or other than the automatic perfection of a security interest created by a broker or a securities intermediary, the effect of perfection and nonperfection and priority is determined by the law of the jurisdiction where the certificated security is located. UCC § 9–305(a)(1), (c).

g. Exception for Uncertificated Security

If the security interest in an uncertificated security is perfected by a method other than filing a financing statement or other than the automatic perfection of a security interest created by a broker or a securities intermediary, the effect of perfection and nonperfection and priority is determined by the law of the jurisdiction where the issuer is located. UCC § 9–305(a)(2), (c).

h. Exception for Securities Entitlement or Securities Account

If the security interest in a securities entitlement or a securities account is perfected by a method other than filing a financing statement or other than the automatic perfection of a security interest created by a broker or a securities intermediary, the effect of perfection and nonperfection and priority is determined by the law of the jurisdiction where the securities intermediary is located. UCC § 9–305(a)(3), (c).

i. Exception for Commodity Contract or Commodity Account

If the security interest in a commodity contract or commodities account is perfected by a method other than filing a financing statement or other than the automatic perfection of a security interest created by a commodity intermediary, the effect of perfection and nonperfection and priority is determined by the law of the jurisdiction where the commodity intermediary is located. UCC § 9–305(a)(4), (c).

j. Exception for Letter-of-Credit Rights

If a security interest is in a letter-of-credit right and is perfected other than through automatic perfection as a supporting obligation for a right to payment, the law of the location of the issuer or nominated person will govern priority and the effect of perfection or nonperfection of that security interest as long as the issuer or nominated person is located in a state of the United States. UCC § 9–306.

H. POST-CLOSING CHANGES AND EFFECT ON PRIORITY

Post-closing events will have an effect on the priority of the security interest or agricultural lien, particularly as priority is determined by the first to file or perfect rule which requires that the secured party either have an effective filing covering the collateral or perfection of the security interest or agricultural lien in order to preserve the date of filing or perfection as the applicable priority date. UCC § 9–322(a).

1. Security Interest or Agricultural Lien Perfection Lapses

If the secured party fails to maintain perfection of its security interest or agricultural lien in the collateral and an interest of a transferee arises in the collateral while the security interest or agricultural lien is unperfected, the priority rules may result in the interest of the secured party being subordinated to the transferee's interests. UCC § 9–317.

2. **Security Interest or Agricultural Lien Deemed Not Perfected as Against Previous Purchasers if Failure to File Effective Continuation Statement**

   If a secured party fails to file an effective continuation statement so that the effectiveness of the filed financing statement lapses and that financing statement was the method of perfection of a security interest or agricultural lien in the collateral, the security interest or agricultural lien is deemed unperfected as against prior purchasers of the collateral for value (including other secured parties). UCC § 9–515(c).

3. **Security Interest Deemed Not Perfected as Against Previous Purchasers If Governing Law Changes**

   a. **Change in Debtor's Location**

      If the secured party must take action to maintain its perfection of a security interest when the debtor moves location from one jurisdiction to another jurisdiction and the secured party fails to take the required action in the new jurisdiction during the applicable time period, the security interest becomes unperfected. The security interest is also deemed unperfected as against purchasers for value that had previously acquired interests in the collateral. UCC § 9–316(a), (b), (h).

   b. **Change in Identity of Debtor**

      If the secured party must take action to maintain its perfection of a security interest when the debtor transfers collateral to a debtor located in a new jurisdiction or a new debtor becomes bound to the old debtor's security agreement, UCC § 9–203(d), (e), and the secured party fails to take the required action in the new jurisdiction during the applicable time period, the security interest becomes unperfected. The security interest is also deemed unperfected as against purchasers for value that had previously acquired interests in the collateral. UCC § 9–316(a)(3), (b), (i).

   c. **Goods Covered by a Certificate of Title**

      If a security interest is perfected in goods in any manner and the goods become covered by a certificate of title issued by a jurisdiction, the secured party has four months to obtain perfection of its security interest by noting it on the certificate of title or by taking possession of the goods. If the secured party fails to do so during the four-month time period, its security interest becomes unperfected and is deemed unperfected as against a previous purchaser for value. UCC § 9–316(d), (e).

d. Change in Third Party's Location

If the security interest is in deposit accounts, letter-of-credit rights, or investment property whereby the governing law is determined by the jurisdiction of the bank, issuer, nominated person, securities intermediary, or commodity intermediary as the case may be, and if that entity's location is moved to another jurisdiction, the secured party has four months to obtain perfection of its security interest in the new jurisdiction. If the secured party fails to do so during the four-month time period, its security interest becomes unperfected and is deemed unperfected as against a previous purchaser for value. UCC § 9–316(f), (g).

4. Transfers of Collateral

As noted in the priority rules explored above, a secured party may find that a transfer of collateral effectively subordinates the secured party's security interest or agricultural lien to the transferee's interest in the collateral or results in the transferee taking the collateral free of the security interest or agricultural lien.

I. FEDERAL TAX LIENS

1. Attachment of the Federal Tax Lien

The federal tax lien arises when the taxpayer refuses to pay the tax, interest, and penalties after demand. 26 U.S.C. § 6321. The lien is considered attached to the taxpayer's property and interests in property as of the date of assessment of the tax liability and also attaches to any property the taxpayer later acquires. 26 U.S.C. § 6322. Assessment usually precedes the demand for payment and does not require any notice to the taxpayer. The tax lien attaches to all of the taxpayer's property or interests in property without regard to any state or federal exemptions from execution on judgments. Whether a taxpayer has an interest in property is determined by state law. The tax lien exists until it is satisfied or until the underlying assessment of taxes may not be collected by reason of lapse of time. The general time period for collection of the tax is 10 years from assessment although there are several exceptions to that general rule. 26 U.S.C. §§ 6322, 6502.

2. Filing a Notice of the Tax Lien

Even though it is not necessary for the federal government to file a notice of tax lien in the public records to take action to enforce the lien, the filing of a notice of tax lien will set the priority position of the federal tax lien as against certain types of other lien claims that have attached to the taxpayer's property. The notice must identify the taxpayer, the tax liability giving rise to the form, and the date of assessment of the tax liability. 26 C.F.R. § 301.6323(f)–1(d). The tax lien notice must be filed in the state in which the property is located. Real estate is considered located at its physical location. Personal property is considered located at the residence of the taxpayer at the time the tax lien notice is filed. 26 U.S.C. § 6323(f). A notice of tax lien can be refiled to extend its period of effectiveness beyond 10 years after assessment of the tax. The notice may be refiled within a one-year period that expires 30 days after the 10-year period expires or if it is a second or subsequent refiling of the tax lien notice, within the one-year period after the expiration of the previous 10-year period. 26 U.S.C. § 6323(g)(3).

3. General Priority Rule

The priority of the federal tax lien as against four types of claimants is determined based upon the timing of the filing of the tax lien notice and time in which the claimant's interests are considered to have affixed to the taxpayer's property under the federal tax lien statute. 26 U.S.C. § 6323(a). Whatever is first, the tax lien notice filing or the affixing of the claimant's interest in the taxpayer's property, will have priority. Those four claimants are a holder of a security interest, a purchaser, a mechanic's lienor, and a judgment lien creditor.

a. Holder of a Security Interest

To be a holder of a security interest within the meaning of the federal tax lien statute, the creditor must fulfill the following criteria. First, the creditor must obtain its interest in the taxpayer's property by contract for the purpose of securing payment or performance of an obligation. Second, the property must be "in existence," which means that the taxpayer has to have rights in the property. Third, the creditor must have priority under other law over the rights of a hypothetical lien creditor whose claim is deemed to arise as of the moment of the tax lien filing. Fourth, the creditor must have parted with money or money's worth at the time of the tax lien filing and the security interest is only effective to the extent that money or money's worth has been given. Only when all of those criteria are met, is the creditor considered to be a holder of a security interest. 26 U.S.C. § 6323(h)(1). An agricultural lien holder is not a holder of a security interest within this federal definition as its lien arises by statute and not by contract.

b. Purchaser

To qualify as a purchaser, the person must meet all of the following criteria. First, the person must not acquire its interest in the property because of a security interest or lien. Second, the person must give adequate and full consideration in money or money's worth in exchange for the interest in property. Third, the person must have priority for its interest in property under other law as against subsequent purchasers that did not have notice of the person's purchase. 26 U.S.C. § 6323(h)(6). Whether an Article 9 secured party that is a buyer of accounts, chattel paper, payment intangibles and promissory notes will be treated as a purchaser under this definition or as a holder of a security interest under the above definition is an open question. An agricultural lien holder is not a purchaser under this definition because its interest is a lien interest.

c. Judgment Lien Creditor

This term is not defined in the federal tax lien statute but is defined in the IRS regulations. To qualify as a judgment lien creditor, the claimant must meet the following criteria. The claimant must obtain a valid court judgment for recovery of specific property or a specified sum of money and perfect that judgment under other law. The judgment is not considered perfected under other law until all of the following are established: the identity of the lienor, the identity of the property subject to the lien, and the amount of the lien. 26 C.F.R. § 301.6323(h)–1(g). An Article 9 secured party could be a judgment lien creditor if it obtained a valid court judgment for recovery of the collateral subject to its security interest.

d. Mechanic's Lienor

A mechanic's lienor is a person that has a lien on real estate to secure the value of services or material furnished to construct an improvement on the real estate. The mechanic's lienor's interest arises no earlier than when it first furnished the services or material to the real estate and no earlier than when the lien becomes valid under other law against subsequent purchasers of the real estate without actual notice of the lienor's interest. 26 U.S.C.§ 6323(h)(2). An Article 9 secured party is not a mechanic's lienor.

4. Choateness Doctrine

If the creditor's claim to the taxpayer's property does not qualify as one of the four types of protected claimants as defined above, the federal common law rule of choateness may apply to determine priority of the claim as against the federal tax lien. That rule is that the competing claimant's interest must be choate before the tax lien becomes effective with respect to the taxpayer's property, that is, prior to *assessment* of the tax liability. To be choate, the "identity of the lienor, the property subject to the lien, and the amount of the lien" must all be established. IRS v. McDermott, 507 U.S. 447, 449 (1993).

5. Exceptions to General Priority Rules For Tax Liens

a. Transactions Covered by 26 U.S.C. § 6323(b)

Even though notice of a federal tax lien has been duly filed, a creditor or purchaser may be able to obtain priority for its interest that attaches to the property after the tax lien filing. Ten such exceptions are found in 26 U.S.C. § 6323(b). The following exceptions are most relevant to the priority contests involving a secured party.

(1) Securities
If a person either becomes a purchaser of a security or becomes a holder of a security interest in a security after the tax lien notice is filed and without actual notice or knowledge of the tax lien, the purchaser or holder of the security interest will have priority in the securities over the federal tax lien. 26 U.S.C. § 6323(b)(1).

(2) Motor Vehicles

If a person purchases a motor vehicle after the filing of notice of a federal tax lien against its seller, made the purchase and took possession of the motor vehicle without actual notice or knowledge of the tax lien, and has not relinquished possession of the motor vehicle thereafter, the purchaser's interest in the motor vehicle will have priority over the federal tax lien. 26 U.S.C. § 6323(b)(2).

(3) Purchasers of Tangible Personal Property Sold at Retail

If a person purchases tangible personal property from a seller in a retail sale in the ordinary course of the seller's trade or business after notice of a tax lien has been filed against the seller, that purchaser's interest in the tangible personal property sold will be superior to the federal tax lien unless the purchaser intended to or knows the purchase will hinder, evade or defeat the collection of the tax. 26 U.S.C. § 6323(b)(3).

(4) Purchasers of Tangible Household Goods or Consumer Goods Sold in Casual Sales

If a person purchases tangible personal property that is household goods, personal effects, or certain types of consumer goods (listed in 26 U.S.C. § 6334(a)) in a casual sale, not for resale, and for less than $1,000 after notice of a tax lien is filed against the seller, the purchaser's interest in that property will be superior to the federal tax lien unless the purchaser has actual notice or knowledge of the tax lien or the sale is one of a series of sales. 26 U.S.C. § 6323(b)(4).

(5) Possessory Liens

If a person has a lien on tangible personal property that arises under other law to secure the price of repair or improvement of that property and is continuously in possession of the property, that person will have priority over a federal tax lien even if the lien arises after notice of the federal tax lien is filed against the owner of the property. 26 U.S.C. § 6323(b)(5).

b. Transactions Covered by 26 U.S.C. § 6323(d)

If all of the following are true, the security interest that secures a future advance will have priority over a federal tax lien to the extent of the advance.

First, the secured party must have made the advance within 45 days after the federal tax lien notice was filed. Second, the secured party must have made the advance without actual notice or knowledge of the tax lien filing. Third, the advance must be secured by property that the debtor had an interest in at the time of tax lien filing pursuant to a written security agreement entered into before the tax lien filing. Fourth, under other law, the security interest that secures that advance must have priority over the rights of a hypothetical lien creditor that is deemed to arise at the time of the tax lien filing.

c. Transactions Covered by 26 U.S.C. § 6323(c)

If all of the following criteria are met, the security interest in collateral that arises after the filing of a federal tax lien notice (either because of a future advance or because the collateral was acquired by the debtor after the filing of the tax lien notice) will have priority over the federal tax lien. First, the collateral must be "paper of a kind ordinarily arising in commercial transactions" (such as chattel paper and instruments), accounts, or inventory. Second, the secured party must have a security agreement that provides for creation of a security interest in such types of collateral (either through making loans or purchasing the collateral types other than inventory) that predates the tax lien notice filing. Third, the collateral of the designated type must be acquired by the debtor within 45 days after the tax lien notice was filed. Fourth, the advances that are secured by the security interest in that type of collateral must be made without actual notice or knowledge of the tax lien filing and within 45 days after the tax lien filing.

J. EFFECT OF BANKRUPTCY ON PRIORITY

Distribution of a debtor's assets in bankruptcy, for the most part, respects the rules of priority found in Article 9. Several Bankruptcy Code sections, however, affect the priority of security interests or agricultural liens that would otherwise have priority over other interests in the debtor's assets.

1. Future Advances

Any future advances the secured party makes to a debtor or debtor in possession after commencement of the bankruptcy case will not automatically be secured by any collateral that is part of the bankruptcy estate even if the secured party has a valid future advances clause in its security agreement. The court may, after notice and hearing, approve the granting of a security interest in property of the estate to secure advances made after the bankruptcy petition is filed. 11 U.S.C. § 364.

2. After-Acquired Property

Even if a holder of a security interest has an after-acquired property clause in the security agreement, 11 U.S.C. § 552(a) provides that such a clause is not effective to attach a security interest to property acquired by the bankruptcy estate or the debtor after commencement of the case, unless the prepetition security agreement is sufficient to attach a security interest to postpetition "proceeds, products, offspring, or profits" of property in which the secured party had an interest in before the filing of the bankruptcy case. 11 U.S.C. § 552(b)(1). The terms "proceeds, products, offspring or profits" are not defined in the Bankruptcy Code. Whether the meaning of "proceeds" in Article 9 will apply as the meaning of "proceeds" in this context is not clear.

3. Lien Avoidance

The bankruptcy trustee has several alternatives to use to attempt to avoid a security interest or agricultural lien.

a. Hypothetical Lien Creditor

When the debtor files bankruptcy, the trustee assumes the status of a hypothetical lien creditor that is deemed to arise as of the time of the bankruptcy filing. 11 U.S.C. § 544(a). If an agricultural lien is unperfected at the time of the bankruptcy filing, the bankruptcy trustee will be able to avoid the agricultural lien. UCC § 9–317(a)(2). With one exception, the bankruptcy trustee will be able to avoid a security interest if the secured party has not prior to the bankruptcy filing qualified for priority over a lien creditor under UCC § 9–317(a)(2). If the security interest is a purchase money security interest in the collateral, the secured party may be able to take advantage of UCC § 9–317(e) that permits the security interest to have priority over the rights of a lien creditor that arises after the debtor receives delivery of the collateral if the secured party files an effective financing statement covering the collateral within 20 days after the debtor receives delivery of the collateral.

b. Statutory Liens

A bankruptcy trustee may avoid an agricultural lien if it was not perfected at the time the case was commenced and a hypothetical purchaser of the property that purchased the property as of bankruptcy filing could take priority over the agricultural lien. 11 U.S.C. § 545(2); UCC § 9–317(b), (c).

c. Preferences

(1) Requirements to Find a Preference

The bankruptcy trustee may avoid a transfer of an interest in the debtor's property made to or for the benefit of a creditor on account of antecedent debt made while the debtor was insolvent, made within 90 days preceding the bankruptcy filing (1 year if the transfer is made to or for the benefit of an insider), and that enables the creditor to obtain more than it would in a Chapter 7 liquidation if the transfer had not been made. 11 U.S.C. § 547.

(2) Exceptions to Preference Liability

Even if all of the requirements for preference liability are met, a creditor may attempt to prevent the bankruptcy trustee from avoiding the transfer of the debtor's property to or for the benefit of the creditor by attempting to bring the transaction within one of the exceptions to preference liability found in 11 U.S.C. § 547(c).

(a) Contemporaneous Exchange for New Value Exception

If the transfer of the debtor's interest in property was intended by both the debtor and the creditor to be a contemporaneous exchange of the interest in property for new value given to the debtor and the exchange was indeed "substantially" contemporaneous, the transfer of the debtor's interest in property may not be avoided as a preference. 11 U.S.C. § 547(c)(1).

(b) Ordinary Course Payment Exception

If the transfer of the debtor's interest in property is a payment of a debt that was incurred in the ordinary course of business or financial affairs of the debtor and the transfer was either made (i) in the ordinary course of business or financial affairs of the debtor or (ii) made according to ordinary business terms, the transfer is not avoidable as a preference. 11 U.S.C. § 547(c)(2).

(c) Purchase Money Security Interest Exception

If the transfer of the debtor's interest in property is a purchase money security interest in collateral, the transfer is not avoidable as a preference if all of the following requirements are met. First, the security interest must secure new value the secured party gives to the debtor at or after the time a security agreement granting the security interest is signed. Second, the new value must enable the debtor to acquire the property. Third, the debtor must use the new value to acquire the property. Fourth, the security interest must be perfected on or before 30 days after the debtor receives possession of the collateral. 11 U.S.C. § 547(c)(3).

(d) New Value Exception

If the debtor makes a transfer of its interest in property to a creditor and subsequent to that transfer, the creditor gives new value to the debtor that is unsecured and did not result in the debtor making an unavoidable transfer of an interest in the debtor's property to the creditor, the previous transfer of the debtor's interest in property is not avoidable as a preference to the extent of the amount of the new value given subsequently. 11 U.S.C. § 547(c)(4).

(e) Security Interests in Inventory and Receivables Exception

If the transfer of the debtor's interest in property is the creation of a security interest in inventory and receivables, the transfer is not avoidable unless the secured party to whom the transfer is made improved its position because of the transfer. To determine whether the secured party improved its position, compare the secured party's unsecured position at a set date prior to the bankruptcy filing to the its unsecured position on the date of the filing of the bankruptcy petition. The way in which the secured party improves its position is by lessening the amount by which its debt is unsecured. That set date for the first date is either 90 days prior to the bankruptcy filing or, if the creditor is an insider, one year prior to the bankruptcy filing. If the first grant of value took place during the 90-day time period or the one-year time period (whichever is applicable), the date on which the first grant of value took place is the comparative date. 11 U.S.C. § 547(c)(5). This exception to preference liability only protects transfers of the security interests. It does not protect payments to the secured party.

(f) Statutory Lien Exception

If the statutory lien is not avoidable under 11 U.S.C. § 545, the creation of the statutory lien during the prebankruptcy preference period (90 days or, if an insider, one year) is not avoidable as a preference. 11 U.S.C. § 547(c)(6).

(g) Small Value Transfer Exceptions

If the debtor is an individual debtor who has primarily consumer debts, transfers of the debtor's interest in property that are less than $600 in value are not avoidable as a preference. 11 U.S.C. § 547(c)(8). If a debtor does not have primarily consumer debts, transfers of the debtor's interest in property that are less than $5,850 in value are not avoidable as a preference. 11U.S.C. § 547(c)(9).

d. Fraudulent Transfers

The bankruptcy trustee may use either the state law fraudulent transfer provisions (under 11 U.S.C. § 544(b)) or 11 U.S.C. § 548 to avoid transfers of the debtor's property made prior to bankruptcy that were made with the actual intent to hinder or defraud creditors or that were made for less than reasonably equivalent value and made while the enterprise was undercapitalized, the debtor was unable to pay debts when they came due, or the debtor was insolvent or rendered insolvent.

4. Effect of Transfer Avoidance

The usual effect of avoiding a security interest or agricultural lien is that the secured party will no longer be considered to have a secured claim in the bankruptcy proceeding because the trustee recovers the property transferred (i.e. effectively nullifying the grant of the security interest or the agricultural lien). 11 U.S.C. § 550(a). The secured party will still be able to make an unsecured claim in the bankruptcy for the amount of the debt that is owed according to the claims allowance procedure. 11 U.S.C. §§ 501, 502. The avoided security interest or agricultural lien is preserved for the benefit of the estate. 11 U.S.C. § 551. The bankruptcy trustee may also recover, in most circumstances, the value of the transferred property from the initial transferee or a subsequent transferee from the initial transferee. 11 U.S.C. § 550(a). The trustee is entitled to only a single satisfaction so that if the transfer is avoidable and the trustee recovers the property transferred, the trustee may not then, in addition, recover the property's value from the transferee. 11 U.S.C. § 550(d).

5. Equitable Subordination

A secured party must be sensitive to equitable considerations a court may invoke to subordinate its otherwise perfected security interest or agricultural lien. 11 U.S.C. § 510. Grounds for equitable subordination include exercising too much influence and control over the affairs of the debtor that result in an unfair detriment to the debtor's other creditors.

■ VI. ENFORCEMENT OF A SECURITY INTEREST OR AGRICULTURAL LIEN

A. GENERAL PRINCIPLES OF ENFORCEMENT

Enforcement refers to the concept of realizing value from the collateral to apply against the debt that the obligor owes to the secured party.

1. Relationship to Scope of Article 9

The enforcement provisions of Article 9 only apply to the enforcement of a security interest or agricultural lien that is within the scope of Article 9.

2. Relationship to Attachment of Security Interest and Agricultural Lien

In order to enforce a security interest or agricultural lien against collateral, the security interest or agricultural lien must have attached to the collateral.

3. Relationship to Perfection and Priority

Perfection of the security interest or agricultural lien is **not** required in order to enforce the security interest or agricultural lien in the collateral. Having first priority in the collateral is **not** required in order to enforce the security interest or agricultural lien in the collateral.

4. Cumulative Rights and Variation by Agreement

The secured party has the right to enforce its security interest or agricultural lien as provided in the agreement of the parties and as provided in Part 6 of Article 9. The debtor and the obligor have the rights after default as provided in the agreement of the parties and as provided in Part 6 of Article 9. All of these rights are cumulative. UCC § 9–601(c), (d).

5. Judicial Enforcement

Part 6 of Article 9 does not preclude the secured party from engaging in a judicial enforcement process. UCC § 9–601(a). Thus a secured party may sue the obligor on the debt and sue the debtor to foreclose on the security interest or agricultural lien pursuant to a process that a court decrees. If the secured party obtains a judgment against the obligor on the debt and then pursuant to that judgment levies on the collateral that is subject to the secured party's security interest or agricultural lien, the levy lien has priority dating from the earlier of the three following dates: (i) the date of perfection of the security interest or agricultural lien; (ii) the date the financing statement covering the collateral was filed; or (iii) the date the agricultural lien statute specifies. UCC § 9–601(e). If the secured party sells the collateral pursuant to an execution sale after obtaining a judgment and a levy and the secured party purchases at the sale, the secured party holds the collateral without the need to comply with any requirements of Article 9. UCC § 9–601(f).

6. Consignments and Sales of Accounts, Chattel Paper, Payment Intangibles, and Promissory Notes

Generally, a secured party that has a security interest that is created by a true consignment or a sale of accounts, chattel paper, payment intangibles, or promissory notes is not subject to the duties imposed in Part 6 of Article 9. UCC § 9–601(g).

7. Default

Upon default, the secured party has the rights provided in Article 9 and in the parties' agreement to enforce its security interest or agricultural lien by the process described in Part 6 of Article 9 or by judicial process. UCC § 9–601(a). The security agreement generally defines default in the case of a security interest. A security agreement may also provide for acceleration of the debt obligation on default or if the secured party deems itself insecure in its confidence that the debt will be repaid. UCC § 1–309. Once the obligation to pay the debt is accelerated, whether the obliogor may reinstate the original due dates for payment of the debt by curing the default depends on the terms of the security agreement or other agreements between the parties. Default for purposes of enforcing an agricultural lien is defined as the time when the secured party is entitled to enforce the agricultural lien as specified in the statute creating the agricultural lien. UCC § 9–606. Buyers of accounts, chattel paper, promissory notes, and payment intangibles have a right to collect on the obligations owed by the account debtors and other parties obligated on these assets once the sale of the asset to the buyer/secured party is completed. *See* UCC § 9–607(a).

8. Deficiency and Surplus

If the transaction is not a sale of accounts, chattel paper, promissory notes, or payment intangibles, the obligor is liable to the secured party for any deficiency and the secured party is liable to the debtor for any surplus. UCC §§ 9–608(a)(4), (b), 9–615(d), (e). If the transaction is a sale of accounts, chattel paper, promissory notes, or payment intangibles, the obligor is not liable for any deficiency and the secured party is not liable for the surplus. UCC §§ 9–608(b), 9–615(e).

9. Secured Party in Possession or Control of Collateral

If the secured party is in possession or control of the collateral, the secured party has the rights and obligations provided in UCC § 9–207 regarding that collateral. UCC § 9–601(b).

10. Duties of Secured Party to Debtor, Obligor, Other Secured Party, and Lienholder

In enforcement of a security interest or agricultural lien, the secured party owes duties to debtors and obligors, including secondary obligors, and to other secured parties and lienholders with rights in the collateral. A secured party will not owe duties to a debtor or obligor unless the secured party knows (i) that the person is a debtor or obligor with respect to the collateral or obligation, (ii) the identity of that person, and (iii) how to communicate with that person. UCC § 9–605(1). The secured party enforcing its security interest or agricultural lien will not owe a duty to another secured party or lienholder that has filed a financing statement against the debtor unless the secured party knows that the person is a debtor in relation to the collateral at issue and the identity of that person. UCC § 9–605(2).

B. REAL ESTATE RELATED COLLATERAL

1. Obligation Secured by Both Personal Property and Real Estate

If the obligation owed to the secured party is secured by both real and personal property, the secured party may enforce its rights as against the personal property only without prejudicing its right to enforce the obligation against the real estate collateral. UCC § 9–604(a)(1). Alternatively, the secured party may enforce its rights against the personal property and the real property by using the rules regarding real property foreclosure. UCC § 9–604(a)(2).

2. Obligation Secured by Fixtures

If the obligation is secured by fixtures, the secured party may enforce its security interest in the fixtures pursuant to the provisions of Part 6 of Article 9 or may elect to use the rules regarding enforcement of liens against real property. UCC § 9–604(b). If the secured party has priority in the fixtures over the rights of all of the owners and encumbrancers of the real estate, the secured party may remove the fixtures from the real property after the obligor's default. UCC § 9–604(c). The secured party has an obligation to reimburse the owner or encumbrancer for the repair of any physical injury to the real property but not for the reduction in value of the real property caused by the removal of the fixture. UCC § 9–604(d).

3. Rights to Payment Secured by a Mortgage in Real Estate

If a right to payment is secured by a mortgage, deed of trust, or other lien in real estate, the process for enforcing the real estate lien is determined by law other than Article 9. See UCC § 9–607(a), (e), and cmt. 6.

C. DISPOSITION OR RETENTION OF COLLATERAL

1. Obtaining Possession of Tangible Collateral

Upon default, the secured party has the right to obtain possession of the collateral and the right to render equipment unusable if the secured party does not remove the equipment from the debtor's premises. UCC § 9–609(a). To obtain possession of the collateral, the secured party has two choices; judicial process or self help repossession without breach of the peace. The obligation of the secured party to take possession without breach of the peace cannot be varied by the agreement of the parties. UCC § 9–602(6). The secured party may not obtain an agreement of the debtor or obligor about the standard of behavior that will be deemed to not breach the peace. UCC § 9–603. The secured party and the debtor may agree to standards that will govern assembly of the collateral or disabling the equipment and disposing of it without removing it from the debtor's premises as long as those standards are manifestly reasonable and do not attempt to define what is or is not a breach of the peace. UCC §§ 9–603, 9–609, cmt. 8. Even though a secured party may not have first priority in the collateral, the secured party still has the right to take possession of the tangible collateral upon a default, although it may have to give up possession of the collateral to a secured party with a senior position, if the senior secured party so demands. UCC § 9–609, cmt. 5.

2. Disposition Process

After default, the secured party is able to sell, lease, license or otherwise dispose of the collateral. The secured party may dispose of the collateral in its current condition or may prepare the collateral for disposition in any commercially reasonable manner. UCC § 9–610(a). This disposition process may be used for all collateral, not just tangible collateral that can be repossessed.

a. Commercial Reasonableness

Every aspect of the disposition must be commercially reasonable, including the method, manner, time, place, and terms of the disposition. UCC § 9–610(b). The disposition of the collateral may be by a public disposition, such as an auction, or a private disposition, such as a private agreement between the secured party and the transferee. UCC § 9–610(b). The fact that a better price may have been obtained if the secured party had conducted the disposition in another manner does not mean the secured party's disposition of the collateral was commercially unreasonable. UCC § 9–627(a). Article 9 deems the following dispositions commercially reasonable: (i) disposing of collateral in the usual manner or the current price in a recognized market; (ii) disposing of collateral in compliance with reasonable commercial practices of dealers of the type of collateral; or (iii) a disposition that has been approved by a court, a creditor's committee, an assignee for the benefit of creditors, or a representative of creditors. UCC § 9–627(b), (c). Failure to obtain the approval specified in alternative (iii) does not mean the disposition is commercially unreasonable. UCC § 9–627(d). The debtor or obligor may not waive the obligation to dispose of collateral in a commercially reasonable manner. UCC § 9–602(7). The secured party may obtain the debtor's and obligor's agreement to standards that govern the determination of commercial reasonableness as long as those standards are not manifestly unreasonable. UCC § 9–603(a).

b. Notice of the Disposition

Prior to the disposition, the secured party must give a reasonable and authenticated notice of the disposition. UCC § 9–611(b). The content, the manner, and the time of the notice must all be reasonable. UCC § 9–611, cmt. 2. The requirement to give this notice does not apply if the collateral is perishable, threatens to decline in value quickly, or is of a type ordinarily sold in a recognized market. UCC § 9–611(d).

(1) Sending Notice

The secured party is required to send the notice in a manner that is reasonably calculated to arrive at the recipient's destination but is not required to ensure that the recipient actually receives it. UCC § 9–102(a)(75).

(2) The Time of Giving the Notice

The notice must be sent after default and a reasonable amount of time before the disposition. The reasonableness of the timing of the notice is a question of fact. In transactions other than consumer transactions, a notice of disposition sent after default and at least ten days before disposition is sent within a reasonable time. UCC § 9–612.

(3) Waiver of the Right to Notice

The right to notice of the disposition cannot be waived by the debtor and any obligor prior to a default, UCC § 9–602(7), but the debtor and a secondary obligor may waive the right to notice in an agreement that is entered into and authenticated after default. UCC § 9–624(a).

(4) To Whom the Notice Must Be Given

The notice must be sent to the debtor and any secondary obligor, unless they have entered into and authenticated an agreement after default waiving the right to notice. UCC §§ 9–611 (c)(1), (2), 9–624(a). Notice need not be given to a primary obligor that is not the debtor (i.e., that does not have a property right in the collateral that is subject to the disposition). UCC § 9–611, cmt. 3. If the collateral is not consumer goods, the secured party that is conducting the disposition must send the notice to any party from whom the secured party has received an authenticated request for notice as long as two conditions are true. First, the party that gave the request for notice to the secured party must assert an interest in the collateral. Second, the request for notice must be received prior to the date the secured party sent out the notice of disposition to the debtor and secondary obligor or the date the debtor and any secondary obligor waived the right to notice. UCC § 9–611(c)(3). If the collateral is not consumer goods, the secured party that is conducting the disposition must send the notice to certain other secured parties and lienholders that have filed in the prescribed office a financing statement to perfect their security interests or liens or perfected a security interest in a filing system governed by UCC § 9–311. UCC § 9–611.

(5) Content of the Notice: Nonconsumer Goods Transaction

In a nonconsumer goods transaction, the notification of the disposition must describe the debtor, the secured party, the collateral that is being disposed of, the method of disposition, the right of the debtor to an accounting of the debt and the charge for the accounting, and the time and place of a public disposition or the time after which a private disposition will take place. UCC § 9–613(1). A model form is included in the statute that, if used, is deemed to provide sufficient information when filled out completely and accurately. UCC § 9–613(4).

(6) Content of the Notice: Consumer-Goods Transaction

If the transaction was a consumer-goods transaction, the notification of disposition must describe the debtor, the secured party, the collateral that is being disposed of, the method of disposition, the right of the debtor to an accounting of the debt and the charge for the accounting, the time and place of a public disposition or the time after which a private disposition will take place, the person's liability for any deficiency, a telephone number to call to determine the amount necessary to redeem the collateral, and a telephone number or mailing address from which additional information concerning the disposition and the debt secured can be obtained. UCC § 9–614(1). A model form is included in the statute that, if used and properly filled out, is deemed to be a sufficient notification. UCC § 9–614(3).

(7) Variation by Agreement

Although the debtor and any obligors may not vary the notice requirements by agreement prior to default, other parties may agree to vary these notification requirements. UCC § 9–602(7). The debtor and obligor may agree with the secured party as to the standards to use to measure the secured party's compliance with the notification requirements as long as those standards are not manifestly unreasonable. UCC § 9–603.

c. Warranties in Dispositions

A secured party that sells, leases, licenses, or otherwise disposes of collateral will give the same warranties of title, possession, and quiet enjoyment that a voluntary disposition of that type of collateral would entail. The secured party may disclaim those warranties by the same method used in voluntary dispositions of that type of collateral or by communicating an express disclaimer of the warranty to the purchaser in a record. A secured party has adequately disclaimed the warranty imposed by Article 9 if the secured party states in connection with the disposition "There is no warranty relating to title, possession, quiet enjoyment, or the like in this disposition." UCC § 9–610(d), (e), (f).

d. Ability of Secured Party to Be the Transferee in the Disposition

If the disposition is a public disposition, the secured party that is conducting the disposition is a permissible transferee of the collateral. If the disposition is of collateral of a type that is normally sold on a recognized market or is the type that is subject to widely distributed standard price quotations, the secured party that is conducting the disposition is a permissible transferee of the collateral. UCC § 9–610(c). The secured party that is conducting the disposition is not otherwise a permissible transferee of the collateral pursuant to the disposition, including pursuant to a private disposition. Instead the secured party must comply with the provisions of retention of collateral in full or partial satisfaction of debt. UCC § 9–610, cmt. 7.

e. Distribution of Proceeds

(1) Payment of Costs of Disposition Process
The proceeds of disposition are first applied to the expenses of sale. If the parties' agreement provides for it, the secured party is also entitled to reasonable attorney's fees and other legal expenses incurred in connection with the disposition.

(2) Application to Obligation for Which Disposition is Taking Place
The proceeds are then applied to the debt obligation that is owed to the secured party conducting the disposition.

(3) Distribution of Proceeds to Subordinate Obligations

If the collateral is not goods in a true consignment, the remaining proceeds are applied to any subordinate security interests or liens in the order of their priority if the secured party conducting the disposition has received from the holder of that subordinate lien or security interest an authenticated demand for payment before the distribution of proceeds is complete. UCC § 9–615. If the goods are the subject of a true consignment and the interest that is subordinate to the secured party conducting the disposition demands payment, the secured party may pay proceeds to that subordinate interest only if that subordinate interest is superior to the rights of the consignor. UCC § 9–615(a)(3)(B). If the person demanding proceeds is the consignor, the secured party must pay the consignor the remaining proceeds if the consignor makes an authenticated demand for payment before distribution of the proceeds is complete. UCC § 9–615(a)(4).

(4) Distribution of Noncash Proceeds

If the proceeds of the disposition are noncash proceeds, the secured party conducting the disposition need not pay over those noncash proceeds unless failure to do so is commercially unreasonable. UCC § 9–615(c). The parties may not vary this rule by agreement, UCC § 9–602(4), but they may specify standards for complying with this rule if the standards are not manifestly unreasonable. UCC § 9–603.

(5) Senior Security Interests or Liens

Proceeds are not distributed to entities holding security interests or liens that are senior in priority to the security interest or agricultural lien in the collateral disposed of by this process. Even though the identifiable proceeds of a disposition of collateral may be subject to the security interest or lien of a senior secured party (UCC § 9–315), a junior secured party that receives cash proceeds in good faith and without knowledge that the junior secured party's receipt of those proceeds violates the rights of the senior secured party or lienholder is able to take those cash proceeds free of the senior security interest or lien, is not obligated to turn those proceeds over to the holder of the senior security interest or lien, and is not obligated to account to the holder of the senior security interest or lien for any surplus from the disposition. UCC § 9–615(g).

f. Surplus or Deficiency

Once the collateral is disposed of and the value received applied in the manner specified above, the obligor is liable for any deficiency remaining unless the parties have agreed that the obligor is not liable for the deficiency. The parties may vary the obligor's liability for a deficiency pursuant to an agreement entered into before default. UCC § 9–602. The debtor is entitled to any surplus unless the secured party was required to pay the surplus to the consignor as specified above. UCC § 9–615(d). The parties may not vary the debtor's entitlement to the surplus. UCC § 9–602(5). If the transaction creating the security interest was a sale of accounts, chattel paper, payment intangibles or promissory notes, the debtor is not entitled to the surplus and the obligor is not liable for the deficiency. UCC § 9–615(e). This rule may be varied by the agreement of the debtor or obligor. UCC § 9–602. If (i) the disposition is made to the secured party, a person related to the secured party, or the secondary obligor, and (ii) the disposition that occurred resulted in proceeds that were significantly below the range of proceeds that a disposition complying with Article 9 to a transferee other than the secured party, a person related to the secured party, or a secondary obligor would have brought, then the surplus or deficiency is calculated by determining the amount that the disposition would have brought if it complied with Article 9 and was made to a person other than the secured party, a person related to the secured party, or the secondary obligor. UCC § 9–615(f). In a consumer-goods transaction, the secured party must send to the debtor and consumer obligor a notice subsequent to the disposition regarding the calculation of the surplus and deficiency. If there is a surplus, the debtor must get a notice. If there is a deficiency, the consumer obligor must get a notice. UCC 9–616(b). This rule may not be varied by the agreement of the parties. UCC § 9–602(9).

g. Rights of Transferee of Collateral After a Disposition

The transferee of collateral pursuant to a disposition succeeds to the debtor's rights in the collateral, takes the collateral free of the security interest under which the disposition was made and free of any subordinate security interests or liens. UCC § 9–617(a). If the transferee is in good faith, the transferee has those rights even if the disposition did not comply with the Article 9 requirements. UCC § 9–617(b). If the transferee does not act in good faith, the transferee takes the collateral subject to the debtor's rights, the security interest or agricultural lien under which the disposition is made and any other security interests or liens. UCC § 9–617(c). If promissory notes or payment intangibles are sold in a disposition pursuant to UCC § 9–610, the buyer of those rights will have the right to enforce those obligations against the obligor on the promissory note or payment intangible as provided in UCC § 9–406(d) in spite of anti-assignment terms contained in the agreement between the account debtor or obligor on the note. UCC §§ 9–406(e), 9–408(b).

3. Retention of Collateral in Full or Partial Satisfaction of Obligation Owed

In some circumstances, the secured party may desire to retain the collateral in full or partial satisfaction of the obligation owed to the secured party and not conduct a disposition of the collateral. This provision applies to all types of collateral, not just collateral that may be subject to a repossession. UCC § 9–620, cmt. 3.

a. Variation by Agreement

The duties of the secured party in this process may not be varied by the agreement of the debtor and obligors, UCC § 9–602(10), although the parties may agree to standards regarding fulfillment of the secured party's duties as long as the standards are not manifestly unreasonable. UCC § 9–603. The secured party's attempt to obtain the collateral by a private sale to itself is in effect a retention in full or partial satisfaction of the debt and is subject to these provisions. UCC §§ 9–610, cmt. 7, 9–602, cmt. 3.

b. Debtor Consent

For the retention to be allowed, the debtor must consent to the secured party's retention of the collateral for credit against the obligation owed. UCC § 9–620(a)(1). If the secured party is only giving partial credit against the obligation owed, the debtor's consent must be in a record that specifies the terms on which the secured party proposes to retain the collateral and that the debtor authenticates after default. UCC § 9–620(c)(1). If the secured party is giving full satisfaction of the obligation owed in return for the secured party's retention of the collateral, the debtor's consent must be evidenced either (i) by a record that specifies the terms on which the secured party proposes to retain the collateral and that the debtor authenticates after default or (ii) by the debtor's failure to object to the secured party's unconditional proposal (other than a condition to preserve the collateral not in the secured party's possession) of the full satisfaction of the debt within 20 days after the secured party sent the proposal. UCC § 9–620(c)(2).

c. Notice to Other Interested Parties

For the retention to be allowed, the secured party must send notice of its proposal to retain the collateral in full or partial satisfaction of the obligation owed to other interested parties. UCC 9–102(a)(66). Notice must be sent to the following: (i) any person that has an interest in the collateral that is subordinate to the security interest that is the subject of the proposal; (ii) any person that sends an authenticated notice of an interest in the collateral to the secured party before the debtor has consented to the secured party's proposal; (iii) any secured party or lienholder that has filed a financing statement against the debtor regarding that collateral in the correct filing office as of 10 days before the debtor has consented to the secured party's proposal; (iv) any person that held a security interest perfected by compliance with another statute or treaty specified in UCC § 9–311 as of 10 days before the debtor has consented to the secured party's proposal; and (v) any secondary obligor if the proposal is to retain the collateral in partial satisfaction of the obligation owed. UCC §§ 9–620, 9–621.

d. Failure to Receive Timely Objections to Proposal

For the retention to be allowed, the secured party must not receive timely objections to the proposal to retain collateral in full or partial satisfaction of the obligation owed. UCC § 9–620(a)(2). Persons to whom the secured party sent the proposal to retain the collateral in full or partial satisfaction of the obligation owed must object within 20 days after the notification was sent to the objector. Other persons claiming an interest in collateral must object within 20 days after the secured party sent its last notification or, if no notifications were sent, before the debtor consents. In any case, the objection is only effective if received by the secured party within the specified time period. UCC § 9–620(d).

e. Secured Party's Consent

For the retention to be allowed, the secured party must consent to the retention of collateral in partial or full satisfaction of the obligation owed. That consent must be either in a record that the secured party authenticates or in a proposal that the secured party sent to the debtor. UCC § 9–620(b).

f. Good Faith of the Secured Party

While a secured party's proposal to retain collateral in full or partial satisfaction of the obligation owed must be made in good faith, good faith is not determined merely by looking at the value of the collateral in relationship to the obligation owed. UCC § 9–620, cmt. 11.

g. Not Precluded by Statute From Engaging in the Retention

Article 9 limits the ability of a secured party to retain the collateral in partial or full satisfaction of the obligation owed in three situations. If the collateral is consumer goods, the collateral may not be in the possession of the debtor when the debtor consents to the retention of collateral in partial or full satisfaction of the debt. UCC § 9–620(a)(3). If a secured party has a purchase money security interest in consumer goods and more than 60% of the price or the debt has been paid, the secured party may not retain the consumer goods in full or partial satisfaction of the debt. UCC § 9–620(e). The secured party must dispose of the consumer goods pursuant to the disposition process described above within 90 days of the secured party taking possession or within a longer period that the debtor and any secondary obligor have agreed to in an authenticated agreement entered into after default. UCC § 9–620(f). The debtor may enter into an authenticated agreement after default that waives its right that the secured party dispose of this collateral pursuant to UCC § 9–610. UCC § 9–624(b). If the transaction was a consumer transaction, the secured party may not accept the collateral in partial satisfaction of the obligation secured. UCC § 9–620(g).

h. Effect on Debt

The retention of collateral in partial or full satisfaction of the obligation discharges the obligation to the extent of the debtor's and secured party's consent. UCC § 9–622(a)(1).

i. Rights of Secured Party in the Collateral Retained

The secured party that has retained the collateral succeeds to the debtor's rights in the collateral. The security interest or agricultural lien that is the subject of the debtor's consent and any subordinate security interests or liens are discharged. UCC § 9–622(a). The secured party will have the collateral subject to security interests or liens in the collateral that are superior in priority to the secured party's security interest or lien. The retention has this effect even if the secured party fails to comply with the provisions of Article 9 in retaining the collateral. UCC § 9–622(b). If the collateral retained consists of promissory notes or payment intangibles, the secured party will have the right to enforce those obligations against the obligor on the promissory note or payment intangible as provided in UCC § 9–406(d) in spite of anti-assignment terms contained in the agreement between the account debtor or obligor on the note. UCC §§ 9–406(e), 9–408(b).

4. Title Clearing Mechanism

In some circumstances, a transferee of collateral pursuant to the enforcement process will need to obtain a record from a filing or registration office that it has title to the collateral. In order for the transferee to obtain that record evidence of title to the transferred collateral, the secured party may authenticate a transfer statement that the transferee will provide to the filing or registration office that issues the record title document. UCC § 9–619. If the registration or title system for the collateral is governed by federal law, this section may be preempted by the applicable provisions of the federal law. UCC § 9–619, cmt. 2.

D. ENFORCEMENT OF OBLIGATIONS OWED TO DEBTOR

If the collateral consists of an obligation owed to the debtor, a secured party may collect that obligation from the person that owes the obligation to the debtor. UCC

§ 9–607(a). The secured party is not required to use this collection mechanism and may instead conduct a disposition or a retention of the collateral.

1. Obligors on Collateral

"Account debtors" are persons that owe obligations to the debtor on accounts, chattel paper (but not instruments that are part of chattel paper), or general intangibles. UCC § 9–102(a)(3). Examples of other types of collateral in which persons owe obligations to the debtor include instruments (such as notes) where the debtor is the payee or holder, documents of title where the goods covered by the document are deliverable to the debtor, deposit accounts of the debtor, letter-of-credit rights where the debtor is the beneficiary of the letter of credit, or investment securities of the debtor.

2. Collection

A secured party may exercise its enforcement against collateral as to "any person obligated on collateral to make payment or otherwise render performance to or for the benefit of the secured party." UCC § 9–607(a). The rights of the obligor on the collateral as against the secured party will depend upon the terms of the contract or right assigned to the secured party, the rules of Article 9 (including UCC § 9–401 through § 9–409), and the rules of other law governing assignment of the type of obligation involved. UCC § 9–607(e), cmt. 6.

a. Special Rules for Deposit Accounts

If the secured party has a security interest in a deposit account perfected by control, the secured party may apply the balance of the deposit account to the obligation that the debtor owes the secured party. UCC § 9–607(a)(4), (5). If the security interest in the deposit account is unperfected or perfected by a manner other than control, the secured party's ability to collect against the bank holding the deposit account will be determined by other law. UCC §§ 9–607, cmt. 7, 9–341.

b. Special Rule for Enforcement of Mortgages

Under applicable mortgage foreclosure process, the obligor on the mortgage must generally be in default under the mortgage in order for the mortgagee to foreclose the mortgage. UCC § 9–607, cmt. 8. If a secured party has a security interest in a mortgage held by the debtor (i.e. the mortgagee) and desires to exercise the debtor's right to foreclose that mortgage without judicial process (assuming that right exists under applicable mortgage foreclosure process), the secured party may need to record documents in the real estate recording office that evidence its right to conduct the foreclosure. Article 9 authorizes the secured party to file in the real estate recording office a copy of the security agreement creating a security interest in the mortgage and a sworn affidavit declaring that a default under the mortgage exists and the secured party has a right to conduct the foreclosure through nonjudicial process. UCC § 9–607(b).

3. Timing of Collection From Person Obligated on Collateral

A secured party may collect on collateral consisting of obligations owed to the debtor if the obligor has defaulted on its obligation owed to the secured party. Even if the obligor is not in default on its obligations to the secured party, the secured party may also collect on obligations owed to the debtor if the obligor has so agreed. UCC §§ 9–607(a), 9–602.

4. Notice to Person Obligated on the Collateral

The secured party will notify the person obligated on the collateral to render its performance to the secured party. UCC § 9–607(a)(1).

5. Defenses of Person Obligated on the Collateral

a. Account Debtor's Ability to Raise Defenses Against Secured Party

Unless an account debtor has agreed otherwise, the account debtor may assert against the secured party whatever defenses or claims in recoupment (essentially a counterclaim) the account debtor could assert against the debtor arising out of the contract between the account debtor and the debtor. UCC § 9–404(a)(1). An account debtor may also assert against the secured party any other defense or claim of the account debtor against the debtor that accrues before the account debtor received notice of the assignment in a record authenticated either by the debtor or the secured party. UCC § 9–404(a)(2). An account debtor may only assert a counterclaim against the secured party to reduce the amount owed to the secured party, not to obtain an affirmative recovery against the secured party. UCC § 9–404(b). These rules allowing defenses and claims and recoupment to be asserted against the secured party do not apply to an account that is a health-care-insurance receivable. UCC § 9–404(e). Other law governs the ability of an insurer (the account debtor) to raise claims and defenses against the secured party. If a rule of law provides a different rule for an account debtor that is an individual and the obligation that the account debtor owes is a consumer obligation, these rules regarding the account debtor's ability to raise defenses or claims against the secured party are subject to that other rule. UCC § 9–404(c).

b. Waiver of the Account Debtor's Ability to Assert Defenses and Claims Against Secured Party

In the agreement between the account debtor and the debtor, the account debtor may waive its right to assert its claims and defenses that it has against the debtor in the event the contract is assigned to a third party, such as a secured party. That waiver is enforceable if the assignee took the assignment of the contract for value, in good faith, without notice of any property claims to the rights under the contract, and without notice of any defenses or counterclaims. UCC § 9–403(b). Even if there is an enforceable waiver of defenses and claims by the account debtor, the account debtor's waiver does not waive certain defenses that are of the type that could be asserted against a holder in due course of a negotiable instrument. UCC § 9–403(c). If other law establishes rules regarding the ability of a individual account debtor that incurred the obligation for consumer purposes to waive claims and defenses, the Article 9 rules regarding waiver of claims and defenses are subject to those other rules. UCC § 9–403(e). If other law validates the account debtor's waiver of the right to assert claims and defenses against an assignee, Article 9 does not displace that other law. UCC § 9–403(f). If other law requires the record evidencing the account debtor's obligation to have a statement that any assignee (including a secured party) is subject to claims and defenses of the account debtor and the record does not have that statement included, the record is treated as if it did have that statement. Thus, the account debtor may assert the claims and defenses against the secured party as if the record contained that statement. UCC §§ 9–403(d), 9–404(d).

c. Ability of Person Obligated on Collateral Other Than Account Debtor to Raise Defenses or Claims Against Secured Party

Article 9 does not address the ability of obligors on collateral, other than account debtors, to raise defenses or claims in recoupment against the secured party. UCC § 9–404, cmt. 5. The law of contract assignment, negotiable instruments, or other law controls the ability of obligors on collateral, other than account debtors, to raise defenses or claims against the secured party and the waiver of the right to do so. *See* UCC § 9–403, cmt. 2.

d. Modification of Underlying Contract

An account debtor may assert that the contract between the account debtor and the debtor has been modified and that the secured party should be subject to that modification. The modification is effective against the secured party to which the contract has been assigned if (i) the modification is made in good faith and (ii) the right to payment that the secured party has been assigned is not yet fully earned by performance or the right to payment has been fully earned by performance and the account debtor has not yet been notified of the assignment. UCC § 9–405. If other law establishes rules regarding the ability of an individual account debtor that incurred the obligation for consumer purposes to modify the agreement and have the assignee be subject to that modification, the Article 9 rules regarding modification of assigned contracts are subject to those other rules. UCC § 9–405(c). This rule regarding modification does not apply to modification of the obligation of the health care insurer. UCC § 9–405(d). Other law addresses this issue.

e. Protection of Certain Persons Obligated on Collateral

Generally, anti-assignment clauses in the contracts between the person obligated on collateral and the debtor or anti-assignment laws also do not preclude the secured party from enforcing its rights in the collateral assigned against the person obligated on the collateral. UCC §§ 9–406(d), (f), 9–407(a). However, the secured party is not entitled to exercise its enforcement rights against the person obligated on the collateral if the assignment of the obligation to the secured party is a transaction in which (i) a payment intangible is sold, a security interest in a general intangible is created, a promissory note is assigned, a health-care-insurance receivable is assigned, or letter-of-credit rights are assigned, *and* (ii) the anti-assignment clause or anti-assignment law would otherwise render the assignment unenforceable. In other words, the person obligated on the collateral need not render its performance to the secured party in the event the secured party seeks to enforce its security interest in the collateral. UCC §§ 9–408, 9–409. However, if a payment intangible or promissory note has been sold in a UCC § 9–610 disposition or retained pursuant to the process in UCC § 9–620, an anti-assignment clause will not be effective to prevent enforcement of the obligation of the obligor on the payment intangible or promissory note. UCC §§ 9–406(e), 9–408(b). An account debtor that is an individual and that has incurred the obligation to the debtor for consumer purposes may also avail itself of other law that establishes a different rule for that individual. UCC § 9–406(h).

6. Account Debtor Discharge by Payment

An account debtor on chattel paper, accounts other than health-care-insurance receivables, and payment intangibles may pay the debtor until the secured party or debtor gives the account debtor an authenticated and effective notice directing payment to the secured party. After receipt of that authenticated and effective notice, the account debtor will not be discharged on its obligation to pay if it pays the debtor instead of the secured party. UCC § 9–406(a), (i). The effect of notification to a person obligated on collateral (other than an account debtor on chattel paper, accounts other than health-care-insurance receivables, and payment intangibles) on that person's ability to discharge its obligation by payment to the debtor is governed by other law. UCC § 9–406, cmt. 2. If a payment intangible has been sold and either an anti-assignment clause or anti-assignment rules of law would be given effect under other law in the absence of the Article 9 rules, then the account debtor need not pay the secured party even if the account debtor receives an authenticated notice to do so. UCC § 9–406(b)(2). However, if a payment intangible has been sold in a UCC § 9–610 disposition or retained pursuant to the process in UCC § 9–620, an anti-assignment clause will not be effective to prevent enforcement of the obligation. UCC §§ 9–406(e), 9–408(b). If the notice to the account debtor requires the account debtor to make less than full payment of the obligation owed (or full payment on any installment that is due), the account debtor has the option of ignoring the notification as ineffective. UCC § 9–406(b)(3).

7. Notice to Debtor or Other Lienholders

The secured party is not required to give notice to any other party (including the debtor, holders of other security interests in the collateral, or persons with liens in the collateral) of its actions taken in collection of obligations owed to the debtor.

8. Commercially Reasonable Collection Efforts

The secured party has an obligation to engage in collection from the obligors in a commercially reasonable manner if the secured party is entitled to full or limited recourse for uncollected obligations against the debtor or a secondary obligor. UCC § 9–607(c). Secured parties that are consignors and buyers of accounts, chattel paper, payment intangibles or promissory notes are subject to this commercial reasonableness obligation. UCC § 9–601(g). The debtor and obligors may not waive this "commercial reasonableness" duty of the secured party. UCC § 9–602(3).

9. Expenses and Fees Incurred in Collection

The secured party has a right to deduct from the amounts collected from obligors on the collateral the reasonable expenses of collection incurred in collecting from the obligors on the collateral, including reasonable attorney's fees and legal expenses. UCC § 9–607(d), cmt. 10.

10. Application of Proceeds of Collection

Once the funds are collected from the obligors on the collateral, after deduction of the expenses of collection against the obligors on the collateral, the proceeds are applied in the following order: (i) to the expenses of collection and if provided in the security agreement, or contract with the debtor or obligor on the secured debt, reasonable attorney's fees and legal expenses incurred in taking action against the debtor or obligor; (ii) to the satisfaction of the obligation that is secured and owed to the secured party doing the collection, and (iii) the satisfaction of liens or security interests subordinate to the security interest or lien being enforced if the secured party doing the collection has received an authenticated demand for payment before the proceeds are completely distributed. UCC § 9–608(a)(1). The debtor and any obligors may not waive the obligations of the secured party to deal with the proceeds of collection in accordance with these principles. UCC § 9–602(4).

11. Surplus or Deficiency

Unless the transaction between the secured party and the debtor is a sale of accounts, chattel paper, payment intangibles or promissory notes, the obligor is liable for any deficiency and the debtor is entitled to any surplus after application of the proceeds as outlined above. UCC § 9–608(a)(4), (b). The obligation of the secured party to account for the surplus to the debtor in a transaction that is not a sale of accounts, chattel paper, payment intangibles or promissory notes may not be altered by agreement. UCC § 9–602(5).

12. Effect of the Collection Process on Junior and Senior Lien Holders

The priority of a lien or security interest that is senior to the lien or security interest that is being enforced is not affected by the enforcement process. UCC § 9–608, cmt. 5. The holder of a senior security interest in the obligation owed will have its interest attach to the proceeds of the collection. UCC § 9–315. Whether the senior secured party will have priority in the proceeds as against the collecting secured party will depend upon application of the rules regarding priority in proceeds. UCC §§ 9–322, 9–607 cmt. 5.

E. REDEMPTION

A debtor, secondary obligor, secured party or lienholder may redeem collateral by tendering fulfillment of all obligations that the collateral secures and any reasonable attorney's fees and expenses that are allowed under the agreement with the secured party prior to collection of obligations that are the collateral, disposition of the collateral, or retention of the collateral in full or partial satisfaction of the obligation owed. UCC § 9–623. The right to redeem may not be varied by an agreement between the secured party and debtor or obligor except that a debtor or secondary obligor, in a transaction other than a consumer-goods transaction, may waive their right to redeem in an agreement that is entered into and authenticated after default. UCC §§ 9–624(c), 9–602(11).

F. EFFECT OF ENFORCEMENT PROCESS ON SECONDARY OBLIGOR

When a secured party enforces its security interest or agricultural lien against collateral, the secondary obligor's liability to the secured party for any remaining debt will be determined by principles of suretyship law, the agreements between the secondary obligor and the secured party, and the rules of Article 9 regarding enforcement of the security interest or agricultural lien. Under suretyship law, if the secondary obligor fulfills the obligation of the primary obligor to the secured party, the secondary obligor succeeds to the rights of the secured party to enforce its lien against the collateral, and would then be obligated to comply with Article 9's enforcement rules as if it was the secured party. The secured party may assign its security interest to the secondary obligor. That action is not a disposition of the collateral requiring the secured party to comply with the rules regarding disposition of collateral found in UCC § 9–610. UCC § 9–618. In this situation, the secondary obligor would then have the duties of a secured party in enforcement of the security interest. On the other hand, if the secondary obligor is the purchaser of the collateral at an Article 9 disposition, the secured party must have complied with the rules of Article 9 and the secondary obligor is free to further deal with the collateral without compliance with the Article 9 disposition rules.

G. OTHER LAW AND EFFECT ON ENFORCEMENT OF SECURITY INTEREST AND AGRICULTURAL LIEN

Common law doctrines and other statutory law may come into play in the enforcement process.

1. Waiver and Estoppel

Principles of common law and equity will supplement the Article 9 enforcement rules to the extent not displaced by the Article 9 rules. UCC § 1–103. Unless waiver of the right is prohibited, UCC § 9–602, a court may apply the doctrines of waiver or estoppel in particular cases subject to the principles found in UCC § 1–103. In addition, the obligations of "good faith, diligence, reasonableness, and care" may not be waived by agreement. UCC §§ 1–302, 9–602, cmt. 2.

2. Marshaling

Marshaling refers to the equitable doctrine that a court may impose to require a secured party to obtain value to apply against the obligation from collateral in a manner that does not disadvantage another secured creditor. This doctrine is subject to numerous caveats which are explored in the cases in which the doctrine is invoked. A full exploration of this doctrine is beyond the scope of these materials.

3. Lender Liability

Another set of equitable doctrines revolves around the factual scenario of a secured party "taking control" of a debtor's operation to the detriment of other creditors of the debtor. If a court determines that the secured party has acted in a manner that unfairly disadvantages other creditors of the debtor, the court may subordinate the secured party's claim under principles of equitable subordination, hold the secured party liable to the other creditors as an undisclosed principal under agency law, or may find that the secured party has failed to act in good faith, resulting in a breach of its agreement with the debtor.

4. Bankruptcy of the Debtor

a. Automatic Stay

The automatic stay will prevent the secured party from taking any action to collect on its security interest or agricultural lien from the debtor, from property of the debtor, or from the property of the estate. 11 U.S.C. § 362(a). Actions stayed include sending the debtor default notices, sending requests for payment, repossession of the collateral, collection against obligations owed the debtor, and disposition of collateral. The secured party may request that the bankruptcy court grant relief from the automatic stay based upon two alternate grounds. The first ground is that the value of the secured party's interest in the collateral is not adequately protected. The second ground is that the debtor does not have any equity in the collateral and the collateral is not necessary for an effective reorganization. 11 U.S.C. § 362(d). If the bankruptcy court grants the secured party relief from the automatic stay, the court order will generally allow the secured party's enforcement process to go forward pursuant to the provisions of Article 9. If the court does not grant relief from the stay, the secured party is subject to liability for damages and contempt of court proceedings for proceeding with its enforcement process. In addition, the rights of the transferee will be subject to being avoided by the bankruptcy court. 11 U.S.C. § 549.

b. Turnover

If the secured party is already in possession of the collateral but has not completed the enforcement process when the debtor files bankruptcy, the automatic stay bars the secured party's ability to continue the disposition or retention process. 11 U.S.C. § 362(a). In addition, the secured party has an obligation to turn over to the estate the debtor's property that is in its possession unless the property is of inconsequential value to the estate. 11 U.S.C. § 542(a). Generally, a secured party will ask for adequate protection of its interest in the collateral in response to the estate's motion for turnover of property. 11 U.S.C. § 363(e).

■ VII. LIABILITY FOR VIOLATION OF ARTICLE 9

If a secured party fails to follow the rules provided in Article 9, the secured party is liable for actual damages caused by the violation to any person that is injured by reason of the violation. UCC § 9–625(b). The secured party's' liability for noncompliance with Article 9 may not be waived by an agreement with the debtor or obligor. UCC § 9–602(13).

A. OBTAINING AN INJUNCTION

A court may enter an injunction against a secured party requiring the secured party to dispose of the collateral on appropriate terms and conditions. UCC § 9–625(a).

B. ADDITIONAL RECOVERY IF COLLATERAL IS CONSUMER GOODS

If the collateral is consumer goods, a debtor or secondary obligor may recover, in addition to actual damages caused by the secured party's failure to comply with Article 9, a return of the interest charges (credit service or time price differential) and

10% of either the principal amount of the debt or the cash price of the consumer goods. UCC § 9–625(c)(2). A secured party is not liable for this penalty more than once with respect to any secured obligation. UCC § 9–628(e). This remedy is not available for the secured party's failure to comply with the requirement to send the calculation of the surplus or deficiency in a consumer-goods transaction under UCC § 9–616. UCC § 9–628(d).

C. EFFECT OF NONCOMPLIANCE WITH ARTICLE 9 ENFORCEMENT RULES ON THE RECOVERY OF A DEFICIENCY JUDGMENT OR ENTITLEMENT TO A SURPLUS

If the obligor or debtor puts into issue the secured party's compliance with the Article 9 enforcement rules, the secured party bears the burden of proving that the secured party complied with the Article 9 requirements. UCC § 9–626(a)(1), (2).

1. Calculating the Deficiency: Rebuttable Presumption Rule

If a secured party has failed to comply with the Part 6 rules regarding enforcement of the security interest or agricultural lien, the obligor's liability for the deficiency may be eliminated or reduced instead of awarding actual damages caused by the failure to comply. UCC § 9–625(d). If it is determined that the secured party did not comply with the requirements of Article 9 in enforcing its security interest or agricultural lien, there is a rebuttable presumption that the collateral's value that would have been obtained in a complying enforcement process was exactly the amount of the debt plus recoverable costs of enforcement, resulting in no liability for any deficiency. UCC § 9–626(a)(4). The rebuttable presumption rule does not apply to consumer transactions. Thus, the courts are free to apply court-developed rules, including the rebuttable presumption rule or the rule that if there is a violation of the Article 9 enforcement rules, the secured party is absolutely barred from collection of any deficiency. UCC § 9–626(b), cmt. 4.

2. Obtaining a Surplus

If the debtor demonstrates that a secured party's compliance with the enforcement rules of Article 9 would have resulted in a surplus instead of a deficiency, the debtor may recover damages for failure to obtain the surplus even if the deficiency is eliminated as set forth above. UCC § 9–625(d).

D. STATUTORY DAMAGES

In addition to the remedy for actual damages, a debtor (or person named as debtor in a filed record) or a consumer obligor may also recover statutory damages of $500 from the secured party if the secured party fails to comply with several listed requirements: (i) the duties of a secured party stated in UCC § 9–208 when in control of collateral; (ii) the duties of a secured party if the account debtor has been notified of an assignment as stated in UCC § 9–209; (iii) the duty to file a financing statement only with authorization as stated in UCC § 9–509(a); (iv) failure to cause the secured party of record to file a financing statement as provided in UCC § 9–513(a) and (c); (v) failure to send the explanation of the calculation of the surplus or deficiency as required in UCC § 9–616(b)(1) if that failure is part of a pattern or practice of noncompliance; (vi) failure to send a waiver of its right to collect the deficiency in a timely manner as required in UCC § 9–616(b)(2); (vii) failure to comply with a request regarding listing the collateral claimed or obligations secured as required in UCC § 9–210. UCC § 9–625(e), (f). A secured party that does not claim an interest in collateral or claim that obligations are secured has a reasonable excuse for failing to respond to the request under UCC § 9–210 and thus would not be liable for the statutory damages. UCC § 9–625(f). If the secured party fails to respond to such a request under UCC § 9–210 and should have, the secured party may claim a security interest only as shown in the list or statement included with the request as against a person that is reasonably mislead by the failure to respond. UCC § 9–625(g).

E. PROTECTION OF SECURED PARTY

A secured party may not be liable for violations of the provisions of Article 9 unless the secured party knows that the person is a debtor or obligor, knows the identity of that person, and knows how to communicate with that person. UCC § 9–628(a), (b). If the secured party has a reasonable belief that a transaction is not a consumer transaction or a consumer-goods transaction or a reasonable belief that the collateral is not consumer goods, the secured party will not be liable for violations of the requirements of Article 9 that are directed toward those types of transactions or consumer goods. UCC § 9–628(c).

Perspective

Secured Transactions is a difficult subject to learn. For many students, this will be the first time studying an intensive scrutiny of statutory provisions. Even if a student has had experience learning another statutory scheme, Secured Transactions, as embodied in Uniform Commercial Code Article 9, has its own vocabulary that must be understood, digested, and mastered. Article 9 is also a complex statute where there are many cross-references to other sections, or informed by an understanding of rules from another section. Part of the challenge of learning the law of secured transactions is understanding the interrelationship of all of the sections of Article 9.

Article 9 also does not exist in isolation from other areas of law. At the state level, Article 9 is a huge part of the law governing the relationship between debtors and creditors and between creditors. Chapter I of these materials puts Article 9 into that context. Article 9 is also a part of the Uniform Commercial Code (UCC) and must be understood in the context of those other Articles. Information about those other UCC Articles is also contained in Chapter I. Principles of consumer law and equitable doctrines may also affect the debtor or creditor in a transaction that is covered by Article 9. At the federal level, bankruptcy law has an effect on the rights of an Article 9 creditor. Each Chapter provides some discussion of these other bodies of law that may affect an Article 9 transaction.

So how should a student go about using these materials to learn the law of secured transactions? These materials are intended to provide a guide for reading and studying the statutory text and comments of Article 9. This outline is **NOT** a substitute for actually reading and studying the statutory text and comments of Article 9. One should not, however, try and read Article 9 from cover to cover like a good novel. It is too complex to be digested in that manner. The most effective way to use these materials to learn secured transactions is to read a discrete section of the full outline in conjunction with the assigned readings from your secured transactions course. Use the table of contents and table of statutes cited to help you correlate the material from this book to your assigned course materials.

Thus, for every assignment in your secured transactions course, follow this methodology. Read the assigned materials from your course book and all the statutory sections and comments that the course book references. Then read the material from this book that correlates to that assigned material. Then reread the assigned course book material and referenced statutory sections and comments. Read each sentence slowly, carefully, and word by word.

As you read the statutory sections and comments, think about the following questions. Is the section stating a permissive or mandatory rule? Is it stating elements to consider in the disjunctive or conjunctive? Does it cross reference other sections of Article 9 or other articles of the UCC? Does it contain words that are defined in other sections of Article 9 or other articles of the UCC? What situation is the section addressing? Can you imagine the scenario that the statute was intended to capture? How do you apply the statutory language to the fact situation and make arguments about how the statute should be applied? Are there arguments that it could be applied in a different way? Then use what you have learned from that careful study and class discussion to make your own outline of the legal principles that reflects your understanding.

As you progress through the course, relate each new principle to the material that you have studied previously. As you approach each new segment of material, think about how it is related to what you have already studied. Constant review and integration of new material with the old material is necessary to arrive at a complete understanding of the law of secured transactions.

The law of secured transactions is but one piece of commercial and business law. In addition to the first year courses in property and contracts, a student seeking a well-rounded knowledge of this area of law should also study debtor and creditor law, sales and leases of goods, payments, tax, business associations, products liability, bankruptcy, real estate transactions, and international business transactions.

I

Introduction to Secured Transactions

A secured transaction is the creation of an interest in personal property to secure an obligation, usually a debt. To begin to understand the area of secured transactions in personal property, it is necessary to start with the concept of debt. In this Chapter, we will consider the definition of debt, the creation of debt, the process for collection of debt, and the risk of nonpayment of debt given that process. We will then consider how the risk of nonpayment may be reduced through certain mechanisms including the granting of consensual liens in property. Finally, we will consider the history and structure of the Uniform Commercial Code, and its role as a set of legal rules that govern the creation and collection of debt.

A. Debt Defined

Debt may be created in an almost infinite variety of ways. Black's Law Dictionary (9th ed. 2009) defines debt as "liability on a claim; a specific sum of money due by agreement or otherwise ... a nonmonetary thing that one person owes another, such as goods or services." The person who owes the debt is the obligor and the person to whom the debt is owed is the obligee.

1. Contingent or Fixed

A debt may be contingent or fixed. A contingent debt is a "debt that is not presently fixed but that may become fixed in the future with the occurrence of some event." Black's Law Dictionary (9th ed. 2009). A fixed debt is a debt that is actually owed.

Example: A sues B for negligence. Until there is an adjudication of liability of B to A for negligence, the debt is contingent. Once there is a final adjudication of B's liability for negligence, B's debt is fixed.

2. Liquidated or Unliquidated

A debt may be liquidated or unliquidated. A liquidated debt is "a debt whose amount has been determined by agreement of the parties or by operation of law." Black's Law Dictionary (9th ed. 2009). An unliquidated debt is "a debt that has not been reduced to a specific amount." Black's Law Dictionary (9th ed. 2009).

Example: A sues B for negligence. B's debt to A is unliquidated as well as contingent until an adjudication of liability. Once the final adjudication of liability takes place, B's debt will be fixed and once damages are adjudicated, the debt will also be liquidated.

3. Matured or Unmatured

A debt may also be mature or unmature. A mature debt is a debt that is due. An unmature debt is a debt that is owed but not yet due.

Example: A has agreed to pay B $500 in one year. The debt is fixed and liquidated but it is not yet mature. The debt will be mature one year from now, when the debt is due.

4. Disputed or Undisputed

A debt may be disputed or undisputed. If the obligor has a legal or equitable basis for asserting that it does not owe the obligation, the debt is disputed. If the obligor does not have a legal or equitable basis for asserting that it does not owe the obligation, the debt is undisputed.

Example: A sues B for negligence. B has a factual or legal basis for arguing that B is not negligent. The debt is disputed.

5. Secured or Unsecured

A debt may also be secured or unsecured. A secured debt is where the obligation to pay the debt is secured on a consensual or nonconsensual basis by an interest in specific property. This interest in specific property allows the creditor to obtain that property to satisfy the debt. An unsecured debt is one in which the obligation to pay is not secured by an interest in specific property.

Example: A has agreed to pay B $500 in one year. A, by contract, grants B an interest in A's car to secure the obligation to pay. This is a grant of a consensual interest in A's property to secure A's obligation to pay B the $500. The debt is a "secured debt." If A fails to pay B the $500 in one year, B will have a right to obtain the car and sell it to satisfy the debt.

Example: Under state law, the state assesses taxes due on real estate that are due each year. If the tax is not paid when due, by operation of law, a tax lien is created on the real estate in order to secure the obligation to pay the tax debt. Once the tax lien arises, the debt for taxes is a secured debt. The state taxing authority has the right to sell the real estate to satisfy the amount of the tax debt.

B. How Debt Is Created

Debt can be created in a variety of ways. Three main methods for debt creation are obligations arising under contract law, obligations arising under tort law, and obligations arising under statutes.

1. Contracts Create Debt

Agreements to pay a specific sum of money include agreements to repay a loan and to pay for services or property purchased, leased or licensed. Agreements to provide something of value other than money also create a debt.

Example: A agrees to sell a car to B for a sum of money. A owes a debt to B (the obligation to provide the car) and B owes a debt to A (the obligation to pay money for the car). Agreements such as these are governed by the law of contracts. Contract law is thus a significant source for determining when a debt is created.

2. Tort Liability Creates Debt

A debt may also be created through incurring liability for a tort.

Example: Under applicable principles of negligence, A was negligent and caused a car accident injuring B. Under principles of tort liability of negligence, A would owe a debt to B.

Example: If A assaulted B, A would owe a debt to B based upon principles of liability for the intentional tort of assault.

3. Statutes May Create Debt

We have already considered one example of a type of statute that may create debt, statutes prescribing liability for taxes (Chapter I, Section A.5). Other examples of statutes that may create debt obligations are antitrust law, environmental laws, worker's compensation laws, employment laws, and intellectual property laws.

C. Regulation of Debt Creation

If the debt is created by tort law, creation of the debt is based upon the substantive elements of tort law. If the debt is created by statute, creation of the debt is based upon the requirements of the statutory scheme. If the debt is created by contract, the creation of the debt is based upon the substantive elements of contract law. When the debt is created through contract, however, there are sources, other than merely the substantive elements of contract law, that regulate that creation of debt.

1. Usury

Usury refers to charging more than the legal rate of interest for a debt. Black's Law Dictionary (9th ed. 2009). Most states have statutes that specify the maximum rate of interest that may be charged for some types of debtors or transactions. Different transactions and different debtors may be subject to different maximum rates of interest. Federal banking law also determines the maximum rate of interest that can be charged by federally regulated entities. What constitutes the legal rate of interest for particular transactions and debtors is a complex subject and beyond the scope of these materials. Usury laws thus presents a source of regulation of debt creation that is apart from the basic contract law that governs creation of the debt.

2. Consumer Protection Law

Under both state and federal law, numerous statutes provide regulation of the debt creation process or govern terms of the debt. These statutes generally operate through prohibiting or requiring certain terms in the contract creating the debt or requiring disclosure of certain types of information concerning the debt. A catalogue of all of these statutes is beyond the scope of these materials but some of the typical examples are explained below.

a. Prohibition of Particular Terms

Examples of provisions that prohibit particular terms concerning the debt can be found in the Federal Trade Commission Practice Rules, 16 C.F.R. Part 444, and the Uniform Consumer Credit Code. For certain types of consumer debts, the FTC rules make it an unfair practice to obtain a wage assignment or a nonpossessory security interest in certain types of household goods to secure the debt. 16 C.F.R. § 444.2. The Uniform Consumer Credit Code (UCCC), promulgated by the National Conference of Commissioners on Uniform State Laws (NCCUSL), has been enacted in part in several states in order to regulate some types of terms. For example, the UCCC prohibits certain charges in consumer leases, UCCC § 3.401, and regulates the premium for insurance charged in certain types of consumer transactions, UCCC § 4.107. These examples obviously do not cover all types of term regulation in consumer contracts. A careful review of applicable state and federal law is required to determine what terms are acceptable in consumer contracts.

b. Disclosure of Information

Other types of consumer regulation focus on disclosure of terms to the consumer so that the consumer can make an informed decision about whether to engage in the transaction. The paradigm example of this type of regulation is the Truth in Lending Act, 15 U.S.C. §§ 1601–1649, and its implementing regulations, Regulation Z, 12 C.F.R. Part 226, Part 1026. The Truth in Lending Act and Regulation Z focus on the terms relating to the cost of credit such as the finance charge, costs and fees, and payment schedules. The Act and regulation require disclosure of the cost of credit at specified times and using a specified method of calculation and a specified manner of presentation. Similar federal legislation applies to leases. Consumer Leases Act, 15 U.S.C. §§ 1667–1667f, and Regulation M, 12 C.F.R. Part 213, Part 1013. A thorough review of relevant state and federal law that applies to the transaction is required to determine adequate compliance with disclosure requirements.

c. Regulating Particular Types of Contracts

Some types of contracts are disfavored and thus state or federal law may specifically regulate those types of contracts and the entities that engage in such contracts. One example is payday lending, which involves a person obtaining a loan based upon personal checks held for future deposit if the loan is not repaid. See Oregon Stat. Ch. 725 for an example of such regulation.

3. Prohibiting Discrimination

Another type of regulation of the debt creation process is the regulation of the permissible basis for declining to enter into a transaction. The Equal Credit Opportunity Act, 15 U.S.C. §§ 1691–1691f, and its implementing regulation, Regulation B, 12 C.F.R. Part 202, Part 1002, prohibit a creditor from discrimination against an applicant in a credit transaction on the basis of prohibited grounds, such as "race, color, religion, national origin, sex or marital status, or age,", the applicant derives its income from public assistance, or the applicant has exercised a right under the federal Consumer Protection Act. This Act applies to all transactions in which a person in the business of extending credit is the creditor, not just consumer transactions. Again, a thorough review of relevant state and federal law is required to determine whether there is regulation of factors that may be taken into account in determining whether to enter into the transaction.

D. Collecting Debt Through Informal Methods

Once a debt is created, the creditor will, at some point, try to collect the debt. Many debts are paid without any difficulty. Sometimes the creditor will have to engage in more effort to collect the debt. That effort may ultimately result in the creditor suing the debtor to obtain a judgment on the debt. Before the creditor sues the debtor, however, the creditor has several other methods for encouraging the debtor to pay the debt, such as by sending a billing notice.

Example: A incurs a debt for use of electricity. When the power company sends the invoice for the usage, A pays the debt by tendering a check before the due date of the invoice. The check is paid in due course by A's bank.

1. Repeated Requests for Payment

Many times the creditor will repeatedly request payment from a debtor that has failed to pay a debt when it is due. This process will often become increasingly "threatening" as time passes without payment and may eventually produce payment of the debt.

Example: A incurs a debt for use of electricity. A fails to pay in response to the invoice of the usage from the power company. The power company sends repeated notices demanding payment.

2. Withholding Needed Goods or Services

If the debtor and creditor have multiple occasions for interaction, the creditor has an additional tool to obtain payment from the debtor. The creditor may threaten to withhold goods or services in the future to encourage the debtor to pay what is owed. In some circumstances, state or federal law may prevent the creditor from withholding certain types of goods or services.

Example: A incurs a debt for use of electricity at A's residence. A fails to pay in response to repeated invoices from the power company showing the usage and the amounts owed. The power company sends a final notice stating that electricity will be shut off at A's residence in ten days unless full payment is received by that time. In some cold weather states, the power company is prohibited from shutting off power to residences in some circumstances during designated winter months even if the debtor fails to pay. *See e.g.*, Minn. Stat. § 216B.097.

3. Setoff

A setoff refers to "a debtor's right to reduce the amount of a debt by any sum the creditor owes the debtor." Black's Law Dictionary (9th ed. 2009). In order to exercise a setoff, the debts between the debtor and creditor must be both mutual and mature. Mutual means that the each party has the same capacity as the debtor on one debt and the creditor on the other debt. Mature means that both debts must be due and owing.

Example: A, a corporation, owes $1,000 to B, an individual. B owes $700 to A. The debt of $1,000 is due in 6 months and the debt of $700 is currently due. Neither A or B can exercise a setoff as the debts are not *both* mature. The debt of $1,000 is not currently due.

Example: A, a corporation, owes $1,000 to B, a partnership. C, one of the partners in B, owes A $700. The two debts cannot be set off as the debts are not mutual. C, a partner in B, is a different entity than B.

4. Obtaining the Debtor's Property to Satisfy the Debt

Other than when a permissible setoff is involved, the usual rule is that a creditor that does not already have a lien in the debtor's asset has no legal right to help itself to the debtor's asset to satisfy the debt that is owed to the creditor. Even if the creditor has a lien, the law governing the lien will specify the circumstances under which the creditor may rightfully seize possession or control of the property subject to the lien or otherwise realize value from the asset subject to the lien. This subject will be addressed in great detail in Chapter VI on enforcement of security interests and agricultural liens.

E. Collecting Debt Through Judicial Process

If the creditor is not able to obtain payment of the debt through an informal collection process, the creditor will have to resort to court process to pursue collection of the debt. What follows is a general description of the process and does not substitute for a thorough study of the applicable state or federal law that governs the process of collection of the judgment at issue.

1. Obtaining a Judgment

Obtaining a judgment against a debtor requires that the creditor file a complaint and pursue the civil process for obtaining a judgment that the defendant is liable for a certain sum of money. All that you have learned in your civil procedure course is relevant and will not be repeated here. Once a judgment is entered by a court, the creditor must engage in additional process to actually turn that entry of judgment into money in the creditor's pocket.

2. Executing on Judgments

Executing a judgment means the process that is used in collecting the judgment amount from the debtor's assets. Each state has statutes and rules that govern this process. The federal government also has a process for collecting certain types of debts owed to the federal government. Federal Debt Collection Procedure Act, 28 U.S.C. §§ 3001–3308.

a. Overview of the Process of Execution

The process of execution involves obtaining a writ of execution from the court clerk and giving that writ to the local law enforcement officer, typically a sheriff, and having the sheriff levy on, that is, seize possession of, the debtor's assets. The sheriff then advertises the property seized and sells the property at public auction. After paying the costs of the seizure, advertisement, and sale process, the remaining value received at the sale is distributed to the creditor whose judgment is being executed. The creditor may continue obtaining writs of execution, levying on property, and conducting execution sales until the judgment is satisfied.

b. Obtaining an Execution Writ

Generally a creditor submits to the clerk of the court that issued the judgment a request for a writ of execution. That request for a writ will specify the judgment that has been entered and the assets of the debtor that will be seized pursuant to the writ. The court clerk will then issue the writ of execution to the creditor and the creditor will take that writ to the sheriff of the county. There is usually a state statute or rule that provides for a procedure that allows a clerk from one county to issue a writ of execution based upon a judgment from a state court that is located in another county. The writ of execution is merely a court document that provides that the sheriff is directed to seize and sell the property of the debtor listed on the writ.

c. Levy

Levy refers to the process that the sheriff follows in seizing possession of the debtor's property. State statutes or rules will usually prescribe what acts constitute a sufficient levy. Those statutes or rules or applicable common law principles usually provide that a levy takes place when the sheriff obtains possession or control of the asset. Some times, such as for bulky personal property or real estate assets, the sheriff will levy by filing a public notice in the applicable state records noting that the asset has been levied on. What constitutes a sufficient levy on a particular asset will vary by state and by type of asset.

d. Execution Lien

Usually once the levy takes place, the property is then subject to an execution lien. An execution lien is a property interest in the particular piece of property on which there has been a levy that sets the priority of the creditor's claim to that asset as against other persons with claims to that particular asset in accordance with a priority rule prescribed by statute or the common law. We will discuss priority rules in Chapter V. Sometimes the lien arises when the levy takes place but the time that the priority of the lien is set relates back to an earlier point of time such as when the writ of execution was delivered to the sheriff. The time the execution lien arises and the priority rule that will apply to that lien will vary from state to state.

e. Conducting the Execution Sale

Once the sheriff levies on the property, the sheriff will then follow the process prescribed by statute for selling the asset at public auction. The statute may require advertising and that the sale take place in a certain format (usually a public auction) and at a specified place (such as on the courthouse steps). The advertising required may not be all that effective in maximizing bidders and the sale price. For instance, the required advertising may be a posting at the courthouse and four weeks published notice in the legal notices section of the local newspaper. Predictably, the sale price at execution sales is usually relative low in comparison to what the asset might bring if sold in a manner more effectively calculated to maximize the price. Having said that, it is relatively difficult for a debtor to successfully obtain a nullification of the execution sale based upon inadequate price. The typical court statements are that the price must be so low as to "shock the conscience of the court." A court may be more willing to nullify an execution sale and require a new sale if the price is very low and there have been procedural irregularities in the sale process.

f. Bidding at the Execution Sale

Given the structure of the usual sale process and the minimal amount of advertising, in many instances, the creditor enforcing the judgment is the only bidder. If the judgment creditor is the winning bidder, that creditor will be able to credit the amount of its bid against the judgment owed. The judgment creditor's bid is credited against the amount of the judgment and the judgment creditor will then be the owner of the sold property and be able to capture any increase in value that it can obtain in a subsequent sale without having to credit that increase against the amount of the judgment. The judgment creditor may then continue to execute against the judgment debtor's property until the judgment is satisfied. If someone other than the judgment creditor is the winning bidder, the bidder must generally pay cash or certified funds for the amount of the winning bid price.

g. Purchaser's Title After the Execution Sale

Generally, the execution sale purchaser's title regarding the purchased asset is subject to any liens on that asset that are superior in priority to the execution lien that is foreclosed by the execution sale. The execution sale generally discharges the execution lien being foreclosed and any liens on the property that are subordinate to that execution lien. The state statutes governing the execution sale may protect the purchaser's title from being set aside even if there are irregularities in the sale process. The precise effect of the execution sale on the purchaser's title in the asset is prescribed by the statute governing the execution process.

h. Post-Sale Redemption

In some circumstances and for some type of property, usually real property, the debtor and other creditors with liens subordinate to the execution lien being foreclosed may redeem the property from the execution sale purchaser after the sale. This post-sale right to redeem is often called "statutory redemption" as the types of property subject to post-sale redemption, the amount necessary to redeem, the persons entitled to redeem and the process for redeeming are all specified by the state statute. Most states *do not* provide for post-sale redemption from execution sales of personal property.

i. Time Limits on Writs of Execution

Historically, there have been time limits on obtaining writs of execution to execute on a judgment. At common law, a writ of execution could be issued within a year and a day of entry of judgment. After that time period, the judgment was considered dormant. To obtain a writ of execution on a dormant judgment, the judgment creditor had to obtain a court order to "revive" the judgment. Today, state statutes or rules usually provide the relevant time period for obtaining a writ of execution after entry of judgment.

j. Statute of Limitations on Enforcement of Judgments

Each judgment entered has a period of effectiveness that is determined by a statute of limitations for that judgment. In order to enforce the judgment beyond the statute of limitations period, the judgment creditor must bring an action on the judgment to "renew" the judgment for another period of time. In essence, the judgment creditor obtains a new judgment on the old judgment that is effective for the additional time period allowed by the new statute of limitations time period that applies to the new judgment.

Example: The court enters a judgment on March 1, 2010. Under state law, a writ of execution must be issued within two years of entry of that judgment and the statute of limitations on a judgment is 15 years. The judgment becomes dormant after March 1, 2012. To obtain a writ of execution after March 1, 2012, the judgment creditor must apply to the court to revive the judgment and to authorize issuance of a writ of execution. The judgment is unenforceable after March 1, 2025 because the statute of limitations will have expired. The creditor should start a lawsuit on the original judgment before March 1, 2025 in order to obtain a new judgment on the original judgment. The new judgment when entered would have a new period of 15 years before the statute of limitation on the new judgment expires.

k. Finding the Debtor's Assets

Obviously, to use the execution process to obtain payment of a judgment, the judgment creditor must be able to find out about the debtor's assets. Most states have post-judgment procedures similar to civil discovery procedures that allow the judgment creditor to obtain information about the debtor's assets. In some states, these post-judgment processes are called "supplemental proceedings." The basic concept of these proceedings is to require the debtor to answer questions under oath about the location of assets. These processes may not be very effective in allowing the judgment creditor to find the debtor's assets when the debtor is uncooperative. Often a judgment creditor will find that the assets have disappeared between the time the debtor answers questions and the judgment creditor can persuade the sheriff to attempt a levy. A creditor may also engage a private investigator or examine public records in an effort to find the debtor's assets.

l. Post-Judgment Garnishment Process

Sometimes, the asset the debtor owns is an obligation that is owed to the debtor by a third party. Most states have a process, usually denominated garnishment, in which the judgment creditor is able to serve process on the third party (the garnishee), directing the garnishee to pay to the sheriff or the judgment creditor the obligation that the garnishee owes to the debtor instead of paying that obligation to the debtor. If the garnishee in fact owes a mature obligation to the debtor but does not pay that obligation to the sheriff or the judgment creditor after the garnishee is served the garnishment summons, the judgment creditor may obtain a judgment against the garnishee for at least the amount of the obligation that the garnishee owed the debtor. In some states, the judgment creditor may obtain a judgment against the nonresponsive garnishee for the amount of the judgment the creditor has against the debtor even if that is more than the garnishee owes the debtor.

m. Exemptions From Judgment Enforcement Process

Many states provide that certain types of property are exempt from the judgment enforcement process.

(1) Exemptions by Individuals

Exemptions for individual debtors vary widely from state to state. The exemptions are usually of a certain type of property and are in many cases capped by a value amount or other limitation. For example, many states have a homestead exemption for property that is owned by a debtor and used as the debtor's principal residence. In some states, the homestead exemption is limited by value or by the amount of real estate involved or both. In a few states, the homestead exemption is not limited by value or amount. The personal property subject to exemption is exceedingly varied and again may be capped by value or by item. One limitation that is imposed by federal law is to protect a certain amount of wages from garnishment or any judgment enforcement process. See 15 U.S.C. §§ 1671–1677.

(2) Exemptions by Non-Individuals

Under most state laws, corporations or other business entities, such as partnerships, are not entitled to claim property as exempt from execution of a judgment against that entity. The entities that may claim property exempt from execution in a state are determined by the specific terms of that state's law.

(3) Effect of Exemption

When an asset is entirely exempt from execution, that asset may not be seized through the execution or garnishment process. If the exemption is limited by value, often the asset may be seized and sold and the nonexempt value of the asset applied to the amount of the judgment and the exempt value returned to the debtor. If the exemption is subject to a nonmonetary limitation, such as an area limitation for a homestead exemption, if feasible, the nonexempt portion may be separated and sold in order to enforce the judgment. Even if an asset is exempt from execution, that does not usually prevent the debtor from granting a contractual lien interest in the asset to secure a debt. Thus, a debtor may grant a mortgage in a homestead to secure a loan for the purchase price of the homestead. The effect of granting a consensual lien interest in the asset is that the asset may be sold pursuant to the contract to satisfy the debt that the lien interest secures. We will consider this further in Chapter VI when we discuss enforcement of security interests and agricultural liens in personal property.

n. Enforcement of Judgments Across State Lines

A creditor that obtains a judgment in one state must undertake additional process in order to enforce that judgment against a debtor's property located in another state.

(1) Starting a Lawsuit in the Second State
The creditor that has obtained a judgment in the first state may start a lawsuit in the state in which the debtor has assets. The second state will enter a judgment on the judgment entered in the first state. Once the second state enters a judgment, the judgment creditor will use the execution process in the second state to execute on the debtor's property in that second state.

> *Example:* Judgment Creditor obtained a judgment against Debtor, entered in a New Jersey state court. In order to execute against Debtor's assets located in New York, Judgment Creditor starts a lawsuit in a New York state court, based upon the New Jersey judgment. Once a judgment is obtained in New York, Judgment Creditor uses the execution process as prescribed in New York to execute on the judgment.

(2) Full Faith and Credit
Under the full faith and credit clause of the United States Constitution, art. IV, § 1, cl. 1, each state must give full faith and credit to a valid judgment from another state. The basis for challenging the judgment from the first state in the lawsuit in the second state is limited to issues,

such as lack of jurisdiction or due process in obtaining the first judgment, that would make the judgment in the first state unenforceable or void.

(3) Uniform Enforcement of Foreign Judgments Act

The Uniform Enforcement of Foreign Judgments Act, promulgated by NCCUSL and enacted by many states, provides an alternative to filing a lawsuit and obtaining a judgment in the second state based upon the judgment from the first state. Under this act, the judgment creditor registers the judgment from the first state with the clerk of a court in the second state and gives notice of that registration to the debtor. After a brief waiting period, the judgment creditor is able to use the execution process of the second state to execute against property in the second state.

3. Pre-Judgment Remedies

In some circumstances, a creditor may be able to obtain a court order that allows it to seize the debtor's assets prior to obtaining a judgment of liability against the debtor. Pre-judgment remedies present a serious risk to a debtor as its property is tied up in court processes even though there has been no adjudication that the debtor in fact owes a debt to the creditor. Pre-judgment remedies are typically set forth in state statutes and vary widely from state to state.

a. Grounds for Issuing a Pre-Judgment Remedy

Given that there has been no judgment that the debtor even owes the creditor a debt, state statutes typically provide that in order to obtain a pre-judgment order directing the sheriff to seize the debtor's property, the creditor must show some sort of extraordinary circumstances to a judge. Typical extraordinary circumstances are that the debtor is dissipating assets or transferring assets with an intent to hinder creditors. Many states require that the debtor be given notice and a hearing prior to issuance of an order for a pre-judgment remedy. Sometimes the creditor will be required to post a bond to protect the debtor against harm caused by the property seizure in the event judgment is not entered against the debtor. In extreme circumstances, a judge may issue an order authorizing seizure of a debtor's asset without a prior notice to the debtor and a hearing. In that circumstance, a prompt post-seizure hearing is required.

b. Attachment

Pre-judgment attachment process is in many respects similar to post-judgment execution process directed at tangible assets. Once the judge issues the order allowing pre-judgment attachment, the clerk's office issues a writ of attachment to the sheriff (or other law enforcement officer), who then levies on the debtor's asset. After the levy, the law enforcement officer maintains possession of the asset until judgment is entered in the creditor's favor. If judgment is entered in the creditor's favor, the asset is then sold pursuant to the execution sale process. If the judgment is not entered in the creditor's favor within a specified period of time, the judge will order the asset released to the debtor.

c. Garnishment

Pre-judgment garnishment process is in most respects the same as post-judgment garnishment process. The garnishment process is directed at third parties that owe obligations to the debtor. Once the judge issues the order allowing pre-judgment garnishment, the garnishee that owes the obligation to the debtor is directed to pay the obligation to the sheriff or the court. The sheriff or court then holds the money until judgment is entered in favor of the creditor. If the judgment is not entered in the creditor's favor within a specified period of time, the judge will order the money released to the debtor.

F. Constitutional Issues

As we have seen, in both the pre-judgment and post-judgment debt collection processes, state actors, such as judges and law enforcement officers, will be involved. Because state actors are participating in seizing a person's assets, some debtors have made successful arguments that the government has violated the constitutional rights of the debtor. The primary constitutional arguments that have been made are as follows.

1. Violation of Procedural Due Process

Under the 5th and 14th amendments to the United States Constitution, states are prohibited from depriving persons of property without due process of law. Through a series of cases culminating in Connecticut v. Doehr, 501 U.S. 1 (1991), the United States Supreme Court has given content to the concept of procedural due process as it relates to pre-judgment remedies. The Court considered "the private interest that will be affected by the prejudgment measure," the "risk of erroneous deprivation through the procedures under attack and the probable value of additional or alternative safeguards," the interest of the creditor seeking the remedy, and the government's interest "in providing the procedure or forgoing the added burden of providing greater protections." Using that balancing test, the Court held that a pre-judgment attachment violated due process when the state statute allowed attachment of real estate without (i) a notice and hearing to the debtor, (ii) a requirement of extraordinary circumstances, and (iii) a bond. The underlying lawsuit was an assault and battery with no connection to the real property subject to the attachment order. The procedural due process problem is peculiarly one related to pre-judgment remedies. Courts have routinely held that the debtor's procedural due process rights in post-judgment collection have been respected if a judgment has been duly entered against a debtor according to the valid state civil procedure process, and the state process regarding post-judgment execution has been followed.

2. Improper Search and Seizure

The 4th amendment of the United States Constitution (as incorporated by the 14th amendment) prohibits state actors from engaging in unreasonable search and seizures. In Soldal v. Cook County, Illinois, 506 U.S. 56 (1992), the United States Supreme Court held that an eviction proceeding in which a mobile home was seized could result in a violation of the 4th amendment protection from unreasonable search and seizures. The Court did not decide whether the eviction at issue did result in a violation of the 4th amendment and remanded to the lower court for a determination. The mobile home seizure took place prior to entry of a judgment that the home owners should be evicted. The Court stated in dicta that it doubted whether the 4th amendment right would be violated if a court ordered seizure following a judgment. Even in the post-judgment collection process, however, a law enforcement officer has to be careful in seizing property pursuant to a writ of execution. The law enforcement officer may not have the right to enter the debtor's residence unless the writ or some other provision of law so provides.

3. Private Creditor's Liability for Violation of Constitutional Rights

Even though the rights guaranteed in the 4th, 5th and 14th amendments are guarantees against deprivation by government actors, under the civil rights law, notably 42 U.S.C. § 1983, private actors have been held to be liable for damages for violation of an individual's constitutional rights if they act in concert with state actors in depriving a person of their constitutional rights. Moreover, the United States Supreme Court has held that the private actors are not entitled to a qualified immunity from liability for damages based upon good-faith compliance with existing law, such as a pre-judgment attachment process, that is subsequently determined to be unconstitutional. Wyatt v. Cole, 504 U.S. 158 (1992).

G. Regulation of the Debt Collection Process

Because of the danger of overzealous collection efforts, a variety of sources regulate the debt collection effort. A thorough review of applicable state and federal regulation is necessary to determine what terms and practices regarding debt collection are permissible. The following are examples of the regulation of the debt collection process.

1. Prohibited Collection Terms or Practices

Some consumer protection statutes prohibit some types of terms related to the collection process from being part of the contract creating the debt. One example is prohibiting terms that allow the creditor to confess judgment in court against a debtor upon any default in payment of the debt by the consumer debtor. Uniform Consumer Credit Code (UCCC) § 3.306. Another example is prohibiting taking a negotiable note as evidence of an obligation in certain types of transactions. UCCC § 3.307. Both of these types of terms or practices involve attempts by the creditor to shorten the collection process through preventing the debtor from having an opportunity to present defenses to liability. A confession of judgment does so by preventing the debtor from being heard before entry of judgment by a court. A negotiable note does so by negotiation of the note to a holder in due course which has the effect of cutting off many of the usual defenses to the obligation to pay. Uniform Commercial Code (UCC) § 3–305.

2. The Fair Debt Collection Practices Act

The Fair Debt Collection Practices Act, 15 U.S.C. §§ 1692–1692p, regulates debt collectors in their actions to collect consumer debts. States may also regulate debt collectors. The following discussion is based upon the federal act.

a. Debt Collector

A debt collector, as defined in the Act, is any entity that uses interstate commerce in "any business the principal purpose of which is the collection" of debts or "who regularly collects or attempts to collect" such debts owed to another entity. 15 U.S.C. § 1692a(6). Attorneys may be "debt collectors" when they collect debts in the course of their law practice. "Debt" are debts incurred by an individual primarily for personal, family or household purposes. 15 U.S.C. § 1692a(3), (5). A debt collector does not include, among others, a person acting as an employee or officer of the creditor, a person serving legal process, and nonprofit consumer credit counseling services in certain situations. 15 U.S.C. § 1692a(6).

b. Communication With the Debtor

The Act specifies the manner in which the debt collector may communicate with the debtor and others about the debt that is owed.

(1) Prohibited Communications
Generally, the Act prohibits communicating with the debtor before 8 a.m. and after 9 p.m. If the debt collector knows that the debtor is represented by an attorney, the debt collector should not communicate with the debtor directly unless the attorney directs otherwise. If the debt collector knows that the debtor's employer prohibits communication with the debtor at the place of employment, the debt collector may not do so. The debt collector generally may not communicate with third parties regarding the debtor's debt. The debt collector must cease communicating with the debtor if the debtor so directs. This direction to cease

communication, however, does not prevent the debt collector from pursuing judicial action to collect the debt. 15 U.S.C. § 1692c.

(2) Required Communications

Within five days after the debt collector contacts the debtor, the debt collector must send to the debtor in writing a validation of the amount of the debt, that includes among other things, the name of the creditor, a statement that the debtor must dispute the debt within 30 days or the debt will be considered valid, and a statement that a dispute about the debt will result in the debt collector obtaining a verification of the debt. This required initial communication cannot be satisfied by a pleading in a civil action. If the debtor complies with the process for disputing the debt, the debt collector must cease collection until it obtains verification of the debt. The debtor's failure to dispute the debt, however, does not equal an admission in court that the debtor is liable for the debt. 15 U.S.C. § 1692g.

c. Prohibition of Harassment or Abuse

The debt collector may not harass or abuse the debtor. Behavior that is considered harassing or abusive includes, but is not limited to, threatening violence, using profanity, causing a telephone to ring continuously, calling without identifying the caller's identity, and publishing a list of debtors that have failed to pay other than to a consumer credit reporting agency. 15 U.S.C. § 1692d.

d. Prohibition of False or Misleading Representations

A debt collector may not make false, deceptive or misleading representations in connection with the collection of a consumer debt. Behavior that is considered in violation of this prohibition includes, but is not limited to, (i) making a false representation that the debt collector is affiliated with the federal government, is an attorney, or is part of a consumer reporting agency, (ii) making a false representation about the character, amount or legal status of the debt, (iii) making a false statement that the debtor has committed a crime, and (iv) threatening to take action not allowed to be taken or not intended to be taken. 15 U.S.C. § 1692e.

e. Prohibition of Unfair Practices

A debt collector is prohibited from using unfair or unconscionable methods to collect a debt. Behavior that is considered to be in violation of this prohibition includes, but is not limited to, (i) collection of an amount that the debt collector is not allowed to collect under applicable law, (ii) soliciting a post-dated check for purposes of threatening criminal prosecution for issuing a bad check, (iii) calling the debtor collect, and (iv) threatening to take property that the creditor does not have a right to take. 15 U.S.C. § 1692f.

f. Civil Liability

A debt collector that acts in violation of the Act is liable for actual damages, statutory damages ($1,000 maximum in individual case, $500,000 maximum in a class action case), and reasonable attorneys' fees and costs. 15 U.S.C. § 1692k.

3. Fair Credit Reporting Act

The Fair Credit Reporting Act, 15 U.S.C. §§ 1681–1681x, regulates consumer reporting agencies and consumer reports in order to increase the accuracy of credit reports used in the granting of credit to consumers. In the debt collection process, the threat of an adverse credit report is leverage that the creditor may use to extract payment from the debtor. The Act applies to consumer credit reports, consumer credit reporting agencies, users of consumer credit reports, and persons that furnish information to consumer credit reporting agencies. See 15 U.S.C. § 1681a. The Act has several distinct facets.

a. Permissible Disclosure and Uses of Consumer Credit Reports

The Act requires that consumer reporting agencies control access to credit reports for the purposes specified in the Act. The primary purposes are the granting of credit, screening of potential employees, screening applicants for government licenses (such as the license to practice law), collection of child support, and underwriting insurance involving the consumer. 15 U.S.C. § 1681b. The credit reporting agency is required to have procedures to ensure that persons requesting credit reports have a legitimate right to do so. 15 U.S.C. § 1681e.

b. Permissible Disclosures in Consumer Credit Reports

The Act specifies what information may not be included in a consumer credit report. For example, a consumer credit report should not contain a bankruptcy case that is more than 10 years old, civil suits or judgments where the statute of limitations has expired, accounts placed for collection more than 7 years before, and other adverse information that is older than 7 years. These limitations do not apply in all cases, including when the consumer has applied for credit that involves more than $150,000 or employment with an annual salary of more than $75,000. 15 U.S.C. § 1681c.

c. Identity Theft

Several provisions allow the consumer to place information in a credit report to alert creditors that the consumer is a victim of identity theft or other fraudulent activity. 15 U.S.C. § 1681c–1. The credit reporting agency also is required to not report information that is the result of the identity theft or fraudulent activity. The credit reporting atency is required to notify the entity that provided the information that the information has been blocked from reporting due to the alleged identity theft or fraudulent activity. 15 U.S.C. § 1681c–2.

d. Disclosure of Credit Report to Consumer

The Act requires credit reporting agencies to make a consumer's credit report available to the consumer upon the consumer's request. 15 U.S.C. §§ 1681g, 1681h. The charge for making the report available to the consumer is limited and, in certain circumstances, the report must be provided to the consumer for free. 15 U.S.C. § 1681j.

e. Disputed Information

The Act provides a procedure for credit reporting agencies to reinvestigate in the case of disputed information and for the consumer to put information in the credit report regarding disputed information. 15 U.S.C. § 1681i.

f. Users of Credit Reports

Users of credit reports are required to notify consumers if the user takes adverse action based upon information in a credit report. 15 U.S.C. § 1681m.

g. Obligation of Information Providers

Persons that provide information to consumer credit reporting agencies have an obligation to furnish correct information and to update and correct inaccurate information. 15 U.S.C. § 1681s–2.

h. Civil Liability

Persons that willfully violate the Act are liable for actual damages, punitive damages, attorneys' fees, and costs. 15 U.S.C. § 1681n. For negligent noncompliance, a person is liable for actual damages, attorneys' fees, and costs, but not punitive damages. 15 U.S.C. § 1681o.

4. Tort Law

In addition to the statutory regimes and constitutional protections that control creditor behavior, tort law also protects debtors. A creditor that engages in trespass, threatening behavior, defamation, invasion of privacy and other tortious behavior will be liable for damages based upon principles of tort law. In other words, in collecting the debt, the creditor must act in accord with the standards of behavior as required by tort law principles.

5. Lender Liability Issues in Debt Collection

If a creditor takes action in collecting debt that had the effect of misleading other creditors or breaches contractual obligations that the creditor owed to the debtor, the creditor may be liable for harm caused by that activity. One of the main issues in litigation concerning misleading other creditors was whether the creditor exerted impermissible control of the debtor in order to maximize collection of its debt to the detriment of other creditors of the debtor. The courts disagree about what are permissible and impermissible methods of control. Compare In re American Lumber Co., 5 B.R. 470 (D. Minn. 1980) with In re Clark Pipe and Supply Co., 893 F.2d 693 (5th Cir. 1990).

H. Fraudulent Transfers

A creditor may only seek to obtain property that is the debtor's property in order to satisfy the debtor's debt. One of the risks of debt collection activity is that the debtor will try to protect its property from the creditor by transferring its property to other persons. Fraudulent transfer law responds to that situation. The principles of fraudulent transfer law arose at common law and are now enshrined in statutes such as the Uniform Fraudulent Transfer Act (UFTA), promulgated by NCCUSL. References below are to that Act.

1. Actual Intent to Hinder, Defraud, or Delay Creditors

If the creditor can prove that the debtor had actual intent to hinder, defraud or delay creditors through a transfer of the debtor's interest in property, the transfer may be set aside as fraudulent. UFTA § 4(a)(1). Because the debtor will not often admit fraud, circumstantial evidence is often used to prove actual fraud. Circumstantial evidence is referred to in the cases as "badges of fraud." Some of the "badges of fraud" are the debtor transferred property to persons with a relationship to the debtor, the debtor retained possession of the property even after the transfer, the debtor concealed the transfer, or the debtor made the transfer in response to a pending suit. UFTA § 4(b).

2. Constructive Fraud

The more usual case is for the creditor to attempt to prove the transfer was fraudulent by proving one or more of three types of constructive fraud. Constructive fraud is proved if the transfer is made for less than reasonably equivalent value and one of three other circumstances are true: (i) the debtor's enterprise was undercapitalized; (ii) the debtor's debts were beyond the debtor's ability to pay as they became due, or (iii) the transfer was made while the debtor was insolvent or rendered the debtor insolvent. UFTA §§ 4(a)(2), 5(a).

3. Effect of Finding a Fraudulent Transfer

The remedy in a fraudulent transfer action is not against the debtor that transferred the asset but is against the transferee and the property in the hands of the transferee. If a court finds that a transfer is fraudulent, there are two remedial options. First, the transfer is nullified, enabling the creditor to obtain a levy or other process against the asset as described above. UFTA § 7. Second, the creditor may obtain a judgment for the value of the transferred asset against the transferee. UFTA § 8(b). A transferee that took the asset in good faith may have a lien on the asset for the value of the consideration it paid for the asset. UFTA § 8(d).

I. Effect of Debtor's Bankruptcy on Debt Collection

A debtor may react to a creditor's debt collection efforts by filing a bankruptcy petition, which will have a significant effect on the ability of a creditor to collect the debt that is owed to the creditor. A full explanation of bankruptcy law and process is beyond the scope of these materials.

1. Filing a Bankruptcy Petition

A debtor need not be in financial distress or insolvent to file a bankruptcy petition. A debtor may file under one of five chapters. Chapter 7 provides for liquidation of the debtor's assets to pay the debtor's debts as set forth in the Bankruptcy Code, 11 U.S.C. § 101 *et seq.* Chapters 11, 12, and 13 allow for reorganization of the debtor's financial affairs through court approval of plans of reorganization according to certain criteria contained in the Bankruptcy Code. 11 U.S.C. §§ 1129, 1225, 1325. Chapter 12 proceedings are restricted to family farmers or family fisherman. 11 U.S.C. § 109. Chapter 13 proceedings are restricted to debtors who are individuals with regular income that have debts under a maximum specified amount. 11 U.S.C. § 109. Either individuals or business entities such as corporations or partnerships may file a petition under Chapters 7, 11, and 12. 11 U.S.C. § 109. However, individual debtors with primarily consumer debts who file a Chapter 7 petition may be forced to proceed under Chapter 11 or 13 unless they meet the means test provided in 11 U.S.C. § 707. Chapter 9 addresses adjustment of debts of a municipality, and provides for a reorganization process. 11 U.S.C. §§ 109, 901–946.

2. The Bankruptcy Estate

Filing the bankruptcy petition creates an estate that consists of all of the debtor's legal and equitable interests in property. 11 U.S.C. § 541. The representative of the bankruptcy estate is the trustee in a Chapter 7 case and the "debtor in possession" in a reorganization case.

3. The Automatic Stay

The automatic stay arises upon the filing of the bankruptcy petition. The automatic stay stops all actions to collect a debt from the debtor, the debtor's property, and the property of the bankruptcy estate. 11 U.S.C. § 362. A creditor that takes any action, no matter how small, to collect a debt after the debtor files bankruptcy is in violation of the automatic stay even if the creditor has no idea that a bankruptcy petition has been filed. Violations of the stay may be punished by contempt of court citations, liability for actual damages, and punitive sanctions in addition to nullifying the action taken in violation of the stay.

4. Discharge of Debts

An individual debtor that files for bankruptcy is often seeking a discharge of his or her personal obligation to pay debts. In a Chapter 7 proceeding, the assets of the bankruptcy estate are used to satisfy the debts the debtor owes. An individual debtor will obtain a discharge of the obligation to pay debts that were incurred prior to the filing of the bankruptcy petition. 11 U.S.C. § 727. In a Chapter 11, 12, or 13 proceeding, the debtor will propose a plan of reorganization and will receive a discharge of all debts provided for in the plan upon confirmation of the Chapter 11 plan in the case of an individual debtor, 11 U.S.C. § 1141, or upon completion of payments under a Chapter 12 or 13 plan, 11 U.S.C. §§ 1228, 1328. Certain types of debts are excepted from the discharge, either automatically or as a result of filing an objection to discharging the debt. 11 U.S.C. § 523. A creditor may also object to the granting of a discharge of all of the debts of the debtor upon specified grounds. 11 U.S.C. §§ 727, 1141, 1228, 1328. If a debt is discharged, the creditor may not take action to collect that debt as a personal obligation of the debtor. 11 U.S.C. § 524.

5. Effect on Liens

The creditor with a lien in specific assets is able to generally retain its lien in the property even if the debtor files bankruptcy. Although the debtor's personal obligation to pay the debt may be discharged, 11 U.S.C. § 524, the discharge does not strip the lien from the property. A creditor with the lien may be subject to claims of the bankruptcy trustee or the debtor in possession to avoid the lien based upon the failure of the creditor to perfect its lien, 11 U.S.C. § 544, or because granting the lien was a preference to the creditor, 11 U.S.C. § 547. We will consider the issues of the treatment of liens in bankruptcy more fully in Chapter V.

J. Reduction of Risk in Debt Collection

Given the difficulty of debt collection as outlined above, it should not be surprising that creditors have invented mechanisms for reducing the risk of nonpayment.

1. Guarantees

One method of reducing risk is to obtain more than one person that is obligated to pay a particular debt. At a very basic level, that is the function of a guarantee contract. A guarantee contract is an agreement from an entity to answer for the debt of another person. Black's Law Dictionary (9th ed. 2009). A creditor is not entitled to more than one satisfaction of the debt. A guarantee is a contract that is subject to all of the common law rules of contract law except to the extent statutes may have altered those rules in a particular state. A guarantee is also subject to another body of law commonly known as suretyship law. A guarantor who has paid the debt of another has a right of recourse against the person whose debt is paid. The two primary effects of suretyship principles are (i) to allow some additional defenses for a guarantor to assert against the creditor regarding the obligation to pay, and (ii) to govern the rights as between the person primarily obligated on the debt and the person secondarily obligated on the debt (guarantor). Many guarantee contracts deal with the first issue by containing a clause that is a waiver of suretyship-based defenses. The principles of suretyship law are well stated in the Restatement of Suretyships and Guarantees and beyond the scope of these materials.

> *Example:*   A loans money to B and B promises to repay the loan. As a condition to making the loan to B, A required that B obtain a guarantor. C signed a contract promising to pay the obligation that B owes A. B is obligated on the debt to A and C is liable on the debt to A as a guarantor. C will have rights against B to reimbursement of any payment that C makes to A. A is entitled to no more than full satisfaction of the debt, even if it collects from both B and C.

2. Obtaining Liens by Contract

Another method of reducing the risk of nonpayment is to obtain a lien in specific items of the debtor's property through a contract with the debtor. Examples of obtaining a lien by contract include obtaining a mortgage on real property and a security interest in personal property. The remainder of these materials will consider security interests in personal property.

a. Collection

In the event the debtor does not pay, the creditor with the lien will be able to use a more summary process for obtaining possession of the asset that is subject to the lien and in some instances, may do so without any court process at all. We will consider the collection process more fully in Chapter VI.

b. Priority

The creditor with a lien in a specific asset also has an advantage in terms of setting its priority position in the asset as it relates to the claims of other creditors to that asset. Generally, the higher the creditor's priority for its lien claim in the asset, the more likely the debt obligation secured by that lien will be paid from the asset value in the event the creditor initiates collection activity. We will consider the concept of priority more fully in Chapter V.

c. Bankruptcy

As noted above, a creditor with a lien in assets enjoys some advantages in the bankruptcy process because the bankruptcy discharge does not strip the lien from the property. We will consider the issues of the treatment of liens in bankruptcy more fully in Chapter V.

K. Overview of the Uniform Commercial Code

The Uniform Commercial Code (UCC) contains Article 9 which governs security interests and agricultural liens in personal property. It is the study of Article 9 that the rest of these materials will address.

1. History

The UCC was promulgated in the 1950s with the stated purpose of simplifying, clarifying, and modernizing commercial law. UCC § 1–103. The original UCC consisted of eight substantive articles each addressing a certain aspect of commercial law and one article of general provisions. The UCC gained widespread adoption in the United States during the 1960s and has been revised several times in piecemeal fashion after that time. In the mid 1980s, a wholesale revision process was undertaken article by article. That revision process was finally completed in 2003.

2. Enactment

The UCC is promulgated by the National Conference of Commissioners on Uniform State Laws (NCCUSL) and the American Law Institute (ALI) through a process of drafting committee meetings and consideration by the general membership of both organizations. All meetings are open to the public and draw participation by interested parties. Once the two sponsoring organizations approve an article of the UCC, the article is proposed to a state for adoption by the normal legislative process in that state. In the adoption process, the state may make nonuniform amendments to the proposed article. The UCC is not law. The law is the relevant article of the UCC as enacted by a particular state. Having said that, most law school curriculums study the UCC in its uniform form as proposed by NCCUSL and the ALI with the caveat that in solving any real issue of a client, the UCC as enacted in the relevant state must be consulted.

3. Overview of Each Article of the UCC

a. Article 1

Article 1 contains several provisions with statements of general principles and definitions. These general provisions and definitions apply to transactions within the scope of the other articles of the UCC. Article 1 was revised in 1999.

b. Article 2

Article 2 applies to transactions in goods and typical transactions covered by the article are contracts for the sale of goods. Article 2 was revised in 2003. Those 2003 amendments were withdrawn by NCCUSL and the ALI in 2011.

c. Article 2A

Article 2A applies to leases of goods and was originally promulgated in 1987 and revised in 1990. Article 2A was again revised in 2003. Those 2003 amendments were withdrawn by NCCUSL and the ALI in 2011.

d. Article 3

Article 3 applies to negotiable instruments. Negotiable instruments are usually either promissory notes or drafts, such as checks. Article 3 was revised in 1990 and in 2002.

e. Article 4

Article 4 applies to bank deposits and the process of collecting items, including checks, through the banking system. Article 4 was revised in 1990 and in 2002.

f. Article 4A

Article 4A was added in 1989 and covers commercial funds transfers through the banking system. A federal law and regulation (the Electronic Fund Transfers Act, 15 U.S.C. §§ 1693–1693r, and Regulation E, 12 C.F.R. Part 205, Part 1005) govern consumer funds transfers in the banking system.

g. Article 5

Article 5 covers a letter of credit issued by a bank that obligates the bank to pay a certain sum of money in response to a complying documentary presentation. Article 5 was revised in 1990.

h. Article 6

Article 6 covers bulk transfers. A bulk transfer is a transfer by a debtor of the bulk of all of its inventory in a single transaction. Article 6 was revised in 1989 with two recommendations. The primary recommendation was repeal of the article with the secondary option of enacting a revised version of the article. Most states have repealed this article.

i. Article 7

Article 7 covers documents of title and bailments of goods with warehouses and carriers. Article 7 was revised in 2003. As part of that revision, amendments were made to other articles of the UCC, including Articles 2 and 2A. The 2011 withdrawal of the 2003 amendments to Articles 2 and 2A does not affect these conforming amendments arising out of the Article 7 revision.

j. Article 8

Article 8 deals with the transfer of interests in investment securities. It does not deal with the regulations regarding issuing securities but rather with the process of transfer of the investment securities after issuance. Article 8 was last revised in 1994.

k. Article 9

Article 9 covers contracts granting security interests in personal property and agricultural liens that arise under state law in farm products. Article 9 was extensively revised in 1999. In 2010, a few additional amendments were promulgated. The remainder of these materials will cover Article 9 as revised in 1999 and amended in 2010.

L. Overview Of UCC Article 9

UCC Article 9 is a statutory scheme that governs attaching, perfecting, and enforcing security interests and agricultural liens in personal property. Article 9 also governs the relative priority of those interests as against other property-based claims to personal property. This text will first discuss the scope of Article 9 in Chapter II. Chapter III will address the process for attachment of security interests and

REVIEW QUESTION FOR CHAPTER I

agricultural liens in personal property. Chapter IV will discuss the process for perfection of security interests and agricultural liens. Chapter V will address priority of security interests and agricultural liens against other claims to the debtor's assets. Chapter VI will discuss enforcement of security interests and agricultural liens. Finally Chapter VII will discuss the liability of a party for violating the mandatory rules of Article 9.

M. Review Questions for Chapter I

Determine whether the following statements are true or false.

1. A debt may not be both contingent and mature.

2. A debt may not be both contingent and disputed.

3. A debt may not be both unmature and secured.

4. A debtor must be insolvent to file bankruptcy.

5. A creditor may not collect a debt by seizing a consumer debtor's personal property.

6. A creditor without a lien in the debtor's property must obtain a court order in order to seize the debtor's property without the debtor's consent to satisfy a debt owed to the creditor.

7. A private creditor may incur civil liability for violating a debtor's constitutional rights if the procedure the creditor uses to seize the debtor's property is found to violate the United States Constitution.

8. An attorney collecting a debt may be a debt collector under the Fair Debt Collection Practices Act.

9. The Fair Credit Reporting Act prohibits reporting a consumer's bankruptcy filing if that filing is more than 10 years previous to the date of the credit report.

10. When a debtor files bankruptcy, a creditor is still entitled to send the debtor a notice of the debt owed.

11. A debtor that transfers its property in order to avoid a creditor's collection actions has made a fraudulent transfer that may be avoided even if the debtor receives reasonably equivalent value for the transferred asset.

12. A debtor may grant an enforceable consensual lien in property that is exempt from execution.

13. A bankruptcy discharge extinguishes a lien in the debtor's property.

II

The Scope of UCC Article 9

UCC Article 9 covers two primary types of lien interests in personal property. First, it covers consensual security interests that arise by a contract between a creditor and a debtor. Second, it covers nonconsensual security interests and agricultural liens that arise by operation of law. UCC § 9–109. UCC Article 9 also covers some sales of certain types of rights to payment.

A. Consensual Security Interests

UCC § 9–109(a)(1) states that Article 9 applies to "a transaction, regardless of its form, that creates a security interest in personal property or fixtures by contract."

1. Security Interest

A security interest is "an interest in personal property or fixtures which secures payment or performance of an obligation." UCC § 1–201(b)(35).

a. Personal Property or Fixtures

The property that is the subject of the security interest must be personal property or fixtures. Personal property is a very broad category and is usually used to distinguish that type of property from real property. Fixtures are a type of property located on real estate that is classified as both real property and personal property. UCC § 9–102(a)(41). The various types of personal property as defined in Article 9 are set forth in Section G of this Chapter II, *infra*. A quick perusal of that list might be helpful to the discussion that follows.

Example: A contracted to buy a new furnace for A's commercial office building. A agreed to grant a security interest in the furnace to secure payment of the purchase price. Under applicable real estate principles in that state, if A sold the building after the furnace was installed, the furnace would pass to the real estate buyer under the real estate deed. Under applicable personal property principles, installation of the furnace in the building does not make the furnace lose its status as personal property that may be the subject of a separate contract, apart from a contract concerning the real estate. The furnace is a fixture because it retains its personal property nature even after affixation to the real estate and even though the real estate owner could alienate its rights to the furnace under applicable real estate law.

b. The Meaning of the Term "Property"

A question that lurks within the concept of "personal property" is whether the asset in question qualifies as "property" in the first instance. This issue has come up most often in the context of licenses, such as liquor licenses or broadcasting licenses. The issuing authority often takes the position that a license is a grant of a privilege to engage in the conduct licensed but the license itself is not property. Article 9 does not determine whether the asset qualifies as "property." One of the questions to consider concerning security interests is whether the asset in question is in fact "property" under the statutes, regulations, and applicable court decisions.

Example: A is the owner of a bar and a licensee of a liquor license granted by the appropriate state agency. A desires to borrow funds from a bank to fund operation of its bar and purports to grant a security interest to the bank in the liquor license to secure the debt. The state agency regulations provide that the licensee of a liquor license has no property interest in the license and is not allowed to transfer the licensee's interest under the license to any other person. The question is whether the liquor license will be treated as personal property for the purpose of allowing the bank to have a security interest in the licensee's rights under the license.

c. Lien Interest and Personal Liability

An interest in property to secure a debt is often referred to as a "lien" in property. The creditor is the obligee of two distinct obligations. The obligor has an obligation to pay the debt to the obligee. That obligation is often referred to as the "in personam" obligation. When there is a lien in property to secure the debt, the property subject to the lien is obligated for the amount of the debt. That obligation is often referred to as the "in rem" obligation. A security interest is an "in rem" obligation of the personal property or fixture to secure an "in personam""obligation of the obligor to pay the debt.

> *Example:* A borrows funds from a bank and grants a security interest in A's inventory to secure the debt. A has an "in personam" obligation to pay the debt to the bank. The inventory is subject to the "in rem" obligation by virtue of the security interest.

d. Secured Party

A secured party is the person in whose favor the security interest is created. UCC § 9–102(a)(73).

e. Debtor

A debtor is the person that has a property interest, other than a lien interest, in the personal property or fixtures that is subject to the security interest. UCC § 9–102(a)(28).

f. Obligor

An obligor is the person that owes performance of the obligation that is secured by a security interest or agricultural lien or a person that has supplied collateral, other than the collateral at issue, to secure the obligation. A bank that issues a letter of credit is not an obligor within this definition. UCC § 9–102(a)(59).

g. Collateral

Collateral is defined as the "property subject to the security interest." UCC § 9–102(a)(12).

Example: A borrows money from Bank. Bank insists on collateral. B grants a security interest in B's car to secure the loan made to A. A is the obligor and not the debtor and B is the debtor but not the obligor. The car is the collateral.

Example: A borrows money from Bank. Bank insists on collateral. B grants a security interest in B's car to secure the loan Bank made to A. A grants a security interest in A's truck to secure the loan as well. A is an obligor. As to A's car, A is a debtor and B is an obligor, and A's car is the collateral. As to B's car, B is the debtor and not an obligor, and B's car is the collateral.

2. Created by Contract

The primary coverage of UCC Article 9 is of security interests created by contract. Except as discussed below in Section D, security interests in personal property or fixtures arise by virtue of the consent of a person with a property interest in the property to create an in rem obligation of the property to secure the debt that is owed to the creditor. In addition to the principles explored in Chapter III regarding attachment of a security interest, all of the principles of contract law are applicable to determine whether the debtor has validly created a security interest by contract.

3. Form of the Transaction

The creation of a security interest by contract happens regardless of the characterization of the transaction by the parties. For a variety of reasons that will become clear as we explore the provisions of UCC Article 9, parties will sometimes not want Article 9 to apply to the transaction. The parties' desires or subjective intentions, however, do not determine this issue. A court will look through the form of the transaction to its substance to determine whether the contract "creates an interest in property to secure an obligation." UCC § 9–109, cmt. 2.

a. Sale or Lease of Goods

One of the most litigated issues concerning whether a transaction falls within Article 9 is to determine whether a transaction that is denominated a lease of goods is in fact a transaction that is a sale of the goods with a security interest retained by the seller. A lease of goods is the right to the use and possession of goods for a period of time. UCC § 2A–103(1).

(1) Consequences

The consequences of the determination that the transaction is a lease or a sale with a retained security interest are quite stark.

(a) True Lease

If the transaction is in fact a lease, called a "true lease," the parties' obligations to each other and the rights of third parties are determined by the rules of UCC Article 2A. The lessee's creditors are generally unable to obtain rights in the goods that are superior to the rights of the lessor and the lessor need not take any action constituting public notice of its claim to the property as lessor in order to obtain that result.

(b) Sale and Security Interest

If the transaction denominated a lease is in fact a sale of the goods with a retained security interest, the transaction is governed by UCC Article 2 regarding the quality of the goods in the sale and by UCC Article 9 regarding collection of the debt obligation and the rights of third parties to the goods. The rights of the lessee/buyer's creditors as against the lessor/seller of the goods will be governed by Article 9. The seller/lessor must give public notice of its claim in order to preserve a priority position that would have a chance to be superior to the rights of the creditors of the buyer/lessee.

(2) Determination

The determination of whether the transaction is a "true lease" or a transaction that creates a security interest is a factual determination that is governed by UCC § 1–203. The primary focus of that complicated provision is to determine as an economic matter whether the buyer/lessee is in fact purchasing more than merely the right to possess or use the good for a particular period of time and whether the lessor is retaining a meaningful residual interest in the goods. Given the fact intensive nature of this inquiry, it is often very difficult to determine whether a transaction is a "true lease" or a disguised security transaction (that is, a sale with a retained security interest).

(a) Baseline Rule

The baseline rule is that to determine whether the transaction creates a true lease or a disguised security interest depends on all the facts and circumstances of the case. UCC § 1–203(a). Under this test, the following factors do not determine that the transaction is a disguised security interest. Many true leases typically have one or more of these characteristics and these characteristics do not necessarily indicate that the lessee is buying the entire economic interest in the goods and that the lessor is not retaining a meaningful residual interest.

(i) Value of the Consideration

The transaction is not creation of a security interest merely because the present value of the consideration under the lease is greater than the fair market value of the goods. UCC § 1–203(c)(1).

(ii) Risk of Loss

The transaction is not creation of a security interest merely because the lessee has the risk of loss for the goods. UCC § 1–203(c)(2).

(iii) Lessee Payment of Certain Costs

The transaction is not creation of a security interest merely because the lessee pays certain costs such as taxes, registration fees, insurance, and service or maintenance fees. UCC § 1–203(c)(3).

(iv) Option to Renew or Own

A transaction is not the creation of a security interest if the contract merely has a renewal option or purchase option. UCC § 1–203(c)(4).

(v) **Option to Renew for Fixed Rent**
A transaction is not the creation of a security interest if the contract merely has an option to renew the lease for a fixed rent that is equal to or greater than the fair market value of the goods predicted for the time the option was to be performed. UCC § 1–203(c)(5).

(vi) **Option to Own for Fixed Price**
A transaction is not the creation of a security interest if the contract merely has an option to buy the goods for a fixed price that is equal to or greater than the fair market value of the goods predicted for the time the option was to be performed. UCC § 1–203(c)(6).

(b) **Presumption of Creation of a Security Interest**
A transaction that is in the form of the lease is presumed to created a security interest if *both* of the following two elements exist. If both of the two elements of the presumption are not met, the "facts and circumstances" test controls.

(i) **First Element**
The first element is that the lessee must be obligated to pay the consideration for the entire lease term and have no legal ability prior to the end of the lease term to terminate that obligation to pay. UCC § 1–203(b).

(ii) **Second Element**
The second element is that one of the following four circumstances must also be true in addition to the first element given above.

(a) *Term of the Lease*
The term of the lease must be equal to or greater than the remaining economic life of the good. UCC 1–203(b)(1).

(b) *Renewal or Ownership*
The contract requires the lessee to renew the lease for the remaining economic life of the goods or to become the owner of the goods. UCC § 1–203(b)(2).

(c) *Option to Renew Lease for Nominal Consideration*
The contract gives the lessee an option to renew the lease for the remaining economic life of the goods without additional consideration or only nominal consideration. UCC § 1–203(b)(3).

(d) *Option to Own for Nominal Consideration*
The contract gives the lessee an option to become the owner of the goods for no additional consideration or nominal consideration. UCC § 1–203(b)(4).

(iii) Relevant Definitions
UCC § 1–203 also provides for some definitions to use in determining whether these two elements are met.

(a) *Nominal Consideration*
Consideration is not nominal in a renewal option if the rent is stated to be the fair market rent at the time the option is to be performed. Consideration is not nominal in a purchase option if the price is stated to be the fair market value of the goods at the time the option is to be performed. UCC § 1–203(d).

(b) *Economic Life of the Goods*
The economic life of the goods should be determined in light of the facts and circumstances at the time the transaction was entered into. UCC § 1–203(e).

(c) *Fair Market Value or Rent*
The fair market value or the rent for the goods should be determined at the time the transaction was entered into. UCC § 1–203(e).

b. Consignments for Sale

A consignment for sale is typically a transfer of possession of the goods from the owner of the goods to a merchant that sells the goods on behalf of the owner with the obligation to return the goods if they are not sold. A consignment for sale is typically a type of bailment.

(1) "True Consignment" or Disguised Security Interest

Often it is very difficult to determine whether the transaction that is denominated a consignment by the parties is in fact such a bailment for sale (a "true consignment") or whether the owner has in reality sold the goods to the merchant and in effect retained a security interest in those goods to secure the merchant's obligation to pay the price.

(2) Determination

Unlike the lease/sale distinction discussed above, however, the UCC does not contain any statutory provision that provides guidance in distinguishing a "true consignment" from a disguised security interest. The courts must continue to do so based upon their assessment of the "true" nature of the transaction.

(3) Consequence

If the transaction that is denominated a consignment in substance actually creates a security interest in the goods, the transaction is within the scope of Article 9 by virtue of the general rule that Article 9 governs security interests created by contract. UCC § 9–109(a)(1). If the transaction is a "true consignment," the transaction may still be within the scope of Article 9 as discussed below.

c. Other Transactions

The rule of UCC § 9–109(a)(1) is very broad. The variety of transaction forms that may exist or are yet to be invented by commercial parties is almost infinite. This provision allows the court to examine the substance of the transaction to determine whether the transaction in fact creates an interest in personal property to secure payment or performance of an obligation.

Example: A sells a good to B. As part of the transaction, B agrees that if A pays B a specified sum of money by a certain time that B will reconvey the good to A. This transaction that is structured as an outright sale with an option to repurchase is in fact a transaction that creates an interest in the good to secure an obligation to pay. *See* UCC § 9–203, cmt 3.

B. True Consignments

As discussed above, a consignment in form that is in substance a creation of a security interest is within the scope of Article 9 under UCC § 9–109(a)(1). As part of the 1999 revision of Article 9, the scope of Article 9 was expanded to cover many true consignments for sale because it is very difficult to tell whether a transaction is a true consignment or a transaction that is really a disguised security interest. Thus, Article 9 defines the term "consignment" and applies to transactions that would otherwise be "true consignments." UCC § 9–109(a)(4).

1. Consignment Defined

A "consignment" as defined in Article 9, UCC § 9–102(a)(20), is a consignment that does not create an interest that secures an obligation and that has *all* of the following five characteristics. A consignment in form that is a disguised security interest is not a "consignment" as defined in Article 9.

a. Delivery to a Merchant for Sale

The goods must be delivered to a merchant for the purpose of sale of the goods. UCC § 9–102(a)(20). Goods are defined in UCC § 9–102(a)(44). *See also* Section G, definition of goods. Merchant is defined in UCC § 2–104. UCC § 9–102(b).

b. Merchant Criteria

The merchant must deal in goods of that kind under a name other than the person making delivery, must not be an auctioneer, and must not be generally known by the merchant's creditors as substantially engaged in selling the goods of others. UCC § 9–102(a)(20)(A).

c. Value of the Goods

The aggregate value of the goods at the time of delivery must be $1,000 or more. UCC § 9–102(a)(20)(B).

d. Not Consumer Goods

The goods must not be consumer goods immediately prior to delivery. UCC § 9–102(a)(20)(C). Consumer goods are goods that are used or bought for use primarily for family, personal, or household purposes. UCC § 9–102(a)(23).

2. Effect of Inclusion

If a transaction meets the definition of "consignment," the interest of the consignor (defined in UCC § 9–102(a)(21)) is deemed to be a security interest in the goods delivered to the merchant, the consignee (defined in UCC § 9–102(a)(19)). UCC § 1–201(b)(35), second sentence. The consignee is the "debtor," UCC § 9–102(a)(28)(c), and the consignor is the "secured party," UCC § 9–102(a)(73)(C). The goods subject to the consignment is the "collateral." UCC § 9–102(a)(12).

3. Effect of Exclusion

If the transaction is in substance a true consignment but is not within the definition of consignment as described *supra*, the transaction is not governed by Article 9 and is in effect a bailment. UCC § 9–109, cmt. 6.

Example: A, a consumer, delivers used household goods to B, a store in the business of selling second hand goods. A and B agree that B will sell the goods and remit the proceeds minus a 10% commission to A. If B fails to sell the goods, B will return them to A. Assume that based upon the facts, a court finds this a true consignment and not a consignment intended as security. The transaction is excluded from the scope of Article 9 as the goods were consumer goods immediately prior to their delivery to B. Law other than Article 9 controls the rights of A and B as against each other and the rights of B's creditors to A's goods while in the possession of B.

C. Sales of Certain Types of Assets

Article 9 also applies to four types of transactions that are sales transactions, not the creation of an interest in property to secure an obligation. Those four types of sales are sales of accounts, chattel paper, promissory notes, and payment intangibles. UCC § 9–109(a)(3). The definitions of these terms are explored in Section G, *infra*.

1. Secured Party and Debtor

The interest of the buyer of accounts, chattel paper, promissory notes, and payment intangibles is treated as a security interest under Article 9, even though the buyer is the outright owner of the asset, and the seller retains no interest in the asset. UCC § 1–201(b)(35), second sentence. The buyer of these types of assets is denominated a "secured party," UCC § 9–102(a)(73)(D), and the seller of these types of assets is denominated a "debtor," UCC § 9–102(a)(28)(B).

Example: A sells an item of equipment to B. B promises to pay the price for that equipment in 10 days. The obligation that B owes A is an account (as defined in UCC § 9–102(a)(2)). A sells that account to C. The transaction between A and C, sale of the account, is subject to Article 9 (exclusions from Article 9 are discussed in Section F, *infra*). A is the debtor and C is the secured party.

Example: A leased goods from B. The lease contract is an asset of B and chattel paper (as defined in UCC § 9–102(a)(11)). B sold the lease contract to C. The sale of the lease contract from B to C is a sale of chattel paper governed by Article 9 (exclusions from Article 9 are discussed in Section F, *infra*). B is a debtor and C is a secured party.

Example: A, a large commercial lending entity, is the payee of approximately 2000 negotiable and nonnegotiable notes that qualify as promissory notes as defined in Article 9 (UCC § 9–102(a)(65)). A sells all of the notes to B. The sale of the notes from A to B is a transaction subject to Article 9 (exclusions from Article 9 are discussed in Section F, *infra*). A is the debtor and B is the secured party.

Example: A makes a loan to B of $1,000,000. A sells a $100,000 participation in that loan to another lender, C. In effect C is the owner of the right to receive payment of $100,000 of the loan that B owes. A's sale of that participation right to C is a sale of a payment intangible (UCC § 9–102(a)(61)) and covered by Article 9 (exclusions from Article 9 are discussed in Section F, *infra*). A is the debtor and C is the secured party.

2. Why Include

Sales of these types of assets are included within the scope of Article 9 because it is difficult to distinguish sales of these types of assets from transactions that create a lien interest to secure an obligation. UCC § 9–109, cmt. 4. Nothing in Article 9 helps determine whether the transaction creates a sale of these types of assets or a lien interest to secure an obligation. The ultimate characterization of the transaction is based upon all the facts and circumstances of the case. UCC § 9–109, cmt. 4.

3. Effect of Including

If the buyer (the secured party, UCC § 9–102(a)(73)(D)), fails to take the proper action to "perfect" its interest in the account or chattel paper it has purchased, a subsequent buyer or a creditor could obtain an interest in the account or chattel paper that is superior to the first buyer's interest. We will study what the buyer must do to perfect in Chapter IV and the consequences of failure to perfect in Chapter V when we discuss priority of interests in personal property and fixtures. (The security interest of a buyer of promissory notes or payment intangibles is automatically perfected. UCC § 9–309.)

D. Security Interest Arising Under Other Articles of the UCC

Other provisions of the UCC provide for a security interest to arise in certain circumstances. If a security interest arises under those other articles, Article 9 will apply to the security interest. UCC § 9–109(a)(5) and (6). Even though a security interest may arise in the circumstances described below, that does not prevent the parties from agreeing by contract to grant a security interest in the asset.

1. Articles 2 and 2A

In three circumstances described in Article 2 and one circumstance described in Article 2A, a security interest arises by operation of law, not the parties' agreement. These four security interests are governed by Article 9 as provided in UCC § 9–110. UCC § 9–109(a)(5).

a. Retention of Title in Goods Sold

A seller of goods may have agreed to sell the goods to the buyer on credit, that is, agreed to deliver the goods in return for payment of the price some period of time thereafter. When the seller does so, the seller will often state in the purchase agreement with the buyer that the seller "retains title" to the goods until the purchase price is paid in full. The seller's retention of title does not prevent title from passing to the buyer upon delivery of the goods to the buyer and is treated as the seller obtaining a security interest in the goods to secure payment of the price. UCC §§ 2–401, 1–201(b)(35), 9–110.

Example: A sells goods to B on credit. The purchase agreement between A and B states that A retains title to the goods until full payment of the price. A delivers the goods to B. A has a security interest in the goods to secure the price that B owes. B has title to the goods subject to A's security interest. A's security interest is governed by Article 9.

b. Shipment Under Reservation

(1) Defined

"Shipment under reservation" means that the seller has obtained a bill of lading made out in a particular manner so as to take a security interest in the goods to secure the price. UCC § 2–505(1), 1–201(b)(35), 9–110. The carrier is not to release the goods to the buyer until the buyer has paid the price for the goods.

(2) Bill of Lading

When a seller ships goods to a buyer using a carrier, the seller will often obtain from the carrier a bill of lading covering the goods. The bill of lading typically describes the goods in some fashion and indicates the delivery point of the goods. The bill of lading is a document of title covered by UCC Article 7. *See* Section G on definition of "document of title." A bill of lading will be either negotiable or nonnegotiable (UCC § 7–104) and the form of the bill of lading will determine how the seller effectuates a shipment under reservation.

(a) Negotiable Bill of Lading

The seller will have shipped under reservation when the carrier has issued a negotiable bill of lading to the seller's own order or otherwise. UCC § 2–505(1)(a). A negotiable bill of lading states on its face that the goods are deliverable "to the order of" a named person or "to bearer." UCC § 7–104.

> *Example:* A sold goods to B with the price due upon delivery. A deposited the goods with C, the carrier, and obtained a negotiable bill of lading stating that the goods are to be delivered to bearer. A has shipped under reservation and has a security interest in the goods. That security interest is subject to Article 9. C should not release the goods to B until B remits the price owed to A, and A provides the bill of lading to B, who can present it to C.

(b) Nonnegotiable Bill of Lading

The seller will have shipped under reservation when a nonnegotiable bill of lading states the seller or the seller's nominee as the person to whom the goods should be delivered. A nonnegotiable bill of lading that states the buyer as the person to whom the goods are to be delivered is not a shipment under reservation. UCC § 2–505(1)(b).

> *Example:* A sold goods to B with the price due upon delivery. A obtained a nonnegotiable bill of lading from C, the carrier, stating that the goods should be delivered to D, A's agent in the city where B is located. A has shipped under reservation and has a security interest in the goods that is subject to Article 9. C should not release the goods to B until B remits the price to A, and D gives the bill of lading to B, who then presents it to C.

> *Example:* A sold goods to B with the price due upon delivery. A obtained a nonnegotiable bill of lading from C, the carrier, stating that the goods should be delivered to B. A has not shipped under reservation and does not have a security interest in the goods. Under Article 2, A is obligated to

provide the bill of lading to B. UCC § 2–503. C may release the goods to B pursuant to the bill of lading.

(3) Shipment Under Reservation as Breach of Contract With Buyer

Even if the seller's shipment under reservation breaches the contract of sale with the buyer of the goods, the seller's rights under the documents are not impaired. UCC § 2–505(2).

c. Buyer's Security Interest

The buyer of goods has a security interest arising in goods in the buyer's possession in one circumstance. If goods have been delivered to a buyer under a contract for the sale of goods governed by Article 2 and the buyer has rightfully and effectively rejected the goods or justifiably revoked acceptance of the goods, the buyer has a security interest in goods in its possession or control to secure the debt that the seller will owe the buyer for refund of the price the buyer has already paid and for expenses related to the transportation, care and custody of the goods. UCC § 2–711(3). Exploring whether the buyer has rightfully and effectively rejected the goods or justifiably and effectively revoked acceptance of the goods is beyond the scope of these materials. *See* UCC §§ 2–601, 2–602, 2–612, 2–608.

> *Example:* A sold goods to B. B made a down payment of 25% of the price. A delivered the goods to B. The goods were not in conformity with the contract between A and B and B rightfully and effectively rejected the goods. *See* UCC §§ 2–601, 2–602. B has a security interest in the goods in B's possession to secure the return of the 25% down payment. To the extent B incurs expenses in taking reasonable care of the goods, the security interest secures A's obligation for those amounts as well. B's security interest is governed by Article 9.

d. Lessee's Security Interest

The lessee of goods has a security interest arising in goods in the lessee's possession in one circumstance. A lessee that has rightfully and effectively rejected goods or justifiably and effectively revoked acceptance of goods delivered under a lease contract governed by Article 2A will have a security interest in those goods in its possession or control to secure the debt the lessor will owe for rent already paid and security deposits made and for expenses in the transportation, care and custody of the goods. UCC § 2A–508. Exploring whether the lessee has rightfully and effectively rejected the goods or justifiably and effectively revoked acceptance of the goods is beyond the scope of these materials. *See* UCC §§ 2A–509, 2A–510, 2A–517.

2. Collecting Bank Security Interest in Items and Documents

During the bank collection process, items, such as checks and drafts, and accompanying documents, such as documents of title, will be in the bank's possession. A bank has a security interest in those items and accompanying documents in its possession until it receives a final settlement for those items or releases possession of the items for a purpose other than collection of the items. The security interest secures amounts given as withdrawable credit against the item. UCC § 4–210.

Example: A, a customer of Bank, deposited a check for credit to A's account. The Bank gave a credit to A for the item. A withdrew cash from its account against the credit from the check. As long as Bank has possession of the check or has released possession solely for the purpose of collection of the check from the drawee bank, Bank has a security interest in the check to secure the amount withdrawn from the account. Bank's security interest is subject to Article 9.

3. Security Interest of Letter of Credit Issuer or Nominated Person

When a presentation of documents is made under a letter of credit, the issuer (defined in UCC § 5–102(a)(9)) or nominated person (defined in UCC § 5–102(a)(11)) will take possession of the documents. The issuer or nominated person has a security interest in those documents to the extent it has given value for the presentation or honored the presentation by paying under the terms of the credit and has not been reimbursed for its payment. UCC § 5–118.

Example: Bank issued a letter of credit at the request of applicant for the benefit of Beneficiary. Beneficiary made a presentation of documents pursuant to the terms of the letter of credit. Bank paid Beneficiary the amount due under the letter of credit. Upon a rightful payment on a letter of credit, applicant has an obligation to reimburse Bank for its payment. UCC § 5–108(i). Bank has a security interest in the documents that Beneficiary presented as long as Bank has not been reimbursed for its payment under the letter of credit by applicant. Bank's security interest is subject to Article 9.

E. Agricultural Liens

In the 1999 revision, the scope of Article 9 was expanded to include a type of nonconsensual lien called an agricultural lien. An agricultural lien is a subset of a type of lien that exists in all of the states called a statutory lien. Agricultural liens are included within the scope of Article 9 under UCC § 9–109(a)(2).

1. Statutory Liens Generally

A statutory lien arises by virtue of a statute that provides that if some specified obligation incurred by the debtor is not paid, a lien arises automatically in specified assets. The scope of a statutory lien can be narrow (such as a lien on clothes deposited for dry cleaning if the dry cleaning bill is not paid) to exceedingly broad (a federal tax lien on all assets of the debtor to secure any federal tax obligation).

2. Agricultural Lien Defined

An agricultural lien is a lien interest arising under a statute other than Article 9 in one particular type of property, "farm products," to secure the obligation to pay for certain obligations that arise in the context of a farming operation. The definition of agricultural lien is found in UCC § 9–102(a)(5) and has several component parts.

a. Creating the Obligation to Pay

The agricultural lien must secure payment or performance of an obligation for goods or services that are furnished to a debtor in the course of the debtor's farming operation or for rent on real property that the debtor leases as part of the debtor's farming operation. UCC § 9–102(a)(5)(A). Generally this obligation to pay arises through a contract between the debtor and the agricultural lien holder.

Example: S sells feed to A for A's dairy herd. A has agreed to pay for the feed pursuant to the contract for sale of the feed between S and A. A's obligation to pay for the feed is the type of obligation that may be secured by an agricultural lien.

Example: L rents 640 acres of land to A for A to use to plant soybeans and wheat. A's obligation to pay the rent pursuant to the lease is the type of obligation that may be secured by the agricultural lien.

b. Creating the Lien

The agricultural lien is created by virtue of a statute other than Article 9. That statute must provide for a lien to arise (i) in favor of a person that supplies goods or services to the debtor in the ordinary course of the supplier's business to the debtor's farming operation or (ii) in favor of a person that leased real property to the debtor in connection with the debtor's farming operation. UCC § 9–102(a)(5)(B).

(1) Farm Products and Farming Operations

The lien must be in "farm products." Farm products as defined in UCC § 9–102(a)(34) consist of "goods" (defined in UCC § 9–102(a)(44)) that are "crops grown, growing or to be grown, ... livestock, born or unborn, ... supplies used or produced in a farming operation," and "products of crops or livestock in their unmanufactured states." Farm products must be "goods with respect to which the debtor is engaged in a farming operation." A farming operation is "raising, cultivating, propagating, fattening, [or] grazing," livestock, crops, or any other activity that is considered farming. UCC § 9–102(a)(35). Farm products does not include standing timber.

Example: A plants and harvests corn. The growing corn and the harvested corn are farm products.

Example: A keeps dairy cows and harvests their milk. A uses the milk to produce cheese. The cows and milk are farm products. The cheese is not a "farm product" as it is not a product of livestock that is in an "unmanufactured state." The cheese may be A's inventory. UCC § 9–102(a)(48).

(2) Lien Arises Without Lienholder's Possession of Farm Products

The effectiveness of the agricultural lien under the other statute must not depend upon the agricultural lienholder's possession of the farm products. UCC § 9–102(a)(5)(C).

> *Example:* S sells feed to A for A's dairy herd. A has agreed to pay for the feed pursuant to the contract for sale of the feed between S and A. Under applicable state law other than Article 9, A's obligation to pay for the feed is secured by a lien in the livestock which eats the feed. The lien arises automatically pursuant to the state law. S need not have possession of the dairy herd which ate the feed in order to have the lien. This lien is an agricultural lien under Article 9.

> *Example:* L rents 640 acres of land to A for A to use to plant soybeans and wheat. Under applicable state law other than Article 9, A's obligation to pay the rent pursuant to the lease is secured by a lien on the crops raised on the land. The lien arises automatically pursuant to the state law. L need not have possession of the crops in order to have the lien. This lien is an agricultural lien under Article 9.

3. Effect of Including

An agricultural lien is not included within the definition of a security interest, UCC § 1–201(b)(35). Thus, Article 9's provisions directed to security interests do not apply to agricultural liens. Nonetheless, the agricultural lienholder is a "secured party," UCC § 9–102(a)(73)(B), and the person that has a property interest, other than a security interest or lien, in the farm products is the "debtor," UCC § 9–102(a)(28)(A). The property subject to the agricultural lien is the "collateral." UCC § 9–102(a)(12).

> *Example:* L rents 640 acres of land to A for A to use to plant soybeans and wheat. Under an applicable state statute other than Article 9, A's obligation to pay the rent pursuant to the lease is secured by a lien on the crops raised on the land. The lien is an agricultural lien under Article 9. L is the secured party, A is the debtor, and the crops are the collateral.

F. Exclusions From Article 9

Article 9 has two subsections, UCC § 9–109(c) and (d), that specify a range of exclusions of certain transactions from the scope of Article 9. The mode of analysis is to first determine if the transaction would be included under the scope provisions discussed earlier in this Chapter. Then work through the exclusions to see if any of the exclusions apply to the particular transaction at issue. If a transaction is excluded from the scope of Article 9, that does not mean an interest in the type of asset to secure a debt is not allowed. The only effect of excluding the particular transaction from Article 9's scope is that other law will control creating an interest in that type of asset to secure a debt.

1. Federal Law Preemption

Article 9 is enacted at the state level. Thus, to the extent that federal law governs a transaction that would otherwise be within the scope of Article 9 as discussed above, there is always an issue of whether Article 9 is preempted. UCC § 9–109(c)(1) recognizes this fact and provides that Article 9 does not apply "to the extent" paramount federal law "preempts" Article 9. The mere existence of a federal statute, regulation or treaty on the subject does not mean that Article 9 is preempted. Rather, the exclusion requires analysis of whether Article 9 is preempted under principles of constitutional law governing federal preemption of state law. Under that analysis, the federal law may not preempt Article 9 at all, it may preempt Article 9 only in part, or it may occupy the field and preempt Article 9 entirely. Article 9 does not govern "only to the extent" that Article 9 is preempted as a matter of federal law.

Example:　The federal Ship Mortgage Act provides for mortgages in ships and foreclosure of those mortgages. The extent to which Article 9 is preempted by the provisions of the Ship Mortgage Act depends upon an analysis of the Ship Mortgage Act under the federal preemption doctrine. The portions of Article 9 that are not preempted would govern a transaction in which an interest is granted in a ship to secure a debt.

2. State Governmental Units and Foreign Countries as Debtors

States, state governmental units, and foreign governments may be debtors in transactions covered by Article 9. If the state or foreign country has a statute that expressly governs creation, perfection, priority or enforcement of security interests granted by a governmental entity, Article 9 does not apply to the extent the issue is governed by that other statute. UCC § 9–109(c)(2) and (3).

Example: A state utility commission grants a security interest in its accounts in order to obtain financing for an expansion of its services. That transaction will be governed by Article 9 unless the relevant state law provides another mechanism for creating, attaching, perfecting, or enforcing that security interest. The other state law will govern the aspects of the transaction that are covered by that other state law. To the extent an aspect of the transaction is not covered by that other state law, Article 9 will apply.

3. Transferee Beneficiary of a Letter of Credit

Article 9 excludes from its scope the right of a transferee beneficiary of a letter of credit to the extent its rights are superior to the rights of an assignee of a letter of credit. UCC § 9–109(c)(4).

a. Letter of Credit Transaction

A letter of credit is an obligation of a bank to pay money according to the terms stated in the letter of credit. UCC § 5–102(a)(10). The terms of a letter of credit typically require the beneficiary of the letter of credit (the person to whom payment is made) to present specified documents to the bank. If those documents strictly comply with the terms of the letter of credit, the bank is obligated to honor the letter of credit by paying the money to the beneficiary. UCC § 5–108.

b. Transfer of Right to Demand Payment Under Letter of Credit

The only person that may rightfully make a demand on the issuing bank for payment under the letter of credit is the beneficiary of the letter of credit. If the terms of the letter of credit allow it, a beneficiary of a letter of credit may transfer its right to draw on the letter of credit to another person. UCC § 5–112.

c. Assignee of Right to Proceeds of Letter of Credit

That transfer of the right to be a beneficiary (i.e. draw on the letter of credit) must be distinguished from the transfer of a right to proceeds of the letter of credit. Article 9 allows for a security interest in a type of collateral called letter-of-credit rights (UCC § 9–102(a)(51)), which is the right to the proceeds of the letter of credit, not the right to be a beneficiary of the letter of credit. That letter-of-credit right assignment is called an assignment of the proceeds of the letter of credit. UCC § 5–114.

d. Priority of Transferee Beneficiary Over Assignee of Letter-of-Credit Rights

The right of a transferee beneficiary to draw on the letter of credit is superior to the right of a person that is assigned the right to proceeds of the letter of credit. UCC § 5–114(e). This provision will make more sense once we work our way through the priority rules that are contained in Chapter V.

Example: Bank issued a letter of credit for the benefit of A, the beneficiary. The letter of credit was transferable and A properly transferred its rights as beneficiary to C. A also granted a security interest in the proceeds of the letter of credit to D. The transfer from A to C is a transaction that is not within the scope of Article 9. The transfer from A to D is a transaction that is within the scope of Article 9. The priority between the rights of C and the rights of D to Bank's payment under the letter of credit is determined under UCC § 5–114.

4. Nonconsensual Liens Other Than Agricultural Liens

Except for agricultural liens as described above, Article 9 does not apply to nonconsensual liens arising under law other than Article 9.

a. Landlord's Lien

Article 9 does not apply to landlord's liens that are not agricultural liens. UCC § 9–109(d)(1). Landlord's liens are nonconsensual liens granted under state statutes or common law that give the landlord an interest in defined personal property to secure rent that is due from the tenant. A landlord's lien that also qualifies as an agricultural lien under the definition contained in UCC § 9–102(a)(5) is governed by Article 9. If the landlord's lien is not also an agricultural lien under that definition, Article 9 does not apply.

Example: Landlord rents an apartment to tenant. Under applicable state law other than Article 9, if tenant fails to pay rent as required by the lease, the landlord has a right to evict the tenant and maintain possession of all personal property of the tenant in the apartment to secure the tenant's obligation to pay the rent. The landlord's lien is not an agricultural lien and thus is not subject to Article 9.

Example: Landlord rents 100 acres of land to A for A to use to plant corn as part of A's farming operation. Under applicable state law other than Article 9, A's obligation to pay the rent pursuant to the lease is secured by a lien on the crops raised on the land. The lien is a landlord's lien and qualifies as an agricultural lien under UCC § 9–102(a)(5). The landlord's lien is governed by Article 9.

b. Other Nonconsensual Liens

State statutes or common law also often allow persons that provide services or materials to a debtor to claim a nonconsensual lien on personal property to secure the debtor's obligation to pay for the services or materials. An example of such a lien is called an artisan's lien. An artisan's lien is often granted to secure the obligation to pay for services or materials used to repair or service goods. The state statute or common law in a particular state may allow the artisan to retain possession of the goods that are repaired or serviced until the debt for the repair or service is paid. Article 9 does not apply to these nonconsensual liens except to govern priority as between those type of liens and an Article 9 security interest. UCC § 9–109(d)(2). If the nonconsensual lien is an agricultural lien (UCC § 9–102(a)(5)), however, Article 9 applies to the agricultural lien in all respects.

Example: A, a person that is in the business of repairing equipment, repairs B's tractor. B is in the business of farming and uses the tractor in B's farming operation. The tractor is also subject to a consensual security interest that B granted to Bank to finance acquisition of the tractor. Under applicable state law other than Article 9, A has a lien on the tractor to secure B's obligation to pay for the repairs as long as A keeps possession of the tractor. A's lien on the tractor is not governed by Article 9 except to govern the priority dispute between A's lien for repairs and Bank's Article 9 security interest in the tractor. A's lien is not an agricultural lien because the tractor is not "farm products."

5. Wage Assignment

Article 9 does not apply to any transaction that is an assignment of wages, salary, or employee compensation. Contractual assignment of wages or compensation may be circumscribed or prohibited by state or federal law. UCC § 9–109, cmt. 11. To the extent such assignments are allowed, Article 9 does not prescribe the rules for obtaining an interest in wages, salary, or employee compensation. UCC § 9–109(d)(3).

Example: A agreed to assign 10% of A's monthly salary to B for one year to pay a debt that A owes B. Whether A is allowed to make such an assignment to B is governed by other law. Even if A's salary assignment is allowed under other law, Article 9 does not govern the transaction between A and B.

6. Assignment of Certain Rights to Payment

As discussed above, Article 9 applies to any transaction that creates a security interest in personal property. Personal property of a debtor includes the right of a debtor to receive payment or performance of an obligation from another person. As discussed above, Article 9 also applies to transactions that are sales of some of those types of rights to receive payment, that is, the rights to receive payment that Article 9 denominates as accounts, chattel paper, promissory notes, and payment intangibles. In spite of that broad coverage, some types of assignments of rights to payment are excluded from the scope of Article 9 because they have been deemed not to be of a financing nature. UCC § 9–109, cmt. 12. The effect of this exclusion is that for the particular described type of assignment, law other than Article 9 will provide the rules for creating, perfecting, and enforcing an interest in that described right to payment.

a. Sale of Right to Payment as Part of Sale of Business

Article 9 does not apply to a transaction that is a sale of accounts, chattel paper, payment intangibles, or promissory notes as part of the sale of the business that generated those rights to payment. UCC § 9–109(d)(4).

Example: A owns a hardware store and sold the hardware store to B. As part of the sale of the hardware store to B, A also transferred to B all of A's rights to payment from all accounts owed by A's hardware store customers. Although Article 9 would normally apply to that sale of accounts from A to B, because the sale of the accounts was in connection with the sale of A's business to B, the sale of the accounts from A to B is not covered by Article 9.

b. Assignment of Right to Payment for Collection Purposes

If a debtor assigns accounts, chattel paper, payment intangibles, or promissory notes to another for the purpose of collection only, that assignment is not covered by Article 9. UCC § 9–109(d)(5).

Example: A is owed payment from B for services that A has rendered to B. B has failed to pay A after repeated requests for payment. A hires C to collect the obligation from B and assigns the account to C to facilitate the collection process. The assignment of the account from A to C is excluded from the scope of Article 9.

c. Assignment of Right to Payment and Performance

Article 9 does not cover an assignment of a right to payment (in whatever form it is held) if the assignee is also required to perform under the contract. UCC § 9–109(d)(6).

Example: A enters into a contract to provide services to B in exchange for payment from B. A assigns the contract to C. Under the assignment, C is to provide the services A contracted to provide and receive the payment from B. Article 9 does not apply to the assignment of the contract from A to C.

d. Assignment of Single Right to Payment

Article 9 does not cover the assignment of a single account, payment intangible, or promissory note to an assignee in full or partial satisfaction of a preexisting debt. UCC § 9–109(d)(7).

Example: A is the obligee of 100 accounts owed by A's customers to A for goods provided to the customers. A owes B an obligation. After discussion with B, A and B agree that A will assign one account to B to satisfy the obligation that A owes B. The assignment of that one account from A to B is excluded from the scope of Article 9.

7. Assignment of Rights Under Insurance Policies

Article 9 does not apply to an assignment of a right under an insurance policy except in two circumstances, when it is proceeds or when it is a "health-care-insurance receivable." UCC § 9–109(d)(8). We will discuss proceeds when we consider attachment of security interest in proceeds in Chapter III. A health-care-insurance receivable exists when a person assigns rights under a health care insurance policy to a health care provider for services rendered or a health care provider assigns its rights under a health care insurance policy to another. UCC § 9–102(a)(46).

Example: A has a life insurance policy with a cash value. A assigns the right to payment of that cash value of the policy to B. The assignment of the right to payment under the life insurance policy from A to B is not covered by Article 9.

Example: A visits a doctor for a checkup and as part of the paperwork, signs a document assigning A's rights under A's health care insurance to the doctor. The assignment of that right to payment under the health care insurance policy is a health-care-insurance receivable and subject to Article 9.

8. Assignment of a Judgment

Article 9 does not apply to an assignment of a right under a judgment unless the judgment was on a right to payment that was already subject to a security interest. UCC § 9–109(d)(9).

Example: A owes B payment for goods that B provided to A. B obtains a judgment against A for the amount that A owes B. B then assigns that judgment to C to secure a debt that B owes C. The assignment of the judgment from B to C is not covered by Article 9.

Example: A owes B payment for goods that B provided to A. B grants to C a security interest in that right to payment from A. B obtains a judgment against A for the amount that A owes B. B assigns that judgment to C. The assignment of the judgment from B to C is covered by Article 9.

9. Recoupment or Setoff

A right of recoupment or setoff is basically an offset of a claim owed by party A to party B against a claim that party B owes party A. The distinction between recoupment and setoff is that in recoupment, the offsetting claims arise out of the same transaction but in setoff the offsetting claims may arise out of different transactions. Article 9 does not apply to the right of recoupment or setoff except for two circumstances. First, Article 9 will apply to the priority of the rights of recoupment and setoff as against a security interest when the asset is a deposit account. Second, Article 9 will apply to setoff and recoupment rights of someone that is obligated on a right to payment where that right to payment is an account, chattel paper, or general intangible that is subject to a security interest. UCC §§ 9–109(d)(10), 9–102(a)(3).

Example: Bank holds a deposit account for its customer, A. A owes an obligation to Bank based upon a loan that Bank made A. A defaults on its loan obligation to Bank and Bank sets off the balance in the deposit account against the loan obligation. Article 9 does not apply to the setoff.

Example: Bank holds a deposit account for its customer, A. A owes an obligation to Bank based upon a loan that Bank made A. A granted a security interest in the deposit account to C. The grant of that security interest to C in the deposit account is covered by Article 9. A defaults on its loan obligation to Bank and Bank sets off the balance in the deposit account against the loan obligation. The priority of Bank's setoff as against C's security interest in the deposit account is governed by Article 9.

Example: A owes B an obligation to pay the price of goods that B sold to A. That obligation is an account. B granted a security interest in the account to C to secure an obligation that B owes to C. The transaction in which B grants a security interest to C in the account is covered by Article 9. B fails to pay C the obligation that B owes C and C requests that A pay C. A asserts a right of recoupment against C based upon a defect in the goods that A purchased from B. Article 9 governs A's ability to assert that right of recoupment against C. UCC § 9–404.

10. Real Estate Interests

Article 9 does not apply to the creation or transfer of interests in real property, including a lease and rents under a lease, except for fixtures and certain enforcement rights when the secured party has lien interests in both real and personal property. UCC § 9–109(d)(11). This provision is tricky as contracts that create interests in real estate are still contracts, that is, the obligation under the contract that is owed to an obligee is the obligee's personal property. Examples of such types of contracts are contracts for deed, leases, and mortgages. For example, a secured party that wants to obtain an interest in a contract right, such as a security interest in the mortgagee's rights under a mortgage, is not attempting to get an interest in the real estate, only in the mortgagee's contract rights, the obligation that the mortgagor owes to the mortgagee. That attempt is subject to Article 9. However, for the secured party to enforce its rights as an assignee of the mortgage against the real estate, the secured party would have to do so using real property law. The enforcement rights will be explained in Chapter VI.

Example: A owns real property and leases that real property to B. The rights and obligations of the parties under the lease of the real estate are not subject to Article 9. A grants an interest in the right to rental payments under the lease to C to secure an obligation that A owes to C. The right of A to rental payments under the lease would be an account and governed by Article 9, absent the exclusion from Article 9 of a transfer a real estate lease and the rents thereunder.

Example: A owns real property. Bank makes a loan to A, evidencing that loan with a promissory note that A signs, and secures the loan by taking a mortgage on A's real property. The transaction in which A issues the note and mortgage to Bank is not governed by Article 9.

11.   Assignment of Tort Claims

Article 9 does not apply to transactions that are assignments of tort claims with two exceptions. First, Article 9 applies to tort claims that are proceeds of other collateral in which there is a security interest. UCC § 9–109(d)(12). The concept of attachment of security interests to proceeds of collateral will be covered in Chapter III. Second, Article 9 applies to commercial tort claims. A commercial tort claim (UCC § 9–102(a)(13)) is one of two things. First, it is any claim arising in tort in which the claimant is an organization. An organization is any entity that is not an individual person. UCC § 1–201(b)(25). Second, it is any claim arising in tort in which the claimant is an individual and the tort claim arose in the course of the claimant's profession or business and is not based upon a claim for damages arising from the personal injury or death of an individual.

Example: A, an individual, is in a car accident while on vacation in which B is liable for negligence. A grants an interest in her negligence claim against B, to C to secure a debt that A owes to C. That transaction between A and C is not within the scope of Article 9 and will be covered by other law.

Example: A, an individual, is in a car accident in which B is liable for negligence. A had the accident with B while A was engaged in delivering goods to D in the course of A's delivery business. A grants an interest in her negligence claim, to C to secure a debt that A owes to C. As long as the claim that A has against B is not for personal injury or death, the transaction in which A granted an interest to C in the negligence claim against B is covered by Article 9.

Example: A, an organization, has a negligence claim against B for damages caused in an accident with one of A's employees. A grants an interest to C in its negligence claim against B to secure a debt that A owes to C. The transaction in which A grants an interest to C in that negligence claim against B is subject to Article 9.

12.   Assignment of Deposit Accounts in Consumer Transactions

Article 9 does not apply to an assignment of an interest in a deposit account in a consumer transaction unless that deposit account is proceeds of other collateral in which there is a security interest. UCC § 9–109(d)(13). A deposit account is a demand account, such as a checking or savings account, maintained with a bank. UCC § 9–102(a)(29). A bank is an entity that is engaged in the business of banking and so does not include nonbank entities, such as securities brokerages. UCC § 9–102(a)(8). A consumer transaction is a transaction where an individual incurs an obligation primarily for personal, family or household purposes, a security interest secures the obligation, and the collateral that secures that obligation is held or acquired for primarily personal, family, or household purposes. UCC § 9–102(a)(26).

Example: A, an individual, maintains a personal checking account at Bank. A obtains a loan from C to use in operating A's business. A grants a security interest in the checking account to C to secure the loan. The transaction between A and C is not a consumer transaction because the loan is for business purposes. The grant of the security interest to C in the deposit account is within the scope of Article 9.

Example: A, an organization, maintains a checking account at Bank. A obtains a loan from C to use in operating A's business. A grants a security interest in the checking account to C to secure the loan. The grant of the security interest to C is within the scope of Article 9.

Example: A, an individual, maintains a personal checking account at Bank. A obtains a loan from C to use to go on vacation. A grants an interest in the checking account to C to secure the loan. The grant of the interest in the checking account to C is not within the scope of Article 9 but is governed by other law. Exclusion from Article 9 does not mean that C's interest in the deposit account is void, rather, other law will control the effectiveness of A's grant of an interest in the deposit account to C.

13. Security Interests in Secured Obligations

Article 9 applies to security interests in obligations that are secured by collateral in a transaction that is not within the scope of Article 9. UCC § 9–109(b).

Example: A owns real estate and obtains a loan from B. A signs a promissory note payable to B evidencing A's obligation to pay the loan and grants B a mortgage in that real estate to secure the loan obtained from B. The transaction between A and B is not within the scope of Article 9. B grants a security interest in the note and mortgage to C to secure a loan that B obtained from C. That transaction between B and C is within the scope of Article 9, although C may have to obtain other documentation under applicable real estate law to enforce the mortgage against A's real estate.

G. Importance of Definitions

As can be seen merely through the analysis of the scope provision of Article 9, there are three categories of definitions that must be mastered in order to understand the law in this area. The first and most important category of definitions is the various collateral types. The second category is the transaction types. The third category is actor types. Spend some time studying these definitions, and other definitions as discussed throughout these materials, in order to become familiar with them. Every rule in Article 9 is affected by the definitions. If you do not understand the definitions, you will not understand Article 9.

1. Collateral Types

The rules in Article 9 for creating, perfecting, and enforcing security interests and agricultural liens in personal property and the application of priority rules for determining the hierarchy of security interests and agricultural liens in that personal property depend upon the type of collateral that is subject to the security interest or lien.

a. Goods

A "good" is a thing that is movable at the time the security interest attaches. A "thing movable" is a term used to differentiate personal property from real property. Black's Law Dictionary (9th ed. 2009) (definition of "thing"). The definition of "goods" in Article 9 differs in some respect from the definition of "goods" found in other articles of the UCC. Compare UCC §§ 2–105, 7–102.

(1) Inclusions

Several "things" are listed as belonging in the category of "goods" in addition to the general test set forth in the definition: fixtures, standing timber to be cut and removed under a sales contract, unborn young of animals, crops growing or to be grown and manufactured homes.

(2) Computer Programs

Computer programs that are embedded in goods are considered to be part of the "goods." A computer program is considered embedded in the goods if the program is associated with the goods in such a manner that it is customarily considered to be part of the goods or if by becoming the owner of the goods, the person acquires a right to use the program in connection with the goods. If the computer program is embedded in goods as described, then the computer program and its supporting information is considered to be "goods." If the computer programs are affixed to a movable thing that is merely the medium for the program, such as discs, CDs, DVDs, or thumb drives, the computer programs are not "goods." UCC § 9–102(a)(44).

Example: A owns five boxes of the latest CD of the music group "Canned Noise." Even though a CD is a movable thing, the computer programs contained on the CDs are not "goods" as the CDs are merely the medium for the computer programs that are contained on the CDs. The computer programs are the music and the programming necessary for the music to play on a CD player.

Example: A owns a car that contains many different computer programs that run among other things, the antilock braking system, the climate control system, and the fuel mix system. The car is a "good" and all of the computer programs contained in the car and the supporting information concerning the computer programing is a "good."

(3) Exclusions

The definition of goods explicitly excludes several types of personal property from its ambit, even if it would otherwise fit the idea of a movable thing, including chattel paper, documents of title, instruments, investment property, letters of credit, money, and oil, gas and other minerals before extraction. Other types of personal property excluded from the definition are accounts, commercial tort claims, deposit accounts, general intangibles, and letter-of-credit rights.

b. Subcategories of Goods

There are many types of "goods" that fall within subcategories and defined in Article 9. In each instance, the item is thus both a "good" and one or more of these various subcategories. These subcategories are necessary because Article 9 includes rules that differentiate between these various types of goods.

(1) Accession

An accession is a good that is united physically with another good so that the identity of the original good is not lost. UCC § 9–102(a)(1).

Example: A owns a tractor. The tractor needs a new engine which is installed in the tractor. The new engine is an accession to the tractor and the tractor is an accession to the new engine.

(2) As-Extracted Collateral

Oil, gas, or other minerals that are extracted from the ground become "goods" upon extraction. If the debtor creates the security interest to attach to those items upon extraction, the oil, gas or other mineral is "as-extracted collateral." UCC § 9–102(a)(6)(A).

Example: A owns oil that is still underground. A grants a security interest in the oil to attach to the oil as it is pumped from the ground. The oil is "as-extracted collateral."

(3) Consumer Goods

Consumer goods are goods "that are used or bought for use primarily for personal, family, or household purposes." UCC § 9–102(a)(23).

Example: A, an individual, purchased a new refrigerator for use in her kitchen in her home. The refrigerator is consumer goods.

Example: A purchased a new refrigerator for use in the break room at A's business. The refrigerator is a "good" but is not "consumer goods."

(4) Equipment

Equipment is a catch-all category that means any goods that do not fall into the categories of inventory, farm products, or consumer goods. UCC § 9–102(a)(33).

(5) Farm Products

Farm products are goods that a debtor engaged in farming operations uses or produces that are either crops or livestock, supplies used or produced in the farming operation, or products of crops or livestock in their unmanufactured state. Crops or livestock include items produced in aquacultural farming and crops produced on trees, vines and bushes. UCC § 9–102(a)(34). A debtor is engaged in a farming operation if it is "raising, cultivating, propagating, fattening, [or] grazing," livestock or crops or engaging in any other activity that is considered farming. UCC § 9–102(a)(35). The term farm products does not include standing timber.

Example: A owns a Christmas tree farm in which customers come and cut down trees at Christmas time. While A may be engaged in a "farming operation," the trees are not farm products as the trees are "standing timber."

Example: A owns an apple orchard. The apples produced by the orchard are farm products. Apple cider, produced from the apples raised by the orchard, is not a farm product.

(6) Fixtures

Fixtures are goods that are considered to be related to the real estate in such a way that an interest in the goods may be granted under real estate law. UCC § 9–102(a)(41). They must fall within the category of "goods" so they must also be a "movable thing" at the time the security interest attaches.

Example: A purchased a furnace and had it installed in A's house. The furnace is a fixture if when A sells the house, title to the furnace will pass to the new owner of the house under real estate law and, under personal property law, the furnace is still considered a "movable thing." The classification of the furnace as a "movable thing" may vary from state to state, depending upon that state's real property law.

Example: A builds a house and incorporates all manner of building materials such as lumber, sheet rock, tile, and plumbing pipes into the construction. The building materials are not fixtures as they do not retain their character as personal property, that is, as a movable thing. See UCC § 9–334(a).

(7) Inventory

Inventory is a type of "good" that does not meet the definition of farm products and that falls into one of the following categories: (i) leased by the debtor as the lessor; (ii) held by the debtor for sale or lease or to be furnished under service contracts; or (iii) furnished by the debtor under a contract of service. The debtor's raw materials, works in process, or materials used up or consumed in the debtor's business are also inventory. UCC § 9–102(a)(48).

Example: A owns a hardware store. All items that A holds for sale that fall within the definition of "goods" are also "inventory." A has paper, pens, computer toner cartridges and other office supplies that A uses in running its business. Those supplies are also "inventory." A has cash registers, computers, and desks that are used in the hardware store. Those items are not inventory, but "equipment."

Example: A owns a manufacturing facility in which it produces cars and trucks which are then sold to dealers. All the parts that are "goods" that A uses to produce the finished cars and trucks are "inventory." All of the finished cars and trucks are "inventory."

(8) Manufactured Home

A manufactured home is a type of good that is a transportable structure meeting certain dimension requirements, built upon a permanent chassis, and designed to be used as a dwelling when connected to the required utilities. The dimension requirements are that it is more than 8 feet wide, more than 40 feet long, and has a minimum of 320 square feet when erected. A manufactured home also includes any structure that meets those requirements except for the dimension requirements and for which the manufacturer files the certification with the Department of Housing and Urban Development and complies with the federal standards for a manufactured home. UCC § 9–102(a)(53). A manufactured home may or may not be a fixture under relevant state law.

c. Money

Money is defined in UCC Article 1, not Article 9. As a general matter, definitions from Article 1 apply in Article 9. UCC § 9–102(c). Money is a "medium of exchange" adopted or authorized by a domestic or foreign government. UCC § 1–201(b)(24). Thus, in the United States, money would be currency bills and coins authorized by the federal government.

d. Obligations Owed

A debtor's personal property assets also consist of obligations that other persons owe the debtor. An obligation owed to the debtor may be unmature, disputed, unliquidated, and contingent. Review Chapter I. Nonetheless, these obligations are still assets of the debtor that a secured party may want to take a security interest in to secure an obligation that the debtor owes the secured party. These obligations owed to the debtor may in some instances be represented by paper contracts that in business practice are treated as embodying the obligation owed, such as a promissory note. In other instances, the obligations that are owed are not, as a historical business practice, embodied in any particular piece of paper, even though there may be a memorialization of the obligation on a piece of paper, such as for an account.

(1) Electronic Commerce

Even though an obligation has historically been embodied in a particular piece of paper, in order to facilitate electronic commerce Article 9 has allowed for electronic representations of these "embodied" obligations of what was once on paper for some, but not all, types of obligations.

(a) Record

"Record" is the term that is used in the UCC to refer to items either in their tangible form or in their electronic form and is defined as "information that is inscribed on a tangible medium or which is stored in an electronic or other medium and is retrievable in perceivable form." UCC § 9–102(a)(70).

(b) Authenticate

"Authenticate" is the term used to refer to signing a paper record or to attach an electronic symbol or process to an electronic record for the same purpose as signing a paper record. UCC § 9–102(a)(7).

(c) Tangible or Electronic

If the rule refers to a type of obligation that is embodied in a "record," the embodiment may be in either a tangible or electronic medium. In some circumstances, the provisions of Article 9 distinguish between the "tangible" form and the "electronic" form of the embodiment of the obligation. If the rule applies only when the information is inscribed on a tangible medium, such as paper, the term "tangible" is used. If the rule applies only when the information is stored in an electronic medium, the term "electronic" is used.

(2) Chattel Paper

Chattel paper refers to a record or group of records that contain both an obligation to pay money and a property interest in specific goods or in specific goods and software used in those goods. Thus an oral agreement cannot be "chattel paper." That property interest may be a security interest in the specific goods or in the specific goods and the software used in the goods. That property interest may be a lessor's rights under a lease of the specific goods or under a lease of the specific goods and a license of the software. The security interest in the specific goods and software (if applicable) secures the obligation to pay that is stated in the records. If it is a lease of specific goods and software (if applicable), the obligation to pay is the rent owed under the lease. Chattel paper does not include contracts involving the use or hiring of a vessel (such as a ship) and does not include the obligation to pay arising out of use of a credit or charge card. UCC § 9–102(a)(11). Chattel paper may be either tangible, UCC § 9–102(a)(79), or electronic, UCC § 9–102(a)(31).

Example: A purchased a car from Dealer and authenticated a record in which he promised to pay for the car and granted a security interest in the car to Dealer. The record is chattel paper.

Example: A purchased a car from Dealer and paid Dealer for the car with a loan from Bank. A signed a promissory note promising to pay Bank the amount of the loan and a separate record that granted a security interest in the car to secure the loan. The promissory note and the record together constitute chattel paper.

Example: A leased a car from Dealer. A signed a lease promising to pay Dealer the monthly lease payments. The lease is chattel paper.

(3) Document of Title

A document of title is a record that is considered, based upon business and financing practice, to be evidence that the person holding the record is entitled to hold the record and entitled to the goods described in the record. A document of title must be issued by a bailee or to a bailee and cover identified goods in the bailee's possession. A bailee is a person that is entitled to have possession of goods for a specified purpose, such as storage or transportation. A document of title may be either electronic or tangible. UCC § 1–201(b)(16). Article 9 refers to documents of title as "documents." UCC § 9–102(a)(30).

(a) Negotiable or Nonnegotiable

A document of title may be either negotiable or nonnegotiable. UCC § 7–104. A document of title is negotiable if by the terms stated in the document the goods are to be delivered "to the order of" a named person or to "bearer." Any other document of title is nonnegotiable.

(b) Types of Documents of Title

Typical examples of documents of title are warehouse receipts issued by warehouses in the business of storing goods, UCC § 1–201(b)(42), and bills of lading issued by carriers in the business of transporting goods, UCC § 1–201(b)(6). A certificate of title for a motor vehicle is not a document of title because it is not issued by or to a bailee.

Example: A stored goods with Warehouse, Inc. Warehouse issued a warehouse receipt describing the goods and stating the goods are to be delivered to "bearer." The warehouse receipt is a negotiable document of title.

Example: A gave goods to Carrier, Inc. to transport to a stated destination. Carrier issued a bill of lading describing the goods and stating that the goods are to be delivered "to A." The bill of lading is a nonnegotiable document of title.

(4) Instrument

An instrument refers to a "writing" that falls within one of two categories, a negotiable instrument, UCC § 3–104, or a writing that evidences an obligation to pay money and is of the type that in the ordinary course of business is transferred through delivery of possession and any necessary indorsement by the transferor. UCC § 9–102(a)(47).

(a) Negotiable Instrument

Whether a "writing" falls within the classification of a negotiable instrument requires an indepth analysis of the terms stated in the writing based upon the criteria stated in UCC § 3–104. Consideration of all that is required to be a negotiable instrument is beyond the scope of these materials. Two types of negotiable instruments that you may be familiar with are notes and checks. A note embodies a promise to pay money to the payee. A check embodies an order to a bank to pay money to the payee.

(b) Tangible Only

An instrument as defined in Article 9 may not be "electronic" but must be in a "writing." A "writing" refers to a tangible form that embodies the obligation and is defined as "printing, typewriting or any other intentional reduction to tangible form." UCC § 1–201(b)(43).

Example: A signed a piece of paper promising to pay "to the order of B" $1,000. Assume the terms stated on the piece of paper render the paper a negotiable instrument under UCC § 3–104. The paper is an "instrument" under Article 9 and a "promissory note" as discussed below.

Example: A signed a piece of paper promising to "pay to B" the sum of $1,000. The paper is not a negotiable instrument because it does not meet one of the requirements for being a negotiable instrument, namely it is not payable to order or to bearer. UCC §§ 3–104, 3–109. The paper may still be an instrument under Article 9 if it is customarily transferred by delivery of the paper and indorsement by B. If it is an "instrument," it is also a "promissory note" "as discussed *infra*.

Example: A authenticated an electronic record promising to pay "to the order of B" $1,000. The record is not a "writing" and thus does not qualify as an instrument under Article 9.

(5) Promissory Note

A promissory note is a subset of the category of instrument. It is an instrument (either negotiable or not) that contains a promise to pay, not an order to pay. The term does not include a certificate of deposit in which a bank acknowledges the receipt of a deposit. UCC § 9–102(a)(65). An order to pay is a written instruction to another to pay money. UCC § 3–103(a)(8). A promise to pay is a written undertaking to pay money. UCC § 3–103(a)(12).

Example: A signed a piece of paper ordering C to "pay $1,000 to bearer." Assume the paper qualifies as a negotiable instrument under UCC § 3–104 and thus an instrument under Article 9. It is not a "promissory note" as it is an order to pay and not a promise to pay.

(6) Account

The term "account" has a very broad definition. An account is a right to payment for (i) all types of property (both real and personal) that has been or is to be disposed of in any manner, (ii) services that were or are to be rendered, (iii) policies of insurance to be or actually issued, (iv) incurring a secondary obligation, (v) energy to be or actually provided, (vi) the use or hire of a vessel, (vii) the use of a credit card, or (viii) lottery winnings. The definition makes clear that the term refers to rights to payment under wholly executory contracts in the above-listed categories. If the right to payment is evidenced by an instrument or chattel paper, it is not an account. The term account also does not include commercial tort claims, deposit accounts, investment property, letter-of-credit rights, letters of credit, and rights to payment arising out of money advanced, except for credit card receivables. UCC § 9–102(a)(2). The term "account" has two defined subsets: "as-extracted collateral" and "health-care-insurance receivable."

Example: A buys a good on credit from B. A's obligation to pay B is an "account" and an asset of B.

Example: A buys real estate from B on credit. A signs a negotiable note evidencing that obligation to pay B. The right to payment is not an account, but an "instrument" and a "promissory note." The note is an asset of B.

Example: A promises to render services over the course of a year to B in return for B's promise to pay for those services. B's obligation to pay A is an "account," regardless of whether A has performed any services. B's obligation to pay A is an asset of A.

Example: A sells a piece of real estate to B. B promises to pay the price in installments over a period of 10 years. The obligation that B owes A is an account.

(7) As-Extracted Collateral

We encountered this term as a subset of "goods." This term "as-extracted collateral" also refers to accounts that arise from the sale of oil, gas, or other minerals that the debtor had an interest in prior to extraction from the ground if those accounts arise from the sale of oil, gas or other minerals at the wellhead or minehead. UCC § 9–102(a)(6)(B).

Example: A owns oil that is still in the ground. A agrees to sell the oil to B upon extraction of the oil in return for B's obligation to pay A money. B's obligation to pay A is an "account" and "as-extracted collateral."

(8) Health-Care-Insurance Receivable

A health-care-insurance receivable is a type of account that is an interest or claim under a health insurance policy for health-care goods or services that are or are to be provided to the insured. UCC § 9–102(a)(46).

Example: A is hospitalized and under A's health care insurance policy is entitled to reimbursement for the reasonable value of medical services A has received from the hospital. The right to payment under the health care insurance policy is an "account" and a "health-care-insurance receivable."

(9) Commercial Tort Claim

A commercial tort claim is one of two things. First, it is any claim arising in tort in which the claimant is an organization. An organization is any entity that is not an individual person. UCC § 1–201(b)(25). Second, it is any claim arising in tort in which the claimant is an individual and the tort claim arose in the course of the claimant's profession or business and is not based upon a claim for damages arising from the personal injury or death of an individual. UCC § 9–102(a)(13).

(10) Deposit Account

A deposit account is a demand account, such as a checking or savings account, maintained with a bank. UCC § 9–102(a)(29). A bank is an entity that is engaged in the business of banking and so does not include nonbank entities, such as securities brokerages. UCC § 9–102(a)(8).

Example: A maintains a money market account at Brokerage Inc. The account is not a deposit account because Brokerage Inc. is not a bank.

(11) Letter-of-Credit Right

A letter of credit is an obligation of a bank to pay money according to the terms in the letter of credit. UCC § 5–102(a)(10). The terms of a letter of credit typically require the beneficiary of the letter of credit to present specified documents to the bank. If the presentation of documents strictly complies with the terms of the letter of credit, the bank is obligated to honor the letter of credit by paying the money to the beneficiary. UCC § 5–108. A letter-of-credit right is a right to payment or performance of the bank's obligation under a letter of credit but does not include the right of a beneficiary to demand payment. UCC § 9–102(a)(51).

(12) Mortgage

A mortgage is an interest in real property that secures payment or performance of an obligation and is granted by consent of a person that has a property interest in the real estate. UCC § 9–102(a)(55).

Example: A owns real estate. A borrows money from C and grants to C an interest in the real estate to secure the loan. The interest of C in the real estate is a mortgage.

(13) Supporting Obligation

In some circumstances, a right to payment or performance may itself be supported by an additional right such as a guarantee of the obligation or a letter of credit. A "supporting obligation" is a letter-of-credit right or a secondary obligation, such as a guarantee, that supports a right to payment or performance that is an account, chattel paper, a document of title, a general intangible, an instrument, or investment property. UCC § 9–102(a)(78).

Example: A buys goods on credit from B. As a condition to allowing B to buy the goods on credit, B requires A to obtain a guarantor for the obligation that A owes B. C signs a document guaranteeing to pay the debt that A owes B in the event A does not pay. The guarantee is a supporting obligation in relationship to the account, the obligation that A owes B.

(14) General Intangible

This is the overall catchall category for any right that is considered personal property but does not fall into any of the other categories of collateral. Thus, a general intangible is personal property that is not an account, chattel paper, a commercial tort claim, deposit account, document of title, goods, an instrument, investment property, a letter-of-credit right, money, or oil, gas or other minerals before extraction. UCC § 9–102(a)(42). The category of "general intangible" has two defined subsets: "payment intangibles" and "software."

Example: A promises to sell goods to B on credit. B's obligation to pay A is an account and an asset of A. A's promise to sell the goods to B is a "general intangible" and an asset of B.

(a) Payment Intangible

A payment intangible is a general intangible in which the obligor's principal obligation is to pay money. UCC § 9–102(a)(61).

Example: A buys a new TV from Dealer, using a credit card issued by Argon Bank to A. Dealer's Bank processes the charge through the credit card system. Dealer's Bank obligation to make funds available to Dealer based upon the credit card transaction is a payment intangible. The obligation of A to pay Argon Bank is an account.

(b) Software

If a computer program is not embedded in goods as provided for in the definition of "goods," the computer program and its supporting information is a general intangible and falls within the definition of software. UCC § 9–102(a)(76).

> *Example:* A has a box of CDs that contain the latest computer game. The computer programs contained on those CDs are not goods but are "software."

e. Investment Property

Investment property is a broad category that includes several subsets: a certificated or uncertificated security, a securities entitlement, securities account, commodity contract, and commodity account. UCC § 9–102(a)(49). Some of these types of collateral are further defined in UCC Article 8. The relevant Article 8 definitions are incorporated into Article 9. UCC § 9–102(b).

(1) Security

A security is an interest in the issuer that is represented by a certificate or that is registered on the books maintained by the issuer. It must be issued as part of a class or series of interests in the issuer and must be of a type that is normally traded in securities markets or is a medium of investment which the parties expressly agree will be a security under UCC Article 8. UCC § 8–102(a)(15).

(a) Certificated Security

A certificated security is a security that is represented by a certificate issued to represent an interest in the issuer. UCC § 8–102(a)(4), (16).

> *Example:* ABC Corp. issued common stock in a manner that each share is represented by a certificate issued by ABC Corp. Z purchased a share of the common stock and received the stock certificate. Z has a certificated security.

(b) Uncertificated Security

An uncertificated security is a security that is not represented by a certificate but is noted on the books of the issuer as an interest in the issuer held by another. UCC § 8–102(a)(18).

> *Example:* ABC Corp. issued common stock. Z purchased a share of that common stock and ABC Corp. noted Z's ownership of that share in ABC's records. Z has an uncertificated security.

(2) Securities Account

A securities account is an account to which an interest in an issuer held by another is noted. UCC § 8–501. The entity holding the securities account is typically referred to as the securities intermediary. UCC § 8–102(a)(14).

(3) Securities Entitlement

A securities entitlement is the right of the person against the securities intermediary regarding an interest in an issuer that is noted in a securities account. UCC §§ 8–102(a)(17), 8–501(b). The person that has the right against the securities intermediary is called the entitlement holder. UCC § 8–102(a)(7).

> *Example:* ABC Corp. issued 1000 shares of common stock. All of the shares were issued to D Holding Co. D's interest was noted on ABC's records. D's interest in ABC Corp. is an "uncertificated" security. Brokerage Inc. purchased 10 shares of ABC from D. D notes on its records that Brokerage has a claim to the 10 shares of ABC. D is a securities intermediary and Brokerage's right to the 10 shares of ABC is a "securities entitlement" against D. The record of Brokerage's interest as noted by D on its records is a "securities account."

(4) Commodity Account

A commodity account is an account maintained with a commodity intermediary in which an interest in a commodity contract is noted for the customer. UCC § 9–102(a)(14). A commodity intermediary is a person that is registered as a commodity merchant under federal commodities law or that in the ordinary course of business provides settlement services for a board of trade designated under federal commodities law. UCC § 9–102(a)(17). This definition is analogous to the concept of securities account except that it deals with commodity markets instead of securities markets. A commodity is typically things such as grain, livestock, gold, silver, or other items that are traded in public markets called boards of trade.

(5) Commodity Contract

A commodity contract is a futures contract, an option on a commodity contract or futures contract, or any other type of contract or option that is traded on the board of trade as designated pursuant to federal commodities law or traded on a foreign board of trade and held in a commodities account. UCC § 9–102(a)(15). This definition is analogous to the definition of securities entitlements except that it involves interests in commodities.

f. Proceeds

This category of collateral need not be, but often is, a type of personal property. In order to have something that is "proceeds," as defined in Article 9, a security interest or agricultural lien must first arise in an item of "collateral." Proceeds falls into the following categories: (i) whatever rights are acquired upon disposition of the collateral including disposition by sale, lease, or license of the collateral; (ii) whatever is collected or distributed on account of collateral; (iii) rights arising out of collateral; (iv) claims arising out of loss, defects, infringement, or other impairment of the value of collateral; and (v) insurance payable by reason of claims arising out of loss, defects, infringement of other impairment of the value of the collateral. UCC § 9–102(a)(64). Something that is proceeds of an item of collateral will often fall into the category of another type of collateral as described above.

Example: A granted a security interest in its car to B. The car was damaged in a car accident. The claim against the other party for damage to the car and any insurance payable based upon damage to the car are "proceeds" of the car, and a "general intangible."

Example: A owes B an obligation to pay for goods that B sold A. B granted to C a security interest in A's obligation to pay, an account. A pays B the amount owed in cash. A's cash payment to B is "money" and a proceed of the account.

Example: A granted a security interest in its car to B. A sold the car to C in exchange for a check made payable to A. The check is an "instrument" and a proceed of the car.

Example: A owns an item of equipment and sold that equipment to B in exchange for a check made payable to A. The check is not "proceeds" as defined under Article 9 as no party has a security interest in the item of equipment. To be proceeds under Article 9, the original property that generates an additional item of property must be "collateral."

(1) Cash Proceeds

If proceeds are in the category of "money, checks, deposit accounts, or the like," the proceeds are denominated "cash proceeds." UCC § 9–102(a)(9).

(2) Noncash Proceeds

Proceeds other than cash proceeds are denominated "noncash proceeds." UCC § 9–102(a)(58).

2. Transaction Types

Just as Article 9's provisions differentiate among the types of collateral that are subject to the security interest and agricultural lien, Article 9's provisions also provide different rules for different types of transactions. We have already considered several types of transactions for which Article 9 makes some different rules: agricultural liens and consignments. Consider the definitions of these additional types of transactions.

a. Consumer Transaction

A consumer transaction is a transaction where an individual incurs an obligation primarily for personal, family or household purposes, the secured party has a security interest in the collateral, and the collateral that secures that obligation is held or acquired for primarily personal, family or household purposes. UCC § 9–102(a)(26).

Example: A, an individual, has 10 shares of ABC Corp. held in a personal investment account at Brokerage, Inc. A's interest is a securities entitlement. A grants to Bank a security interest in its securities entitlements held by Brokerage Inc. to secure a loan for a new deck added on to A's house. The transaction between A and Bank is a consumer transaction and not a consumer-goods transaction as described *infra*.

b. Consumer-Goods Transaction

A consumer-goods transaction is a subset of a consumer transaction and so those elements must be met. In addition, the collateral subject to the security interest must be consumer goods. UCC § 9–102(a)(24). In contrast, in a consumer transaction, the collateral may be any assets that are held for personal, family or household purposes.

Example: A, an individual, has a car that A uses for personal purposes. A grants to Bank a security interest in its car to secure a loan for a new deck added on to A's house. The transaction between A and Bank is both a consumer transaction and a consumer-goods transaction.

c. Manufactured-Home Transaction

A manufactured-home transaction is one where the manufactured home (UCC § 9–102(a)(53)) is the collateral, the manufactured home is not inventory of the debtor, and the security interest in the manufactured home is either a purchase money security interest (a security interest given in the manufactured home to secure an obligation that enabled the debtor to acquire the manufactured home, UCC § 9–103) or where the manufactured home is the primary collateral. UCC § 9–102(a)(54).

Example: A purchased a mobile home from Dealer and granted Dealer a security interest in the mobile home to secure the price owed. The mobile home meets the definition of a "manufactured home." The transaction between A and Dealer is a manufactured-home transaction.

d. Public-Finance Transaction

A public-finance transaction is transaction in which a security interest is created in some form of collateral, debt securities are issued with an initial maturity of 20 years or more, and the debtor, obligor, or secured party are a state or a governmental unit of the state. UCC § 9–102(a)(67).

Example: State A issues bonds for sale to the public that are secured by an interest in the property tax revenues that State A receives from taxpayers. The bonds have a maturity date of 25 years. The transaction in which State A grants a security interest in the tax revenues is a public-finance transaction.

3. Actor Types

Article 9 also creates a scheme of rules that apply differently depending upon what role an entity is playing. We have already considered the role of a debtor, UCC § 9–102(a)(28), obligor, UCC § 9–102(a)(59), a secured party, UCC § 9–102(a)(73), a consignee, UCC § 9–102(a)(19), and a consignor, UCC § 9–102(a)(21). Now consider these additional types of actors.

a. Consumer Debtor

A consumer debtor is a person that falls within the definition of debtor (UCC § 9–102(a)(28)) in a transaction that is a consumer transaction (UCC § 9–102(a)(26)). UCC § 9–102(a)(22).

Example: A, an individual, has 10 shares of ABC Corp. held in a personal investment account at Brokerage, Inc. A's interest is a securities entitlement. A grants to Bank a security interest in its securities entitlements held by Brokerage Inc. to secure a loan for a new deck added on to A's house. The transaction between A and Bank is a consumer transaction and A is a consumer debtor.

b. Consumer Obligor

A consumer obligor is an individual obligor that incurred the obligation as part of a transaction that was entered into primarily for personal, family or household purposes. UCC § 9–102(a)(25).

Example: A borrows money from Bank to finance construction of a new bathroom in A's house. Bank insists on collateral. B grants a security interest in B's car to secure the loan made to A. A is a consumer obligor. B is a debtor and not an obligor. B may also be a consumer debtor.

c. Secondary Obligor

A secondary obligor has incurred an obligation in a manner that suretyship law indicates is secondary to the person that has incurred the obligation as a primary obligation. An obligor will also be a secondary obligor if it has a right of recourse against the debtor, another obligor, or their property. UCC § 9–102(a)(72).

Example: A borrows money from Bank and signs a note promising to repay the loan. Bank insists on securing the loan and on a guarantor. A grants a security interest in A's car to secure the loan. B guarantees the loan by signing a contract promising to pay Bank in the event A does not repay the loan. A is an obligor (promise to repay the loan) and a debtor (grant of security interest in car). B is a secondary obligor on the loan and is not a debtor.

d. Account Debtor

An account debtor is the person obligated on a right to payment that constitutes an account, chattel paper, or general intangible but not on a negotiable instrument. UCC § 9–102(a)(3). Thus the use of the term "debtor" in this context means a person obligated on a right to payment, and not with an interest in collateral.

Example: A purchased goods on credit from B. A's obligation to pay B is an account and an asset of B. B grants a security interest in the account to C. A is the "account debtor."

Example: A purchased goods on credit from B. A's obligation to pay B is evidenced by a negotiable promissory note, an instrument. A is not an "account debtor" but is an obligor on the note.

4. Other Definitions

We will address other definitions set forth in UCC § 9–102, UCC Article 1, and in other UCC articles that apply to Article 9 transactions in the context in which they come up. See UCC §§ 1–201, 9–102(b), (c).

H. Review Questions For Chapter II

Determine whether the following statements are true or false.

1. Contracting parties may prevent Article 9 from applying to the transaction by explicitly agreeing that Article 9 does not apply.

2. Article 9 does not apply to transactions in which an interest in personal property is given to secure a debt if the debtor is a state governmental unit.

3. A right to payment, that is not memorialized in an "instrument," arising from the sale of real estate is an "account."

4. Article 9 applies to all sales of accounts without exception.

5. Chattel paper may consist of an aggregation of two or more records in which the debtor promises to pay an obligation and grants an interest in goods to secure the obligation.

6. Article 9 applies to all interests in personal property given to secure loans made to consumers and commercial entities.

7. A true lease of personal property is not within the scope of Article 9.

8. A true consignment is not within the scope of Article 9.

9. The category of goods may include a computer program.

10. If an item is farm products, it is not equipment.

11. A promissory note may be either tangible or electronic.

12. Chattel paper may be either tangible or electronic.

13. Article 9 does not apply to a right to payment if that right to payment is secured by an interest in real estate.

14. Article 9 does not apply to security interests in deposit accounts.

15. Article 9 does not apply to security interests in consumer goods.

16. Article 9 does not apply to a security interest in rights under an insurance policy.

17. A sale of goods in which the seller retains title to the delivered goods is subject to Article 9.

18. A right to payment can be both an account and a payment intangible.

19. A consumer-goods transaction is not a consumer transaction.

20. A person cannot be both a debtor and an obligor in the same transaction.

III

Attachment of a Security Interest or Agricultural Lien

In this Chapter we will consider the legal requirements that must be fulfilled to attach a security interest or agricultural lien to a specific asset of the debtor. As we learned in Chapter II, Article 9 applies to consensual grants of security interests in the debtor's personal property. In this Chapter we will learn the manner in which those consensual grants must take place in order for the security interest to be attached to the personal property. We will also consider those few circumstances covered by Article 9 where a security interest attaches to particular items of property through operation of law. Finally, we will consider what is required to attach an agricultural lien to farm products in a transaction covered by Article 9. For any transaction that is not covered by Article 9, such as those transactions excluded from its coverage by UCC § 9–109(c) or (d) (as discussed in Chapter II), law other than Article 9 will determine how to attach a consensual or nonconsensual lien interest to that item of property.

A. Attachment and Enforceability

Understanding attachment of a security interest or agricultural lien to the specific item of property is a necessary step to understanding Article 9. Attachment refers to fulfilling the necessary legal requirements to create the "in rem" obligation of an item of personal property that secures an "in personam" obligation to pay a debt. As we know from the material covered in Chapter II, security interests and agricultural liens are two types of "in rem" interests in personal property.

1. Attachment of an Agricultural Lien

An agricultural lien attaches to farm products according to the terms of the statute that allows the agricultural lien to arise. See UCC § 9–102(a)(5)(B). Thus, in order to determine the legal requirements for attachment of an agricultural lien, the statute that provides for the lien must be consulted. The statute that creates the agricultural lien will also provide when the lien is considered attached to the farm products.

Example: Under state law other than Article 9, a landlord that rents land to a farmer has a lien in the crops grown on the land to secure rental payments. When that lien arises, it qualifies as an "agricultural lien" under Article 9. The state statute providing for the lien states that the lien attaches to the crops upon harvesting for all rental payments for the land that produced the crop that are due and unpaid at the time of harvest of the crop. The lien attaches to the crop when the farmer harvests the crop if any amount for rent is due and unpaid at that time. Once the lien attaches to the crop, it is an agricultural lien under Article 9.

2. Attachment of a Security Interest

A security interest attaches to the collateral when the security interest becomes enforceable against the debtor. UCC § 9–203(a). The requirements for enforceability of the security interest are contained in UCC § 9–203(b) through (i). These requirements will be considered in this Chapter.

3. Enforcement

Once the security interest or agricultural lien attaches to the specific item of property, the security interest or agricultural lien is enforceable against the property. Enforcement means that the property to which the security interest or lien is attached may be seized by the creditor, using a prescribed process, in order to apply the value of that property to the "in personam" obligation. In Chapter VI, we will consider the enforcement mechanisms of Article 9 in regard to security interests and agricultural liens.

4. Secured Party not Liable for Debtor's Acts or Omissions

The existence of a security interest or agricultural lien does not make the secured party liable for the debtor's acts or omissions in contract or tort. UCC § 9–402.

B. Three Requirements for Attachment of a Security Interest

In order to attach a security interest by agreement of the parties, subject to some limited exceptions, three basic requirements must be met. The debtor must agree to grant the security interest to the creditor, value must be given, and the debtor must have the right, as a matter of property law, to grant a security interest in the collateral. UCC § 9–203(b). These three requirements apply to both interests in collateral to secure a debt and sales of rights to payment that are within the scope of Article 9, as discussed in Chapter II. The security interest attaches when all three of the requirements for attachment of the security interest are fulfilled. The agreement between the secured party and the debtor may postpone the time of attachment to a time later then when all three of the requirements are met. UCC § 9–203(a).

1. Debtor's Agreement to Grant a Security Interest, Generally

Most security interests are created by an agreement between a debtor and a creditor. A "security agreement" is an "agreement that creates or provides for a security interest." UCC § 9–102(a)(74). An "agreement" is the "bargain of the parties in fact, as found in their language or inferred from other circumstances." UCC § 1–201(b)(3). Putting those two definitions together with the definition of "security interest" (UCC § 1–201(b)(35)) that we considered in Chapter II, the debtor will, through an agreement, grant the secured party an interest in personal property that will secure payment or performance of an obligation owed to that secured party, or, alternatively, sell accounts, chattel paper, payment intangibles, or promissory notes to a buyer who is denominated a "secured party," UCC § 9–102(a)(73). The agreement of the parties that creates that security interest is the "bargain in fact" of the parties and is the "security agreement."

a. Evidencing the Security Agreement

The terms of a security agreement may or may not be memorialized in a record, such as a piece of paper. Article 9 does not require that the terms of the security agreement be written down in order for a security interest to attach. The security agreement must be evidenced by one of the following three methods: an authenticated record with an adequate collateral description, possession of specified types of collateral, or control of specified types of collateral.

b. Security Agreement as a Contract

The security agreement between the secured party and the debtor is a contract under typical contract law analysis. Compare UCC § 1–201(b)(3) with UCC § 1–201(b)(12). As a contract, the security agreement is subject to all of the usual doctrines of the common law concerning contracts except as those doctrines are altered by a provision of Article 9 or other statute.

Example: A signed a security agreement granting a security interest in described collateral to B to secure a loan. A signed that security agreement due to B's exercise of undue influence. If a court finds that B exercised undue influence on A and that undue influence resulted in A signing the security agreement, the court may hold that the security agreement is unenforceable under principles of contract law.

(1) Effectiveness as to Third Parties

A security agreement grants a security interest in the debtor's property. That security interest is effective as to third parties except as otherwise provided in Article 9. UCC § 9–201(a). The exceptions to that general principle of effectiveness against third parties will occupy us in Chapter

V on priority of security interests as against other property-based claims to the debtor's property.

(2) Effect of Other Law

A transaction subject to Article 9 may also be subject to other law that regulates certain classes of transactions. Such regulation might be protective of consumer debtors or obligors or regulate the cost of credit. Article 9 does not displace that other regulatory law or change the effect of that other law on the transaction it regulates. UCC § 9–201(b), (c), (d).

Example: A, a consumer, borrows funds from Bank and grants Bank a security interest in certain described goods owned by A to secure that loan. Under applicable state and federal law, Bank is required to make certain disclosures concerning the cost of the loan, including the interest rate and all applicable fees. Article 9 does not alter Bank's obligation to comply with that other law.

c. Debtor's Use, Possession, and Control of Collateral

The debtor's mere grant of a security interest in the debtor's property does not prevent the debtor from using, possessing, controlling, collecting, or disposing of the collateral. The debtor's continued actions of that sort in regard to the collateral are not fraudulent as to the debtor's other creditors. UCC § 9–205(a). The terms of the agreement between the debtor and the secured party may, as a matter of contractual agreement, restrict the debtor's ability to deal with the collateral, but the mere grant of the security interest does not.

Example: A granted a security interest to B in A's inventory to secure a loan. Unless the security agreement with B provides otherwise, A may sell items of inventory to purchasers. Whether the security interest remains attached to those items of inventory after the sale of the items to a purchaser depends upon application of the Article 9 priority rules discussed in Chapter V.

Example: A sold to B rights to payment that obligors owe to A. Those rights to payment are "accounts" and the sale to B is a transaction covered by Article 9. Unless the sale contract (i.e., security agreement) with B provides otherwise, A may collect the amounts owed on the accounts from the obligors on the accounts.

2. Debtor's Security Agreement Memorialized in a Record

Unless the secured party has possession or control of the collateral pursuant to a security agreement as described *infra*, in order to fulfill the first requirement for attachment of the security interest, the debtor must authenticate a record that constitutes the security agreement and that authenticated record must provide an adequate collateral description. UCC § 9–203(b)(3)(A).

a. Record and Debtor Authentication

The terms of the security agreement may be memorialized in either a tangible or electronic record. UCC § 9–102(a)(70). A security agreement contained in a record is authenticated when the debtor attaches or executes a symbol or process with the record with the present intent to adopt or accept the record. UCC § 9–102(a)(7). It is important that the debtor authenticate the record containing the security agreement. The debtor is the person with a property interest (other than a lien or security interest) in the collateral, the consignee in a consignment, or the seller of accounts, chattel paper, payment intangibles, and promissory notes. UCC § 9–102(a)(28).

Example: A signed a paper record that stated "A grants to B a security interest in all of A's goods" to secure a loan. A, the debtor, has authenticated a security agreement in favor of B.

Example: A sent an email to B that stated "A grants to B a security interest in all of A's goods" to secure a loan. A's name is automatically added at the bottom of the email. A, the debtor, has authenticated a security agreement in favor of B.

Example: A signed a paper record that stated "A grants to B a security interest in all of A's goods" to secure a loan. The good that B wants to assert is subject to the security interest is actually owned by C and C has not granted A permission to encumber C's goods.

As to these goods, C is the debtor, and thus B has not obtained a security agreement authenticated by the debtor.

b. Collateral Description

The authenticated security agreement must contain an adequate description of the collateral and, if the collateral is timber to be cut, a description of the land that contains the timber. UCC § 9–203(b)(3)(A).

(1) General Rule

The general rule for an adequate collateral description of the collateral or the described real estate in the security agreement is that it must "reasonably identify what it describes." UCC § 9–108(a). The description need not be "exact and detailed," and any requirement that specific item serial numbers be used is rejected. UCC § 9–108, cmt. 2.

(2) Reasonably Identifying What It Describes

A collateral description is deemed to meet the test of reasonably identifying what it describes if it falls into one of the following types of description: a specific listing, a category, a type of collateral defined in the UCC, a quantity, a formula or procedure, or any other method where the "identity of the collateral is objectively determinable." UCC § 9–108(b).

(a) Importance of UCC Collateral Classifications

The practice of secured parties and debtors is to use the collateral classification terms, as defined in Article 9, in the authenticated security agreement. Thus, understanding collateral classification is critical to understanding the rules of Article 9. Review the definition of the terms for collateral as discussed in Chapter II.

Example: A authenticated a security agreement in favor of B that described the collateral subject to the security interest as "all goods." The collateral description of "goods" is sufficient to attach the security interest to A's car. The collateral description need not contain the VIN of the car or a further description of the car by make or model.

(b) Meaning of Terms in Security Agreement

When a security agreement describes the collateral using the same terms as are used in Article 9 for types of collateral, a contract interpretation question arises as to whether the parties meant to adopt the Article 9 definition as their definition of the types of collateral. The parties are free in the security agreement to provide their own definitions of terms used to describe collateral. In the absence of the parties' own definitions in a memorialized agreement, however, most courts use the Article 9 definitions to determine what collateral is described in the security agreement when the parties use the same terms as are used in Article 9.

(c) "All Assets" Descriptions

A description of the collateral in the security agreement using "all assets" or "all personal property" of the debtor is deemed to be an inadequate description of the collateral for purposes of attachment of the security interest to the collateral. UCC § 9–108(c). Even though the description in the security agreement may not merely state "all assets" or "all personal property," the secured party may achieve the same effect (getting a security interest in all of the debtor's personal property) by listing all of the UCC types of collateral, subject to the specialized description rules stated below.

(3) Description of Investment Property

In a nonconsumer transaction, to describe collateral that constitutes a securities account, a securities entitlement, or a commodity account, the security agreement may use those terms, may describe the collateral as "investment property," or may describe the underlying asset. UCC § 9–108(d).

Example: A holds 30 shares of XYZ Corp. in an account with Brokerage, Inc. The account is a "securities account" and A's interest in the shares in the account, a "securities entitlement." In a nonconsumer transaction, A authenticates a security agreement that grants a security interest to C in all of A's "investment property." The description of "investment property" is a sufficient description to attach the security interest to A's securities account and securities entitlement.

Example: A holds 30 shares of XYZ Corp. in an account with Brokerage, Inc. The account is a "securities account" and A's interest in the shares in the account is a "securities entitlement." In a nonconsumer transaction, A authenticates a security agreement that grants a security interest to C in A's "rights in shares of XYZ Corp." That description is a sufficient description to attach the security interest to those 30 shares.

(4) More Specific Descriptions Required in Some Circumstances

Even though using the types of collateral as defined in the UCC is an adequate description of collateral in most circumstances, there are two exceptions to that principle.

(a) Commercial Tort Claims

Describing the collateral as a "commercial tort claim" is an inadequate description of the collateral in the security agreement. More specific information about the commercial tort claim must be included in order to have an adequate description. That specific information need not be much more specific, but must include some information that identifies the claim beyond merely a designation of "commercial tort claim." UCC § 9–108(e)(1). This requirement for a more specific description applies regardless of whether the transaction is a consumer or nonconsumer transaction.

Example: A authenticates a security agreement granting to B a security interest in all of A's "commercial tort claims." That description is an insufficient description of the collateral. The description would be sufficient if it stated all of A's "commercial tort claims arising out of the explosion of Manufacturing Facility."

(b) Certain Collateral Types in a Consumer Transaction

In a consumer transaction, a description of some types of collateral by the UCC-designated descriptor is not an adequate description of collateral. Review Chapter II on the definition of consumer transaction. The types of collateral that must be described by more than type alone in a consumer transaction are "consumer goods," "security entitlements," "securities accounts," and "commodity accounts." UCC § 9–108(e).

Example: A holds 30 shares of XYZ Corp. in an account with Brokerage, Inc. In a consumer transaction, A authenticates a security agreement that grants a security interest to C in all of A's "securities entitlements." That description is not a sufficient description to attach the security interest to those 30 shares.

Example: A holds 30 shares of XYZ Corp. in an account with Brokerage, Inc. In a consumer transaction, A authenticates a security agreement that grants a security interest to C in all of A's "securities entitlements held at Brokerage Inc." That description is a sufficient description of collateral that will attach the security interest to the 30 shares as it is not by "type alone" but adds information about where the securities entitlements are held.

Example: In a consumer transaction, A authenticates a security agreement that grants a security interest to B in all of A's "consumer goods." That description is not a sufficient description to attach the security interest to any of A's goods that are consumer goods.

Example: In a consumer transaction, A authenticates a security agreement that grants a security interest to B in all of A's "consumer goods located at A's cabin in Wisconsin." That description should be a sufficient description of the collateral as it is not by type alone.

Example: A, an individual, borrows funds from B to secure a loan that funds A's business. A authenticates a security agreement that grants B a security interest in all of A's "consumer goods" to secure that loan. The collateral description is sufficient as the transaction is not a consumer transaction.

c. Composite Document Doctrine

Although it appears to be a simple requirement, that the debtor authenticate a record that creates or provides for a security interest in collateral that is adequately described in the record, inevitably mistakes will be made. If the three critical components, debtor authentication, the provision for the security interest, and the description of the collateral, are not all contained in one record, the courts may construe a number of records together to find that this requirement is met. This court construction is called the "composite document doctrine." The essence of the court's inquiry in this situation is whether, based upon the composition of the records in evidence before the court, the records evidence an intent of the debtor and secured party to grant a security interest in the described collateral. A secured party should not count on a court applying the doctrine to rescue the secured party's attempt to attach a security interest to collateral. Thus, the better practice is to make sure one record contains all three items: the debtor authentication, the provision for a security interest, and an adequate description of the collateral.

Example: A signed a promissory note agreeing to pay B $10,000. The promissory note stated that it was "secured by a security interest in collateral as provided in the security agreement." The lending agreement between A and B provided that A would grant a security interest in collateral to secure all obligations owed to B but that lending agreement did not contain a description of the collateral. B filed a financing statement in the relevant filing office (see the form following UCC § 9–521 as an example) listing A as the debtor and the collateral as "all accounts and inventory." A has authenticated two records (the note and the lending agreement) which could be read to "provide for a security interest" but neither of those documents contain a description of the collateral. The document containing the description of the collateral (the financing statement) is not authenticated by A and does not "provide for a security interest." [A financing statement may be filed before a security interest is created, UCC § 9–502(d), and is a step typically taken to "perfect" a security interest.] A court might construe these three records together as an authenticated security agreement that contains a collateral description, but that outcome is far from certain.

3. Secured Party's Possession Pursuant to a Security Agreement

As an alternative to a debtor-authenticated security agreement with an adequate collateral description, the secured party may take possession of certain types of collateral pursuant to an *agreement* with the debtor that the collateral is subject to a security interest. This security agreement need not be memorialized in a record but must be an agreement of the debtor and secured party that the property in the secured party's possession is subject to the security interest. UCC §§ 9–203(b)(3)(B), 1–201(b)(3).

> *Example:* A borrowed $5,000 from B. B is worried about A's repayment of the loan and so takes possession of A's motorcycle without A's permission, planning to return the motorcycle to A when the loan is repaid. Even though B has possession of A's motorcycle to secure A's obligation to repay the loan, B does not have the motorcycle pursuant to an agreement with A that the motorcycle will be subject to B's possession as security for the loan. B does not have a security interest in the motorcycle and may be liable to A for conversion of the motorcycle.

a. Types Of Collateral That May Be Possessed

Not all types of collateral may be possessed for the purpose of attachment of a security interest. Some types of collateral, such as accounts, have no tangible embodiment that is considered representative of the obligation owed. The types of collateral that may be possessed, and thus subject to attachment of a security interest through the secured party's possession pursuant to the debtor's oral agreement to grant a security interest, are tangible negotiable documents of title, goods, instruments, money, and tangible chattel paper. UCC §§ 9–203(b)(3)(B), 9–313(a). Although this is an acceptable method of attaching a security interest, the better practice is to memorialize a security agreement in a record as discussed *supra*.

> *Example:* A and B agree that B will have a security interest in A's accounts to secure A's obligation to repay a loan of $10,000 from B to A. A and B have an oral security agreement. A and B agree that B may take possession of A's accounts ledger and B does so. B has not attached a security interest to the accounts as accounts are not a

type of collateral where possession pursuant to an oral agreement is sufficient to fulfill a requirement for attachment of the security interest.

Example: A and B orally agree that B will have a security interest in A's promissory notes to secure A's obligation to repay a loan of $10,000 from B to A. A and B agree that B may take possession of promissory notes in which A is the payee and B does so. B has an attached security interest in the promissory notes in B's possession. A need not authenticate a security agreement that describes the collateral.

b. Possession Defined

Possession is not defined in Article 9, although the concept is that the secured party or its agent has dominion over the collateral and the debtor is excluded from access to the collateral. UCC § 9–313, cmt. 3. See UCC § 9–205(b).

Example: A and B agree that B will have a security interest in a painting that A owns to secure A's obligation to pay B $100,000. A agrees that B may take possession of the painting as security for that obligation. B takes possession of the painting. B has possession of the painting pursuant to an oral security agreement and thus has a security interest in the painting. A decides to sell the painting and asks B to give the painting to A. B does so. B no longer has a security interest in the painting as B has released possession of the painting to A and A has not authenticated a security agreement that describes the collateral.

4. Secured Party Taking Delivery of a Certificated Security Pursuant to a Security Agreement

As an alternative to a debtor-authenticated security agreement with an adequate collateral description, the secured party may take delivery of a certificated security pursuant to the debtor's agreement to grant a security interest in the certificated security. UCC §§ 9–203(b)(3)(C), 8–102(a)(4), (16). Delivery of a certificated security to a secured party takes place in one of several ways. The first way is for the secured party to acquire possession of the certificate. The second way is for the secured party to obtain the acknowledgment of the possessor, other than a securities intermediary, that the possessor holds the certificate for the benefit of the secured party. The third way is if a securities intermediary has possession of the certificate in registered form and the certificate is registered, payable to, or indorsed to the secured party. UCC § 8–301. Although delivery of the certificated security pursuant to an oral agreement to grant a security interest is an acceptable method of attaching a security interest to a certificated security, the better practice is to memorialize a security agreement in a record as discussed *supra*.

Example: A and B agreed that B would have a security interest in a certificated security owned by A to secure a loan that B made to A. The certificated security was in the possession of C, not a securities intermediary. Pursuant to B's request, C acknowledged to B that C was holding the certificate for the benefit of B. B has an attached security interest in the certificated security.

Example: A and B agreed that B would have a security interest in a certificated security owned by A, to secure a loan that B made to A. C, a securities intermediary, had possession of the certificate. The certificated security was in registered form. Pursuant to B's request, A indorsed the certificate to B and left the certificate in C's possession. B has taken delivery of the certificated security.

5. Secured Party Control Pursuant to a Security Agreement

As an alternative to a debtor-authenticated security agreement with an adequate collateral description, the secured party may "control" certain types of collateral pursuant to the debtor's agreement to grant a security interest in that type of collateral. UCC § 9–203(b)(3)(D). The types of collateral that may be "controlled" by a secured party in order to attach a security interest, in the absence of a security agreement memorialized in an adequate record, are deposit accounts, electronic chattel paper, investment property, letter-of-credit rights, and electronic documents of title. Although control of these types of collateral pursuant to an oral security agreement is an acceptable method of attaching a security interest, the better practice is to memorialize a security agreement in a record as discussed *supra*.

a. Control

Control is a concept that is a substitute for the idea of possession of tangible collateral. Unlike the concept of possession, however, control does not mean that the debtor must be excluded from access to the collateral. Rather, control is defined for each type of collateral for which a secured party can obtain control. What is necessary to have control of one type of collateral, such as deposit accounts, is not the same as what is necessary to have control of another type of collateral, such as electronic chattel paper.

b. Control of Deposit Accounts

A secured party may obtain control of a deposit account in one of three ways described below. If the secured party has control using one of the three described methods, the debtor may still withdraw and deposit funds in the deposit account without affecting the determination regarding the secured party's control of the deposit account. UCC § 9–104(b).

(1) Secured Party as Depositary Bank
The secured party will have control of a deposit account of the debtor if the secured party is also the depositary bank where the account is maintained. No further steps need be taken for the depositary bank to have control. UCC § 9–104(a)(1).

> *Example:* A orally agreed that Bank would have a security interest in A's savings account held at Bank to secure an obligation that A owed Bank. Bank has control and an attached security interest in the savings account.

(2) Secured Party Obtains Control Agreement
A secured party that is not the depositary bank may obtain control of the deposit account by obtaining a control agreement, which is a record authenticated by the debtor, the secured party, and the depositary bank that the depositary bank will agree to the secured party's directions regarding disposition of funds from the account without any further consent of the debtor. UCC § 9–104(a)(2).

> *Example:*   A orally agreed that C would have a security interest in A's savings account held at Bank. Bank, C, and A executed a document that provided that Bank would comply with C's instructions regarding the savings account without any further consent of A. C has control and an attached security interest in the savings account.

(3) Secured Party Becomes Depositary Bank's Customer on the Deposit Account

A secured party that is not the depositary bank may obtain control of the deposit account by becoming an additional customer of the bank on the deposit account. The bank need not be the exclusive customer on the deposit account, and the debtor may remain a customer on the deposit account. UCC § 9–104(a)(3).

> *Example:*   A orally agreed that C would have a security interest in A's savings account held at Bank. With A's agreement, C becomes an additional signatory on the savings account and a customer of Bank on that savings account. C has control and an attached security interest in the savings account.

(4) Further Rules on Control Agreements with Depositary Bank

A depositary bank is not obligated to enter into a control agreement. If the depositary bank enters into a control agreement, the depositary bank is not required to confirm the existence of that control agreement to another person unless the bank's customer requests the bank to do so. UCC § 9–342. Unless the depositary bank undertakes a duty to the secured party or otherwise agrees, the attachment of a security interest to the bank account does not alter the depositary bank's rights or duties in regard to the deposit account. UCC § 9–341.

c. Control of Electronic Chattel Paper

To obtain control of electronic chattel paper, the records comprising that chattel paper must be created and stored in a database or other electronic medium in a manner that reliably establishes that the secured party is the person to whom the chattel paper was assigned. UCC § 9–105(a). This test must be met as a matter of factual proof regarding the creation and storage of the records. In other words, the secured party and the debtor *cannot* merely agree that the secured party has control of the records that constitute electronic chattel paper. UCC § 9–105, cmt. 3. UCC 9–105(b) provides a safe harbor for satisfying the test. Other methods of satisfying the test set forth in UCC § 9–105(a) could be developed. UCC § 9–105(b) sets forth six criteria. The records constituting the chattel paper must be designated in some manner as the "authoritative copy" which is "unique, identifiable, and [subject to certain exceptions] unalterable." UCC § 9–105(b)(1). Any copy of the authoritative copy must be readily identifiable as a copy that is not authoritative. UCC § 9–105(b)(5). The authoritative copy must identify the secured party as the assignee of the records. UCC § 9–105(b)(2). The authoritative copy must be maintained by the secured party or a designated custodian. UCC § 9–105(b)(3). Copies or revisions to the authoritative copy that add or change the assignee must be made with the consent of the secured party. UCC § 9–105(b)(4). Any amendments to the authoritative copy must be readily identifiable as authorized or unauthorized. UCC § 9–105(b)(6).

Example: A and B orally agree that B has a security interest in electronic chattel paper which A owns and that is stored by R in a database system. A makes arrangements with R to indicate in the database system that B is the assignee of the electronic chattel paper and the only one allowed to make changes to the chattel paper records. If R's system operates in a manner that meets either the general test in UCC § 9–105(a) or the safe harbor in UCC § 9–105(b), B will have control of the electronic chattel paper and an attached security interest in that chattel paper.

d. Control of Investment Property

How a secured party obtains control of investment property depends upon the type of investment property at issue. UCC §§ 9–106, 8–106. Thus correctly classifying the type of investment property is critical to determining the appropriate steps to establish control.

(1) Control of a Certificated Security in Bearer Form

A secured party will have control of a certificated security in bearer form if the secured party has taken delivery of the certificate. UCC §§ 9–106(a),

8–106(a). Taking delivery of the certificate in bearer form means either the secured party taking possession of the certificate or a person, other than a securities intermediary, holding possession of the certificate and acknowledging to the secured party that it holds possession on behalf of the secured party. UCC § 8–301(a).

(2) Control of a Certificated Security in Registered Form

A secured party will have control of a certificated security in registered form if the secured party takes delivery of the certificate and the certificate is indorsed to the secured party or in blank or the certificate is registered in the name of the secured party. UCC §§ 9–106(a), 8–106(b). A secured party takes delivery of a certificated security in registered form if it obtains possession of the certificate or obtains an acknowledgment from a person, other than a securities intermediary, that it holds possession on behalf of the secured party. If a securities intermediary has possession of the certificate and the certificate is registered to, payable to, or indorsed to the secured party, it has been delivered to the secured party. UCC § 8–301(a).

(3) Control of an Uncertificated Security

A secured party has control of an uncertificated security if the security is delivered to the secured party or the issuer of the security has agreed to comply with the secured party's instructions without the further consent of the registered owner of the security (i.e., entered into a control agreement). UCC §§ 9–106(a), 8–106(c). An uncertificated security is delivered to a secured party if the issuer registers the secured party as the owner of the security or a person, other than a securities intermediary or the debtor, is the registered owner and acknowledges that it holds the security for the benefit of the secured party. UCC § 8–301(b).

(a) Right of the Debtor to Deal With Uncertificated Security

The secured party has control even if the debtor has a right to deal with the uncertificated security. UCC § 8–106(f).

(b) Entering Into Control Agreement

The issuer has no obligation to enter into an agreement with the secured party to comply with the secured party's instructions even if the registered owner so directs. The issuer may not enter into such an agreement without the registered owner's consent. The issuer has no obligation to confirm the existence of a control agreement to any other party unless the registered owner so directs. UCC § 8–106(g).

Example: A and B orally agree that B will have a security interest in A's uncertificated security in XYZ Corp. to secure a loan that B made to A. A obtains a change in the registration with XYZ Corp. showing that B is now the registered owner of the uncertificated security. B has control of the uncertificated security and an attached security interest in that uncertificated security.

Example: A and B orally agree that B will have a security interest in A's uncertificated security in XYZ Corp. to secure a loan that B made to A. The security is registered to A in the records of XYZ Corp. A and B obtain an agreement with XYZ Corp. that it will comply with B's instructions regarding the uncertificated security without need for A's consent. B has control of the uncertificated security and an attached security interest in that uncertificated security.

(4) Control of a Security Entitlement

A secured party may control a securities entitlement in one of three ways: (i) the secured party becomes the entitlement holder; (ii) the secured party obtains a control agreement in which the securities intermediary has agreed to comply with the instructions of the secured party without further agreement of the entitlement holder; or (iii) another person has control of the securities entitlement on behalf of the secured party, or acknowledges that it holds the securities entitlement on behalf of the secured party. UCC §§ 9–106(a), 8–106(d). If the secured party is the securities intermediary that is holding the securities entitlement, the securities intermediary automatically has control without taking any other action beyond obtaining the debtor's agreement that grants the security interest. UCC §§ 9–106(a), 8–106(e).

(a) Right of the Debtor to Deal With the Security Entitlement

The secured party has control even if the debtor retains the right to deal with the securities entitlement. UCC § 8–106(f).

(b) Entering Into Control Agreement

The securities intermediary has no obligation to enter into an agreement with the secured party to comply with the secured party's instructions even if the entitlement holder so directs. The securities intermediary may not enter into such an agreement without the entitlement holder's consent. The securities intermediary has no obligation to confirm the existence of the control agreement to a third party unless the entitlement holder so requests. UCC § 8–106(g).

> *Example:* A and C orally agree that C will have a security interest in A's securities entitlements held by Brokerage to secure a loan that C made to A. A, C, and Brokerage enter into an agreement that Brokerage will comply with C's instructions regarding all of A's securities entitlements held by Brokerage without further consent of A. C has control of the securities entitlements and an attached security interest in the securities entitlement.

> *Example:* A opens a securities account at Brokerage. A and Brokerage orally agree that Brokerage will have a security interest in any securities entitlement held in the account to secure any amounts that A will owe Brokerage. Brokerage has control of any securities entitlements in the account and an attached security interest in those securities entitlements.

(5) Control of a Securities Account

If a secured party has control over all of the securities entitlements in a securities account, the secured party has control of the securities account. UCC § 9–106(c).

(6) Control of a Commodity Contract

A secured party has control of a commodity contract if it is the commodity intermediary that holds the commodity contract. UCC § 9–106(b)(1). If the secured party is not the commodity intermediary that is holding the commodity contract, the secured party has control of the commodity contract if the commodity customer, the secured party, and the commodity intermediary have agreed that the commodity intermediary will apply any value derived from the commodity contract as directed by the secured party without any further consent of the commodity customer (i.e., a control agreement). UCC § 9–106(b)(2).

(7) Control of a Commodity Account
If a secured party has control over all commodity contracts in a commodity account, the secured party has control of the commodity account. UCC § 9–106(c).

e. Control of Letter-of-Credit Rights

A secured party will have control of letter-of-credit rights if the secured party obtains the consent of the issuer or any nominated person to the assignment of the proceeds of the letter of credit. UCC §§ 9–107, 5–114 . The issuer is the bank that issues the letter of credit to the beneficiary. UCC § 5–102(a)(9). A nominated person is a person that agrees with an issuer that the nominated person will pay or give value pursuant to the letter of credit. UCC § 5–102(a)(11). Consent to the assignment of proceeds of the letter of credit is an agreement of the issuer or nominated person to recognize the secured party's claim to the proceeds. Consent to the assignment is not the same as recognizing the right of a transferee beneficiary to make a demand for payment under the letter of credit. UCC § 9–107, cmts. 1, 4. See the discussion of the difference between an assignee of a letter-of-credit right and a transferee beneficiary in Chapter II as part of the discussion of the scope of Article 9.

Example: A and Z orally agree that Z will have a security interest in A's right to payment as a beneficiary of a letter of credit issued by Bank to secure a loan that Z made to A. Bank consents to the assignment of the proceeds of the letter of credit to Z. Z has no right to demand payment under the letter of credit but does have a right to payment of the proceeds when A makes a demand for payment under the letter of credit. Z is not a transferee beneficiary of the letter of credit.

f. Control of Electronic Documents of Title

A secured party will have control of an electronic document of title when the secured party is designated by the system used to evidence interests in the electronic document of title as the person entitled to the goods under the electronic document of title. UCC §§ 7–106(a), 9–314. This test must be met as a matter of factual proof regarding the creation and storage of the records. In other words, the secured party and the debtor *cannot* merely agree that the secured party has control of the record that constitutes the electronic document of title. UCC § 7–106(b) provides a safe harbor for satisfying the test. Other methods of satisfying the test set forth in UCC § 7–106(a) could be developed. UCC § 7–106(b) sets forth six criteria. The records constituting the electronic document of title must be designated in some manner as the "authoritative copy" which is "unique, identifiable, and [subject to certain exceptions] unalterable." UCC § 7–106(b)(1). Any copy of the authoritative copy must be readily identifiable as a copy that is not authoritative. UCC § 7–106(b)(5). The authoritative copy must identify the secured party as the assignee of the records. UCC § 7–106(b)(2). The authoritative copy must be maintained by the secured party or a designated custodian. UCC § 7–106(b)(3). Copies or revisions to the authoritative copy that add or change the assignee must be made with the participation of the secured party. UCC § 7–106(b)(4). Any revisions to the authoritative copy must be readily identifiable as authorized or unauthorized. UCC § 7–106(b)(6).

6. Value Has Been Given

If the debtor has authenticated the security agreement with an adequate collateral description, or the secured party has possession or control of the designated types of collateral pursuant to the debtor's security agreement as described *supra*, the second requirement for attachment of a consensual security interest in the collateral is that value must be given. UCC § 9–203(b)(1).

a. Value Defined

Value must consist of one of four things. First, value may be any consideration that is sufficient to support a contract. Second, value may be a binding commitment to extend credit. Third, value may be security for or total or partial satisfaction of a preexisting claim. Fourth, value may be accepting delivery under a preexisting purchase contract. UCC § 1–204.

b. Giving and Getting Value

The debtor need not receive the value and the secured party need not be the one who parts with the value. Having said that, normally, the secured party is giving value to the debtor in exchange for the debtor's grant of the security interest in the debtor's property.

Example: A authenticates a security agreement granting B a security interest in all of "A's inventory" to secure a loan that B made to C. Value has been given in the form of the loan that B made to C sufficient to attach a security interest in A's inventory.

7. Rights in Collateral or Power to Transfer Rights in Collateral

If the debtor has authenticated the security agreement with an adequate collateral description, or the secured party has possession or control of the designated types of collateral pursuant to the debtor's security agreement as described *supra*, and value has been given, the third requirement for attaching a consensual security interest in collateral is that the debtor that has made the security agreement must actually have rights in the collateral or power to transfer rights in the collateral to the secured party. UCC § 9–203(b)(2).

a. Derivative Rights Concept

Granting a security interest in collateral is, in effect, granting a property interest in the collateral to the secured party. Under principles of property law, a person may only transfer the property rights that the person actually has in that property or the rights that the person has power to transfer. Article 9 follows this principle. A security interest attaches to whatever property rights in the collateral the debtor actually has or has power to transfer. UCC § 9–203, cmt. 6.

Example: A granted a security interest in all of A's "goods" to B to secure a loan that B made to A. A is the lessee of several items of equipment from C. B's security interest in the leased equipment attaches to A's limited property rights in the equipment as a lessee.

b. Role of Title

A debtor need not have full title to the collateral in order to grant a security interest in the collateral to a secured party. The provisions of Article 9 apply no matter who holds the title to the property at issue. UCC § 9–202.

c. Power to Transfer Rights

In certain circumstances, a debtor may transfer to a secured party more property rights than what the debtor actually has in the collateral because a statute or other legal rule gives the debtor power to transfer such rights. If a statute or other legal rule allows the debtor to grant more rights than what it has in the collateral to another person and the secured party is a person that may take advantage of that other law, the debtor may grant those greater rights to the secured party. UCC § 9–203(b)(2), cmt. 6.

(1) Good Faith Purchasers of Goods

In most circumstances, a person with an interest in goods may only transfer the rights that person has in the goods to another person, including a secured party. A buyer of goods may have "voidable title" to the goods, and may transfer "good title" to a person that purchases for value those goods in good faith from the buyer. UCC § 2–403(1). This is a circumstance where a buyer of goods has the power to transfer greater property rights to a qualifying purchaser than the buyer actually has. The buyer's secured party may qualify as a good faith purchaser under this provision.

(a) Voidable Title

The circumstances in which the buyer has voidable title to goods are determined by common law principles. UCC Article 2 specifies four circumstances in which the buyer is deemed to have voidable title. First, if the buyer takes possession of the goods in a transaction in which the buyer deceived its seller about the buyer's identity, the buyer has voidable title to the goods. Second, if the buyer takes possession of the goods in a transaction in which the buyer issued a check to its seller and that check was dishonored when presented for payment, the buyer has voidable title to the goods. Third, if the buyer takes possession of the goods in a transaction in which the buyer and its seller agreed that the transaction was to be a "cash sale," the buyer has voidable title to the goods. Fourth, if the transferor takes possession of the goods in a transaction in which the transferor committed criminal fraud in relation to its seller, the transferor has voidable title to the goods. UCC § 2–403(1).

Example: B purchased goods from S in a transaction where B told S that B was Q, an employee of XYZ Corp. B is not an employee of that company and is not Q. B took possession of the goods and has voidable title to the goods.

Example: B purchased goods from S in a transaction where B gave S a check and B took possession of the goods. The check was dishonored when S presented it to the bank on which the check was drawn. B has voidable title to the goods.

Example: B purchased goods from S in a transaction where B gave S an envelope full of currency and B took possession of the goods. The currency was counterfeit. B has voidable title to the goods.

Example: B purchased goods from S in a transaction where B represented to S that B was purchasing the goods for use in a product that complied with applicable regulatory law. B took possession of the goods. The product did not comply with applicable regulatory law and under the law of the state, B's conduct amounts to criminal fraud. B has voidable title to the goods.

(b) Secured Party as Good Faith Purchaser for Value

A secured party may qualify as a good faith purchaser for value of the goods from the buyer when the buyer grants a security interest in the goods to the secured party. A grant of a security interest is a purchase, making the secured party a purchaser. UCC § 1–201(b)(29), (30). A secured party gives value even if the secured party advances no new value at the time it obtains the security interest. UCC § 1–204. A secured party acts in good faith as long as it acts with honesty in fact and in accord with reasonable commercial standards of fair dealing. UCC §§ 1–201(b)(20), 2–103.

Example: B purchased goods from S in a transaction where B told S that B was Q, an employee of XYZ Corp. B is not an employee of that company and is not Q. B took possession of the goods and has voidable title to the goods. B granted a security interest in those goods to C. C qualifies as a good faith purchaser for value and has "good title" to the goods consistent with its rights as a secured party. In a priority contest between S and C as to the goods, C will win. See Chapter V *infra*.

Example: B purchased goods from S in a transaction where B gave S a check and B took possession of the goods. The check was dishonored for insufficient funds when S presented it to the bank on which the check was drawn. B has voidable title to the goods. B granted a security interest in those goods to C. C qualifies as a good faith purchaser for value and has "good title" to the goods consistent with its rights as a secured party. In a priority contest between S and C as to the goods, C will win. See Chapter V *infra*.

(2) Sellers of Accounts, Chattel Paper, Payment Intangibles, and Promissory Notes

As we learned in Chapter II, Article 9 covers many sales of accounts, chattel paper, payment intangibles, and promissory notes. UCC § 9–109(a)(3), (d). After a seller sells these types of payment rights, the seller does not retain any property interest in the payment rights. UCC § 9–318(a). In a transaction covered by Article 9, however, the buyer of these four types of collateral is treated as having a security interest in these rights to payment. UCC §§ 1–201(b)(35), 9–102(a)(73). In certain circumstances, the rights of such a buyer can be defeated and thus the sellers of these payment rights in effect have the power to transfer greater rights than what they have to a secured party that arises subsequent to the first sale of the payment right.

(a) Sellers of Accounts and Chattel Paper

In some circumstances, a seller that has sold accounts or chattel paper may actually sell them again or grant a security interest in them even though the seller does not retain any property interest in the account or chattel paper after the first sale. If the buyer at the first sale of accounts or chattel paper does not "perfect" its security interest in the accounts or chattel paper that it purchased, the seller of the accounts or chattel paper can in effect sell the accounts or chattel paper again or grant a security interest in the accounts and chattel paper to another secured party. UCC § 9–318(b). To the extent that a subsequent party has priority over the rights of a first buyer of the accounts or chattel paper, the seller (the debtor) of the accounts or chattel paper is transferring more rights to the second buyer/secured party than what the seller (debtor) had at the time of the second transfer. What action is required for the buyer/secured party to perfect its interest in accounts and chattel paper will be considered in Chapter IV. The priority rules that will apply between the first buyer and other parties claiming an interest in the accounts and chattel paper will be considered in Chapter V.

> *Example:*   A sells its accounts to B. B fails to perfect its interest in the accounts. A sells the same accounts to C. C perfects its interest in the accounts. Under the applicable priority rule in a priority contest in the accounts as between B and C, C will win. Because of Article 9, A had power to transfer to C more rights than it actually had after the sale of the accounts to B.

(b) Sellers of Promissory Notes

Although the buyer's security interest in a sold promissory note is automatically perfected, UCC § 9–309(4), in some circumstances, a seller of promissory notes may be able to grant an interest in the already sold promissory note to a subsequent buyer or secured party and that subsequent buyer or secured party will have priority over the rights of the first buyer. UCC §§ 9–330, 9–331. To the extent that a subsequent party has priority over the rights of a first buyer of the promissory notes, the seller of the promissory note is transferring more rights to the second buyer/secured party than what the seller had at the time of the second transfer. We will consider these priority rules in Chapter V.

(c) Sellers of Payment Intangibles

Although a buyer's security interest in a payment intangible that is sold is automatically perfected, UCC § 9–309(3), a seller of the payment intangible may be able to sell the payment intangible again or grant a security interest that would have priority over the first buyer's interest under the Article 9 priority rules. To the extent that a subsequent party has priority over the rights of a first buyer of the payment intangible, the seller of the payment intangible is transferring more rights to the second buyer/secured party than what the seller had at the time of the second transfer. We will study the Article 9 priority rules concerning payment intangibles in Chapter V.

(3) Consignees in an Article 9 Consignment

As we learned in Chapter II, a true consignment as defined in UCC § 9–102(a)(20) is within the scope of Article 9. In a true consignment, the consignor retains title to the goods and the consignee is granted a right to sell the goods. If the consignor has not "perfected" its interest in the goods, the consignee has the ability to transfer the consignor's rights in the goods to the consignee's creditors and purchasers. UCC § 9–319. To the extent that a consignee is able to grant superior rights in the goods to another party, the consignee is transferring more rights to the goods than what the consignee has under principles of property law. What it takes to perfect the consignor's interest will be discussed in Chapter IV. The priority rules applicable to the consignor's security interest will be discussed in Chapter V.

C. After-Acquired Property and Future Advances Clauses in the Security Agreement

A security agreement usually provides that the secured party will have a security interest in described collateral to secure an obligation owed to the secured party. As a matter of contract construction, two issues commonly arise. First, does the security interest attach to collateral of the same type as described in the security agreement that the debtor acquires rights in after the security agreement is authenticated?

Second, does the security interest secure obligations owed to the secured party that arise after the security agreement is authenticated?

1. After-Acquired Property Clause

Article 9 allows the security agreement to contain an after-acquired property clause. UCC § 9–204(a). A typical after-acquired property clause provides that "the security interest attaches to all of the debtor's (insert collateral description here such as "goods, chattel paper, accounts") in which the debtor currently has rights or acquires rights hereafter." Such a clause is effective to attach a security interest to items that the debtor acquires rights in after the execution of the security agreement as long as those items fall within the collateral description.

Example: A authenticates a security agreement granting a security interest to B in all of A's "accounts, inventory, chattel paper now owned or hereafter acquired" to secure a loan that B made to A for A's business. The day after the security agreement is signed, A acquires a new item of inventory. B's security interest attaches to that new item of inventory.

a. Inference From Type of Collateral

On occasion, a security agreement may not have a well-drafted after-acquired property clause. In that situation it will be necessary to convince a court as a matter of contract interpretation that the court should infer that the parties intended that the security interest attach to collateral of the type described in the security agreement which is acquired after the security agreement was authenticated. Some courts have been amenable to that contract construction argument as long as the collateral was of a type that turns over frequently, such as inventory or accounts, but not amenable to that argument if the collateral was of the type that is not quickly turned over, such as equipment. Expecting to have the security interest attach to collateral acquired after the signing of the security agreement but omitting the after-acquired property clause from the security agreement is an invitation to litigation.

Example: A authenticates a security agreement granting a security interest to B in all of A's "equipment" to secure a loan that B made to A. The day after the security agreement is signed, A acquires a new item of equipment. B's security interest does not attach to that new item of equipment.

b. Restrictions on Effectiveness of the After-Acquired Property Clause

Article 9 contains two restrictions on the general effectiveness of an after-acquired property clause. First, such a clause does not effect an attachment of the security interest in either a consumer or nonconsumer transaction to a commercial tort claim that arises after the authentication of the security agreement. Second, such a clause does not effect an attachment of the security interest to consumer goods, other than an accession, unless the debtor acquires rights in the consumer goods within 10 days after the secured party gives value. UCC § 9–204(b).

Example: In a nonconsumer transaction, A authenticates a security agreement granting a security interest to B in all of A's "consumer goods now owned or hereafter acquired" to secure a loan that B made to A. (Review UCC § 9–108 regarding the effectiveness of the description). The day after the security agreement is signed and value is given, A acquires a new item that is a consumer good. B's security interest attaches to that new item of consumer goods. If A had acquired the new item of consumer goods 11 days after B gave the value to A, B's security interest would not attach to the new item of consumer goods.

2. Future Advances Clause

Article 9 gives effect to a future advances clause in the security agreement. UCC § 9–204(c). A typical future advances clause provides that the security interest in the described collateral secures "all obligations that the debtor owes the creditor now or hereafter." Without a future advances clause, the security interest in the collateral does not secure value provided after the authentication of the security agreement. Article 9 rejects the line of cases that held that even a broadly-drafted future advances clause was not sufficient to secure a future advance unless that future advance was of the same type or classification as the original advance. UCC § 9–204, cmt. 5.

Example: A authenticated a security agreement granting a security interest to B in all of A's goods to secure a loan of $50,000 made that same day. One month later, B lent A an additional $10,000. The additional loan is not secured as the security agreement did not specify that future advances would be secured by A's goods.

Example: A authenticated a security agreement granting a security interest to B in all of A's goods to secure a loan of $50,000 made that same day and any other obligations that A may owe to B in the future. One month later, B lent A an additional $10,000. The additional loan is secured by a security interest in A's goods given the future advances clause in the security agreement.

3. Cross Collateralization

The effect of a well-drafted after-acquired property clause and a well-drafted future advances clause in the same security agreement is to provide for cross collateralization of all of the debtor's obligations owed to the same secured party. Such cross collateralization is not considered an unusual or unconscionable practice in commercial transactions. The best way to explain cross collateralization is with an example.

Example: A, an antique dealer, authenticated a security agreement that provides "A grants to B a security interest in all of A's goods then owned or thereafter acquired to secure all obligations that A currently or hereafter owes to B." On the date that A signed the security agreement, A owed B $10,000 and owned an antique dresser that A held for sale. The next month B lent A $5,000 and A subsequently purchased an antique chest. Without either the future advances or after-acquired property clauses, the initial $10,000 obligation would be secured by the antique dresser. With only the after-acquired property clause and not a future advances clause, the initial $10,000 obligation would be secured by the antique desk in addition to the antique dresser. The $5,000 obligation would be unsecured. With only the future advances clause and not the after-acquired property clause, the total debt of $15,000 would be secured by the antique dresser, and not the antique desk. With both a future advances clause and an after-acquired property clause, the total debt of $15,000 is secured by the antique dresser and the antique desk.

D. Exceptions to the Rule Regarding Collateral Description

In six circumstances that are all defined in the provisions of Article 9, attachment of a security interest in one type of collateral will result in the attachment of the security interest to a different specified type of collateral. This is in effect an exception to the collateral description rule that the description must "reasonably identify what is described." UCC § 9–108(a).

1. Attachment of a Security Interest to Proceeds of Collateral

When a secured party obtains an attached security interest in any type of collateral, the security interest automatically attaches to any identifiable proceeds of that collateral. UCC §§ 9–203(f), 9–315(a)(2). The security agreement need not state that the collateral includes "proceeds" of collateral types that are described in the security agreement. In order to be identifiable, the proceeds must fall into one of the categories of proceeds set forth in the definition and result, in a factual sense, from the original collateral.

a. Proceeds Defined

The term proceeds means: (i) whatever rights are acquired upon disposition of the collateral including disposition by sale, lease, or license of the collateral; (ii) whatever is collected or distributed on account of collateral; (iii) rights arising out of collateral; (iv) claims arising out of loss, defects, infringement, or other impairment of the value of collateral; and (v) insurance payable by reason of claims arising out of loss, defects, infringement or other impairment of the value of the collateral. UCC § 9–102(a)(64).

Example: A authenticates a security agreement giving B a security interest in all of A's "equipment" to secure a loan that B made to A. A sells that equipment and receives money from the purchaser. B has an attached security interest in the money as long as it is identifiable as proceeds of the sale of the equipment even though the security agreement does not use the word "proceeds" or "money" in the collateral description.

b. Commingled Property

Courts sometimes determined that if the proceeds that resulted from the original collateral were commingled with other property, the identifiable nature of the proceeds was lost. Article 9 rejects that result by providing that if proceeds are commingled with other property, the proceeds are still "identifiable" in some circumstances.

(1) Commingled Goods

If the proceeds are goods that are commingled with other goods, then the rules on commingled goods determine the continued attachment of the security interest in the commingled goods. UCC § 9–315(b)(1).

(2) Commingled Personal Property That Is Not Goods

If the proceeds are not goods, then the secured party may use equitable methods of tracing the proceeds to identify what portion of the commingled property is considered to be proceeds. UCC § 9–315(b)(2). The most commonly applied tracing method is called the "lowest intermediate balance" rule. This rule provides that if funds that are proceeds are commingled with funds that are not proceeds, the lowest balance in the total fund between the time of the commingling to the time of the tracing is presumed to be identifiable proceeds of the collateral.

Example: B has an attached security interest in A's equipment. A sells an item of equipment to C and receives $100 as proceeds. A deposits that $100 in A's checking account at Bank. Prior to the deposit, the account contained $500 and after the deposit, the account contained $600. A withdrew $550 and then deposited an additional $200, for a balance of $250. The identifiable proceeds under the lowest intermediate balance rule is $50.

2. Attachment of a Security Interest to the Product or Mass of Commingled Goods

If a security interest is attached to goods and then those goods are commingled with other goods, a security interest will attach to the product or mass of commingled goods, even if the security agreement does not describe the product or mass. UCC § 9–336(c). Goods are considered commingled goods when the goods are united in such a way that the individual identity of the goods is subsumed within the product or mass that results from the commingling. UCC § 9–336(a).

Example: A authenticates a security agreement granting B a security interest in A's inventory of sand to secure a loan that B made to A. A uses the sand to make glass. B's security interest attaches to the glass.

3. Attachment of a Security Interest to Supporting Obligations of Other Collateral

When a secured party obtains an attached security interest in any right to payment which is supported by another obligation that qualifies as a supporting obligation, the security interest automatically attaches to the supporting obligation. UCC § 9–203(f). A description of the collateral in the security agreement as either a supporting obligation or the underlying type of supporting obligation is not required.

Example: A authenticated a security agreement granting B a security interest in all of A's "accounts." At A's insistence, C, one of the account debtors, obtained a letter of credit for the benefit of A that allowed A to draw on the letter of credit to satisfy C's obligation to A on the account. B's security interest attaches to A's rights as a beneficiary of the letter of credit, as a supporting obligation of the account. The collateral description in the security agreement between A and B need not specify a "supporting obligation" or a "letter-of-credit right."

4. Attachment of a Security Interest to a Security Interest, Mortgage, or Lien Interest

When a secured party obtains an attached security interest in any right to payment that is secured by a security interest, mortgage, or any other type of lien interest, the secured party also obtains an attached security interest in the security interest, mortgage, or lien interest. UCC § 9–203(g). The security interest, mortgage, or other lien interest need not be specifically described in the security agreement that describes the right to payment.

5. Attachment of a Security Interest to Securities Entitlements in a Securities Account

If a secured party attaches a security interest to a securities account, the security interest attaches to all securities entitlements carried in the securities account. The collateral description need not state "securities entitlement" or a description of the underlying financial asset. UCC § 9–203(h).

Example: A, a consumer, authenticates a security agreement granting B a security interest in "A's securities account held at Brokerage Inc." (Review UCC § 9–108(e).) B's security interest attaches to all securities entitlements held in the securities account.

6. Attachment of a Security Interest to Commodity Contracts in a Commodity Account

If a secured party attaches a security interest to a commodity account, the security interest attaches to all commodity contracts carried in the commodity account. The collateral description need not state "commodity contract." UCC § 9–203(i).

E. Attachment of a Security Interest Without the Debtor's Security Agreement

Article 9 recognizes some security interests that arise by operation of law, not agreement. Thus, in these circumstances, a security interest attaches to collateral without the debtor's security agreement.

1. Security Interests Arising Under UCC Articles 2 and 2A

A seller's security interest that arises through retention of title, UCC § 2–401, and shipment under reservation, UCC § 2–505, and a buyer's or lessee's security interest in rightfully rejected goods or goods as to which acceptance has been justifiably revoked, UCC §§ 2–711(3), 2A–508, are subject to Article 9. As long as the debtor does not have possession of the goods, however, the secured party does not have to have a debtor-authenticated security agreement that describes the collateral or have possession of the goods pursuant to the debtor's security agreement. UCC § 9–110(1). The security interest attaches as specified in UCC §§ 2–401, 2–505, 2–711(3) and 2A–508. Review Chapter II, Section D.

2. Security Interest of a Collecting Bank Under Article 4

The security interest of a collecting bank in items in its possession attaches when withdrawable credits are given against the item. UCC § 4–210(a). No security agreement is necessary to make the security interest enforceable as long as the collecting bank does not receive final settlement for the item or give up possession or control of the item for purposes other than collection of the item through the banking system. UCC § 4–210(c)(1). Review Chapter II, Section D.

3. Security Interest of Bank Issuing Letter of Credit

The letter of credit issuer's security interest in documents in its possession presented under a letter of credit attaches when the issuer gives value for the presentation or honors the presentation. UCC § 5–118(a). "Documents" in Article 5 are defined more broadly than just documents of title. UCC § 5–102(a)(6). A security agreement is not necessary to attach the security interest to these documents as long as the issuer has not been reimbursed for or otherwise recovered the value given under the letter of credit. UCC § 5–118(b)(1). Review Chapter II, Section D.

4. Attachment of a Security Interest in Cases of Successor Liability

If a debtor enters into a security agreement with a creditor and that debtor transfers substantially all of its assets to a new debtor and the new debtor becomes generally obligated for the obligations of the original debtor, that new debtor, UCC § 9–102(a)(56), is bound by the security agreement entered into by the original debtor, UCC § 9–102(a)(60). UCC § 9–203(d)(2). The new debtor's liability occurs by operation of law based upon principles of successor liability. Article 9 recognizes that the original security agreement between the original secured party and original debtor is sufficient to create a security interest in the new debtor's assets that are within the description contained in that security agreement without the new debtor executing a new agreement. UCC § 9–203(e).

Example: A authenticates a security agreement granting B a security interest in all of A's equipment then owned or thereafter acquired to secure a loan that B made to A. A sells the entire business to C and under principles of successor liability, C is obligated on A's obligations. C is bound to the security agreement with B and the security agreement is sufficient to attach a security interest to all of C's equipment.

5. Security Interest of Securities Intermediary in Securities Entitlement

If a securities intermediary allows a person to buy a financial asset (defined in UCC § 8–102(a)(9)) through a securities intermediary under an agreement to pay for the asset at the time of purchase, and the securities intermediary credits the asset to the person's securities account before the person actually makes the payment (thereby creating a securities entitlement), the securities intermediary has a security interest in the securities entitlement to secure the person's obligation to pay the purchase price. UCC § 9–206(a), (b).

6. Security Interest of Person Delivering Certificated Security or Financial Asset Represented by a Writing

If a person in the business of dealing with securities or financial assets delivers a certificated security or other financial asset that is represented by a writing to another person also in the business of dealing with securities or financial assets under an agreement in which the transferee is to pay for the delivery, the transferor has a security interest in the certificates or financial asset represented by a writing to secure the transferee's obligation to pay for the certificated security or financial asset. UCC 9–206(c), (d).

F. Effect of Dispositions of Collateral on Attachment of a Security Interest Or Agricultural Lien

The disposition of the collateral to another person does not strip off a security interest or agricultural lien that has attached to the item of collateral unless the secured party authorizes the disposition of the collateral free of the security interest or agricultural lien or a priority rule in Article 9 specifies otherwise. UCC § 9–315(a)(1). The secured party's authorization to dispose of the collateral free of the security interest or agricultural lien may be express or implied. The fact that the secured party has a right to the proceeds obtained upon disposition of the collateral, UCC § 9–315(a)(2), is not an express or implied authorization to dispose of the collateral free of the security interest. UCC § 9–315, cmt. 2.

> *Example:*   A authenticates a security agreement giving B a security interest in all of A's equipment. A sold a piece of equipment to C. Absent the express or implied authorization of B to sell the equipment free of the security interest, the security interest remains attached to the piece of equipment in C's possession unless a priority rule of Article 9 specifies otherwise.

G.   Ability to Stop Attachment of a Security Interest

Article 9 approaches attachment of security interests from the perspective that the debtor should be free to create a security interest in the debtor's assets even if the debtor by contract or the legal rules governing that type of asset provide that the debtor cannot transfer its rights in the asset. Article 9 does not address any restrictions on the ability to attach an agricultural lien. Whether an agricultural lien attaches depends upon the provisions of law other than Article 9.

1. Contractual Agreements Not to Create a Security Interest or Transfer Rights in the Property

Article 9 contains several rules that make contractual agreements by the debtor to not transfer its rights in the asset to another person ineffective to prevent attachment of a security interest.

a. Agreements Between the Debtor and Secured Party

An agreement between the debtor and secured party that prohibits the debtor from transferring its rights in the collateral or makes such a transfer a default under the agreement is not effective to prevent the transfer from being effective. One type of transfer is the creation of another security interest in the collateral. UCC § 9–401(b).

Example: A authenticates a security agreement granting B a security interest in A's equipment to secure a loan that B made to A. In the security agreement, B has prohibited A from transferring any collateral or allowing any liens or security interests to attach to the collateral and making such actions a default. A authenticates a security agreement granting C a security interest in A's equipment to secure a loan that C made to A. C's security interest attaches to the equipment in spite of the prohibition contained in the security agreement between A and B.

b. Agreements Between the Debtor and an Account Debtor or an Obligor on a Promissory Note

A term in an account, chattel paper (other than a lease), a general intangible, or a promissory note that requires that the obligor on that collateral to consent to the debtor granting a security interest in that collateral or that purports to prevent the creation of a security interest in that collateral is not effective to prevent the attachment of the security interest that the debtor grants to the secured party. UCC § 9–406(d), 9–408(a). This rule may be subject to other law to the extent that the other law establishes a different rule for an account debtor or obligor when that obligor incurred that obligation primarily for family, personal, or household purposes. UCC § 9–406(h). The effect of the attachment of the security interest on the ability of the secured party to engage in enforcement actions against the obligor on the collateral will be considered in Chapter VI.

Example: S sold goods to B in exchange for B's promise to pay for the goods in 30 days. In the contract between S and B, S agreed not to assign S's rights to payment (an account) to any other person. S authenticated a security agreement granting to D a security interest in all of S's accounts then owned or thereafter acquired to secure a loan that D made to S. D's security interest in the account (the obligation that B owes S) attaches in spite of S's promise to B to not assign the right to payment to anyone.

c. Term in a Lease Agreement

A term in a lease that prohibits the creation of a security interest in either party's rights under the lease or requires the consent of one party to the lease contract to the creation of the security interest in the other party's rights under the lease is not effective to prevent attachment of the security interest to the debtor's rights under the lease or the debtor's residual rights in the leased property. UCC § 9–407(a). The effect of the attachment of the security interest on the ability of the secured party to engage in enforcement actions against the obligor on the collateral will be considered in Chapter VI.

d. Term in a Letter of Credit

A term in the letter of credit that purports to prohibit or to require the consent of the issuer, applicant, or nominated person to the creation of a security interest in a letter-of-credit right is ineffective to prevent attachment of a security interest to the letter-of-credit right. UCC § 9–409(a). The effect of the attachment of the security interest on the ability of the secured party to engage in enforcement actions against the obligor on the collateral will be considered in Chapter VI.

2. Legal Rules Prohibiting Assignment of Personal Property

Under some bodies of law other than Article 9, certain principles have developed that prohibit assignments of certain types of rights even in the absence of an agreement that purports to prohibit assignment. Article 9 respects that other body of law in small part, UCC § 9–401(a), but then provides an immense set of exceptions to that principle. For most assignments of rights, those other bodies of law that prohibit assignment of rights are ineffective to prevent attachment of a security interest. The effect of the attachment of the security interest on the ability of the secured party to engage in enforcement actions against the obligor on the collateral will be considered in Chapter VI.

a. Legal Rules Prohibiting Assignment of Accounts, Chattel Paper, Promissory Notes, and General Intangibles

If a legal rule prohibits or conditions assignment of the debtor's rights in accounts, chattel paper (including a lease), promissory notes, or general intangibles, that legal rule is not effective to prevent attachment of a security interest in the debtor's rights in that collateral. UCC §§ 9–406(f), 9–407, 9–408(c). This rule may be subject to other law to the extent that the other law establishes a different rule for an obligor on a right to payment who incurred that obligation primarily for family, personal or household purposes. UCC § 9–406(h).

Example: S sold goods to B in exchange for B's promise to pay for the goods in 30 days. Assume under other law governing contract assignments, B cannot assign its right to receive S's performance (delivery of the goods, a general intangible) to any other person. B authenticated a security agreement granting to D a security interest in all of B's general intangibles then owned or thereafter acquired to secure a loan that D made to B. D's security interest in the general intangible (the obligation that S owes B) attaches in spite the law prohibiting assignment of this type of right.

b. Legal Rules Affecting Letter-of-Credit Rights

If letter of credit legal rules, customs, or practices prohibit or condition the assignment of a letter-of-credit right on the consent of the issuer, applicant, or nominated person, those rules, customs and practices are ineffective to prevent attachment of a security interest in those letter-of-credit rights. UCC § 9–409(a).

H. Obligations of Secured Party Regarding Collateral

Once a security interest attaches, a security agreement is entered into, or an agricultural lien attaches, the secured party has certain rights and obligations to a debtor. The secured party also has obligations to an obligor that owes an obligation to the debtor when that obligation is subject to or potentially subject to a security interest. Recall that while the definition of "secured party" includes both a holder of a security interest and an agricultural lienholder (UCC § 9–102(a)(73)), the definition of "security interest" does not include an agricultural lien (UCC § 1–201(b)(35)). The definition of "collateral" includes property subject to a security interest or an agricultural lien. UCC § 9–102(a)(12).

1. Secured Party in Possession of Collateral

A secured party in possession of collateral has several rights and obligations specified in UCC § 9–207. The secured party has the obligation to take reasonable care of the collateral. UCC § 9–207(a). This obligation does not apply to a secured party who is a buyer of accounts, chattel paper, payment intangibles, or promissory notes or a consignor unless the secured party is entitled to recourse against the debtor or a secondary obligor on account of uncollected collateral. UCC § 9–207(d). The remaining provisions of UCC § 9–207 do not apply if the secured party is a buyer of accounts, chattel paper, payment intangibles, or promissory notes or if the secured party is a consignor. UCC § 9–207(d). In these circumstances, other law will control this issue. UCC § 9–207, cmt. 7. The secured party may charge the reasonable expenses of taking care of the collateral to the debtor and secure those expenses with the collateral. UCC § 9–207(b)(1). If the insurance coverage for the collateral is inadequate, the debtor has the risk of loss from accidental loss or damage to the collateral. UCC § 9–207(b)(2). The secured party has the obligation to keep the collateral identified, but may commingle fungible collateral. UCC § 9–207(b)(3). The secured party may use or operate the collateral in order to preserve the collateral and its value or as permitted by court order. In a nonconsumer transaction, the secured party may use or operate the collateral as agreed to by the debtor. UCC § 9–207(b)(4). A secured party may hold any proceeds, other than money or funds, received from the collateral as additional security. UCC § 9–207(c)(1). A secured party shall apply any proceeds that are money or funds to reduce the secured obligation or remit those proceeds to the debtor. UCC § 9–207(c)(2). A secured party may create a security interest in the collateral. UCC § 9–207(c)(3).

2. Secured Party in Control of Collateral

A secured party that is in control of an electronic document of title, a deposit account, electronic chattel paper, investment property, or a letter-of-credit right has several rights and obligations.

a. Dealing with the Collateral and Proceeds

A secured party may hold any proceeds, other than money or funds, received from the collateral as additional security. UCC § 9–207(c)(1). A secured party shall apply any proceeds that are money or funds to reduce the secured obligation or remit those proceeds to the debtor. UCC § 9–207(c)(2). A secured party may create a security interest in the collateral. UCC § 9–207(c)(3). These provisions do not apply if the secured party is a buyer of accounts, chattel paper, payment intangibles, or promissory notes or if the secured party is a consignor. UCC § 9–207(d). Other law will control this issue. UCC § 9–207, cmt. 7.

b. Obligations When There Is No Outstanding Obligations or Commitment to Give Value

If there is no obligation outstanding or any commitment to give value and the secured party has control of collateral, the secured party must take the specified action within ten days of receiving an authenticated demand from the debtor to release the rights the secured party has obtained by virtue of control of the debtor's asset. UCC § 9–208. The required action depends upon the collateral that the secured party controls.

(1) Deposit Account

If the secured party has control of a deposit account through a control agreement, the secured party must send an authenticated record to the bank that releases the bank from any obligation to comply with the secured party's instructions. UCC § 9–208(b)(1). If the secured party has become the bank's customer on the deposit account, the secured party either has to pay the debtor the balance on deposit in the deposit account or transfer the deposit account to be held in the debtor's name. UCC § 9–208(b)(2).

(2) Electronic Chattel Paper

If the secured party has control of electronic chattel paper, the secured party must either give the debtor the authoritative copy or communicate in an authenticated record with the custodian of the authoritative copy that the custodian need no longer comply with the secured party's instructions and take action that allows the debtor or the designated custodian to add or change an assignee without the consent of the secured party. These obligations do not apply if the secured party is a buyer of chattel paper. UCC § 9–208(b)(3).

(3) Investment Property

If the secured party has control of investment property that is held by a securities intermediary or a commodity intermediary, the secured party must send an authenticated record to the intermediary releasing the intermediary from any obligation to comply with instructions of the secured party. UCC § 9–208(b)(4).

(4) Letter-of-Credit Right

If the secured party has control of a letter-of-credit right, the secured party must send to any person that was obligated to pay or deliver proceeds of the letter of credit to the secured party an authenticated release providing that the person has no obligation to the secured party to pay or deliver the proceeds of the letter of credit. UCC § 9–208(b)(5).

(5) Electronic Document of Title

A secured party must transfer control of the electronic document of title to the debtor or its designated custodian, provide an authenticated record releasing the custodian from acting pursuant to the secured party's instructions, and take appropriate action to allow the debtor to add or change assignees of the electronic document of title without the secured party's consent. UCC § 9–208(b)(6).

3. Secured Party That Has Notified Account Debtor of Its Interest in Accounts, Chattel Paper, or Payment Intangibles

If a transaction is not a sale of an account, chattel paper or payment intangible, there is no outstanding secured obligation or any commitment to give value, and the secured party has notified an account debtor of the assignment to the secured party of the account, chattel paper, or payment intangible, the secured party has an obligation to send an authenticated notice to the account debtor that it has no obligation to the secured party. That notice must be sent within 10 days after the debtor makes an authenticated demand on the secured party to release the account debtor. UCC § 9–209.

4. Debtor's Request for Statements of Collateral and for an Accounting of the Secured Obligation

In transactions other than consignments and other than sales of accounts, chattel paper, payment intangibles, or promissory notes, the secured party has an obligation to respond to the debtor's requests for an accounting of the obligations remaining unpaid and a list of collateral subject to the security interest. The secured party must respond within 14 days after receiving the debtor's authenticated request. UCC § 9–210(a), (b).

a. Listing of Collateral

The debtor's request for a listing of collateral must ask the secured party to correct or approve a list of collateral. UCC § 9–210(a)(3). If the secured party claims an interest in all of a particular type of collateral, the secured party's statement of that fact to the debtor in an authenticated record is sufficient. UCC § 9–210(c). If the secured party does not currently claim an interest in the collateral on the list, the secured party's response must indicate that fact and, if applicable and known, the name and mailing address of any assignee of the secured party's previous interest in the collateral. UCC § 9–210(d).

b. Request for an Accounting or Statement of Account

The debtor's statement for an accounting regarding the amount of the unpaid secured obligation may either ask for an accounting from the secured party or may ask the secured party to approve or correct a statement of the unpaid secured obligation that the debtor has indicated. UCC § 9–210(a)(2), (3). If the secured party no longer asserts that any unpaid secured obligation is owed to the secured party, the secured party's response must indicate that fact and, if applicable and known, the name and mailing address of any assignee of the secured party's right to payment. UCC § 9–210(e).

c. Charges for Provision of Statements

The debtor is entitled to one response to one of the types of request stated above within a six month period without any charge. The secured party may require payment of a charge that cannot exceed $25 for any additional response within the six month period. UCC § 9–210(f).

I. Effect of Debtor's Bankruptcy on Attachment of Security Interest and Agricultural Lien

As briefly covered in Chapter I, the debtor's bankruptcy filing has a significant effect on a creditor's ability to collect debts. A debtor's bankruptcy filing also has a significant effect on the attachment of a security interest or agricultural lien.

1. Automatic Stay

The automatic stay prevents the secured party from taking any action to create a security interest or agricultural lien in the property of the estate or in the debtor's property. 11 U.S.C. § 362(a). Thus if the security interest or agricultural lien has not already attached to the collateral by the time the debtor files bankruptcy, any action by the secured party that results in the attachment of the security interest or agricultural lien after the bankruptcy filing violates the automatic stay.

2. Collateral Part of Bankruptcy Estate

If the security interest or agricultural lien has attached prior to the filing of the bankruptcy petition, that attachment does not prevent the collateral itself from becoming part of the bankruptcy estate. 11 U.S.C. § 541.

3. Effect on Security Interest in After-Acquired Property Including Proceeds

If the debtor acquires property after the filing of the bankruptcy petition to which the secured party's security interest would attach under an after-acquired property clause or the rule allowing for automatic attachment of the security interest in proceeds, the security interest will not attach to that after-acquired property that is not proceeds of collateral that was subject to the security interest. 11 U.S.C. § 552. Proceeds under the Bankruptcy Code may not be the same as "proceeds" as defined in Article 9.

Example: A authenticated a security agreement granting B a security interest in A's inventory then owned or thereafter acquired to secure a loan that B made to A. A filed bankruptcy. A then acquired a new piece of inventory. Unless B can show the new piece of inventory is proceeds of inventory that A had prior to the filing of the bankruptcy petition, B's security interest will not attach to that new piece of inventory acquired after the bankruptcy filing.

4. Debtor Use, Sale, or Lease of Collateral

The debtor in possession or the bankruptcy trustee may use, sell, or lease collateral that is part of the bankruptcy estate in the ordinary course of the debtor's business without the need for court approval. Court approval is required for the use, sale or lease of collateral that is part of the bankruptcy estate if that use, sale, or lease is not in the ordinary course of the debtor's business or the collateral is cash collateral. 11 U.S.C. § 363(b), (c). Cash collateral refers to collateral such as cash, negotiable instruments, documents of title, deposit accounts, or cash equivalents. 11 U.S.C. § 363(a).

5. Adequate Protection

A secured party with a security interest or agricultural lien in the collateral may request that the bankruptcy court order the debtor to adequately protect the value of the secured party's interest in the collateral. 11 U.S.C. § 363(e), 362(d). Adequate protection of the value of the secured party's interest in collateral requires that the bankruptcy court determine the value of the secured party's secured claim in bankruptcy, determine what risks to that value are present, and determine the additional rights the secured party should be granted in order to protect that value.

a. Valuing the Secured Claim

Once a security interest or agricultural lien has attached to an item of collateral, the secured party has a property interest in that item of collateral. (For present purposes, we are assuming that the property interest is not avoidable. Avoiding property interests in collateral that is property of the bankruptcy estate will be discussed in Chapter V.) The Bankruptcy Code recognizes the secured party's property interest and provides that the value of that property interest is a secured claim in the debtor's bankruptcy. 11 U.S.C. § 506. In order to determine the amount of the secured claim, the value of the item of the collateral which is subject to the security interest or agricultural lien and the amount of debt that the security interest or agricultural lien secures must be determined.

Example: A authenticates a security agreement granting B a security interest in A's equipment then owned or thereafter acquired. At the date of the bankruptcy filing, A owed B $1,000. The equipment that A had an interest in at the time of the bankruptcy filing was valued at $700. B's secured claim is $700. B has an unsecured claim for $300. If the equipment was valued at $1,200, A would have a secured claim of $1,000 and no unsecured claim.

b. Risks to the Value of the Secured Claim

In a request to adequately protect the value of the secured claim, the secured party must identify the risk to that value. Risks to the value of the secured claim include depreciation, dissipation, destruction of the collateral, and failure to keep the collateral insured. Measures employed to protect against decreases in value of the secured claim include granting replacement liens on other collateral, requiring periodic payments to the secured party, obtaining insurance on the collateral, or prohibiting use of the collateral. 11 U.S.C. § 361.

Example: A authenticates a security agreement granting B a security interest in A's equipment then owned or thereafter acquired. At the date of the bankruptcy filing, A owed B $1,000. The equipment that A had an interest in at the time of the bankruptcy filing was valued at $700. B's secured claim is $700 and B's unsecured claim is $300. A continues to use the equipment so that it depreciates in value to $500. B would seek adequate protection against the $200 decline in value of B's secured claim.

6. Right to Post-Petition Interest as Part of a Secured Claim

If the value of the collateral that is subject to the secured party's security interest or agricultural lien is more than the amount of the obligation owed, the post-petition interest that accrues on the obligation is added to the amount of the secured claim until the value of the collateral is exhausted. 11 U.S.C. § 506. If the value of the collateral is less than the amount of the obligation owed, the post-petition interest is not added to the secured claim and is not even allowed as an unsecured claim. 11 U.S.C. § 502(b)(2).

Example: A authenticates a security agreement granting B a security interest in A's equipment then owned or thereafter acquired to secure all obligations then or thereafter owed. At the date of the bankruptcy filing, A owed B $1,000. The equipment that A had an interest in at the time of the bankruptcy filing was valued at $700. B's secured claim is $700 and its unsecured claim is $300. Interest that accrues after the bankruptcy petition is filed is not part of B's allowable claim in A's bankruptcy. If the collateral had been valued at $1,200, the accruing interest on the loan could be added to the value of the secured claim until the value of the collateral is exhausted. Thus, if the collateral was valued at $1,200, B would have a secured claim of $1,000 plus accruing interest to a maximum secured claim of $1,200 (assuming no collateral depreciation or devaluation).

7. Future Advances

Even if the security agreement contains a future advances clause, if the secured party advances value to the debtor after the debtor files bankruptcy, that new value will be unsecured unless the bankruptcy court approves the advance on a secured basis. 11 U.S.C. § 364.

J. Review Questions for Chapter III

Determine whether the following statements are true or false.

1. A security interest always attaches to the described collateral when a debtor authenticates a security agreement containing that collateral description.

2. A security agreement must always be in writing.

3. Using the collateral descriptors defined in the Uniform Commercial Code is considered to be an adequate description of the collateral in all cases.

4. To control a certificated security, the secured party must always take possession of the certificate.

5. To control a deposit account, the secured party must prevent the debtor from having access to the funds in the account.

6. A secured party and debtor may enter into an agreement that the secured party has control of electronic chattel paper.

7. A debtor must have title to the collateral in order to grant a security interest in the collateral.

8. A security agreement must provide that it covers proceeds in order for the security interest to attach to proceeds.

9. A security interest never attaches unless there is a security agreement providing for the security interest.

10. Filing a bankruptcy petition has the effect of stripping off an attached security interest from collateral.

11. If the agreement between the debtor and secured party provides that the debtor may not grant a subsequent security interest in the collateral, the debtor's subsequent grant of a security interest in that collateral to another creditor is void.

12. A rule of law that provides that a right to payment may not be assigned is sufficient to prevent attachment of a security interest to that right to payment.

13. A secured party that has control of collateral pursuant to a security agreement with the debtor has an obligation to release control if the debtor no longer owes an obligation to the secured party and the secured party has no further obligation to give value.

14. Filing a bankruptcy petition prevents a security interest from attaching to the debtor's assets acquired after the filing of the bankruptcy petition unless the assets are proceeds of collateral subject to the security interest prior to the filing of the bankruptcy petition.

15. Any consideration sufficient to support a contract constitutes value for purposes of attachment of a security interest.

16. To attach a security interest, the secured party must advance value to the person who grants the security interest in personal property.

17. Article 9 provides that an agricultural lien will attach to farm products to secure value advanced to a farmer.

18. A person may not grant a security interest in personal property it does not own.

19. A consumer cannot grant a security interest in the consumer's investment property.

20. A secured party must take possession of an instrument in order to attach a security interest to the instrument.

IV

Perfection of a Security Interest or Agricultural Lien

In this Chapter we will consider what it takes to perfect a security interest or agricultural lien in a transaction that is subject to Article 9. Understanding the concept of perfection is critical to understanding the priority rules that we will study in Chapter V. In many circumstances, the priority of a security interest or agricultural lien as against another claim to the item of personal property will depend upon whether the security interest or agricultural lien is considered "perfected" and when perfection was obtained. Perfection of a security interest is not usually critical, however, to the ability of a secured party to enforce its security interest or agricultural lien in the personal property as against the debtor. We will discuss enforcement of the security interest and agricultural lien in Chapter VI.

A. Perfection Overview

In a transaction that is subject to Article 9 (review Chapter II) perfection of a security interest or agricultural lien means that the security interest or agricultural lien has attached (as discussed in Chapter III) and that a required perfection method has been completed. UCC § 9–308(a), (b). The idea behind most, but not all, of the perfection methods permitted under Article 9 is that the method will give notice to interested parties that the secured party has an interest in the debtor's collateral.

1. Types of Perfection Methods

Article 9 provides for five different perfection methods: filing a financing statement, taking possession of collateral, taking control of collateral, merely attaching a security interest to the collateral (known as automatic perfection), or complying with other law. Each of these perfection methods will be explored in this Chapter.

2. Perfection Methods and Collateral Types

Whether one or more of the five types of perfection methods is effective in a transaction depends upon the type of collateral that is the subject of the security interest. For some types of collateral, there may be several permissible methods of perfection. For other types of collateral, there may be only one permissible method of perfection. If a security interest may be perfected by more than one method of perfection, the priority of the security interest may be better if the secured party uses one method instead of another method of perfection.

3. Continuous Perfection

Many of the priority rules we will cover in Chapter V set the priority of the security interest or agricultural lien from the date perfection was obtained or the perfection method was completed. If the secured party fails to maintain perfection of the security interest or agricultural lien, the secured party may lose that priority position. If the security interest or agricultural lien in the collateral is perfected by one method allowed under Article 9 and subsequently perfected by another allowed method, and there is no time in which the security interest or agricultural lien was unperfected, the security interest or agricultural lien is continuously perfected. UCC § 9–308(c).

Example: Secured Party appropriately perfects its security interest by taking possession of a good. Secured Party loses possession of the good. Two days later, Secured Party files a financing statement sufficient to perfect its security interest in the good. Secured Party's security interest is not continuously perfected as there were two days in which Secured Party had taken no act sufficient to perfect its security interest in the good.

Example: Secured Party appropriately perfects its security interest by taking possession of a good. Secured Party then files a financing statement sufficient to perfect its security interest in the good. Secured Party then loses possession of the good. Secured Party's security interest in the good is continuously perfected because at the time Secured Party lost possession of the good, Secured Party had engaged in another sufficient perfection method as to the good, properly filing a financing statement.

4. Choice of Law Issues in Determining Compliance With a Perfection Method

Article 9 is enacted by each state. To determine how to perfect a security interest or agricultural lien, one must first determine what state's version of Article 9 should be consulted to instruct what must be done to perfect a security interest or agricultural lien in the collateral. To the extent action, such as filing a financing statement, must be accomplished in a particular state in order to perfect the security interest or agricultural lien, the choice of law issue is critical. The choice of law issues will be explored in Section G of this Chapter after we have learned the intricacies of the Article 9 perfection rules.

5. Post-Initial Perfection Events That May "Unperfect" a Security Interest or Agricultural Lien

Yet another complication of the perfection scheme of Article 9 is that even though a secured party has properly perfected its security interest or agricultural lien in the collateral, events that take place subsequent to that initial perfection may have the effect of "unperfecting" the security interest or agricultural lien. The secured party, therefore, must be diligent in maintaining perfection of its security interest or agricultural lien in order to give itself the best possible priority position in the collateral. We will explore the events that may result in "unperfection" of a security interest or agricultural lien in Section H of this Chapter.

B. Filing a Financing Statement as a Perfection Method

The dominant method for perfection of a security interest or agricultural lien is filing a financing statement. Unless there is an exception provided in Article 9, filing a financing statement is the only acceptable method for perfecting a security interest or agricultural lien. UCC § 9–310(a). A financing statement is a record filed in a particular state office (such as the Secretary of State) which gives notice of the fact that a secured party may have a security interest in or agricultural lien on collateral of the stated debtor. The requirements of a financing statement are reviewed in this Section B.

1. Agricultural Liens

Because there are no exceptions to the filing of a financing statement to perfect an agricultural lien that falls within the scope of Article 9, filing a financing statement to perfect an agricultural lien is the only method of perfection of that lien in the farm products covered by the lien.

2. Timing of Filing a Financing Statement

A financing statement may be filed before the security interest attaches, UCC § 9–502(d), and will be effective as long as the filing is authorized. UCC §§ 9–510(a), 9–509. A financing statement to perfect an agricultural lien is not authorized to be filed until the agricultural lien actually exists. UCC § 9–509.

3. Collateral Types Where Filing a Financing Statement is Not an Allowed Perfection Step

Filing a financing statement is the required perfection step for perfecting a security interest unless Article 9 states it is not. For a few types of collateral, filing a financing statement is not a permissible method of perfection of a security interest and some other method must be used.

a. Deposit Accounts and Money

A filed financing statement is not a permitted perfection method for security interests in deposit accounts or money, subject to one exception. If the deposit account or money is proceeds of other collateral as to which a secured party has perfected its security interest, the secured party will also be perfected in deposit accounts and money that are identifiable proceeds of that original collateral. Thus if a filed financing statement is a sufficient perfection method for the original collateral, that filing as to the original collateral is a sufficient perfection method as to a security interest in deposit accounts and money that are identifiable proceeds of that original collateral. UCC §§ 9–312(b), 9–315(d)(2).

b. Letter-of-Credit Rights

A filed financing statement is not a permitted perfection method for a security interest in letter-of-credit rights, subject to two exceptions. First, if a letter-of-credit right constitutes identifiable proceeds of other collateral in which a security interest is perfected by a properly-filed financing statement, that filing is sufficient perfection as to the letter-of-credit right as identifiable proceeds of the original collateral for a short period of time. UCC §§ 9–312(b), 9–315(c), (d). Second, if the letter-of-credit right is a supporting obligation as to a right to payment as to which a filed financing statement is a sufficient method of perfection, then that filing as to the right to payment is a sufficient perfection method as to the letter-of-credit right as the supporting obligation. UCC §§ 9–312(b); 9–308(d).

c. Collateral Subject to Another Type of Filing System

Article 9 explicitly provides that a filed financing statement under Article 9 is not sufficient to perfect a security interest in collateral if some other law already provides a system for perfecting the security interest. If so, compliance with the other law is equivalent to the filing of a financing statement to perfect the security interest and the security interest is otherwise subject to Article 9. UCC § 9–311(b), (c).

(1) Federal Law

The first circumstance in which Article 9 defers to other filing systems is when a federal statute, treaty, or regulation provides a method for a secured party to obtain priority over the rights of a lien creditor and that method preempts Article 9. UCC § 9–311(a)(1). This type of federal preemption is narrower than the federal preemption provided for in UCC § 9–109(c)(1). The federal preemption in UCC § 9–109(c)(1) preempts all of Article 9. (Review material in Chapter II.) The federal preemption in UCC § 9–311(a)(1) preempts only the filing system of Article 9, leaving the remaining rules in Article 9 as governing law. UCC § 9–311(c). An example of this type of statute that preempts the filing rules in Article 9 but not the rest of Article 9 is the federal aviation act for registration of interests in aircraft. UCC § 9–311, cmt. 2.

(2) Certificate of Title Systems

The second circumstance in which Article 9 defers to another filing system is when a certificate of title law of a state provides that security interests are to be noted on the certificate of title as a condition to or result of perfection. UCC § 9–311(a)(2), (3).

(a) Certificate of Title Defined

A certificate of title law refers to a statute in which the notation on the certificate (including an electronic record if maintained by the same governmental unit that issues a certificate of title) is a condition to or result of a secured party obtaining priority over the rights of a lien creditor regarding the collateral covered by the certificate of title. UCC § 9–102(a)(10). If the relevant certificate of title law does not require that notation on the certificate (or the electronic record) as a condition to or result of perfection, it is not a certificate of title law to which Article 9 defers.

(b) Typical Coverage

Certificates of title are generally issued by a state's department of motor vehicles. While automobiles and trucks are generally subject to certificate of title laws, coverage of other motorized vehicles, such as snowmobiles, motorcycles, all terrain vehicles, boats, construction equipment, or farm equipment, varies widely from state to state.

(c) Exception to the Deference to Certificate of Title Laws

Even if the motorized vehicle is subject to the right kind of certificate of title law, during any period where that motorized vehicle is held as inventory for sale or lease, compliance with the certificate of title law is not the applicable perfection step for perfecting a security interest in that vehicle. UCC § 9–311(d).

Example: Dealer holds automobiles for sale. Bank has a security interest in Dealer's inventory pursuant to an authenticated security agreement. To perfect its security interest in Dealer's automobiles held for sale (the inventory), Bank cannot do so through noting its security interest on the automobiles' certificates of title but must use one of the other permissible perfection steps. Bank will likely file a financing statement covering the inventory of automobiles as its perfection step.

(3) Other Central Filing Systems

The third circumstance in which Article 9 defers to another filing system is when the state law provides for a central filing system other than Article 9 for a particular type of collateral. UCC § 9–311(a)(2). Obviously the other types of collateral where this exception is applied varies widely from state to state.

4. The Requirements of the Financing Statement

A financing statement is a record that is filed in a designated office. The financing statement may be in paper form, or if the designated office permits, electronic form. If it is in paper form and the filing office accepts paper forms, the filing office must accept the prescribed standard form set out in UCC § 9–521. The first filed record is referred to as the initial financing statement.

a. Sufficiency to Perfect as Opposed to Requirement of Additional Information to Prevent Rejection of the Record

That record must contain certain information in order to be sufficient as the perfection method. UCC § 9–502. Other information is included in the record, some of which, if not included, provides a basis for the filing office to reject the record. UCC § 9–516. We will first discuss the requirements of the financing statement for sufficiency as a perfection method and then discuss the other information as it relates to the ability of the filing office to reject the record.

b. Philosophy of Notice Filing

The Article 9 filing system is a system for providing notice that someone might have an interest in some of the debtor's personal property. It is not expected to be a system that functions like the real estate recording system where the state of the title as to a particular item of real estate can be determined through an examination of the public record. It is expected that in order to determine the state of interests in the debtor's personal property, the person that searches and finds a financing statement filed against the debtor will have to make a further inquiry into more facts than are shown on the public record in order to determine the nature and extent of interests in the debtor's personal property. UCC § 9–502, cmt. 2.

c. Requirements for Sufficiency of the Financing Statement as a Method Of Perfection

To be sufficient to perfect a security interest or agricultural lien, the financing statement must not only be appropriate for the type of collateral at stake, the financing statement must also provide for three items of information: (i) the debtor's name; (ii) the secured party's name or the name of the secured party's representative; and (iii) an indication of the collateral. UCC § 9–502(a). If there is a mistake in any of these three items and the filed financing statement is the only method of perfection the secured party has used, the secured party is subject to an argument that its security interest or agricultural lien is unperfected.

(1) Real Estate Related Collateral
If the collateral is as-extracted collateral, timber to be cut, or fixtures where a fixture financing statement is to be filed, the financing statement must contain the three requirements for a financing statement and several additional items. Those additional items are: (i) an indication that the type of collateral is as-extracted collateral, timber to be cut, or fixtures; (ii) an indication that the statement is to be filed in the real estate records; (iii) a real property description for the real estate that is related to the as-extracted collateral, timber to be cut, or fixtures; and (iv) the name of the record owner of the real estate if the debtor does not have an interest in the real estate. UCC § 9–502(b). A mortgage may satisfy these requirements as to as-extracted collateral, timber to be cut, and fixtures related to the real estate that is subject to the mortgage as long as the mortgage indicates the goods or accounts it covers and the mortgage is properly recorded in the real estate records. UCC § 9–502(c).

(2) **The Debtor's Name**

The financing statement must provide the debtor's name in order to be sufficient to perfect a security interest or agricultural lien. Whether the debtor's name is correct on the financing statement depends upon whether the name meets the standard set forth in UCC § 9–503. The financing statements are indexed by the debtor's name in the filing office. UCC § 9–519(c). For searchers, knowing the debtor's correct name in order to find financing statements filed against that debtor is critical. Article 9 places the burden of getting the name correct on the filer of the financing statement. In any situation where the name of the debtor is not stated correctly on the financing statement under the standards set forth in UCC § 9–503, the secured party seeking to maintain perfected status will argue that the debtor's name on the financing statement is nonetheless sufficient for purposes of perfection because the name is not seriously misleading under UCC § 9–506. That argument will be considered *infra*.

(a) **Identification of the Debtor**

The entities listed on the financing statement as the debtors must be the persons that have a property interest (other than a lien interest) in the collateral covered in the financing statement. UCC § 9–102(a)(28) (definition of debtor).

(b) **Entity Type**

The correct name of the debtor depends upon what type of entity the debtor is: a registered organization, a nonregistered organization, a decedent, a trust, or an individual. The rules regarding the correct name of the debtor are found in UCC § 9–503 and explored *infra*.

(c) **Organizations**

An organization is a corporation, business trust, estate, trust, partnership, limited liability company, association, joint venture, government, government agency or subdivision, or any other legal or commercial entity. UCC § 1–201(b)(25), (27). Organizations are either "registered organizations" or nonregistered organizations.

(i) Registered Organizations

A registered organization is an organization that is "formed or organized" under the law of one state or of the United States by one of three methods: (i) by filing a "public organic record" with a governmental entity; (ii) by a government entity issuing a "public organic record"; or, (iii) by an enactment of a state or the United States. UCC § 9–102(a)(71). A registered organization can include a business trust if a state statute requires the trust's organic public record be filed with the state. The typical registered organization is a corporation.

(a) Public organic record

A public organic record is a record available for public inspection and which is one of three things, depending upon the method by which the organization is formed or organized. If the organization is "formed or organized" by filing a record with a governmental entity, the "public organic record" is that initial record and any filing that amends or restates the initial record. If the organization is "formed or organized" by a governmental entity issuing a record, the "public organic record" is the initial record issued by the governmental entity and any filing that amends that initial record or any record issued by the governmental entity that amends the initial record. If the organization is "formed or organized" by the enactment of a state or the United States, the "public organic record" is the initial enactment, any subsequent amending enactment, and any record filed with or issued by the state or the United States which "amends or restates the name of the organization." If the statute of a state requires a business trust to file its organizational documents, the "public organic record" is the initial record so filed, and any subsequent filed record which amends or restates the initial record. UCC § 9–102(a)(68).

(b) Name of a Registered Organization

The financing statement must show the debtor's name as the name is stated in the debtor's most recently filed, issued, or enacted public organic record which purports to state, amend or restate the debtor's name. UCC § 9–503(a)(1).

Example: ABC Corporation is incorporated in the state of Minnesota. In the public organic record filed in the Minnesota Secretary of State's office, the name of the corporation is "ABC Corporation." The debtor's correct name which should be on the financing statement to comply with the requirement of the debtor's name is "ABC Corporation." "ABC Corp." or "ABC Inc." would not satisfy the requirement of showing the debtor's correct name under the test of UCC § 9–503(a)(1).

(ii) Nonregistered Organizations

If the debtor is an organization but is not a registered organization, the correct name of the debtor is the "organizational name" of the debtor. UCC §§ 9–503(a)(6) (Alt. A), 9–503(a)(5) (Alt. B). Exactly how to determine this name is left to the secured party without any guidance in the text or comments. If the debtor does not have an "organizational name," the financing statement must provide the names of the partners, members, associates or persons that comprise the debtor. UCC §§ 9–503(a)(6) (Alt. A), 9–503(a)(5) (Alt. B). These names must meet the standard for names of that type as set forth in UCC § 9–503.

Example: The debtor is a partnership of two brothers, Joe and Al Jones, engaged in the business of running a plumbing service. Under relevant state law, a partnership is not a registered organization as defined in Article 9. On the side of the truck and on the store front, the name of the business is "Plumbing Brothers." That may be the partnership name. If it is, that name is the name of the debtor. If it is not the partnership name, then the names of the individuals making up the partnership are the correct name of the debtor. The names of the individuals must comply with the rules regarding how to state an individual's name on a financing statement.

(d) Decedent's Name

If collateral is being administered by a decedent's personal representative, the correct name of the debtor on the financing statement is the name of the decedent. UCC § 9–503(a)(2). The name of the decedent is the name indicated on the order appointing the personal representative. UCC § 9–503(f). The financing statement must also indicate that a personal representative is administering the decedent's assets. UCC § 9–503(a)(2).

(e) Trust

If collateral is held in a trust that is a registered organization, then the rules regarding the name of a registered organization as discussed *supra* will control. UCC § 9–503(a)(1). If the trust is not a registered organization, the correct name of the debtor on the financing statement is the name of the trust in its organic record. If the trust does not have a name specified in the organic record, the name of the settlor or testator of the trust is the debtor's name.

(i) Name of Settlor or Testator

If the settlor is a registered organization, the name of the settlor is the name as stated on the public organic record most recently filed, issued, or enacted which purports to state, amend or restate the settlor's name. In all other cases, the name of the settlor or testator is the name indicated in the trust's organic record. UCC § 9–503(h).

(ii) Additional Information Required

If the debtor's name is the name of the settler or testator, the financing statement must also provide any information necessary to distinguish the debtor from other trusts of the same settlor or testator. In any case in which the trust is not a registered organization, the financing statement must also indicate that the collateral is held in a trust. UCC § 9–503(a)(3).

(f) Individuals

If the debtor is an individual, the individual's name must be provided on the financing statement. Article 9 provides the states two alternatives (Alternative A or Alternative B) for enactment regarding what constitutes an individual debtor's name for purpose of the financing statement. UCC § 9–503(a)(4).

(i) Alternative A

If the state in which the financing statement must be filed to perfect as to the collateral (see *infra* Section G regarding choice of law) chose Alternative A, has issued a driver's license to the debtor, and that license is unexpired, the debtor's name is the name on the license. If the state has issued more than one license, then the most recently issued license is the one to use. UCC § 9–503(g). If the state has not issued a driver's license to the debtor, or the issued license is expired, the debtor's name is either the debtor's "individual name" or the debtor's surname and first personal name.

Example: The debtor is an individual with a driver's license that shows her name as "Mary K. Smith," a social security card that shows her name as "Mary Kay Smith," and tax returns filed with the name "Mary Smith." She signs her name "M. Kay Smith" when she is acting in her capacity as a professional accountant. She is married and in social circles is known as either "Kay Smith" or "Kay Smith Johnson." Johnson is her husband's name. If the driver's license is issued by the state in which the financing statement must be filed as to that particular collateral type, and that license is not expired, the name for the financing statement is "Mary K. Smith", with "Smith" as the surname, "Mary" as the first personal name and "K." as the initial. If another state has issued the driver's license or the issued driver's license has expired, then the debtor's name is her "individual name" (which is difficult to discern with any certainty) or her "surname" and first personal name. Her surname is either "Smith" or "Johnson" and her first personal name is "Mary."

(ii) **Alternative B**

If the state in which the financing statement must be filed to perfect as to the collateral (see *infra* Section G regarding choice of law) choose Alternative B, a secured party may use any one of three alternatives as the debtor's name: the "individual name"; the surname and first personal name; or the name indicated on the driver's license issued by that state in and that is not expired. If the state has issued more than one license, then the most recently issued license is the one to use. UCC § 9–503(g).

Example: The debtor is an individual with a driver's license that shows her name as "Mary K. Smith," a social security card that shows her name as "Mary Kay Smith," and tax returns filed with the name "Mary Smith." She signs her name "M. Kay Smith" when she is acting in her capacity as a professional accountant. She is married and in social circles is known as either "Kay Smith" or "Kay Smith Johnson." Johnson is her husband's name. The debtor's name is one of the following: her "individual name" (which is difficult to discern with any certainty); her "surname" and first personal name (surname is either "Smith" or "Johnson" and her first personal name is "Mary"); or if the driver's license is issued by the state in which the financing statement must be filed as to that particular collateral type, and that license is not expired, "Mary K. Smith" ("Smith" as the surname, "Mary" as the first personal name and "K." as the initial).

(iii) **Mortgage Filed as to Fixtures, As-Extracted Collateral, or Timber to be Cut**

For a mortgage that is filed for fixtures, as-extracted collateral, or timber to be cut, the name of a debtor that is an individual must be either the "individual name" of the debtor, or the surname and first personal name of the debtor. This is an exception to the requirements stated in UCC § 9–503(a)(4) in either an Alternative A or B state. UCC § 9–502(c)(3)(B).

(g) Trade Names

Trade names are not part of the debtor's correct name. UCC § 9–503(b)(1). A financing statement that lists only the debtor's trade name as the name of the debtor has not sufficiently provided the name of the debtor. UCC § 9–503(c).

Example: The debtor is a partnership of two brothers, Joe and Al Jones, engaged in the business of running a plumbing service. Under relevant state law, the partnership is not a registered organization under Article 9. On the side of the truck and on the store front, the name of the business is "Plumbing Brothers." That name may be a trade name or it may be the name of the partnership (see *supra* regarding "organizational name"). If it is a trade name, using that name as the name of the debtor will not be sufficient to perfect an interest in the partnership's property.

(h) Multiple Debtors

A financing statement may provide more than one debtor on the financing statement. UCC § 9–503(e).

(i) Seriously Misleading Financing Statements Due to Errors in the Debtor's Name

If a financing statement contains errors in the debtor's name so that it is seriously misleading, the financing statement is insufficient to perfect the security interest or agricultural lien. UCC § 9–506(a). The "correct name" must be on the financing statement at the time someone searches for the financing statement. A financing statement that does not provide the debtor's correct name as provided in UCC § 9–503(a) is per se seriously misleading. UCC § 9–506(b). That "per se seriously misleading" rule is subject to one exception. If a search of the records at the filing office under the debtor's correct name turns up the financing statement with the incorrect name on it, that financing statement with the incorrect name is deemed to not be seriously misleading and thus deemed to be sufficient to perfect, providing the other requirements of Article 9 as related to that financing statement are met. UCC § 9–506(c). The search has to be in accordance with the filing office's standard search logic. The standard search logic will vary from filing office to filing office depending upon the computer technology and procedures utilized. The seriously misleading test also applies to the additional information that is required in UCC § 9–503(a)(2) regarding collateral being administered by a personal representative and in UCC § 9–503(a)(3) regarding collateral held in a trust that is not a registered organization. UCC § 9–506, cmt. 2.

Example: The debtor is a registered organization with the name "ABC Corporation" shown in the public organic record filed with the Secretary of State of the jurisdiction of organization. The financing statement was filed using "ABC Corp." as the name of the debtor. Under the filing office's standard search logic, a search of the records under "ABC Corporation" turned up the financing statement listing "ABC Corp." The use of the name "ABC Corp." on the financing statement was not seriously misleading.

Example: The debtor is a registered organization with the name "ABC Corporation" shown in the public organic record filed with the Secretary of State of the jurisdiction of organization. The financing statement was filed using "ABC Corp." as the name of the debtor. Under the filing office's standard search logic, a search of the records under "ABC Corporation" did not turn up the financing statement listing "ABC Corp." The use of the name "ABC Corp." on the financing statement was seriously misleading and thus the financing statement will be insufficient to perfect the security interest or agricultural lien (as applicable).

Example: The debtor is an individual with a driver's license that shows her name as "Mary K. Smith," a social security card that shows her name as "Mary Kay Smith," and tax returns filed with the name "Mary Smith." She signs her name "M. Kay Smith" when she is acting in her capacity as a professional accountant. She is married and in social circles is known as either "Kay Smith" or "Kay Smith Johnson." Johnson is her husband's name. The secured party filed a financing statement listing the debtor's name as "Mary Kay Smith."

In an Alternative A state, the "correct name" was "Mary K. Smith" as shown on her unexpired driver's license issued by that state. Under the standard search logic of the filing office, a search under "Mary K. Smith" does not reveal the financing statement that provided the debtor's name as "Mary Kay Smith." The financing statement is per se seriously misleading and thus insufficient to perfect a security interest or agricultural lien (as applicable).

In an Alternative B state, the court may find that the debtor's "individual name" is "Mary Kay Smith" and thus the filed financing statement is sufficient.

(3) The Secured Party's Name

To be sufficient to perfect a security interest or agricultural lien, the financing statement must also provide the name of the secured party or a representative of the secured party. UCC § 9–502(a)(2). The financing statement may provide more than one secured party's name. UCC § 9–503(e). If the financing statement names a representative of the secured party, failure to indicate the representative status of that person does not render the financing statement insufficient to perfect. UCC § 9–503(d).

(a) Function of Listing the Secured Party's Name on the Financing Statement

The financing statements are not indexed by the secured party's name. The function of the secured party's name on the financing statement is to provide information to searchers about who to contact to determine the extent of the secured party's claim to the collateral.

(b) **Seriously Misleading Financing Statements Due to Errors in the Secured Party's Name**

If the financing statement contains errors in the secured party's name, those errors could conceivably be seriously misleading under the general standard stated in UCC § 9–506(a). The comments to that section indicate, however, that "an error in the name of the secured party or its representative will not be seriously misleading" although it may give rise to an estoppel argument in an appropriate case. UCC § 9–506, cmt. 2.

(4) **The Indication of Collateral**

To be sufficient to perfect a security interest or an agricultural lien, the financing statement must also contain an indication of the collateral. UCC § 9–502(a)(3). To properly indicate the collateral, the financing statement must meet one of two tests. Either it must follow the rules for collateral description in UCC § 9–108 discussed in Chapter III, or it must indicate that the financing statement covers "all assets" or "all personal property." UCC § 9–504.

(a) **Distinguished From Security Agreements**

Although an "all assets" or "all personal property" description is not a sufficient description of collateral in a security agreement, UCC § 9–108(c), it may be a sufficient indication of collateral in a financing statement.

(b) **Seriously Misleading Financing Statements Due to Errors or Omissions in Collateral Indication**

A financing statement may be seriously misleading if there are errors or omissions in the collateral indication. UCC § 9–506(a). If there are seriously misleading errors or omissions in the collateral indication, the financing statement is insufficient to perfect a security interest or agricultural lien in the misdescribed or undescribed collateral.

(5) **Future Advances and After-Acquired Property Clauses**

A financing statement is sufficient to perfect even if it does not indicate that the collateral secures future advances or that the financing statement covers after-acquired collateral. UCC § 9–502, cmt. 2.

d. Other Information Required in the Financing Statement

Article 9 provides that a filing office must refuse to accept a financing statement if it does not have certain types of information or for other reasons specified in UCC § 9–516(b) but only for those specified reasons. UCC §§ 9–516(b), 9–520(a). The idea of the Article 9 filing system is that it is an "open drawer." That is, the filing office does not screen financing statements for correctness or sufficiency, but rather takes the filing as offered with a limited number of very specific grounds for rejecting the filing.

(1) Distinguished From Requirements for Sufficiency to Perfect Under UCC § 9–502

Accurate information of the type listed in UCC § 9–516(b) is not required in order for a financing statement to be sufficient to perfect. If the filing office accepts the financing statement, even if the filing office should have refused the financing statement, the sufficiency of the financing statement for purposes of perfection is tested under UCC § 9–502 as described *supra*, not the requirements of UCC § 9–516(b). UCC § 9–520(c).

(2) Grounds for the Filing Office to Refuse to Accept the Financing Statement Stated in UCC § 9–516(b)

Under UCC § 9–516(b), a filing office may refuse to accept a filing if any of the following occurs: (i) the method or manner of communication of the filing is not allowed; (ii) the applicable fee is not tendered; (iii) the filing office is not able to index the record because the debtor's name is not provided on an initial financing statement, the filing of an amendment or correction statement does not reference the initial financing statement or the initial financing statement has lapsed, an individual debtor's surname is not provided, or a real estate related filing does not provide an adequate real estate description; (iv) the record does not provide a secured party's mailing address; (v) the record does not provide the debtor's mailing address; (vi) the record does not indicate that the debtor is an individual or organization; (vii) the record is an assignment of an initial financing statement and does not indicate the name and mailing address of the assignee; and (viii) the record is a continuation statement that is not filed during the time period permitted for continuation statements.

Example: SP tenders a financing statement that correctly lists the debtor's name, SP's name and the collateral. The financing statement does not contain a mailing address for the debtor. The filing office refuses to accept the financing statement. That refusal is rightful as the debtor's mailing address is one of those items of information that is listed in UCC § 9–516(b).

Example: SP tenders a financing statement that correctly lists the debtor's name, SP's name and the collateral. The financing statement does not contain a mailing address for the debtor. The filing office accepts the financing statement even though it should have refused the financing statement under UCC § 9–516(b) and § 9–520(a). The sufficiency of the filing depends upon whether the debtor's name, SP's name and the collateral indiction comply with UCC § 9–502. The absence of the debtor's mailing address does not affect the sufficiency of the financing statement as the perfection method.

(3) Inability to Read or Decipher Information

If the filing office cannot read or decipher the information, the information is considered not provided. UCC § 9–516(c)(1).

(4) Effect of a Wrongfully-Refused Financing Statement

If the filing office refuses to accept a financing statement for a reason other than as allowed under UCC § 9–516(b), the filing is still considered effective except as to a purchaser of the collateral that gives value in reasonable reliance upon the absence of the financing statement from the files. UCC § 9–516(d).

Example: SP tenders a financing statement that correctly lists the debtor's name, SP's name and the collateral and contains the information specified in UCC § 9–516(b). The filing office rejects the filing and that rejection is wrongful. The financing statement is effective as a filed financing statement except as to a purchaser of the described collateral that gives value in reliance on the fact that the financing statement is not in the filed records for that debtor.

5. Authority to File

In order for a financing statement to be effective to perfect a security interest or agricultural lien, the secured party must have authority to file the financing statement. UCC §§ 9–510(a), 9–509. If the secured party does not have authority to file the financing statement, the financing statement is not effective to perfect a security interest or agricultural lien in the indicated collateral.

a. To Perfect a Security Interest

In order to file an effective initial financing statement, the debtor must authorize the filing in an authenticated record. UCC § 9–509(a)(1). The debtor's authentication of the security agreement automatically authorizes the secured party to file a financing statement covering the collateral described in the security agreement and any collateral that is identifiable proceeds of that original collateral. UCC § 9–509(b). The debtor also automatically authorizes the filing of a financing statement as to collateral the debtor acquires that is subject to a security interest. UCC § 9–509(c). Because a secured party may file a financing statement before the security interest attaches, UCC § 9–502(d), the secured party may get authority for that filing by having the debtor sign an authenticated record with the authority to file the financing statement before the debtor signs the security agreement.

b. To Perfect an Agricultural Lien

In order to file an effective initial financing statement covering farm products subject to an agricultural lien, the secured party must actually have an agricultural lien in the farm products at the time of the filing and the financing statement may cover only those farm products that are subject to the agricultural lien. UCC § 9–509(a)(2).

c. Ratification

If the secured party does not have authority to file a financing statement at the time it filed the statement, subsequent acts of the debtor may ratify the secured party's act of filing the financing statement, rendering it an authorized filing. Comment 3 to UCC § 9–509 and Comment 4 to UCC § 9–322 state that the filing should be given retroactive effect for purposes of establishing priority of the security interest or agricultural lien. Whether courts will agree is unclear.

Example: SP and Debtor discuss a possible loan transaction. In light of the discussion, SP files a financing statement against Debtor that complies with UCC § 9–502 and § 9–516. Debtor did not authenticate a record giving SP authority to file the financing statement. The financing statement is ineffective.

Example: SP and Debtor discuss a possible loan transaction. In light of the discussion, SP files a financing statement against Debtor that complies with UCC § 9–502 and § 9–516. Debtor did not authenticate a record giving SP authority to file the financing statement. Several days later, Debtor signs a security agreement granting SP a security interest in the collateral. The collateral description in the security agreement is the same as the description in the financing statement and complies with UCC § 9–108. Debtor's signing of the security agreement gives SP the authority to file the financing statement. The comments suggest that the financing statement is retroactively effective on the date it was filed for purposes of determining the priority of the security interest.

6. The Process of Filing

Each filing office will set protocols for filing of financing statements. The filing office will determine whether it takes electronic filings and the form of those filings. If the filing office takes paper financing statements, it must accept the standard form set forth in UCC § 9–521, although a significant number of states have provided an exception to that rule.

a. Determining the Correct Filing Office

Determining the correct filing office within a state is relatively easy once it is determined in which state the filing should take place. The determination of the correct state in which to file is a matter of choice of law principles that will be discussed in Section G *infra*. Once the correct state is determined, the next question is which office within the state is the correct place to file the financing statement.

(1) Central Filing

Article 9 adopted a central filing office rule, that is, most filings will be within one office within a state. The correct state office is designated by the state and is usually the state's secretary of state's office. A secured party will file a financing statement in the designated state office for all collateral except for three types of real estate related collateral. UCC § 9–501(a).

(2) Local Filing

When the collateral is fixtures and the secured party files a fixture financing statement as set forth in UCC § 9–502(b) (discussed in Section B.4. *supra*), as-extracted collateral, or timber to be cut, the correct office in which to file the financing statement is the office where a real estate mortgage would be recorded for the real estate that is described in the financing statement. UCC § 9–501(a)(1). This is referred to as local filing. Local filing for this type of collateral is subject to two exceptions.

(a) Perfecting in Fixtures as Goods Without a Fixture Filing

If a secured party wants to perfect in fixtures as goods and not file a fixture financing statement in the real estate recording office, the correct office in which to file the financing statement is the central filing office, that is, the state's secretary of state's office. UCC § 9–501(a)(2). Filing a fixture financing statement gives the secured party the opportunity to assert priority over some types of real estate claimants, such as mortgagees. UCC § 9–334. Priority in fixtures will be discussed in Chapter V.

(b) Perfecting in Fixtures of a Transmitting Utility

To perfect a security interest in the collateral of a transmitting utility, including fixtures located in that state, the financing statement will be filed in the state's central filing office. The filing of the financing statement in the central office will satisfy the requirement of a fixture financing statement for fixtures located in that state without being filed in the local real estate recording office. UCC § 9–501(b). A transmitting utility is defined as a person operating a railroad or similar railway system such as a subway, transmitting communications, transmitting goods by pipeline or sewer, or transmitting electricity, steam, water, or gas. UCC § 9–102(a)(81).

b. What Constitutes Filing

Tender of the financing statement and applicable fee to the filing office constitute filing of the financing statement. UCC § 9–516(a). The financing statement is filed unless the filing office rightfully rejects the financing statement for the reasons stated in UCC § 9–516(b). UCC § 9–516(d).

c. Rejection of a Financing Statement

The filing office may rightfully reject a financing statement only for the reasons stated in UCC § 9–516(b) (Section B.4 *supra*). The filing office is not supposed to review the financing statement to determine if it is sufficient to perfect a security interest or agricultural lien or whether the debtor has authorized it to be filed. UCC § 9–520(a), cmt. 2.

(1) Notification of Rejection
If the filing office rejects the financing statement, the filing office must notify the secured party that the financing statement has been rejected, the reasons for the rejection, and the date and time the financing statement would have been filed if not rejected. UCC § 9–520(b).

(2) Partial Rejections
Whether a financing statement fulfills the requirements of UCC § 9–516(b) is evaluated for each debtor. If the information required by UCC § 9–516(b) is given for one debtor but not another, the filing office must accept the financing statement for the debtor whose information is complete and reject it for the debtor whose information is not complete. UCC § 9–520(d).

7. Time Period That a Filed Financing Statement is Effective

A filed financing statement that is sufficient under UCC § 9–502 as to the type of collateral as to which a filed financing statement is a sufficient perfection method is generally effective for five years from the date of filing. UCC § 9–515(a). This general rule is subject to several exceptions for certain types of financing statements.

a. Public-Finance Transactions

If an initial financing statement is filed with respect to a public-finance transaction, the financing statement is effective for a period of 30 years from the date of filing if the financing statement indicates it is filed in connection with a public-finance transaction. UCC § 9–515(b). A public-finance transaction is defined as a secured transaction in which debt securities are issued, the securities have an initial stated maturity of 20 years or more, and any of the parties (debtor, obligor, secured party, or a person obligated on collateral) are a state or governmental unit of a state. UCC § 9–102(a)(67).

b. Manufactured-Home Transactions

If an initial financing statement is filed with respect to a manufactured-home transaction, the financing statement is effective for a period of 30 years from the date of filing if the financing statement indicates it is filed in connection with a manufactured-home transaction. UCC § 9–515(b). A manufactured-home transaction is defined as a secured transaction that creates a purchase money security interest in the manufactured home in which the manufactured home is the primary collateral. A manufactured-home transaction does not include a secured transaction where the manufactured home is the debtor's inventory. UCC § 9–102(a)(54).

c. Transmitting Utility

If the debtor is a transmitting utility and an initial filed financing statement indicates that the debtor is a transmitting utility, the financing statement is effective until the financing statement is terminated through another filing. UCC § 9–515(f). Termination statements are described in Section B.10, *infra*.

d. Mortgages

If a creditor files a mortgage that qualifies as a fixture financing statement, the mortgage is effective as a fixture financing statement until the mortgage is released or terminated as to the real property it covers. UCC § 9–515(g).

8. Lapse and Continuation of Period of Effectiveness of a Financing Statement

A financing statement lapses at the end of the 5-year or 30-year term, as applicable. UCC § 9–515(c).

a. Effect of Lapse

Upon lapse, the financing statement is ineffective to perfect a security interest or agricultural lien rendering the security interest or agricultural lien unperfected. The lapsed financing statement is also deemed ineffective to perfect a security interest or agricultural lien as against a person that purchased the collateral for value prior to its lapse. UCC § 9–515(c). This retroactive unperfection is important when determining priority of the security interest or agricultural lien as against other interests in the collateral. Priority issues are considered in Chapter V.

b. Continuation Statement Extends Effectiveness of Financing Statement

In order to continue the effectiveness of the financing statement beyond the 5-year or 30-year term as indicated above, a secured party must file a continuation statement within the last six months of either the 5-year or 30-year time period, as applicable. UCC § 9–515(d). A continuation statement filed outside that six-month window is ineffective to continue the effectiveness of the financing statement. UCC § 9–510(c).

(1) Continuation Statement Defined
   A continuation statement is an amendment of a financing statement that contains a reference to the unique filing number assigned to the initial financing statement and indicates that it is filed as a continuation statement or that it is filed to extend the effectiveness of the initial financing statement. UCC § 9–102(a)(27).

(2) Authority to File Continuation Statement
   A continuation statement is effective only if the secured party has authority to file it. UCC § 9–510(a). A secured party has authority to file a continuation statement, which is a type of amendment of the initial financing statement, in the same circumstances in which the secured

party has authority to file the initial financing statement. UCC § 9–509(a) and (b).

(3) Effect of Continuation Statement

If the continuation statement is timely filed, it continues the effectiveness of the financing statement for 5 years from the date the initial financing statement that was continued would have otherwise lapsed. UCC § 9–515(e).

> *Example:* Bank properly filed the original financing statement on June 1, 2007. The financing statement will lapse after June 1, 2012. The Bank filed a proper continuation statement on May 1, 2012. The effectiveness of the original financing statement is continued for another five years from June 1, 2012, that is until June 1, 2017.

(4) Successive Continuation Statements

A secured party may file successive continuation statements to continue the effectiveness of a financing statement indefinitely as long as the secured party has the authority to file the continuation statements. Each successive continuation statement must be filed in the six-month window prior to the end of the period of effectiveness of the currently effective financing statement. UCC § 9–515(e).

9. Duties of Filing Officers

As already noted, the filing officer has an obligation to accept a financing statement that complies with the requirements of UCC § 9–516(b). UCC § 9–520(a). In addition, as already noted, the filing office also has the duty to accept the standard form if the filing office accepts paper forms. UCC § 9–521. The filing office may charge a fee for accepting filings, indexing, searching, and other services the filing office provides. UCC § 9–525. The filing office may prescribe administrative rules that regulate its operation. Those rules must be consistent with the rules found in Article 9. UCC §§ 9–526, 9–527. The standard search logic that was discussed in connection with errors in the debtor's name is an example of the type of information that is contained in the filing office's administrative rules. Article 9 prescribes certain other duties for filing officers. As with the requirement to accept the standard form provided in UCC § 9–521, a state may not have adopted some of these requirements.

a. Acknowledge Filings

If the person that files a paper financing statement with the filing office requests, the filing office must provide an acknowledgment of the filing that contains the unique filing number and the date and time of the filing. UCC § 9–523(a). If the person filing a financing statement files a non-paper financing statement, the filing office must acknowledge the information in the record, the number assigned to the record, and the date and time the record was filed. UCC § 9–523(b).

b. Assign a Unique Number to the Initial Financing Statement

When an initial financing statement is filed, the filing office assigns a unique number to that record. UCC § 9–519(a)(1), (b). That unique number must then be placed on all subsequent amendments of that financing statement, including continuation statements, so that the initial financing statements and all associated records can be retrieved based upon that unique number. UCC § 9–519(f).

c. Maintain a Public Record of Financing Statements Filed

The filing office must maintain a record showing the financing statements filed, the number assigned to the financing statements, and the date and time the financing statements were filed. The financing statements must be available for public inspection, UCC § 9–519(a), and must be offered for sale or license to the public on a regular basis, UCC § 9–523(f). Financing statements include not only the initial financing statement but any record related to the initial financing statement, including all amendments. UCC § 9–102(a)(39). The filing office must maintain a record of the information in a financing statement for at least one year after the lapse of the effectiveness of the financing statement. UCC § 9–522(a). The filing office may destroy the "original" financing statement if allowed to do so under state statutes regarding maintenance of public records, but if the filing office does destroy the "original" financing statement, the filing office must maintain a copy of the information from the "original" financing statement. UCC § 9–522(b).

d. Index the Financing Statements by the Debtor's Name

The filing office must index all financing statements and related records by the debtor's name. UCC § 9–519(c). The filing office may not remove the debtor's name from the index until after one year after the financing statement lapses. UCC § 9–519(g). If the collateral is as-extracted collateral, timber to be cut, or fixtures, and the secured party has filed the financing statement in the real estate records, the filing must also be indexed under the name of the record owner of the real estate. If the real estate record system allows for it, the real estate related filing must also be indexed under the secured party's name as if the secured party was the mortgagee, and under the description of the real estate. UCC § 9–519(d), (e). The filing office's failure to correctly index a financing statement does not render the financing statement insufficient to perfect the security interest or agricultural lien. UCC § 9–517. The filing office may have immunity from liability for mistakes in maintaining the public record. *See e.g.* Minn. Stat. § 336.9–531.

e. Allow for Search and Retrieval of Financing Statements

The filing office must maintain the capability of retrieving the financing statement and all associated records by the debtor's name and by the unique filing number. UCC § 9–519(f).

(1) Time for Response
The filing office must respond to a search request for all financing statements filed as to a specific debtor within two business days of the filing office receiving the request. UCC § 9–523(e).

(2) Content of Response
The filing office search response must consist of the information from all of the financing statements that identify the specific debtor as a debtor on the financing statement and the date and time that each financing statement was filed. The searcher may request all financing statements that have not lapsed as to that debtor or all financing statements, including lapsed financing statements, that are still in the filing office records. The filing office must indicate a date and time at which the records were on file, but not more than 3 days before the search request. UCC § 9–523(c).

Example: On June 5, 2005, a person requested a search from the filing office of all financing statements on file against Debtor. Two days later, the filing office sent a response to the requesting person that indicated as of June 2, 2005, no records were on file against Debtor.

f. Time for Filing and Indexing

The filing office has to file and index all financing statements no later than two business days after it receives the financing statement. UCC § 9–519(h).

g. Delay

The filing office will be excused from compliance with the time deadlines set forth in the statute if it encounters circumstances beyond its control, such as computer failure or war, if the filing office exercises reasonable diligence under the circumstances. UCC § 9–524.

10. Amendments of an Initial Financing Statement

A financing statement may be amended. A continuation statement, discussed *supra*, is one type of amendment. Amendments may also add or delete collateral, add or delete a debtor, or add or delete a secured party. An amendment may also terminate the effectiveness of a financing statement. The amendment must identify the initial financing statement by its file number in order to relate the two filings together. UCC § 9–512(a). If the amendment does not do so, the amendment is treated as an initial financing statement. UCC § 9–516(c)(2). To be effective, amendments must be authorized. UCC § 9–510(a).

a. Additions of Collateral or Debtor

An amendment that adds collateral or adds a debtor to a financing statement must be authorized. If the amendment relates to a security interest, the debtor must authorize that amendment in an authenticated record. If the amendment relates to an agricultural lien, the agricultural lien must be attached to the collateral that is added to the financing statement. UCC § 9–509(a). By authenticating a security agreement, the debtor automatically authorizes the filing of an amendment that adds collateral that is identifiable proceeds of original collateral. UCC § 9–509(b)(2). If a debtor acquires collateral that is already subject to a security interest or agricultural lien, the debtor is deemed to authorize the filing of an amendment that covers that acquired collateral. UCC § 9–509(c).

b. Authority of Secured Party

As to all amendments, other than the ones that add collateral or a debtor or a termination statement in a particular circumstance discussed below, the secured party of record must authorize the filing. UCC § 9–509(d). The secured party of record is the person that is named as the secured party on the initial financing statement. UCC § 9–511(a). If more than one person is a secured party of record, all secured parties of record must authorize the filing. UCC § 9–509(e). The secured party's authorization need not be in an authenticated record.

c. Assignments to a New Secured Party of Record

An amendment of an initial financing statement may reflect an assignment of the secured party's authority to amend an initial financing statement by identifying an assignee and providing the mailing address of the assignee. UCC § 9–514.

d. Time of Effectiveness of Amendments

Authorized amendments that add a debtor or add collateral are effective as to that added debtor or added collateral only from the time the amendment is filed. UCC § 9–512(c), (d). Amendments, other than continuation statements that are appropriately filed as discussed *supra*, do not extend the time period of effectiveness of the initial financing statement. UCC § 9–512(b). Amendments filed by one secured party of record do not affect the rights of another secured party of record. UCC § 9–510(b).

e. Deletion of all Debtors and Secured Parties

Amendments that purport to delete all debtors or all secured parties of record without providing for at least one remaining debtor and one remaining secured party of record are ineffective. UCC § 9–512(e).

f. Termination Statements

A termination statement is an amendment of an initial financing statement that identifies the initial financing statement and indicates that the effectiveness of the initial financing statement is terminated. UCC § 9–102(a)(80).

(1) Requirement to File Termination Statement if Collateral is Consumer Goods

If the financing statement covers consumer goods as collateral and there is no obligation owed or any commitment to give value or if the debtor did not authorize the filing of the initial financing statement, the secured party of record must file a termination statement within the earlier of one month after there is no outstanding obligation or any commitment to give value or within 20 days after the secured party receives an authenticated demand for a termination statement from the debtor. UCC § 9–513(a), (b). If the secured party of record has assigned its rights to payment of the obligation to another secured party, the secured party that is not of record has the obligation to cause the secured party of record to file the termination statement. UCC § 9–513(a).

(2) Requirement to File Termination Statement if Collateral Other Than Consumer Goods

If the collateral indicated in the financing statement is not consumer goods and either there is no outstanding obligation or commitment to give value or the debtor did not authorize the filing of the initial financing statement, the secured party of record must file a termination statement within 20 days after the debtor makes an authenticated demand for termination. This requirement to file a termination statement does not apply if the collateral is accounts or chattel paper that have been sold (unless the account debtor has discharged its obligation on the collateral) or goods that are subject to a consignment. UCC § 9–513(c).

Example: ABC Corp. sold its accounts receivable to Factoring Inc. Factoring Inc. filed an authorized initial financing statement against ABC Corp. in the proper place. ABC Corp. requested that Factoring Inc. terminate the financing statement.

Factoring Inc. need not do so until all of the accounts that it purchased are collected.

(3) Authority to File

Generally, a secured party of record must authorize an amendment that is a termination statement. UCC § 9–509(d). If the secured party of record does not file a termination statement when required as described above, the debtor may authorize the filing of a termination statement as long as that statement indicates that the debtor has authorized the filing. UCC § 9–509(d)(2).

(4) Effect of Termination Statement

A termination statement that is appropriately filed terminates the effectiveness of the initial financing statement. UCC § 9–513(d). If the termination statement is not authorized by the secured party or allowed to be filed by the debtor as described above, it is not effective to terminate the effectiveness of the financing statement.

11.   Information Statements

Sometimes initial financing statements are filed against debtors that have not authorized the filing of the financing statement. Article 9 allows a filing called an information statement that identifies the initial financing statement and states the basis for the person's belief that the record is inaccurate or wrongfully filed. The information statement does not affect the effectiveness of the initial financing statement or any amendments to that initial financing statement nor does the failure to file an information statement have any effect. UCC § 9–518.

C. Possession of Collateral as a Perfection Method

As noted *supra*, filing of a financing statement is the dominant method of perfection for a security interest and the only method of perfection of an agricultural lien. For some types of collateral a secured party has an option to perfect its security interest by possession of the collateral. UCC § 9–310(b)(6).

1. Collateral Types

Article 9 restricts the type of collateral in which a security interest may be perfected by possession. To perfect a security interest by possession, the collateral must be tangible negotiable documents of title, goods, instruments, money, or tangible chattel paper. UCC § 9–313(a). A secured party may not perfect its security interest in any other collateral types by possession of that collateral. If the collateral is money, possession is the only method of perfecting a security interest in that collateral unless the money is identifiable proceeds of original collateral in which the secured party has a perfected security interest. UCC § 9–312(b)(3). If the collateral is a good that is covered by a certificate of title law, the secured party ordinarily cannot perfect its security interest in that good by taking possession of the good. UCC § 9–313(b). This principle is subject to an exception discussed in Section H *infra*.

2. Possession Defined

Article 9 does not define possession. Based upon comment 3 to UCC § 9–313, if a debtor has unfettered access to the collateral, the secured party will not be in possession for purposes of perfection of the security interest. But the debtor may have some access, such as when the collateral is with an escrow agent, without defeating the secured party's possession. The concept of possession for perfection is the same as the concept of possession for purposes of attachment as discussed in Chapter III, Section B.3.

> *Example:* Bank has a security interest in a painting to secure a debt that ABC Corp. owes to Bank. Bank and ABC Corp. agree that Bank has "possession" of the painting but the painting is displayed in ABC Corp.'s lobby. Bank does not have possession of the painting that is sufficient to perfect its security interest.

a. Possession by an Agent

An agent of the secured party, other than the debtor, may have possession on behalf of the secured party. The agent would have to have possession, however defined, of the collateral.

b. Possession by a Third Party of Collateral Other Than a Certificated Security or Goods Covered by a Document of Title

If a third party (other than the debtor, the secured party, an agent of the secured party, or a lessee of goods from the debtor) has possession of the collateral, the secured party may perfect its security interest in the collateral based upon that third party's possession of the collateral through a notification and acknowledgment process. This process does not apply to all types of collateral however. This process is permitted only for collateral for which perfection by possession is allowed and if the collateral is not a certificated security or goods covered by a document of title. In those circumstances, the secured party may obtain an authenticated record from the third party that the third party holds the collateral for the benefit of the secured party. That authenticated acknowledgment may be obtained either from a third party that already has possession of the collateral or from a third party that takes possession of the collateral after the acknowledgment is authenticated. UCC § 9–313(c). When the secured party obtains that acknowledgment, the secured party's security interest is perfected.

(1) Acknowledgment

The acknowledgment is effective even if it violates the rights of the debtor. The acknowledgment does not impose any duties on the third party absent the third party's agreement to undertake a duty to the secured party. The third party is not required to confirm the acknowledgment to another person. UCC § 9–313(g). A third party in possession of collateral has no obligation to render an acknowledgment to the secured party. UCC § 9–313(f).

Example: Warehouse Inc. is in possession of several containers of goods that belong to Debtor. Warehouse Inc. has not issued any document of title that covers the goods. Debtor granted a security interest in all of Debtor's goods to secure all obligations owed to Bank. Bank sent a notice and request for acknowledgment of Bank's security interest in Debtor's goods to Warehouse Inc. Warehouse Inc. signed and returned the requested acknowledgment. Bank has perfected its security interest in the goods in Warehouse Inc.'s possession. Warehouse Inc. is under no duty to Bank regarding the goods in its possession although Warehouse Inc. will have duties to Debtor regarding care of the goods. Those duties of care arise under other law. UCC § 7–204.

Example: Warehouse Inc. is in possession of several containers of goods that belong to Debtor. Warehouse Inc. has not issued any document of title covering the goods. Debtor granted a security interest in all of Debtor's goods to secure all obligations owed to Bank. Bank sent a notice and request for acknowledgment of Bank's security interest in Debtor's goods to Warehouse Inc. Warehouse Inc. does not return the requested acknowledgment. Warehouse Inc. has no obligation to render an acknowledgment to Bank. Bank has not perfected its security interest in the goods in Warehouse Inc.'s possession. Bank must perfect its security interest in another manner, such as by filing an effective financing statement against Debtor covering the goods.

(2) Delivery of Collateral to Third Party With Notice

In some industries, the practice developed that allowed the secured party to deliver the collateral to a third party in the ordinary course of the secured party's business with a notice to the third party that the third party is holding possession of the collateral for the secured party's benefit or the third party has to redeliver the collateral to the secured party. Article 9 recognizes this practice and allows the secured party to be deemed to remain in possession of the collateral even if it has delivered possession to a third party in accordance with the above process. UCC § 9–313(h). This is an effective manner of perfection even if delivery of the collateral violates the rights of the debtor. The third party does not owe any duty to the secured party or have any obligation to confirm the delivery unless the third party agrees to assume a duty or confirm the delivery. UCC § 9–313(i).

Example: Debtor granted a security interest in all of Debtor's instruments to secure all obligations that Debtor owes Bank. Bank has possession of several boxes of promissory notes payable to Debtor and thus has a perfected security interests in the notes by its possession. Bank delivered 2 boxes of these notes to Warehouse Inc. instructing Warehouse Inc. to hold the notes for Bank's benefit or redeliver the notes to Bank. Warehouse Inc. stored the notes. Bank has maintained perfection of the security interest in the notes by possession.

3. Effectiveness of Possession as a Perfection Method

As to the collateral types where possession is a potentially effective perfection method, possession is effective as a perfection method only as long as the secured party, its agent, or the third party (as described *supra*) has possession of the collateral. If possession of the collateral is lost, the perfection of the security interest is lost unless the secured party has perfected in another permissible method before the loss of possession. UCC §§ 9–313(d), 9–308(c).

Example: Bank has a security interest in a painting to secure a debt that ABC Corp. owes to Bank. Bank has possession of the painting and it is stored in the Bank's vault. Bank agreed to allow ABC Corp. to retrieve the painting for display in the lobby of ABC Corp. during an art show. ABC Corp took the painting and displayed it in the lobby of its headquarters. Bank's security interest is no longer perfected.

4. Delivery of a Certificated Security

A secured party may perfect its security interest in a certificated security by taking delivery of the certificated security. UCC §§ 9–310(b)(7), 9–313(a). Delivery of a certificated security occurs in one of several ways. First, the secured party may obtain possession of the certificate. UCC 8–301(a)(1). Second, a third party, other than a securities intermediary, may obtain possession of the security certificate on behalf of the secured party or if the third party is already in possession of the security certificate, acknowledge that it holds the certificate on behalf of the secured party. UCC § 8–301(a)(2). If the third party is a securities intermediary, the secured party takes delivery of a certificated security in registered form if the securities intermediary is acting on behalf of the secured party and the certificated security is registered to, payable to the order of, or specifically indorsed to the secured party. UCC § 8–301(a)(3). A security interest in the certificated security in registered form is perfected when the delivery takes place and remains perfected until the debtor obtains possession of the certificate. UCC § 9–313(e).

5. Possession by a Third Party of Goods Covered by a Document of Title

If the goods are covered by a document of title, the secured party may not use the notice or acknowledgment process described *supra* to perfect its security interest in the goods covered by the document of title. Rather, the secured party must use a different process, depending on whether the document of title is negotiable or nonnegotiable, when attempting to perfect a security interest in the goods using possession as the perfection method. Of course, the secured party may perfect its security interest by filing a financing statement instead.

a. Negotiable or Nonnegotiable

A document of title is negotiable if by the terms contained in the document the goods are either deliverable to "bearer" or to "the order of a named person." UCC § 7–104.

b. Goods Covered by Negotiable Document of Title

If the goods are in the possession of a bailee and covered by a negotiable document of title, title to the goods is considered locked up in the document. That is, by dealing with the document, the secured party is in effect dealing with the goods. While the goods are covered by the negotiable document of title, the secured party should perfect its security interest in the goods by perfecting a security interest in the negotiable document of title. UCC § 9–312(c). Negotiable documents of title may be either tangible (paper) or electronic. UCC § 1–201(b)(16). Perfection in the negotiable tangible document of title may be by taking possession of the document of title. UCC § 9–313(a). Perfection in an electronic negotiable document of title may be by obtaining control, discussed in Section D, *infra*.

Example: Warehouse Inc. has stored some of Debtor's goods and has issued tangible negotiable warehouse receipts (a type of document of title) covering those goods. Debtor signed a security agreement granting Bank a security interest in Debtor's goods and documents of title to secure a loan made to Debtor. Bank took possession of the tangible negotiable warehouse receipts. Bank has perfected its security interest in the tangible negotiable warehouse receipts and in the goods covered by those receipts.

c. Goods Covered by a Nonnegotiable Document of Title

If the goods are in possession of a bailee and covered by nonnegotiable documents of title, the secured party will perfect its security interest in the goods, by perfecting as to the goods, not as to the document of title. A nonnegotiable document of title does not represent title to the goods. In this circumstance, the secured party may perfect its security interest in the goods in one of three ways. The secured party may (i) obtain a document of title issued to the secured party, (ii) send a notice to the bailee of the secured party's interest which the bailee receives, or (iii) file a financing statement as to the goods. If the secured party sends a notice to the bailee, the bailee does not need to acknowledge the secured party's interest in order for the secured party's security interest in the goods covered by the nonnegotiable document to be perfected. UCC § 9–312(d).

Example: Warehouse Inc. has stored some of Debtor's goods and has issued tangible nonnegotiable warehouse receipts covering those goods. Debtor signed a security interest granting Bank a security interest in Debtor's goods and documents of title to secure a loan made to Debtor. Bank sent a notice to Warehouse Inc. of the Bank's security interest in Debtor's goods. Warehouse Inc. received the notice and did not take any action. Bank's security interest in the goods covered by the nonnegotiable warehouse receipt is perfected.

6. Secured Party's Obligations While in Possession

While a secured party has possession of collateral in which it has a security interest to perfect a security interest, the secured party has the same obligations as to the collateral that it has if it has possession of the collateral in order to attach the security interest. See Chapter III, Section H.

D. Control of Collateral as a Perfection Method

A secured party may perfect its security interest in deposit accounts, electronic chattel paper, electronic documents of title, investment property, and letter-of-credit rights through control of the collateral. UCC §§ 9–310(b)(8), 9–314(a).

1. Relationship to Other Perfection Methods

As to electronic chattel paper, electronic documents of title, and investment property, the secured party may also perfect its security interest by filing an effective financing statement. Control is the exclusive method of perfection for deposit accounts unless the deposit accounts are identifiable proceeds of other collateral in which the secured party has a perfected security interest. UCC § 9–312(b)(1). As to letter-of-credit rights, control is the exclusive method of perfection unless the letter-of-credit rights are identifiable proceeds of other collateral in which the secured party has a perfected security interest or the letter-of-credit rights are a supporting obligation of a right to payment in which the secured party has a perfected security interest. UCC § 9–312(b)(2).

2. Control Defined

Control for these types of collateral for perfection purposes is the same as control for the purpose of establishing attachment of a security interest. See Chapter III, Section B.5.

3. Effect of Control on Perfection

As to deposit accounts, electronic chattel paper, electronic documents of title, and letter-of-credit rights, a secured party is perfected in that type of collateral by control from the time the secured party obtains control until the secured party no longer has control. UCC § 9–314(b). As to investment property, a secured party is perfected by control from the time the secured party obtains control until the secured party does not have control and one of three things is true: (i) if the collateral is a certificated security, the debtor acquires possession of the certificate; (ii) if the collateral is an uncertificated security, the debtor becomes the registered owner; or (iii) if the collateral is a securities entitlement, the debtor becomes the entitlement holder. UCC § 9–314(c).

4. Obligations While in Control

While a secured party has control of collateral in which it has a security interest, the secured party has the same obligations as to the collateral that it has if it has control of the collateral in order to attach the security interest. See Chapter III, Section H.

E. Compliance With Other Law as a Method of Perfection

Article 9 defers to other law to control perfection of a security interest in three situations: when a federal law preempts the Article 9 filing system, when a state certificate of title law provides for security interests to be noted on the certificate of title as a condition or result of perfection, and when a state law provides for a central filing statute regarding particular types of collateral. UCC §§ 9–310(b)(3), 9–311.

1. Effect of Compliance

Compliance with the non-Article 9 law is treated as the equivalent of filing the Article 9 financing statement. The security interest in all other respects is still subject to Article 9. UCC § 9–311(b), (c).

2. Exception for Collateral Covered by Certificate of Title Law That is Held for Sale or Lease by a Person in the Business of Selling Goods of the Kind

When goods covered by a certificate of title law are held for sale or lease by someone in the business of selling goods of that kind (i.e. inventory), the proper method of perfection in that inventory is not through notation of the security interest on the certificates of title, but rather through using one of the other methods of perfection permitted for goods that are inventory, such as filing an effective financing statement. UCC § 9–311(d).

F. Automatic Perfection

In some circumstances, Article 9 does not require that the secured party take any action other than attachment to perfect its security interest in collateral. This is referred to as "automatic perfection." In other words, the security interest is automatically perfected upon attachment of the security interest to the collateral. The category of collateral and transactions in which the security interest is automatically perfected is an eclectic mix without a general unifying theme except that the drafters of Article 9 surmised it would be inefficient or unwise to subject the secured party to the requirement of filing a financing statement, taking possession, or taking control of that type of collateral in the situation designated.

1. Purchase Money Security Interest in Consumer Goods Not Covered by a Certificate of Title

A purchase money security interest in consumer goods is automatically perfected upon attachment as long as the consumer goods are not subject to a certificate of title law that requires perfection of a security interest to be accomplished through notation of the security interest on the certificate of title. UCC §§ 9–310(b)(2), 9–309(1). The purpose of this exception is to avoid clogging the filing system with filings that would really serve no purpose as it is extremely unlikely that there will be multiple security interests on collateral of this type.

a. Purchase Money Security Interest

A purchase money security interest in consumer goods means that the security interest is granted to secure the value given or the obligation incurred in order for the debtor to obtain rights in the collateral. UCC § 9–103(b)(1). The seller of the goods may give the value, that is, the seller may sell the goods on credit to the buyer and the buyer grant the seller a security interest in the goods to secure the purchase price. A person other than the seller may also give the value, that is, a third party may give the debtor value to purchase the goods and may take a security interest in the goods purchased to secure the loan. The value must be used by the debtor to acquire the rights in the purchased goods.

Example: Debtor, a consumer, desires to purchase a new washing machine and dryer from Big Box Appliance Inc. On Friday, Debtor borrowed $1,000 from Bank to finance the purchase granting Bank a security interest in the yet to be purchased washing machine and dryer. On Saturday, Debtor played poker at the local casino, losing all but $10 of the $1,000 loan proceeds before winning $2,000. On Monday, Debtor used the poker winnings to purchase the washing machine and dryer from Big Box Appliance Inc. Bank has a security interest in the washing machine and dryer (*see* UCC § 9–204) but does not have a purchase money security interest as the value that Bank gave was not used to purchase the items.

Example: Debtor Inc., a laundry service business, purchased a new washing machine and dryer from Big Box Appliance Inc. on credit and granted Big Box a security interest in the two items to secure the purchase price obligation. Big Box Appliance Inc. has a purchase money security interest but not in consumer goods. The two items purchased would be Debtor Inc.'s equipment and Debtor Inc. is not a consumer. The automatic perfection rule does not apply to this situation.

b. Consumer Goods Not Covered by Certificate of Title Law

The automatic perfection rule only covers consumer goods (UCC § 9–102(a)(23)), not all goods, and the consumer goods must not be covered by a certificate of title law that governs perfection of a security interest in those goods. UCC § 9–311.

Example: Debtor, a consumer, purchased a new car from Dealer Inc. for Debtor's personal use. Debtor borrowed from Bank the necessary funds to purchase the new car and granted Bank a security interest in the car to secure the loan. Bank directly remitted the loan proceeds to Dealer and Dealer delivers the car to Debtor. Bank's security interest is not automatically perfected even though Bank has a purchase money security interest and the collateral is consumer goods. Bank must perfect its security interest by complying with the applicable certificate of title law.

2. Insignificant Assignments of Accounts and Payment Intangibles

An assignment of accounts or payment intangibles within the scope of Article 9 creates a security interest whether the assignment is a sale or voluntary creation of a lien to secure an obligation. UCC § 9–109(a)(1), (3), (d)(4)–(8). The security interest created by an assignment of accounts or payment intangibles that does not effect a transfer to the same assignee of a significant part of the assignor's outstanding accounts or payment intangibles, either standing alone or in conjunction with other assignments, is automatically perfected upon attachment without the need to file a financing statement. UCC §§ 9–310(b)(2), 9–309(2). The purpose of this exception is to protect a casual or isolated assignment where the secured party may not realize that it should have filed a financing statement to perfect its security interest. What constitutes a "significant part" of the debtor's outstanding accounts or payment intangibles is not defined.

Example: A owes B money. A assigned to B an obligation that C owes to A. That obligation is an "account" and created a security interest with B as the secured party, A as the debtor, and C as the account debtor. The assignment was not excluded from the scope of Article 9 under UCC § 9–109(d)(4)–(8). B did not file a financing statement to perfect its interest in the obligation that C owes to A. B would argue that its security interest in the account is automatically perfected as it is an insignificant amount of the accounts that are owed to A.

3. Sales of Payment Intangibles and Promissory Notes

A security interest created by a sale of a payment intangible or a sale of a promissory note, UCC § 9–109(a)(3), and which is not excluded from the scope of Article 9, UCC § 9–109(d)(4)–(8), is automatically perfected upon attachment of the security interest. UCC §§ 9–310(b)(2), 9–309(3), (4). The security interest created by an assignment of a payment intangible or a promissory note that is not a sale, that is, the assignment is a transfer of the payment intangible or promissory note to secure an obligation, is not automatically perfected. The secured party will have to file an effective financing statement as to the payment intangible or promissory note or take possession of the promissory note in order to perfect its security interest in the non-sale situation. Article 9 provides no guidance on distinguishing between transactions that create a security interest to secure an obligation and transactions that are sales.

4. Assignment of Health-Care-Insurance Receivable to the Health Care Provider

An insured that has a right to payment under a health care insurance policy creates a security interest in that right to payment when it assigns the right to payment to a health care provider. UCC §§ 9–102(a)(46), 9–109(d)(8). The health-care-insurance receivable is a type of account. UCC § 9–102(a)(2). Absent automatic perfection of the security interest created by the assignment, the health care provider would have to file a financing statement against the insured (the patient). Article 9 provides that the security interest created by the assignment of the insured's rights under the health care insurance policy to the health care provider is automatically perfected. UCC §§ 9–310(b)(2), 9–309(5). The health care provider's further assignment of that right to payment to a secured party is not automatically perfected. UCC § 9–309, cmt. 5.

Example: Insured visits her local doctor and as part of the visit signs a form assigning to her doctor her rights under her health care insurance policy to pay the doctor for the visit. That assignment creates a security interest in the right to payment under the insurance policy. The doctor is the secured party and Insured is the debtor. That security interest is automatically perfected. The doctor has granted a security interest in all of her accounts to Bank to finance the doctor's practice. Bank's collateral will include the right to payment under Insured's health care policy. Bank's security interest in that right to payment is **not** automatically perfected.

5. Security Interests Arising Under Other UCC Articles

Article 9 applies to security interests created under other articles of the UCC (Chapter II, Section D). The provisions of the other articles that create the security interest and Article 9 provide the rules on attachment of the security interest (Chapter III, Section E). Article 9 governs the manner of perfection of those security interests.

a. Security Interests Arising Under Articles 2 and 2A

A seller's security interest that arises through retention of title, UCC § 2–401, and shipment under reservation, UCC § 2–505, and a buyer's or lessee's security interest in rightfully rejected goods or goods as to which acceptance has been justifiably revoked, UCC §§ 2–711(3), 2A–508, are automatically perfected upon attachment until the debtor obtains possession of the goods. UCC §§ 9–310(b)(2), 9–309(6), 9–110. Once the debtor obtains possession of the goods, however, those security interests are no longer automatically perfected and the secured party must take the appropriate perfection step for that type of collateral in order for the security interest to be perfected.

b. Security Interest of a Collecting Bank Under Article 4

A collecting bank's security interest in items taken for collection through the banking system is automatically perfected when it is attached. UCC §§ 4–210, 9–310(b)(2), 9–309(7).

c. Security Interest of Issuer or Nominated Person on a Letter of Credit Under Article 5

The letter of credit issuer's or nominated person's security interest in documents (UCC 5–102(a)(6)) in its possession that were presented under a letter of credit is automatically perfected when it is attached if those documents are not in tangible form. If those documents are in tangible form and are not certificated securities, chattel paper, documents of title, instruments, or a letter of credit, the security interest of the issuer or nominated person is perfected when attached as long as the debtor does not obtain possession of the documents. UCC §§ 5–118, 9–310(b)(2), 9–309(8).

6. Security Interest Created When Delivery of a Financial Asset

As explained in Chapter III, Section E, if a person in the business of dealing with securities or financial assets delivers a certificated security or other financial asset that is represented by a writing to another person that is also in the business of dealing with securities or financial assets and the transferee is to pay for the delivery, the transferor has a security interest in the securities or financial assets delivered to secure the purchase price. UCC § 9–206(c), (d). That security interest is automatically perfected upon attachment. UCC §§ 9–310(b)(2), 9–309(9).

7. Security Interest in Investment Property Created by Broker or Securities Intermediary

If a broker or securities intermediary grants a security interest in investment property it holds, the security interest is automatically perfected upon attachment. UCC §§ 9–310(b)(2), 9–309(10).

8. Security Interest in Commodity Contracts or Commodity Account Created By Commodity Intermediary

If a commodity intermediary grants a security interest in commodity contracts or commodity accounts it holds, the security interest created is automatically perfected upon attachment. UCC §§ 9–310(b)(2), 9–309(11).

9. Assignments for Benefit of Creditors

Many states allow for a common law or statutory process in which all of the debtor's assets are transferred to an assignee and the assignee has the obligation to use the assets to satisfy the claims of the debtor's creditors. This process is called an assignment for benefit of creditors. An assignment for the benefit of creditors is automatically perfected when it takes place and all subsequent transfers by the assignee are also automatically perfected. UCC §§ 9–310(b)(2), 9–309(12).

10. Assignment of Beneficial Interest in Decedent's Estate

A security interest created by an assignment of a beneficial interest in a decedent's estate is automatically perfected when it is attached. UCC §§ 9–310(b)(2), 9–309(13).

11. Sale of Right to Payment From Game of Chance

A right to payment from a game of chance authorized or run by a state is an account. UCC § 9–102(a)(2). A sale of that right to payment by an individual creates a security interest that is automatically perfected when it has attached. UCC §§ 9–310(b)(2), 9–309(14).

12. Perfection in One Type of Collateral Results in Perfection in Related Type of Collateral

For certain types of collateral, perfection of a security interest in that collateral results in automatic perfection of a security interest in related collateral. This is not a general rule but is restricted to specific types of original collateral and specific types of collateral related to the original collateral. UCC § 9–310(b)(1).

a. Perfection in a Right to Payment and a Supporting Obligation

A secured party that has perfected a security interest, using any permitted method of perfection, in a right to payment has also automatically perfected a security interest in a supporting obligation for that right to payment. UCC § 9–308(d).

Example: State Bank has a perfected security interest in Debtor's accounts. For the account ABC Corp. owes to Debtor, Debtor also has rights as a beneficiary under a letter of credit issued by National Bank. State Bank's security interest automatically attaches to the letter-of-credit right, UCC § 9–203(f), and is automatically perfected, UCC § 9–308(d).

b. Perfection in a Right to Payment and a Lien Securing That Right to Payment

A secured party that has perfected a security interest, using any permitted method of perfection, in a right to payment that is secured by a security interest, mortgage or other lien in property that secures that right to payment has also automatically perfected its security interest in the security interest, mortgage or other lien in property. UCC § 9–308(e).

Example: Debtor is the payee of a note secured by a mortgage on real estate. Debtor granted a security interest in the note to Bank. Bank perfected its security interest in the note by taking possession of the note. Bank's security interest in the mortgage attached automatically, UCC § 9–203(g), and is automatically perfected, UCC § 9–308(e).

c. Perfection in a Securities Account and Securities Entitlements

A secured party that has perfected a security interest in a securities account, using any permitted method of perfection, has automatically perfected a security interest in all security entitlements carried in the securities account. UCC § 9–308(f).

d. Perfection in a Commodity Account and Commodity Contracts

A secured party that has perfected a security interest in a commodity account, using any permitted method of perfection, has automatically perfected a security interest in all commodity contracts carried in the commodity account. UCC § 9–308(g).

13. Periods of Temporary Perfection

Article 9 also allows automatic perfection of security interests for short periods of time as to certain types of collateral in defined circumstances. UCC § 9–310(b)(5). Allowing for these temporary periods of perfection accommodates certain longstanding industry practices.

a. Security Interest Given in Exchange for New Value

If a security interest attaches to certificated securities, negotiable documents of title, or instruments in exchange for new value under an authenticated security agreement, the security interest is automatically perfected for a period of 20 days from the time it attaches. UCC § 9–312(e). After that period of time expires, the security interest will be unperfected unless the secured party utilizes one of the permissible methods of perfection for that type of collateral. UCC § 9–312(h). New value means money, money's worth, or a release of rights already transferred that is not the substitution of a new obligation for an old obligation. UCC § 9–102(a)(57).

b. Security Interest in Negotiable Documents of Title or Goods in Possession of Bailee That Are Not Covered by a Negotiable Document of Title and Are Made Available to Debtor for Limited Purposes

If the secured party has already perfected its security interest in either a negotiable document of title or in goods that are in the possession of a bailee that has not issued a negotiable document of title covering those goods and in a manner other than filing an effective financing statement concerning the collateral, the security interest remains perfected for 20 days if the secured party makes the document of title or goods available to the debtor for the purpose of ultimate sale or exchange or dealing with the goods in a manner preliminary to sale or exchange. UCC § 9–312(f). After the 20-day period expires, the security interest will be unperfected unless the secured party utilizes one of the permissible methods of perfection for that type of collateral. UCC § 9–312(h).

Example: Debtor granted Bank a security interest in its goods and documents of title. Bank has possession of a negotiable document of title covering goods stored in Warehouse Inc. in order to perfect a security interest in those goods. Debtor needs to get possession of the goods in order to prepare the goods for sale. Bank allowed Debtor to take the negotiable document of title in order to present the document to Warehouse Inc. to obtain the goods. Bank's security interest in the goods remains perfected for 20 days even though it no longer has possession of the negotiable document of title and Bank has not filed any financing statement to perfect it security interest in the document of title. If the goods are no longer covered by the document of title because Warehouse releases the goods to Debtor, this temporary perfection rule does not help Bank remain perfected in the goods. See UCC § 9–312(c).

c. Security Interest in Certificated Securities and Instruments Made Available to Debtor for Limited Purposes

If the secured party has already perfected its security interest in a certificated security or an instrument through a manner other than the filing of an effective financing statement concerning that collateral, the security interest remains perfected for 20 days even if the secured party delivers the security certificate or the instrument to the debtor for the purpose of ultimate sale or exchange or for presentment, collection, enforcement, renewal or registration or transfer. UCC § 9–312(g). After the 20-day period expires, the security interest must be perfected using one of the permissible methods of perfection for that type of collateral. UCC § 9–312(h).

G. Choice of Law Rules

As noted in Chapter II, Article 9 is enacted by state legislatures, not by Congress. One of the results of state enactment is that there is always an initial issue of which state's version of Article 9 will control the analysis of the issues in any given transaction. To the extent the enacted versions of Article 9 are uniform from state to state, this issue will only have real bite if the court decisions or administrative practices of the various filing offices vary. Unfortunately, Article 9 was not enacted in a totally uniform manner across all 50 states and court decisions and administrative practices of the filing offices do differ. These differences necessitate paying some attention to choice of law issues.

1. Choice of Law Regarding Which State's Article 9 Applies

The first choice of law question is to determine which state's Article 9 controls. This question is not determined by Article 9 but rather by other choice of law principles that govern in the state where any litigation concerning the parties' transaction may be commenced. An example of a choice of law statute that a court should consult is found in UCC § 1–301.

> *Example:* Litigation concerning a secured transaction is brought in State A. The court in State A will decide whether State A's Article 9 or another state's Article 9 provides the governing law. That decision will be made using choice of law principles such as whether the transaction and the parties bear a reasonable relationship to State A or another state.

2. Choice of Law Regarding Perfection of the Security Interest or Agricultural Lien

After the court determines which state's Article 9 controls, that state's Article 9 is consulted to determine the question of which state's law governs perfection of the security interest or agricultural lien. That state's Article 9 will contain several sections that set forth choice of law rules concerning the perfection method. UCC § 9–301 through § 9–307. Fortunately, the choice of law rules in Article 9 were uniformly enacted across the country.[1]

> *Example:* Litigation concerning a secured transaction is brought in State A. The court in State A will decide whether State A's Article 9 or another state's Article 9 provides the governing law. That decision will be made using choice of law principles such as whether the transaction and the parties bear a reasonable relationship to State A or another state. The court decides that State A's Article 9 provides the governing law. The court will then look at Article 9 as enacted in State

---

[1] Thus, many times, but not always, the initial choice of law rule (which state's Article 9) can be safely ignored. An example of when the choice of which state's Article 9 should be consulted makes a difference is when the state has enacted a nonuniform scope section to Article 9. That scenario leads to a quite complex analysis which we will not explore but that is discussed in a Permanent Editorial Board Report issued December 1, 2004.

A. Article 9 as enacted in State A contains choice of law provisions for perfection purposes in UCC § 9–301 through § 9–307.

a. Perfection of an Agricultural Lien

The law of the location of the farm products will govern perfection of an agricultural lien in those farm products. UCC § 9–302.

Example: Under the law of State A, Seed Supply Inc. has an agricultural lien on Debtor's crops to secure the price of the seed used to plant the crops. Debtor's crop is located in State A and Debtor is located in State B. State A's Article 9 will govern the perfection of the agricultural lien. Because an agricultural lien may only be perfected by filing a financing statement where the farm products are located, the proper place to file the financing statement to perfect the agricultural lien is in State A. UCC § 9–302. In State A, the proper place to file the financing statement is at the central filing office, not the local filing office. UCC § 9–501.

b. Dominate Rule: Law of the Debtor's Location Governs Perfection of a Security Interest

For most types of collateral and transactions, the law of the debtor's location will govern the perfection of a security interest. UCC § 9–301(1), (2). This means that unless an exception applies, the jurisdiction in which the debtor is located will be the correct jurisdiction in which to file a financing statement to perfect the security interest.

Example: Bank has a security interest in Debtor' crops to secure a loan made to Debtor. Debtor is located in State B and Debtor's crops are located in State A. State B's law, where Debtor is located, provides the governing law for perfection of the security interest in the crops located in State A. Bank will file its financing statement in State B to perfect its interest in the crops. UCC § 9–301(1). Bank will file its financing statement in the central office in State B, not the local filing office. UCC § 9–501.

c. Determining the Debtor's Location

The location of the debtor depends upon what type of debtor is involved. The rules provided in Article 9 regarding the location of the debtor apply only for purposes of the perfection rules in Article 9. UCC 9–307(k).

(1) Location of Registered Organization

In an effort to simplify the determination of the debtor's location, Article 9 provides for the concept of a registered organization. UCC § 9–102(a)(71). Review Section B.4. *supra.* A corporation will typically be a registered organization.

(a) Location if Organized Under State Law

A registered organization organized under state law is located in the state in which it is organized. UCC § 9–307(e).

(b) Location if Organized Under Federal Law

A registered organization organized under the law of the United States is located in the state the federal law designates as the location or in the state the registered organization designates, if the law allows the registered organization to make a designation. If neither of these circumstances apply, the registered organization is located in the District of Columbia. UCC § 9–307(f).

(c) Effect of Lapse of Status or Ceasing Affairs

The demise of the registered organization or the lapse, suspension or revocation of its registration in its jurisdiction of organization does not affect the location of the organization as previously determined above. UCC § 9–307(g). This circumstance should be distinguished from the situation of the registered organization moving its location as discussed in Section H *infra.*

(2) Foreign Banks

If a branch of a bank is not organized under the law of a state or the law of the United States (and thus is not a registered organization) and it has a license to do business in only one state, the branch bank is located in that state in which it is licensed. UCC § 9–307(i). When the bank is licensed to do business in more than one state, a bank that is not organized under the laws of the United States or a state (and thus not a registered organization) is located in the state a federal law designates as the location or in the state the bank designates, if the law allows the bank to make a designation. If none of these circumstances apply, the bank is located in the District of Columbia. UCC § 9–307(f).

(3) Foreign Air Carrier

A foreign air carrier is located at the place at which it has designated its agent for purposes of service of process. UCC § 9–307(j).

(4) United States

The United States is located in the District of Columbia. UCC § 9–307(h).

(5) Location of Individual Debtors and Organizations Other Than Those Specifically Provided For

An individual debtor's location is the location of the individual's principal residence. UCC 9–307(b)(1). An organization that is the debtor, that is not a registered organization, a foreign bank, a foreign air carrier, or the United States, and that has only one place of business is located at the place of business. If such an organization has more than one place of business, the organization is located at its chief executive office. UCC § 9–307(b)(2), (3). The debtor's place of business is where the debtor conducts its affairs. UCC § 9–307(a).

(a) Exception Based Upon Lack of a Filing System in That Location

For individual debtors or organization that are not registered organizations, foreign banks, foreign air carriers, or the United States, if the law of the debtor's location does not have a filing or public notice system in place for giving notice of nonpossessory security interests in order to obtain priority over lien creditors with respect to the collateral, the debtor is deemed to be located in the District of Columbia. UCC § 9–307(c). The purpose of this exception is to avoid a determination that the law governing perfection of the security interest results in affording no public notice of security interests generally. This exception will have its possible effect only if the debtor's location is determined to not be in one of the states of the United States, or in the District of Columbia. Article 9 is a system that generally affords some sort of public notice through a filing system. UCC § 9–307, cmt. 3.

Example: D, an individual, lives in Paris, France. If France does not have a public notice system for nonpossessory security interests, D will be deemed to be located in the District of Columbia.

(b) **Effect of Ceasing to Exist, Having a Residence or Having a Place of Business**

For individual debtors or organization that are not registered organizations, foreign banks, foreign air carriers, or the United States, if a debtor is dissolved or dies, an individual ceases to have a residence, or an organization no longer has a place of business, that does not affect the determination of the debtor's location previously made. UCC § 9–307(d). This situation should be distinguished from the situation of the debtor moving locations which is discussed in Section H *infra*.

d. Exceptions to the Debtor-Location Rule

Article 9 contains several exceptions to the requirement that the law of the debtor's location governs perfection of the security interest.

(1) **Possessory Security Interests**

If the security interest is perfected through possession of collateral (and possession of collateral is an effective method of perfection as to that type of collateral), the law of the jurisdiction where the collateral is located will govern perfection of the security interest. UCC § 9–301(2).

(2) **Fixture Filing**

If the security interest is in goods that are fixtures and perfection is through filing a fixture financing statement, then the law of the jurisdiction where the fixtures are located governs perfection. UCC § 9–301(3)(A).

(3) **Timber to Be Cut**

If the security interest is in timber to be cut, the law of the jurisdiction where the timber to be cut is located governs perfection. UCC § 9–301(3)(B).

(4) As-Extracted Collateral

If the security interest is in as-extracted collateral, the law of the jurisdiction where the minehead or wellhead is located governs perfection. UCC § 9–301(4).

(5) Goods Covered by Certificate of Title

If the security interest is in goods that are covered by a certificate of title (as defined in UCC § 9–102(a)(10)) and the goods are not inventory held for sale or lease by the debtor, then the law of the jurisdiction that issued the certificate of title governs perfection until the goods cease to be covered by the certificate of title. UCC § 9–303(c), cmt. 5.

(a) No Need for Relationship With the Jurisdiction Issuing Certificate Of Title

Goods are covered by a certificate of title even if the jurisdiction that issued the certificate of title has no relationship to the goods or the debtor. UCC § 9–303(a).

(b) Start of Coverage

Goods become covered by a certificate of title when a valid application for the certificate of title and the applicable fee are delivered to the appropriate authority. UCC § 9–303(b).

(c) End of Coverage

Goods stop being covered by a certificate of title at the earlier of (i) the certificate ceases to be effective under the law of the jurisdiction issuing the certificate or (ii) the goods become covered by a certificate of title issued by another jurisdiction. UCC § 9–303(b).

(6) Deposit Accounts

If the security interest is in a deposit account, the law of the jurisdiction where the depositary bank is located governs the perfection of the security interest. UCC § 9–304(a). The bank's location is determined by the following hierarchy of choices in this order: (i) the location specified as the bank's location in the bank-customer agreement for purposes of Article 9; (ii) the location specified as providing the governing law for the bank-customer agreement for any purpose; (iii) the location specified in the bank-customer agreement as the place where the deposit account is maintained; (iv) the location of the bank's office identified in an account statement regarding the deposit account; or (v) the location of the bank's chief executive office. UCC § 9–304(b).

(7) Investment Property

The law governing perfection of a security interest in investment property depends upon the manner of perfection.

(a) Perfection by Filing

If a security interest in investment property is perfected by filing, the law of the debtor's location will govern perfection of the security interest. UCC § 9–305(c).

(b) Automatic Perfection of Security Interest of Broker, Securities Intermediary, or Commodity Intermediary

The law of the debtor's location will govern perfection of a security interest through automatic perfection under UCC § 9–309(10) and (11) when the security interest is created by the broker or securities intermediary in investment property or by a commodity intermediary in a commodity contract or commodity account. UCC § 9–305(c).

(c) Security Interests Perfected by Other Methods

If the security interest in investment property is perfected by a method other than filing a financing statement and other than automatically perfected under UCC § 9–309(10) and (11), the law that governs perfection of a security interest in investment property depends upon the type of investment property that is subject to the security interest.

(i) Certificated Security

The law of the location of the certificated security will govern perfection of a security interest in the certificated security. UCC § 9–305(a)(1).

(ii) Uncertificated Security

The law of the location of the issuer will govern perfection of a security interest in an uncertificated security. UCC § 9–305(a)(2). An issuer is located in the jurisdiction of its organization unless the law of that jurisdiction allows the issuer to designate another jurisdiction as the location of the issuer. If the law so allows and the issuer so designates, the law of the jurisdiction designated is the location of the issuer. UCC § 8–110(d).

(iii) Securities Account or Securities Entitlement

The law of the location of the securities intermediary will govern perfection of a security interest in a customer's securities account or securities entitlement. UCC § 9–305(a)(3). The securities intermediary's location is determined by the following hierarchy of choices in this order: (i) the location specified as the intermediary's location in the intermediary-customer agreement for purposes of Article 9; (ii) the location specified as providing the governing law for the intermediary-customer agreement for any purpose; (iii) the location specified in the intermediary-customer agreement as the place where the securities account is maintained; (iv) the location of the intermediary's office identified in an account statement regarding the securities account; or (v) the location of the intermediary's chief executive office. UCC § 8–110(e).

Example: A granted a security interest to State Bank in A's security account held at Brokerage Inc. If State Bank perfects its security interest by filing a financing statement, the law of the state where A is located will govern perfection of the security interest and State Bank should file its financing statement in that state. If State Bank perfects its security interest by control, the law of the state where the securities intermediary is located will govern the perfection of the security interest and State Bank must comply with the Article 9 in the state where the securities intermediary is located to perfect through control of the securities account.

(iv) Commodity Account or Commodity Contract

The law of the location of the commodity intermediary will govern perfection of a security interest in a customer's commodity account or commodity contract. UCC § 9–305(a)(4). The commodity intermediary's location is determined by the following hierarchy of choices in this order: (i) the location specified as the intermediary's location in the intermediary-customer agreement for purposes of Article 9; (ii) the location specified as providing the governing law for the intermediary-customer agreement for any purpose; (iii) the location specified in the intermediary-customer agreement as the place where the commodity account is maintained; (iv) the location of the intermediary's office identified in an account statement regarding the commodity account; or (v) the location of the intermediary's chief executive office. UCC § 9–305(b).

(8) Letter-of-Credit Rights

Unless the security interest in the letter-of-credit right is automatically perfected because it is a supporting obligation to a right to payment in which a security interest has been perfected, the law of the location of the issuer of the letter of credit or the law of the location of the nominated person as to the letter of credit will govern perfection of a security interest in a letter-of-credit right as long as the issuer or nominated person is located in a state in the United States. UCC § 9–306(a). If the issuer or nominated person is not located in a state of the United States, the general rule that the law of the debtor's location governs perfection will apply. UCC § 9–306, cmt. 2. An issuer or a nominated person is located at the location specified in the letter of credit. If there is more than one address specified, the issuer or nominated person is located at the address from which the letter of credit or undertaking issued. UCC § 5–116(b).

Example: A grants a security interest to State Bank in A's rights as a beneficiary under a letter of credit issued by Nations Bank. The address listed in the letter of credit for Nations Bank is Munich, Germany. The law of the state where A is located will determine whether State Bank has taken sufficient steps to perfect its security interest in the letter-of-credit right. If the address for Nations Bank as stated in the letter of credit was New York, New York, the law of the state of New York would determine whether State Bank has taken the appropriate steps for perfection of the security interest in the letter-of-credit right.

3. Choice of Law Regarding Priority and the Effect of Perfection and Nonperfection

The choice of law rules just studied also contain provisions for the choice of law concerning application of priority rules and the effect of taking or not taking a perfection step. In some circumstances, the law of one jurisdiction will govern the acts necessary to perfect the security interest and the law of a different jurisdiction will govern the priority of the security interest. See Chapter V, Section G.

H. Post-Closing Issues and Effect on Perfection

Once a security interest or agricultural lien attaches and is properly perfected, the secured party cannot rest easy thinking that its position in regard to the collateral is protected. The secured party must think about and take appropriate action to maintain perfection of its security interest or agricultural lien as events unfold.

1. Passage of Time

As discussed previously, the secured party will need to file a continuation statement in a timely manner in order to continue the effectiveness of the financing statement beyond its initial term. UCC § 9–515. Thus a security interest and agricultural lien can become unperfected by the mere passage of time.

2. Loss of Possession or Control

If perfection is accomplished through possession of collateral and the secured party loses possession of the collateral or if perfection is accomplished through control and the secured party loses control of the collateral, the perfection of the security interest is ended. UCC §§ 9–313(d), 9–314(b), (c).

3. Change in Use or Characterization of Goods

In a financing statement, the collateral must be adequately described. If the collateral is described as one type of goods, such as inventory, and subsequently the use of the good changes, such as to equipment, the effectiveness of the financing statement to perfect the security interest in the item of inventory is not affected even though that item is now equipment. UCC § 9–507(b). An exception to this principle, that changes in use of the collateral after perfection does not matter to maintaining perfection, is if the effect of the change in use is to require a different manner of perfection or a different place of perfection be used to perfect the security interest.

Example: A operates an appliance store and has granted a security interest in the inventory to secure an operating loan obtained from State Bank. State Bank properly perfected its security interest by filing a financing statement against A in the state of A's location listing the collateral as "inventory." A takes a stove out of inventory and starts to use it in the employee's break room. The stove is now being used as equipment. State Bank's security interest in the stove is still perfected.

Example: A operates a car dealership and has granted a security interest in the inventory to secure an operating loan obtained from State Bank. State Bank properly perfected its security interest by filing a financing statement against A in the state of A's location listing the collateral as "inventory." A takes a car out of inventory and starts to use it as a loaner for customers that need a car while the customers' cars are being serviced. The car is not being held for sale or lease and is now being used as equipment. State Bank's security interest in the car is no longer perfected because to perfect a security interest in the car requires compliance with the state's certificate of title law. UCC § 9–311(d).

4. Loss of Purchase Money Status

A purchase money security interest in consumer goods is automatically perfected, unless the consumer goods are covered by a certificate of title. Subsequent to the initial transaction, the loan may be refinanced, additional nonpurchase money collateral could be used to secure the original purchase money debt, or additional nonpurchase money obligations could be secured by the purchase money collateral. In a consumer goods transaction, a court may find that these types of events destroy the purchase money status of the original transaction, rendering the original automatic perfection no longer effective. In a nonconsumer goods transaction, Article 9 provides that these types of events do not destroy purchase money status of the original security interest. UCC § 9–103(f).

Example: A purchases a new stove on credit from Appliance Giant, Inc. for A's personal use and grants Appliance Giant a security interest in the new stove to secure the purchase price. Appliance Giant's security interest is automatically perfected. One week later, A purchases a new dishwasher on credit from Appliance Giant and grants a security interest in the dishwasher to secure the price. Under the two contracts with Appliance Giant, the two appliances secure all debts due to Appliance Giant, that is, the security interest in the stove secures the debt for the stove and the dishwasher and the security interest in the dishwasher secures the debt for the stove and the dishwasher. This cross collateralization may result in the security interest in both the stove and the dishwasher as not being considered purchase money security interests rendering Appliance Giant's security interests unperfected unless Appliance Giant files an effective financing statement covering the collateral against A in the proper location.

5. Sale or Disposition of Collateral

As stated in Chapter III, Section F, a security interest generally continues in collateral even though it has been sold or otherwise disposed of. Assuming the security interest or agricultural lien remains attached to the collateral after disposition, a financing statement remains effective as to collateral disposed of even if after a disposition the original debtor is no longer the debtor with respect to that collateral. UCC § 9–507(a). By acquiring collateral subject to a security interest or agricultural lien, the acquiring debtor authorizes the secured party to file a financing statement against the acquiring debtor covering that collateral and its proceeds. UCC § 9–509(c). If the transfer is to a debtor located in another jurisdiction the law governing perfection changes and thus the secured party would have to take steps to achieve perfection in the second state. See UCC § 9–316(a)(3) discussed *infra*.

Example: State Bank properly perfected a security interest in A's equipment by filing a financing statement against A in the proper location. A sold a piece of equipment to B, who was located in the same state as A, and under the attachment rules of Article 9 the security interest continues in that equipment. The financing statement filed against A is sufficient to maintain perfection of the security interest in the collateral even though B is now the debtor with respect to that collateral. State Bank is authorized to file a financing statement against B, if State Bank chooses to do so.

6. Perfection in Proceeds

As stated in Chapter III, Section D, a security interest attaches automatically to identifiable proceeds of collateral that was subject to the security interest. If the security interest in the original collateral was perfected, the security interest in the identifiable proceeds is automatically perfected for a period of 20 days. UCC § 9–315(c). To maintain perfection of the security interest in identifiable proceeds beyond the 20-day time period, one of three circumstances must be true. Article 9 does not address perfection of an agricultural lien in proceeds of farm products subject to the lien. UCC § 9–315, cmt. 9.

a. Security Interest in Original Collateral Perfected by a Filed Financing Statement

If a filed financing statement covers the original collateral and is effective to perfect a security interest in the original collateral, the identifiable proceeds are not acquired with cash proceeds, and the proceeds are the type of collateral that could be perfected by filing a financing statement in the same office as the filed financing statement that already exists, the security interest in the identifiable proceeds is perfected. UCC § 9–315(d)(1). The security interest in identifiable proceeds that is perfected due to the effectiveness of the financing statement as to the original collateral is perfected until the financing statement lapses or is terminated. UCC § 9–315(e).

Example: State Bank properly filed a financing statement covering A's inventory to perfect a security interest in the inventory. A sold a piece of inventory receiving in return a good that A used as equipment that is not subject to a certificate of title law. State

Bank's security interest in the equipment is perfected for a period of 20 days as identifiable proceeds of the sold inventory. State Bank's security interest is perfected beyond the 20 days because a financing statement perfecting a security interest in equipment could be filed to perfect a security interest in the same place as the filed financing statement that covers inventory. State Bank need not amend its financing statement to cover equipment.

Example: State Bank properly filed a financing statement covering A's inventory to perfect a security interest in the inventory. A sold a piece of inventory receiving in return a car that A used as equipment. State Bank's security interest in the car is perfected for a period of 20 days as identifiable proceeds of the sold inventory. State Bank's security interest is not perfected beyond the 20 days because a financing statement perfecting a security interest in car could not be filed to perfect a security interest in the car used as equipment. Rather State Bank must comply with the relevant state's certificate of title law.

b. Security Interest in Identifiable Cash Proceeds

If the security interest in the original collateral is perfected by any method and the proceeds are identifiable cash proceeds, the security interest in the identifiable cash proceeds is perfected as long as the proceeds remain identifiable cash proceeds. UCC § 9–315(d)(2). Cash proceeds are defined as "money, checks, deposit accounts, or the like." UCC § 9–102(a)(9).

c. Security Interest in Proceeds Perfected as if Proceeds Were Original Collateral

If neither of the above two provisions apply, the secured party has to take the appropriate perfection step as to the identifiable proceeds of the type involved in order to perfect its security interest in the identifiable proceeds beyond the 20-day time period of temporary perfection. UCC § 9–315(d)(3).

7. Debtor Name Change: Security Interest

If a security interest is perfected by a filed financing statement, UCC § 9–503 provides what name is sufficient on that financing statement. If a debtor's name does not meet the requirements of UCC § 9–503, and that noncompliance makes the financing statement seriously misleading, the filed financing statement will not be effective to perfect a security interest in collateral acquired after four months after the financing statement became seriously misleading unless within the four-month period the financing statement is amended to reflect the debtor's name as required under UCC § 9–503. The debtor's name on the financing statement will be considered seriously misleading if a search of the filing records under the debtor's correct name does not turn up the filing under the debtor's old name. UCC § 9–506(c). As to collateral acquired by the debtor within that four-month period, the financing statement with the debtor's seriously misleading name is still effective to perfect the security interest. UCC § 9–507(c). The debtor's authentication of the security agreement provides the authority for the secured party to file an amendment to reflect the debtor's correct name. UCC § 9–509(b).

Example: In a state that has adopted Alternative A of UCC § 9–503(a)(4), State Bank properly filed a financing statement with the surname "Smith" and the first personal name of "James" and middle initial of "A." as provided on the unexpired driver's license of the individual debtor issued by the debtor's state of residence, to perfect a security interest in all the debtor's equipment. A year later, the state reissues all driver's licenses so that they provide for the full middle name of the driver, making the correct name of the debtor to be surname "Smith," the first personal name of "James" and middle name of "Allen." Under the filing office's standard search logic, an exact match is required, and a search under the new correct name (with the full middle name) does not bring up the filing that has only the debtor's middle initial. State Bank's security interest will not be perfected as to collateral acquired after four months after the reissuance of the debtor's driver's license.

Example: In a state that has adopted Alternative B of UCC § 9–503(a)(4), State Bank properly filed a financing statement with the surname "Smith" and the first personal name of "James" to perfect a security interest in all the debtor's equipment. The unexpired driver's license of the individual debtor issued by the debtor's state of residence provides that debtor's name is "James A. Smith." A year later, the state reissues all driver's licenses providing for the full middle name of the driver, so that the driver's license shows the name "James Allen Smith." Under the filing office's standard search logic, an exact match is required. Under Alternative B, either the name on the driver's license or the debtors first personal name and surname are correct names. A search under "James Smith" which is one of the possible correct names, brings up the financing statement. State Bank's security interest continues perfected regardless of the name change on the driver's license.

8. Debtor Name Change: Agricultural Lien

A debtor's name change does not affect the effectiveness of a financing statement filed to perfect an agricultural lien. UCC § 9–507(b).

9. Debtor Structural Changes

When a new debtor becomes bound by an old debtor's security agreement, review Chapter III, Section E, the effectiveness of the filed financing statement against the collateral depends upon when the new debtor acquired the collateral. If a debtor changes its structure such as by reincorporation or converting from a partnership structure to a corporation structure, other state law may treat that as a change creating a "new debtor" or it may treat that as merely a debtor name change. See UCC § 9–512, cmt. 5. For purposes of this discussion, assume that the old and new debtor are both located in the same jurisdiction so that a change in the governing law is not implicated.

a. Collateral Acquired From the Old Debtor

The financing statement filed against the old debtor remains effective as to the collateral the new debtor acquires from the old debtor. UCC § 9–507(a).

b. Collateral Acquired by the New Debtor After Becoming the New Debtor

The financing statement filed against the old debtor is effective as to collateral the new debtor acquires subsequently to becoming the new debtor. UCC § 9–508(a). That rule is subject to an exception if the difference between the name of the new debtor and the old debtor is such that the filed financing statement as to the old debtor becomes seriously misleading. In that circumstance, the financing statement filed against the old debtor continues to be effective as to collateral acquired by the new debtor within four months after becoming the new debtor. As to collateral acquired after the four-month time period, the financing statement against the old debtor is not effective unless within the four-month time period a new initial financing statement is filed against the new debtor. UCC § 9–508(b). A financing statement against the old debtor will be seriously misleading if a search of the system under the new debtor's name does not reveal the filing under the old debtor's name. UCC § 9–506(c), (d).

c. Authority to File New Financing Statement

By becoming bound as a new debtor, the new debtor authorizes the filing of a financing statement covering the collateral. UCC § 9–509(b).

10. Secured Party Name Change, Structural Change, or Change in Location

Even though the secured party's name must be on a financing statement to make it effective to perfect, UCC § 9–502(a), and an address must be given as required in UCC § 9–516(b), a change in the secured party's name, business structure, or location does not affect the effectiveness of a filed financing statement. UCC § 9–507(b).

11. Assignment of Security Interest or Agricultural Lien

A secured party may assign its rights to another person. While the secured party may file an amendment to a financing statement in order to reflect the assignment, UCC § 9–514, the secured party is not required to do so in order to maintain the effectiveness of the perfection of the security interest or agricultural lien. UCC § 9–310(c).

12. Change in Governing Law

Because the debtor's location, the collateral's location, or a third party's location, determines the law that governs perfection of a security interest or agricultural lien, a change in the location of the debtor, collateral, or third party, as applicable, may have the effect of undoing the perfection of the security interest or agricultural lien.

a. Relocation of Debtor

If the location of the debtor determines the law governing perfection, the change in location of the debtor to another jurisdiction will require the secured party to take action to keep its security interest perfected.

(1) Collateral in Which the Security Interest Has Attached at the Time of Relocation

The law of the debtor's old jurisdiction will continue to govern questions regarding the perfection of the security interest in collateral to which the security interest has attached at the time the debtor relocates until the earlier of the following three events: (i) the expiration of the old financing statement by its own terms; (ii) four months after the debtor's location changed to the new jurisdiction; or (iii) one year after the collateral has been transferred to a person that is located in another jurisdiction and that is a debtor with respect to that collateral. UCC § 9–316(a). If the secured party takes the necessary perfection step in the jurisdiction of the debtor's new location within the applicable time period, the security interest is perfected by that new step. If the secured party does not take the necessary perfection step in the jurisdiction of the debtor's new location within that time period, the security interest becomes unperfected and is deemed to be retroactively unperfected as against a purchaser of the collateral for value. UCC § 9–316(b). The debtor's authentication of the security agreement is authority for the secured party to file an initial financing statement in the new jurisdiction to perfect a security interest in collateral covered by the security agreement and its proceeds. UCC § 9–509(b).

Example: State Bank has properly perfected its security interest in collateral by filing a financing statement in the state of the

Debtor's location, State 1. Debtor moves from State 1 to State 2. State Bank has the shorter of four months or when the financing statement in State 1 would have lapsed to file a new financing statement against Debtor in State 2 to maintain continuous perfection of its security interest in the collateral to which the security interest had attached prior to the move from State 1 to State 2.

Example: State Bank properly filed a financing statement against Debtor A in State 1 to perfect a security interest in equipment. Debtor A sold a piece of equipment to B, located in State 2. Assume under the rules of Article 9, State Bank's security interest continues in the piece of equipment. UCC § 9–315(a). State Bank has the shorter of one year or when the financing statement against Debtor A would have lapsed to file a financing statement in State 2 against Debtor B.

(2) After-Acquired Collateral

Assume the security interest attaches to collateral acquired by the debtor after relocation to a new jurisdiction under a properly constructed after-acquired property clause. As to collateral acquired within four months after the debtor's relocation, the financing statement filed in the first jurisdiction continues to control for the shorter of the time of four months or when the statement would have lapsed. If the secured party files a proper financing statement as to the collateral in the second jurisdiction during that time period, the security interest will remain continuously perfected. If the secured party does not file in the new jurisdiction within the time period, the security interest as to that after-acquired collateral becomes unperfected and is deemed retroactively unperfected against a purchaser for value. UCC § 9–316(h).

b. New Debtor

As explained above, when a new debtor becomes bound to the old debtor's security agreement, the filed financing statement against the old debtor continues to be effective to perfect a security interest in the assets of both the old and new debtor for a period of time. UCC § 9–508. If the new debtor is located in a jurisdiction that is different than the jurisdiction of the old debtor, additional rules apply.

(1) Assets Transferred from Old Debtor to New Debtor

As to the assets transferred from the old debtor to the new debtor in the new jurisdiction, the secured party must perfect its security interest in the new jurisdiction within the time period of effectiveness of the financing statement against the old debtor or one year after the assets were transferred to the new debtor in the new jurisdiction (whichever is shorter). UCC § 9–316(a).

(2) All Other Assets of New Debtor

As to the assets of the new debtor that were not the assets of the old debtor and the assets that the new debtor acquires within four months after becoming the new debtor, the law of the old jurisdiction will provide the governing law for perfection purposes for four months or the period of effectiveness of the old jurisdiction financing statement. If the secured party files an effective financing statement against the new debtor in the new jurisdiction within that time period, the security interest in the new debtor's collateral that did not come from the original debtor will remain continuously perfected. If the secured party does not file in the new jurisdiction against the new debtor within that time period, the security interest in the new debtor's collateral that did not come from the original debtor is deemed retroactively unperfected against a purchaser for value. UCC § 9–316(i).

Example: State Bank has properly perfected its security interest in collateral by filing a financing statement in the state of Debtor A's location, State 1. Debtor A reincorporates in State 2 under the name A Plus and all of the assets of Debtor A are transferred to A Plus, located in State 2. Debtor A is the original debtor and "A Plus" is the new debtor. As to assets of A Plus acquired from Debtor A, State Bank has one year to refile its financing statement in State 2 (assuming that the financing statement filed against Debtor A in State 1 does not lapse prior to that time). As to assets that A Plus acquires otherwise than from Debtor A, State 1 provides the governing law for perfection for four months after A Plus became the new debtor (assuming that the financing statement filed against Debtor A in State 1 does not lapse prior to that time). If State Bank files a financing statement against A Plus in State 2 within that four month time period, State Bank will be continuously perfected in the assets of A Plus acquired before and within four months after it became a new debtor.

c. Relocation of Collateral

Perfection of an agricultural lien, and in some circumstances, perfection of a security interest is governed by the location of the collateral. In that circumstance, if the location of the collateral moves to another jurisdiction, the law of that new jurisdiction will control perfection.

(1) Agricultural Liens

Perfection of agricultural liens requires filing a financing statement in the jurisdiction where the farm products are located. UCC §§ 9–302, 9–310(a). If the farm products move from one jurisdiction where the secured party has filed a financing statement to another jurisdiction where the secured party has not filed a financing statement (assuming the agricultural lien continues to exist once the farm products leave the jurisdiction in which the lien arose), the agricultural lien immediately becomes unperfected as there has been no perfection step in the new jurisdiction. Article 9 does not provide any grace period for the agricultural lienholder to refile. UCC § 9–316, cmt. 9.

(2) Possessory Security Interests

The law of the jurisdiction where the collateral is located governs the perfection of possessory security interests. UCC § 9–301(2). If the collateral moves from one jurisdiction to another, as long as the security interest in the collateral is perfected in the old jurisdiction and, under the law of the new jurisdiction, the security interest is perfected in the collateral when it enters the new jurisdiction, the security interest was continuously perfected. UCC § 9–316(c).

d. Certificate of Title Goods

When goods are covered by a certificate of title, the law of the jurisdiction issuing the certificate of title controls perfection of a security interest in the good. UCC § 9–303. If a certificate of title is issued for a good, the law governing perfection will change from the debtor's location (if perfection is by any method other than possession of the good) or the collateral's location (if perfection is by possession of the good) to the law of the jurisdiction that issued the certificate of title. Similarly, if one jurisdiction issues a certificate of title covering a good and then another jurisdiction issues a certificate of title covering the same good, the law governing perfection of the security interest will change from the first jurisdiction to the second jurisdiction. UCC § 9–303(b).

(1) General Rule

Article 9 provides that if a security interest in a good is perfected in any manner in one jurisdiction and the good becomes covered by a certificate of title issued by another jurisdiction, the security interest remains perfected based upon the law of the first jurisdiction as if the certificate of title was not issued by the second jurisdiction. UCC § 9–316(d).

(2) Exception to General Rule

The security interest that was perfected by the appropriate action in the first jurisdiction when the good becomes covered by a certificate of title in the second jurisdiction is deemed unperfected as to a purchaser for value unless the secured party takes the appropriate action in the second jurisdiction within the earlier of four months after the goods become covered by the certificate of title issued by the second jurisdiction or the time perfection would have expired of its own force in the first jurisdiction. UCC § 9–316(e).

Example: State Bank perfects a security interest in a boat by properly filing a financing statement covering the boat in Debtor's location, State 1. Debtor subsequently obtains a certificate of title covering the boat in State 2. State Bank's security interest remains perfected for a period of four months. State Bank needs to perfect under the certificate of title law in State 2 within the four months in order to maintain perfection of its security interest in the boat as against a purchaser for value.

Example: State Bank perfects a security interest in a boat by properly obtaining notation of its security interest on the boat certificate of title in State 1. Debtor subsequently obtains a certificate of title covering the boat in State 2. State Bank's security interest remains perfected for a period of four months. State Bank needs to perfect under the certificate of title law in State 2 within the four months in order to maintain perfection of its security interest in the boat as against a purchaser for value.

Example: State Bank perfects a security interest in a boat by properly obtaining notation of its security interest on the boat certificate of title in State 1. Debtor subsequently cancels the certificate of title under the law of State 1. The law of State 1 no longer governs perfection. State Bank's security interest is unperfected as the law of the Debtor's location will now govern perfection of the security interest and under that law, State Bank has not taken the applicable perfection steps of either filing a financing statement or taking possession of the boat. The four month rule does not apply as the boat has not become covered by another certificate of title law.

(3) Perfection by Possession

If the goods are subject to a security interest that is perfected in any manner and the goods become covered by a certificate of title issued by another jurisdiction, the secured party may perfect its security interest in the goods by possession even though the goods are now covered by the new certificate of title. UCC § 9–313(b).

e. Relocation of Third Party

The law governing perfection of a security interest in deposit accounts, letter-of-credit rights, and investment property when perfection is by a nonfiling method is determined by the law where the bank, issuer, nominated person, securities intermediary, or commodity intermediary (as the case may be) are located. If those entities move jurisdictions so as to implicate a different governing law, the security interest remains perfected until the earlier of the time the security interest would be unperfected under the law of the first jurisdiction or four months after the relevant entity moves to the second jurisdiction. UCC § 9–316(f). If the security interest becomes perfected in the new jurisdiction within that time period, the security interest is perfected thereafter. If the security interest is not perfected within that time period, the security interest is unperfected and deemed retroactively unperfected against a purchaser for value of the collateral. UCC § 9–316(g).

13. Effect of Bankruptcy on Perfection of Security Interest or Agricultural Lien

Generally, if the security interest or agricultural lien is perfected when the debtor files bankruptcy, the Bankruptcy Code does not effect the perfection of the security interest or agricultural lien. Collateral that is subject to a perfected security interest or agricultural lien becomes property of the debtor's bankruptcy estate, 11 U.S.C. § 541, and the secured party is subject to the automatic stay preventing the secured party from taking any further action with respect to the collateral and its security interest, 11 U.S.C. § 362. Two special situations deserve special mention.

a. Turnover

If the secured party has perfected its security interest by possession or control of the collateral, the secured party may be faced with a difficult issue. If the secured party loses possession or control of the collateral, the secured party faces the risk that its security interest will become unperfected. UCC §§ 9–313, 9–314. On the other hand, persons with possession or control of property of the estate (which the collateral would be) are under an obligation to turn the collateral over to the bankruptcy trustee, 11 U.S.C. §§ 542, 543, and may be subject to liability for contempt of court for failing to do so.

b. Continuation Statements and the Automatic Stay

The automatic stay prevents the secured party from taking any action to create, perfect or enforce its security interest or agricultural lien in the collateral. 11 U.S.C. § 362. An exception to the automatic stay allows the secured party to file a continuation statement during the pendency of the bankruptcy case to continue the effectiveness of a filed financing statement. 11 U.S.C. § 362(b)(3).

I. Review Questions for Chapter IV

Question 1

Barley Feed Company supplied feed to Farmer for Farmer's chickens. Farmer did not pay for the feed. Under state law, Barley Feed Company has a lien in the chickens to secure the obligation of Farmer to pay for the feed. Barley comes to you to ask whether it needs to do anything else to protect its lien in the chickens. Advise Barley.

Question 2

For each type of collateral listed below, identify the proper method or methods of perfection of a security interest in that collateral. Review the material in Chapter II as well to determine whether Article 9 will govern the answer to that question.

A. Electronic chattel paper
B. Goods not covered by a certificate of title or a document of title
C. Goods covered by certificate of title
D. Documents of title and goods covered by such documents but are not covered by a certificate of title law
E. Accounts
F. Tangible chattel paper
G. Instruments
H. Certificated security
I. Payment intangibles

J. Inventory
K. Consumer goods
L. General intangibles
M. Letter-of-credit right
N. Equipment
O. Farm products
P. Fixtures
Q. As-extracted collateral
R. Deposit accounts
S. Uncertificated security
T. Securities entitlement
U. Securities account
V. Manufactured home
W. Proceeds

Question 3

For each type of collateral listed above in Question 2, determine the choice of law rule in Article 9 that will govern the attempt to perfect a security interest in that collateral.

Question 4

Albert wants to borrow money from Bank. Bank insists on collateral to secure the loan. Albert lists the following items on his loan application. Advise Bank as to how to perfect an enforceable security interest in each of these items and any items of personal property that Albert acquires in the future to secure all obligations that Albert may ever owe Bank. Review all the material covered in Chapters I through IV to give a complete analysis.

A. Checking account held at National Bank
B. Pickup truck
C. Riding lawnmower
D. Mobile home
E. Amounts owed Albert by his next door neighbor stemming from the sale of a car to the neighbor
F. Bonds held in an account at Brokerage Inc.
G. Produce from Albert's garden
H. Items such as furniture and household goods stored at Warehouse Inc.

Question 5

Based upon the facts of Question 4, advise Bank as to the steps it should take to ensure that it remains perfected in the list of collateral even if Albert moves location, moves the location of the collateral, or disposes of any item of collateral.

V

Priority of Security Interests and Agricultural Liens

Priority of a security interest or agricultural lien requires attachment of the security interest or agricultural lien to the debtor's assets. Unless the security interest or agricultural lien has attached, the secured party has no specific property claim to the debtor's asset. Thus, familiarity with the provisions of Chapters II and III on the scope of Article 9 and attachment of a security interest and agricultural lien is necessary in order to make sense of the priority rules. The perfection or lack of perfection of a security interest and agricultural lien in many circumstances will determine the priority of the security interest and agricultural lien as against other parties that make claims to the debtor's assets. Thus, familiarity with the methods of perfection as set forth in Chapter IV is necessary to understand the priority rules. This Chapter will consider the priority rules found in UCC Article 9 concerning the priority of property claims to the debtor's assets as against security interests and agricultural liens within the scope of Article 9. This Chapter does not consider other priority rules found in other law, such as real estate law.

A. Basic Concept of Priority

The concept of priority of security interests and agricultural liens in the debtor's assets is the concept of the hierarchy of property claims (i.e. security interests or agricultural liens) as against specific assets of the debtor. Application of the priority rules will determine the relative priority of that creditor's property claim to a specific asset. Generally, a creditor will want as high a priority as possible for its property claim against the debtor's asset as that high priority will increase the likelihood of the creditor being able to realize value out of the asset.

Example: Under the applicable priority rules, SP–1 has a first priority claim for $5,000 in an item of debtor's equipment. SP–2 has a second priority claim for $2,000 in that same piece of equipment. The equipment is sold for $10,000. SP–1 collects $5,000 from the sale proceeds in full satisfaction of its claim and SP–2 collects $2,000 in full satisfaction of its claim. The debtor receives the $3,000 excess.

Example: Under the applicable priority rules, SP–1 has a first priority claim for $5,000 in an item of debtor's equipment. SP–2 has a second priority claim for $2,000 in that same piece of equipment. The equipment is sold for $5,500. SP–1 receives $5,000 from the sale in full satisfaction of its claim and SP–2 receives $500 in partial satisfaction of its claim, leaving an unpaid claim for $1,500. SP–2 would have to try and collect that unpaid claim for $1,500 (the deficiency) from the debtor through other means.

1. Fundamental Priority Principle

Many priority rules are based upon a fundamental property principle that the priority of interests in property will be based upon the time the interest is sufficiently attached to the property. This basis principle is called "first-in-time" and is subject to much further definition and refinement. The time at which a property right is sufficiently attached to an asset to count for purposes of the first-in-time principle varies among bodies of law. For example, in some systems, an interest may not be considered to be sufficiently attached to property until some public notice is given of the attachment of the interest. Article 9 uses a type of first-in-time principle subject to many exceptions and refinements.

2. Security Agreement Effective Against Third Parties

Article 9 provides that a security agreement is effective against purchasers of the collateral and creditors of the parties. UCC § 9–201(a). This is a basic statement of a first-in-time principle that a security agreement creating a security interest is effective against third parties that deal with the property. This general rule is subject to numerous exceptions that will take the rest of this Chapter to explore.

3. Priority Is Determined by Asset

The priority hierarchy requires that the analysis concerning priority be considered on an asset-by-asset basis. Thus it is misleading and inaccurate to talk about a particular creditor's priority position in regard to all of the debtor's assets. The precise question that must be answered is what is this creditor's priority position for its property claim in this particular asset of the debtor. One creditor may have a first priority property claim in Asset A and a second priority property claim in Asset B. In some circumstances, the priority rules will differ depending upon the type of asset. Thus, for example, some priority rules will apply to goods and other priority rules will apply to instruments and chattel paper.

4. Priority Is Determined by Type of Creditor

The priority positions of the creditor's property claims to the debtor's asset will also be determined by what type of creditor is involved in the priority contest as against the security interest or agricultural lien. Thus, Article 9 will state a priority rule that will control the priority contest as between a secured party with a security interest and a lien creditor with a lien created by execution on property pursuant to a judgment. Article 9 will state a different priority rule to govern the contest as between two secured parties with security interests in the same asset. If there are three creditors with claims to an asset, there will be three priority contests with possibly three different rules involved.

Example: Creditors A, B, and C all have property claims against one of the debtor's assets. Creditor A has a security interest. Creditor B has an execution lien. Creditor C has a statutory lien. To determine the hierarchy of the three property claims to the asset, the following priority disputes must be considered: Creditor A's security interest against Creditor B's execution lien, Creditor A's security interest against Creditor C's statutory lien, and Creditor B's execution lien as against Creditor C's statutory lien.

5. Priority May Be Determined by the Method of Perfection

If a secured party has alternative methods of perfection of its security interest, such as by either filing a financing statement covering the collateral or by taking possession of the collateral, the priority of the security interest as against other claims to the same asset may be different depending upon the method the secured party used to perfect its security interest.

6. Methodology

The methodology for determining the hierarchy of property claims to an asset is as follows. First, determine the asset and its type (inventory, chattel paper, etc.). Second, determine what creditors have property claims to the asset. As to each creditor that has a property claim to the asset, determine the type of property claim (execution lien, agricultural lien, statutory lien, security interest). Third, determine the relative priority of that creditor's type of property claim as against each of the other creditor's property claims to the asset by selecting and applying the appropriate priority rule. After making that determination for each creditor's property claim, place the property claims to that asset in their order of priority as determined by the priority rules.

7. Subordination

Even though application of the priority rules results in a determination of the priority of a creditor's property claim, the creditor may agree with another creditor that its property claim will be subordinated in priority to the other creditor's property claim. UCC § 9–339.

B. Security Interest and Agricultural Lien as Against Lien Creditor

A lien creditor is a creditor that has obtained a lien on the debtor's personal property by execution, attachment or levy. Those processes were briefly described in Chapter I. A lien creditor also includes an assignee for the benefit of creditors, an equity receiver, and the trustee in bankruptcy. UCC § 9–102(a)(52).

1. Basic Priority Rule

Subject to two exceptions, a security interest or agricultural lien that is attached but unperfected at the time the lien creditor becomes a lien creditor is subordinate in priority to the lien created by the lien creditor. UCC § 9–317(a)(2)(A). Perfection means the security interest or agricultural lien has attached and the secured party has taken the applicable perfection step regarding the security interest or agricultural lien. UCC § 9–308(a), (b).

Example: Debtor authenticated a security agreement giving SP–1 a security interest in Debtor's securities account held at Brokerage Inc. in exchange for a loan. On Monday, SP–1 funded the loan. SP–1's security interest has attached to the securities account. On Tuesday, Lien Creditor levied on the securities account at Brokerage Inc. in execution of a judgment obtained against Debtor. On Wednesday, SP–1 filed a financing statement against Debtor indicating the securities account as collateral. SP–1's security interest in the securities account will be subordinate to the lien created by Lien Creditor's levy because SP–1's security interest was attached but not perfected when Lien Creditor levied and thereby obtained its execution lien.

Example: Debtor authenticated a security agreement giving SP–1 a security interest in Debtor's securities account held at Brokerage Inc. in exchange for a loan. On Monday, SP–1 funded the loan. SP–1's security interest has attached to the securities account. On Tuesday, Lien Creditor 1 levied on the securities account at Brokerage Inc. in execution of a judgment obtained against Debtor. On Wednesday, SP–1 filed a financing statement against Debtor indicating the securities account as collateral. On Thursday, Lien Creditor 2 levied on the securities account in execution of a different judgment against Debtor. As between Lien Creditor 1 and SP–1, Lien Creditor 1's lien has priority over SP–1's security interest in the securities account. As between SP–1 and Lien Creditor 2, SP–1's security interest has priority over Lien Creditor 2's lien in the securities account. The priority contest between Lien Creditor 1 and Lien Creditor 2 will not be determined by Article 9 but by state law governing priority between lien creditors. Assuming that other law employs the priority rule of first to levy has priority, the ranking of the three interests in order of priority of claims to the securities account would be: 1st priority-Lien Creditor 1, 2nd priority-SP–1, and 3rd priority-Lien Creditor 2.

Example: Debtor obtained feed from Feed Supplier Inc. and fed it to Debtor's livestock. Under state law, Feed Supplier Inc. has a lien on the livestock to secure the price of the feed which qualifies as an agricultural lien under Article 9. After Feed Supplier delivered the feed to Debtor and Debtor gave the feed to its livestock, Lien Creditor levied on the livestock. Feed Supplier then filed a financing statement against Debtor to perfect its agricultural lien, indicating livestock as collateral. Lien Creditor's lien created by the levy has first priority and Feed Supplier's agricultural lien has second priority in the livestock.

2. Exception to the Basic Priority Rule: No Value as the Only Missing Step to Perfection of a Security Interest

The basic lien creditor priority rule is subject to the following exception. If the secured party has filed an effective financing statement against the debtor and has obtained the debtor's authenticated security agreement with an adequate collateral description but has not yet given value at the time the lien creditor's lien arises, the secured party's security interest created subsequently, through the giving of value after the lien creditor's lien arises, will be superior to the lien creditor's lien. UCC § 9–317(a)(2)(B).

Example: On Monday, SP–1 filed an effective financing statement against Debtor covering inventory and Debtor signed a security agreement granting SP–1 a security interest in inventory to secure a loan. On Tuesday, Lien Creditor levied on Debtor's inventory. On Wednesday, SP–1 funded the loan to Debtor. SP–1's security interest was not perfected at the time the Lien Creditor levied and obtained its lien because value had not yet been given by SP–1. UCC § 9–308. Nonetheless, SP–1's security interest in the inventory will have priority over the Lien Creditor's lien created by the levy.

3. Exception to the Basic Priority Rule: Purchase Money Security Interests

The basic rule is also subject to an exception for purchase money security interests that have attached but are not perfected prior to the lien creditor's obtaining of the lien, as long as the secured party files a financing statement against the debtor covering the collateral within 20 days after the debtor receives delivery of the collateral subject to the purchase money security interest. UCC §§ 9–317(e), 9–103 (definition of purchase money security interest). In that situation, the security interest is not subordinate to a lien creditor's lien that arises between the time the security interest is attached and the secured party files the financing statement. The same result should obtain if the creditor complies with an applicable certificate of title law instead of filing a financing statement. UCC § 9–317, cmt. 8.

Example: Debtor bought a new piece of equipment for Debtor's factory and granted Seller a security interest in that piece of equipment to secure the purchase price. Seller delivered the equipment to Debtor on Monday. Seller has a purchase money security interest in the piece of equipment. On the following Friday, Lien Creditor levied on the equipment. On the following Tuesday (8 days after the equipment was delivered to Debtor), Seller filed a financing statement against Debtor covering the equipment. Seller's purchase money security interest is superior to Lien Creditor's lien created by the levy.

Example: Debtor bought a new piece of equipment for Debtor's factory and granted Seller a security interest in that piece of equipment to secure the purchase price. Seller delivered the equipment to Debtor on Monday. Seller has a purchase money security interest in the piece of equipment. On the following Friday, Lien Creditor levied on the equipment. Three weeks later (22 days after the equipment was delivered to Debtor), Seller filed a financing statement against Debtor covering the equipment. Seller's purchase money security interest is subordinate to Lien Creditor's lien created by the levy.

Example: Debtor bought a new truck as equipment for Debtor's business and granted State Bank a security interest in the truck to secure the loan given for the purchase price. The truck is delivered to Debtor on

Monday. State Bank has a purchase money security interest in the truck. On the following Friday, Lien Creditor levied on the truck. On the following Tuesday (8 days after the equipment was delivered to Debtor), State Bank filed an application with the state department of motor vehicles to obtain notation of its security interest on the truck's certificate of title. UCC §§ 9–303, 9–311. State Bank's purchase money security interest will be superior to the Lien Creditor's lien on the truck created by the levy.

4. Treatment of Future Advances

A secured party may make additional extensions of value under a future advances clause after the lien creditor's lien arises. If the secured party does so and the secured party's security interest is otherwise superior to the lien creditor's lien, the lien creditor's lien will be subordinate to the security interest that secures those advances unless the advance is made more than 45 days after the date of the lien creditor's obtaining of the lien. Even if the advance is made more than 45 days after the lien creditor's lien arose, the security interest securing the advance may still have priority over the lien creditor's lien if the advance is made without knowledge of the lien creditor's lien or made pursuant to a commitment entered into without knowledge of the lien creditor's lien. UCC § 9–323(b). This rule subordinating some security interests securing future advances does not apply to secured parties that are buyers of accounts, chattel paper, payment intangibles, or promissory notes or a secured party that is a consignor of goods. UCC § 9–323(c). Knowledge means "actual knowledge" and not mere of notice facts and circumstances that may give reason to know of the lien. UCC § 1–202.

Example: Debtor, a nonconsumer, authenticated a security agreement giving SP–1 a security interest in Debtor's securities account held at Brokerage Inc. to secure a loan of $5,000 and any future loans. On Monday, SP–1 funded the loan. SP–1 has a security interest in the securities account. On Tuesday, SP–1 filed a financing statement against Debtor indicating securities account as the collateral. SP–1 has a perfected security interest in the securities account. On Wednesday, Lien Creditor levied on the securities account at Brokerage Inc. in execution of a judgment for $1,000 obtained against Debtor. On the following Friday, SP–1 gave additional value of $2,000 to Debtor that was secured by a security interest in the securities account at Brokerage Inc. The securities account is worth $6,500. Lien Creditor's lien in the securities account is subordinate to the security interest that secures both the $5,000 initial advance and the subsequent $2,000 advance. SP–1's knowledge or lack of knowledge of the levy does not impact the result.

Example: Debtor, a nonconsumer, authenticated a security agreement giving SP–1 a security interest in Debtor's securities account held at Brokerage Inc. to secure a loan of $5,000 and any future loans. On Monday, SP–1 funded the loan. SP–1 has a security interest in the securities account. On Tuesday, SP–1 filed a financing statement against Debtor indicating securities account as the collateral. SP–1 has a perfected security interest in the securities account. On Wednesday, Lien Creditor levied on the securities account at Brokerage Inc. in execution of a judgment for $1,000 obtained against Debtor. Fifty days after the levy, SP–1 gave additional value of $2,000 to Debtor that was secured by a security interest in the securities account at Brokerage Inc. The securities account is worth $6,500. The additional loan of $2,000 was made *with* knowledge of the levy. The order of priority of interests in the securities account is: 1st priority-SP–1 for $5,000; 2nd priority-Lien Creditor for $1,000; and 3rd priority- SP–1 future advance of $2,000.

Example: Debtor, a nonconsumer, authenticated a security agreement giving SP–1 a security interest in Debtor's securities account held at Brokerage Inc. to secure a loan of $5,000 and any future loans. On Monday, SP–1 funded the loan. SP–1 has a security interest in the securities account. On Tuesday, SP–1 filed a financing statement against Debtor indicating securities account as the collateral. SP–1 has a perfected security interest in the securities account. On Wednesday, Lien Creditor levied on the securities account at Brokerage Inc. in execution of a judgment for $1,000 obtained against Debtor. Fifty days after the levy, SP–1 gave additional value of $2,000 to Debtor that was secured by a security interest in the securities account at Brokerage Inc. The securities account is worth $6,500. The additional loan of $2,000 was made *without* knowledge of the levy. The order of priority of interests in the securities account is: 1st priority-SP–1 for $7,000 and 2nd priority-Lien Creditor for $1,000.

Example: Debtor, a nonconsumer, authenticated a security agreement giving SP–1 a security interest in Debtor's securities account held at Brokerage Inc. to secure a loan of $5,000 and any future loans. On Monday, SP–1 funded the loan for $5,000. SP–1 has a security interest in the securities account. On Tuesday, Lien Creditor levied on the securities account at Brokerage Inc. in execution of a judgment for $1,000 obtained against Debtor. On Wednesday, SP–1 filed a financing statement against Debtor indicating securities account as the collateral. On Friday, SP–1 loaned an additional $2,000 to Debtor that is also secured by a security interest in the securities account. SP–1's security interest in the securities account securing the $7,000 loan (both the initial and subsequent advance) will be subordinate to the lien created by Lien Creditor's levy.

Example: Debtor signed an agreement in which it sold accounts worth $5,000 to SP–1 for a purchase price of $4,000. On Monday, SP–1 paid Debtor $2,000. The sale of the accounts was covered by Article 9 and created a security interest. On Tuesday, SP–1 filed a financing statement against Debtor covering the accounts. On Friday, Lien Creditor levied on the accounts. Fifty days later, SP–1 paid Debtor the remaining balance of $2,000 for the accounts even though it knew of the levy. SP–1's security interest as a buyer of accounts is superior to the Lien Creditor's lien created by the levy. UCC § 9–323 does not subordinate SP–1's security interest created by the sale of accounts to Lien Creditor's lien.

C. Security Interest as Against Possessory Statutory or Common Law Lien

Sometimes law other than Article 9 will create nonconsensual liens in the debtor's property in favor of a person that performs services or furnishes materials to the debtor and its property. If such a lien is created under other law and there is also a security interest on that property, Article 9 provides that in some circumstances the lien created under other law will have priority over the security interest even if the security interest attached to the property first and was perfected prior to the other lien attaching to the property. In order for the lien created under other law to be superior in priority to the security interest, the other lien must be a possessory lien in goods that secures payment or performance of an obligation for services and materials that the lienholder furnishes with respect to the goods in the ordinary course of the lienholder's business. That possessory lien must be created by a statute or rule of law other than Article 9 and the effectiveness of the lienholder's lien must depend upon the lienholder's possession of the goods. If all of those criteria are true, the possessory lien will have priority over the security interest even if the security interest was attached and perfected before the possessory lien arose, unless the statute creating the possessory lien expressly provides otherwise. UCC § 9–333.

Example: SP–1 has an attached and perfected security interest in Debtor's equipment. Debtor took the equipment to Repair Shop Inc. for service and repairs. Under state law, Repair Shop Inc. may assert a possessory lien for the value of the repairs to the equipment. Repair Shop did so and refused to relinquish possession of the equipment until paid for the repairs. In a priority dispute between SP–1 and Repair Shop regarding the equipment, Repair Shop's possessory lien will have priority over SP–1's security interest as long as Repair Shop does not lose possession of the equipment.

Example: SP–1 has an attached and perfected security interest in Debtor's equipment. Debtor took the equipment to Repair Shop Inc. for service and repairs. Under state law, Repair Shop Inc. may assert a possessory lien for the value of the repairs to the equipment. Repair Shop did so and refused to relinquish possession of the equipment until paid for the repairs. While the equipment was in Repair Shop's possession, Lien Creditor levied on the equipment in execution of a judgment obtained against Debtor. In the priority dispute between SP–1 and Repair Shop regarding the equipment, Repair Shop's possessory lien will have priority over SP–1's security interest. UCC § 9–333. In the priority dispute between SP–1 and Lien Creditor, SP–1 will have priority. UCC § 9–317. The priority dispute between Lien Creditor and Repair Shop will be determined by non-Article 9 law. Assuming under that non-Article 9 law Repair Shop will have priority over Lien Creditor's lien under a first-in-time principle, the order of priority of interests will be: 1st priority-Repair Shop's possessory lien; 2nd priority-SP–1's security interest; and 3rd priority-Lien Creditor's lien.

D. Security Interest or Agricultural Lien as Against Another Security Interest or Agricultural Lien

The majority of the priority rules in Article 9 address the rights of secured parties with security interests or agricultural liens in collateral as against other secured parties with security interests or agricultural liens in the same collateral.

1. General Rules

Article 9 contains three general rules for determining the priority of security interests and agricultural liens as against other security interests and agricultural liens: (i) first to file a financing statement or perfect beats another perfected interest; (ii) perfected interest beats unperfected; and (iii) when both the competing interests are unperfected, first to attach has priority. These three general rules are subject to numerous exceptions detailed in this Chapter.

a. First to File or Perfect

The general priority rule for determining the priority of *perfected* security interests or *perfected* agricultural liens as against other *perfected* security interests or *perfected* agricultural liens in the same asset is that priority dates from the time an effective financing statement covering the collateral is first filed against the collateral or the time a security interest or agricultural lien is first perfected as long as there is no time thereafter when there is neither an effective financing statement filed as to the collateral nor perfection of the security interest or agricultural lien. UCC § 9–322(a)(1). Perfection means attachment plus an applicable perfection method. UCC § 9–308.

Example: On Monday, SP–1 filed an effective financing statement against Debtor covering accounts. On Tuesday, SP–2 filed an effective financing against Debtor covering accounts and obtained Debtor's signed security agreement granting a security interest in accounts then owned or thereafter acquired to secure a loan from SP–2. SP–2 funded the loan that day. On Wednesday, SP–1 obtained

Debtor's signed security agreement granting a security interest in accounts then owned or thereafter acquired to SP–1 to secure a loan from SP–1. SP–1 funded the loan that day. Even though SP–2's security interest was attached and perfected first as to accounts existing at the time, SP–1 filed its effective financing statement first. Even though both SP–1's and SP–2's security interests attached to after acquired accounts at the same time (when the debtor acquires rights in them), SP–1 filed its effective financing statement first. In a priority contest between SP–1 and SP–2 regarding accounts (whether owned at the time or thereafter acquired), SP–1 has priority under the first to file or perfect rule.

Example: SP–1 obtained Debtor's signed security agreement granting SP–1 a security interest in Debtor's equipment in exchange for a loan funded the same day. SP–1's security interest in the equipment is attached. The next week, SP–2 obtained Debtor's signed security agreement granting SP–2 a security interest in Debtor's equipment in exchange for a loan funded the same day. SP–2 filed an effective financing statement against Debtor in the correct place covering equipment the same day. SP–2's security interest in the equipment is perfected. SP–2 knew about Debtor's arrangement with SP–1 at the time SP–2 made the loan and filed its financing statement. SP–1 then filed an effective financing statement against Debtor in the correct place covering the equipment. SP–2's knowledge of SP–1's security interest is irrelevant to application of the priority rule. SP–2's security interest in the equipment has priority as its security interest was perfected first and its financing statement was filed first.

Example: On Monday SP–1 obtained Debtor's signed security agreement granting SP–1 a security interest in Debtor's chattel paper in exchange for a loan. SP–1 funded the loan and took possession of the chattel paper. SP–1's security interest in the chattel paper in its possession is perfected. On Tuesday, SP–2 filed an effective financing statement against Debtor listing chattel paper as the collateral. SP–2 also obtained Debtor's signed security agreement giving a security interest in chattel paper to SP–2 in exchange for a loan. SP–2 funded the loan. SP–2's security interest in the chattel paper is perfected. SP–1 has priority in the chattel paper as it perfected its security interest before SP–2 filed its financing statement or perfected its security interest.

Example: On Monday SP–1 obtained Debtor's signed security agreement granting SP–1 a security interest in Debtor's equipment in exchange for a loan. SP–1 funded the loan. SP–1's security interest in the equipment is attached. On Tuesday, SP–2 filed an effective financing statement against Debtor listing equipment as the collateral. SP–2 also obtained Debtor's signed security agreement giving a security interest in equipment to SP–2 in exchange for a loan. On Wednesday, SP–1 took possession of the equipment. On Thursday, SP–2 funded the loan. SP–1's security interest was perfected on Wednesday and SP–2's security interest was perfected on Thursday. Under the first to file or perfect rule, however, SP–2's security interest in the equipment has priority over SP–1's security interest because SP–2 filed its financing statement before SP–1 perfected its security interest.

Example: In May, SP–1 filed a financing statement against Debtor listing farm products as the collateral, had Debtor sign a security agreement granting SP–1 a security interest in farm products to secure all obligations then owed or thereafter owed, and funded the loan. SP–1's security interest is perfected. In June, Chemical Supply Inc. provided chemicals to Debtor to spray on Debtor's crops to combat an insect infestation. Under state law, Chemical Supply has a lien Debtor's crops to secure payment of the price of the chemicals. Chemical Supply filed a financing statement listing crops as the collateral on June 15. SP–1's security interest in Debtor's crops (farm products) has priority over Chemical Supply's agricultural lien.

Example: On Monday, SP–1 obtained Debtor's signed security agreement granting SP–1 a security interest in Debtor's chattel paper in exchange for a loan. SP–1 funded the loan and took possession of the chattel paper that same day. SP–1's security interest is perfected. On Tuesday, SP–2 filed an effective financing statement against Debtor listing chattel paper as the collateral. SP–2 also obtained Debtor's signed security agreement giving a security interest in chattel paper to SP–2 in exchange for a loan. On Wednesday, SP–2 funded the loan. At this point, SP–1's security interest in the chattel paper has priority over SP–2's security interest in the chattel paper. Two weeks later, SP–1 relinquished possession of the chattel paper to Debtor. Two days after that, SP–1 filed an effective financing statement against Debtor covering the chattel paper. Because SP–1 had a two-day period in which its security interest was unperfected and there was no effective filed financing statement covering the chattel paper, SP–2's security interest in the chattel paper will have priority over SP–1's security interest.

Example: On Monday, SP–1 obtained Debtor's signed security agreement granting SP–1 a security interest in all of Debtor's instruments in exchange for a new loan. SP–1 funded the loan the same day. Under UCC § 9–312(e), SP–1's security interest is perfected for 20 days from attachment of the security interest. On Wednesday, SP–2 obtained Debtor's signed security agreement granting SP–2 a security interest in all of the Debtor's instruments to secure an already existing loan. SP–2 filed an effective financing statement against Debtor covering instruments that same day. SP–2's security interest is perfected. Nineteen days after funding the loan, SP–1 filed an effective financing statement against Debtor covering instruments. SP–1's perfection of its security interest by filing the financing statement took place prior to the expiration of the 20-day period of temporary perfection and thus SP–1's security interest was continually perfected. UCC § 9–308(c). SP–1's security interest will have priority over SP–2's security interest in the instruments.

Example: On Monday, SP–1 purchased Debtor's accounts pursuant to a written purchase agreement adequately describing the accounts, paying Debtor the purchase price. SP–1 is the owner of the accounts, which ownership interest is defined as a "security interest" covered by Article 9. On Wednesday, Debtor signed a security agreement granting a security interest in accounts to SP–2 in exchange for a loan which was funded that day. That same day

SP–2 filed a financing statement against Debtor covering accounts. SP–2's security interest is perfected. On Friday, SP–1 filed a financing statement against Debtor covering accounts. Under the first to file or perfect rule, SP–2's security interest has priority over SP–1's security interest in the accounts.

(1) When the Perfection Method Is Governed by Other Law

Because compliance with a federal preemptive filing system or a certificate of title system is deemed to be the filing of a financing statement, the first to file or perfect rule also applies to situations in which the secured party complies with those systems. UCC § 9–311(b).

(2) Application of Rule to Proceeds and Supporting Obligations

For purposes of applying the first to file or perfect rule, the time of filing or perfection as to the original collateral is deemed to be the time of filing or perfection as to proceeds of the original collateral and supporting obligations to the original collateral. UCC § 9–322(b). The proceeds and supporting obligations priority rules are very complex and best explored after explaining the many exceptions to the first to file or perfect priority rule in the rest of this Section D.

Example: On Monday, SP–1 filed an effective financing statement against Debtor covering accounts. On Tuesday, SP–2 filed an effective financing against Debtor covering accounts and obtained Debtor's signed security agreement granting a security interest in accounts to secure a loan from SP–2. SP–2 funded the loan that day. SP–2's security interest is perfected. On Wednesday, SP–1 obtained Debtor's signed security agreement granting a security interest in accounts to SP–1 to secure a loan from SP–1. SP–1 funded the loan that day. SP–1's security interest is perfected. In a priority contest between SP–1 and SP–2 regarding accounts, SP–1 has priority under the first to file or perfect rule. The account debtor on an account then made payment by giving money to Debtor. SP–1 and SP–2 both have perfected security interests in that money as identifiable proceeds of an account in which both have perfected security interests. UCC § 9–315(a)-(d). SP–1's security interest has first priority in that money as long as it remains identifiable as proceeds of the account.

b. Perfected Has Priority Over Unperfected

If the security interest or agricultural lien is unperfected, it will be subordinate to a perfected security interest or agricultural lien. UCC § 9–322(a)(2).

Example: On Monday, SP–1 obtained Debtor's signed security agreement granting SP–1 a security interest in all of Debtor's inventory in exchange for a loan which SP–1 funded. SP–1 filed the financing statement in the state where the inventory was located, not where the Debtor was located. SP–1's security interest is attached but unperfected due to filing the financing statement in the wrong state. On Wednesday, SP–2 obtained Debtor's signed security agreement granting SP–2 a security interest in all of Debtor's inventory in exchange for a loan which SP–2 funded the same day. SP–2 filed an effective financing statement in the state where Debtor was located. SP–2's security interest is perfected. SP–2's perfected security interest will have priority in the inventory over SP–1's unperfected security interest.

c. When Both Unperfected, First to Attach

If conflicting security interests and agricultural liens are unperfected, the first security interest or agricultural lien to attach will have priority. UCC § 9–322(a)(3).

2. Exceptions to Three General Priority Rules: Methodology

Numerous exceptions to these three basic priority rules are detailed in the rest of this Section D. To analyze the priority of a security interest or agricultural lien as against other security interests or agricultural liens, first determine who would have priority in the asset based upon the three general rules given above. Then determine if any of the following exceptions to the general rules apply. If the exception applies, the exception will control the priority of the security interest or agricultural lien as against another security interest or agricultural lien.

3. Exception: Subordination Due to Error in Financing Statement

Even though a financing statement is sufficient to perfect under UCC § 9–502 by providing the correct name of the debtor, an indication of the collateral and the name of the secured party, the financing statement may have errors in the information required under UCC § 9–516(b)(5). In the event the financing statement is sufficient to perfect but has errors in the debtor's mailing address or does not indicate whether the debtor is an individual or organization, the security interest or agricultural lien perfected by that financing statement with the errors is subordinated to a conflicting perfected security interest if the holder of that conflicting perfected security interest gave value in reasonable reliance on the incorrect information. UCC §§ 9–322(f)(1), 9–338(1).

Example: SP–1 obtained the Debtor's signed security agreement granting SP–1 a security interest in Debtor's accounts then owned or thereafter acquired to secure a loan that SP–1 funded the same day. SP–1 filed an effective financing statement covering Debtor's accounts. That financing statement contained an error in Debtor's mailing address. SP–2, reasonably determined, based upon the error in the Debtor's mailing address on SP–1's filed financing statement, that the debtor it was dealing with was not the same debtor as the one listed in SP–1's financing statement. SP–2 was in error on this point. SP–2 obtained Debtor's signed security agreement granting SP–2 a security interest in Debtor's accounts and filed an effective financing statement against Debtor covering accounts. SP–2 has an argument that SP–1's security interest should be subordinated to SP–2's security interest in the accounts as SP–2 gave value to Debtor in reasonable reliance on the inaccurate information regarding Debtor's mailing address.

4. Exception: A Different Priority Rule Stated in an Agricultural Lien Statute

If the statute creating an agricultural lien expressly provides, a perfected agricultural lien will have priority over a conflicting security interest or agricultural lien even if the perfected agricultural lien would otherwise be subordinate under the first to file or perfect rule. UCC § 9–322(g).

Example: In May, SP–1 filed a financing statement against Debtor listing farm products as the collateral, had Debtor sign a security agreement granting SP–1 a security interest in farm products to secure all obligations now or hereafter owed, and funded the loan. In June, Chemical Supply Inc. provided chemicals to Debtor to spray on Debtor's crops to combat an insect infestation. Under state law, Chemical Supply has a lien on Debtor's crops to secure payment of the price of the chemicals. Chemical Supply filed a financing statement listing crops as the collateral on June 15. Under the first to file or perfect rule, SP–1's security interest in Debtor's crops (farm products) would have priority over Chemical Supply's agricultural lien. The statute that grants Chemical Supply an agricultural lien, however, provides that a perfected lien under that statute has priority over all other security interests no matter when perfected. Chemical Supply's agricultural lien will have priority over SP–1's security interest in the crops.

5. Exception: Purchase Money Security Interests

In some circumstances, a perfected purchase money security interest will have priority over a conflicting perfected security interest in the same collateral even though that conflicting security interest would otherwise have priority under the first to file or perfect rule. UCC §§ 9–322(f)(1), 9–324.

a. In Goods or Software Only

Purchase money security interests must either be in goods or software as described below. Security interests in other types of collateral are not purchase money security interests even if the secured party gives value to enable the debtor to acquire the collateral and takes a security interest in the collateral to secure repayment of that value.

(1) Purchase Money Security Interest in Goods Defined
A security interest in goods is a purchase money security interest if one or more of three situations is present: (i) the security interest in goods secures the value given to enable the debtor to acquire rights in the goods; (ii) the security interest in goods secures value given to enable the debtor to acquire rights in software in the same transaction in which it

acquired rights in the goods and for software that is for use in the goods; or (iii) the security interest is in inventory and secures value given to enable the debtor to acquire other items of inventory that the secured party also has a purchase money security interest in. UCC § 9–103(b). In each situation, the value given must actually be used by the debtor to acquire rights in the goods or software that is for use in the goods.

Example: SP–1 extended a loan to Debtor to enable Debtor to acquire a new piece of equipment. SP–1 obtained Debtor's signed security agreement granting SP–1 a security interest in the new equipment. Debtor used the loan proceeds to acquire the equipment. SP–1 has a purchase money security interest in the equipment.

Example: Seller obtained Debtor's signed security agreement granting Seller a security interest in all of Debtor's inventory now owned or hereafter acquired to secure all obligations that Debtor owes Seller now and hereafter. Seller sold Item 1 of inventory to Debtor on credit. Seller has a purchase money security interest in Item 1 to secure the price of Item 1. Seller sold Debtor Item 2 of inventory to Debtor on credit. Seller has a purchase money security interest in Item 2 of inventory to secure the price of Item 2. Seller also has a purchase money security interest in Item 1 of inventory to secure the price of Item 2 and a purchase money security interest in Item 2 of inventory to secure the price of Item 1.

(2) Purchase Money Security Interest in Software Defined

A security interest in software is a purchase money security interest if the secured party has given value to enable the debtor to acquire goods, the secured party has a purchase money security interest in those goods, the software was acquired in the same transaction in which the debtor acquired the goods, and the software was acquired for the principal purpose of using it in the goods. UCC § 9–103(c).

Example: Seller obtained Debtor's signed security agreement granting Seller a security interest in a computer and the software in the computer to secure the purchase price of the computer and software. Seller has a purchase money security interest in the computer to secure the purchase price of the computer and the purchase price of the software. UCC § 9–103(b)(1) and (3). Seller has a purchase money security interest in the software to secure the purchase price of the software and the computer. UCC § 9–103(c).

(3) Consignor's Interest

The consignor's security interest in the goods in a consignment is deemed to be a purchase money security interest in inventory. UCC § 9–103(d).

(4) Effect of Subsequent Events on Purchase Money Security Interest Status

In a transaction other than a consumer-goods transaction, the secured party has the burden to demonstrate the extent of the purchase money status of the security interest. UCC § 9–103(g). In such a transaction, a purchase money security interest remains a purchase money security interest even though it is refinanced, the goods or software secures nonpurchase money debt, or the purchase money debt is secured by collateral other than what was purchased. UCC § 9–103(f). In such a transaction, if payments are made on the debt, the payments are applied in accordance with the following hierarchy of preference: (i) any reasonable method to which the parties have agreed; (ii) in accord with the payor's direction at the time of payment; (iii) to obligations that are not secured; or (iv) to obligations secured by purchase money security interests in the order those obligations were secured. UCC § 9–103(e). In a consumer-goods transaction, courts are directed to apply their own established approaches to these issues. UCC § 9–103(h).

b. Priority in Goods Other Than Inventory and Livestock

If the collateral is goods other than inventory and livestock, a perfected purchase money security interest in those goods has priority over a conflicting security interest in the same goods as long as the purchase money security interest is perfected when the debtor receives possession of the collateral or within 20 days thereafter. UCC §§ 9–322(f)(1), 9–324(a).

Example: SP–1 has a security interest in Debtor's equipment then owned or thereafter acquired to secure all obligations Debtor owes SP–1.

SP–1 filed a financing statement against Debtor covering equipment. Seller sold a new piece of equipment to Debtor retaining a security interest in the equipment to secure the purchase price. Seller delivered the new equipment to Debtor on October 1. SP–1 has a perfected security interest and Seller has an attached but unperfected security interest in the new equipment. On October 15, Seller filed a financing statement against Debtor covering the equipment. Seller's security interest in the new equipment is perfected. Under the first to file or perfect priority rule, SP–1's security interest would have priority over Seller's security interest. However, because of the rule granting priority to perfected purchase money security interests in goods other than inventory and livestock, Seller's perfected purchase money security interest will have priority over SP–1's perfected security interest in the new equipment.

Example: SP–1 has a security interest in Debtor's equipment then owned or thereafter acquired to secure all obligations Debtor owes SP–1, and perfected by a filed financing statement covering equipment. SP–2 financed the Debtor's purchase of a new piece of equipment obtaining a security interest in the equipment to secure a loan for the purchase price. Seller delivered the new equipment to Debtor on October 1. On October 25, SP–2 filed a financing statement against Debtor covering the equipment. Both SP–1 and SP–2 have perfected security interests in the new equipment. SP–2 perfected its security interest after 20 days after delivery of the equipment to Debtor and thus SP–2's security interest does not qualify for priority over SP–1's security interest even though SP–2's security interest is a purchase money security interest. Under the first to file or perfect priority rule, SP–1's security interest will have priority over SP–2's security interest in the new equipment.

c. Priority in Inventory

If the collateral is inventory, a perfected purchase money security interest has priority over a conflicting security interest in the same inventory if (i) the purchase money security interest is perfected when the debtor receives possession of the inventory, (ii) the purchase money secured party has sent an authenticated notice to the holder of the conflicting security interest, and (iii) that holder has received that notice within five years before the debtor receives possession of the inventory. UCC §§ 9–322(f)(1), 9–324(b).

(1) Content of the Notice

The notice must state that the purchase money secured party has or will have a purchase money security interest in the inventory and describe the inventory that will be subject to the purchase money security interest. UCC § 9–324(b)(4).

(2) Holders of Conflicting Security Interests

The holders of conflicting security interests in the same inventory that must receive the notice are those that have filed a financing statement against the debtor covering inventory before the date the purchase money secured party filed its financing statement or the date that starts the temporary 20-day perfection period described in UCC § 9–312(f). UCC § 9–324(c).

Example: SP–1 has a properly perfected security interest in inventory then owned or thereafter acquired. SP–1 filed its effective financing statement to perfect its security interest on June 1. In July, Debtor purchased more inventory from Seller and granted Seller a security interest in that purchased inventory to secure the purchase price. Seller filed an effective financing statement to perfect its security interest in the new inventory *prior* to delivery of the new inventory to the Debtor. Seller sent a notice to SP–1 describing its purchase money security interest in the new inventory. SP–1 received the notice *prior* to Seller's delivery of the new inventory to Debtor. Seller's perfected purchase money security interest will have priority over SP–1's perfected security interest in the new inventory.

Several months later, Seller sold more inventory to Debtor, and Debtor granted Seller a security interest in that new inventory to secure the purchase price. Seller's security interest in the second batch of inventory is perfected by its previously filed financing statement. SP–1's security interest is perfected in this second batch of new inventory. If the notice to SP–1 sufficiently describes the second batch of new inventory, Seller's perfected purchase money security interest will have priority over SP–1's perfected security interest in the second batch of new inventory.

Example: SP–1 has a properly perfected security interest in inventory then owned or thereafter acquired. SP–1 filed its effective financing statement to perfect its security interest on June 1. In July, Debtor purchased more inventory from Seller and granted Seller a security interest in the purchased inventory to secure the purchase price. Seller filed an effective financing statement to perfect its security interest prior to delivery of the new inventory to the Debtor. Seller sent a notice to SP–1 describing its purchase money security interest in the new inventory. SP–1 received the notice *after* Seller's delivery of the new inventory to Debtor. Seller's perfected purchase money security interest will *not* have priority over SP–1's perfected security interest in the new inventory.

Example: SP–1 has a properly perfected security interest in inventory then owned or thereafter acquired. SP–1 filed its effective financing statement to perfect its security interest on June 1. In July, Debtor purchased more inventory from Seller and granted Seller a security interest in the purchased inventory to secure the purchase price. Seller filed an effective financing statement to perfect its security interest *after* delivery of the new inventory to the Debtor. Seller sent a notice to SP–1 describing its purchase money security interest in the new inventory. SP–1 received the notice *before* Seller's delivery of the new inventory to Debtor. Seller's perfected purchase money security interest in the new inventory will *not* have priority over SP–1's perfected security interest.

d. Priority in Software

If the collateral is software, a perfected purchase money security interest in the software has priority over a conflicting security interest in the same software if the perfected purchase money security interest in the goods in which the software is used has priority over conflicting perfected security interests in those goods. UCC §§ 9–322(f)(1), 9–324(f).

> *Example:* SP–1 has a security interest in all of Debtor's equipment and software in which Debtor currently has rights or in which Debtor acquires rights thereafter. SP–1 filed its effective financing statement covering equipment and software in June. On August 10, Seller sold Debtor a new computer with software for use in the computer and Debtor granted a security interest to Seller in the computer and software to secure the purchase price of the computer and software. Debtor will use the computer in its office operations. Seller delivered the computer and software to Debtor on August 20. Seller filed an effective financing statement on August 30 to perfect its security interest in the computer and software. Seller's perfected purchase money security interest in the computer has priority over SP–1's perfected security interest in the computer under UCC § 9–324(a) and thus Seller's perfected purchase money security interest in the software has priority over SP–1's perfected security interest in the software. UCC § 9–324(f).

e. Priority in Livestock

If the collateral is livestock that are farm products, a perfected purchase money security interest in the livestock has priority over a conflicting perfected security interest in the livestock if (i) the purchase money security interest is perfected when the debtor receives possession of the livestock, (ii) the purchase money secured party has sent an authenticated notice to the holder of the conflicting security interest, and (iii) that holder has received that notice within six months before the debtor receives possession of the livestock. UCC §§ 9–322(f)(1), 9–324(d).

(1) Content of the Notice
The notice must state that the purchase money secured party has or will have a purchase money security interest in the livestock and describe the livestock that will be subject to the purchase money security interest. UCC § 9–324(d)(4).

(2) Holders of Conflicting Security Interests

The holders of conflicting security interests in the same livestock that must receive the notice are those that have filed a financing statement against the debtor covering livestock before the date the purchase money secured party filed its financing statement or the date that starts the temporary 20-day perfection period described in UCC § 9–312(f). UCC § 9–324(e).

> *Example:*   SP–1 has a properly perfected security interest in Farmer's livestock then owned or thereafter acquired. SP–1 filed its effective financing statement covering livestock in June. In August, SP–2 loaned Farmer money to allow Farmer to buy cows. SP–2 obtained Farmer's signed security agreement granting SP–2 a security interest in the cows to secure the purchase price. SP–2 sent a notice to SP–1 that SP–2 had a security interest in the new cows to secure the purchase price and SP–1 received that notice *before* the seller delivered the cows to Farmer. SP–2 filed its financing statement to perfect its security interest in the cows *before* the seller delivered the cows to Farmer. SP–2's perfected purchase money security interest has priority over SP–1's perfected security interest in the cows.

f. Conflicting Purchase Money Security Interests

Occasionally, more than one purchase money security interest will exist in goods or software. If both purchase money security interests would qualify for priority over other security interests under the rules stated above, the seller's purchase money security interest will have priority over the non-seller secured party's purchase money security interest. UCC § 9–324(g)(1). If neither of the conflicting purchase money security interests are held by the seller, the general rules of UCC § 9–322(a) apply. UCC § 9–324(g)(2).

> *Example:*   Seller agreed to sell an item of equipment to Debtor on credit and take a security interest in the equipment to secure part of the purchase price. Seller, however, insisted that Debtor make a 20% down payment on the purchase price. Debtor borrowed the 20%

down payment from SP–1 and granted SP–1 a security interest in the new item of equipment to secure that amount. Both Seller and SP–1 filed financing statements to perfect their respective security interests within 20 days after Debtor received possession of the equipment. Seller's perfected purchase money security interest has priority over SP–1's perfected purchase money security interest in the new equipment.

Example: Seller agreed to sell an item of equipment to Debtor on credit and take a security interest in the equipment to secure part of the purchase price. Seller, however, insisted that Debtor make a 20% down payment on the purchase price. Debtor borrowed the down payment from SP–1 and granted SP–1 a security interest in the new item of equipment to secure that amount. SP–1 filed a financing statement to its security interest within 20 days after Debtor received possession of the equipment. Seller filed its financing statement to perfect its security interest 30 days after Debtor received possession of the equipment. SP–1's perfected purchase money security interest has priority over Seller's perfected purchase money security interest in the new equipment.

6. Exception: Priority in an Accession

An accession is a good that is physically united with another good in such a manner that the identity of the two goods is not lost after the unification. UCC § 9–102(a)(1). The good that is added to another good is the accession. The good that the accession is added to is called the "other goods." The good with the accession added is called the "whole."

Example: A new engine is added to a backhoe. The new engine is an accession to the backhoe, the other goods. The backhoe is an accession to the engine, the other goods. The backhoe with the new engine is the "whole."

a. Attachment of a Security Interest in the Accession

A secured party with a security interest in a good may have its security interest attach to an accession if the description in the security agreement is sufficient to cover the accession. UCC §§ 9–203, 9–108. A secured party with a security interest in the accession will have its security interest continue in the accession even after the accession is united with the "other goods." UCC § 9–335(a). Whether the secured party with a security interest in the accession will have its security interest attach to the other goods depends upon whether the collateral description in the security agreement is sufficient to cover the other goods.

> *Example:* SP–1 has a security interest in a backhoe. SP–2 has a security interest in a new engine. When the engine is added to the backhoe, whether SP–1's security interest also attaches to the engine depends upon the description of the collateral in SP–1's security agreement and whether SP–2's security interest also attaches to the backhoe depends upon the description of the collateral in SP–2's security agreement. The uniting of the engine with the backhoe does not affect SP–1's security interest in the backhoe or SP–2's security interest in the new engine. If SP–1's collateral description specifies that its security interest is in "equipment then owned or thereafter acquired," the description is broad enough to encompass the engine when it is added to the backhoe.

b. Perfection of a Security Interest in the Accession

If the security interest is perfected in the accession before the accession is united with the other good, the uniting of the accession with the other good does not affect the perfection of the security interest in the accession. UCC § 9–335(b).

> *Example:* SP–1 has a security interest in a backhoe and has filed a financing statement to perfect that security interest. SP–2 has a security interest in a new engine and has filed a financing statement to perfect that security interest. The new engine is installed in the backhoe. The uniting of the engine with the backhoe does not affect SP–1's perfection of its security interest in the backhoe or SP–2's perfection of its security interest in the new engine.

c. Priority Rule

With one exception for certificate of title goods, the other rules in Article 9 that govern priority will determine priority of a security interest in the accession. UCC § 9–335(c). If the goods are covered by a certificate of title, any security interest in an accession is subordinate to a security interest in the whole (the other good and the accession) if the security interest in the whole is perfected by compliance with a certificate of title statute. UCC § 9–335(d).

Example: SP–1 has a security interest in all equipment of Debtor which includes a backhoe. On June 1, SP–1 filed a financing statement to perfect its security interest in equipment. Debtor purchased a new engine for the backhoe on June 20, financed by a loan from SP–2. SP–2 has a security interest in the new engine to secure the purchase price for the new engine and on July 1 filed a financing statement covering the new engine. When the engine is added to the backhoe, SP–1's security interest also attached to the engine because the collateral description in SP–1's security agreement covered all "equipment and accessions thereto." SP–2 has a purchase money security interest in the new engine which qualifies for priority over SP–1's perfected security interest in the new engine under the rules for purchase money security interests in UCC § 9–324(a).

Example: SP–1 has a security interest in all equipment of Debtor, including a backhoe, perfected by a financing statement filed on June 1. On June 20, Debtor purchased a new engine for the backhoe, financed by a loan from SP–2. The engine was delivered the same day. SP–2 has a security interest in the new engine for the backhoe to secure the purchase price for the new engine and on July 30 filed a financing statement covering the new engine. When the engine is added to the backhoe, SP–1's security interest also attached to the engine because the collateral description in SP–1's security agreement covered all "equipment and accessions thereto." Under the first to file or perfect rule of UCC § 9–322(a), SP–1's perfected security interest has priority over SP–2's perfected purchase money security interest in the new engine because SP–2 failed to file its financing statement with the time period required under UCC § 9–324(a) to qualify for purchase money priority over SP–1's security interest.

> *Example:* SP–1 has a security interest in all equipment of Debtor which includes a truck, perfected by a notation on the truck's certificate of title on June 1. On June 20, Debtor purchased a new engine for the truck financed by a loan from SP–2. The engine was delivered the same day. SP–2 has a security interest in the new engine to secure the purchase price for the new engine and on July 1 filed a financing statement covering the new engine. When the engine is added to the truck, SP–1's security interest also attached to the engine because the collateral description in SP–1's security agreement covered all "equipment and accessions thereto." Under the priority rule for accessions to goods covered by a certificate of title, SP–1's perfected security interest in the truck and the new engine has priority over SP–2's perfected security interest in the new engine.

7. Exception: Priority in Commingled Goods

Commingled goods are goods that are united with other goods in such a manner that the identity of the original goods is lost in the united product or mass. UCC § 9–336(a).

a. Attachment and Perfection of Security Interests in Commingled Goods

If a secured party has attached and perfected a security interest to goods before they become commingled, the security interest will be attached and perfected in the product or mass after commingling. UCC § 9–336(c), (d).

> *Example:* SP–1 has a perfected security interest in Debtor's Lot A of corn. SP–2 has a perfected security interest in Debtor's Lot B of corn. Lots A and B are commingled creating Mass AB. SP–1 and SP–2 each have an attached and perfected security interest in Mass AB.

> *Example:* SP–1 has a perfected security interest in Debtor's wood chips. SP–2 has a perfected security interest in Debtor's paper. Debtor used the wood chips to make paper by pulverizing the wood

chips and mixing them with water. SP–1 has a perfected security interest in the resulting paper due to UCC § 9–336. SP–2 has an attached and perfected security interest in the paper based upon its collateral description covering "paper," not due to UCC § 9–336.

b. Priority Rule

The priority rules for security interests in commingled goods are governed by the other Article 9 rules for priority, with the following exception. UCC § 9–336(e). If more than one security interest attaches to the product or mass because the security interests were in the goods before the goods were commingled, the following two rules apply: (i) a perfected security interest in the product or mass has priority over an unperfected security interest in the product or mass; and (ii) if both security interests are perfected in the product or mass, the security interests rank equal in priority according to the proportion of value of the collateral at the time it was commingled up to the amount of the secured party's debt. UCC § 9–336(f), cmt. 4.

Example: SP–1 has a perfected security interest in Debtor's Lot A of corn and filed its financing statement on May 1. Lot A of corn is worth $1,000 and secures a debt of $800. SP–2 has a perfected security interest in Debtor's Lot B of corn and filed its financing statement on June 1. Lot B of corn is worth $2,000 and secures a debt of $1,200. Lots A and B are commingled creating Mass AB. SP–1 and SP–2 both have an attached and perfected security interest in Mass AB. The security interests of SP–1 and SP–2 have co-equal priority in proportion to the value of the goods at the time the two lots of corn became commingled goods. In this case, SP–1 would be able to recover 1/3 times the value of Mass AB up to a total of $800 and SP–2 would be able to recover 2/3 times the value of Mass AB up to a total of $1,200.

Example: SP–1 has a perfected security interest in Debtor's wood chips and filed its financing statement on June 1 to perfect its security interest in the wood chips. SP–2 has a perfected security interest in Debtor's paper and filed its financing statement on May 1 to perfect its security interest in paper. Debtor used the wood chips to make paper by pulverizing the wood chips and mixing them with water. SP–1 has a perfected security interest in the resulting paper. SP–2's security interest has priority over SP–1's security interest under the first to file or perfect rule as the conflicting security interests were not *both* in the goods prior to commingling.

Example: SP–1 has a perfected security interest in Debtor's Lot A of corn and filed its financing statement on May 1. SP–2 has a security interest in Debtor's Lot B of corn and did not perfect its security interest. Lots A and B are commingled to create Mass AB. Both SP–1 and SP–2 have a security interest in Mass AB. SP–1's security interest is perfected and SP–2's security interest is not perfected. SP–1's security interest in Mass AB has priority over SP–2's security interest in Mass AB, under UCC § 9–322(a).

8. Exception: Priority of Security Interests Noted First on a Clean Certificate of Title

If a secured party has perfected a security interest in goods by any method and a state issues a certificate of title for those goods, the security interest remains perfected even though the law governing perfection of the security interest is changed to the law of the jurisdiction issuing the certificate. UCC §§ 9–303, 9–316(d). The secured party has the lesser of four months or the time perfection would lapse in the first jurisdiction to obtain perfection of its security interest by notation on the certificate of title or the security interest is deemed unperfected as against a pre-existing purchaser of the good. UCC § 9–316(e). Review Chapter IV, Section H. If that new certificate of title does not show the goods are subject to the existing security interest or contain a notation that the goods may be subject to security interests not shown on the certificate of title, the secured party's unnoted security interest is subordinated to a security interest that is perfected on the clean certificate by a secured party that did not have knowledge of the first security interest. UCC § 9–337(2).

Example: SP–1 perfected its security interest in a truck covered by a certificate of title by notation of the security interest on the certificate of title issued by State A. Debtor obtained a new certificate of title for the truck from State B which did not show any security interests or any indication that the truck may be subject to security interests not shown on the certificate of title. SP–1's security interest is perfected and SP–1 has four months from issuance of the new certificate of title from State B to obtain notation of its security interest on the new certificate of title to continue perfection beyond the four-month period. Approximately one month after State B issued the new certificate of title, Debtor obtained a loan from SP–2 and granted a security interest in the truck to SP–2. SP–2 did not have knowledge of SP–1's security interest. SP–2 obtained notation of its security interest on the State B certificate of title. SP–2's security interest in the truck has priority over SP–1's security interest in the truck, even if SP–1 subsequently obtains notation of its interest on the certificate of title within the four-month period as specified in UCC § 9–316(e).

9. Exception: Priority in Goods Covered by a Negotiable Document of Title

If goods are covered by a negotiable document of title, a secured party should perfect a security interest in the goods by perfecting its security interest in the document of title. That perfection may be by filing a financing statement covering the document of title, taking possession of a tangible document of title, or having control of an electronic document of title. UCC §§ 9–312, 9–314. If a secured party perfects a security interest directly in goods while the goods are covered by a negotiable document of title, that security interest perfected directly in the goods is subordinate to a security interest in the goods that is perfected by perfection of a security interest in the negotiable document of title. UCC §§ 9–322(f), 9–312(c). The priority of security interests in the negotiable document of title, and thus in the goods covered by the document of title, will be determined by the three general rules of UCC § 9–322(a), as it applies to filing or perfection in the negotiable document of title, subject to two exceptions.

Example: Debtor stored goods with Warehouse Inc. which issued to Debtor a negotiable warehouse receipt covering the stored goods. Debtor granted SP–1 a security interest in Debtor's goods, including those stored in the warehouse, to secure a loan from SP–1. On May 1, SP–1 filed a financing statement against Debtor listing "goods" as the collateral. Debtor granted SP–2 a security interest in the warehouse receipt to secure a loan SP–2 made to Debtor. On June 1, SP–2 filed a financing statement against Debtor listing the warehouse receipt as collateral. SP–2's security interest in the stored goods has priority over SP–1's security interest.

a. Protection of Holders of Negotiable Documents of Title That Take the Document by Due Negotiation

If a secured party becomes a holder of a negotiable document of title by "due negotiation," that secured party will take the negotiable document of title and the goods covered by the document of title free of a security interest perfected in the document of title by a different method, such as by filing a financing statement. UCC §§ 7–502, 9–322(f), 9–331. Subsection to one exception noted below, a holder to whom a negotiable document of title is negotiated by due negotiation has title to the document and title to the goods that is superior to the rights of a person to whom previous rights under the document have been transferred. UCC § 7–502.

(1) Holder of a Negotiable Document of Title

A secured party becomes a holder of a negotiable document of title when the document is negotiated to the secured party. Negotiation of the negotiable document of title will take place in the following manner. If the negotiable document of title is tangible and payable to bearer, the document of title is negotiated by voluntary transfer of physical possession. UCC § 7–501(a)(2). If the negotiable document of title is tangible and payable to order, the document of title is negotiated by indorsement of the named person to whom it is payable and voluntary transfer of physical possession. UCC § 7–501(a)(1). If the negotiable document of title is electronic, it is negotiated to the secured party by a voluntary transfer of control to the secured party. UCC §§ 7–501(b)(1), 7–106.

(2) Due Negotiation of a Negotiable Document of Title

A secured party will take a negotiable document of title by "due negotiation" if the document of title is negotiated to the secured party that takes the document of title in good faith, without notice of any defense or claim to it on the part of any person, for value, and in the regular course of business and financing as long as it is not in settlement or payment of a monetary obligation. UCC § 7–501(a)(5), (b)(3). A filed financing statement covering documents of title is not notice of a claim or defense to a negotiable document of title. UCC § 9–331(c).

Example: Debtor stored goods with Warehouse Inc. which issued to Debtor a negotiable warehouse receipt payable to bearer covering the stored goods. Debtor granted SP–1 a security interest in Debtor's documents of title to secure a loan from SP–1. On May 1, SP–1 filed a financing statement against Debtor listing documents of title as the collateral. Debtor granted SP–2 a security interest in the warehouse receipt to secure a loan SP–2 made to Debtor. On June 1, Debtor gave possession of the negotiable warehouse receipt to SP–2. Given the warehouse receipt was payable to bearer, Debtor's voluntary transfer of possession of the warehouse receipt to SP–2 was a negotiation to SP–2. SP–2 gave value in the form of a loan and did not have any notice of a claim or defense to the warehouse receipt. The loan and grant of security interest in the document of title was in the regular course of business and financing. SP–2 took the negotiable warehouse receipt by "due negotiation." SP–2's security interest in the stored goods has priority over SP–1's security interest even though SP–1's financing statement covering the document of title was filed before SP–2 perfected its security interest through taking possession of the negotiable warehouse receipt.

b. Rights of a Secured Party With a Security Interest in Goods Prior to the Goods Being Covered by a Negotiable Document of Title

If a secured party has a perfected security interest in goods prior to the goods being covered by a document of title and the goods subsequently become covered by a negotiable document of title, the rights of a holder of that negotiable document of title are not superior to the first secured party's rights in the goods. However, if the first secured party entrusted the goods or the document of title to the debtor with actual or apparent authority to ship, store, sell, or otherwise dispose of the goods or the first secured party acquiesced in the debtor's procurement of the document of title, the holder of the negotiable document of title who took the document by due negotiation will have rights in the goods superior to the rights of the first secured party whose rights arose prior to the issuance of the negotiable document of title covering the goods. UCC § 7–503.

> *Example:* Debtor granted SP–1 a security interest in Debtor's goods to secure a loan from SP–1. On May 1, SP–1 filed a financing statement against Debtor listing "goods" as the collateral. Debtor then stored goods with Warehouse Inc. which issued a negotiable warehouse receipt payable to bearer covering the stored goods. Debtor granted SP–2 a security interest in the warehouse receipt to secure a loan SP–2 made to Debtor. On June 1, Debtor gave SP–2 possession of the negotiable warehouse receipt, which was a negotiation of the receipt to SP–2. SP–2 gave value in the form of a loan and did not have any notice of a claim or defense to the warehouse receipt. The loan and grant of security interest in the document of title was in the regular course of business and financing. Thus, SP–2 took the negotiable warehouse receipt by "due negotiation." SP–2's security interest in the stored goods does not have priority over SP–1's security interest if the court finds that SP–1 did not entrust the goods to Debtor with authority to store, sell, or ship the goods or acquiesce in Debtor's procurement of the document of title.

10.   Exception: Priority in Chattel Paper

Conflicting security interests in chattel paper will normally be governed by the three general rules in UCC § 9–322(a). In some circumstances, however, a secured party will be able to take advantage of the priority given to purchasers of chattel paper. UCC §§ 9–322(f), 9–330(a), (b). A secured party is a purchaser of chattel paper because the definitions of purchase and purchaser in Article 1 include any voluntary transfer of a property right in an asset, including the creation of a lien or security interest in the asset. Giving "new value" for the property interest in the asset is not required in order to be a "purchaser." UCC § 1–201(b)(29), (30).

a.   Purchaser's Priority Over Security Interest in Chattel Paper That Is Claimed Merely as Proceeds of Inventory

If a purchaser takes possession in good faith of tangible chattel paper or control of electronic chattel paper in the ordinary course of the purchaser's business and gives new value for the chattel paper, the purchaser will have priority over a security interest in the chattel paper that is claimed merely as proceeds of inventory subject to a security interest if the chattel paper does not indicate that it has been assigned to an identified assignee other than the purchaser. UCC § 9–330(a). If a secured party has a security interest in specific items of inventory, gives value against those specific items of inventory and expects payment on the sale of those items, the secured party's security interest in chattel paper that is proceeds of those items of inventory is claimed "merely as proceeds" of inventory unless the secured party gives value against the chattel paper that is generated from sale of the inventory. PEB Commentary No. 8.

Example: SP–1 has a security interest in Debtor's inventory to secure all obligations then or thereafter owed to SP–1, perfected by an effective financing statement indicating inventory as the collateral. Debtor sells an item of inventory to Buyer on credit and takes a security interest in the item to secure the purchase price. The contract between Buyer and Debtor is chattel paper. SP–1 has a perfected security interest in the chattel paper because the chattel paper is identifiable proceeds of the inventory. UCC § 9–315(a), (c), (d). Debtor sold the chattel paper to SP–2 for new value and SP–2 took possession of the chattel paper in the ordinary course of its business and in good faith. The sale to SP–2 creates a security interest in favor of SP–2. UCC § 9–109(a)(3). SP–2 has perfected its interest in the chattel paper through taking possession of the chattel paper. UCC § 9–313(a). Under the first to file or perfect rule, SP–1's security interest in the chattel paper would be superior to SP–2's security interest. UCC § 9–322(a)(1), (b)(1). SP–1's security interest in the chattel paper is claimed merely as proceeds of its security interest in inventory and the chattel paper did not contain a legend that it had been assigned to a specific assignee. Under UCC § 9–330(a), SP–2's security interest will have priority over SP–1's security interest.

b. Purchaser's Priority Over Security Interest in Chattel Paper That Is Not Claimed as Merely Proceeds of Inventory

If a purchaser takes possession in good faith of tangible chattel paper or control of electronic chattel paper and in the ordinary course of the purchaser's business and gives new value for the chattel paper, the purchaser will have priority over a security interest in the chattel paper that is claimed other than as merely proceeds of inventory subject to a security interest if the purchaser is without knowledge that the purchase violates the rights of the secured party with the conflicting security interest. UCC § 9–330(b). If a secured party claims a security interest in the chattel paper because it advances credit against the value of the chattel paper, that secured party has a security interest in chattel paper that is claimed more than merely as proceeds of inventory. PEB Commentary No. 8.

Knowledge means "actual knowledge" of a fact, not notice or reason to know of a fact. UCC § 1–202. If the chattel paper indicates that it has been assigned to an identified secured party other than the purchaser, the purchaser has knowledge that the purchase violates the rights of that secured party. UCC § 9–330(f). Mere knowledge that a financing statement lists chattel paper as collateral does not constitute knowledge that the purchase violates the rights of a secured party. However, if the secured party places on the financing statement an indication that purchase of chattel paper will violate the rights of the secured party and the purchaser actually sees that financing statement, the purchaser would have knowledge that the purchase violates the rights of the secured party. UCC § 9–330, cmt. 6.

Example: SP–1 has a perfected security interest in Debtor's inventory, accounts and chattel paper then or thereafter owned to secure all obligations then or thereafter owed to SP–1. SP–1 has filed an effective financing statement against Debtor listing inventory, accounts and chattel paper as the collateral. SP–1 gives credit to the Debtor each month based upon the collective value of the inventory, accounts and chattel paper. Debtor sells an item of inventory to Buyer on credit and takes a security interest in the item to secure the purchase price. The contract between Buyer and Debtor is chattel paper. SP–1 has a perfected security interest in the chattel paper based upon either the after-acquired property clause in its security agreement or as proceeds of inventory. UCC

§§ 9–204, 9–315. SP–1's security interest in the chattel paper is not claimed merely as proceeds of its security interest in inventory. Debtor sold the chattel paper to SP–2 for new value and SP–2 took possession of the chattel paper in the ordinary course of its business. The sale to SP–2 creates a security interest in favor of SP–2. UCC § 9–109(a)(3). SP–2 perfected its interest in the chattel paper through taking possession of the chattel paper. UCC § 9–313(a). Under the first to file or perfect rule, SP–1's security interest in the chattel paper would be superior to SP–2's security interest. UCC § 9–322(a)(1). Under UCC § 9–330(b), SP–2 will have priority over SP–1's security interest if SP–2 acted in good faith, and did not have knowledge that its purchase of the chattel paper violated SP–1's rights. SP–1's filed financing statement did not give SP–2 knowledge that the purchase violated SP–1's rights.

c. Possession or Control

Possession of tangible chattel paper or control of electronic chattel paper in this context has the same meaning as discussed in Chapters III on attachment and Chapter IV on perfection. Because chattel paper as a whole may consist of more than one record, one record may be tangible and the other record may be electronic, in which case, a purchaser may qualify under this priority rule by possessing the tangible record and controlling the electronic record. Similarly, an electronic record may constitute electronic chattel paper and be converted to tangible form (or from tangible form to electronic form), and as long as the purchaser controls the electronic form or possesses the tangible form, the purchaser may qualify for priority under this rule.

d. New Value

A purchase is for new value when new money, property, services or credit is granted in exchange for the voluntary transfer of an interest in property and does not include the substitution of one obligation for another. UCC § 9–102(a)(57).

e. Good Faith

"Good faith" means honesty in fact and the observance of reasonable commercial standards of fair dealing. UCC § 1–201(b)(20). The purchaser is not required to search the public records for financing statements related to the chattel paper being purchased in order to be in good faith. UCC § 9–330, cmt. 6.

11. Exception: Priority in Instruments

The three general rules in UCC § 9–322(a) for priority of conflicting security interests in instruments normally will apply except in two circumstances.

a. Priority for Purchasers of Instruments

If a person purchases an instrument for value, takes possession of the instrument in good faith, and does not have knowledge that the purchase violates the rights of the secured party, the purchaser will take priority over a conflicting security interest perfected by a method other than possession. UCC §§ 9–322(f), 9–330(d).

(1) Secured Party as a Purchaser
A secured party is a purchaser of an instrument because the definitions of purchase and purchaser in Article 1 include any voluntary transfer of a property right in an asset, including the creation of a lien or security interest in the asset. UCC § 1–201(b)(29), (30).

(2) Value, Not New Value
The purchaser must give value, which includes any consideration necessary to support a contract and, in addition, includes past consideration. UCC § 1–204. New value is not required.

(3) Knowledge That the Purchase Violates the Rights of a Secured Party
Knowledge means "actual knowledge" of a fact, not notice or reason to know of a fact. UCC § 1–202. Knowledge that a financing statement lists instruments as collateral does not constitute knowledge that the purchase violates the rights of a secured party. If the instrument indicates that it has been assigned to an identified secured party other than the purchaser,

the purchaser who takes possession of the instrument has knowledge that the purchase violates the rights of that secured party. UCC § 9–330(f). If the secured party places on the financing statement an indication that purchase of instruments will violate the rights of the secured party and the purchaser actually sees that financing statement, the purchaser would have knowledge that the purchase violates the rights of the secured party. UCC § 9–330, cmt. 6.

(4) Good Faith

"Good faith" means honesty in fact and the observance of reasonable commercial standards of fair dealing. UCC § 1–201(b)(20). Good faith of the purchaser may require the purchaser to search the public records for financing statements related to the instrument being purchased. UCC § 9–330, cmt. 7; UCC § 9–331, cmt. 5. The difference between the good faith standard as applied to instrument purchasers and as applied to chattel paper purchasers stems from the expectations of the parties in the relevant industries that deal with these types of obligations.

(5) Perfection by a Nonpossession Method

The conflicting security interest in the instrument must be perfected by a nonpossession method such as by filing a financing statement covering the instrument or by one of the periods of automatic perfection such as automatic perfection of proceeds (UCC § 9–315(c), (d)) or temporary perfection of a security interest in instruments under UCC § 9–312(e) or (g).

Example: SP–1 has a security interest in instruments owned by Debtor whether then owned or thereafter owned to secure all obligations Debtor owes or may thereafter owe to SP–1, properly perfected by an effective financing statement against Debtor listing instruments as the collateral. Debtor granted a security interest in an instrument to SP–2 to secure an obligation owed to SP–2. SP–2 took possession of the instrument which perfects SP–2's security interest. SP–2's security interest perfected by possession in that instrument will have priority over SP–1's security interest in that instrument as long as SP–2 did not have knowledge that the purchase violated SP–1's rights in the instrument and SP–2 acted in good faith. The mere filing of SP–1's financing statement listing instruments does not give SP–2 such knowledge or mean that SP–2 lacks good faith.

b. Priority for Holders in Due Course of Negotiable Instruments

A holder in due course of a negotiable instrument takes the instrument free of property claims of third parties, such as secured parties with perfected security interests in the instrument. UCC §§ 3–306, 9–322(f), 9–331(a). This rule does not apply to nonnegotiable instruments.

(1) Negotiable Instrument

A negotiable instrument is a written promise to pay or order to pay that meets all of the requirements stated in UCC § 3–104. Those requirements are that there be a written unconditional promise or order to pay a fixed amount of money that is payable to order or bearer, on demand or at a definite time and that does not state any other undertaking or instruction by the person promising or ordering to pay money except as permitted in UCC § 3–104(a)(3). To fully understand these requirements one must study the statute and comments contained in UCC § 3–104 through UCC § 3–117 and all applicable definitions. Such an in-depth study is beyond the scope of these materials. Recall that an "instrument" as defined in Article 9 includes a "negotiable instrument" but includes writings that do not qualify as negotiable instruments. UCC § 9–102(a)(47). Chapter II, Section G.

(2) Holder in Due Course

If the instrument is a negotiable instrument as defined in UCC § 3–104, a transferee of that instrument may qualify as a holder in due course of the instrument. In order to be a holder in due course, the person must meet all of the requirements of UCC § 3–302. Those requirements are that the person must be a holder of the negotiable instrument (which means that the person must at least be in possession) and take the instrument for value, in good faith, without notice of numerous defenses to the obligation to pay, and without notice of claims to the instrument. The negotiable instrument must also not bear apparent evidence of forgery, alteration, or irregularity or incompleteness that calls into question its authenticity. These requirements are very complex and to fully understand them requires study of the text and comments of UCC § 3–302 through § 3–308 and all applicable definitions. Such an in-depth study is beyond the scope of these materials. The filing of a financing statement listing instruments as the collateral is not notice of a claim or defense to the negotiable instrument. UCC § 9–331(c). In some limited circumstances, failure to search the public record for financing statements may mean that the holder of the negotiable instrument has not taken the instrument in good faith. UCC § 9–331, cmt. 5.

Example: SP–1 has a properly perfected security in instruments owned by Debtor whether then owned or thereafter owned to secure all obligations Debtor owes or may thereafter owe to SP–1. SP–1 filed an effective financing statement against Debtor listing instruments as the collateral. Debtor sold a negotiable promissory note to SP–2. That sale creates a security interest in the promissory note. UCC § 9–109(a)(3). SP–2 took possession of the note even though SP–2's security interest was automatically perfected. UCC § 9–309(4). Under UCC § 3–302, SP–2 met all of the requirements to be a holder in due course of the promissory note. Under the first to file or perfect rule, SP–1's security interest would have priority over SP–2's security interest. However, SP–2's security interest will have priority over SP–1's security interest because SP–2 qualified as a holder in due course of the promissory note.

12. Exception: Priority in Deposit Accounts

Conflicting security interests in a deposit account are governed by the following rules. If none of these following specific rules apply, priority in the deposit account will be governed by the three general rules in UCC § 9–322(a).

a. Paramount Priority for Security Interests Perfected by Control

A security interest in a deposit account perfected by control will have priority over a security interest that is not perfected by control. UCC §§ 9–322(f), 9–327(1).

Example: SP–1 has a perfected security interest in Debtor's equipment. SP–1 filed an effective financing statement against Debtor listing the collateral as equipment. Debtor sold a piece of equipment and placed the cash proceeds from that sale into a deposit account maintained at Bank. Subsequently, SP–2 obtained a security interest in the deposit account to secure a loan to Debtor and perfected its security interest in the deposit account at Bank by obtaining a control agreement between Debtor, Bank and SP–2 that Bank would follow SP–2's instructions regarding the deposit account without further consent of Debtor. UCC § 9–104(a)(2). SP–2's security interest in the deposit account perfected by control has priority over SP–1's security interest in the deposit account perfected by its perfection against the equipment, with automatic perfection of its security interest in cash proceeds. UCC § 9–315.

b. Two or More Security Interests Perfected by Control

If more than one secured party has perfected its security interests by control, the security interests rank in priority based upon the time control was obtained unless one of the two following rules apply. UCC §§ 9–322(f), 9–327(2). The security interest of the depository bank in the deposit account (which is automatically perfected by control, UCC § 9–104(a)(1)) has priority over a conflicting security interest held by another secured party except as provided by the next rule. UCC § 9–327(3). If the secured party perfects its security interest in the deposit account by becoming the depositary bank's customer on the account (UCC § 9–104(a)(3)), that security interest will have priority over the depositary bank's security interest in the deposit account. UCC § 9–327(4).

Example: SP–1 has a security interest in Debtor's deposit accounts which it perfected by obtaining a control agreement between Debtor, Bank and SP–1 that Bank would follow SP–1's instructions regarding the deposit account without further consent of Debtor. UCC § 9–104(a)(2). SP–2 subsequently obtained a security interest in Debtor's deposit accounts and also obtained a control agreement between Debtor, SP–2 and Bank that Bank would follow SP–2's instructions regarding the deposit account without further consent of Debtor. UCC § 9–104(a)(2). The order of priority as between SP–1 and SP–2 is the order in which the control agreements were obtained.

Example: Debtor maintains a deposit account at Bank. In the Debtor-Bank agreement in opening the deposit account, Debtor granted a security interest to Bank in all deposit accounts to secure any obligations then or thereafter owed to Bank. Debtor has a loan from Bank. Bank has a security interest in the deposit account which is perfected by control. UCC § 9–104(a)(1). SP–1 attached a security interest in Debtor's deposit accounts to secure a loan that SP–1 made to Debtor. SP–1 obtained a control agreement between Bank, Debtor and SP–1 that Bank would follow SP–1's instructions regarding the deposit account without further consent of Debtor, thus perfecting its security interest in the deposit account by control. UCC § 9–104(a)(2). Bank's security interest has priority over SP–1's security interest in the deposit account because a depository bank's security interest has priority over a security interest perfected by a control agreement.

Example: Debtor maintains a deposit account at Bank. In the Debtor-Bank agreement in opening the deposit account, Debtor granted a security interest to Bank in all deposit accounts to secure any obligations then or thereafter owed to Bank. Debtor has a loan from Bank. Bank has a security interest in the deposit account which is perfected by control. UCC § 9–104(a)(1). SP–1 has a security interest in Debtor's deposit accounts. SP–1 became an additional customer on the deposit account held at Bank, and thus has control of the deposit account. UCC § 9–104(a)(3). SP–1's security interest in the deposit account has priority over Bank's security interest.

Example: SP–1 has a perfected security interest in Debtor's equipment. On June 1, SP–1 filed an effective financing statement against Debtor listing the collateral as equipment. SP–2 also has a perfected security interest in Debtor's equipment that is perfected by an effective financing statement against Debtor listing equipment as collateral, filed on June 10. Thereafter, Debtor sold a piece of equipment and placed the cash proceeds from that sale into a deposit account maintained at Bank. Both SP–1 and SP–2 have a perfected security interest in the deposit account as identifiable cash proceeds of perfected security interests in the sold equipment. UCC § 9–315(a)-(d). Neither SP–1 nor SP–2 have perfected a security interest in the deposit account by control. Thus the first to file or perfect rule will govern the priority of the security interests in the deposit account. The date of filing or perfection as to the equipment is the date of filing or perfection as to the proceeds. UCC § 9–322(b)(1). SP–1's security interest in the deposit account has priority over SP–2's security interest in the deposit account.

c. Setoff

A depositary bank may have a right of setoff against its bank customer either through a contractual agreement or through the common law rules governing setoff. *See* Chapter I. If the depositary bank has a right of setoff against the deposit account, that right of setoff will have priority over a secured party with a perfected security interest in the deposit account unless the secured party is a customer on the deposit account and the bank's setoff is exercised based upon the bank's claim against the debtor. UCC § 9–340.

Example: Debtor has a deposit account at Bank. Bank has a contractual right of setoff that is set forth in the Debtor-Bank agreement governing the deposit account. SP–1 perfects a security interest in the deposit account to secure a loan to Debtor by obtaining a control agreement between Debtor, Bank and SP–1 that Bank would follow SP–1's instructions regarding the deposit account without further consent of Debtor. UCC § 9–104(a)(2). Debtor defaults on a loan from Bank and Bank exercises its right of setoff. Bank's right of setoff is superior in priority to SP–1's security interest perfected by control.

Example: Debtor has a deposit account at Bank. Bank has a contractual right of setoff that is set forth in the Debtor-Bank agreement governing the deposit account. SP–1 perfects a security interest in the deposit account to secure a loan to Debtor by becoming an additional customer on the deposit account. UCC § 9–104(a)(3). Debtor defaults on a loan from Bank and Bank exercises its right of setoff. Bank's right of setoff is not superior in priority to SP–1's security interest perfected by control.

d. Funds From Deposit Account

A transferee of funds from a deposit account will take those funds free of any security interest in the deposit account even if the security interest is perfected, unless the transferee acted in collusion with the debtor in violating the rights of the secured party with a security interest in the deposit account. UCC § 9–332(b). Collusion to violate rights of the secured party requires more than mere knowledge or notice of the security interest. UCC § 9–332, cmt. 4; UCC § 8–503, cmt. 2. A transferee need not give value or be without knowledge or notice of the security interest in the deposit account. The debtor is not a transferee of funds so if the debtor withdrew funds from the deposit account, this rule does not apply.

Example: SP–1 has a first priority perfected security interest and SP–2 has a second priority perfected security interest in a deposit account Debtor maintains at Bank to secure all obligations Debtor owes to SP–1 and SP–2. Debtor directs Bank to transfer funds from the deposit account to SP–2 to pay part of the debt owed to SP–2. As long as SP–2 does not act in collusion with Debtor to violate SP–1's rights, SP–2 takes the funds free of SP–1's security interest.

13. Exception: Priority in Money

Unless money (as defined in UCC § 1–201(b)(24)) is identifiable proceeds of other collateral, a secured party may only perfect a security interest in money by taking possession of it. UCC § 9–312(b). If money is not proceeds of other collateral, the three general priority rules in UCC § 9–322(a) apply. Priority in money as proceeds will be considered *infra* in this Chapter. Regardless of whether money is proceeds, a transferee of money takes the money free of a security interest in the money even if the security interest is perfected unless the transferee acts in collusion with the debtor in violating the rights of the secured party. UCC §§ 9–322(f), 9–332(a). Collusion to violate rights of the secured party requires more than mere knowledge or notice of the security interest. UCC § 9–332, cmt. 4; UCC

§ 8–503, cmt. 2. A transferee need not give value or be without knowledge or notice of the security interest in the money.

Example: SP–1 has a security interest in Debtor's inventory to secure a loan made to Debtor. On June 1, SP–1 filed its effective financing statement against Debtor describing the collateral as inventory. SP–2 also has a security interest in Debtor's inventory to secure a loan made to Debtor. On June 5, SP–2 filed its effective financing statement against Debtor describing the collateral as inventory. Debtor sold an item of inventory generating money as identifiable proceeds of that inventory. Debtor gave the money from the sale to SP–2 to apply against the debt Debtor owed SP–2. SP–2 took the money free of SP–1's security interest unless SP–2 acted in collusion with Debtor to violate SP–1's rights. Mere knowledge of SP–1's security interest is insufficient to render SP–2 in collusion with Debtor.

14.   Exception: Priority in a Letter-of-Credit Right

Priority of conflicting perfected security interests in a letter-of-credit right is determined by the three general rules in UCC § 9–322(a) with the following exceptions.

a.   Perfection of Security Interest by Control of Letter-of-Credit Right Has Priority Over Security Interest Perfected in Another Manner

A security interest perfected by control of a letter-of-credit right will have priority over a security interest in the letter-of-credit right which is not perfected by control. UCC §§ 9–322(f), 9–329(1).

Example: SP–1 has a security interest in Debtor's accounts and has perfected its security interest in accounts by filing an effective financing statement against Debtor listing the collateral as accounts. Debtor is the beneficiary of a letter of credit issued by Nations Bank at the request of Account Debtor to support payment of an account owed to Debtor. The letter of credit is a supporting obligation of the account. SP–1 has a perfected security interest in the letter-of-credit right as a supporting obligation of the account. UCC § 9–308(d). SP–2 obtains a security interest in the letter-of-credit right to secure an obligation that Debtor owes SP–2. SP–2 obtains control of the letter-of-credit right by obtaining Nations Bank's consent to the assignment of proceeds of the letter of credit to SP–2. UCC § 9–107. SP–2's security interest has priority over SP–1's security interest in the letter-of-credit right. SP–2 does not have a security interest in the account which the letter-of-credit right supports.

b. Conflicting Security Interests Perfected by Control

If the conflicting security interests in a letter-of-credit right are all perfected by control, the priority is based upon the time that control is obtained. UCC §§ 9–322(f), 9–329(2).

Example: SP–1 has a security interest in Debtor's accounts and has perfected its security interest in accounts by filing an effective financing statement against Debtor listing the collateral as accounts. In *payment* of an account owed to Debtor, Debtor is the beneficiary of a letter of credit issued by Nations Bank at the request of Account Debtor. The letter of credit is proceeds of the account. SP–1 has a temporarily perfected security interest in the letter-of-credit right as identifiable proceeds of the account. UCC § 9–315(a)-(d). SP–2 obtains a security interest in the letter-of-credit right to secure an obligation that Debtor owes SP–2. SP–2 obtains control of the letter-of-credit right by obtaining Nations Bank's consent to the assignment of proceeds of the letter of credit to SP–2. UCC § 9–107. Prior to the expiration of the 20-day period of temporary perfection for identifiable proceeds of the account but after SP–2 obtains control of the letter-of-credit right, SP–1 obtains control of the letter-of-credit right by obtaining Nations Bank's consent to the assignment of the right to proceeds of the letter of credit. UCC § 9–107. SP–2's security interest in the letter-of-credit right has priority over SP–1's security interest.

c. Rights of a Transferee Beneficiary

The rights of a secured party that is a transferee beneficiary under a letter of credit has priority over the rights of a secured party that has merely obtained a security interest in the letter-of-credit rights. UCC §§ 9–109(c)(4), 5–114.

Example: Debtor is the beneficiary of a letter of credit issued by Nations Bank at the request of Account Debtor who is the obligor on an account. Debtor granted a security interest in the letter-of-credit right to SP–1 and SP–1 perfected its security interest by obtaining Nation Bank's consent to assignment of the proceeds to SP–1. Debtor then obtained Nations Bank's consent to transfer the rights as beneficiary under the letter of credit to SP–2 as security for a loan. SP–2's rights as transferee beneficiary of the letter of credit are superior to SP–1's perfected security interest in the letter-of-credit right.

15. Exception: Priority in Investment Property

Priority of security interests in investment property will be determined by the three general priority rules in UCC § 9–322(a) subject to several exceptions. UCC §§ 9–322(f), 9–328.

a. Security Interests Perfected by Control Have Priority Over Security Interests Perfected by Means Other Than Control

A security interest in investment property that is perfected by control has priority over a security interest in investment property perfected by a method other than control. UCC § 9–328(1).

Example: SP–1 has a security interest in Debtor's investment property to secure a loan made to Debtor. SP–1 perfected its security interest by filing an effective financing statement against Debtor listing investment property as collateral. Debtor subsequently grants a security interest in a securities entitlement to SP–2 to secure a loan to Debtor from SP–2. SP–2 obtained control of the securities entitlement by obtaining a control agreement with the Debtor and the securities intermediary that the intermediary would comply with entitlement orders issued by SP–2 without further consent of the Debtor. UCC §§ 9–106(a), 8–106(d). SP–2's security interest in the securities entitlement has priority over SP–1's security interest in the securities entitlement.

b. Priority of Security Interests That Are All Perfected by Control

Priority between conflicting security interests in investment property which are each perfected by control are determined according to the following rules.

(1) Priority of Security Interests of Securities Intermediary in Securities Entitlements or Securities Accounts Maintained by the Intermediary

A securities intermediary's security interest in the debtor's securities entitlements held by the intermediary is perfected by control. UCC §§ 9–106(a), 8–106(e). If the securities intermediary has a perfected security interest in all securities entitlements in a securities account, the securities intermediary has control over the securities account. UCC § 9–106(c). A securities intermediary's security interest in securities entitlements or securities accounts maintained by the intermediary has priority over any conflicting security interest held by a secured party even if that secured party has obtained control of the securities account or securities entitlement. UCC § 9–328(3).

> *Example:* SP–1 has a security interest in Debtor's securities account held by Brokerage Inc. to secure a loan that SP–1 made to Debtor. SP–1 has perfected its security interest by obtaining a control agreement with Brokerage Inc. and Debtor that Brokerage Inc. would comply with entitlement orders issued by SP–1 without further consent of the Debtor. UCC §§ 9–106(a), 8–106(d). SP–1's perfected security interest in the securities account perfects its security interest in all securities entitlements held in the account. UCC §§ 9–203(h), 9–308(f). In the agreement between Brokerage and Debtor, Debtor granted a security interest in the securities account and all securities entitlements in the securities account maintained by Brokerage to secure any amounts that Debtor may owe Brokerage. Brokerage's security interest in the securities account and the securities entitlements in that account is superior in priority to SP–1's

security interest in the securities account and the securities entitlements held in that account.

(2) Priority of Security Interests of Commodity Intermediary in Commodity Contract or Commodity Account Maintained by the Intermediary

A commodity intermediary's security interest in the debtor's commodity contracts held by the intermediary is perfected by control. UCC § 9–106(b). If the commodity intermediary has a perfected security interest in all commodity contracts in a commodity account, the commodity intermediary has control over the commodity account. UCC § 9–106(c). A commodity intermediary's security interest in commodity contracts or commodity accounts maintained by the intermediary has priority over any conflicting security interest held by a secured party even if that secured party has obtained control of the commodity account or commodity contracts. UCC § 9–328(4).

(3) Priority of Security Interests Perfected by Control Other Than Those Held by Securities or Commodity Intermediaries

When the conflicting security interests in a security, a securities entitlement, or a commodity contract are each perfected by control but neither secured party is a securities intermediary or a commodities intermediary, the priority of the conflicting security interests is determined by the order in which the secured parties obtained control. UCC § 9–328(2).

Example: SP–1 obtained a security interest in Debtor's securities entitlements held by Brokerage Inc. and perfected its security interest by obtaining a control agreement with Brokerage and Debtor. SP–2 obtained a security interest in Debtor's securities entitlements held by Brokerage Inc. and perfected its security interest by obtaining a control agreement with Brokerage and Debtor. The order of priority of SP–1's and SP–2's security interests in the securities entitlements will be determined by the order in which they obtained the control agreements.

c. Priority of Security Interests in Certificated Security in Registered Form

A security interest in a certificated security may be perfected by the secured party taking delivery of the certificated security. UCC § 9–313(a). Delivery of a certificated security in registered form, to a person other than a securities intermediary, occurs when the secured party takes possession of the certificated security. UCC § 8–301(a). Control of a certificated security in registered form requires not only that the secured party take possession of it but that it be indorsed to the secured party or in blank or be registered in the name of the secured party. UCC §§ 9–106(a), 8–106(b). If the secured party takes delivery of the certificated security in registered form but does not have control of the certificated security (because it is lacking the necessary indorsement or registration), the secured party will have priority over a conflicting security interest in the certificated security that is perfected by a method other than control, such as by filing a financing statement. UCC § 9–328(5).

Example: SP–1 has a security interest in Debtor's certificated security in registered form. SP–1 filed an effective financing statement against Debtor listing the collateral as the certificated security. SP–2 obtained a security interest in the same certificated security and took possession of the certificated security. SP–2 does not obtain an indorsement or registration of the certificated security to SP–2. SP–1 has both filed first and perfected its security interest in the certificated security first. SP–2 has perfected second by taking delivery, but not control, of the certificated security. SP–2's security interest has priority over SP–1's security interest.

d. Priority of Security Interests Created by Broker, Securities Intermediary, or Commodity Intermediary

A security interest in investment property that is created by the broker, securities intermediary, or commodity intermediary is automatically perfected without the secured party having to do anything other than obtain attachment of the security interest. UCC § 9–309(10), (11).

(1) Conflicting Security Interests

If there are conflicting security interests created by a broker, securities intermediary, or commodity intermediary and those interests are not perfected by control, the security interests will have co-equal rank. UCC § 9–328(6). If the conflicting security interests are both perfected by control, then the time of obtaining control will determine priority. UCC § 9–328(2). If one of the conflicting security interests is perfected by control and the other security interest is perfected in a manner other than control, then the security interest perfected by control will have priority. UCC § 9–328(1).

(2) Priority of a Secured Party of a Securities Intermediary as Against Entitlement Holders of the Securities Entitlements

When the securities intermediary grants to a creditor a security interest in the securities entitlements it holds, the securities intermediary is supposed to have enough securities entitlements to satisfy both the claims of the entitlement holders and the claims of the securities intermediary's creditors to those securities entitlements. If the securities intermediary does not have enough securities entitlements to satisfy both types of claims, the priority rule as between the security interest of the secured party of the securities intermediary and the claims of the entitlement holders depends upon whether the secured party has obtained control, that is, not relied upon automatic perfection of its security interest under UCC § 9–309(10). If the secured party has perfected its security interest in the securities entitlements held by the securities intermediary by control, the secured party's security interest will have priority over the claims of the entitlement holders. UCC §§ 9–331(b), 8–511(b). If the secured party has not perfected its security interest in the securities entitlements by control, the entitlement holders claims will have priority over the secured party's claims.

16. Exception: Priority of Security Interests Created Under Other Articles

If a security interest is created based upon a rule found in the other articles of the UCC, the priority rule stated in those other articles governing those security interests controls. UCC § 9–322(f). If the priority rules as stated below do not apply and none of the other exceptions to the three general priority rules apply, then the three general priority rules in UCC § 9–322(a) apply to determine priority between conflicting security interests.

a. Security Interest of Collecting Bank in Items Sent for Collection

A collecting bank has a security interest in items sent for collection and accompanying documents and proceeds of the item for credit given against the item until the bank receives final settlement for the item or the bank gives up possession of the item and documents for a purpose other than collection. The collecting bank's security interest has priority over conflicting perfected security interests in the item, accompanying documents, and proceeds. UCC § 4–210.

Example: SP–1 has a security interest in Debtor's instruments. SP–1 filed an effective financing statement against Debtor listing instruments as the collateral. Debtor was the payee on several checks (instruments) and deposited those checks for collection with Bank. Bank gave Debtor credit for those checks which was available for withdrawal from Debtor's account held by Bank. Bank has a security interest in those checks for the amount of the credit given to Debtor. Bank's security interest in the checks is superior to SP–1's security interest.

b. Security Interest of Letter of Credit Issuer or Nominated Person

An issuer or nominated person under a letter of credit has a security interest in the documents presented if the issuer or nominated person gives value or honors the presentation and that security interest continues as long as the issuer or nominated person is not reimbursed for the value given. If the documents are in tangible form and *are not* a certificated security, chattel paper, a document of title, an instrument, or a letter of credit, the security interest of the issuer or nominated person will have priority over a conflicting security interest as long as the debtor does not obtain possession of the documents. UCC § 5–118. If the documents are in intangible form or are tangible documents that *are* a certificated security, chattel paper, a document of title, an instrument, or a letter of credit, then the priority rules of Article 9 are applicable.

Example: SP–1 has a security interest in Debtor's documents of title and commercial paper, perfected by filing an effective financing statement against Debtor listing documents of title and commercial paper as collateral. Debtor purchased some goods from Seller and obtained a letter of credit from Nations Bank issued to Seller as the beneficiary. As required by the letter of credit, Seller submitted to Nations Bank a tangible document of title, invoice, and insurance certificate. Nations Bank honored the presentation of the documents under the letter of credit by paying Seller. Nations Bank took possession of the three documents. Nations Bank has a security interest in the document of title, invoice, and insurance certificate as security for the obligation of Debtor to reimburse Nations Bank for honoring the letter of credit. Nations Bank's security interest in the tangible document of title is perfected by possession and in the tangible invoice and insurance certificate by virtue of the rule of UCC § 5–118(b)(3). The priority rule governing the priority of security interests in the document of title is the first to file or perfect priority rule and SP–1 has priority as it filed before Nations Bank perfected by possession (assuming Nations Bank does not qualify for priority in the document title under UCC § 9–331). The priority rule governing the priority of security interests in the invoice and insurance certificate is the rule of UCC § 5–118(b)(3) and Nations Bank's security interest has priority in those items.

c. Security Interests Created Under Articles 2 and 2A

Under Article 2, a seller has a security interest in goods sold for the price if the seller retains title to delivered goods or ships the goods under reservation. UCC §§ 2–401, 2–505. Under Article 2, a buyer has a security interest for a refund of the price paid and certain incidental damages if the buyer has possession of goods it has rightfully and effectively rejected or as to which it has effectively and justifiably revoked acceptance. UCC § 2–711(3). Under Article 2A, a lessee has a similar security interest for a refund of rent already paid, security deposits, and certain incidental damages if the lessee has possession of goods it has rightfully and effectively rejected or as to which it has effectively and justifiably revoked acceptance. UCC § 2A–508. These security interests will have priority over conflicting security interests in the goods created by the debtor as long as the debtor does not obtain possession of the goods. UCC § 9–110.

Example: SP–1 has a security interest in all of Buyer's goods then owned or thereafter acquired and filed an effective financing statement against Buyer listing goods as the collateral. Seller shipped goods under reservation to Buyer. The goods are in the possession of the carrier that transported the goods. Seller's security interest created by shipment under reservation has priority over SP–1's security interest in Buyer's goods as long as Buyer does not obtain possession of the goods. Once Buyer obtains possession of the goods, the priority of Seller's security interest as against SP–1's security interest will be determined by the purchase money priority rules of UCC § 9–324, if Seller perfects its security interest in the goods by filing or possession, or the general priority rules of UCC § 9–322(a).

17. Exception: Priority in Proceeds

For purposes of the first to file or perfect priority rule, the filing or perfection as to the original collateral is the time of filing or perfection as to the identifiable proceeds of that original collateral. UCC § 9–322(b). Because part of the first to file or perfect rule is that in order to use that time to establish the priority of the security interest that there be no time thereafter when there is neither an effective filing or perfection as to that collateral, continuous perfection or filing as to the collateral, including proceeds is critical. Review the materials in Chapter IV on perfection of security interests in proceeds.

Example: SP–1 has a security interest in Debtor's equipment which it has perfected by filing an effective financing statement against Debtor listing equipment as collateral. SP–2 also has a security interest in Debtor's equipment which it has perfected by filing an effective financing statement against Debtor listing equipment as collateral. SP–1 filed its financing statement first and thus its security interest in the equipment has priority over SP–2's security interest in the equipment. Debtor then sold the equipment and received in exchange a used pickup truck. The pickup truck is identifiable proceeds of the sold equipment and both SP–1's and SP–2's security interests attach to the pickup truck and are temporarily perfected for 20 days from attachment. UCC § 9–315(a)-(c). On the 19th day after attachment, SP–2 obtained notation of its security interest on the pickup truck's certificate of title. On the 22nd day after attachment, SP–1 obtained notation of its security interest on the pickup truck's certificate of title. Under the state's certificate of title law, perfection occurs when the security interest is actually noted on the certificate of title. SP–2's security interest in the pickup truck was continuously perfected and the date for determining the priority of its security interest is the date of the filing of its financing statement against Debtor. SP–1's security interest in the pickup truck was not continuously perfected (a gap of 2 days) and its filed financing statement was not effective to perfect a security interest in the truck given the certificate of title law. UCC § 9–311. Thus, the priority date for purposes of the first to file or perfect rule of UCC § 9–322(a) and (b) as applied to the pickup truck is the date SP–1's security interest was noted on the certificate of title. SP–2's security interest in the pickup truck has priority over SP–1's security interest in the pickup truck.

This first to file or perfect rule for priority in proceeds is only applied if none of the following three exceptions apply: (i) the security interest qualifies for priority in collateral under any of the previously explored exceptions to the three general rules in UCC § 9–322(a); (ii) the security interest is in deposit accounts, investment property, letter-of-credit rights, chattel paper, instruments, or negotiable documents of title and the proceeds are cash proceeds or proceeds that are the same type as the original collateral; or (iii) the security interest is perfected by a nonfiling method and the collateral is chattel paper, deposit accounts, negotiable documents of title, instruments, investment property or letter-of-credit rights and the proceeds are not cash proceeds, chattel paper, negotiable documents of title, instruments, investment property, or letter-of-credit rights.

a. Qualified for Priority in Collateral Under Any of the Exceptions to the Three General Rules in UCC § 9–322(a)

If a security interest in the type of proceeds qualifies for priority against a conflicting security interest in that same type of proceeds under any of the priority rules that are exceptions to three general rules in UCC § 9–322(a) as outlined *supra*, then the security interest that has priority under the exception has priority in that type of proceeds. If this rule applies, then it governs priority in the proceeds and the other two exceptions to the first to file or perfect rule as applied to proceeds, explored *infra*, do not apply. UCC § 9–322(a), (f).

(1) Subordination Due to Error in Financing Statement Information

Review Section D.3. *supra* where this rule is explained, and consider the following example as it applies to proceeds. The subordination rule is not limited in terms of the type of collateral to which it applies. UCC § 9–338.

Example: SP–1 obtained the Debtor's signed security agreement granting SP–1 a security interest in Debtor's accounts then owned or thereafter acquired. SP–1 funded the loan and filed an effective financing statement covering Debtor's accounts. That financing statement contained an error in Debtor's mailing address. SP–2, upon examining the financing statement, reasonably determined based upon the error in the mailing address that the debtor it was dealing with was not the same debtor as the one listed in SP–1's financing statement. SP–2 was in error on this point. SP–2 obtained Debtor's signed security agreement granting SP–2 a security interest in Debtor's accounts then owned or thereafter acquired and filed an effective financing statement against Debtor covering accounts. Debtor received a payment of money from an account debtor on the account. Both SP–1 and SP–2 have a perfected security interest in the money as identifiable cash proceeds of the account, UCC § 9–315(a)-(d), and SP–1 would have priority in those proceeds under UCC § 9–322(a), (b). SP–2 has an argument that SP–1's security interest in the money (identifiable proceeds) should be subordinated to SP–2's security interest in the money as SP–2 gave value to Debtor in reasonable reliance on the inaccurate information regarding Debtor's mailing address.

(2) Proceeds of Perfected Purchase Money Security Interests in Goods Other Than Inventory and Livestock

Review Section D.5. *supra*. If a secured party has a perfected purchase money security interest in goods, other than inventory and livestock, with priority over a conflicting security interest in those goods and the purchase money security interest in identifiable proceeds is perfected, the perfected purchase money security interest in the proceeds will also have priority over a conflicting security interest in those same proceeds as long as the purchase money security interest in the proceeds remains perfected. UCC § 9–324(a). That priority rule is subject to an exception if the identifiable proceeds of the goods is a deposit account. In that situation, the priority in the deposit account will be determined by the special rules for deposit accounts in UCC § 9–327. Review Section D.12, *supra*.

Example: SP–1 has a security interest in Debtor's equipment now owned and hereafter acquired and has perfected its security interest in the equipment by filing an effective financing statement against Debtor listing equipment as collateral. SP–2 sold Debtor an item of new equipment and retained a security interest to secure the price. SP–2 filed an effective financing statement covering the new equipment against Debtor within 20 days of delivery of the new item of equipment to Debtor. SP–2 has a perfected purchase money security interest in the new equipment that qualifies for priority over SP–1's perfected security interest in the new equipment. Debtor then sold the new equipment to Buyer on credit, creating an account. SP–1's and SP–2's security interests in the account are attached and perfected as identifiable proceeds of the equipment under UCC § 9–315(a)-(d). SP–2's security interest has priority in the account over SP–1's security interest.

Example: SP–1 has a security interest in Debtor's equipment now owned and hereafter acquired and has perfected its security interest in the equipment by filing an effective financing statement against Debtor listing equipment as collateral. SP–2 sold Debtor an item of new equipment and retained a security interest to secure the price. SP–2 filed an effective financing statement covering the new equipment against Debtor within 20 days of delivery of the new item of equipment to Debtor. SP–2 has a perfected purchase money security interest in the new equipment that qualifies for priority over SP–1's security interest in the new equipment. Debtor then sold the piece of new equipment to Buyer in exchange for a funds transfer to Debtor's deposit account at Bank. SP–1's and SP–2's security interests in the deposit account are attached and perfected as identifiable proceeds of the equipment under UCC § 9–315(a)-(d). SP–1 obtains control of the deposit account by obtaining a control agreement with Bank and Debtor. SP–1's security interest in the deposit account is superior to SP–2's security interest in the deposit account. UCC § 9–327.

Example: SP–1 has a security interest in Debtor's equipment now owned and hereafter acquired and has perfected its security interest in the equipment by filing an effective financing statement against Debtor listing equipment as collateral. SP–2 sold Debtor an item of new equipment and retained a security interest to secure the price. SP–2 filed an effective financing statement covering the new equipment against Debtor within 20 days of delivery of the new item of equipment to Debtor. SP–2 has a perfected purchase money security interest in the new equipment that qualifies for priority over SP–1's security interest in the new equipment. Debtor then sold the new equipment to Buyer in exchange for a pickup truck. Both SP–1's and SP–2's security interests are perfected in the pickup truck for a period of 20 days. UCC § 9–315(a)-(d). During that time, SP–2's security interest in the pickup truck is superior to SP–1's security interest in the pickup truck. After the 20 days expire, SP–1 perfects its security interest in the pickup truck by obtaining notation of its security interest on the certificate of title for the truck. SP–1's security interest in the truck has priority over SP–2's now unperfected security interest in the truck.

(3) Proceeds of Perfected Purchase Money Security Interests in Inventory

Review Section D.5 *supra.* If a perfected purchase money security interest in inventory has priority in the inventory, the perfected security interest in identifiable proceeds of that inventory will have the same priority as the purchase money security interest in the inventory only as to certain types of proceeds. UCC § 9–324(b).

(a) Proceeds That Are Chattel Paper and Instruments

If the identifiable proceeds of inventory are chattel paper or instruments, the purchase money security interest in the chattel paper or instruments will have priority over a conflicting security interest in the chattel paper or instruments only if the secured party qualifies for priority in the chattel paper and instruments under the special priority rules for purchasers of chattel paper and instruments in UCC § 9–330. Review Section D.10 and D.11 *supra.* UCC § 9–324(b). A secured party with a perfected purchase money security interest in inventory is deemed to give new value for chattel paper that is identifiable proceeds of the inventory. UCC § 9–330(e). Presumably, a purchase money secured party could also qualify for priority in negotiable instruments as a holder in due course of that instrument. UCC § 9–331.

Example: SP–1 has a properly perfected security interest in inventory then owned or thereafter acquired. SP–1 filed its effective financing statement to perfect its security interest on June 1. In July, Debtor purchased more inventory from Seller and granted Seller a security interest in the purchased inventory to secure the purchase price. Seller filed an effective financing statement to perfect its security interest prior to delivery of the new inventory to the Debtor. Seller sent a notice to SP–1 describing its purchase money security interest in the new inventory. SP–1 received the notice prior to Seller's delivery of the new inventory to Debtor. Seller's purchase money security interest in the new inventory has priority over SP–1's perfected security interest in the new inventory. Debtor sold an item of the new inventory to Buyer in exchange for the Buyer's written agreement to pay for the item and

Buyer's grant of a security interest in the new item to Debtor. The Debtor/Buyer contract is chattel paper. Both Seller and SP–1 have perfected security interests in the chattel paper as identifiable proceeds of the new item of inventory that was sold to Buyer. UCC § 9–315(a)-(d). Seller is deemed to have given new value for the chattel paper given its perfected purchase money security interest in the inventory. Seller will have priority in that chattel paper over SP–1 only if Seller takes possession of the chattel paper in good faith and in the ordinary course of the Seller's business and if the chattel paper does not indicate that it has been assigned to an identified assignee other than Seller.

(b) Proceeds That Are Cash Proceeds

If the proceeds are identifiable cash proceeds that are received by the debtor on or before the inventory is delivered to a buyer, the secured party with a perfected purchase money priority security interest in the inventory will have priority over conflicting security interests in those cash proceeds unless the cash proceeds are a deposit account and a secured party qualifies for priority in the deposit account under the rules of UCC § 9–327. Review Section D.12 *supra*.

Example: SP–1 has a properly perfected security interest in inventory then owned or thereafter acquired. SP–1 filed its effective financing statement to perfect its security interest on June 1. In July, Debtor purchased more inventory from Seller and granted Seller a security interest in the purchased inventory to secure the purchase price. Seller filed an effective financing statement to perfect its security interest prior to delivery of the new inventory to the Debtor. Seller sent a notice to SP–1 describing its purchase money security interest in the new inventory. SP–1 received the notice prior to Seller's delivery of the new inventory to Debtor. Seller's purchase money security interest in the new inventory has priority over SP–1's perfected security interest in the new inventory. Debtor sold an item of the new inventory to Buyer for money.

Buyer delivered that money to Debtor at the time Buyer took delivery of the item. Both Seller and SP–1 have perfected security interests in the money as identifiable cash proceeds. UCC § 9–315(a)-(d). Seller's security interest in the money has priority over SP–1's security interest in the money.

Example: SP–1 has a properly perfected security interest in inventory then owned or thereafter acquired. SP–1 filed its effective financing statement to perfect its security interest on June 1. In July, Debtor purchased more inventory from Seller and granted Seller a security interest in the purchased inventory to secure the purchase price. Seller filed an effective financing statement to perfect its security interest prior to delivery of the new inventory to the Debtor. Seller sent a notice to SP–1 describing its purchase money security interest in the new inventory. SP–1 received the notice prior to Seller's delivery of the new inventory to Debtor. Seller's purchase money security interest in the new inventory has priority over SP–1's perfected security interest in the new inventory. Debtor sold an item of the new inventory to Buyer for money to be paid upon delivery. Debtor delivered the item of inventory to Buyer and 2 days later, Buyer delivered the money to Debtor. Both SP–1 and Seller have perfected security interests in the money. UCC § 9–315(a)-(d). The priority of the conflicting security interests in the money is determined by the first to file or perfect rule. UCC § 9–322(a), (b). SP–1 filed first as to the original collateral and thus its security interest in the money has priority over Seller's security interest in the money.

Example: SP–1 has a properly perfected security interest in inventory then owned or thereafter acquired. SP–1 filed its effective financing statement to perfect its security interest on June 1. In July, Debtor purchased more inventory from Seller and granted Seller a security interest in the purchased inventory to secure the purchase price. Seller filed an effective financing statement to perfect its security interest prior to delivery of the new inventory to the Debtor. Seller sent a notice to SP–1 describing its purchase money security interest in the new inventory. SP–1 received the notice prior to Seller's delivery of the new inventory to Debtor. Seller's purchase money security interest in the new inventory has priority over SP–1's perfected security interest in the new inventory. Debtor sold an item of the new inventory to Buyer in exchange for a wire transfer of funds to Debtor's deposit account at Bank prior to delivery of the purchased item to Buyer. Both SP–1 and Seller have perfected security interests in the deposit account as identifiable cash proceeds of the item of inventory sold. Seller has priority in the deposit account. UCC §§ 9–315(a)-(d), 9–324(b). SP–1 then obtains a control agreement with Bank and Debtor concerning the deposit account. SP–1's security interest in the deposit account now has priority over Seller's security interest in the deposit account.

(c) Proceeds That Do Not Meet the Tests Above

As to any proceeds of inventory that do not fall within those two categories above, the other priority rules in Article 9 apply, including the three general rules of UCC § 9–322(a) and the exceptions to those three general rules, if applicable, discussed in this Section D.

Example: SP–1 has a properly perfected security interest in inventory then owned or thereafter acquired. SP–1 filed its effective financing statement to perfect its security interest on June 1. In July, Debtor purchased more inventory from Seller and granted Seller a security interest in the purchased inventory to secure the purchase price. Seller filed an effective financing statement to perfect its security interest prior to delivery of the new inventory to the Debtor. Seller sent a notice to SP–1 describing its purchase money security interest in the new inventory. SP–1 received the notice prior to Seller's delivery of the new inventory to Debtor. Seller's purchase money security interest in the new inventory has priority over SP–1's perfected security interest in the new inventory. Debtor sold an item of the new inventory to Buyer in exchange for Buyer's promise to pay for the item, creating an account. Seller's and SP–1's security interests in the account are perfected. UCC § 9–315(a)-(d)(1). Under the first to file or perfect rule, SP–1's security interest in the account has priority over Seller's security interest in the account. UCC § 9–322(a), (b).

(4) Proceeds of Perfected Purchase Money Security Interests in Livestock
If a perfected purchase money security interest in livestock has priority over a conflicting security interest in the livestock, the purchase money secured party's security interest will also have priority in a perfected security interest in identifiable proceeds of all types and identifiable products in their unmanufactured state. If the identifiable proceeds are a deposit account, the priority of conflicting security interests in the deposit account is determined under UCC § 9–327. Review Section D.12 *supra*. UCC § 9–324(d).

    Example: SP–1 has a properly perfected security interest in Farmer's livestock then owned or thereafter acquired and filed its effective financing statement covering livestock in June. In August, SP–2 lent Farmer money to allow Farmer to buy cows. SP–2 obtained Farmer's signed security agreement granting SP–2 a security interest in the cows to secure the purchase price. SP–2 sent a notice to SP–1 that SP–2 had a security interest in the new cows to secure the purchase price and SP–1 received that notice before the seller delivered the cows to Farmer. SP–2 filed its financing statement to perfect its security interest in the cows before the seller delivered the cows to Farmer. SP–2's perfected purchase money security interest in the cows has priority over SP–1's perfected security interest in the cows. Farmer then sold the cows to Buyer and obtained Buyer's promise to pay for the cows, creating an account. Both SP–1's and SP–2's security interests in the account are perfected. UCC § 9–315(a)-(d). SP–2's security interest in the account has priority over SP–1's security interest in the account.

Example: SP–1 has a properly perfected security interest in Farmer's livestock then owned or thereafter acquired and filed its effective financing statement covering livestock in June. In August, SP–2 lent Farmer money to allow Farmer to buy cows. SP–2 obtained Farmer's signed security agreement granting SP–2 a security interest in the cows to secure the purchase price. SP–2 sent a notice to SP–1 that SP–2 had a security interest in the new cows to secure the purchase price and SP–1 received that notice before the seller delivered the cows to Farmer. SP–2 filed its financing statement to perfect its security interest in the cows before the seller delivered the cows to Farmer. SP–2's perfected purchase money security interest in the cows has priority over SP–1's perfected security interest in the cows. Farmer then sold the new cows to Buyer and Buyer wire transferred the funds to Farmer's deposit account at Bank in payment for the cows. Both SP–1's and SP–2's security interests in the deposit account are perfected as identifiable cash proceeds of their security interests in the new cows. UCC § 9–315(a)-(d). SP–2's security interest has priority in the deposit account. UCC § 9–324(d). SP–1 then obtained a control agreement with Bank and Farmer concerning the deposit account. SP–1's security interest in the deposit account will now have priority over SP–2's security interest in the deposit account.

Example: SP–1 has a properly perfected security interest in Farmer's livestock and products of livestock then owned or thereafter acquired and filed its effective financing statement covering livestock and their products in June. In August, SP–2 lent Farmer money to allow Farmer to buy cows. SP–2 obtained Farmer's signed security agreement granting SP–2 a security interest in the new cows and products of the those cows to secure the purchase price. SP–2 sent a notice to SP–1 that SP–2 had a security interest in the new cows to secure the purchase price and SP–1 received that notice before the seller delivered the new cows to Farmer. SP–2 filed its financing statement to perfect its security interest in the new cows and their products before the seller delivered the new cows to Farmer. SP–2's perfected purchase money security interest in the new cows has priority over SP–1's perfected security interest in the new cows. The new cows produced milk. Both SP–1 and SP–2 have perfected security interests in the milk as a product of the new cow based upon the descriptions in the security agreements and financing statements. SP–2's security interest in the milk has priority over SP–1's security interest in the milk.

Example: SP–1 has a properly perfected security interest in Farmer's livestock and products of livestock then owned or thereafter acquired and filed its effective financing statement covering livestock and their products in June. In August, SP–2 lent Farmer money to allow Farmer to buy cows. SP–2 obtained Farmer's signed security agreement granting SP–2 a security interest in the new cows and products of those cows to secure the purchase price. SP–2 sent a notice to SP–1 that SP–2 had a security interest in the new cows to secure the purchase price and SP–1 received that notice before the seller delivered the new cows to Farmer. SP–2 filed its financing statement to perfect its security interest in the new cows and their products before the seller delivered the new cows to Farmer. SP–2's perfected purchase money security interest in the new cows has priority over SP–1's perfected security interest in the new cows. The new cows produced milk which Farmer used to make cheese. Both SP–1 and SP–2 have perfected security interests in the cheese assuming that cheese falls into the category of "products" of the cows. The priority of security interests in the cheese will be determined by the first to file or perfect rule as the cheese is not in an unmanufactured state. SP–1 filed first and thus its security interest in the cheese will have priority over SP–2's security interest in the cheese.

(5) Proceeds of Perfected Purchase Money Security Interests in Software

If the secured party's purchase money security interest in software has priority over a conflicting security interest in the software, the secured party's perfected security interest in any type of identifiable proceeds of the software will have priority over a conflicting security interest in the same proceeds if the perfected purchase money security interest in the goods in which the software is used and in proceeds of the goods has priority over conflicting security interests in the goods and the proceeds of the goods. If the proceeds are a deposit account, the rules on priority of a security interest in a deposit account control, UCC § 9–327. Review Section D.12 *supra*. UCC § 9–324(f).

Example: SP–1 has a perfected security interest in all of Debtor's equipment and software in which Debtor currently has rights or in which Debtor acquires rights thereafter and filed its effective financing statement covering equipment and software in June. On August 10, Seller sold Debtor a new computer with software for use in the computer and Debtor granted a security interest to Seller to secure the purchase price of the computer and software. Debtor will use the computer in its office operations. Seller delivered the computer and software to Debtor on August 20. Seller filed an effective financing statement on August 30 to perfect its security interest in the computer and software. Seller's perfected purchase money security interest in the computer has priority over SP–1's perfected security interest in the computer under UCC § 9–324(a) and thus Seller's perfected purchase money security interest in the software has priority over SP–1's perfected security interest in the software. UCC § 9–324(f). Debtor then sold the computer and software to Buyer in exchange for Buyer's promise to pay for both, creating an account. Both Seller's and SP–1's security interests are perfected in the account as identifiable proceeds of the computer and software. UCC § 9–315(a)-(d). Seller's perfected security interest in the account has priority over SP–1's perfected security interest in the account.

(6) Conflicting Purchase Money Security Interests and Proceeds

If two or more secured parties qualify for purchase money priority in goods or software, or any proceeds, a seller's perfected purchase money security interest in goods or software and the proceeds in which it has priority will have priority over a non-seller's perfected purchase money security interest in the same proceeds. UCC § 9–324(g).

> *Example:* Seller agreed to sell an item of equipment to Debtor on credit and take a security interest to secure part of the purchase price. Seller, however, insisted that Debtor make a 20% down payment on the purchase price. Debtor borrowed the 20% down payment from SP–1 and granted SP–1 a security interest in the new item of equipment to secure that amount. Both Seller and SP–1 filed financing statements to perfect their respective security interests within 20 days after Debtor received possession of the equipment. Seller's perfected purchase money security interest in the equipment has priority over SP–1's perfected purchase money security interest in the equipment. Debtor then sold the equipment to Buyer in exchange for Buyer's promise to pay for the equipment, creating an account. Seller's perfected security interest in the account has priority over SP–1's perfected security interest in the account.

(7) Priority in Proceeds That Are Negotiable Documents of Title

If the proceeds of collateral consist of negotiable documents of title, a secured party that becomes a holder of the negotiable document of title by due negotiation will take the document free of a conflicting security interest in that document of title. UCC §§ 9–331, 7–502. Review Section D.9 *supra*.

> *Example:* SP–1 has a security interest in Debtor's equipment and has perfected its security interest by filing an effective financing statement against Debtor stating equipment as collateral. Debtor also granted a security interest in its equipment to SP–2 and SP–2 perfected its security interest in the equipment by filing an effective financing statement against Debtor stating equipment as collateral. Under the first to file or

perfect rule, SP–1's security interest in equipment has priority over SP–2's security interest in equipment. Debtor then sold a piece of equipment to Buyer and as payment for that equipment purchase, Buyer gave Debtor a negotiable document of title deliverable to bearer covering goods stored with Warehouse Inc. The negotiable document of title is identifiable proceeds of the sold equipment and both SP–1 and SP–2 have perfected security interests in the negotiable document of title. UCC § 9–315(a)-(d). Under the first to file or perfect rule, SP–1's security interest in the negotiable document of title would have priority over SP–2's security interest in the negotiable document of title. Debtor then delivered the negotiable document of title to SP–2 in a due negotiation. SP–2 takes the negotiable document of title free of SP–1's perfected security interest in the negotiable document. UCC § 9–331.

(8) Priority in Proceeds That Are Chattel Paper

If the proceeds of collateral consist of chattel paper and a secured party obtains possession or control of the chattel paper as set forth in UCC § 9–330, the secured party will have priority over a conflicting security interest in the chattel paper. Review Section D.10 *supra*.

Example: SP–1 has a security interest in Debtor's inventory and perfected its security interest by filing an effective financing statement against Debtor covering inventory. SP–2 also has a security interest in Debtor's inventory and perfected its security interest by filing an effective financing statement against Debtor covering inventory. Under the first to file or perfect rule, SP–1's security interest in inventory has priority over SP–2's security interest in inventory. Debtor sold an item of inventory to Buyer in a transaction in which Buyer agreed in writing to pay the price and granted a security interest to Debtor in the item to secure the price. That agreement is chattel paper and identifiable proceeds of the item of inventory sold. Both SP–1's and SP–2's security interests in the chattel paper are perfected. UCC § 9–315(a)-(d). Under the first to file or perfect rule, SP–1's security interest in the chattel paper would be superior to SP–2's security interest in the chattel paper. SP–2 then took possession of the chattel paper in the ordinary course of its business, in good faith, and gave new value for the chattel paper. The chattel paper did not indicate it was assigned to a specific assignee and SP–2 had no knowledge that SP–2's purchase of the chattel paper violated SP–1's rights. SP–2's security interest in the chattel paper is superior to SP–1's security interest in the chattel paper.

(9) Priority in the Specific Goods Covered by the Chattel Paper

If a secured party has priority in chattel paper under the rule of UCC § 9–330, then the secured party has priority in the proceeds of the chattel paper that consist of the specific goods covered by the chattel paper if those goods are returned to the debtor in a transaction in which the debtor acquires rights in the goods even if the secured party's security interest in those returned goods is unperfected. UCC § 9–330(c). Review Section D.10 *supra*.

Example: SP–1 has a security interest in Debtor's inventory and perfected its security interest by filing an effective financing statement against Debtor covering inventory. SP–2 also has a security interest in Debtor's inventory and perfected its security interest by filing an effective financing statement against Debtor covering inventory. Under the first to file or perfect rule, SP–1's security interest in inventory has priority over SP–2's security interest in inventory. Debtor sold an item of inventory to Buyer in a transaction in which Buyer agreed in writing to pay the price and granted a security interest to Debtor in the item to secure the price. That agreement is chattel paper and identifiable proceeds of the item of inventory sold. Both SP–1's and SP–2's security interests in the chattel paper are perfected. UCC § 9–315(a)-(d). Under the first to file or perfect rule, SP–1's security interest in the chattel paper would be superior to SP–2's security interest in the chattel paper. SP–2 then took possession of the chattel paper in the ordinary course of its business, in good faith, and gave new value for the chattel paper. The chattel paper did not indicate it was assigned to a specific assignee and SP–2 had no knowledge that SP–2's purchase of the chattel paper violated SP–1's rights. SP–2's security interest in the chattel paper is superior to SP–1's security interest in the chattel paper. Buyer returned the goods to Debtor because Buyer rightfully rejected the goods as defective. Both SP–1's and SP–2's security interests attach to and are perfected in the returned goods as proceeds of the chattel paper. UCC § 9–315(a)-(d). Because SP–2 has priority in the chattel paper, SP–2's security interest in the goods covered by the chattel paper has priority over SP–1's security interest in those goods.

Example: SP–1 has a security interest in Debtor's inventory and perfected its security interest by filing an effective financing statement against Debtor covering goods. SP–2 also has a security interest in Debtor's inventory but that security interest is not perfected. Debtor sold an item of inventory to Buyer in a transaction in which Buyer agreed in writing to pay the price and granted a security interest in the item to Debtor to secure the price. That agreement is chattel paper and identifiable proceeds of the item of inventory sold. Both SP–1's and SP–2's security interests in the chattel paper are attached but only SP–1's security interest is perfected. UCC § 9–315(a)-(d). SP–1 has priority in the chattel paper under the rule that perfected security interests have priority over unperfected security interests. UCC § 9–322(a). SP–2 then took possession of the chattel paper in the ordinary course of its business, in good faith, and gave new value for the chattel paper. The chattel paper did not indicate it was assigned to a specific assignee and SP–2 had no knowledge that SP–2's purchase of the chattel paper violated SP–1's rights. SP–2's security interest in the chattel paper is superior to SP–1's security interest in the chattel paper. Buyer returned the goods to Debtor because Buyer rightfully rejected the goods as defective. Both SP–1's and SP–2's security interests attach to the goods as proceeds of the chattel paper, but only SP–1's security interest in the goods is perfected beyond the 20-day time period of temporary perfection for proceeds. UCC § 9–315(a)-(d). Because SP–2 has priority in the chattel paper,

SP–2's security interest in the goods covered by the chattel paper has priority over SP–1's security interest in those goods even though SP–2's security interest in the goods is unperfected.

(10) Priority in Proceeds That Are Instruments

If the proceeds of collateral are instruments, a secured party that qualifies for priority over conflicting security interests in instruments under UCC § 9–330(d) or as a holder in due course of a negotiable instrument under UCC § 9–331 will have priority over conflicting security interests in the instrument. Review Section D.11 *supra*.

Example: SP–1 has a security interest in debtor's equipment that is perfected by filing an effective financing statement against debtor listing the collateral as equipment. SP–2 also has a security interest in debtor's equipment that is perfected by filing an effective financing statement against debtor listing the collateral as equipment. Under the first to file or perfect rule, SP–1's security interest has priority over SP–2's security interest in the equipment. Debtor sold a piece of equipment to buyer in exchange for a nonnegotiable promissory note that is an instrument under Article 9. Both SP–1 and SP–2 have perfected security interests in the promissory note as identifiable proceeds of the equipment. UCC § 9–315(a)-(d). Under the first to file or perfect rule, SP–1 would have priority for its security interest in the promissory note over SP–2's security interest in the promissory note. SP–2 then took possession of the promissory note in good faith and without knowledge that the transaction violated the rights of SP–1 in the promissory note. SP–2 gave value because of the outstanding debt that debtor owed to SP–2. SP–2's security interest has priority in the promissory note over SP–1's security interest. UCC § 9–330(d).

Example: SP–1 has a security interest in Debtor's equipment and perfected its security interest by filing an effective financing statement against Debtor listing the collateral as equipment. SP–2 also has a security interest in Debtor's equipment that is perfected by filing an effective financing statement against Debtor listing the collateral as equipment. Under the first to file or perfect rule, SP–1's security interest in the equipment has priority over SP–2's security interest in the equipment. Debtor sold a piece of equipment to Buyer in exchange for a negotiable promissory note that is an instrument under Article 9. Both SP–1 and SP–2 have perfected security interests in the promissory note as identifiable proceeds of the equipment. UCC § 9–315(a)-(d). Under the first to file or perfect rule, SP–1 would have priority for its security interest in the promissory note over SP–2's security interest in the promissory note. SP–2 then took possession of the promissory note and qualified as a holder in due course of the negotiable promissory note by fulfilling all the criteria under UCC § 3–302. SP–2 takes the promissory note free of SP–1's security interest in the promissory note. UCC §§ 9–331, 3–306.

(11)   Priority in Proceeds That Are Deposit Accounts

If the proceeds of collateral are a deposit account, and a secured party has control of the deposit account, UCC § 9–104, the rules on priority of conflicting security interests in deposit accounts controls. UCC § 9–327. Review Section D.12 *supra*.

Example: SP–1 has a security interest in Debtor's equipment and has perfected that security interest by filing an effective financing statement against Debtor listing equipment as the collateral. SP–2 has a security interest in Debtor's equipment and has perfected that security interest by filing an effective financing statement against Debtor listing equipment as the collateral. Under the first to file or perfect rule, SP–1's security interest in the equipment has priority over SP–2's security interest in the equipment. Debtor sold a piece of equipment in exchange for a wire transfer of funds into the Debtor's deposit account held by Bank. Both SP–1's and SP–2's security interests in the deposit account are perfected as the deposit account is identifiable cash proceeds of the sold equipment. UCC § 9–315(a)-(d). Under the first to file or perfect rule, SP–1's security interest in the deposit account would have priority over SP–2's security interest in the deposit account. SP–2 then obtains a control agreement with Bank and Debtor giving SP–2 control of the deposit account. SP–2's security interest in the deposit account has priority over SP–1's security interest. UCC § 9–327(1).

(12)   **Priority in Proceeds That Are Money or Funds From a Deposit Account**

If the proceeds are money or a transfer of funds from a deposit account, a transferee (other than the debtor) takes those proceeds free of a security interest unless the transferee acts in collusion with the debtor to violate the rights of the secured party. UCC § 9–332. Review Section D.12 and 13 *supra*.

Example: SP–1 has a security interest in Debtor's equipment and has perfected its security interest in the equipment by filing an effective financing statement against Debtor listing equipment as the collateral. SP–2 has a security interest in Debtor's equipment and has perfected its security interest in the equipment by filing an effective financing statement against Debtor listing equipment as the collateral. Under the first to file or perfect rule, SP–1's security interest in the equipment has priority over SP–2's security interest in the equipment. Debtor sold a piece of equipment to Buyer in exchange for money. Both SP–1 and SP–2 have perfected security interests in the money as identifiable proceeds of the sold equipment. UCC § 9–315(a)-(d). Debtor then took the money and paid it to SP–2. SP–2 has the money free of SP–1's security interest unless SP–2 acted in collusion with Debtor to violate SP–1's security interest.

(13)   **Priority in Proceeds That are a Letter-of-Credit Right**

If the proceeds of collateral consist of a letter-of-credit right, the special priority rules for letters of credit will control priority in the letter-of-credit right. UCC §§ 5–114, 9–109(c)(4), 9–329. Review Section D.14 *supra*.

Example: SP–1 has a security interest in Debtor's accounts and has perfected that security interest by filing an effective financing statement against Debtor listing accounts as collateral. SP–2 has a security interest in Debtor's accounts and has perfected that security interest by filing an effective financing statement against Debtor listing accounts as collateral. Under the first to file or perfect rule, SP–1's security interest in the accounts has priority over SP–2's security interest in the accounts. An account debtor pays its obligation on the account by making Debtor a beneficiary under a letter of credit issued by Nations Bank. The letter-of-credit right is proceeds of the account. Both SP–1 and SP–2 have perfected security interests in the letter-of-credit right for a period of 20 days after attachment of the security interests to the letter-of-credit right. UCC § 9–315(a)-(d). During that time, under the first to file or perfect rule, SP–1's security interest in the letter-of-credit right has priority over SP–2's security interest in the letter-of-credit right. With the cooperation of Debtor, SP–2 obtains Nations Bank's consent to an assignment of the right to proceeds under the letter of credit to SP–2. SP–2 has perfected its interest in the letter-of-credit right by control. UCC § 9–107. SP–2's security interest in the letter-of-credit right has priority over SP–1's security interest in the letter-of-credit right.

(14)   Priority in Proceeds That Are Investment Property

If the proceeds of collateral are investment property, then the special priority rules for investment property will determine priority in the investment property. UCC § 9–328. Review Section D.15 *supra.*

Example: SP–1 has a security interest in Debtor's accounts that is perfected by filing an effective financing statement against Debtor listing accounts as collateral. SP–2 has a security interest in Debtor's accounts that is perfected by filing an effective financing statement against Debtor listing accounts as collateral. Under the first to file or perfect rule, SP–1's security interest has priority over SP–2's security interest in the accounts. To pay the obligation owed on an account, the account debtor transferred to Debtor a certificated security in registered form. Both SP–1 and SP–2 have perfected security interests in the certificated security as identifiable proceeds of an account. UCC § 9–315(a)-(d). Under the first to file or perfect rule, SP–1's security interest in the certificated security will have priority over SP–2's security interest in the certificated security. SP–2 then obtained delivery of the certificated security from Debtor. SP–2's security interest in the certificated security will have priority over SP–1's security interest in the certificated security. UCC § 9–328(5).

(15)   Collecting Bank's Priority in Proceeds of Items and Accompanying Documents

A collecting bank has priority in the proceeds of an item and accompanying documents in which it has a security interest as against other secured parties with security interests in those proceeds. UCC §§ 4–210, 9–322(f). Review Section D.16 *supra*.

b. If the Collateral Is Deposit Accounts, Investment Property, Letter-of-Credit Rights, Chattel Paper, Instruments, Negotiable Documents Of Title and the Proceeds Are Cash Proceeds or Proceeds of Same Type as the Original Collateral

If a security interest in deposit accounts, investment property, letter-of-credit rights, chattel paper, instruments or negotiable documents of title qualifies for priority over a conflicting security interest in the same collateral under UCC § 9–327 through UCC § 9–331, then the security interest with priority in that collateral also has priority in proceeds of that collateral if the following criteria are met. First the security interest in the proceeds of the collateral must be perfected. Second, the proceeds must either be cash proceeds or proceeds of the same type as the original collateral. Third, if the proceeds are proceeds of proceeds, all intervening proceeds are either cash proceeds, proceeds of the same type as the original collateral, or an account relating to the collateral. UCC § 9–322(c). This rule is subject to being trumped by the first exception (Section D.17.a, *supra*), that is, if a particular rule provides for priority of a security interest in the type of collateral that is proceeds. UCC § 9–322(f).

Example: SP–1 has a security interest in Debtor's inventory that is perfected by filing an effective financing statement against Debtor listing inventory as collateral. SP–2 has a security interest in Debtor's inventory that is perfected by filing an effective financing statement against Debtor listing inventory as collateral. Under the first to file or perfect rule, SP–1's security interest in the inventory has priority over SP–2's security interest in the inventory. Debtor sold an item of inventory to Buyer generating chattel paper as proceeds. Both SP–1 and SP–2 have perfected security interests in the chattel paper as identifiable proceeds of the sold inventory. UCC § 9–315(a)-(d). SP–2 then took possession of the chattel paper in a transaction in which SP–2's security interest had priority over SP–1's security interest in the chattel paper under UCC § 9–330. Buyer then made a payment in money to Debtor pursuant to Buyer's obligation to pay under the chattel paper. Both SP–1 and SP–2 have perfected security interests in the money as identifiable cash proceeds of the chattel paper. UCC § 9–315(a)-(d). SP–2's security interest in the money is superior to SP–1's security interest in the money. UCC §§ 9–330(c), 9–322(c). Debtor then deposited the money in its deposit account at Bank. Both SP–1 and SP–2 have perfected security interests in the deposit account as identifiable cash proceeds of the money. UCC § 9–315(a)-(d). SP–2's security interest in the deposit account has priority over SP–1's security interest in the deposit account. UCC § 9–322(c). Thereafter, SP–1 obtained a control agreement with Debtor and Bank concerning the deposit account. SP–1's security interest in the deposit account is now superior to SP–2's security interest in the deposit account. UCC § 9–327.

Example: SP–1 has a security interest in Debtor's investment property and has perfected its security interest by filing an effective financing statement against Debtor listing the collateral as investment property. SP–2 subsequently obtained a security interest in Debtor's securities entitlements held by Brokerage and perfected its security interest by obtaining a control agreement concerning the securities entitlements with Brokerage and Debtor. Under UCC § 9–328(1), SP–2's perfected security interest in the securities entitlements has priority over SP–1's perfected security interest in the securities entitlements. Debtor sold a securities entitlement to Buyer in exchange for a promissory note. SP–1's security interest in the promissory note as identifiable proceeds of the securities entitlement is perfected under UCC § 9–315(d)(1) given its filed financing statement against the original collateral. SP–2's security interest in the promissory note is temporarily perfected for 20 days after attachment of the security interest. UCC § 9–315(a)-(d). The promissory note is not "cash proceeds" nor of the same type of collateral as the original collateral, and thus the priority rule of UCC § 9–322(c) does not apply. SP–1's security interest in the promissory note will have priority over SP–2's security interest in the promissory note under the first to file or perfect rule. If SP–2 took possession of the promissory note, SP–2 could use the priority rules of UCC § 9–330(d) (protection for certain purchasers of instruments) or UCC § 9–331 (protection for holders in due course of negotiable instruments), to establish priority for its security interest in the promissory note over SP–1's security interest in the promissory note.

c. If the Collateral Is Chattel Paper, Deposit Accounts, Negotiable Documents of Title, Instruments, Investment Property, or Letter-of-Credit Rights In Which a Security Interest Is Perfected by a Non-Filing Method and the Proceeds Are Not Cash Proceeds, Chattel Paper, Negotiable Documents of Title, Instruments, Investment Property, or Letter-of-Credit Rights

If a security interest in certain types of collateral is perfected by a non-filing method and the proceeds of that collateral are of a particular type, the priority of conflicting perfected security interests in the proceeds is determined by the order of filing a financing statement covering the type of collateral that is the proceeds. The original collateral must be chattel paper, deposit accounts, negotiable documents of title, instruments, investment property, or letter-of-credit rights. The proceeds must *not* be cash proceeds, chattel paper, negotiable documents of title, instruments, investment property, or letter-of-credit rights. UCC § 9–322(d), (e). This rule is subject to being trumped by the first exception (Section D.17.a, *supra*), that is, if a particular rule provides for priority of a security interest in the type of collateral that is proceeds. UCC § 9–322(f).

Example: SP–1 has a security interest in Debtor's securities entitlements held by Brokerage Inc. and has perfected its security interest by obtaining a control agreement with Brokerage and Debtor. SP–2 subsequently obtained a security interest in Debtor's inventory then owned or thereafter acquired and perfected its security interest by filing an effective financing statement against Debtor listing inventory as the collateral. Debtor sold a securities entitlement to Buyer in exchange for a new item of inventory. SP–1's security interest in the new item of inventory is temporarily perfected under UCC § 9–315(a)-(d) for 20 days from the time it attached to the new item of inventory. Within the 20-day time period, SP–1 filed an effective financing statement against Debtor listing inventory as the collateral. Under the first to file or perfect rule, SP–1's security interest in the new item of inventory would have priority over SP–2's security interest in the new item of inventory. However, under the exception to that rule stated above, the priority of security interests in the new item of inventory is determined by the order of the filed financing statements covering inventory. Thus, SP–2's security interest in the new item of inventory has priority over SP–1's security interest in that item. UCC § 9–322(d), (e).

Example: SP–1 has a security interest in Debtor's securities entitlements held by Brokerage Inc. and has perfected its security interest by filing an effective financing statement against Debtor listing securities entitlements as collateral. SP–2 subsequently obtained a security interest in Debtor's inventory then owned or thereafter acquired and perfected its security interest by filing an effective financing statement against Debtor listing inventory as the collateral. Debtor sold a securities entitlement to Buyer in exchange for a new item of inventory. SP–1's security interest in the new item of inventory is perfected beyond the 20-day period of temporary perfection for identifiable proceeds. UCC § 9–315(a)-(d). The exception to the first to file or perfect rule in UCC § 9–322(d), (e) does not apply as SP–1 perfected its security interest in securities entitlements by a filing method. The exception to the first to file or perfect rule in UCC § 9–322(c) does not apply as the proceeds (inventory) are not cash proceeds or of the same type of collateral as the original collateral (securities entitlements) and SP–1 has not obtained priority in the securities entitlements by virtue of application of UCC § 9–328. None of the special priority rules previously studied apply to inventory as the type of collateral, leaving the only priority rule to be first to file or perfect rule of UCC § 9–322(a) and (b) for priority in the inventory as proceeds. Under the first to file or perfect rule, SP–1's security interest in the new item of inventory has priority over SP–2's security interest in the inventory.

d. Exceptions to the First to File or Perfect Rule That Do Not Address Proceeds of These Types of Collateral

Some of the exceptions to the first to file or perfect rule as outlined in this Chapter do not address the priority of the secured party's security interest in proceeds of that item. That is, even though the security interest in the particular asset has priority over a conflicting security interest in the same asset, that priority does not appear to carry over to proceeds of that asset. This result seems to be a mistake in the drafting as opposed to an intended result because the purpose of priority in an asset is to give the secured party the value of the asset.

(1) Priority in Proceeds of an Accession When the Whole Is Covered by a Certificate of Title

If goods are covered by a certificate of title and there is an accession to those goods, a secured party that has perfected its security interest in the goods as a whole (including the accession) through notation of its security interest on the certificate of title will have priority over a secured party that has perfected its security interest in the accession. UCC § 9–335(d). Review Section D.6 *supra*. If the goods covered by the certificate of title are sold, the priority rule does not state that the secured party that has perfected by notation on the certificate of title will have priority in the proceeds of the goods as a whole over the security interest perfected in the accession as to the proceeds attributable to the accession.

(2) Priority in Proceeds of Commingled Goods When Security Interests Have Co-Equal Priority

If conflicting perfected security interests in a product or mass both attached to the product or mass because they were attached to goods before they were commingled, the conflicting perfected security interests in the product or mass have co-equal priority based upon the value of the goods commingled at the time of commingling. UCC § 9–336(f). Review Section D.7 *supra*. The section does not state that the co-equal priority extends to the proceeds.

(3) Priority in Proceeds of Goods Covered by Clean Certificate of Title
A secured party's security interest that was perfected in goods and as to which a clean certificate of title is issued is subordinated to a secured party's security interest that is subsequently perfected on that clean certificate of title without knowledge of the previously perfected security interest. UCC § 9–337(2). Review Section D.8 *supra*. The priority rule does not state that the priority for the second secured party extends to proceeds of the good covered by the certificate of title.

(4) Priority in Proceeds of Goods Covered by a Negotiable Document of Title When Conflicting Security Interest Perfected Directly in Goods
If goods are covered by a negotiable document of title and a security interest is perfected in the document of title, that security interest will have priority in the goods over a security interest perfected directly in the goods while the goods are covered by that negotiable document of title. UCC § 9–312(c). Review Section D.9 *supra*. The rule does not specify that the priority carries over to the proceeds of the goods.

(5) Priority in Proceeds of Documents Presented Under a Letter of Credit
The priority for an issuer or nominated person in certain documents presented under a letter of credit does not specify that it applies to proceeds. UCC § 5–118. Review Section D.16 *supra*.

(6) Priority in Proceeds of Goods Subject to a Security Interest Created Under Articles 2 and 2A
The priority for a seller, buyer or lessee that is provided under UCC § 9–110 does not specify that it applies to proceeds of the goods subject to the security interest. Review Section D.16 *supra*.

18. Exception: Priority In Proceeds Of Collateral Subject To Agricultural Liens

Article 9 leaves to other law the priority rules for proceeds of collateral that are subject to agricultural liens. Whether the agricultural lien attaches to proceeds of farm products subject to the agricultural lien (assuming the proceeds are not farm products), how to perfect the agricultural lien in proceeds of the farm products, and the priority of the agricultural lien in the proceeds of the farm products, assuming it does attach, are all left to other law. UCC § 9–315, cmt. 9.

19. Exception: Priority in Supporting Obligations

With two exceptions, the time of filing or perfection as to the original collateral is the time of filing or perfection as to a supporting obligation for that original collateral. UCC § 9–322(b)(2). The first exception is that if a security interest in deposit accounts, investment property, letter-of-credit rights, chattel paper, instruments or negotiable documents of title qualifies for priority over a conflicting security interest in the same collateral under UCC § 9–327 through UCC § 9–331, then the security interest with priority in that collateral also has priority in supporting obligations of that collateral. UCC § 9–322(c). The second exception is that both of these rules will be trumped by a particular rule that provides for priority in that type of collateral, such as UCC § 9–329 which provides for priority in letter-of-credit rights. UCC § 9–322(f).

Example: SP–1 has a security interest in Debtor's accounts and perfected that security interest by filing on May 1 an effective financing statement against Debtor listing accounts as the collateral. SP–2 has a security interest in Debtor's accounts and perfected its security interest by filing on June 1 an effective financing statement against Debtor listing accounts as collateral. For one of the accounts, Nations Bank has issued a standby letter of credit with Debtor as beneficiary. Both SP–1 and SP–2 have perfected security interests in the letter-of-credit right as a supporting obligation for the account. Under the first to file or perfect rule, SP–1's security interest in the letter-of-credit right has priority over SP–2 security interest in the letter-of-credit right.

Example: SP–1 has a security interest in Debtor's accounts and perfected that security interest by filing on May 1 an effective financing statement against Debtor listing accounts as the collateral. SP–2 has a security interest in Debtor's accounts and perfected its security interest by filing on June 1 an effective financing statement against Debtor listing accounts as collateral. For one of the accounts, Nations Bank has issued a standby letter of credit with Debtor as beneficiary. Both SP–1 and SP–2 have perfected security interests in the letter-of-credit right as a supporting obligation for the account. SP–2 obtains Nations Bank's consent to assignment of the proceeds of the letter of credit to SP–2. SP–2's perfection in the letter-of-credit right by control gives SP–2's security interest priority in the letter-of-credit right over SP–1's security interest in the letter-of-credit right. UCC §§ 9–322(f)(1), 9–329.

Example: SP–1 has a security interest in Debtor's chattel paper and perfected that security interest by filing on May 1 an effective financing statement against Debtor listing chattel paper as the collateral. SP–2 has a security interest in Debtor's chattel paper and perfected its security interest by obtaining possession of the chattel paper in a transaction that gives SP–2's security interest in that chattel paper over SP–1's security interest in that chattel paper. UCC § 9–330. For that item of chattel paper, Nations Bank has issued a standby letter of credit with Debtor as beneficiary. Both SP–1 and SP–2 have perfected security interests in the letter-of-credit right as a supporting obligation. SP–2's security interest in the letter-of-credit right has priority over SP–1's security interest in the letter-of-credit right. UCC § 9–322(a), (b). Thereafter, SP–1 obtained control of the letter-of-credit right. SP–1's security interest in the letter-of-credit right has priority over SP–2's security interest in the letter-of-credit right. UCC §§ 9–322(f), 9–329.

20. Exception: Future Advances

For purposes of the priority rules, it generally does not matter when an advance is made. The priority of the security interest that secures the future advance has the same priority as the first advance. UCC § 9–323, cmt. 3. This rule is subject to an exception if the security interest secures an advance that is made when the security is perfected automatically under UCC § 9–309 or UCC § 9–312(e), (f), and (g) and while the secured party has taken no other perfection step as against the collateral. In that case, the security interest that secures the future advance has priority from the date the future advance was made. UCC § 9–323(a). This exception does not apply if the secured party has made a binding commitment to give value (i.e. the future advance) while the security interest is perfected by a method other than perfection under UCC § 9–309 or § 9–312(e), (f), or (g). UCC § 9–323(a)(2). In the case of a sale of accounts, chattel paper, payment intangibles, or a promissory notes or in a consignment subject to Article 9, only the general rule applies, that is, the priority of a security interest for subsequent advances is the same as the priority for the security interest securing the first advance. UCC § 9–323(c).

Example: SP–1 has a security interest in Debtor's instruments to secure any existing and future obligations owed to SP–1. SP–1 made an original advance of $5,000. SP–1 perfected its security interest by filing an effective financing statement against Debtor listing instruments as collateral. SP–1 then makes an additional $1,000 advance to Debtor. The security interest in the instruments that secures both the $5,000 and the $1,000 advance will have priority dating from the time SP–1 filed the financing statement.

Example: SP–1 has a security interest in Debtor's instruments to secure any existing and future obligations owed to SP–1. SP–1 perfected its security interest by possession of the instruments. SP–1 advanced $5,000 to Debtor. SP–1 released possession of one instrument to Debtor for the purposes permitted under UCC § 9–312(g) and thus maintained temporary perfection of its security interest for an additional 20 days without filing a financing statement or possession of the instrument. While the instrument is in Debtor's possession and during the 20-day time period, SP–1 made a $1,000 advance to Debtor. The priority of the security interest that secures the original $5,000 advance will date from the date SP–1 took possession of the instrument. The priority of the security interest that secures the $1,000 future advance will date from the date the future advance was made.

21. Exception: Double Debtor

Article 9 provides for a special subordination rule that protects a secured party of the transferor when the collateral is transferred to a transferee and the transferee has granted a security interest in that transferred collateral to another secured party. If the transferee acquires collateral that is subject to a security interest, UCC § 9–315(a)(1), that existing security interest is perfected when the transferee acquires the collateral, and that existing security interest remains perfected thereafter, any security interest created by the transferee is subordinate to the security interest created by the transferor. UCC § 9–325(a). This subordination rule operates whenever the security interest created by the transferee would otherwise have priority over the pre-existing security interest under three general rules in UCC § 9–322(a) or the purchase money priority rules in UCC § 9–324. The security interest of a buyer or lessee created under Articles 2 or 2A is also subordinated to the pre-existing security interest under this rule. UCC § 9–325(b).

Example: SP–1 has a security interest in Debtor's equipment that is perfected by an effective financing statement filed against Debtor listing equipment as collateral. Debtor transferred an item of equipment to Transferee. SP–1's security interest remained attached and perfected in the transferred equipment and did not become unperfected by the transfer to Transferee because Transferee is located in the same jurisdiction as Debtor. UCC §§ 9–315(a)(1), 9–507(a), (b). To finance acquisition of the equipment, Transferee granted a security interest to SP–2 to secure the purchase price that Transferee paid to Debtor. SP–2 perfected its security interest in the equipment by filing an effective financing statement against Transferee listing equipment as collateral. Under the purchase money priority rule, SP–2's security interest would have priority over SP–1's security interest in the equipment that Transferee purchased. UCC § 9–324(a). Under the rule of UCC § 9–325, however, SP–1's security interest will have priority over SP–2's security interest.

Example: SP–1 has a security interest in Debtor's equipment that is perfected by an effective financing statement filed against Debtor listing equipment as collateral. That financing statement was filed in December 2014. Debtor transferred an item of equipment to Transferee. SP–1's security interest remained attached and perfected in the transferred equipment and did not become unperfected by the transfer to Transferee. UCC §§ 9–315(a)(1), 9–316, 9–507(a), (b). Transferee had previously granted a security interest to SP–2 in all of Transferee's equipment then owned or thereafter acquired and SP–2 had perfected its security interest by filing an effective financing statement against Transferee listing equipment as the collateral. That financing statement was filed in June 2014. Under the first to file or perfect rule, SP-2's security interest in the transferred equipment would have priority over SP-1's security interest in the equipment. Under the subordination rule of this section, however, SP-1's security interest in the transferred equipment will have priority over SP-2's security interest.

22. Exception: New Debtor

Assume a new debtor becomes bound to an old debtor's security agreement. UCC § 9–203(d), (e). In some circumstances, a security interest in collateral that is perfected pursuant to UCC § 9–508 or § 9–316(i) (review Chapter IV, Section H) will be subordinated to security interests perfected in another manner.

a. Both Old and New Debtor Located in Same Jurisdiction

Assume the old and new debtor are located in the same jurisdiction so as to not implicate a change in governing law for perfection purposes. UCC §§ 9–203(d), 9–316. As to existing collateral that is transferred to the new debtor, the secured party's financing statement against the old debtor remains effective to perfect its security interest in that collateral. UCC § 9–507. As to collateral that the new debtor acquires within four months after new debtor became bound to the security agreement that the old debtor had entered into with the secured party, the financing statement filed against the old debtor is effective to perfect the secured party's security interest in that newly-acquired collateral. UCC § 9–508. A secured party of the old debtor may need to take action to obtain perfection of a security interest in collateral that the new debtor acquires more than four months after the new debtor becomes the new debtor if the difference between the name of the old and new debtor is seriously misleading. In that case, the secured party of the old debtor must file a new initial financing statement against the new debtor. UCC § 9–508. If there are conflicting security interests in the collateral in the hands of the new debtor, the following priority rules apply.

(1) Financing Statements Effective Solely Under UCC § 9–508

If the filed financing statements against the new debtor are effective solely because of the rule of UCC § 9–508 that allows the financing statement against the old debtor to be effective to perfect a security interest against the new debtor's collateral that the new debtor has or acquires after becoming the new debtor, the priority rules that are set forth in Section D, *supra*, control the priority of the conflicting security interests unless the security agreements were entered into by different original debtors. UCC § 9–326(b).

> *Example:* SP–1 has a security interest in Old Debtor's inventory then owned or thereafter acquired perfected by an effective financing statement against Old Debtor listing inventory as collateral. SP–2 also has a security interest in Old Debtor's inventory then owned or thereafter acquired perfected by an effective financing statement against Old Debtor listing inventory as collateral. Under the first to file or perfect rule, SP–1's security interest in inventory has priority over SP–2's security interest in inventory. Old Debtor merged into New Debtor. New Debtor becomes bound by Old Debtor's security agreements. UCC § 9–203(d). The financing statements filed against Old Debtor are effective to perfect SP–1's and SP–2's security interests in the inventory New Debtor acquired from Old Debtor, UCC § 9–507, the items of inventory that New Debtor owned at the time of the acquisition, and the items of inventory that New Debtor acquired within four months after the acquisition of Old Debtor, UCC § 9–508. As to all of these items of inventory, the priority of SP–1's and SP–2's conflicting security interests will be determined by the first to file or perfect rule.

(2) Financing Statements Not Effective Solely Under UCC § 9–508

If the filed financing statement of a secured party against the new debtor is effective solely because of the rule of UCC § 9–508 that allows the financing statement against the old debtor to be effective to perfect a security interest against the new debtor's collateral that the new debtor has or acquires after becoming the new debtor, that secured party's security interest is subordinate to a security interest that is perfected against the new debtor by a method other than under UCC § 9–508. UCC § 9–326(a).

Example: SP–1 has a security interest in Old Debtor's inventory then owned or thereafter acquired and perfected by an effective financing statement against Old Debtor listing inventory as collateral. SP–2 also has a security interest in Old Debtor's inventory then owned or thereafter acquired and perfected by an effective financing statement against Old Debtor listing inventory as collateral. Under the first to file or perfect rule, SP–1's security interest in inventory has priority over SP–2's security interest in inventory. Old Debtor merged into New Debtor. New Debtor becomes bound by Old Debtor's security agreements. UCC § 9–203(d). The financing statements filed against Old Debtor are effective to perfect SP–1's and SP–2's security interests in the inventory New Debtor acquired from Old Debtor, UCC § 9–507, the items of inventory that New Debtor owned at the time of the acquisition, and the items of inventory that New Debtor acquired within four months after the acquisition of Old Debtor, UCC § 9–508. One week after the merger, SP–2 filed an initial effective financing statement against New Debtor covering inventory. SP–2's security interest in the items of inventory New Debtor had an interest at the time of the merger and as to the items of inventory acquired after the merger will have priority over SP–1's security interest. As to the items of inventory that the New Debtor acquired from Old Debtor, the first to file or perfect rule continues to control giving SP–1 priority because SP–1's financing statement as to these items of collateral is effective due to UCC § 9–507, not UCC § 9–508. UCC § 9–326, cmt. 2.

(3) Different Original Old Debtors

If the conflicting security interests are perfected solely by filed financing statements that are effective under UCC § 9–508 and the security agreements that the new debtor is bound to were entered into by different old debtors, then the conflicting security interests have priority in the order in which the new debtor became bound to the security agreements. UCC § 9–326(b).

Example: SP–1 has a security interest in OD–1's inventory then owned or thereafter acquired and perfected by an effective financing statement against OD–1 listing inventory as collateral. SP–2 has a security interest in OD–2's inventory then owned or thereafter acquired and perfected by an effective financing statement against OD–2 listing inventory as collateral. OD–1 and OD–2 merged to form New Debtor. New Debtor becomes bound by OD–1's and OD–2's security agreements. UCC § 9–203(d). SP–1's financing statement is effective to perfect a security interest in the inventory transferred from OD–1 to New Debtor, UCC § 9–507, and that New Debtor acquired at the merger from OD–2 and within the four months after the merger, UCC § 9–508. SP–2's financing statement is effective to perfect a security interest in the inventory transferred from OD–2 to New Debtor, UCC § 9–507, and that New Debtor acquired from OD–1 and within four months after the merger, UCC § 9–508. The priority of SP–1's and SP–2's security interests in the inventory are determined by the order in which New Debtor became bound to the security agreements of OD–1 and OD–2.

b. New Debtor Located in Different Jurisdiction Than Old Debtor

Assume a new debtor becomes bound to the old debtor's security agreement. UCC § 9–203(d), (e). If a new debtor is located in a jurisdiction that is different than the old debtor, a secured party's financing statement filed against the old debtor in the old jurisdiction will be effective for one year to perfect a security interest in collateral that the old debtor transferred to the new debtor. UCC § 9–316(a). As to collateral that the new debtor has and acquires within four months after it becomes the new debtor, the financing statement filed against the old debtor in the old jurisdiction will remain effective to perfect the security interest of the old debtor's secured party in those assets. UCC § 9–316(i). Review Chapter IV, Section H. 12. If there are conflicting security interests in the collateral in the hands of the new debtor, the following priority rules apply.

(1) Financing Statements Effective Solely Under UCC § 9–316(i)(1)

If the filed financing statements against the new debtor are effective solely because of the rule of UCC 9–316(i)(1) that allows the financing statement against the old debtor to be effective to perfect a security interest against the new debtor's collateral that the new debtor has or acquires within four months after becoming the new debtor, the priority rules that are set forth in Section D, *supra*, control the priority of the conflicting security interests unless the security agreements were entered into by different original debtors. UCC § 9–326(b).

Example: SP–1 has a security interest in Old Debtor's inventory then owned or thereafter acquired perfected by an effective financing statement against Old Debtor listing inventory as collateral. SP–2 has a security interest in Old Debtor's inventory then owned or thereafter acquired perfected by an effective financing statement against Old Debtor listing inventory as collateral. Under the first to file or perfect rule, SP–1's security interest in inventory has priority over SP–2's security interest in inventory. Old Debtor merged into New Debtor, which is located in a different jurisdiction than Old Debtor. New Debtor becomes bound by Old Debtor's security agreements. UCC § 9–203(d). Under UCC § 9–316(a) and § 9–316(i), the financing statements filed against Old Debtor are effective for one year to perfect SP–1's and SP–2's security interests in the inventory New Debtor acquired from Old Debtor, and for 4 months, the items of inventory that New Debtor owned at the time of the acquisition, and the items of inventory that New Debtor acquired within 4 months after the acquisition of Old Debtor. As to all of these items of inventory, the priority of SP–1's and SP–2's conflicting security interests will be determined by the first to file or perfect rule.

(2) Financing Statements Not Effective Solely Under UCC § 9–316(i)(1)

If the filed financing statement of a secured party against the new debtor is effective solely because of the rule of UCC § 9–316(i)(1) that allows the financing statement against the old debtor to be effective to perfect a security interest against the new debtor's collateral that the new debtor has or acquires after becoming the new debtor, that secured party's security interest is subordinate to a security interest that is perfected against the new debtor by a method other than under UCC § 9–316(i)(1). UCC § 9–326(a).

Example: SP–1 has a security interest in Old Debtor's inventory then owned or thereafter acquired and perfected by an effective financing statement against Old Debtor listing inventory as collateral. SP–2 has a security interest in Old Debtor's inventory then owned or thereafter acquired and perfected by an effective financing statement against Old Debtor listing inventory as collateral. Under the first to file or perfect rule, SP–1's security interest in inventory has priority over SP–2's security interest in inventory. Old Debtor merged into New Debtor, which is located in a different jurisdiction. New Debtor becomes bound by Old Debtor's security agreements. UCC § 9–203(d). The financing statements filed against Old Debtor are effective to perfect SP–1's and SP–2's security interests in the inventory New Debtor acquired from Old Debtor, UCC § 9–316(a), the items of inventory that New Debtor owned at the time of the acquisition, and the items of inventory that New Debtor acquired within four months after the acquisition of Old Debtor, UCC § 9–316(i). One week after the merger, SP–2 filed an initial effective financing statement against New Debtor in the new jurisdiction covering inventory. SP–2's security interest in the items of inventory New Debtor had an interest at the time of the merger and as to the items of inventory acquired after the merger will have priority over SP–1's security interest. As to the items of inventory that the New Debtor acquired from Old Debtor, the first to file or perfect rule continues to control giving SP–1 priority because SP–1's financing statement as to these items of collateral is effective due to UCC § 9–316(a), not UCC § 9–316(i)(1). UCC § 9–326, cmt. 2.

(3) Different Original Old Debtors

If the conflicting security interests are perfected solely by filed financing statements that are effective under UCC § 9–316(i)(1) and the security agreements that the new debtor is bound to were entered into by different old debtors, then the conflicting security interests have priority in the order in which the new debtor became bound to the security agreements. UCC § 9–326(b).

E. Priority of Security Interests Against Real Estate Claimants Regarding Fixtures

If there are two conflicting security interests in fixtures, the priority rules governing conflicting security interests as explained in Section D of this Chapter govern. If the priority dispute is between a security interest in a fixture and a person whose claim in the fixtures arises under real estate law, Article 9 contains a special priority rule in UCC § 9–334.

1. Real Estate Interests

The interests arising under real estate law are those of the owner of the real estate (as long as the owner is not the debtor), the person with a property interest in the fixture, and an encumbrancer of the real estate. An encumbrancer is a person with a property interest, but not an ownership interest, in real property. UCC § 9–102(a)(32). An example of an encumbrancer is the mortgagee under a real estate mortgage.

2. Fixtures

A fixture is a good that is considered to be related to the real estate in such a way that an interest in the good can be granted under real estate law as well as personal property law. UCC § 9–102(a)(41). Building materials that are incorporated into an improvement on real estate are not considered to be fixtures (i.e. not personal property) but rather are part of the real estate. UCC § 9–334(a).

3. Perfection of a Security Interest in Fixtures

To perfect a security interest in fixtures (a type of a "good", UCC § 9–102(a)(44)), the secured party may perfect either by filing a financing statement against the goods in the central filing office of the debtor's location or by filing a fixture financing statement in the real estate recording office for the real estate where the fixture is located. UCC §§ 9–301, 9–501. The fixture financing statement has additional requirements in order to file it in the real estate records, including a description of the real estate on which the fixtures are located. UCC § 9–502. Review Chapter IV, Section B.4.

4. General Priority Rule

A security interest in fixtures is subordinate to the conflicting claim of an encumbrancer or owner of the real estate (other than the debtor). UCC § 9–334(c). This rule is subject to several exceptions.

Example: Debtor owns a house subject to a mortgage in favor of State Bank which is properly recorded in the county real estate records. The mortgage covers fixtures on the real estate. SP–1 financed Debtor's acquisition of a new furnace for Debtor's house. Under applicable state law, the furnace when installed is a fixture. SP–1 filed an effective fixture financing statement against Debtor in the real estate recording office for the county where the house is located 30 days after the furnace was installed. None of the following exceptions apply. State Bank's interest in the fixture as a mortgagee is superior to SP–1's security interest in the fixture.

5. Exception for Purchase Money Security Interests in Fixtures

If the secured party has a purchase money security interest in the fixture and perfected its security interest in fixtures by filing an effective fixture financing statement in the real estate records before the goods become fixtures or within 20 days thereafter, the security interest will have priority over the conflicting interest of the real estate owner and an encumbrancer if the interests of the owner and encumbrancer arise in the real estate prior to the goods becoming fixtures and the debtor has an interest of record or is in possession of the real estate. UCC § 9–334(d). The secured party with a purchase money security interest in fixtures is not entitled to priority in the fixture over the interests of a construction mortgage holder if the construction mortgage holder recorded its mortgage prior to the filing of the fixture financing statement and the goods become fixtures before the construction project is complete. A construction mortgage is a mortgage that secures an obligation incurred for construction of an improvement to land, including the cost of acquisition of the land, if the mortgage denotes itself as a construction mortgage. UCC § 9–334(h).

Example: Debtor owns a house subject to a mortgage in favor of State Bank which extends to fixtures, and which is properly recorded in the applicable real estate recording office. Thereafter, SP–1 financed Debtor's acquisition of a new furnace for Debtor's house. Under applicable state law, the furnace when installed is a fixture. SP–1 filed an effective fixture financing statement against Debtor in the real estate recording office where the house is located 15 days after the furnace was installed. SP–1's purchase money security interest in the furnace has priority over State Bank's interest in the furnace pursuant to the mortgage.

Example: Debtor is building a house. The house is subject to a construction mortgage in favor of State Bank to finance construction of the house. The mortgage extends to fixtures on the real estate and is labeled as a construction mortgage. State Bank recorded its mortgage on the house in the applicable real estate recording office. Thereafter, SP–1 financed Debtor's acquisition of a new furnace for the house. The new furnace was installed during the construction process. Under applicable state law, the furnace when installed is a fixture. SP–1 filed an effective fixture financing statement against Debtor in the real estate recording office for the county where the house is located 15 days after the furnace was installed. SP–1's purchase money security interest in the furnace does not have priority over State Bank's interest in the furnace pursuant to the construction mortgage.

6. Exception for First-Filed Interest

The security interest in the fixture will have priority over the interests of the owner of the real estate or the encumbrancer in the fixture if (i) the secured party has perfected its security interest in the fixture by a filed fixture financing statement prior to the recording in the real estate records of the interest of the encumbrancer or owner of the real property, (ii) the security interest has priority over the interest of the predecessor in title to the owner or encumbrancer, and (iii) the debtor has an interest in the real estate or is in possession of the real estate. UCC § 9–334(e)(1).

Example: SP–1 financed Debtor's acquisition of a new furnace for Debtor's house which Debtor owns. Under applicable state law, the furnace when installed is a fixture. Twenty-five days after the furnace was installed, SP–1 filed an effective fixture financing statement against Debtor in the real estate recording office where the house is located. Five weeks later, Debtor obtained a mortgage on the house from Bank. The mortgage extends to fixtures located on the property. SP–1's security interest in the furnace has priority over Bank's interest in the furnace.

7. Exception for Security Interests in Particular Types of Fixtures

A perfected security interest in the fixtures will have priority over the conflicting interest of the owner of the real estate or encumbrancer in those fixtures if (i) the goods that become fixtures are readily removable factory or office machines, equipment that is not primarily used or leased for operation of the real estate, or replacements of domestic appliances that are consumer goods and (ii) the secured party perfects its security interest in those goods in any manner (including filing a financing statement that is not a fixture financing statement or automatic perfection, if applicable) before the goods become fixtures. UCC § 9–334(e)(2).

Example: SP–1 finances Consumer's purchase of a new dishwasher in Consumer's home to replace the old dishwasher and takes a security interest in the new dishwasher to secure the purchase price. SP–1's security interest in the new dishwasher is automatically perfected as a purchase money security interest in consumer goods. UCC § 9–309(1). Consumer's house is subject to a mortgage in favor of State Bank which operates to give State Bank an interest in the dishwasher as a fixture. SP–1's security interest in the dishwasher has priority over State Bank's interest.

8. Exception for Legal or Equitable Liens

If the security interest is perfected through any method permitted under Article 9 (including the filing of a non-fixture financing statement or automatic perfection) and the holder of the conflicting interest obtained its lien in the fixture through equitable or legal proceedings as against the real estate after the security interest was perfected, the security interest will have priority over the legal or equitable lien. UCC § 9–334(e)(3).

Example: SP–1 has a security interest in Debtor's equipment and perfected its security interest by filing an effective financing statement against Debtor listing equipment as the collateral. SP–1 filed that financing statement in the central filing office of the state of Debtor's location. Under the applicable state law, some of the items of equipment are considered fixtures to a parcel of Debtor's real estate. A creditor of Debtor obtained a judgment against Debtor and levied against the real estate. Under the state's law on judgments, the lien of the judgment that attached to the real estate by virtue of the levy also attached to fixtures located on that real estate. SP–1's security interest in the equipment that is fixtures has priority over the judgment lien creditor's levy lien on the real estate and the fixtures even though SP–1 has not filed a fixture financing statement.

9. Exception for Manufactured-Home Transactions Governed by Certificate Of Title Law

If a manufactured home (UCC § 9–102(a)(53)) is a fixture, a security interest that is perfected in the manufactured home under an applicable certificate of title law (UCC § 9–311) has priority over the interests of the real estate owner or encumbrancer in the manufactured home. UCC § 9–334(e)(4).

10. Exception Based Upon Consent of Real Estate Claimant

A security interest will have priority over the conflicting interest of the encumbrancer or owner of the real estate if the encumbrancer or owner has consented, in an authenticated record, to the security interest or disclaimed an interest in the fixture. UCC § 9–334(f)(1). The security interest in the fixture need not be perfected for this rule to apply.

11. Exception Based Upon Debtor's Right to Remove the Goods

If as against the owner of the real estate or the encumbrancer, the debtor has a right to remove the fixture from the real estate, a security interest in that fixture will have priority over the rights in the fixture of the encumbrancer or real estate owner. UCC § 9–334(f)(2). The security interest in the fixture need not be perfected for this rule to apply. This priority for the security interest will continue for a reasonable time to allow removal of the fixture if the debtor's right to remove the fixture as against the owner or encumbrancer expires. UCC § 9–334(g).

12.   Exception for Crops

A security interest in crops has priority over the interest of the encumbrancer or owner of the real estate if (i) under real estate law the interests of an encumbrancer or owner of real estate extends to the crops growing on the land, (ii) the debtor has an interest of record or possession of the real estate where the crops are grown, and (iii) the security interest in the crops is perfected in any manner permitted under Article 9. UCC § 9–334(i).

F. Priority of a Security Interest or Agricultural Lien as Against Transferees

Mere attachment of a security interest or agricultural lien does not prevent the debtor from transferring its rights in the collateral to other parties. When the debtor transfers collateral to another person, Article 9 governs the secured party's rights as against the transferee's rights in the transferred collateral. If the transferee is another secured party (that is the transfer creates a security interest), the rights of parties with conflicting security interests or an agricultural lien are generally governed by the rules set forth previously in this Chapter regarding priority. In some circumstances, however, the transferee that is a secured party may be able to use the rules that follow to establish its priority position in the transferred collateral.

1. General Rule

The general rule is that collateral that is subject to a security interest remains subject to that security interest even after the collateral is transferred to another person, and that the security interest remains effective as against transferees. UCC §§ 9–201, 9–315(a)(1). Similarly, an agricultural lien stays attached to transferred collateral subject to the lien. That general rule is subject to several exceptions as set forth *infra*.

2. Exception Based Upon Secured Party's Consent

If the secured party that holds the security interest or agricultural lien consents to the disposition of the collateral free from the security interest or agricultural lien, then the transferee will take the collateral free of the security interest or agricultural lien. UCC § 9–315(a)(1). That consent may be express or implied. Whether the secured party has consented to a disposition of the collateral free of the security interest or agricultural lien depends upon the facts and circumstances of the case. An agreement that provides that a secured party has a right to proceeds should not be interpreted to be an authorization of a disposition of the collateral free of the security interest. UCC § 9–315, cmt. 2.

3. Exception for Transferees in Ordinary Course of Business

As to some types of collateral, even if the secured party has not consented to a transfer of the collateral free of the security interest, Article 9 protects some types of transferees of the collateral from a security interest that would otherwise continue in the collateral. These transferees are protected from the security interest in the transferred collateral based upon the usual expectations of these types of transferees in the marketplace.

a. Buyer of Goods in Ordinary Course of Business

A buyer in ordinary course of business of goods (other than farm products) from a seller that has created the security interest in the goods (that is, the seller is the debtor) takes the goods free of a perfected security interest in the goods even if the buyer knows that the security interest exists. UCC § 9–320(a). The buyer in ordinary course of business also takes the goods free of an unperfected security interest. UCC § 9–320, cmt. 2. Article 9 does not contain any rule that provides that a buyer in ordinary course of business will take free of a perfected or unperfected agricultural lien. The priority of an agricultural lien as against a buyer in ordinary course of business of farm products will be governed by the statute creating the agricultural lien.

Example: SP–1 has a security interest in Manufacturer's inventory then owned or thereafter acquired to secure all obligations then or thereafter owed by Manufacturer and has perfected its security interest by filing an effective financing statement against

Manufacturer listing inventory as the collateral. Manufacturer transferred some items of inventory to Retailer in satisfaction of a pre-existing obligation that Manufacturer owed Retailer. Retailer thus does not qualify as a buyer in ordinary course of business as to those items of inventory and takes the items of inventory subject to SP–1's security interest as SP–1 has not consented to the disposition to Retailer. Retailer then makes a sale of one of the items to Buyer who qualifies as a buyer in ordinary course of business from Retailer. Buyer takes the item subject to SP–1's security interest because the buyer in ordinary course of business rule only protects buyers from security interests created by the buyer's seller (Retailer), not by another seller. In this case, the security interest was created by Manufacturer, not Retailer.

(1) Buyer in Ordinary Course of Business Defined

To qualify as a buyer in ordinary course of business the buyer and the transaction must meet certain criteria. When all of the criteria are fulfilled the buyer is a buyer in ordinary course of business. UCC § 1–201(b)(9).

(a) The Type of Transaction

The buyer must buy the goods (i) in good faith (UCC §§ 9–102(a)(43), 1–201(b)(20)), (ii) without knowledge (UCC § 1–202)) that the sale violates the rights of another person in the goods, and (iii) in the ordinary course from a person in the business of selling goods of that kind. The transaction is in the ordinary course if the sale is in accord with the usual and customary practices in the seller's kind of business or in accord with the seller's usual and customary practices.

Example: SP–1 has a security interest in Debtor's inventory then owned or thereafter acquired to secure all obligations then or thereafter owed by the Debtor and has perfected its security interest by filing an effective financing statement against Debtor listing inventory as the collateral. Debtor is an electronics retail business. Debtor sold a stereo to Buyer. Buyer happened to know that SP–1 had a security interest in Debtor's inventory but had no knowledge of the terms of the security agreement. Buyer paid for the stereo using a credit card. Buyer took possession of the stereo. Buyer has knowledge of the security interest but not knowledge that the sale of the stereo to Buyer violated SP–1's rights. Buyer will qualify as a buyer in ordinary course of business and take the stereo free of SP–1's security interest as long as Buyer acted in good faith.

(b) Qualifications of the Seller

The seller must be a person in the business of selling goods of the kind. The seller may not be a pawn broker. A seller that sells oil, gas or minerals from the wellhead or minehead is in the business of selling those kinds of goods.

(c) The Consideration for the Buy

The buyer may buy the goods with cash, with other property, on secured or unsecured credit, or pursuant to a pre-existing contract for sale. The buyer may not acquire the goods in a bulk transfer or as security or satisfaction in whole or part of a pre-existing debt.

Example: SP–1 has a security interest in Debtor's inventory then owned or thereafter acquired to secure all obligations then or thereafter owed by the Debtor and perfected its security interest by filing an effective financing statement against Debtor listing inventory as the collateral. Debtor is an electronics retail business. Debtor gave a stereo from its inventory to Buyer to satisfy a debt that Debtor owed Buyer. Buyer is not a buyer in ordinary course of business. If SP–1's security interest continues in the stereo because SP–1 has not consented to the disposition of the stereo free of the security interest, Buyer will take the stereo subject to SP–1's security interest.

(d) The Buyer's Possession or Right to Possession

The buyer must take possession of the goods or have a right to possession of the goods from the seller under UCC Article 2. The buyer will have a right to possession from the seller in three circumstances.

Example: SP–1 has a security interest in Debtor's inventory then owned or thereafter acquired to secure all obligations then or thereafter owed by the Debtor and has perfected its security interest by filing an effective financing statement against Debtor listing inventory as the collateral. Debtor is an electronics retail business. Debtor sold a stereo to Buyer. Buyer paid for the stereo using a credit card. Buyer took possession of the stereo. Buyer will qualify as a buyer in ordinary course of business and take the stereo free of SP–1's security interest as long as Buyer acted in good faith.

(i) **Prepaying Buyer**

If the buyer has paid all or part of the price, the goods are identified to the contract, and the buyer keeps good a tender of the remaining purchase price owed, the buyer will have the right to obtain the goods from the seller in two defined circumstances. First, in all cases, if the seller becomes insolvent (UCC § 1–201(b)(23)) within 10 days after the seller received the first installment on the price, the buyer will have the right to recover the identified goods from the seller. UCC § 2–502(1)(b). Second, if the seller repudiates or fails to deliver and the buyer has purchased the goods for family, personal, or household purposes, the buyer has a right to obtain the identified goods from the seller. UCC § 2–502(1)(a). Generally, goods are identified to the contract when they are designated as pertaining to the particular contract. UCC § 2–501.

Example: SP–1 has a security interest in Debtor's inventory then owned or thereafter acquired to secure all obligations then or thereafter owed by the Debtor and has perfected its security interest by filing an effective financing statement against Debtor listing inventory as the collateral. Debtor is an electronics retail business. Debtor sold a stereo to Buyer in exchange for a down payment of $100 and a promise by Buyer to pay the remaining purchase price within one month. Buyer left the stereo in Debtor's possession until Buyer was able to pay the full purchase price. Buyer is not a buyer in ordinary course of business because Buyer does not have possession of the stereo. If Buyer purchased the stereo for personal, family or household use, and tendered the remaining purchase price to Debtor and Debtor refused to deliver the stereo, Buyer would have a right to possession of the stereo under UCC § 2–502 and would then qualify as a buyer in ordinary course of business as long as Buyer bought the stereo in good faith.

(ii) **Buyer's Right to Specific Performance**
The buyer may obtain specific performance of the seller's contract to deliver the goods if the goods are unique or the court decides that it is proper to order specific performance of the contract for sale. The court has discretion to not award specific performance. UCC § 2–716(1). Because specific performance is a type of injunctive relief, the usual rules on granting injunctive relief apply.

(iii) **Buyer's Right to Replevin**
The buyer has a right to replevin (i.e. the right to possession) for goods identified to the contract (UCC § 2–501) if the buyer is unable to obtain substitute goods from another source after a reasonable effort or the circumstances indicate that such an effort will be unsuccessful. The buyer also has a right to replevin for identified goods shipped under reservation (UCC § 2–505) if the buyer keeps good a tender of the price for the goods in order to satisfy the security interest created by the shipment under reservation. UCC § 2–716(3).

(2) **Buyers of Farm Products**
The Article 9 protection for a buyer of goods in ordinary course of business does not apply to buyers of farm products. A federal law, the Food Security Act of 1985, 7 U.S.C. § 1631, protects certain buyers of farm products. If the following criteria are met, the buyer will take the farm products free of the security interest even if it perfected and even if the buyer knows the security interest exists unless the buyer and secured

party have complied with a federal notification scheme. For the buyer to take the farm products free of the security interest, the buyer must buy the farm products in the ordinary course of business, the seller must be a person engaged in farming operations, the seller must sell the farm products in the ordinary course of the seller's business, and the seller must be the person that created the security interest. This protection for the buyer will not exist if the notification scheme prescribed in the Food Security Act is followed. 7 U.S.C. § 1631(d). The notification scheme contains two basic options, a direct notice system or a central filing notice system.

(a) Direct Notice

If the buyer received a notice from the seller or secured party within one year prior to the buyer's purchase of the farm products that contained notice of the security interest, the secured party's name and address, the debtor's name and address, the debtor's tax identification number or other unique identifier, a description of the farm products, the name of the county or parish where the farm products are produced or located, and a description of the payment obligation owed to the secured party, the buyer will take the farm products covered by the notice subject to the secured party's security interest unless the buyer satisfies the payment obligation owed to the secured party. 7 U.S.C. § 1631(e)(1).

(b) Central Filing System

The state may establish a central filing system for notices of security interests in farm products that is separate from the Article 9 filing system. The central filing system must follow certain prescribed criteria and must be certified by the United States Department of Agricultural as a central filing system. 7 U.S.C. § 1631(c)(2). In states with such a central filing system, there are two circumstances in which the buyer will take subject to a security interest. First, the buyer will take the goods subject to the security interest if the secured party has filed its notice in the central filing system and the buyer has failed to register with the central filing system prior to its purchase of the farm products. 7 U.S.C. § 1631(e)(2). Second, the buyer will take the goods subject to the security interest of the secured party if the buyer receives a notice from the central filing system administrator that specifies the debtor and the farm products subject to the security interest and the buyer does not receive a waiver or release from the secured party. 7 U.S.C. § 1631(e)(3).

b. Lessee in Ordinary Course of Business

A lessee in ordinary course of business of goods will take its leasehold interest in the goods free of a security interest created by the lessor. This protection applies even if the security interest is perfected and the lessee knows that the security interest exists. UCC § 9–321(c). A lessee in ordinary course of business is defined similarly to a buyer in ordinary course of business. The lessee must lease the goods (i) in good faith, (ii) without knowledge that the lease violates the rights of another person in the goods, and (iii) in the ordinary course from a person in the business of selling or leasing goods of that kind. The lessor may not be a pawn broker. The lessee may lease the goods for cash, for exchange of other property, on secured or unsecured credit, or pursuant to a pre-existing lease contract. The lessee may not acquire the goods in a bulk transfer or as security or satisfaction in whole or part of a pre-existing debt. UCC § 2A–103(1).

c. Licensees in Ordinary Course of Business

A licensee in ordinary course of business under a nonexclusive license takes its rights free of a security interest in the general intangible that is being licensed if that security interest was created by the licensor. This protection applies even if the security interest is perfected and the licensee knows that the security interest exists. UCC § 9–321(b). A licensee in ordinary course of business must become the licensee of a general intangible (i) in good faith, (ii) without knowledge that the license violates the rights of another person in the general intangible, and (iii) in the ordinary course from a person in the business of licensing general intangibles of that kind. The transaction is in the ordinary course if the license is in accord with the usual and customary practices in the licensor's kind of business or in accord with the licensor's usual and customary practices. UCC § 9–321(a).

d. Security Interest that Secures Future Advances

A buyer in ordinary course of business or lessee in ordinary course of business that takes the goods free of a security interest created by the seller or lessor also take the goods free of a security interest that secures an advance made after the sale or lease. UCC § 9–323, cmt. 6. Presumably the licensee in ordinary course of business has the same protection but the comment does not explicitly state that rule.

4. Exception for Transferees When the Security Interest or Agricultural Lien Is Unperfected

A transferee of collateral in which there is an existing security interest or agricultural lien that continues in the collateral, UCC § 9–315(a), may take free of those security interests and agricultural liens that are unperfected. The specific priority rule depends upon the type of collateral transferred.

a. Buyers of Certain Tangible Collateral

A buyer of tangible chattel paper, tangible documents of title, goods, instruments, or a certificated security takes those items free of a security interest if the buyer gives value (UCC § 1–204) for the item and takes delivery of the item without knowledge (UCC § 1–202) of the security interest or agricultural lien and at a time when the security interest or agricultural lien is unperfected. UCC § 9–317(b). A buyer that is a secured party may not use this rule to take the collateral free of the security interest. UCC § 9–317(b). As to a buyer of tangible chattel paper and promissory notes (a type of instrument), if the transaction is within the scope of Article 9, the buyer will be a secured party as the transaction creates a security interest. UCC § 9–109(a). Thus a buyer of tangible chattel paper and promissory notes will be able to use this priority rule only if the sale of chattel paper and promissory notes are excluded from Article 9 under UCC § 9–109(d). UCC § 9–317, cmt. 6.

Example: SP–1 has an attached but unperfected security interest in Debtor's goods. Debtor sold a good to Buyer and delivered the good to Buyer in exchange for a promise to pay Debtor for the good. Buyer took delivery of the good. Assume Buyer is not a buyer in ordinary course of business. At the time Buyer took delivery, Buyer had no knowledge of SP–1's security interest. Buyer took the good free of SP–1's security interest.

Example: SP–1 has a security interest in Debtor's goods. SP–1 filed an effective financing statement against Debtor listing goods as collateral. Debtor sold a good to Buyer and delivered the good to Buyer in exchange for a promise to pay Debtor for the good. Assume Buyer is not a buyer in ordinary course of business. At the time Buyer took delivery, Buyer had no knowledge of SP–1's security interest. Buyer took the good subject to SP–1's security interest because SP–1's security interest is perfected and Buyer is not a buyer in ordinary course of business.

Example: SP–1 has an unperfected agricultural lien in Debtor's farm products. Debtor sold some of the farm products to Buyer and delivered the farm products to Buyer in exchange for a promise to pay Debtor. Assume Buyer is not a buyer in ordinary course of business and thus does not qualify for protection under the Food Security Act. At the time Buyer took delivery, Buyer had no knowledge of SP–1's agricultural lien. Buyer took the farm products free of SP–1's agricultural lien.

(1) Buyer Subject to a Later-Perfected Purchase Money Security Interest in Goods

Even if a buyer takes possession of goods at the time the security interest in the collateral is unperfected, if the security interest is a purchase money security interest and the secured party perfects its security interest by filing a financing statement within 20 days after the debtor received delivery of the goods, the buyer will take the goods subject to that purchase money security interest. UCC § 9–317(e).

Example: Seller sold a good to Debtor on credit and retained a security interest in the good to secure the purchase price. Debtor then sold the good to Buyer in exchange for a check. Assume Buyer is not a buyer in ordinary course of business. Buyer took possession of the good without knowledge of Seller's security interest. Fifteen days later, Seller filed an effective financing statement against Debtor listing goods as collateral. Seller's purchase money security interest is perfected after Buyer took possession. Buyer nonetheless does not take the good free of Seller's security interest.

(2) Security Interest that Secures Future Advances

Presumably if a buyer of collateral takes free of a security interest under this priority rule, it would also take free of any security interest in that collateral that might otherwise secure a future advance. See UCC § 9–323, cmt. 6. If a buyer not in ordinary course of business takes the goods subject to a security interest because the buyer does not qualify to take free of the security interest under UCC § 9–317(b) and the secured party subsequently makes an advance, the buyer will take the goods free of the security interest that secures that future advance if the secured party made the advance with knowledge of the buyer's purchase or made the advance 45 days or more after the purchase. UCC § 9–323(d). The buyer not in ordinary course of business will not take the goods free of the security interest that secures the advance if the secured party made the advance or a commitment to make an advance without knowledge of the purchase and before the end of the 45-day time period. UCC § 9–323(e). This freedom from security interests that secure future advances does not appear to apply to buyers of tangible collateral other than goods and who take the tangible collateral subject to the security interest.

Example: SP–1 has a security interest in Debtor's goods to secure any obligations that Debtor may then or thereafter owe to SP–1. SP–1 filed an effective financing statement against Debtor listing goods as collateral. Debtor sold a good to Buyer and delivered the good to Buyer in exchange for a promise to pay Debtor for the good. Assume Buyer is not a buyer in ordinary course of business. Buyer took delivery of the good. At the time Buyer took delivery, Buyer had no knowledge of SP–1's security interest. Buyer took the good subject to SP–1's security interest because SP–1's security interest is perfected and Buyer is not a buyer in ordinary course of business. Thirty days later, SP–1 made another loan to Debtor. SP–1's security interest in the goods that Buyer purchased secures the future advance as long as SP–1 either made the commitment to make the advance or made the advance without knowledge that Buyer purchased the goods.

b. Lessees of Goods

A lessee of goods that gives value and takes delivery of the goods without knowledge of the security interest or agricultural lien while the security interest or agricultural lien is unperfected takes the goods free of the security interest or agricultural lien. UCC § 9–317(c).

(1) Purchase Money Security Interests

Even if a lessee takes possession of goods at the time the security interest in the collateral is unperfected, if the security interest is a purchase money security interest and the secured party perfects its security interest by filing a financing statement within 20 days after the debtor received delivery of the goods, the lessee will take the goods subject to that purchase money security interest. UCC § 9–317(e).

(2) Future Advances

Presumably if a lessee of goods takes free of a security interest under this priority rule, it would also take free of any security interest in that collateral that might otherwise secure a future advance. See UCC § 9–323, cmt. 6. If a lessee not in ordinary course of business takes goods subject to a security interest and the secured party subsequently makes an advance, the lessee will take the goods free of the security interest that secures that future advance if the secured party made the advance with knowledge of the lease or made the advance 45 days or more after the lease contract becomes enforceable. UCC § 9–323(f). The lessee not in ordinary course of business will not take the goods free of the security interest that secures the advance if the secured party made the advance or a commitment to do so without knowledge of the lease and before the end of the 45-day time period. UCC § 9–323(g).

c. Licensees of General Intangibles

A licensee of a general intangible takes the general intangible free of a security interest in the general intangible if the licensee gives value without knowledge of the security interest and while it is unperfected. UCC §

9–317(d). Unlike a buyer or lessee of goods, a licensee of software does not take subject to later perfected purchase money security interest in the software. UCC § 9–317(e). Presumably if a licensee of general intangibles takes free of a security interest under this priority rule, it would also take free of any security interest in that collateral that might otherwise secure a future advance. See UCC § 9–323, cmt. 6. Unlike a buyer or lessee of goods, a licensee of general intangibles that takes subject to the security interest does not have any protection against future advances that are secured by the security interest in the licensed general intangibles. See UCC § 9–323.

d. Buyers of Certain Intangible Collateral

A buyer of collateral, other than tangible chattel paper, tangible documents, goods, instruments, or a certificated security, takes the collateral free of a security interest in the collateral if the buyer gives value without knowledge of the security interest and while it is unperfected. The buyer must not be a secured party. UCC § 9–317(d). As to a buyer of accounts, electronic chattel paper, and payment intangibles, if the transaction is within the scope of Article 9, the buyer will be a secured party as the transaction creates a security interest. UCC § 9–109(a). Thus a buyer of accounts, electronic chattel paper, and payment intangibles will be able to use this priority rule only if the sale of that collateral is excluded from Article 9 under UCC § 9–109(d). UCC § 9–317, cmt. 6. Presumably if a buyer of this type of collateral takes free of a security interest under this priority rule, it would also take free of any security interest in that collateral that might otherwise secure a future advance. See UCC § 9–323, cmt. 6. Unlike a buyer or lessee of goods, buyers of these types of intangible collateral that take subject to the security interest do not have any protection against future advances that are secured by a security interest in the sold collateral. See UCC § 9–323.

5. Exception for Consumer Buyers of Consumer Goods

If a consumer sells its consumer goods to a buyer who buys the goods primarily for personal, family, or household purposes, the buyer may take free of a perfected security interest in the goods if several criteria are met. First, the buyer must not have knowledge of the security interest at the time it bought the goods. Second, the buyer must give value. Third, the buy must take place before an effective financing statement is filed against the goods. UCC § 9–320(b).

Compliance with a certificate of title statute to perfect the security interest is the equivalent of filing an effective financing statement. UCC § 9–320, cmt. 5.

Example: SP–1 has a purchase money security interest in Seller's new entertainment center purchased for use in Seller's home, perfected automatically as a purchase money security interest in consumer goods. UCC § 9–309(1). Seller sold the entertainment center to her next door neighbor for the neighbor to use in her home. The neighbor takes the entertainment center free of SP–1's security interest.

Example: SP–1 has a purchase money security interest in Seller's new entertainment center purchased for use in Seller's home, automatically perfected. SP–1 filed an effective financing statement against Seller listing the entertainment center as collateral. Seller sold the entertainment center to her next door neighbor for the neighbor to use in her home. The neighbor takes the entertainment center subject to SP–1's security interest.

Example: SP–1 has a security interest in Seller's new automobile, perfected by obtaining notation of the security interest on the automobile's certificate of title. Seller sells the automobile to her next door neighbor for the neighbor's personal use. The neighbor takes the automobile subject to SP–1's perfected security interest.

6. Exception for Buyer of Certificate of Title Goods When Certificate Does Not Note Security Interest

If a state issues a certificate of title when a security interest in the goods covered by that certificate has been previously perfected by any allowed method and that new certificate does not show that security interest or indicate that security interests that are not noted may exist, a buyer of that good covered by that "clean" certificate of title will take the good free of the unnoted security interest if the buyer meets certain criteria. First, the buyer must not be a secured party and must not be in the business of selling goods of the kind. Second, the buyer must give value and receive delivery of the goods after the clean certificate of title was issued. Third, the buyer must give value and receive delivery of the goods without knowledge of the security interest. UCC § 9–337(1).

Example: SP–1 perfected its security interest in Debtor's automobile by obtaining notation of its security interest on the certificate of title issued by State A. Debtor obtained a new title for the automobile in State B and State B issued the certificate without any notation of SP–1's security interest or indication that the automobile may be subject to unnoted security interests. One month later, Debtor sold the automobile to Buyer, a person not in the business of selling goods of the kind. Buyer gave value, took possession of the automobile, and did not have knowledge of SP–1's security interest. Even though SP–1's security interest in the automobile is still perfected, UCC § 9–316(d), and thus Buyer cannot use UCC § 9–317(b) to take free of the security interest, Buyer takes the automobile free of SP–1's security interest. The result would not change even if SP–1 obtained notation of its security interest on the certificate of title issued by State B after the sale of the automobile to Buyer.

7. Exception for Purchasers of Collateral in Reliance on Certain Incorrect Information on a Financing Statement

Even though a financing statement is sufficient to perfect under UCC § 9–502 by providing the correct name of the debtor, an indication of the collateral, and the name of the secured party, the financing statement may have errors in the information required under UCC § 9–516(b)(5). In the event the financing statement is sufficient to perfect but has errors in the debtor's mailing address or does not indicate whether the debtor's name is an individual or organizational name, a purchaser of collateral in reasonable reliance on that incorrect information takes the collateral free of the security interest or agricultural lien that is perfected by that inaccurate financing statement. The purchaser must not be a secured party and must give value in reasonable reliance on the incorrect information. If the collateral is tangible chattel paper, tangible documents of title, goods, instruments, or a certificated security, the purchaser must also take delivery of that collateral in reasonable reliance on the incorrect information. UCC § 9–338(2).

Example: SP–1 has a security interest in Debtor's goods. SP–1 perfected its security interest by filing an effective financing statement against Debtor covering goods. The financing statement had an incorrect Debtor's mailing address but was nonetheless sufficient to perfect

SP–1's security interest in Debtor's goods. UCC § 9–502. Debtor sold a good to Buyer. Buyer is not a secured party. Buyer never looked at the financing statement SP–1 filed. Buyer does not qualify to take the good free of the security interest under UCC § 9–338(2). Buyer will take subject to SP–1's security interest in the good unless Buyer qualifies as a buyer in ordinary course of business to take free of the security interest in the good under UCC § 9–320 or the Food Security Act of 1985 or SP–1 authorized the sale to Buyer free of SP–1's security interest under UCC § 9–315.

Example:　SP–1 has a security interest in Debtor's goods. SP–1 perfected its security interest by filing an effective financing statement against Debtor covering goods. The financing statement had an incorrect Debtor's mailing address but was nonetheless sufficient to perfect SP–1's security interest in Debtor's goods. UCC § 9–502. Debtor sold a good to Buyer. Buyer is not a secured party. Prior to the purchase, Buyer looked at the financing statement SP–1 filed and mistakenly thought that it was buying the good from a different seller than Debtor because of the incorrect mailing address of Debtor noted on the financing statement. Buyer gave value and took delivery of the good after its examination of the financing statement. Buyer has an argument that it should take the good free of SP–1's security interest if Buyer's actions were taken in reasonable reliance on the incorrect mailing address for Debtor in the financing statement.

8. Exception for Certain Transferees of Investment Property

A transferee of investment property that qualifies as a protected transferee under the rules of Article 8 will take the investment property free of a perfected security interest in the investment property. UCC § 9–331. Such transferees must take control of the investment property without notice of an adverse claim. An adverse claim is a claim of a property right in the security such that it is a violation of the rights of the property claimant for another person to deal with the security. UCC § 8–102(a)(1). A person has notice of an adverse claim when it knows of the adverse claim, has reason to know of the adverse claim based upon the facts available, or has a duty to investigate and such investigation would have revealed the adverse claim. UCC § 8–105(a). Filing a financing statement covering the investment property does not constitute notice of an adverse claim. UCC §

9–331(c). Control of investment property is defined in UCC § 8–106. Review Chapter III, Section B. A secured party or a person other than a secured party may qualify for this protection of transferees.

a. Protected Purchaser of a Security

A protected purchaser of a security (whether certificated or uncertificated) that gives value, does not have notice of any adverse claim to the security, and takes control of the security will have priority over a previously perfected security interest in the security. UCC §§ 9–331(a), 8–303(a).

b. Priority of a Person That Becomes an Entitlement Holder of a Securities Entitlement

A person that acquires a securities entitlement for value and without notice of an adverse claim is protected from any assertion of an adverse claim, including a claim of a security interest, in the securities entitlement. UCC §§ 8–502, 9–331(a). A person acquires a securities entitlement when the person becomes the entitlement holder with respect to the securities entitlement. UCC §§ 8–501, 8–102(a)(7).

c. Priority of a Purchaser From a Securities Intermediary of a Securities Entitlement

A purchaser of a securities entitlement from a securities intermediary takes free of the entitlement holder's property claims to the securities entitlement if the purchaser gives value, obtains control of the securities entitlement, and does not act in collusion with the securities intermediary in violating the securities intermediary's obligations to the entitlement holder. UCC §§ 8–503(e), 9–331(a).

d. Priority of a Purchaser From an Entitlement Holder of a Securities Entitlement

A purchaser of a securities entitlement from an entitlement holder takes free of adverse claims, including security interests, to the securities entitlement if the purchaser gives value, does not have notice of an adverse claim, and obtains control of the securities entitlement. UCC §§ 8–510, 9–331(a).

9. Exception for Transferee of Funds From Deposit Account

A transferee of funds from a deposit account will take those funds free of a security interest in the deposit account even if the security interest is perfected unless the transferee acted in collusion with the debtor in violating the rights of the secured party with the security interest in the deposit account. UCC § 9–332(b). This transferee may be a secured party or a person other than a secured party.

10. Exception for Transferees of Money

A transferee of money takes the money free of a security interest in the money even if the security interest is perfected unless the transferee acts in collusion with the debtor in violating the rights of the secured party with a security interest in the money. UCC § 9–332(a). This transferee may be a secured party or a person other than a secured party.

11. Exception for Purchasers of Instruments

A purchaser of an instrument, either a secured party or a purchaser other than a secured party, will have priority over a conflicting security interest in the instrument even if the security interest is perfected if the purchaser meets several requirements. If a person purchases an instrument for value, takes possession of the instrument in good faith, and does not have knowledge at the time it takes possession that the purchase violates the rights of the secured party, the purchaser's rights in the instrument will have priority over the security interest if that security interest is perfected by a method other than possession. UCC § 9–330(d). If the instrument is a negotiable instrument and the holder of the instrument (including a secured party) qualifies as a holder in due course of the instrument, the holder in due course will take the instrument free of the claims of the secured party with a security interest in the instrument even if the security interest is perfected. UCC § 9–331. Review Section D.11 *supra*.

12. Exception for Holders of Negotiable Documents of Title

If a person becomes a holder of a negotiable document of title by due negotiation, the holder will take the document of title and the goods covered by the document free of a security interest in the document and the goods even if that security interest is perfected. UCC § 9–331. A secured party or a person other than a secured party may become a holder of a negotiable document of title by due negotiation. This protection for holders of a negotiable document of title that take the document by due negotiation is subject to an exception if the security interest is perfected in the goods prior to the issuance of the negotiable document of title and the secured party did not entrust the goods or the document to the debtor with apparent or actual authority to dispose of the goods nor acquiesce in the debtor's procurement of the document of title. In that case, the secured party's security interest in the goods is not defeated by the interest of the holder of the negotiable document of title. UCC § 7–503. Review Section D.9 *supra*.

13. Exception for Purchasers of Chattel Paper

A purchaser of chattel paper, whether a secured party or a person other than a secured party will have priority over a conflicting security interest in the chattel paper, even if the security interest in the chattel paper is perfected in the two circumstances set forth in UCC § 9–330(a) and (b). Review Section D.10 *supra*.

G. Choice of Law for Priority and the Effect of Perfection or Nonperfection

Article 9 contains choice of law rules for governing priority and the effect of perfection and nonperfection of security interests or agricultural liens. The "effect of perfection and nonperfection" language is meant to encompass the "take free" types of priority rules that have been explored in this Chapter. In most circumstances, the same choice of law rule that determined perfection of the security interest or agricultural lien will also determine the choice of law for purposes of perfection and the effect of perfection or nonperfection. Chapter IV, Section G. As to some types of collateral, however, the choice of law rule will point to one state's law for the perfection rule and to another state's law for the priority and "take free" rules. To the extent that the law in all jurisdictions is uniform, the choice of law these issues is not troublesome for secured parties.

1. General Rule for Agricultural Liens

The law of the jurisdiction in which the farm products are located will govern the effect of perfection or nonperfection and priority of agricultural liens in the farm products. UCC § 9–302.

2. General Rule for Security Interests

The general rule is that the law of the debtor's location governs the priority and the effect of perfection and nonperfection of a security interest in the collateral. UCC § 9–301(1). That rule is subject to the following exceptions.

a. Exception for Possessory Security Interests

If the security interest is a possessory security interest, the priority and effect of perfection or nonperfection of the security interest will be determined by the law of the state where the collateral is located. UCC § 9–301(2).

b. Exception for Tangible Collateral

If the collateral is tangible negotiable documents of title, goods, instruments, money, or tangible chattel paper, the effect of perfection or nonperfection and priority of the security interest will be determined by the law of the jurisdiction where the collateral is located if the security interest is a nonpossessory security interest. UCC § 9–301(3). For these types of collateral, except for fixtures and timber to be cut, the law of the jurisdiction where the debtor is located will govern perfection whereas the law of the collateral's location will govern priority and the effect of perfection and nonperfection.

c. Exception for As-Extracted Collateral

If the collateral is as-extracted collateral, the effect of perfection or nonperfection and priority of a security interest will be determined by the location of the wellhead or minehead. UCC § 9–301(4).

d. Exception for Goods Covered by a Certificate of Title

If the collateral is goods covered by a certificate of title, the effect of perfection or nonperfection and priority of a security interest in those goods will be determined by the law of the jurisdiction issuing the certificate of title until the goods cease to be covered by that certificate of title. UCC § 9–303.

e. Exception for Deposit Accounts

If the collateral is a deposit account, the effect of perfection or nonperfection and priority of a security interest in the deposit account will be determined by the law of the depositary bank's jurisdiction. UCC § 9–304(a).

f. Exception for Certificated Security

If the security interest in a certificated security is perfected by a method other than filing a financing statement or other than the automatic perfection of a security interest created by a broker or a securities intermediary, the effect of perfection and nonperfection and priority is determined by the law of the jurisdiction where the certificated security is located. UCC § 9–305(a)(1), (c).

g. Exception for Uncertificated Security

If the security interest in an uncertificated security is perfected by a method other than filing a financing statement or other than the automatic perfection of a security interest created by a broker or a securities intermediary, the effect of perfection and nonperfection and priority is determined by the law of the jurisdiction where the issuer is located. UCC § 9–305(a)(2), (c).

h. Exception for Securities Entitlement or Securities Account

If the security interest in a securities entitlement or a securities account is perfected by a method other than filing a financing statement or other than the automatic perfection of a security interest created by a broker or a securities intermediary, the effect of perfection and nonperfection and priority is determined by the law of the jurisdiction where the securities intermediary is located. UCC § 9–305(a)(3), (c).

i. Exception for Commodity Contract or Commodity Account

If the security interest in a commodity contract or commodities account is perfected by a method other than filing a financing statement or other than the automatic perfection of a security interest created by a commodity intermediary, the effect of perfection and nonperfection and priority is determined by the law of the jurisdiction where the commodity intermediary is located. UCC § 9–305(a)(4), (c).

j. Exception for Letter-of-Credit Rights

If a security interest is in a letter-of-credit right and is perfected other than through automatic perfection as a supporting obligation for a right to payment, the law of the location of the issuer or nominated person will govern priority and the effect of perfection or nonperfection of that security interest as long as the issuer or nominated person is located in a state of the United States. UCC § 9–306.

H. Post-Closing Changes and Effect on Priority

As set forth in Chapter IV, Section H, as events unfold, the secured party may find that it has to take action to keep its security interest or agricultural lien perfected. Post-closing events will thus also have an effect on the priority of the security interest or agricultural lien, particularly as priority is determined by the first to file or perfect rule which requires that the secured party either have an effective filing covering the collateral or perfection of the security interest or agricultural lien in order to preserve the date of filing or perfection as the applicable priority date. UCC § 9–322(a). Thus, the material explored in Chapter IV, particularly in Section H, on maintaining continuous perfection is critical to maintaining priority status.

1. Security Interest or Agricultural Lien Perfection Lapses

If the secured party fails to maintain perfection of its security interest or agricultural lien in the collateral and an interest of a transferee arises in the collateral while the security interest or agricultural lien is unperfected, the priority rules studied in this Chapter may result in the interest of the secured party being subordinated to the transferee's interests.

Example: SP–1 has a security interest in Debtor's equipment and perfected that security interest by filing an effective financing statement against Debtor listing equipment as collateral. SP–1 did not file a continuation statement at the end of the five-year period thus allowing its financing statement to lapse and rendering its security interest in the equipment unperfected. UCC § 9–515(c). After the lapse of the financing statement, Debtor's lien creditor levied on an item of equipment. Lien Creditor's lien created by the levy will be superior to the unperfected security interest of SP–1 in that item of equipment. UCC § 9–317(a).

2. Security Interest or Agricultural Lien Deemed Not Perfected as Against Previous Purchasers if Fail to File Effective Continuation Statement

If a secured party fails to file an effective continuation statement so that the effectiveness of the filed financing statement lapses and that financing statement was the method of perfection of a security interest or agricultural lien in the collateral, the security interest or agricultural lien is deemed unperfected as against prior purchasers of the collateral for value. UCC § 9–515(c).

Example: SP–1 has a security interest in Debtor's equipment and perfected that security interest by filing an effective financing statement against Debtor listing equipment as collateral. SP–2 has a security interest in Debtor's equipment and perfected its security interest by filing an effective financing statement against Debtor listing equipment as collateral. Under the first to file or perfect priority rule, SP–1's security interest in the equipment has priority over SP–2's security interest in the equipment. SP–1 did not file a continuation statement at the end of the five-year period and thus its financing statement lapsed, rendering SP–1's security interest unperfected at the moment of lapse of the financing statement. SP–1's security interest is deemed unperfected as to prior purchasers for value. UCC § 9–515(c). SP–2 is a purchaser for value. UCC §§ 1–201(b)(30), 1–204. SP–2's financing statement is still effective to perfect its security interest. SP–2's security interest will have priority over SP–1's security interest under the rule that perfected security interests have priority over unperfected security interests. UCC § 9–322(a).

Example: SP–1 has a security interest in Debtor's equipment and perfected that security interest by filing an effective financing statement against Debtor listing equipment as collateral. While SP–1's security interest in the equipment was perfected, Debtor's lien creditor levied on an item of equipment. Lien Creditor's lien is subordinate to SP–1's security interest. SP–1 did not file a continuation statement at the end of the five-year period thus allowing its financing statement to lapse and rendering its security interest in the equipment unperfected at the moment of lapse of the financing statement. Lien Creditor's lien created by the levy will still be subordinate to the now unperfected security interest of SP–1 in that item of equipment as Lien Creditor is not a purchaser for value and its lien on the equipment arose while SP–1's security interest in the equipment was perfected. UCC § 9–317(a).

Example: SP–1 has a security interest in Debtor's equipment and perfected that security interest by filing an effective financing statement against Debtor listing equipment as collateral. Debtor sold a piece of equipment to a buyer, who is not a secured party and who is not a buyer in ordinary course of business. SP–1 did not file a continuation statement at the end of the five-year period and thus its financing statement lapsed, rendering SP–1's security interest unperfected at the moment of lapse of the financing statement, and deemed unperfected as against a prior purchaser for value. UCC § 9–515(c). Buyer will now have the equipment free of the SP–1's security interest under UCC § 9–317(b) as long as Buyer gave value and received delivery of the equipment without knowledge of the security interest.

3. Security Interest Deemed Not Perfected as Against Previous Purchasers If Governing Law Changes

If the governing law for perfection of the security interest changes so that the secured party must take action within a certain time frame to maintain perfection of its security interest, the secured party that fails to take that required action within the time frame will have its security interest deemed unperfected not only as against claimants whose interests subsequently arise but also as to previous purchasers for value of the collateral that obtained their interests in the collateral prior to the end of the time period. UCC § 9–316. As noted above regarding continuation statements, this deemed retroactive unperfection does not take place as to claimants that are not purchasers for value, such as lien creditors. Review Chapter IV, Section H.12.

a. Change in Debtor's Location

If the secured party must take action to maintain its perfection of a security interest when the debtor moves location from one jurisdiction to another jurisdiction and the secured party fails to take the required action in the new jurisdiction during the applicable time period, the security interest becomes unperfected. The security interest is also deemed unperfected as against purchasers for value that had previously acquired interests in the collateral. UCC § 9–316(a), (b), (h).

Example: SP–1 has a security interest in Debtor's equipment and perfected its security interest by filing an effective financing statement against Debtor in State A, Debtor's location, listing the collateral as equipment. Debtor changed its location to State B. SP–1 has four months to file a financing statement in State B to continue perfection of its security interest in the equipment. Two months after Debtor's move to State B, SP–2 obtained a security interest in Debtor's equipment and filed an effective financing statement against Debtor in State B listing equipment as collateral. SP–1 does not file an effective financing statement against Debtor in State B by the end of the four-month period following Debtor's relocation to State B. SP–1's security interest is unperfected and is deemed to be unperfected as against SP–2, a previous purchaser for value of the collateral. SP–2's security interest in the equipment has priority over SP–1's security interest in the equipment. UCC § 9–322(a).

b. Change in Identity of Debtor

If the secured party must take action to maintain its perfection of a security interest when the debtor transfers collateral to a debtor located in a new jurisdiction or a new debtor becomes bound to the old debtor's security agreement, UCC § 9–203(d), (e), and the secured party fails to take the required action in the new jurisdiction during the applicable time period, the security interest becomes unperfected. The security interest is also deemed unperfected as against purchasers for value that had previously acquired interests in the collateral. UCC § 9–316(a)(3), (b), (i).

Example: SP–1 has a security interest in Debtor's equipment then owned and thereafter acquired and perfected its security interest by filing an effective financing statement against Debtor in State A, Debtor's location, listing the collateral as equipment. Debtor sold an item of equipment to Buyer located in State B. Buyer did not take the equipment free of SP–1's security interest under UCC § 9–315(a)(1), § 9–317(b) or § 9–320. Buyer is now the debtor as to that item of equipment. SP–1 has one year to file a financing statement in State B against Buyer to continue perfection of its security interest in that item of equipment. SP–1 failed to file any financing statement in State B. SP–1's security interest is unperfected and is deemed to be unperfected as against Buyer, a previous purchaser for value of the collateral. Under UCC § 9–317(b), Buyer takes the item of equipment free of the SP–1's security interest as long as Buyer gave value and received delivery of the item of equipment without knowledge of the security interest.

Example: SP–1 has a security interest in Debtor's equipment then owned and thereafter acquired and perfected its security interest by filing an effective financing statement against Debtor in State A, Debtor's location, listing the collateral as equipment. Debtor merged with another entity forming New Debtor located in State B. SP–1 has one year to file a financing statement in State B against New Debtor to continue perfection of its security interest in the equipment that Debtor had an interest in prior to relocation to State B and four months to file a financing statement in State B against New Debtor as to any equipment that New Debtor has or acquires within four months after its formation in State B. Two months after New Debtor was formed in State B, SP–2 obtained a security interest in New Debtor's equipment then owned and thereafter acquired, and filed in State B against New Debtor an effective financing statement listing equipment as collateral. SP–1 does not file an effective financing statement against New Debtor in State B. SP–1's security interest is unperfected and is deemed to be unperfected as against SP–2, a previous purchaser for value of the collateral. SP–2's security interest in all of Debtor's equipment has priority over SP–1's security interest in the equipment. UCC § 9–322(a).

c. Goods Covered by a Certificate of Title

If a security interest is perfected in goods in any manner and the goods become covered by a certificate of title issued by a jurisdiction, the secured party has four months to obtain perfection of its security interest by noting it on the certificate of title or by taking possession of the goods. If the secured party fails to do so during the four-month time period, its security interest becomes unperfected and is deemed unperfected as against a previous purchaser for value. UCC § 9–316(d), (e).

d. Change in Third Party's Location

If the security interest is in deposit accounts, letter-of-credit rights, or investment property whereby the governing law is determined by the jurisdiction of the bank, issuer, nominated person, securities intermediary, or commodity intermediary as the case may be, and if that entity's location is moved to another jurisdiction, the secured party has four months to obtain perfection of its security interest in the new jurisdiction. If the secured party fails to do so during the four-month time period, its security interest becomes unperfected and is deemed unperfected as against a previous purchaser for value. UCC § 9–316(f), (g).

4. Transfers of Collateral

A secured party may find that a transfer of collateral effectively subordinates the secured party's security interest or agricultural lien to the transferee's interest in the collateral or results in the transferee taking the collateral free of the security interest or agricultural lien. See Section F, *supra*.

I. Federal Tax Liens

When the federal government is owed taxes of any kind, the federal tax lien statute allows the federal government to impose a lien on the taxpayer's property as one of the methods for collecting the tax, interest and penalties owed. 26 U.S.C. § 6321. State governments may also have state tax lien statutes that allow the state government to impose liens on the taxpayer's property. Those statutes will vary from state to state. Generally, if the debtor is experiencing financial stress such that a secured party may be seeking to enforce its security interest or agricultural lien against the debtor's property, the secured party may encounter the federal government as a competing creditor with a tax lien on the same property. This section sets forth the rules that govern the priority of the federal tax lien as against a security interest or agricultural lien that is governed by Article 9. These priority rules are not found in Article 9 but in the federal tax lien statute.

1. Attachment of the Federal Tax Lien

The federal tax lien arises when the taxpayer refuses to pay the tax, interest, and penalties after demand. 26 U.S.C. § 6321. The lien is considered attached to the taxpayer's property and interests in property as of the date of assessment of the tax liability. 26 U.S.C. § 6322. Assessment usually precedes the demand for payment and does not require any notice to the taxpayer. These two statutory sections have been construed as if they contained an after-acquired property clause. That is, the federal tax lien also attaches to property or interests in property that the debtor acquires after the assessment of the tax. The tax lien attaches to all of the taxpayer's property or interests in property without regard to any state or federal exemptions from execution on judgments. Whether a taxpayer has an interest in property is determined by state law. The tax lien exists until it is satisfied or until the underlying assessment of taxes may not be collected by reason of lapse of time. The general time period for collection of the tax is 10 years from assessment although there are several exceptions to that general rule. 26 U.S.C. §§ 6322, 6502.

2. Filing a Notice of the Tax Lien

Even though it is not necessary for the federal government to file a notice of tax lien in the public records to take action to enforce the lien, the filing of a notice of tax lien will set the priority position of the federal tax lien as against certain types of other lien claims that have attached to the taxpayer's property.

a. What Is Filed

The Internal Revenue Service agent will file a notice of a federal tax lien which is a paper form denominated Form 668 "Notice of Federal Tax Lien Under Internal Revenue Laws." If the relevant filing office accepts electronic filings, the filing may be electronic. The form must identify the taxpayer, the tax liability giving rise to the form, and the date of assessment of the tax liability. 26 C.F.R. § 301.6323(f)–1(d).

b. Where the Tax Lien Notice Is Filed

To file an effective notice of federal tax lien against the taxpayer's property, the tax lien notice must be filed in the state in which the property is located. Real estate is considered located at its physical location. Personal property is considered located at the residence of the taxpayer at the time the tax lien notice is filed. The residence of a corporate or partnership taxpayer is the principal executive office of the business. If the taxpayer's residence is outside the United States, the taxpayer is considered to have a residence in the District of Columbia. The state where the property is located may designate the relevant state office in which the federal tax lien notices are filed. If the state fails to designate a state office in which federal tax lien notices are filed, the tax lien notice is filed in the United States District Court clerk's office where the property is located. If the taxpayer's property is located in the District of Columbia, the federal tax lien notice must be filed in the District's office of Recorder of Deeds. 26 U.S.C. § 6323(f).

c. Term of Effectiveness of Tax Lien Filing

A notice of tax lien can be refiled to extend its period of effectiveness beyond 10 years after assessment of the tax. The notice may be refiled within a one-year period that expires 30 days after the 10-year period expires or if it is a second or subsequent refiling of the tax lien notice, within the one-year period after the expiration of the previous 10-year period. 26 U.S.C. § 6323(g)(3).

d. Post-Filing Changes

The question of whether the notice of tax lien must be refiled if the residence of the taxpayer changes is a matter of interpretation of the federal tax lien statute and is not governed by the Article 9 principles on that subject. Courts give inconsistent answers to this question.

3. General Priority Rule

The priority of the federal tax lien as against four types of claimants is determined based upon the timing of the filing of the tax lien notice and time in which the claimant's interests are considered to have affixed to the taxpayer's property under the federal tax lien statute. 26 U.S.C. § 6323(a). Whatever is first, the tax lien notice filing or the affixing of the claimant's interest in the taxpayer's property, will have priority. Those four types of claimants are a holder of a security interest, a purchaser, a mechanic's lienor, and a judgment lien creditor. When the interest of one of those claimants is considered to be fixed to the taxpayer's property is determined by the federal tax lien statute and not the rules of other law, such as Article 9.

a. Holder of a Security Interest

To be a holder of a security interest within the meaning of the federal tax lien statute, the creditor must fulfill the following criteria. First, the creditor must obtain its interest in the taxpayer's property by contract for the purpose of securing payment or performance of an obligation. Second, the property must be "in existence," which means that the taxpayer has to have rights in the property. Third, the creditor must have priority under other law over the rights of a hypothetical lien creditor whose claim is deemed to arise as of the moment of the tax lien filing. Fourth, the creditor must have parted with money or money's worth at the time of the tax lien filing and the security interest is only effective to the extent that money or money's worth has been given. Only when all of those criteria are met, is the creditor considered to be a holder of a security interest. 26 U.S.C. § 6323(h)(1). An agricultural lien holder is not a holder of a security interest within this federal definition as its lien arises by statute and not by contract.

Example: SP–1 obtained a signed security agreement granting SP–1 a security interest in Debtor's equipment now owned or hereafter acquired to secure all obligations then or thereafter owed to SP–1. SP–1 filed, in the correct place, its effective financing statement against Debtor listing collateral as equipment. The IRS filed a notice of tax lien in the correct place against Debtor. SP–1 then gave value. Even though under UCC § 9–317 SP–1 would prevail over a judgment lien creditor's lien that arose at the time of the filing of the tax lien notice, SP–1's security interest in Debtor's equipment will be subordinate to the IRS tax lien because SP–1 had not parted with money or money's worth at the time of the tax lien filing.

Example: SP–1 obtained a signed security agreement granting SP–1 a security interest in Debtor's equipment now owned or hereafter acquired to secure all obligations then or thereafter owed to SP–1. SP–1 filed, in the correct place, its effective financing statement against Debtor listing collateral as equipment. SP–1 gave value. The IRS filed a notice of tax lien in the correct place against Debtor. As to all equipment that Debtor has an interest in at the time of the tax lien notice filing, SP–1 will have priority over the federal tax lien. Debtor acquired a new piece of equipment. Even though SP–1's security interest is attached and perfected in that new piece of equipment, SP–1's security interest in that new piece of equipment will be subordinate to the federal tax lien because SP–1's security interest did not come into existence as to that piece of equipment for purposes of the federal tax lien statute priority rule until Debtor acquired rights in the collateral. The federal tax lien notice was on file before that time.

b. Purchaser

To qualify as a purchaser, the person must meet all of the following criteria. First, the person must not acquire its interest in the property because of a security interest or lien. Second, the person must give adequate and full consideration in money or money's worth in exchange for the interest in property. Third, the person must have priority for its interest in property under other law as against subsequent purchasers that did not have notice of the person's purchase. 26 U.S.C. § 6323(h)(6). Whether an Article 9 secured party that is a buyer of accounts, chattel paper, payment intangibles and promissory notes will be treated as a purchaser under this definition or as a holder of a security interest under the above definition is an open question. An agricultural lien holder is not a purchaser under this definition because its interest is a lien interest.

c. Judgment Lien Creditor

This term is not defined in the federal tax lien statute but is defined in the IRS regulations. To qualify as a judgment lien creditor, the claimant must meet the following criteria. The claimant must obtain a valid court judgment for recovery of specific property or a specified sum of money and perfect that judgment under other law. The judgment is not considered perfected under other law until all of the following are established: the identity of the lienor, the identity of the property subject to the lien, and the amount of the lien. 26 C.F.R. § 301.6323(h)–1(g). An Article 9 secured party could be a judgment lien creditor if it obtained a valid court judgment for recovery of the collateral subject to its security interest.

d. Mechanic's Lienor

A mechanic's lienor is a person that has a lien on real estate to secure the value of services or material furnished to construct an improvement on the real estate. The mechanic's lienor's interest arises no earlier than when it first furnished the services or material to the real estate and no earlier than when the lien becomes valid under other law against subsequent purchasers of the real estate without actual notice of the lienor's interest. 26 U.S.C. § 6323(h)(2). An Article 9 secured party is not a mechanic's lienor.

4. Choateness Doctrine

If the creditor's claim to the taxpayer's property does not qualify as one of the four types of protected claimants as defined above, the federal common law rule of choateness may apply to determine priority of the claim as against the federal tax lien. That rule is that the competing claimant's interest must be choate before the tax lien becomes effective with respect to the taxpayer's property, that is, prior to *assessment* of the tax liability. To be choate, the "identity of the lienor, the property subject to the lien, and the amount of the lien" must all be established. IRS v. McDermott, 507 U.S. 447, 449 (1993).

5. Exceptions to General Priority Rules For Tax Liens

The federal tax lien statute has several exceptions to the general priority rules set forth above that are relevant to determining priority of a creditor's claim to property as against a federal tax lien.

a. Transactions Covered by 26 U.S.C. § 6323(b)

Even though notice of a federal tax lien has been duly filed, a creditor or purchaser may be able to obtain priority for its interest that attaches to the property after the tax lien filing. Ten such exceptions are found in 26 U.S.C. § 6323(b). The following exceptions are most relevant to the priority contests involving a secured party.

(1) Securities

If a person either becomes a purchaser of a security or becomes a holder of a security interest in a security after the tax lien notice is filed against the debtor and without actual notice or knowledge of the tax lien, the purchaser or holder of the security interest will have priority in the securities over the federal tax lien. 26 U.S.C. § 6323(b)(1). The definitions given above for purchaser and holder of a security interest apply for purposes of this rule. Securities are defined as stocks, bonds, or other items that typically fall within the category of investment property. The definition also includes negotiable instruments and money. 26 U.S.C. § 6323(h)(4).

Example: SP–1 obtained a signed security agreement granting SP–1 a security interest in Debtor's equipment now owned or hereafter acquired to secure all obligations then or thereafter owed to SP–1. SP–1 filed, in the correct place, its effective financing statement against Debtor listing collateral as equipment. SP–1 then gave value. Thereafter, the IRS filed a notice of tax lien in the correct place against Debtor. Debtor sold an item of equipment in exchange for money. SP–1's security interest in the money as identifiable proceeds is

automatically attached and perfected pursuant to UCC §
9–315. For purposes of the tax lien statute, SP–1's security
interest in the money did not arise until Debtor acquired
rights in the money and that security interest thus arose after
the IRS filed the tax lien notice. If SP–1 did not have actual
notice or knowledge of the tax lien at the time Debtor
acquired rights in the money, SP–1's security interest in the
money will have priority over the IRS tax lien.

(2) Motor Vehicles

If a person purchased a motor vehicle after the filing of notice of a federal
tax lien against its seller, made the purchase and took possession of the
motor vehicle without actual notice or knowledge of the tax lien, and has
not relinquished possession of the motor vehicle thereafter to the seller,
the purchaser's interest in the motor vehicle will have priority over the
federal tax lien. 26 U.S.C. § 6323(b)(2). The definition of purchaser as set
forth above applies. A motor vehicle is a "self-propelled" vehicle that is
registered for use on the highways of a State or another country. 26 U.S.C.
§ 6323(h)(3).

(3) Purchasers of Tangible Personal Property Sold at Retail

If a person purchases tangible personal property from a seller in a retail
sale in the ordinary course of the seller's trade or business after notice of
a tax lien has been filed against the seller, that purchaser's interest in the
tangible personal property sold will be superior to the federal tax lien
unless the purchaser intended to or knows the purchase will hinder,
evade or defeat the collection of the tax. 26 U.S.C. § 6323(b)(3). The
definition of purchaser given above applies to this rule. This protection
is analogous to the protection for buyers in the ordinary course of
business from security interests created by the buyer's seller. UCC §
9–320(a).

**(4) Purchasers of Tangible Household Goods or Consumer Goods Sold in
Casual Sales**

If a person purchases tangible personal property that is household goods,
personal effects, or certain types of consumer goods (listed in 26 U.S.C.
§ 6334(a)) in a casual sale, not for resale, and for less than $1,000 after
notice of a tax lien is filed against the seller, the purchaser's interest in

that property will be superior to the federal tax lien unless the purchaser has actual notice or knowledge of the tax lien or the sale is one of a series of sales. 26 U.S.C. § 6323(b)(4). Purchaser as defined above applies to this priority rule.

(5) Possessory Liens

If a person has a lien on tangible personal property that arises under other law to secure the price of repair or improvement of that property and is continuously in possession of the property, that person will have priority over a federal tax lien even if the possessory lien arises after notice of the federal tax lien is filed against the owner of the property. 26 U.S.C. § 6323(b)(5).

b. Transactions Covered by 26 U.S.C. § 6323(d)

To become a holder of a security interest as defined in the federal tax lien statute, the secured party has a security interest only to the extent it has parted with money or money's worth at the time of the tax lien filing. 26 U.S.C. § 6323(h)(1). That means that even if the security agreement specifies that future advances are secured by a security interest in the described collateral, the secured party's security interest that secures the future advance is not effective as against a federal tax lien if the advance is given subsequent to the filing of the tax lien notice. That general principle is subject to the following exception found in 26 U.S.C. § 6323(d). If all of the following are true, the security interest that secures a future advance will have priority over a federal tax lien to the extent of the advance. First, the secured party must have made the advance within 45 days after the federal tax lien notice was filed. Second, the secured party must have made the advance without actual notice or knowledge of the tax lien filing. Third, the advance must be secured by a security interest in property that the debtor had an interest in at the time of the tax lien filing, pursuant to a written security agreement entered into before the tax lien filing. Fourth, under other law, the security interest that secures that advance must have priority over the rights of a hypothetical lien creditor that is deemed to arise at the time of the tax lien filing. On this last point, review the materials on priority for security interests securing future advances as against a lien creditor. UCC § 9–323. Review Section B, *supra*.

Example: SP–1 obtained a signed security agreement granting SP–1 a security interest in Debtor's equipment now owned or hereafter acquired to secure all obligations then or thereafter owed to SP–1. SP–1 filed, in the correct place, its effective financing statement against Debtor listing collateral as equipment. SP–1 gave value of $10,000. The IRS then filed a notice of tax lien in the correct place against Debtor for a tax assessment of $6,000. *Forty* days later, SP–1 advanced an additional $2,000 to Debtor. The equipment is worth $15,000. SP–1's security interest that secures the initial advance of $10,000 will have priority over the federal tax lien pursuant to 26 U.S.C. § 6323(a). SP–1's security interest that secures the subsequent advance of $2,000 will have priority over the federal tax lien if SP–1 made the advance without actual knowledge of the federal tax lien filing. 26 U.S.C. § 6323(d).

Example: SP–1 obtained a signed security agreement granting SP–1 a security interest in Debtor's equipment now owned or hereafter acquired to secure all obligations then or thereafter owed to SP–1. SP–1 filed, in the correct place, its effective financing statement against Debtor listing collateral as equipment. SP–1 gave value of $10,000. The IRS then filed a notice of tax lien in the correct place against Debtor for a tax assessment of $6,000. *Sixty* days later, SP–1 advanced an additional $2,000 to Debtor. The equipment is worth $15,000. SP–1's security interest that secures the initial advance of $10,000 will have priority over the federal tax lien pursuant to 26 U.S.C. § 6323(a). SP–1's security interest that secures the subsequent advance of $2,000 will *not* have priority over the federal tax lien. The order of priority in the equipment will be SP–1's security interest that secures the $10,000 initial advance, federal tax lien that secures tax liability of $6,000, SP–1's security interest that secures the $2,000 future advance.

Example: SP–1 obtained a signed security agreement granting SP–1 a security interest in Debtor's equipment now owned or hereafter acquired to secure all obligations then or thereafter owed to SP–1. SP–1 filed, in the correct place, its effective financing statement against Debtor listing collateral as equipment. SP–1 gave value of $10,000. The IRS then filed a notice of tax lien in the correct place against Debtor for a tax assessment of $6,000. Debtor acquired a new item of equipment. *Forty* days after the tax lien filing and without actual notice or knowledge of that filing, SP–1 advanced Debtor an additional $2,000. Under Article 9, SP–1's security interest attaches and is perfected in all of Debtor's equipment (both old and new) to secure all obligations (both the initial and the subsequent advance). Under the federal tax lien statute, SP–1's security interest that secures the initial advance (26 U.S.C. § 6323(a)) and the subsequent advance (26 U.S.C. § 6323(d)) in Debtor's equipment that Debtor had rights in at the time of the tax lien filing will have priority over the federal tax lien. SP–1's security interest in the new item of equipment to secure both the initial advance and the subsequent advance will be subordinate to the federal tax lien.

c. Transactions Covered by 26 U.S.C. § 6323(c)

To become a holder of a security interest as defined in the federal tax lien statute, the secured party has a security interest only to the extent it has parted with money or money's worth at the time of the tax lien filing. That means that even if the security agreement specifies that future advances are secured by a security interest in the described collateral, the secured party's security interest that secures the future advance is not effective as against a federal tax lien if the advance is given subsequent to the filing of the tax lien notice with the exception noted under 26 U.S.C. § 6323(d) explained *supra*. In addition, to become a holder of a security interest as defined in the federal tax lien statute, the secured party has a security interest only to the extent the debtor had rights in the collateral as of the time of the tax lien filing. That means that generally security interests that arise in collateral the debtor acquires after the tax lien filing will be subordinate in priority to the federal tax lien. 26 U.S.C. § 6323(h)(1). Both of these principles are subject to an exception found in 26 U.S.C. § 6323(c) for certain types of collateral. The statutory expression of the exception is unduly complex and can be summarized as follows as it relates to Article 9 security interests. If all of the following criteria are met, the security interest in collateral that arises after the filing of a federal tax lien notice will have priority over the federal tax lien. First, the collateral must be "paper of a kind ordinarily arising in commercial transactions" (such as chattel paper and instruments), accounts, or inventory. Second, the secured party must have a security agreement that predates the tax lien notice filing and that provides for creation of a security interest in such types of collateral. Third, the collateral of the designated type must be acquired by the debtor within 45 days after the tax lien notice was filed. Fourth, the advances that are secured by the security interest in that type of collateral must be made without actual notice or knowledge of the tax lien filing and before or within 45 days after the tax lien filing.

Example: SP–1 obtained a signed security agreement granting SP–1 a security interest in Debtor's inventory now owned or hereafter acquired to secure all obligations then or thereafter owed to SP–1. SP–1 filed, in the correct place, its effective financing statement against Debtor listing collateral as inventory. SP–1 gave value of $10,000. The IRS then filed a notice of tax lien in the correct place against Debtor for a tax assessment of $6,000. Under the general priority rule of 26 U.S.C. § 6323(a), SP–1's security interest to secure the initial advance of $10,000 in all inventory that Debtor had rights in at the time of the tax lien filing is superior in priority to the tax lien. The rule of 26 U.S.C. § 6323(c) is unnecessary to give SP–1's security interest priority in that existing inventory. Ten days later, Debtor acquired a new item of inventory. SP–1's security interest in the new item of inventory is attached and perfected under Article 9. Under the exception in 26 U.S.C. § 6323(c), SP–1's security interest in the new item of inventory to secured the $10,000 initial advance has priority over the federal tax lien.

Example: SP–1 obtained a signed security agreement granting SP–1 a security interest in Debtor's inventory now owned or hereafter acquired to secure all obligations then or thereafter owed to SP–1. SP–1 filed, in the correct place, its effective financing statement against Debtor listing collateral as inventory. SP–1 gave value of $10,000. The IRS then filed a notice of tax lien in the correct place against Debtor for a tax assessment of $6,000. Ten days later, Debtor acquired a new item of inventory. SP–1's security interest in the new item of inventory is attached and perfected under Article 9. Five days after the purchase of the new inventory and without actual notice or knowledge of the federal tax lien filing, SP–1 made an advance of $2,000 to Debtor.

Under 26 U.S.C. § 6323(a), SP–1's security interest in the old inventory (inventory that Debtor had rights in at the time the tax lien notice was filed) secures the initial advance of $10,000 with priority over the federal tax lien. Under either 26 U.S.C. § 6323(d) or § 6323(c), SP–1's security interest in the old inventory secures the additional advance of $2,000 with priority over the federal tax lien. Under 26 U.S.C. § 6323(c), SP–1's security interest in the new inventory secures the initial advance of $10,000 with priority over the federal tax lien. Under 26 U.S.C. § 6323(c), SP–1's security interest in the new inventory secures the future advance of $2,000 with priority over the federal tax lien.

J. Effect of Bankruptcy on Priority

Distribution of a debtor's assets in bankruptcy, for the most part, respects the rules of priority found in Article 9. Several Bankruptcy Code sections, however, affect the priority of security interests or agricultural liens that would otherwise have priority over other interests in the debtor's assets.

1. Future Advances

Because the Bankruptcy Code carefully restricts the ability of the debtor to grant security interests in collateral during the pendency of a bankruptcy case, any future advances the secured party makes to a debtor or debtor in possession after commencement of the bankruptcy case will not automatically be secured by any collateral that is part of the bankruptcy estate even if the secured party has a valid future advances clause in its security agreement. The court may, after notice and hearing, approve the granting of a security interest in property of the estate to secure advances made after the bankruptcy petition is filed. 11 U.S.C. § 364.

2. After-Acquired Property

The bankruptcy process provides for distribution to creditors based upon a statutory priority scheme in which secured creditors (such as a holder of a security interest or agricultural lien) are generally allowed to collect the value of their lien interest. See 11 U.S.C. § 506. Even if a holder of a security interest has an after-acquired property clause in the security agreement, 11 U.S.C. § 552(a) provides that such a clause is not effective to attach a security interest to property acquired by the bankruptcy estate or the debtor after commencement of the case. There are two exceptions to that rule, one of which is most applicable to an Article 9 secured party. If the prepetition security agreement is sufficient to attach a security interest to postpetition "proceeds, products, offspring, or profits" of property in which the secured party had an interest in before the filing of the bankruptcy case, the secured party will be able to assert its interest in that the "proceeds, products, offspring or profits" in which the debtor acquires rights postpetition. 11 U.S.C. § 552(b)(1). The terms "proceeds, products, offspring or profits" are not defined in the Bankruptcy Code. Whether the meaning of "proceeds" in Article 9 will apply as the meaning of "proceeds" in this context is not clear. The other exception allows for a valid postpetition interest in rents of property subject to a prepetition security interest and in payments for use or occupancy of lodging facilities. 11 U.S.C. § 552(b)(2).

3. Lien Avoidance

One of the risks a secured party takes when the debtor files bankruptcy is that the bankruptcy trustee will avoid the security interest or agricultural lien. The bankruptcy trustee has several alternatives to use to attempt to avoid a security interest or agricultural lien.

a. Hypothetical Lien Creditor

When the debtor files bankruptcy, the trustee assumes the status of a hypothetical lien creditor that is deemed to arise as of the time of the bankruptcy filing. 11 U.S.C. § 544(a). That hypothetical lien creditor is able to avoid unperfected liens using state law such as UCC § 9–317(a).

(1) Agricultural Lien

If an agricultural lien is unperfected at the time of the bankruptcy filing, the bankruptcy trustee will be able to avoid the agricultural lien. UCC § 9–317(a)(2).

(2) Security Interest

With one exception, the bankruptcy trustee will be able to avoid a security interest if the secured party has not prior to the bankruptcy filing qualified for priority over a lien creditor under UCC § 9–317(a)(2). If the security interest is a purchase money security interest in the collateral, the secured party may be able to take advantage of UCC § 9–317(e) that permits the security interest to have priority over the rights of a lien creditor that arises after the debtor receives delivery of the collateral if the secured party files an effective financing statement covering the collateral within 20 days after the debtor receives delivery of the collateral. Review the discussion of the lien creditor as against security interest and agricultural lien priority rules in Section B, *supra*. In the case of a purchase money security interest, the secured party's filing of the financing statement after the bankruptcy filing, but within that 20-day time period, is not a violation of the automatic stay because of an exception to the stay which allows a financing statement to be filed in this circumstance. 11 U.S.C. §§ 362(b)(3), 546(b).

b. Statutory Liens

An agricultural lien is a statutory lien as defined in the bankruptcy code. 11 U.S.C. § 101(53). A bankruptcy trustee may avoid an agricultural lien if it was not perfected at the time the case was commenced and a hypothetical purchaser of the property that purchased the property as of bankruptcy filing could take priority over the agricultural lien. 11 U.S.C. § 545(2); UCC § 9–317(b), (c); Section F, *supra*. This rule will rarely come into play given the hypothetical lien creditor rule explained above as applied to agricultural liens.

c. Preferences

If a security interest or agricultural lien attaches to the debtor's property before the bankruptcy filing, in certain circumstances, that attachment of the security interest or agricultural lien may be avoidable as a preference. Payments to a secured party prior to the bankruptcy filing may also result in the payment being a preference. In analyzing a secured party's liability for a preference, the first question to ask is whether the transfer of the debtor's interest in property to the secured party meets all of the requirements to be a preference. If the answer to that question is yes, then determine whether one of the exceptions to preference liability prevents the trustee from avoiding the transfer of the interest in the property to the secured party.

(1) Requirements to Find a Preference

All of the following requirements must be met for the transfer to the secured party to be avoidable as a preference. 11 U.S.C. § 547(b).

(a) Transfer of an Interest in the Debtor's Property

A transfer is any voluntary or involuntary parting with an interest in property to another. 11 U.S.C. § 101(54). Thus attaching a security interest or agricultural lien to the debtor's property or making a payment to a secured party is a transfer of an interest in property. Notice that the transfer must be of an interest in the debtor's property. The debtor is the entity that has filed the bankruptcy petition. 11 U.S.C. § 101(13). A transfer of the debtor's interest in property is made when the transfer takes effect as between the transferor and transferee if the transfer is perfected within 30 days after that time. A transfer is perfected when a judicial lien creditor cannot obtain a superior interest in the property. If the transfer is not perfected within 30 days after the transfer takes effect between the transferor and the transferee, the transfer is made at the time it is perfected. If the transfer is not perfected at the time of the bankruptcy filing or within 30 days after the transfer takes effect between the transferor or transferee, the transfer is considered made at the time of the bankruptcy filing. 11 U.S.C. § 547(e). A transfer cannot take place until the debtor has rights in the property. 11 U.S.C. § 547(e)(3).

(b) Transfer To or for Benefit of a Creditor

The transfer of the debtor's interest in property must be to a creditor or for the benefit of a creditor. A secured party is a creditor. 11 U.S.C. § 101(10).

(c) Transfer On Account of Antecedent Debt

The transfer of the debtor's interest of property must be on account of a debt that was owed by the debtor at any time before the transfer was made.

(d) **Transfer Made While the Debtor Was Insolvent**

The transfer of the debtor's interest in property must be made while the debtor was insolvent. In most cases, insolvency is defined as liabilities greater than assets. 11 U.S.C. § 101(32). The debtor is presumed to be insolvent during the 90 days preceding the filing of the bankruptcy petition. 11 U.S.C. § 547(f).

(e) **Transfer Made Within the Specified Time Period**

The transfer of the debtor's interest in property must be made within a certain period of time prior to the bankruptcy filing. That time period is generally 90 days prior to the filing of the bankruptcy petition. If the transfer is made to or for the benefit of a creditor that is an insider, however, the time period is one year prior to the filing of the bankruptcy petition. An insider is defined in the Bankruptcy Code to include relatives of individual debtors and certain related entities of non-individual debtors such as corporations and partnerships. 11 U.S.C. § 101(31).

(f) **Transfer Enabled Creditor to Obtain More Than it Would in a Chapter 7 Case if the Transfer Had Not Been Made**

Finally, the transfer of the debtor's interest in property must enable the creditor to obtain more than it would obtain from a distribution of the debtor's assets in a Chapter 7 if the transfer had not taken place. Generally, attachment of security interests or agricultural liens will result in this requirement being fulfilled if the effect of the attachment is that the secured party has a secured claim in the bankruptcy proceeding rather than an unsecured claim. Generally, payments on the debt to a fully secured creditor will not result in preference liability as the creditor would receive full payment in the bankruptcy from the value of its collateral. Payments to an undersecured creditor could enable the undersecured creditor to obtain more value than it would obtain without the payment. Assuming that the bankruptcy does not result in 100% payment of all unsecured claims, an undersecured creditor being paid on its unsecured claim prior to the bankruptcy will have received a preference because the payment reduces the amount of the unsecured claim that will be allowed in the bankruptcy.

Example: On June 1, SP–1 obtained a signed security agreement granting SP–1 a security interest in Debtor's equipment then owned or thereafter acquired to secure any and all obligations that Debtor then owed or thereafter owed to SP–1. The same day SP–1 made a loan to Debtor. Forty days later, SP–1 filed an effective financing statement against Debtor listing equipment as the collateral. Debtor at all times owned several pieces of equipment. The transfer of the security interest in the equipment took effect between SP–1 and Debtor when the security interest attached on June 1. For purposes of preference analysis, the transfer of the security interest in the equipment took place when it was perfected by filing the financing statement and it was not within 30 days of June 1, when the transfer took effect between the transferor and transferee. The gap in time between June 1 and the filing of the effective financing statement also makes the transfer of the security interest "on account of antecedent debt" (the June 1 loan).

Example: On June 1, SP–1 obtained a signed security agreement granting SP–1 a security interest in Debtor's equipment then owned or thereafter acquired to secure any and all obligations that Debtor then owed or thereafter owed to SP–1. The same day SP–1 loaned money to Debtor. Eight days later, on June 9, SP–1 filed an effective financing statement against Debtor listing equipment as the collateral. Debtor at all times owned several pieces of equipment. The transfer of the security interest in the equipment took effect between SP–1 and Debtor when the security interest attached on June 1 and for purposes of preference analysis that is also the date on which the transfer is considered made because the security interest was perfected within 30 days of when the transfer took effect between SP–1 and Debtor. On June 15, Debtor acquired a new piece of equipment. Pursuant to the after-acquired property clause, a security interest in that new piece of equipment attached to secure the loan from

SP–1 to Debtor. The security interest was perfected when made so a transfer of Debtor's interest in property to SP–1 took place on June 15 when the security interest attached to the new piece of equipment. That transfer (attachment of the security interest to the new equipment) was on account of the antecedent debt incurred on June 1.

Example: SP–1 has an attached and perfected security interest in Debtor's equipment. The security interest secures a debt of $10,000 and the equipment has a value of $7,000. Within the 90 days before Debtor files bankruptcy, Debtor pays SP–1 $1,000. In the bankruptcy case, unsecured claims will be paid at the rate of 10 cents per dollar of claim. If SP–1 keeps the prepetition payment of $1,000, it will be paid on its $10,000 claim the following: $7,000 on account of the value of the equipment, $1,000 on account of the prepetition payment, and $200 on account of the 10% distribution on its remaining unsecured claim of $2,000. If SP–1 did not receive the $1,000 prepetition payment, the distribution to SP–1 in Debtor's bankruptcy would be the following: $7,000 on account of the value of the equipment and $300 on account of the 10% distribution on its remaining unsecured claim of $3,000. The prepetition payment of $1,000 is a preference.

(2) Exceptions to Preference Liability

Even if all of the requirements for preference liability are met, a creditor may attempt to prevent the bankruptcy trustee from avoiding the transfer of the debtor's property to or for the benefit of the creditor by attempting to bring the transaction within one of the exceptions to preference liability found in 11 U.S.C. § 547(c). The exceptions most relevant to an Article 9 secured party are detailed below.

(a) Contemporaneous Exchange for New Value Exception

If the transfer of the debtor's interest in property was intended by both the debtor and the creditor to be a contemporaneous exchange of the interest in property for new value given to the debtor and the exchange was indeed "substantially" contemporaneous, the transfer of the debtor's interest in property may not be avoided as a preference. 11 U.S.C. § 547(c)(1). In determining whether the transfer of the debtor's interest in property was contemporaneous with the giving of new value to the debtor, the timing of the transfer of the debtor's interest in property is determined by the timing rules in 11 U.S.C. § 547(e).

(b) Ordinary Course Payment Exception

If the transfer of the debtor's interest in property is a payment of a debt that was incurred in the ordinary course of business or financial affairs of the debtor and the transfer was either made (i) in the ordinary course of business or financial affairs of the debtor or (ii) made according to ordinary business terms, the transfer is not avoidable as a preference. 11 U.S.C. § 547(c)(2).

(c) Purchase Money Security Interest Exception

If the transfer of the debtor's interest in property is a purchase money security interest in collateral, the transfer is not avoidable as a preference if all of the following requirements are met. First, the security interest must secure new value the secured party gives to the debtor at or after the time a security agreement granting the security interest is signed. Second, the new value must enable the debtor to acquire the property. Third, the debtor must use the new value to acquire the property. Fourth, the security interest must be perfected on or before 30 days after the debtor receives possession of the collateral. 11 U.S.C. § 547(c)(3).

(d) New Value Exception

If the debtor makes a transfer of its interest in property to a creditor and subsequent to that transfer, the creditor gives new value to the debtor that is unsecured and did not result in the debtor making an unavoidable transfer of an interest in the debtor's property to the creditor, the previous transfer of the debtor's interest in property is not avoidable as a preference to the extent of the amount of the new value given subsequently. 11 U.S.C. § 547(c)(4).

(e) Security Interests in Inventory and Receivables Exception

If the transfer of the debtor's interest in property is the creation of a security interest in inventory and receivables, the transfer is not avoidable unless the secured party to whom the transfer is made improved its position because of the transfer. To determine whether the secured party improved its position, compare the secured party's unsecured position at a set date prior to the bankruptcy filing to the its unsecured position on the date of the filing of the bankruptcy petition. The way in which the secured party improves its position is by lessening the amount by which its debt is unsecured. That set date for the first date is either 90 days prior to the bankruptcy filing or, if the creditor is an insider, one year prior to the bankruptcy filing. If the first grant of value took place during the 90-day time period or the one-year time period (whichever is applicable), the date on which the first grant of value took place is the comparative date. 11 U.S.C. § 547(c)(5). This exception to preference liability only protects transfers of the security interests. It does not protect payments to the secured party.

(f) Statutory Lien Exception

If the statutory lien is not avoidable under 11 U.S.C. § 545, the creation of the statutory lien during the prebankruptcy preference period (90 days or, if an insider, one year) is not avoidable as a preference. 11 U.S.C. § 547(c)(6).

(g) Small Value Transfer Exceptions

If the debtor is an individual debtor who has primarily consumer debts, transfers of the debtor's interest in property that are less than $600 in value are not avoidable as a preference. 11 U.S.C. § 547(c)(8). If a debtor does not have primarily consumer debts, transfers of the debtor's interest in property that are less than $5,850 in value are not avoidable as a preference. 11 U.S.C. § 547(c)(9).

d. Fraudulent Transfers

In Chapter I, the concept of transfers of property as fraudulent transfers was briefly discussed. In addition to the Uniform Fraudulent Transfers Act (UFTA) (which the bankruptcy trustee can use pursuant to 11 U.S.C. § 544(b) if there is a creditor of the debtor that would have a cause of action under that statute), the Bankruptcy Code has its own incarnation of fraudulent transfer law in 11 U.S.C. § 548. That statute applies to transfers of the debtor's interest in property during the two-year period prior to the filing of the bankruptcy petition. Like the UFTA, the bankruptcy fraudulent transfer provision in the Bankruptcy Code also focuses on actual intent to hinder or delay creditors (actual fraud) or constructive fraud that is presumed when the transfer is for less than reasonably equivalent value and made while the enterprise was undercapitalized, the debtor was unable to pay debts when they came due, or the debtor was insolvent or rendered insolvent. The Bankruptcy Code also treats transfers not in the ordinary course of business and for less than reasonably equivalent value under an employment contract as an additional subcategory of fraudulent transfer. Unlike the UFTA, the Bankruptcy Code fraudulent transfer law gives the good faith transferee of the property a lien on the property to secure any value that the transferee gave the debtor for the transfer. 11 U.S.C. § 548(c).

4. Effect of Transfer Avoidance

The usual effect of avoiding a security interest or agricultural lien is that the secured party will no longer be considered to have a secured claim in the bankruptcy proceeding because the trustee recovers the property transferred (i.e. effectively nullifying the grant of the security interest or the agricultural lien). 11 U.S.C. § 550(a). The secured party will still be able to make an unsecured claim in the bankruptcy for the amount of the debt that is owed according to the claims allowance procedure. 11 U.S.C. §§ 501, 502. The avoided security interest or agricultural lien is preserved for the benefit of the estate. 11 U.S.C. § 551. What this means is that the trustee is able to assert the priority position of the avoided security interest or lien for the benefit of the estate. The bankruptcy trustee may also recover the value of the transferred property from the initial transferee or a subsequent transferee from the initial transferee. 11 U.S.C. § 550(a). The trustee is entitled to only a single satisfaction so that if the transfer is avoidable and the trustee recovers the property transferred, the trustee may not then, in addition, recover the property's value from the transferee. 11 U.S.C. § 550(d).

Example: SP–1 has a first priority properly perfected security interest in Debtor's equipment worth $50,000 to secure a debt of $30,000. The security interest was granted to SP–1 during the 90 days prior to

Debtor's bankruptcy and was to secure a debt that was incurred a year before Debtor's bankruptcy. SP–1's security interest is avoidable as a preference. Assume SP–2 has a properly perfected *second* priority security interest in the same equipment to secure a debt of $25,000 and its security interest is not avoidable as a preference as it was not given to the secured party on account of antecedent debt. When the bankruptcy trustee avoids SP–1's security interest as a preference, the bankruptcy estate is able to step into SP–1's priority position and take the first $30,000 in value for the benefit of the estate, leaving SP–2 in its second priority position. In effect, this prevents SP–2 from moving up to first priority position on the equipment even though SP–1's first priority security interest was avoided.

a. Protection of Transferees

A subsequent transferee from the initial transferee is protected from having to return the transfer or the value of the transfer to the bankruptcy estate if that subsequent transferee takes the transfer in good faith, for value, and without knowledge of the voidable nature of the transfer to the initial transferee. 11 U.S.C. § 550(b). A good faith transferee (either an initial transferee or a subsequent transferee) that has made improvements on property recovered may have a lien on the property to secure the lesser of the net cost of the improvement or the increase in property value due to the improvement. 11 U.S.C. § 550(e).

b. Recovering From the Person Benefitted

The trustee may also recover the value of the avoided transfer from the person benefitted instead of the person to whom the transfer was made. 11 U.S.C. § 550(a). However, if the person benefitted by a transfer is an insider, the transfer was made during the one-year period prior to bankruptcy but not within the 90 days prior to bankruptcy, and the transfer is an avoidable preference, the trustee may not recover from a noninsider transferee. 11 U.S.C. §§ 550(c), 547(i).

Example: SP–1 has a first priority properly perfected security interest in Debtor's equipment to secure a debt of $30,000. The equipment has a value of $50,000. The transfer of the security interest is not avoidable on any grounds. SP–2 has a properly perfected second priority security interest in the same equipment to secure a debt of $25,000 and its security interest is not avoidable on any grounds. In the 90 days prior to filing bankruptcy, Debtor makes a payment to SP–1 of $4,000, thus reducing the debt owed to SP–1 to $26,000. The payment to SP–1 benefits SP–2 by making SP–2 fully secured instead of partially unsecured and thus is avoidable as a preference as it enables SP–2 to obtain more than it otherwise would in a Chapter 7 without the payment. The trustee could seek to recover the value of the payment from SP–2, the person benefitted. The trustee could also seek to recover the payment from SP–1, the transferee.

Example: SP–1 has a first priority properly perfected security interest in Debtor's equipment to secure a debt of $30,000. The equipment has a value of $10,000. Debtor's president guaranteed the debt. Nine months prior to Debtor's bankruptcy filing, Debtor paid off the loan. That payoff benefitted Debtor's president because it released her from the guarantee. The president is an insider. The payoff is a preference because it enabled the president to recover more than it would have in Debtor's Chapter 7. In Debtor's Chapter 7, the president would have an unsecured claim for $20,000 (the amount of the debt minus the value of the collateral) against Debtor based upon suretyship law. Trustee may not recover the transfer from SP–1 because of 11 U.S.C. § 550(c) and § 547(i).

5. Equitable Subordination

A secured party must be sensitive to equitable considerations a court may invoke to subordinate its otherwise perfected security interest or agricultural lien. 11 U.S.C. § 510. Grounds for equitable subordination include exercising too much influence and control over the affairs of the debtor that result in an unfair detriment to the debtor's other creditors. Exactly where that line is between acceptable conduct and unacceptable conduct for a secured party is somewhat uncertain. See the discussion in Andrew DeNatale and Prudence B. Abram, The Doctrine of Equitable Subrogation as Applied to Nonmanagement Creditors, 40 Bus. Law. 417 (1985).

K. Review Questions for Chapter V

Question 1

On January 4, Evergreen Landscaping and Design, Inc. signed a security agreement with First Bank granting First Bank a security interest in all of Evergreen's inventory and equipment then owned or thereafter acquired to secure all obligations then owed or thereafter owed to First Bank. That same day First Bank lent Evergreen $100,000 and properly perfected its security interest in inventory and equipment by filing a financing statement in the correct place.

On January 5, Blue Spruce Tree Farm, Inc. granted a security interest in its inventory then owned or thereafter acquired to Commercial Finance to secure any obligations then owed or thereafter owed to Commercial Finance. That same day, Commercial Finance lent Blue Spruce $200,000. Commercial Finance properly perfected its security interest in the inventory through a properly filed financing statement on January 5.

On April 1, Evergreen agreed to purchase potted tree seedlings from Blue Spruce Tree Farm, Inc. for delivery on May 1. The seedlings were for sale to customers for whom Evergreen was doing landscaping. On April 20, Blue Spruce started to dig up the tree seedlings and pot them. On April 24, Evergreen defaulted on a payment to First Bank under the loan agreement.

A. On April 25, before any seedlings are delivered to Evergreen, who would have priority in the seedlings as between Commercial Finance and First Bank?

B. Assume that Evergreen gave Blue Spruce a check on May 1 when the seedlings were delivered to pay for the seedlings and the check was dishonored for insufficient funds on May 5. Blue Spruce is asserting that it has a right to get the seedlings back and First Bank is contending that it has a right to the seedlings that is superior to Blue Spruce's claim to the seedlings. Who has priority in the seedlings as between Commercial Finance, First Bank, and Blue Spruce?

Question 2

Secured Party wants to take a security interest in fixtures of the debtor. The fixtures are not a manufactured home. What should Secured Party do to ensure that it will have priority in the fixtures over all other parties, including other secured parties and persons with interests in the real estate where the fixtures are located?

Question 3

Road graders are not subject to any certificate of title law. Larry leased a new road grader to Darla for 10 years for $250,000. Darla cannot terminate the obligation to pay the lease price by returning the goods to Larry. Larry did not file a financing statement or a copy of the lease in the secretary of state's office where Darla is located.

Road graders typically last about 8 to 12 years before they wear out and need replacing. Darla could have purchased a new road grader of the same type for approximately $200,000. Darla runs a construction company as a sole proprietor and uses the leased road grader for use in her construction jobs.

Darla obtained a loan from State Bank and State Bank attached a security interest in Darla's "equipment then owned or thereafter acquired" to secure the obligation. State Bank perfected its security interest by filing a proper financing statement against Darla in the state of Darla's residence.

Darla defaulted on her lease payments to Larry and Larry instructed Darla to return the road grader to Larry. Darla also stopped paying State Bank on the loan. State Bank asserted that it has a security interest in the road grader that is superior to Larry's interest in the road grader. Is State Bank correct?

Question 4

Autoworld, Inc, is a Minnesota corporation in the business of selling automobiles. State Bank, located in Wisconsin, finances Autoworld's inventory acquisitions from the manufacturer. Autoworld's president signed a security agreement granting a security interest in "all of Autoworld's inventory then owned or thereafter acquired to secure all obligations now or hereafter owed to State Bank." State Bank filed a financing statement in the Minnesota Secretary of State's office on June 1, naming Autoworld, Inc. as the debtor, State Bank as secured party, and the collateral as "inventory." Autoworld owes State Bank $100,000.

On July 1, Daniel Boone granted First Bank a security interest in "all of the debtor's goods now owned or hereafter acquired to secure any and all obligations owed to First Bank now or in the future." First Bank filed a financing statement in the Wisconsin Secretary of State's office listing the debtor as Daniel Boone, First Bank as the secured party, and the collateral as "goods." Daniel Boone lives in Wisconsin.

On July 15, First Bank lent Daniel Boone $100,000. Daniel used $20,000 of the money as a down payment on a Chevy SUV and Autoworld, Inc., the dealer that sold the SUV from its inventory to Daniel, granted credit to Daniel for $12,000 to make up the total purchase price of $32,000. In the purchase agreement between Autoworld and Daniel, Autoworld retained title to the SUV until the $12,000 plus interest was paid. On July 30, Autoworld applied for its interest to be noted on the SUV certificate of title and on August 15, the certificate of title for the SUV was issued, listing Autoworld as the secured party.

On September 30, Daniel sold the SUV to his next door neighbor, Ted Williams for $25,000 to be paid in one month. Daniel Boone signed the certificate of title and gave it to Ted.

What is the priority of interests in the SUV?

Question 5

On January 4, Computer Systems, Inc. granted a mortgage to Real Estate Moguls, Inc. to secure a loan to acquire a building that Computer Systems uses for its only retail store in Story County, Iowa. Real Estate Moguls properly recorded the mortgage on January 5 in the real estate records in Story County, Iowa.

On March 1, Computer Systems' president signed a security agreement, on behalf of Computer Systems, Inc., granting a security interest in all inventory, equipment, chattel paper, instruments, investment property, deposit accounts, and accounts then owned or thereafter acquired to secure all obligations then owed or thereafter owed to National Bank. Computer Systems, Inc. Is a Minnesota corporation. On March 2, National Bank filed a financing statement in the Secretary of State's office in Minnesota listing Computer Systems, Inc. as the debtor and the collateral as inventory, equipment, chattel paper, instruments, investment property, deposit accounts and accounts. National Bank was listed as the secured party.

On March 3, Intelligent Gamer, another creditor of Computer Systems, Inc. levied on all the property the sheriff found in Computer Systems' retail store in Iowa. The levy was in support of a judgment for $50,000.

On March 5, National Bank made a loan of $100,000 to Computer Systems, Inc.

On March 6, the IRS filed a notice of tax lien against Computer Systems, Inc. in the correct places for $10,000 in taxes that were assessed on January 6.

On March 28, Computer Systems purchased on credit several printers from Printer's Inc. Printer's Inc. retained title to the printers and sent written notice to National Bank of Printer's Inc. interest in the printers. National Bank received the notice on March 29. The printers were delivered to Computer Systems' retail store on March 30.

On March 30, Computer Systems sold several computers to ABC Industries, which signed a security agreement agreeing to pay the purchase price of $8,000 and granting Computer Systems a security interest in the computers sold to it to secure the price owed.

On April 1, Computer Systems sold the ABC Industries' contract to Second Wind Finance for $5,000. Second Wind Finance took possession of the contract.

On May 1, National Bank made another loan to Computer Systems in the amount of $5,000 when it knew about the execution levy.

It is May 2. What is the priority of interests in the following property of Computer Systems, Inc.?

A. Assorted pre-packaged software on CDs held for sale in Computer Systems' retail store, approximate value of $30,000. These CDs were in the store on March 3 and have not yet been sold.

B. Cash registers, desks, and chairs in Computer Systems' retail store used by the employees, approximate value $15,000. These items were in the store on March 3 as well. Under both Iowa and Minnesota law, these items are not fixtures.

C. Printers acquired on March 30 from Printer's Inc., approximate value $20,000.

D. Built in cupboards and a generator located in Computer Systems' retail store, used to run a network for Computer Systems' customers, approximate value $5,000. Under both Minnesota and Iowa law, these items are considered fixtures.

E. A checking account held at State Bank, located in Story County, Iowa. On March 6, it contained $10,000 and on May 2, it contained $2,000. Computer Systems deposits its daily receipts from the retail store into this account.

F. A $3,000 funds transfer on April 2, from the checking account held at State Bank to the Excellent Utility Company, in payment of Computer Systems' retail store utility bill.

G. The ABC Industries' contract, approximate value $4,000.

H. The computers purchased by ABC Industries, approximate value $8,000.

I. Accounts receivable from items Computer Systems sold from its retail store, on credit, to various buyers (other than ABC Industries) from March 1 to May 1, approximate value $6,000.

J. A brokerage account of Computer Systems held by Churn, Churn, and Churn Brokerage. All securities in the account were purchased on March 5, paid for by a loan from Brokerage to Computer Systems. The brokerage agreement provides that Brokerage has a security interest in all securities held in the account to secure any amounts owed to Brokerage. The amount owed to Brokerage is approximately $7,000. The value of the securities held in the account is currently $10,000.

VI

Enforcement of a Security Interest or Agricultural Lien

In this Chapter, we will explore the process for enforcement of security interests or agricultural liens. Enforcement refers to the concept of realizing value from the collateral to apply against the debt that the obligor owes to the secured party. The process the secured party may use to realize the value of the collateral is set forth in Article 9. This process is a nonjudicial process, that is, it is conducted without court supervision and the secured party need not obtain a court order to engage in the process. The enforcement process is set forth in Part 6 of Article 9. Failure to comply with this process as set forth in Article 9 may result in the secured party being liable to the debtor, a secondary obligor, or any other person harmed by that failure. Liability for violating the provisions of Article 9 is discussed in Chapter VII.

A. General Principles of Enforcement

Before delving into the details of the enforcement process, some discussion of general principles will help put the enforcement provisions in context.

1. Relationship to Scope of Article 9

The enforcement provisions of Article 9 only apply to the enforcement of a security interest or agricultural lien that is within the scope of Article 9. If the transaction that creates a right in a person's property is not covered by Article 9, the rules of Part 6 of Article 9 do not apply to enforcement of the lien. Because of the comprehensive nature of the enforcement provisions, states may, as a matter of nonuniform state statutes, provide that enforcement of liens not covered by Article 9 will be governed by the provisions of Article 9 regarding enforcement.

2. Relationship to Attachment of Security Interest and Agricultural Lien

In order to enforce a security interest or agricultural lien against collateral, the security interest or agricultural lien must have attached to the collateral. If the security interest or agricultural lien is not attached to the collateral at the time that the secured party is seeking to enforce the security interest or agricultural lien, the secured party will not have a right to enforce the security interest or agricultural lien against the collateral. Thus the rules on attachment (Chapter III) and on when certain transferees take free of a security interest or agricultural lien (Chapter V, Section F) are relevant to determining the secured party's rights at the time of enforcement.

3. Relationship to Perfection and Priority

Perfection of the security interest or agricultural lien is **not** required in order to enforce the security interest or agricultural lien in the collateral. Having first priority in the collateral is **not** required in order to enforce the security interest or agricultural lien in the collateral. Perfection and its effect on priority of interests in collateral, however, may have an effect on the rights of the transferee of tangible collateral and may have an effect on the rights of a secured party as it collects on obligations owed to the debtor. Those effects will be explored in this Chapter.

4. Cumulative Rights and Variation by Agreement

The secured party has the right to enforce its security interest or agricultural lien as provided in the agreement of the parties and as provided in Part 6 of Article 9. The debtor and the obligor have the rights after default as provided in the agreement of the parties and as provided in Part 6 of Article 9. All of these rights are cumulative. UCC § 9–601(c), (d). Even though the agreement of the parties may speak to the rights and duties of the secured party, debtor, and obligor regarding enforcement of the security interest or agricultural lien, Article 9 restricts the ability of the parties to alter some of the provisions of Article 9 regarding that enforcement. UCC § 9–602. As the rights and duties are explored in this Chapter, whether that right or duty may be varied or defined by the parties' agreement will be noted.

5. Judicial Enforcement

Even though Part 6 of Article 9 describes a nonjudicial enforcement process, it does not preclude the secured party from engaging in a judicial enforcement process. UCC § 9–601(a). Thus a secured party may sue the obligor on the debt and sue the debtor to foreclose on the security interest or agricultural lien pursuant to a process that a court decrees. If the secured party obtains a judgment against the obligor on the debt and then pursuant to that judgment levies on the collateral that is subject to the secured party's security interest or agricultural lien that secures that debt, the lien arising out of the judgment enforcement process (review Chapter I) has priority dating from the earlier of the three following dates: (i) the date of perfection of the security interest or agricultural lien; (ii) the date the financing statement covering the collateral was filed; or (iii) the date the agricultural lien statute specifies. UCC § 9–601(e). If the secured party sells the collateral pursuant to an execution sale after obtaining a judgment and a levy and the secured party purchases at the sale, the secured party holds the collateral without the need to comply with any requirements of Article 9. UCC § 9–601(f).

6. Consignments and Sales of Accounts, Chattel Paper, Payment Intangibles, and Promissory Notes

With one exception detailed in Section D, *infra*, a secured party that has a security interest that is created by a true consignment, UCC § 9–102(a)(20), or by a sale of accounts, chattel paper, payment intangibles, or promissory notes is not subject to the duties imposed in Part 6 of Article 9. UCC § 9–601(g).

7. Default

Typically, to enforce a security interest that secures payment or performance of an obligation or an agricultural lien, the debtor or obligor must be in default of its obligations to the secured party. Thus the general rule is that upon default, the secured party has the rights provided in Article 9 and in the parties' agreement to enforce its security interest or agricultural lien by the process described in Part 6 of Article 9 or by judicial process. UCC § 9–601(a).

a. Defined for Security Interests

Default in the case of a security interest is not defined in Article 9. Thus in order to determine if there is a default in the case of a security interest, the parties' agreement, usually the security agreement or other lending documents, must be consulted. Typical default clauses include the following events as a default: failure to make payment when payment is due, change in management or organizational structure of the debtor, disposing of collateral without the secured party's permission, failure to remit proceeds of collateral disposition, and failure to maintain insurance on collateral. Typical default clauses focus on the risks to repayment and the risks to collateral value.

b. Defined for Agricultural Liens

Agricultural liens arise by virtue of statutes other than Article 9 and thus the parties will not have defined default through their agreement. Default for purposes of enforcing an agricultural lien is thus defined as the time when the secured party is entitled to enforce the agricultural lien as specified in the statute creating the agricultural lien. UCC § 9–606.

c. Acceleration and Cure

An acceleration clause is a term in an agreement that allows the creditor in a circumstance where the debt is not already payable on demand to accelerate the entire obligation to be due immediately upon the happening of some event.

(1) Acceleration on Incident of Default
Security agreements or lending documents will generally contain an acceleration clause in which an incident of default will result in accelerating the obligation to pay the entire debt.

(2) Acceleration Upon Insecurity of Secured Party

An acceleration clause may provide that the secured party may accelerate the debt obligation in the event the secured party deems itself insecure in its confidence that the debt will be repaid. In this instance, the acceleration of the obligation owed must be exercised in a good faith belief that the prospect of payment or performance is impaired. The debtor or obligor has the burden to prove that the secured party failed to act in good faith. UCC § 1–309.

(3) Reinstatement and Cure

Once the obligation to pay the debt is accelerated, whether the obliogor may reinstate the original due dates for payment of the debt by curing the default depends on the terms of the security agreement or other agreements between the parties. In some states, by law other than Article 9, the obligor's cure of the default may result in a reinstatement of the original payment schedule.

Example: Debtor owes the SP–1 a $10,000 obligation payable in equal monthly installments over the course of a year at 5% per year interest. The debt is secured by a security interest in Debtor's automobile. The security agreement contains a clause that provides: "Debtor's failure to pay pursuant to the payment schedule is a default. Upon default, all amounts due under this agreement are immediately due and payable." The first sentence of the clause is a definition of default. The second sentence is an acceleration clause keyed to the default. Debtor missed one payment and SP–1 demanded payment of the entire principal amount and accrued interest. Whether Debtor may reinstate the original payment terms by paying the one past due payment depends upon whether the security agreement or law other than Article 9 provides for cure of the default and reinstatement of the original installment payment schedule.

d. Buyers of Accounts, Chattel Paper, Promissory Notes, and Payment Intangibles

Buyers of accounts, chattel paper, promissory notes, and payment intangibles are deemed to be secured parties under Article 9, but they are actually the owners of the asset. In that case, the right to collect on the obligations owed by the account debtors and other parties obligated on these assets is not keyed to the idea of default. As an owner of the asset, the owner has the right to collect that asset once the sale of the asset to the buyer/secured party is completed. See UCC § 9–607(a).

8. Deficiency and Surplus

After the value of the collateral is realized and applied to the obligation owed to the secured party, one of three situations will exist. First, the obligation will be fully satisfied and there will be value left over, called a surplus. Second, the obligation will not be fully satisfied and the obligor will owe the remaining amount of the obligation, called the deficiency. Third, the obligation will be fully satisfied and there will be neither a surplus or a deficiency. If the transaction is not a sale of accounts, chattel paper, promissory notes, or payment intangibles, the obligor is liable to the secured party for any deficiency and the secured party is liable to the debtor for any surplus. UCC §§ 9–608(a)(4), (b), 9–615(d), (e). If the transaction is a sale of accounts, chattel paper, promissory notes, or payment intangibles, the obligor is not liable for any deficiency and the secured party is not liable for the surplus. UCC §§ 9–608(b), 9–615(e).

9. Secured Party in Possession or Control of Collateral

If the secured party is in possession or control of the collateral, the secured party has the rights and obligations provided in UCC § 9–207 regarding that collateral. UCC § 9–601(b). Review Chapter III, Section H.

10. Duties of Secured Party to Debtor, Obligor, Other Secured Party, and Lienholder

Part 6 of Article 9 on enforcement of security interests or agricultural liens imposes duties on the secured party in regard to debtors and obligors, including secondary obligors. A secured party will not owe duties to a debtor or obligor unless the secured party knows (i) that the person is a debtor or obligor with respect to the collateral or obligation, (ii) the identify of that person, and (iii) how to communicate with that person. UCC § 9–605(1). The secured party enforcing its security interest or agricultural lien will also owe duties to other secured parties and lienholders with rights in the collateral. The secured party enforcing its security interest or agricultural lien will not owe a duty to another secured party or lienholder that has filed a financing statement against the debtor unless the secured party knows that the person is a debtor in relation to the collateral at issue and the identity of that person. UCC § 9–605(2).

B. Real Estate Related Collateral

Because the rules regarding enforcement of liens against real estate are different than the rules in Article 9 for enforcing security interests and agricultural liens against personal property, Article 9 contains several provisions addressing real estate related issues.

1. Obligation Secured by Both Personal Property and Real Estate

If the obligation owed to the secured party is secured by both real and personal property, the secured party may enforce its rights as against the personal property only without prejudicing its right to enforce the obligation against the real estate collateral. UCC § 9–604(a)(1). Whether enforcement against the real estate prejudices rights against the personal property is determined by the rules regarding enforcement against real estate. UCC § 9–604, cmt. 2. The secured party may enforce its rights against the personal property and the real property by using the rules regarding real property foreclosure. In that circumstance, the secured party will not have to comply with the rules of Part 6 of Article 9 on enforcement of the security interest or agricultural lien. UCC § 9–604(a)(2).

2. Obligation Secured by Fixtures

If the obligation is secured by fixtures, the secured party may enforce its security interest in the fixtures pursuant to the provisions of Part 6 of Article 9 or may elect to use the rules regarding enforcement of liens against real property. UCC § 9–604(b).

a. Ability to Remove the Fixtures From the Real Estate

Only if the secured party has priority in the fixtures over the rights of all of the owners and encumbrancers of the real estate may the secured party remove the fixtures from the real property after the obligor's default. UCC § 9–604(c). Review Chapter V, Section E on priority in fixtures.

b. Liability for Physical Harm Caused by Removal

If the secured party removes the fixtures from the real property, the secured party has an obligation to reimburse the owner or encumbrancer for the repair of any physical injury to the real property but not for the reduction in value of the real property caused by the removal of the fixtures. An owner or encumbrancer entitled to this reimbursement may refuse permission to remove the fixture until the secured party gives adequate assurance of reimbursement. UCC § 9–604(d).

3. Rights to Payment Secured by a Mortgage in Real Estate

If a right to payment is secured by a mortgage, deed of trust, or other lien in real estate, the process for enforcing the real estate lien is determined by law other than Article 9. See UCC § 9–607(a), (e), and cmt. 6.

C. Disposition or Retention of Collateral

When the collateral is tangible assets that can be sold to generate value, the secured party generally obtains possession of the collateral in order to commence the disposition process. Once the secured party obtains possession or control of the collateral, Article 9 prescribes either a disposition process or a retention process for realizing value from the collateral to apply to the debt obligation.

1. Obtaining Possession of Tangible Collateral

Upon default, the secured party has the right to obtain possession of the tangible collateral and, in addition, the right to render equipment unusable, if the secured party does not remove the equipment from the debtor's premises. UCC § 9–609(a). To obtain possession of the tangible collateral, the secured party has two choices, judicial process or self help repossession.

a. Judicial Process

The secured party may use judicial process. Law other than Article 9 governs this judicial process. In effect, the secured party obtains a court order that requires the debtor to turn the collateral over to the secured party. That court order, as with all court orders, is enforceable using the contempt power of the court. Law other than Article 9 governs this judicial process for obtaining possession.

b. Self Help Repossession

The secured party may proceed without a court order to obtain possession of the collateral or render equipment unusable and dispose of the equipment at the debtor's premises if the secured party is able to do so without a breach of the peace. UCC § 9–609(b).

(1) Breach of the Peace

Breach of the peace is not defined in Article 9 but has been explored in a variety of circumstances by the courts. The concern is that the repossession process should not result in violence or the risk of violence. Generally the debtor's or a third party's protest of the repossession while the repossession is being attempted will be enough to render the resulting actions of the secured party a breach of the peace if the secured party persists in repossessing. The secured party is also not empowered to engage in behavior such as breaking into the debtor's house or other enclosures or to enlist law enforcement officers in deceiving the debtor that the repossession is taking place pursuant to court orders. The secured party is responsible for the behavior of third parties it hires to repossess the collateral. UCC § 9–609, cmt. 3.

(2) Assembly of Collateral

Based upon the agreement of the parties, or upon default, the secured party may require the debtor to assemble the collateral and make it available to the secured party at a place reasonably convenient to the parties. UCC § 9–609(c).

(3) Inability to Vary by Agreement

The obligation of the secured party to take possession without breach of the peace cannot be varied by the agreement of the parties. UCC § 9–602(6). The secured party may not obtain an agreement of the debtor or obligor about the standard of behavior that will be deemed to not breach the peace. UCC § 9–603. The secured party and the debtor may agree to standards that will govern assembly of the collateral or disabling the equipment and disposing of it without removing it from the debtor's premises as long as those standards are not manifestly unreasonable and do not attempt to define what is or is not a breach of the peace. UCC §§ 9–603, 9–609, cmt. 8.

c. Priority and Relationship to the Right to Obtain Possession

Even though a secured party may not have first priority in the collateral, the secured party still has the right to take possession of the tangible collateral upon a default. Generally, a secured party with a lower priority interest in the collateral must give up possession of the collateral to a secured party with a senior priority position if the senior secured party so demands. Failure of the junior secured party to do so may result in liability of the junior secured party to the senior secured party for the tort of conversion. UCC § 9–609, cmt. 5.

2. Disposition Process

After default, the secured party is able to sell, lease, license or otherwise dispose of the collateral. The secured party may dispose of the collateral in its current condition or may prepare the collateral for disposition in any commercially reasonable manner. UCC § 9–610(a). This disposition process may be used for all collateral, not just tangible collateral that can be repossessed.

a. Commercial Reasonableness

Every aspect of the disposition must be commercially reasonable, including the method, manner, time, place, and terms of the disposition. UCC § 9–610(b). The timing of the disposition, that is, how long the secured party waits to dispose of the collateral after repossession of the collateral must also be commercially reasonable. UCC § 9–610, cmt. 3. The secured party's decision whether to engage in any preparation of the collateral for disposition must also be commercially reasonable. UCC § 9–610, cmt. 4. A disposition may be conducted over the Internet if that is commercially reasonable. UCC § 9–610, cmt. 2.

(1) Public or Private Disposition

The disposition of the collateral may be by a public disposition, such as an auction, or a private disposition, such as a private agreement between the secured party and the transferee. UCC § 9–610(b). A public disposition is one in which members of the public have a meaningful opportunity for competitive bidding after reasonable advertising. UCC § 9–610, cmt. 7. The choice between a public or a private disposition must be commercially reasonable. In many circumstances, a private disposition will bring a better price for the collateral. UCC § 9–610, cmt. 2.

(2) Price Obtained and Commercial Reasonableness

The fact that a better price may have been obtained if the secured party had conducted the disposition in another manner does not mean the secured party's disposition of the collateral was commercially unreasonable. UCC § 9–627(a). A low price obtained in a disposition generally means a court should scrutinize the disposition carefully to determine that each aspect of the disposition was conducted in a commercially reasonable manner. UCC § 9–627, cmt. 2.

(3) Per se Commercially Reasonable Dispositions

Article 9 deems the following dispositions per se commercially reasonable: (i) disposing of collateral in the usual manner or the current price in a recognized market (meaning a market where there is standardized prices for property that is essentially fungible, UCC § 9–627, cmt. 4); (ii) disposing of collateral in compliance with reasonable commercial practices of dealers of the type of collateral; or (iii) a disposition that has been approved by a court, a creditor's committee, an assignee for the benefit of creditors, or a representative of creditors. UCC § 9–627(b), (c). Failure to obtain the approval specified in alternative (iii) does not mean the disposition is commercially unreasonable. UCC § 9–627(d).

(4) Variation by Agreement

The debtor or obligor may not waive the obligation to dispose of collateral in a commercially reasonable manner. UCC § 9–602(7). The secured party may obtain the debtor's and obligor's agreement to standards that govern the determination of commercial reasonableness as long as those standards are not manifestly unreasonable. UCC § 9–603(a).

b. Notice of the Disposition

Prior to the disposition, the secured party must give a reasonable and authenticated notice of the disposition. UCC § 9–611(b). The content, the manner, and the time of the notice must all be reasonable. UCC § 9–611, cmt. 2. The requirement to give this notice does not apply if the collateral is perishable, threatens to decline in value quickly, or is of a type ordinarily sold in a recognized market. UCC § 9–611(d). Law other than Article 9 may require additional notifications prior to a disposition. UCC § 9–611, cmt. 10. The requirements set forth below only apply to the notice required under Article 9.

(1) Sending Notice

The secured party is required to send the notice in a manner that is reasonably calculated to arrive at the recipient's destination but is not required to ensure that the recipient actually receives it. UCC § 9–102(a)(75).

(2) The Time of Giving the Notice

The notice must be sent after default and a reasonable amount of time before the disposition. The reasonableness of the timing of the notice is a question of fact. If the notice is sent so close to the time that the disposition is scheduled to take place that a reasonable person could not act on the notification, the time of the notice will be unreasonable. UCC § 9–612, cmt. 2. In transactions other than consumer transactions, a notice of disposition sent after default and at least ten days before disposition is sent within a reasonable time. UCC § 9–612.

(3) Waiver of the Right to Notice

The right to notice of the disposition cannot be waived by the debtor and any obligor prior to a default, UCC § 9–602(7), but the debtor and a secondary obligor may waive the right to notice in an agreement that is entered into and authenticated after default. UCC § 9–624(a).

(4) To Whom the Notice Must Be Given

Article 9 specifies what parties must be sent the notice of disposition.

(a) Notice to Debtor and Secondary Obligor

The notice must be sent to the debtor and any secondary obligor, unless they have entered into and authenticated an agreement after default waiving the right to notice. UCC §§ 9–611(c)(1), (2), 9–624(a). Notice need not be given to a primary obligor that is not the debtor. UCC § 9–611, cmt. 3.

> *Example:* SP–1 has a security interest in all of A's equipment to secure a debt that B incurred to SP–1. C has guaranteed the debt that B owes to SP–1. Neither B or C has a property interest in the equipment and A has no liability for the debt. When SP–1 seeks to sell the equipment after B's default on the debt, SP–1 must send notice of the disposition to A, the debtor, and to C, the secondary obligor, not to B, the primary obligor.

(b) Notice to Parties Requesting Notice

If the collateral is not consumer goods, the secured party that is conducting the disposition must send the notice to any party from whom the secured party has received an authenticated request for notice as long as two conditions are true. First, the party that gave the request for notice to the secured party must assert an interest in the collateral. Second, the request for notice must be received prior to the date the secured party sent out the notice of disposition to the debtor and secondary obligor or the date the debtor and any secondary obligor waived the right to notice. UCC § 9–611(c)(3).

(c) **Notice to Other Secured Parties and Lienholders**

If the collateral is not consumer goods, the secured party that is conducting the disposition must send the notice to other secured parties and lienholders that have filed financing statements to perfect their security interests or liens.

(i) **Determining the Office in Which to Search for Filings**

To determine the proper filing office to search for those filed financing statements, the secured party must search in the filing office which was the correct place to file against the debtor regarding that collateral as determined by the applicable choice of law rules as of 10 days before the secured party sent the notice to the debtor and secondary obligor or the date the debtor and secondary obligor waived the right to notice. Thus, the secured party conducting the disposition need not determine if there was a filed financing statement in a different filing office, at an earlier point in time. The secured party also need not search under names that the debtor may have previously had. UCC § 9–611, cmt. 4. The secured party must send the notice of disposition to those secured parties or lienholders so identified after this search. UCC § 9–611(c)(3).

(ii) **Response to Search Request**

In order to send the notice to the secured parties and lienholders that have filed financing statements, the secured party conducting the disposition must obtain a response from the filing office regarding the filings that are on record as to the debtor and the collateral. Because of delays by filing offices in responding to search requests, Article 9 provides that a secured party has satisfied this notice requirement if it requests a search for financing statements indexed under the debtor's name not more than 30 days nor less than 20 days before the secured party sends the notice to the debtor and secondary obligor (or the debtor and secondary obligor waived the notice) and the secured party did not receive the response to the search request before that notice date. The secured party conducting the disposition is also deemed to satisfy this notice requirement if it sends the notice to all parties identified on the filing office's response to the search request. UCC § 9–611(e).

(d) **Notice to Secured Parties That Have Perfected Their Security Interests by Compliance With Law Other Than Article 9**
The secured party conducting the disposition must give notice to any other secured party that has perfected its security interest in the collateral through compliance with a statute or treaty specified in UCC § 9–311(a). UCC § 9–611(c)(3)(C). There is no safe harbor for a secured party conducting the disposition when it is unable to get information from the filing office or system described in that other law.

(5) **Content of the Notice: Nonconsumer Goods Transaction**
In a nonconsumer goods transaction, the notification of the disposition must describe the debtor, the secured party, the collateral that is being disposed of, the method of disposition, the right of the debtor to an accounting of the debt and the charge for the accounting, and the time and place of a public disposition or the time after which a private disposition will take place. UCC § 9–613(1). In the case of a disposition over the Internet, an Internet address such as a URL may be used as the place of sale. Whether failure to include all of that information in the notification renders that notification insufficient is a question of fact. UCC § 9–613(2). The notification may include other information as long as the notification does not mislead the debtor. UCC § 9–613(3). A model form is included in the statute that, if used, is deemed to provide sufficient information when filled out completely and accurately. UCC § 9–613(4).

(6) **Content of the Notice: Consumer-Goods Transaction**
If the transaction was a consumer-goods transaction, the notification of disposition must describe the debtor, the secured party, the collateral that is being disposed of, the method of disposition, the right of the debtor to an accounting of the debt and the charge for the accounting, the time and place of a public disposition or the time after which a private disposition will take place, the person's liability for any deficiency, a telephone number to call to determine the amount necessary to redeem the collateral, and a telephone number or mailing address from which additional information concerning the disposition and the debt secured

can be obtained. UCC § 9–614(1). If any of that information is omitted or incorrect, the notice is deemed insufficient as a matter of law. UCC § 9–614, cmt. 2. A model form is included in the statute that, if used, and properly filled out is deemed to be a sufficient notification. UCC § 9–614(3). The model form of notification, if used by a secured party, may include additional information without affecting the sufficiency of the notice of the disposition, as long as the additional information is not misleading, and the information that is required is accurate. UCC § 9–614(4), (5).

(7) Variation by Agreement

Although the debtor and any obligors may not vary the notification requirements by agreement prior to default, other parties may agree to vary these notification requirements. UCC § 9–602(7). The debtor and obligor may agree with the secured party as to the standards to use to measure the secured party's compliance with the notification requirements as long as those standards are not manifestly unreasonable. UCC § 9–603.

c. Warranties in Dispositions

A secured party that sells, leases, licenses, or otherwise disposes of collateral will give the same warranties of title, possession, and quiet enjoyment that a voluntary disposition of that type of collateral would entail. The secured party may disclaim those warranties by the same method used in voluntary dispositions of that type of collateral or by communicating an express disclaimer of the warranty to the purchaser in a record. A secured party has adequately disclaimed these warranties if the secured party states in connection with the disposition: "There is no warranty relating to title, possession, quiet enjoyment, or the like in this disposition." UCC § 9–610(d), (e), (f). Warranties of title, possession and quiet enjoyment are not warranties related to the quality of the collateral. Law other than Article 9 determines whether a warranty related to the quality of the collateral arises. For example, whether an implied warranty of merchantability will arise in the disposition of goods is determined by whether the seller is a merchant with respect to goods of the kind, UCC § 2–314, not by the provisions of Article 9. UCC § 9–610, cmt. 11.

d. Ability of Secured Party to Be the Transferee in the Disposition

If the disposition is a public disposition, the secured party that is conducting the disposition is a permissible transferee of the collateral pursuant to that disposition. If the disposition is of collateral of a type that is normally sold on a recognized market or is the type that is subject to widely distributed standard price quotations, the secured party that is conducting the disposition is a permissible transferee of the collateral pursuant to the disposition. UCC § 9–610(c). A recognized market is one in which the prices are not subject to individual negotiation and the items sold are fungible, such as stock sold on the New York Stock Exchange. UCC § 9–610, cmt. 9. The secured party that is conducting the disposition is not otherwise a permissible transferee of the collateral pursuant to the disposition, including pursuant to a private disposition. Instead the secured party must comply with the provisions of retention of collateral in full or partial satisfaction of debt. UCC § 9–610, cmt. 7.

e. Distribution of Proceeds

Once the disposition takes place, the proceeds of the disposition are distributed according to the scheme described in Article 9.

(1) Payment of Costs of Disposition Process
The proceeds of disposition are first applied to the expenses of the disposition including the costs of obtaining possession of tangible collateral, storing it until disposition, preparing it for disposition, and the costs of arranging for the disposition. If the parties' agreement provides for it, the secured party is also entitled to reasonable attorney's fees and other legal expenses incurred in connection with the enforcement of the security interest or agricultural lien. UCC § 9–615(a)(1).

(2) Application to Obligation for Which Disposition is Taking Place
After the above-described expenses relating to the disposition process are satisfied, the proceeds of the disposition are applied to the debt obligation that is owed to the secured party conducting the disposition. UCC § 9–615(a)(2).

(3) Distribution of Proceeds to Subordinate Obligations

If there are any proceeds of the disposition remaining after the above two categories are taken care of in full, and the collateral is not goods in a true consignment, the remaining proceeds are applied to any subordinate security interests or liens in the order of their priority if the secured party conducting the disposition has received from the holder of that subordinate lien or security interest an authenticated demand for payment before the distribution of proceeds is complete. UCC § 9–615(a)(3).

(a) True Consignments

If the goods are the subject of a true consignment and the interest that is subordinate to the secured party conducting the disposition demands payment, the secured party may pay proceeds to that subordinate interest only if that subordinate interest is superior to the rights of the consignor. UCC § 9–615(a)(3)(B). If the person demanding proceeds is the consignor, the secured party must pay the consignor the remaining proceeds if the consignor makes an authenticated demand for payment before distribution of the proceeds is complete. UCC § 9–615(a)(4).

(b) Proof of Subordinate Interest in Any Case

The secured party conducting the disposition may ask for reasonable proof of the subordinate interest and if the subordinate holder does not supply that reasonable proof within a reasonable time, the secured party need not pay the proceeds to the subordinate interest. UCC § 9–615(b).

(4) Distribution of Noncash Proceeds

If the proceeds of the disposition are noncash proceeds, the secured party conducting the disposition need not pay over those noncash proceeds unless failure to do so is commercially unreasonable. Applying noncash proceeds to the obligation or paying over those noncash proceeds to subordinate interests must be done in a commercially reasonable manner. UCC § 9–615(c). The parties may not vary this rule by agreement, UCC § 9–602(4), but they may specify standards for complying with this rule if the standards are not manifestly unreasonable. UCC § 9–603.

(5) Senior Security Interests or Liens

Proceeds are not distributed to entities holding security interests or liens that are senior in priority to the security interest or agricultural lien in the collateral disposed of by this process. Even if the identifiable proceeds of a disposition of collateral are subject to the security interest or lien of a senior secured party (UCC § 9–315), a junior secured party that receives cash proceeds in good faith and without knowledge that the junior secured party's receipt of those proceeds violates the rights of the senior secured party or lienholder is able to take those cash proceeds free of the senior security interest or lien, is not obligated to turn those proceeds over to the holder of the senior security interest or lien, and is not obligated to account to the holder of the senior security interest or lien for any surplus from the disposition. UCC § 9–615(g). The mere fact that the junior secured party that has conducted the disposition knows of the senior security interest or lien does not mean that the junior secured party knows that receiving the cash proceeds violates the senior holder's rights.

f. Surplus or Deficiency

Once the collateral is disposed of and the value received applied in the manner specified above, the following rules govern the surplus and deficiency that may result from the disposition process.

(1) Deficiency

The obligor is liable for any deficiency remaining unless the parties have agreed that the obligor is not liable for the deficiency. The parties may vary the obligor's liability for a deficiency pursuant to an agreement entered into before or after default. UCC § 9–602.

(2) Surplus

The debtor is entitled to any surplus (after the payments outlined above) unless the secured party was required to pay the surplus to the consignor as specified above. UCC § 9–615(d). The parties may not vary the debtor's entitlement to the surplus. UCC § 9–602(5).

(3) Transactions That Are Sales That Create Security Interests

If the transaction creating the security interest was a sale of accounts, chattel paper, payment intangibles or promissory notes, the debtor is not entitled to the surplus and the obligor is not liable for the deficiency. UCC § 9–615(e). This rule may be varied by the agreement of the debtor or obligor. UCC § 9–602.

(4) **Disposition Made to a Secured Party, Person Related to the Secured Party, or Secondary Obligor**

To combat the problem of low-disposition prices and perceived conflict of interests when the secured party, a person related to the secured party, or the secondary obligor is the transferee of the collateral, Article 9 protects the debtor and obligor when the collateral is disposed of in a transaction that transfers the collateral to these types of entities. UCC 9–615(f). This rule may not be varied by the agreement of the debtor and obligor. UCC § 9–602(8).

(a) **"Related to the Secured Party" Defined**

If the secured party is an individual, "a person related to the secured party" means the spouse, siblings and siblings in law, ancestors or descendants of the secured party or secured party's spouse, or other relatives by blood or marriage that share the secured party's home. UCC § 9–102(a)(62). If the secured party is an organization, "a person related to the secured party" means a person that is controlled by or controlling the organization, officer or directors of the organization, officers or directors of persons controlled by or controlling the organization, spouses of any of those individuals, and individuals related by blood or marriage to any of the above that share the same home. UCC § 9–102(a)(63).

(b) **Calculating the Surplus or Deficiency**

If (i) the disposition is made to the secured party, a person related to the secured party, or the secondary obligor, and (ii) the disposition that occurred resulted in proceeds that were significantly below the range of proceeds that a disposition complying with Article 9 to a transferee other than the secured party, a person related to the secured party, or a secondary obligor would have brought, then the surplus or deficiency is calculated by determining the amount that the disposition would have brought if it complied with Article 9 and was made to a person other than the secured party, a person related to the secured party, or the secondary obligor. UCC § 9–615(f). The debtor or obligor has the burden to establish that the proceeds generated from the disposition are significantly below the range of prices that a disposition to to a person other than the secured party, a person related to the secured party, or the secondary obligor would have generated. UCC § 9–626(a)(5).

(5) Notice of the Calculation of the Surplus or Deficiency in a Consumer-Goods Transaction

In a consumer-goods transaction, the secured party must send a notice, subsequent to the disposition, to the debtor and consumer obligor regarding the calculation of the surplus and deficiency. If there is a surplus, the debtor must get the notice. If there is a deficiency, the consumer obligor must get the notice. UCC § 9–616(b). This rule may not be varied by the agreement of the parties. UCC § 9–602(9).

(a) Content of Notice

The notice must state the amount of the surplus or deficiency, provide an explanation of how it was calculated, state whether additional credits or debits will affect the amount, and provide a telephone number or mailing address for obtaining additional information. UCC § 9–616(a)(1). In providing the explanation of the calculation of the surplus or deficiency, the notice must provide the aggregate amount of the debt, the amount of proceeds of the disposition, the aggregate amount of the debt after application of the proceeds, the expenses of the disposition process, the amount of all other credits against the debt, and the amount of the surplus or deficiency. UCC § 9–616(c).

(b) Timing of Notice

The secured party must send the notice after the disposition when the secured party accounts for the surplus or before first making a demand for payment of the deficiency or within 14 days after the secured party receives a request for the explanation. If the secured party does not seek a deficiency when a consumer obligor would be liable for the deficiency, the secured party must send a notice to the consumer obligor of the secured party's waiver of the deficiency within 14 days after the secured party receives a request for an explanation of the calculation of the surplus or deficiency. A debtor's or consumer obligor's request for an explanation of the calculation of the surplus or deficiency must be authenticated and sent after the disposition of the collateral in order to trigger the 14-day periods referenced above. UCC § 9–616(b), (a)(2).

(c) Substantial Compliance

An explanation that substantially complies with these requirements is sufficient even if it contains minor errors that are not seriously misleading. UCC § 9–616(d).

(d) Charge for Explanation of Calculation of Surplus or Deficiency

The debtor or consumer obligor is entitled to one response to a request for an explanation of the calculation of the surplus or deficiency during a six-month period if the secured party has not already provided the explanation. The secured party may charge no more than $25 for each additional response. UCC § 9–616(e).

g. Rights of Transferee of Collateral After a Disposition

The transferee of collateral pursuant to a disposition succeeds to the debtor's rights in the collateral and takes the collateral free of the security interest under which the disposition was made and any subordinate security interests or liens. UCC § 9–617(a). Even though the statute is silent regarding the effect of a disposition on an agricultural lien, presumably the disposition of collateral pursuant to an agricultural lien would also discharge the agricultural lien.

(1) Good Faith Transferee

If the transferee is in good faith, the transferee has those rights even if the disposition did not comply with the Article 9 requirements. UCC § 9–617(b). Thus a good faith transferee of collateral pursuant to the disposition will take the collateral subject to security interests or liens that are superior in priority to the security interest or agricultural lien under which the disposition is made, and free of the security interest under which the disposition is made and any subordinate security interests or liens.

(2) **Transferee Not in Good Faith**

If the transferee does not act in good faith, the transferee takes the collateral subject to the debtor's rights, the security interest or agricultural lien under which the disposition is made, and any other security interests or liens. UCC § 9–617(c).

Example: SP–1 has a first priority security interest in A's equipment to secure a debt of $5,000. SP–2 has a second priority security interest in A's equipment to secure a debt of $7,000. SP–3 has a third priority security interest in A's equipment to secure a debt of $8,000. A defaulted on its obligation to SP–2. SP–2 repossessed the equipment without breach of the peace and gave timely notice to A, SP–1 and SP–3 concerning the scheduled disposition. Costs of sale were $500. SP–2 conducted a commercially reasonable disposition of the equipment, selling it to Transferee for $8,000 in cash. SP–2 applied the $8,000 proceeds first to the $500 costs of sale and then to the $7,000 debt owed to SP–2. The remaining $500 proceeds will be distributed either to SP–3, if it made a timely and effective demand for distribution to SP–2, or to A as a surplus. Transferee takes the collateral subject to the security interest of SP–1 and free of the security interest of SP–2 and SP–3. SP–2 has a right to keep the proceeds of the sale free of SP–1's security interest in the proceeds as long as SP–2 is in good faith and without knowledge that the receipt of those proceeds violates SP–1's rights.

(3) **Sale of Promissory Notes or Payment Intangibles in a Disposition**

If promissory notes or payment intangibles are sold in a disposition pursuant to UCC § 9–610, the buyer of those rights will have the right to enforce those obligations against the obligor on the promissory note or payment intangible as provided in UCC § 9–406(d) in spite of anti-assignment terms contained in the agreement between the account debtor or obligor on the note. UCC §§ 9–406(e), 9–408(b).

3. Retention of Collateral in Full or Partial Satisfaction of Obligation Owed

In some circumstances, the secured party may desire to retain the collateral in full or partial satisfaction of the obligation owed to the secured party and not conduct a disposition of the collateral. Article 9 provides for a process to enable the secured party to keep the collateral without a disposition. This provision applies to all types of collateral, not just collateral that may be subject to a repossession. UCC § 9–620, cmt. 3. In order for the secured party to keep the collateral in exchange for full or partial satisfaction of the obligation owed to the secured party, the following requirements must be met.

a. Variation by Agreement

The duties of the secured party in this process may not be varied by the agreement of the debtor and obligors, UCC § 9–602(10), although the parties may agree to standards regarding fulfillment of the secured party's duties as long as the standards are not manifestly unreasonable. UCC § 9–603. The secured party's attempt to obtain the collateral by a private sale to itself is in effect a retention in full or partial satisfaction of the debt and is subject to these provisions. UCC §§ 9–610, cmt. 7, 9–602, cmt. 3.

b. Debtor Consent

For the retention to be allowed, the debtor must consent to the secured party's retention of the collateral for credit against the obligation owed. UCC § 9–620(a)(1). If the secured party is only giving partial credit against the obligation owed, the debtor's consent must be in a record that specifies the terms on which the secured party proposes to retain the collateral and that the debtor authenticates after default. UCC § 9–620(c)(1). If the secured party is giving full satisfaction of the obligation owed in return for the secured party's retention of the collateral, the debtor's consent must be evidenced either (i) by a record that specifies the terms on which the secured party proposes to retain the collateral and that the debtor authenticates after default or (ii) by the debtor's failure to object to the secured party's unconditional proposal (other than a condition to preserve the collateral not in the secured party's possession) of the full satisfaction of the debt within 20 days after the secured party sent the proposal. UCC § 9–620(c)(2).

c. Notice to Other Interested Parties

For the retention to be allowed, the secured party must send notice of its proposal to retain the collateral in full or partial satisfaction of the obligation owed to other interested parties. The secured party's proposal is merely an authenticated record that states the terms on which the secured party is willing to retain the collateral in return for partial or full satisfaction of the obligation owed. UCC § 9–102(a)(66).

(1) Who Must Be Notified

Notice must be sent to the following: (i) any person that has an interest in the collateral that is subordinate to the security interest that is the subject of the proposal, UCC § 9–620(a)(2)(B); (ii) any person that sends an authenticated notice of an interest in the collateral to the secured party before the debtor has consented to the secured party's proposal, UCC §§ 9–620(a)(2)(A), 9–621(a)(1); (iii) any secured party or lienholder that has filed a financing statement against the debtor regarding that collateral in the correct filing office as of 10 days before the debtor has consented to the secured party's proposal, UCC §§ 9–620(a)(2)(A), 9–621(a)(2); (iv) any person that held a security interest perfected by compliance with another statute or treaty specified in UCC § 9–311 as of 10 days before the debtor has consented to the secured party's proposal, UCC §§ 9–620(a)(2)(A), 9–621(a)(3), and (v) any secondary obligor if the proposal is to retain the collateral in partial satisfaction of the obligation owed, UCC §§ 9–620(a)(2)(A), 9–621(b).

(2) No Excuse for Not Sending Notice Based Upon Filing Office Inaction

The secured party is not excused from its obligation to send notice to those who have filed financing statements if the filing office delays in responding to the requested search of the filing records. UCC § 9–621, cmt. 2. Cf. UCC § 9–611(e).

d. Failure to Receive Timely Objections to Proposal

For the retention to be allowed, the secured party must not receive timely objections to the proposal to retain collateral in full or partial satisfaction of the obligation owed. UCC § 9–620(a)(2). Persons to whom the secured party sent the proposal to retain the collateral in full or partial satisfaction of the obligation owed must object within 20 days after the notification was sent to the objector. Other persons claiming an interest in collateral must object within 20 days after the secured party sent its last notification or, if no notifications were sent, before the debtor consents. In any case, the objection is only effective if received by the secured party within the specified time period. UCC § 9–620(d).

e. Secured Party's Consent

For the retention to be allowed, the secured party must consent to the retention of collateral in partial or full satisfaction of the obligation owed. That consent must be either in a record that the secured party authenticates or in a proposal that the secured party sent to the debtor. UCC § 9–620(b). This rule is designed to prevent courts from deeming that the secured party's retention of collateral for a long period of time prior to a disposition as a retention in full satisfaction of the debt. UCC § 9–620, cmt. 5. Whether the secured party has held the collateral for an unreasonable period of time prior to a disposition is determined by the commercially reasonable standard of UCC § 9–610.

f. Good Faith of the Secured Party

While a secured party's proposal to retain collateral in full or partial satisfaction of the obligation owed must be made in good faith, good faith is not determined merely by looking at the value of the collateral in relationship to the obligation owed. UCC § 9–620, cmt. 11.

g. Not Precluded by Statute From Engaging in the Retention

Article 9 limits the ability of a secured party to retain the collateral in partial or full satisfaction of the obligation owed in three situations.

(1) Consumer Goods in Possession of Debtor
If the collateral is consumer goods, the collateral may not be in the possession of the debtor when the debtor consents to the retention of collateral in partial or full satisfaction of the debt. UCC § 9–620(a)(3).

(2) Purchase Money Security Interests in Consumer Goods

If a secured party has a purchase money security interest in consumer goods and more than 60% of the price or the debt has been paid, the secured party may not retain the consumer goods in full or partial satisfaction of the debt. UCC § 9–620(e). The secured party must dispose of the consumer goods pursuant to the disposition process described above within 90 days of the secured party taking possession or within a longer period that the debtor and any secondary obligor have agreed to in an authenticated agreement entered into after default. UCC § 9–620(f). After default, the debtor may enter into an authenticated agreement that waives its right that the secured party dispose of this collateral pursuant to UCC § 9–610. UCC § 9–624(b).

(3) Consumer Transactions

If the transaction was a consumer transaction, the secured party may not accept the collateral in partial satisfaction of the obligation secured. UCC § 9–620(g).

h. Effect on Debt

The retention of collateral in partial or full satisfaction of the obligation discharges the obligation to the extent of the debtor's and secured party's consent. UCC § 9–622(a)(1). If the retention is in full satisfaction of the obligation owed, there will be no surplus or deficiency. If the retention is in partial satisfaction of the obligation owed, there will remain a deficiency that the secured party may seek to collect from other collateral that secures the debt or from the obligor.

i. Rights of Secured Party in the Collateral Retained

The secured party that has retained the collateral succeeds to the debtor's rights in the collateral. The security interest or agricultural lien that is the subject of the debtor's consent and any subordinate security interests or liens are discharged. The secured party will have the collateral subject to security interests or liens in the collateral that are superior in priority to the secured party's security interest or lien. UCC § 9–622(a). The retention has this effect even if the secured party fails to comply with the provisions of Article 9 in retaining the collateral. UCC § 9–622(b). If the collateral retained consists of promissory notes or payment intangibles, the secured party will have the right to enforce those obligations against the obligor on the promissory note or payment intangible as provided in UCC § 9–406(d) in spite of anti-assignment terms contained in the agreement between the account debtor or obligor on the note. UCC §§ 9–406(e), 9–408(b).

Example: SP–1 has a first priority security interest in A's equipment to secure a debt of $5,000. SP–2 has a second priority security interest in A's equipment to secure a debt of $7,000. SP–3 has a third priority security interest in A's equipment to secure a debt of $8,000. A defaulted on its obligation to SP–2. SP–2 repossessed the equipment without breach of the peace and gave timely notice to A, SP–1 and SP–3 of its proposal to retain the equipment in full satisfaction of the debt to SP–2. SP–2 takes the equipment subject to the security interest of SP–1 and free of the security interest of SP–2 and SP–3.

4. Title Clearing Mechanism

In some circumstances, a transferee of collateral pursuant to the enforcement process (in either a disposition or a retention) will need to obtain a record from a filing or registration office that the transferee has title to the collateral. In order for the transferee to obtain that record evidence of title to the transferred collateral, the secured party may authenticate a transfer statement that the transferee will provide to the filing or registration office that issues the record title document.

a. Contents of Transfer Statement

The transfer statement contains a statement that the debtor has defaulted on an obligation secured by the collateral, that the secured party has exercised its postdefault remedies, and the transferee has acquired its interest pursuant to that process. The transfer statement will also contain the names and mailing addresses of the secured party, debtor, and transferee. UCC § 9–619(a).

b. Effect of Transfer Statement

Upon providing the transfer statement and any applicable fees to the filing office, the filing office must accept the transfer statement and amend its records to reflect the transfer to the transferee. If the filing office issues certificates of title regarding the collateral, the filing office must issue a new certificate of title in the name of the transferee. UCC § 9–619(b).

c. Using Transfer Statement to Obtain Title in Secured Party

In some circumstances to facilitate a disposition, the secured party may use a transfer statement to obtain title in the secured party's name prior to disposition of the collateral. The secured party doing so does not result in a disposition of the collateral or alter the secured party's duties to engage in a complying disposition or retention of the collateral under Article 9. UCC § 9–619(c).

d. Federal Preemption

If the registration or title system for the collateral is governed by federal law, this section may be preempted by the applicable provisions of the federal law. UCC § 9–619, cmt. 2.

D. Enforcement of Obligations Owed to Debtor

If the collateral consists of an obligation owed to the debtor, Article 9 provides a mechanism for a secured party to collect that obligation from the person obligated on the collateral. The secured party is not required to use this collection mechanism and may instead conduct a disposition or a retention of the collateral as discussed in Section C, *supra*.

1. Obligors on Collateral

"Account debtors" are persons that owe obligations to the debtor on accounts, chattel paper (but not instruments that are part of chattel paper), or general intangibles. UCC § 9–102(a)(3). Examples of other types of collateral in which persons owe obligations to the debtor include instruments (such as notes) where the debtor is the payee or holder, documents of title where the goods covered by the document are deliverable to the debtor, deposit accounts of the debtor, letter-of-credit rights where the debtor is the beneficiary of the letter of credit, or investment securities of the debtor.

Example: SP–1 has a security interest in accounts owed to A to secure a debt that B owes to SP–1. A is the debtor and B is the obligor. X owes an obligation to A for goods that A sold to X. That obligation is an "account" and X is the "account debtor," the person obligated on the collateral.

2. Collection

A secured party may exercise its enforcement against collateral as to "any person obligated on collateral to make payment or otherwise render performance to or for the benefit of the secured party." UCC § 9–607(a). The rights of the obligor on the collateral as against the secured party will depend upon the terms of the contract or right assigned to the secured party, the rules of Article 9 (including UCC § 9–401 through § 9–409), and the rules of other law governing assignment of the type of obligation involved. UCC § 9–607(e), cmt. 6.

a. Special Rules for Deposit Accounts

If the secured party has a security interest in a deposit account perfected by control, the secured party may apply the balance of the deposit account to the obligation that the debtor owes the secured party. UCC § 9–607(a)(4), (5). If the security interest in the deposit account is unperfected or perfected by a manner other than control, the secured party's ability to collect against the bank holding the deposit account will be determined by other law. UCC §§ 9–607, cmt. 7, 9–341.

b. Special Rule for Enforcement of Mortgages

Under applicable mortgage foreclosure process, the obligor on the mortgage must generally be in default under the mortgage in order for the mortgagee to foreclose the mortgage. UCC § 9–607, cmt. 8. If a secured party has a security interest in a mortgage held by the debtor (i.e. the mortgagee) and desires to exercise the debtor's right to foreclose that mortgage without judicial process (assuming that right exists under applicable mortgage foreclosure process), the secured party may need to record documents in the real estate recording office that evidence its right to conduct the foreclosure. Article 9 authorizes the secured party to file in the real estate recording office a copy of the security agreement creating a security interest in the mortgage and a sworn affidavit declaring that a default under the mortgage exists and the secured party has a right to conduct the foreclosure through nonjudicial process. UCC § 9–607(b).

3. Timing of Collection From Person Obligated on Collateral

The secured party may collect on collateral consisting of obligations owed to the debtor if the obligor on the secured obligation has defaulted. Even if the obligor is not in default on its secured obligation to the secured party, if that obligor has agreed, the secured party may collect on the collateral. UCC §§ 9–607(a), 9–602.

4. Notice to Person Obligated on the Collateral

The secured party will notify the person obligated on the collateral to render its performance to the secured party. UCC § 9–607(a)(1).

Example: SP–1 has a security interest in accounts owed to A to secure a debt that B owes to SP–1. A is the debtor and B is the obligor. X owes an obligation to A for goods that A sold to X. That obligation is an "account" and X is the "account debtor," the person obligated on the collateral. SP–1 may seek to collect from X even if B is not in default on its obligation to SP–1 if B has so agreed with SP–1. To collect from X, SP–1 will notify X to pay SP–1 instead of A.

5. Defenses of Person Obligated on the Collateral

When the person obligated on the collateral is notified to render its performance to the secured party, that person may have defenses to assert against the secured party's enforcement effort.

a. Account Debtor's Ability to Raise Defenses Against Secured Party

Generally, an account debtor may assert against the secured party whatever defenses or claims in recoupment (essentially a counterclaim) the account debtor could assert against the debtor arising out of the contract between the account debtor and the debtor. UCC § 9–404(a)(1). An account debtor may also assert against the secured party any other defense or claim of the account debtor against the debtor that accrues before the account debtor received notice of the assignment in a record authenticated either by the debtor or the secured party. UCC § 9–404(a)(2). An account debtor may only assert a counterclaim against the secured party to reduce the amount owed to the secured party, not to obtain an affirmative recovery against the secured party. UCC § 9–404(c).

Example: SP–1 has a security interest in accounts owed to A to secure a debt A owes to SP–1. A is the debtor and the obligor. X owes an obligation to A for goods that A sold to X. That obligation is an "account" and X is the "account debtor," the person obligated on the collateral. When SP–1 notifies X to pay SP–1 instead of A, X may raise any defenses to payment or counterclaims that X has against A arising out of the contract that generated X's obligation to pay. Such a claim may be that the goods failed to conform to a warranty that A made in the sale of goods transaction between X and A. X may also raise any defenses or counterclaims arising out of other transactions or dealings with A that accrued prior to receiving notice of the assignment of the account to SP–1.

(1) Exception for Health-Care-Insurance Receivables

These rules allowing defenses and claims and recoupment to be asserted against the secured party do not apply to an account that is a health-care-insurance receivable. UCC § 9–404(e). Other law governs the ability of an insurer (the account debtor) to raise claims and defenses against the secured party.

(2) Exception for Consumers

If a rule of law provides a different rule for an account debtor that is an individual and the obligation that the account debtor owes is a consumer obligation, these rules regarding the account debtor's ability to raise defenses or claims against the secured party are subject to that other rule. UCC § 9–404(c).

b. Waiver of the Account Debtor's Ability to Assert Defenses and Claims Against Secured Party

In the agreement between the account debtor and the debtor, the account debtor may waive its right to assert its claims and defenses that it has against the debtor in the event the contract is assigned to a third party, such as a secured party. That waiver is enforceable if the assignee (the secured party) took the assignment of the contract for value, in good faith, without notice of any property claims to the rights under the contract, and without notice of any defenses or counterclaims. UCC § 9–403(b). Even if there is an enforceable waiver of defenses and claims by the account debtor, the account debtor's waiver does not waive certain defenses that are of the type that could be asserted against a holder in due course of a negotiable instrument. UCC § 9–403(c). Those defenses are set forth in Article 3, UCC § 3–305 and include lack of capacity to enter into the contract based upon infancy or other disabling status, unenforceability due to duress, illegality, fraud such that the account debtor did not have a reasonable opportunity to learn of the nature of the contract or its essential terms, and discharge in insolvency proceedings.

Example: SP–1 has a security interest in accounts owed to A to secure a debt A owes to SP–1. A is the debtor and the obligor. X owes an obligation to A for goods that A sold to X. That obligation is an "account" and X is the "account debtor," the person obligated on the collateral. In the contract between A and X governing the sale of the goods, X agreed to waive the right to raise any claims or defenses arising out of the contract or other dealings with A against any assignee of A, such as SP–1. That waiver is enforceable if SP–1 took its security interest in the account in good faith, for value, without notice of any property claims to the account, and without notice of any defenses or counterclaims that X may have had. The waiver will not be enforceable if X has the type of defense that X could assert against a holder in due course under Article 3 on a negotiable instrument.

(1) Waiver by Consumer
If other law establishes rules regarding the ability of a individual account debtor that incurred the obligation for consumer purposes to waive

claims and defenses, the Article 9 rules regarding waiver of claims and defenses are subject to those other rules. UCC § 9–403(e).

(2) Preservation of Other Law

If other law validates the account debtor's waiver of the right to assert claims and defenses against an assignee, Article 9 does not displace that other law. UCC § 9–403(f).

(3) Preservation of the Right to Assert Defenses and Claims Against Secured Party

If other law requires the record evidencing the account debtor's obligation to have a statement that any assignee (including a secured party) is subject to claims and defenses of the account debtor and the record does not have that statement included, the record is treated as if it did have that statement. Thus, the account debtor may assert the claims and defenses against the secured party as if the record contained that statement. UCC §§ 9–403(d), 9–404(d). An example of the type of rule that this principle refers to is found in the Federal Trade Commission rule, 16 C.F.R. pt. 433.

c. Ability of Person Obligated on Collateral Other Than Account Debtor to Raise Defenses or Claims Against Secured Party

Article 9 does not address the ability of obligors on collateral, other than account debtors, to raise defenses or claims in recoupment against the secured party. UCC § 9–404, cmt. 5. The law of contract assignment, negotiable instruments, or other law controls the ability of obligors on collateral, other than account debtors, to raise defenses or claims against the secured party and the waiver of the right to do so. See UCC § 9–403, cmt. 2.

d. Modification of Underlying Contract

An account debtor may assert that the contract between the account debtor and the debtor has been modified and that the secured party should be subject to that modification. Article 9 provides that the modification is effective against the secured party to which the contract has been assigned if (i) the modification is made in good faith and (ii) either the right to payment that the secured party has been assigned is not yet fully earned by performance *or* the right to payment has been fully earned by performance and the account debtor has not yet been notified of the assignment. The agreement between the assignor (the debtor) and the assignee (the secured party) may provide that modification of the contract between the account debtor and the debtor is a breach of assignor-assignee agreement. UCC § 9–405(a), (b).

(1) Exception for Consumer
If other law establishes rules regarding the ability of an individual account debtor that incurred the obligation for consumer purposes to modify the agreement and have the assignee be subject to that modification, the Article 9 rules regarding modification of assigned contracts are subject to those other rules. UCC § 9–405(c).

(2) Exception for Health-Care-Insurance Receivables
This rule regarding modification does not apply to modification of the obligation of the health care insurer. UCC § 9–405(d). Other law addresses this issue.

e. Protection of Certain Persons Obligated on Collateral

As explained in Chapters III and IV, the attachment and perfection of a security interest in obligations that are owed to the debtor is not hampered either by anti-assignment clauses in the contract between the person obligated on the collateral and the debtor or by anti-assignment rules of law. Generally, anti-assignment clauses in the contracts between the person obligated on collateral and the debtor or anti-assignment laws also do not preclude the secured party from enforcing its rights in the collateral assigned against the person obligated on the collateral. UCC §§ 9–406(d), (f), 9–407(a).

(1) Exception
That general rule is subject to an exception in the case of a person obligated on certain types of collateral and transactions where either an anti-assignment clause or anti-assignment law would, if not for the rules of Article 9, be enforceable to prevent assignment of the obligation owed. The secured party is not entitled to exercise its enforcement rights against the person obligated on the collateral if the assignment of the obligation to the secured party is a transaction in which (i) a payment intangible is

sold, a security interest in a general intangible is created, a promissory note is assigned, a health-care-insurance receivable is assigned, or letter-of-credit rights are assigned, *and* (ii) the anti-assignment clause or anti-assignment law would otherwise render the assignment unenforceable. In other words, the person obligated on the collateral need not render its performance to the secured party in the event the secured party seeks to enforce its security interest in the collateral. UCC §§ 9–408, 9–409. However, if a payment intangible or promissory note has been sold in a UCC § 9–610 disposition or retained pursuant to the process in UCC § 9–620, an anti-assignment clause will not be effective to prevent enforcement of the obligation of the obligor on the payment intangible or promissory note. UCC §§ 9–406(e), 9–408(b).

(2) Individual Account Debtors

An account debtor that is an individual and that has incurred the obligation to the debtor for consumer purposes may also avail itself of other law that establishes a different rule for that individual. UCC § 9–406(h).

6. Account Debtor Discharge by Payment

An account debtor on collateral that is chattel paper, accounts other than health-care-insurance receivables, and payment intangibles may pay the debtor until the secured party or debtor gives the account debtor an authenticated and effective notice directing payment to the secured party. After receipt of that authenticated and effective notice, those types of account debtors will not be discharged on their obligation to pay if they pay the debtor instead of the secured party. UCC § 9–406(a), (i). The effect of notification to a person obligated on collateral (other than an account debtor on chattel paper, accounts other than health-care-insurance receivables, and payment intangibles) on that person's ability to discharge its obligation by payment to the debtor is governed by other law. UCC § 9–406, cmt. 2.

a. Effective Notification

In order to be an effective notification, the notice must reasonably identify the rights assigned. UCC § 9–406(b). The account debtor may request proof of the assignment and until reasonable proof is furnished, the account debtor may pay the debtor instead of the secured party. UCC § 9–406(c). The account debtor is not the sole arbiter of what is reasonable proof, and thus must be careful to avoid the risk of double payment. UCC § 9–406, cmt. 3.

b. Exception in the Case of Sale of Payment Intangibles

If a payment intangible has been sold and either an anti-assignment clause or anti-assignment rules of law would be given effect under other law in the absence of the Article 9 rules, then the account debtor need not pay the secured party even if the account debtor receives an authenticated notice to do so. UCC § 9–406(b)(2). However, if a payment intangible has been sold in a UCC § 9–610 disposition or retained pursuant to the process in UCC § 9–620, an anti-assignment clause will not be effective to prevent enforcement of the obligation. UCC §§ 9–406(e), 9–408(b).

c. Exception for Partial Assignments

If the notice to the account debtor instructs the account debtor to make less than full payment of the obligation owed (or less than full payment on any installment that is due), the account debtor has the option of ignoring the notification as ineffective. UCC § 9–406(b)(3).

d. Notice of No Obligation to Pay the Secured Party

If an account debtor has received notification of to pay the secured party instead of the debtor, the secured party has a duty to notify the account debtor that it is not obligated to pay the secured party if: (i) the secured party no longer has a right to that payment because there is no outstanding secured obligation or commitment to give value to the obligor on the secured obligation, *and* (ii) the debtor makes an authenticated demand on the secured party to notify the account debtor. UCC § 9–209. If the debtor makes that authenticated demand, then the secured party has 10 days to send the account debtor an authenticated notice that the account debtor no longer has an obligation to pay the secured party. UCC § 9–209(b). The secured party does not have a duty to send notice to the account debtor if the transaction between the debtor and secured party was a sale of accounts, chattel paper or payment intangibles. UCC § 9–209(c).

7. Notice to Debtor or Other Lienholders

The secured party is not required to give notice to any other party (including the debtor, holders of other security interests in the collateral, or persons with liens in the collateral) of its actions taken in collection of obligations owed to the debtor.

8. Commercially Reasonable Collection Efforts

The secured party has an obligation to engage in collection from the persons obligated on collateral in a commercially reasonable manner if the secured party is entitled to full or limited recourse against the debtor or a secondary obligor for any uncollected obligations. UCC § 9–607(c). This includes the ability to compromise and settle the obligation. UCC § 9–607, cmt. 9. Secured parties that are consignors and buyers of accounts, chattel paper, payment intangibles or promissory notes are subject to this commercial reasonableness obligation. UCC § 9–601(g). The debtor and obligors on the secured transaction may not waive this "commercial reasonableness" duty of the secured party. UCC § 9–602(3).

9. Expenses and Fees Incurred in Collection

The secured party has a right to deduct from the amounts collected from obligors on the collateral the reasonable expenses of collection incurred in collecting from the obligors on the collateral, including reasonable attorney's fees and legal expenses. UCC § 9–607(d), cmt. 10.

10. Application of Proceeds of Collection

Once the funds are collected from the obligors on the collateral, after deduction of the expenses of collection against the obligors on the collateral, the proceeds are applied in the following order: (i) to the expenses of collection from the debtor or obligor on the secured debt, and if provided in the security agreement or contract with the debtor or obligor on the secured debt, reasonable attorney's fees and legal expenses incurred in taking action against the debtor or obligor on the secured transaction; (ii) to the satisfaction of the secured obligation and owed to the secured party doing the collection; and (iii) the satisfaction of liens or security interests subordinate to the security interest or lien being enforced if the secured party doing the collection has received an authenticated demand for payment before the proceeds are completely distributed. UCC § 9–608(a)(1). The debtor and any obligors on the secured obligation may not waive the duty of the secured party to deal with the proceeds of collection in accordance with these principles. UCC § 9–602(4).

a. Proof of Subordinate Interest

A person that claims a subordinate lien or security interest in the collateral must furnish reasonable proof of its interest within a reasonable time if the secured party that is collecting on the collateral (the obligations owed to the debtor) so demands. UCC § 9–608(a)(2).

b. Noncash Proceeds

If the secured party obtains noncash proceeds in the collection process, it need not apply those proceeds to its debt or pay those proceeds to another party unless failure to do so is commercially unreasonable. If it does apply those noncash proceeds to the debt or pay those proceeds over to another party, it must do so in a commercially reasonable manner. UCC § 9–608(a)(3).

11. Surplus or Deficiency

Unless the transaction is a sale of accounts, chattel paper, payment intangibles or promissory notes, the obligor on the secured obligation is liable for any deficiency and the debtor is entitled to any surplus after application of the proceeds as outlined above. UCC § 9–608(a)(4), (b). The duty of the secured party to account for the surplus to the debtor in a transaction that is not a sale of accounts, chattel paper, payment intangibles or promissory notes may not be altered by agreement. UCC § 9–602(5).

12. Effect of the Collection Process on Junior and Senior Lien Holders

The priority of a lien or security interest that is senior to the lien or security interest that is being enforced is not affected by the enforcement process. UCC § 9–608, cmt. 5. The holder of a senior security interest in the obligation owed to the debtor will have its interest attach to the proceeds of the collection. UCC § 9–315. Whether the senior secured party will have priority in the proceeds as against the collecting secured party will depend upon application of the rules regarding priority in proceeds. UCC §§ 9–322, 9–607 cmt. 5. Review Chapter V on priority in proceeds.

> *Example:*   SP–1 has a first priority security interest in A's accounts to secure a $10,000 debt that A owes to SP–1. SP–2 has a second priority security interest in A's accounts to secure a $7,000 debt that A owes to SP–2. SP–3 has a third priority security interest in A's accounts to secure a $5,000 debt that A owes SP–3. SP–2 notifies X, an account debtor on one of the accounts owed to A, to pay SP–2. SP–2's enforcement action does not affect SP–1's first priority security interest in A's accounts. X paid SP–2 and is discharged on its obligation to pay A, effectively extinguishing that account so that if SP–1 or SP–3 sought to collect from X, X would have a viable defense to payment. SP–2's ability to keep the proceeds generated by the collection from X would depend upon whether SP–2 had first priority in those proceeds under the proceeds priority rules.

E. Redemption

Article 9 provides that a debtor, secondary obligor, secured party, or lienholder may redeem collateral prior to collection of obligations that are the collateral, disposition of the collateral, or retention of the collateral in full or partial satisfaction of the secured obligation owed.

1. Full Payment to Redeem

In order to redeem the collateral, the redeeming party must tender fulfillment of all obligations that the collateral secures and any reasonable attorney's fees and expenses that are allowed under the agreement with the secured party. UCC § 9–623.

2. Variation by Agreement

This right to redeem may not be varied by an agreement between the secured party and debtor or obligor, with one exception. UCC § 9–602(11). A debtor or secondary obligor, in a transaction other than a consumer-goods transaction, may waive their right to redeem in an agreement that is entered into and authenticated after default. UCC § 9–624(c).

F. Effect of Enforcement Process on Secondary Obligor

When a secured party enforces its security interest or agricultural lien against collateral, the secured party's enforcement actions may have an effect on the secondary obligor's liability for any remaining debt and on the secondary obligor's duties owed to the debtor.

1. Liability of Secondary Obligor on the Debt

The secondary obligor's liability to the secured party for any remaining debt will be determined by principles of suretyship law, the agreements between the secondary obligor and the secured party, and the rules of Article 9 regarding enforcement of the security interest or agricultural lien.

2. Secondary Obligor's Duty to Debtor

The secondary obligor's rights as against the debtor will also be determined by suretyship law, the agreements between the secondary obligor, the debtor, and the secured party, and the rules of Article 9. Under suretyship law, if the secondary obligor fulfills the obligation of the primary obligor to the secured party, the secondary obligor succeeds to the rights of the secured party to enforce its lien against the collateral, and would then be obligated to comply with Article 9's enforcement rules as if it was the secured party. The secured party may assign its security interest to the secondary obligor. That action is not a disposition of the collateral requiring the secured party to comply with the rules regarding disposition of collateral found in UCC § 9–610. UCC § 9–618. In this situation, the secondary obligor would then have the duties of a secured party in enforcement of the security interest. On the other hand, if the secondary obligor is the purchaser of the collateral at an Article 9 disposition, the secured party has the duty to comply with the rules of Article 9 and the secondary obligor (the transferee at the disposition) is free to further deal with the collateral without compliance with the Article 9 disposition rules. It may be difficult to determine what the nature of the transfer to the secondary obligor is and thus the parties should attempt to be clear about this issue. UCC § 9–618, cmt. 2.

G.   Effect of Other Law on Enforcement of Security Interest and Agricultural Lien

As detailed as the rules of Article 9 are regarding enforcement of security interests or agricultural liens, they do not occupy the field. Common law doctrines and other statutory law may come into play in this process.

1. Waiver and Estoppel

Principles of common law and equity will supplement the Article 9 enforcement rules to the extent not displaced by the Article 9 rules. UCC § 1–103. Sometimes the secured party will engage in conduct or the debtor or obligor will engage in conduct that will be held to be a waiver of rights or an estoppel to assert rights that the party may otherwise have. Unless waiver of the right is prohibited, UCC § 9–602, a court may apply the doctrines of waiver or estoppel in particular cases subject to the principles found in UCC § 1–103. In addition, the obligations of "good faith, diligence, reasonableness, and care" may not be waived by agreement. UCC §§ 1–302, 9–602, cmt. 2.

2. Marshaling

Marshaling refers to the equitable doctrine that a court may impose to require a secured party to obtain value to apply against the obligation from collateral in a manner that does not disadvantage another secured creditor. For example, assume SP–1 had a first priority security interest in Asset A which is worth $10,000 and in Asset B which is worth $20,000 to secure a debt worth $15,000 and SP–2 had a second priority security interest in Asset A only to secure a debt worth $10,000. The court may employ the doctrine of marshaling to require SP–1 to sell Asset B first in order to allow SP–2 to realize value out of Asset A. If SP–1 sold Asset A first, SP–2's security interest would be extinguished and SP–2 would not have a right, absent judgment and execution against the debtor, to pursue Asset B. See UCC § 9–610, cmt. 5. This doctrine is subject to numerous caveats which are explored in the cases in which the doctrine is invoked. A full exploration of this doctrine is beyond the scope of these materials.

3. Lender Liability

Another set of equitable doctrines revolves around the factual scenario of a secured party "taking control" of a debtor's operation to the detriment of other creditors of the debtor. If a court determines that the secured party has acted in a manner that unfairly disadvantages other creditors of the debtor, the court may subordinate the secured party's claim under principles of equitable subordination, hold the secured party liable to the other creditors as an undisclosed principal under agency law, or may find that the secured party has failed to act in good faith, resulting in a breach of its agreement with the debtor. While the use of these doctrines has waned over the years, the secured party in enforcing its security interest or agricultural lien must take care to comply with the terms contained in the documentation of the lending arrangement and the rules of Article 9 and act in good faith in its relationships with the other creditors of the obligor in order to have the best chance of defeating these arguments. Review Chapter I.

4. Bankruptcy of the Debtor

The debtor's bankruptcy proceedings will have an immediate effect on the secured party's ability to enforce its security interest.

a. Automatic Stay

The automatic stay will prevent the secured party from taking any action to collect on its security interest or agricultural lien from the debtor, from property of the debtor, or from the property of the estate. 11 U.S.C. § 362(a). Actions stayed include sending the debtor default notices, sending requests for payment, repossession of the collateral, collection against obligations owed the debtor, and disposition of collateral.

(1) Relief From Stay
The secured party may request that the bankruptcy court grant relief from the automatic stay based upon two alternate grounds. The first ground is that the value of the secured party's interest in the collateral is not adequately protected. This ground generally focuses on depreciation or other risks to the collateral that make its value decline during the pendency of the bankruptcy case. The second ground is that the debtor

does not have any equity in the collateral and the collateral is not necessary for an effective reorganization. 11 U.S.C. § 362(d). If the bankruptcy court grants the secured party relief from the automatic stay, the court order will generally allow the secured party's enforcement process to go forward pursuant to the provisions of Article 9.

(2) Violation of the Stay

If the court does not grant relief from the stay, the secured party is subject to liability for damages and contempt of court proceedings for proceeding with its enforcement process. In addition, the rights of the transferee will be subject to being avoided by the bankruptcy court. 11 U.S.C. § 549.

b. Turnover

If the secured party is already in possession of the collateral but has not completed the enforcement process when the debtor files bankruptcy, the automatic stay bars the secured party's ability to continue the disposition or retention process. 11 U.S.C. § 362(a). In addition, the secured party has an obligation to turn over to the estate the debtor's property that is in its possession unless the property is of inconsequential value to the estate. 11 U.S.C. § 542(a). Generally, a secured party will ask for adequate protection of its interest in the collateral in response to the estate's motion for turnover of property. 11 U.S.C. § 363(e).

H. Review Questions for Chapter VI

Question 1

On January 5, Evergreen Landscaping and Design, Inc. signed a security agreement with First Bank granting First Bank a security interest in all of Evergreen's inventory and equipment then owned or thereafter acquired to secure all obligations then owed or thereafter owed to First Bank. That same day First Bank lent Evergreen $100,000. First Bank did not file a financing statement. On April 24, Evergreen defaulted on a payment to First Bank under the loan agreement.

Advise First Bank as to how to enforce its security interest as to these items of Evergreen's property: (i) flowers and green plants in the greenhouse and (ii) amounts owed to Evergreen by customers who purchased items on unsecured credit from Evergreen.

Question 2

First Bank has an attached security interest in Jamie Smith's car to secure the loan made to Jamie to enable her to buy the car. The loan is payable in equal monthly installments over 5 years. Jamie has paid reliably for two years but has missed the last two payments. Jamie has not communicated with First Bank and the bank officer has asked what it needs to do to enforce First Bank's security interest in the car.

A. Advise the bank officer.
B. In looking at the documents on this loan, you realize that First Bank has not obtained notation of its security interest on the car's certificate of title, does that change your advice?
C. In looking at the documents on this loan, you discover a clause in the security agreement that provides that the debtor agrees that the secured party may keep the collateral in satisfaction of the debt if the secured party repossesses the collateral upon the debtor's default. Does that clause help First Bank in enforcing its security interest?

Question 3

First Bank has an attached security interest in inventory then owned or thereafter acquired of Auto Dealer, Inc. to secure any obligation then or thereafter owed to First Bank. First Bank has filed an effective financing statement in the correct location against Auto Dealer, Inc. indicating inventory as the collateral. Auto Dealer, Inc. sold a car on credit from its inventory to Brice Industries, retaining title in the car until Brice Industries had completed all payments. Auto Dealer sold that purchase agreement with Brice Industries to Commercial Factors, which took possession of the physical copy of the agreement. Thereafter Auto Dealer defaulted on the loan to First Bank. First Bank seeks to repossess the car sold to Brice Industries, in order to apply the proceeds to Auto Dealer's debt owed to First Bank. Advise First Bank. Review the material in Chapter V before giving your advice.

VII

Liability for Violation of Article 9

In general, if a secured party fails to follow the rules provided in Article 9, the secured party is liable for actual damages caused by the violation to any person that is injured by reason of the violation. UCC § 9–625(b). Persons injured by the noncompliance may include the debtor, a secondary obligor, another secured party, or a lien holder. The secured party's liability for noncompliance with Article 9 may not be waived by an agreement with the debtor or obligor. UCC § 9–602(13). The remedies set forth in Article 9 are remedies that are to be applied for any violation of Article 9, not just for violation of the rules for enforcement of security interests or agricultural liens. UCC § 9–625, cmt 2. A secured party may also be required to comply with other law in obtaining and enforcing a security interest or agricultural lien. Liability for failure to comply with that other law will be governed by that other law, not Article 9.

A. Obtaining an Injunction

A court may enter an injunction against a secured party requiring the secured party to dispose of the collateral on appropriate terms and conditions. UCC § 9–625(a).

B. Additional Recovery if Collateral is Consumer Goods

If the collateral is consumer goods, a debtor or secondary obligor may recover, in addition to actual damages caused by the secured party's failure to comply with

Article 9, additional damages for noncompliance with the enforcement rules of Part 6 of Article 9. Those additional damages are twofold: a return of the interest charges (credit service charge or time-price differential) and 10% of either the principal amount of the debt or the cash price of the consumer goods. UCC § 9–625(c)(2). Although the comment states that this remedy is available only in a consumer-good transaction, the statute provides it is available whenever the collateral is consumer goods. UCC § 9–625, cmt. 4. A secured party is not liable for this penalty more than once with respect to any secured obligation. UCC § 9–628(e). This remedy is not available for the secured party's failure to comply with the requirement to send the calculation of the surplus or deficiency in a consumer-goods transaction under UCC § 9–616. UCC § 9–628(d).

C. Effect of Noncompliance with Article 9 Enforcement Rules on the Recovery of a Deficiency Judgment or Entitlement to a Surplus

If the obligor or debtor puts into issue the secured party's compliance with the Article 9 enforcement rules, the secured party bears the burden of proving that the secured party complied with the Article 9 requirements. UCC § 9–626(a)(1), (2).

1. Calculating the Deficiency: Rebuttable Presumption Rule

If a secured party has failed to comply with the Part 6 rules regarding enforcement of the security interest or agricultural lien, the obligor's liability for the deficiency may be eliminated or reduced instead of awarding actual damages caused by the failure to comply. UCC § 9–625(d).

a. Effect of Noncompliance: Presumption

If it is determined that the secured party did not comply with the requirements of Article 9 in enforcing its security interest or agricultural lien, there is a rebuttable presumption that the collateral's value that would have been obtained in a complying enforcement process was exactly the amount of the debt plus recoverable costs of enforcement, resulting in no liability for any deficiency. UCC § 9–626(a)(4).

Example: Secured Party failed to conduct a commercially reasonable disposition of an item of collateral. The debt owed to Secured Party and the costs of the disposition total $15,000, and the collateral was sold for $5,000. The collateral is presumed to have been disposed of for $15,000, resulting in no liability for a deficiency.

b. Burden of Proof on Complying Disposition: Rebutting the Presumption

The secured party has the burden to demonstrate that the value of the collateral that could be obtained in a complying disposition was less than the amount of the debt plus recoverable costs of enforcement. If the secured party does so, then the deficiency is calculated based upon the difference between the amount of the debt plus costs of enforcement and the amount of proceeds that a complying disposition of the collateral would have obtained. UCC § 9–626(a)(3).

Example: Secured Party failed to conduct a commercially reasonable disposition of an item of collateral. The debt owed to Secured Party and the costs of the disposition total $15,000, and the collateral was sold for $5,000. Secured Party demonstrates that the value of the collateral that would be realized in a complying disposition was $8,000. Secured Party may seek a deficiency of $7,000 from the obligor.

c. Restriction on Eliminating the Deficiency

The comment indicates that the rebuttable presumption rule as described above does not apply to repossession of collateral in breach of the peace as that is not part of "enforcement" of the security interest. Rather, the rules on actual damages should apply. UCC § 9–626,cmt. 2. This seems a rather curious limitation on the word "enforcement" as repossessing collateral without breach of the peace has historically been the beginning of the enforcement process against tangible collateral.

d. Calculation of the Deficiency in a Consumer Transaction

The rebuttable presumption rule as stated above does not apply to consumer transactions. The courts are free to apply court-developed rules, including the rebuttable presumption rule or the rule that if there is a violation of the Article 9 enforcement rules, the secured party is absolutely barred from collection of any deficiency. UCC § 9–626(b), cmt. 4.

2. Obtaining a Surplus

If the debtor demonstrates that a secured party's compliance with the enforcement rules of Article 9 would have resulted in a surplus instead of a deficiency, the debtor may recover damages for failure to obtain the surplus even if the deficiency is eliminated as set forth above. UCC § 9–625(d).

D. Statutory Damages

In addition to the remedy for actual damages, a debtor (or person named as debtor in a filed record) or a consumer obligor may also recover statutory damages of $500 from the secured party if the secured party fails to comply with several listed requirements: (i) the duties of a secured party stated in UCC § 9–208 when in control of collateral; (ii) the duties of a secured party if the account debtor has been notified of an assignment as stated in UCC § 9–209; (iii) the duty to file a financing statement only with authorization as stated in UCC § 9–509(a); (iv) failure to cause the secured party of record to file a financing statement as provided in UCC § 9–513(a) and (c); (v) failure to send the explanation of the calculation of the surplus or deficiency as required in UCC § 9–616(b)(1) if that failure is part of a pattern or practice of noncompliance; (vi) failure to send a waiver of its right to collect the deficiency in a timely manner as required in UCC § 9–616(b)(2); (vii) failure to comply with a request regarding listing the collateral claimed or obligations secured as required in UCC § 9–210. UCC § 9–625(e), (f). A secured party that does not claim an interest in collateral or claim that obligations are secured has a reasonable excuse for failing to respond to the request under UCC § 9–210 and thus would not be liable for the statutory damages. UCC § 9–625(f). If the secured party fails to respond to such a request under UCC § 9–210 and should have, the secured party may claim a security interest only as shown in the list or statement included with the request as against a person that is reasonably mislead by the failure to respond. UCC § 9–625(g).

E. Protection of Secured Party

A secured party may not be liable for violations of the provisions of Article 9 in several circumstances.

1. Lack of Knowledge of Identity and How to Communicate

Unless the secured party knows that the person is a debtor or obligor, knows the identity of that person, and knows how to communicate with that person, the secured party will not be liable to a debtor, obligor, or to a lienholder or secured party of the debtor or obligor for violations of the Article 9 requirements. UCC §§ 9–605, 9–628(a), (b).

2. Reasonable Belief That Transaction or Collateral Not Subject to Consumer-based Rule

If the secured party has a reasonable belief that a transaction is not a consumer transaction or a consumer-goods transaction, or a reasonable belief that the collateral is not consumer goods, the secured party will not be liable for violations of the requirements of Article 9 that are directed toward those two types of transactions or consumer goods. The secured party's reasonable belief must be based upon the debtor's representation of what the collateral was going to be used for or the obligor's representation of the purpose of the obligation. UCC § 9–628(c).

F. Review Questions for Chapter VII

1. The secured party fails to conduct a commercially reasonable sale of repossessed equipment. What is the secured party's liability for that failure?

2. The secured party repossesses equipment in a manner that constitutes a breach of the peace. What is the secured party's liability for that action?

3. The secured party fails to properly perfect its security interest in the debtor's goods. What is the secured party's liability for that action?

4. The secured party fails to file a termination statement when the debtor requests the secured party do so. Assuming that the secured party should have filed the termination statement, what is the secured party's liability for that failure?

5. The secured party fail to send the calculation of surplus and deficiency notice after a disposition in a consumer-goods transaction when required to do so under UCC § 9–616(b)(1). What is the secured party's liability for that failure?

Appendix A

Answers to Review Questions

Chapter I

1. True. A contingent debt is a debt that may become fixed in the future based upon an occurrence of some event. A mature debt is a debt that is currently due.

2. False. A contingent debt is a debt that may become fixed in the future based upon an occurrence of some event. A disputed debt is an obligation for which the debtor has a basis for disputing the fact or amount of the obligation.

3. False. A debt that is not mature may be either secured or unsecured.

4. False. The Bankruptcy Code does not require the debtor to be insolvent to be eligible to file a bankruptcy case. 11 U.S.C. § 109.

5. False. If the creditor follows applicable legal process, the creditor may be able to effect a seizure of a consumer debtor's personal property to apply to a debt.

6. True. Absent a court order or a lien that allows the creditor to take an item of the debtor's property to apply to a debt, the creditor has no right to seize the debtor's property without the debtor's consent.

7. True. A creditor may be liable to the debtor by "acting under color of state law" and in conjunction with state actors in violating a debtor's constitutional rights.

8. True. See the definition of "debt collector" in the Act.

9. False. In limited circumstances, that information may be included on a credit report.

10. False. Sending a notice of amount owed violates the automatic stay. 11 U.S.C. § 362.

11. True. A transfer made with intent to hinder, delay or defraud creditors is an avoidable transfer even if the debtor receives reasonably equivalent value for the asset transferred.

12. True. Exemption statutes generally do not prevent granting a consensual lien in property that would otherwise be exempt from execution.

13. False. The bankruptcy discharge operates to discharge the in personam obligation and does not affect any lien on the debtor's property.

Chapter II

1. False. Parties may not prevent Article 9 from applying if the transaction falls within the scope of Article 9. UCC § 9–109.

2. False. This exception is only true if the state has a statutory scheme that displaces Article 9's provisions. UCC § 9–109(c)(2) and (3).

3. True. UCC § 9–102(a)(2), (47).

4. False. UCC § 9–109(d)(4) through (8).

5. True. UCC § 9–102(a)(11).

6. False. UCC § 9–109(a) includes these transactions unless excluded by UCC § 9–109(c) and (d).

7. True. UCC §§ 9–109(a)(1), 1–203, 1–201(b)(35).

8. False. UCC §§ 9–109(a)(4); 9–102(a)(20).

9. True. UCC § 9–102(a)(44).

10. True. UCC § 9–102(a)(33).

11. False. UCC § 9–102(a)(47), (65).

12. True. UCC § 9–102(a)(31), (79).

13. False. UCC § 9–109(b).

14. False. UCC § 9–109(a), (d)(13) and comment 16.

15. False. UCC § 9–109(a).

16. False. Article 9 applies to rights under an insurance policy that are a health-care-insurance receivable. UCC §§ 9–109(d)(8), 9–102(a)(46).

17. True. The seller's retention of title to delivered goods is in effect a security interest, UCC § 2–401, and that security interest is within the scope of Article 9. UCC § 9–109(a)(5).

18. False. These collateral categories are mutually exclusive. UCC § 9–102(a)(2), (42), (61).

19. False. To be a consumer-goods transaction, the transaction must also be a consumer transaction. UCC § 9–102(a)(24), (26).

20. False. If a person both grants a security interest in personal property and also owes repayment of the secured obligation, that person is both the debtor and the obligor. UCC § 9–102(a)(28), (59).

Chapter III

1. False. UCC § 9–203. A security interest attaches only when all three requirements for enforceability have been met.

2. False. UCC §§ 9–203, 9–102(a)(74).

3. False. UCC § 9–108(e).

4. False. UCC §§ 9–106, 8–106, 8–301.

5. False. UCC § 9–104.

6. False. UCC § 9–105.

7. False. UCC §§ 9–202, 9–203.

8. False. UCC §§ 9–203(f), 9–315(a)(2).

9. False. See UCC § 9–203(c) regarding security interests that arise pursuant to operation of law.

10. False.

11. False. UCC § 9–401.

12. False. UCC § 9–406 through § 9–409.

13. True, but only upon a demand by the debtor. UCC § 9–208.

14. True. What constitutes proceeds in this context will be determined pursuant to bankruptcy law. 11 U.S.C. § 552.

15. True. UCC §§ 9–203, 1–204.

16. False. Value must be given, but the secured party need not advance the value. In addition, the value need not be advanced to the debtor. The debtor and the obligor may be two different persons. UCC § 9–102(a)(28), (59).

17. False. An agricultural lien must arise under another statute, not under Article 9. UCC § 9–102(a)(5). That other statute will determine whether the agricultural lien attaches to farm products.

18. False. A debtor need only have rights in the collateral or power to transfer rights in the collateral to the secured party. Those rights do not have to be ownership rights. UCC § 9–203.

19. False. A consumer may grant a security interest in his or her investment property. The fact that the collateral may have to be more specifically described if the transaction is a consumer transaction is not a prohibition on granting a security interest in that property. UCC § 9–108(e).

20. False. UCC § 9–203.

Chapter IV

Question 1

To assert a lien without obtaining the debtor's agreement to grant a security interest, Barley must have an agricultural lien that is created under a *statute* other than Article 9. Thus, if the lien is a common law lien, it is not an "agricultural lien" under Article 9. If there is a state statute that creates that lien, then you must determine whether the lien is an "agricultural lien" as defined in UCC § 9–102. If it is an agricultural lien as defined in Article 9, to perfect that lien Barley must file a financing statement covering the collateral in the jurisdiction where the collateral is located, UCC § 9–302, and in the filing office designated under that state's UCC § 9–501. The financing statement is sufficient to perfect the agricultural lien if it complies with the requirements of UCC § 9–502. To avoid a rejection by the filing office, the financing statement must contain the information required by UCC § 9–516(b). The financing statement is only authorized to be filed if it indicates only the collateral that is subject to the agricultural lien. UCC § 9–509(a).

Question 2

If the collateral type is governed by federal law that preempts Article 9 or by a state statute that governs when a state governmental body is the debtor, UCC § 9–109(c), Article 9 will not control the perfection method of the collateral type. If the transaction falls outside the scope of Article 9, Article 9 will not control the perfection method.

Collateral Type	Perfection Method	Scope of Article 9
A. Electronic chattel paper	Filing, control, and automatic in some circumstances. UCC §§ 9–105, 9–309, 9–310, 9–312, 9–314, 9–315.	Under UCC § 9–109(a), both sales of and obligations secured by electronic chattel paper included unless excluded by UCC § 9–109(d).
B. Goods not covered by a certificate of title or a document of title	Filing, possession, and automatic in some circumstances, UCC §§ 9–313, 9–310, 9–309, 9–312, 9–315.	Obligations secured by goods (including sales with retention of title) and consignments included, UCC § 9–109.
C. Goods covered by certificate of title	Compliance with certificate of title law, UCC 9–311.	Obligations secured by goods (including sales with retention of title) and consignments included, UCC § 9–109.
D. Documents of title and goods covered by such documents but not covered by a certificate of title law	If negotiable and tangible, possession, filing, and automatic in some circumstances, UCC §§ 9–310, 9–313, 9–312, 9–309, 9–315. If negotiable and electronic, control, filing, and automatic in some circumstances, UCC §§ 9–310, 9–314, 9–313, 9–312, 9–309, 9–315. If nonnegotiable, either electronic or tangible, filing, and automatic in some circumstances, UCC §§ 9–310, 9–315.	Obligations secured by documents of title included, UCC § 9–109.

Collateral Type	Perfection Method	Scope of Article 9
E. Accounts	Filing, and automatic perfection in some circumstances, UCC §§ 9–310, 9–309, 9–315.	Under UCC § 9–109(a), both sales of and obligations secured by accounts included unless excluded by UCC § 9–109(d).
F. Tangible chattel paper	Possession, filing, and automatic in some circumstances, UCC §§ 9–310, 9–312, 9–313, 9–315.	Under UCC § 9–109(a), both sales of and obligations secured by tangible chattel paper included unless excluded by UCC § 9–109(d).
G. Instruments	Possession, filing, and automatic in some circumstances, UCC §§ 9–310, 9–309, 9–312, 9–313, 9–315.	Under UCC § 9–109(a), obligations secured by instruments included, unless excluded by UCC § 9–109(d), and sales of promissory notes included, unless excluded by UCC § 9–109(d).
H. Certificated security	Taking delivery, control, filing, and automatic in some circumstances, UCC §§ 9–106, 9–313, 9–310, 9–309, 9–312, 9–314, 9–315.	Obligations secured by certificated security included, UCC § 9–109.
I. Payment intangibles	Filing, and automatic in some circumstances, UCC §§ 9–310, 9–309, 9–315.	Under UCC § 9–109(a), both sales of and obligations secured by payment intangibles included, unless excluded by UCC § 9–109(d).
J. Inventory	Possession, filing, and automatic in some circumstances, UCC §§ 9–313, 9–310, 9–309, 9–312, 9–315.	Obligations secured by inventory (including sales with retention of title) and consignments included, UCC § 9–109.

Collateral Type	Perfection Method	Scope of Article 9
K. Consumer goods	Possession, filing, and automatic in some circumstances, UCC §§ 9–313, 9–310, 9–309, 9–312, 9–315. If covered by certificate of title, compliance with certificate of title law, UCC § 9–311.	Obligations secured by consumer goods (including sales with retention of title) and consignments included, UCC § 9–109, subject to being excluded from definition of consignment, UCC § 9–102.
L. General intangibles	Filing, and automatic in some circumstances, UCC §§ 9–310, 9–315, 9–309.	Under UCC § 9–109(a), obligations secured by interest in general intangibles, and sales of payment intangibles included, unless excluded by UCC § 9–109(d).
M. Letter-of-credit right	Control, and automatic in some circumstances, UCC §§ 9–312, 9–310, 9–308, 9–315, 9–314, 9–107.	Obligations secured by letter-of-credit right included, UCC § 9–109(a), subject to superior rights of transferee beneficiary, UCC § 9–109(c).
N. Equipment	Possession, filing, and automatic in some circumstances, UCC § 9–313, 9–310, 9–309, 9–312, 9–315.	Obligations secured by equipment (including sales with retention of title) and consignments included, UCC § 9–109.
O. Farm products	Possession, filing, and automatic in some circumstances, UCC §§ 9–313, 9–310, 9–309, 9–312, 9–315.	Obligations secured by farm products, and agricultural liens, included, UCC § 9–109.
P. Fixtures	Possession, filing, and automatic in some circumstances, UCC §§ 9–313, 9–310, 9–309, 9–312, 9–315.	Obligations secured by fixtures included, UCC § 9–109(a), subject to UCC § 9–109(d)(11).

Collateral Type	Perfection Method	Scope of Article 9
Q. As-extracted collateral	Filing, possession if goods, and automatic in some circumstances, UCC §§ 9–310, 9–309, 9–313, 9–312, 9–315.	Obligations secured by as-extracted collateral and sales of accounts that are as-extracted collateral included, UCC § 9–109(a), unless excluded by UCC § 9–109(d).
R. Deposit accounts	Control, or automatic in some circumstances, UCC §§ 9–310, 9–312, 9–314, 9–104, 9–315.	Obligations secured by deposit accounts included, UCC § 9–109(a), unless excluded by UCC § 9–109(d)(13).
S. Uncertificated security	Control, filing, or automatic in some circumstances, UCC §§ 9–310, 9–309, 9–314, 9–106, 9–315.	Obligations secured by uncertificated security included, UCC § 9–109.
T. Securities entitlement	Control, filing, or automatic in some circumstances, UCC §§ 9–310, 9–309, 9–308, 9–314, 9–106, 9–315.	Obligations secured by securities entitlement included, UCC § 9–109.
U. Securities account	Control, filing, or automatic in some circumstances, UCC §§ 9–310, 9–309, 9–314, 9–106, 9–315.	Obligations secured by securities account included, UCC § 9–109.
V. Manufactured home	Possession, filing, and automatic in some circumstances, UCC §§ 9–313, 9–310, 9–309, 9–312, 9–315, and compliance with certificate of title law in some circumstances, UCC § 9–311.	Obligations secured by manufactured home included, UCC § 9–109(a), subject to UCC § 9–109(d)(11).
W. Proceeds	Possession, filing, and automatic in some circumstances, UCC §§ 9–310, 9–315, and compliance with certificate of title law in some circumstances, UCC § 9–311.	Obligations secured by proceeds included, UCC § 9–109(a), subject to exclusion by UCC § 9–109(d).

Question 3

If the collateral type is governed by federal law that preempts Article 9 or by a state statute that governs when a state governmental body is the debtor, UCC § 9–109(c), Article 9 will not control the choice of law issue. If the transaction falls outside the scope of Article 9, Article 9 will not control the choice of law issue.

Collateral Type	Choice of law for perfection
A. Electronic chattel paper	Location of debtor, UCC § 9–301.
B. Goods not covered by a certificate of title or a document of title	Location of debtor unless possessory security interest, or fixtures and perfected by a fixture filing, or as-extracted collateral, or timber to be cut, UCC § 9–301.
C. Goods covered by certificate of title	Jurisdiction that issued certificate of title, UCC § 9–303.
D. Documents of title and goods covered by such documents but are not covered by a certificate of title law	Location of debtor unless possessory security interest in tangible negotiable document of title, UCC § 9–301.
E. Accounts	Location of debtor unless as-extracted collateral, UCC § 9–301.
F. Tangible chattel paper	Location of debtor unless possessory security interest, UCC § 9–301.
G. Instruments	Location of debtor unless possessory security interest, UCC § 9–301.
H. Certificated security	Location of debtor if perfect by filing or automatic perfection of security interest created by broker or securities intermediary, otherwise where certificated security is located, UCC § 9–305.
I. Payment intangibles	Location of debtor, UCC § 9–301.
J. Inventory	Location of debtor unless possessory security interest, UCC § 9–301.

Collateral Type	Choice of law for perfection
K. Consumer goods	Location of debtor unless possessory security interest, UCC § 9–301. If subject to certificate of title law, then jurisdiction issuing certificate of title, UCC § 9–303.
L. General intangibles	Location of debtor, UCC § 9–301.
M. Letter-of-credit right	If issuer is located in a state of the United States, location of issuer, unless the security interest is automatically perfected in the letter-of-credit right is a supporting obligation, UCC § 9–306. In all other cases, location of debtor, UCC § 9–301.
N. Equipment	Location of debtor unless possessory security interest or in fixtures in which security interest is perfected by a fixture filing, UCC § 9–301. If subject to certificate of title law, then jurisdiction issuing certificate of title, UCC § 9–303.
O. Farm products	Location of debtor, unless possessory security interest or agricultural lien, then location of farm products, UCC §§ 9–301, 9–302.
P. Fixtures	Location of debtor unless possessory security interest or security interest is perfected by a fixture filing, UCC § 9–301. If subject to certificate of title law, then jurisdiction issuing certificate of title, UCC § 9–303.
Q. As-extracted collateral	Location of wellhead or minehead, UCC § 9–301.
R. Deposit accounts	Location of bank holding deposit account, UCC § 9–304.
S. Uncertificated security	Location of debtor if perfect by filing or automatic perfection of security interest created by broker or securities intermediary, otherwise where issuer of security is located, UCC § 9–305.
T. Securities entitlement	Location of debtor if perfect by filing or automatic perfection of security interest created by broker or securities intermediary, otherwise where securities intermediary is located, UCC § 9–305.

Collateral Type	Choice of law for perfection
U. Securities account	Location of debtor if perfect by filing or automatic perfection of security interest created by broker or securities intermediary, otherwise where securities intermediary is located, UCC § 9–305.
V. Manufactured home	Location of debtor unless possessory security interest or in fixtures in which security interest is perfected by a fixture filing, UCC § 9–301. If subject to certificate of title law, then jurisdiction issuing certificate of title, UCC § 9–303.
W. Proceeds	Depends upon type of proceeds and operation of UCC § 9–315.

Question 4

Perfection. Perfection of the security interest requires attachment of the security interest plus completion of the required perfection step. UCC § 9–308.

Collateral description. To perfect a security interest in the collateral requires a classification of the collateral for purposes of the description of the collateral in the security agreement and to identify the appropriate perfection method. The Bank will also have to know if this is a consumer transaction as that will impact the collateral description. UCC §§ 9–108(e), 9–504.

A. Deposit account, perfect by obtaining control. UCC §§ 9–312(b), 9–104. If consumer transaction, taking an interest in deposit account is excluded from Article 9, UCC § 9–109(d)(13). Investigate other law regarding how to take an interest.

B. Goods, could be consumer goods, equipment, or inventory depending upon its use. If not inventory, it will likely be governed by a certificate of title law and perfection must be by compliance with that law. UCC § 9–311. If inventory, then perfection must be by filing a financing statement, UCC §§ 9–310, 9–311. If a consumer transaction, secured party cannot merely use UCC collateral descriptor to describe "consumer goods." UCC § 9–108(e).

C. Goods, could be consumer goods, equipment, or inventory depending upon its use. Less likely to be covered by a certificate of title law, but that must be investigated. If a consumer transaction, cannot merely use UCC collateral descriptor to describe "consumer goods." UCC § 9–108(e).

D. Goods, could be consumer goods, equipment, or inventory depending upon its use. If not inventory, it may be governed by a certificate of title law and perfection must be by compliance with that law. UCC § 9–311. It may also be a fixture and perfection by a fixture filing in order to perfect as against real estate claimants. UCC §§ 9–310, 9–334. It may be real estate and an interest must be taken under real estate law. UCC § 9–109(d)(11). If a consumer transaction and covered by Article 9 as the mobile home is not considered real estate, secured party cannot merely use UCC collateral descriptor to describe "consumer goods." UCC § 9–108(e).

E. Could be an account, or if the neighbor's obligation to pay is in writing, may be an instrument, or if Albert has a record in which the neighbor has promised to pay and granted a security interest in the car to secure payment, the obligation is chattel paper. Perfect by filing a financing statement and if there is a record, taking possession of the record if it is a tangible instrument or tangible chattel paper, and if electronic chattel paper, take control of the electronic chattel paper. UCC §§ 9–310, 9–314, 9–313. Could be automatically perfected under UCC § 9–309(2) if it is an account.

F. Securities entitlements. Perfect by filing, UCC § 9–310, or by control, UCC § 9–314. If a consumer transaction, secured party cannot merely use UCC collateral descriptor to describe "securities entitlements." UCC § 9–108(e).

G. Goods, could be consumer goods, farm products (if Albert is a farmer engaged in farming operations) or inventory, depending upon its use. Perfect by filing or possession. UCC § 9–310, 9–313. If a consumer transaction, secured party cannot merely use UCC collateral descriptor to describe "consumer goods." UCC § 9–108(e).

H. If covered by a negotiable document of title, perfect by filing as to the document. Should also take possession (if tangible) or control (if electronic) of the negotiable document of title. UCC §§ 9–312, 9–310, 9–313, 9–314. If covered by a nonnegotiable document of title, perfect as to the goods through filing as to the goods, sending a notice to the warehouse, or obtaining the document issued to the Bank. UCC § 9–312. If not covered by a document of title, then perfect as to the goods either by filing as to the goods, or by obtaining the bailee's acknowledgment of security interest. UCC § 9–310, 9–313. If a consumer transaction, secured party cannot merely use UCC collateral descriptor to describe "consumer goods." UCC § 9–108(e).

Future advances and after-acquired property clauses. To secure all future obligations that Albert may owe to the Bank, the security agreement should provide a well-drafted future advances clause such as "Debtor grants an interest in the described collateral to secure any and all obligations that the Debtor may now or hereafter owe Bank." To obtain a security interest in personal property acquired by Albert after the security agreement is signed, the collateral description should contain an after-acquired property clause after the listing of the description of the collateral such as "and all collateral of the same type that the Debtor now has an interest or acquires an interest in the future." To the extent that Bank wants a security interest in after-acquired consumer goods, that interest is subject to limitation by UCC § 9–204.

Rights in collateral and authenticated security agreement with collateral description. Bank should investigate Albert's rights in the collateral and attempt to ascertain whether any other party has rights in the collateral. If a party has rights in the collateral other than a lien interest or security interest, that person is a "debtor" and should authenticate the security agreement. UCC § 9–203, 9–102 (definition of debtor). The security agreement must contain an accurate description of the collateral. UCC §§ 9–203, 9–108. If this is a consumer transaction (as defined in UCC § 9–102), using the UCC collateral descriptors is not a sufficient description for a security interest in consumer goods or securities entitlements. UCC § 9–108(e).

Financing statement. To the extent that the security interest in the collateral will be perfected by filing, the financing statement must have the correct name of the debtor and the secured party and must indicate the collateral. UCC § 9–504. The financing statement must be filed in the correct place, UCC § 9–301 through § 9–307. To avoid a rejection by the filing office, the financing statement must contain the information required by UCC § 9–516(b).

Question 5

The basic answer is that Bank will have to monitor Albert's location, the location of the collateral and whether Albert disposes of the collateral in order to maintain perfection. What has to be monitored depends upon the type of collateral and the perfection method initially used.

A. Checking account. If Albert moves, there is no effect on perfection of a security interest in the checking account as original collateral. UCC § 9–304. If National Bank's jurisdiction changes, the law governing perfection will change. UCC § 9–316(f). If Albert moves the checking account to another bank, or is no longer the customer on the checking account at National Bank, an existing control agreement between Bank and National Bank will no longer be effective. UCC §§ 9–104, 9–314.

B. Pickup truck. If the pickup truck is not inventory, perfection should be through compliance with the certificate of title law and having Bank's interest noted on the certificate of title. UCC §§ 9–303, 9–311. Albert moving, moving the location of the pickup truck, or disposing of the pickup truck, will not matter unless that results in a change in the certificate of title law, or the pickup truck is no longer covered by the same certificate of title law. UCC §§ 9–315, 9–316(d), (e). If the pickup truck is part of the inventory of Albert, and perfected by filing a financing statement, it will be filed in the jurisdiction of the debtor's location. UCC § 9–301. If Albert moves or the pickup truck is sold to another person located in a different jurisdiction, then the filing will have to be made in the new jurisdiction, UCC § 9–316(a). Moving the location of the pickup truck when it is inventory does not affect the perfection issue.

C. Riding lawnmower. Assuming the lawnmower is not covered by a certificate of title statute, perfection will be by filing in Albert's location. If Albert moves or the lawnmower is sold to another person located in a different jurisdiction, then the filing will have to be made in the new jurisdiction, UCC § 9–316(a). Moving the location of the lawnmower inventory does not affect the perfection issue.

D. Mobile home. If the mobile home is real property and not personal property, and Bank has taken a mortgage in the mobile home, what Bank has to do to monitor and make sure its interest stays intact is subject to real property law. There may be a process for removing the mobile home from the real estate, and thus may make the mobile home no longer subject to a real estate mortgage. Assuming the mobile home is personal property and Bank has made a fixture filing, a change in the mobile home's location may change the governing law. UCC § 9–301. Section 9–316 contains no grace period for obtaining perfection in another manner if the fixture filing is no longer effective because the mobile home moved. If the mobile home is personal property, and Bank has perfected through a non-fixture filing, a change in Albert's location or a sale of the mobile home to another person located in another jurisdiction could affect perfection. UCC §§ 9–301, 9–316(a). If the mobile home is covered by a certificate of title law, perfection will be affected only if there is a change in the governing certificate of title law. UCC §§ 9–303, 9–316(d), (e).

E. Amounts owed to Albert by his next door neighbor stemming from the sale of the car to the neighbor. If an account, chattel paper or an instrument, and perfected by filing, a change in Albert's location or a sale of the account, chattel paper, or instrument to another person located in another jurisdiction will affect perfection. UCC §§ 9–301, 9–316(a). If the obligation is represented by an instrument or tangible chattel paper, and perfection was by possession, a loss of possession will end perfection. UCC § 9–313. In addition, a change in the location of the collateral to another jurisdiction may affect perfection. UCC § 9–316(c). If electronic chattel paper and perfection was by control, a loss of control will end perfection, UCC § 9–314. In addition, a change in Albert's location or a sale of the chattel paper to a person located in another jurisdiction will affect perfection. UCC § 9–316(a).

F. Bonds held in an account at Brokerage Inc. If perfected by filing, a change in Albert's location or a sale of the securities entitlement to another person located in another jurisdiction will affect perfection. UCC §§ 9–301, 9–316(a). If perfected by control, and the events specified in UCC § 9–314 take place, perfection will end. If perfected by control and the securities intermediary's jurisdiction changes, perfection may be lost. UCC §§ 9–305(a), 9–316(f), (g).

G. Produce from Albert's garden. If perfected by filing, a change in Albert's location or a sale of the produce to another person located in another jurisdiction will affect perfection. UCC §§ 9–301, 9–316(a). If perfected by possession, a loss of possession will end perfection. UCC § 9–313. In addition, a change in the location of the collateral to another jurisdiction may affect perfection. UCC § 9–316(c).

H. Goods stored at Warehouse Inc. If the goods are covered by a negotiable document of title and perfection is by filing, a major risk to perfection is that the goods are removed from the warehouse and no longer covered by the document of title. In that case, Bank needs to make sure it should file a financing statement that is sufficient to perfect in the goods directly. If there is a filing covering the negotiable document of title, Albert's change in location or disposition of the document of title to a person located in another jurisdiction will affect perfection. UCC §§ 9–301, 9–316(a). If the negotiable document of title is tangible and perfection is by possession, loss of possession will result in loss of perfection, UCC § 9–313, and if the document of title moves location, that may result in the loss of perfection, UCC § 9–316(c). If the negotiable document of title is electronic and perfection is by control, a loss of control will end perfection, UCC § 9–314, and a change in Albert's location or a disposition of the document to another person located in another jurisdiction will change the law governing perfection, UCC § 9–316(a). If perfection is achieved through filing directly as to the goods (either because there is no document of title or the document of title is nonnegotiable), Albert's change in location or disposition of the goods to a person located in another jurisdiction will affect perfection. UCC §§ 9–301, 9–316(a). If perfection is achieved through a notification to the warehouse, or a warehouse's acknowledgment, perfection is maintained only if the warehouse maintains possession of the goods, and thus removing the goods from the warehouse may result in a loss of perfection. UCC §§ 9–312, 9–313.

Chapter V

Question 1

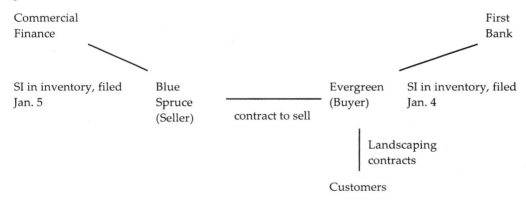

A. The potted trees are inventory of Blue Spruce and Commercial Finance has an attached security interest in inventory. Query whether the trees are "personal property" before they are potted.

Second, First Bank's security interest could attach to those potted trees when they are identified to the contract for sale as between Blue Spruce and Evergreen. Because Evergreen is buying the trees for sale to its Customers, the trees are Evergreen's inventory to the extent that Evergreen has rights in the potted trees.

Third, does Evergreen qualify as a buyer in ordinary course of business before the trees are delivered so that it will take the trees free of Commercial Finance's security interest? In order to qualify as a buyer in ordinary course of business, at a minimum, Evergreen must either have possession or a right to possession of the trees under Article 2. Evergreen does not have possession, but it is possible it may have a right to possession under UCC § 2–502 or § 2–716. Based upon these facts, it is not clear if the criteria of either of those sections is met. If Evergreen qualified as a buyer in ordinary course of business, then it would take the potted trees free of Commercial Finance's security interest and there is no priority contest.

Fourth, assuming Evergreen does not qualify as a buyer in ordinary course of business, and because Commercial Finance has perfected its interest in the trees as inventory, UCC §§ 9–317, 9–320, Evergreen's interest in the trees is subject to Commercial Finance's security interest. Assuming that First Bank's security interest has indeed attached to these trees pursuant to the creation of the special property interest upon identification of the trees to the contract between Blue Spruce and Evergreen, the priority contest is determined by the first to file or perfect rule, UCC § 9–322, with the exception of the double debtor rule in UCC § 9–325. Under that rule, Commercial Finance's security interest would have priority over First Bank's security interest even though First Bank's security interest was filed first.

B. First, Commercial Finance probably lost its security interest in the delivered trees because Evergreen probably qualified as a buyer in ordinary course of business when it took delivery even though the check bounced. At issue would be whether Evergreen bought the trees in good faith if it knowingly tendered a check that bounced. UCC § 1–201(b)(9). If Evergreen was a buyer in ordinary course of business, the priority contest would be between First Bank and Blue Spruce.

Blue Spruce's right to get the trees back is based upon its right to reclaim as a cash seller of goods when the cash payment failed. UCC § 2–507. That right is subject to the right of good faith purchasers for value. First Bank would generally qualify as a good faith purchaser for value given its security interest in the trees as part of Evergreen's inventory (a purchase as defined in UCC § 1–201(b)(29)).

Value need not be "new" value, but may be the outstanding debt and there is not any fact that would lead to doubt about First Bank's good faith. Thus, First Bank's interest in the trees is superior to Blue Spruce's interest in the trees.

If Evergreen was not a buyer in ordinary course of business, so that the trees were subject to Commercial Finance's security interest even though delivered to Evergreen, Commercial Finance's security interest would be superior to First Bank's security interest for the same reason as set forth in Part A above. UCC §§ 9–322, 9–325. Commercial Finance's security interest in the trees would also be superior to Blue Spruce's interest in the trees because of the security agreement it has with Blue Spruce. Thus, the relative order of priority of interests in the trees would be Commercial Finance, First Bank, and Blue Spruce.

Question 2

To obtain a first priority perfected security interest in fixtures, the Secured Party should file a fixture financing statement complying with the requirements of UCC § 9–502 in the real estate recording office for the real estate where the fixtures are located. UCC § 9–301, 9–501. If that filing is made before any other interest in the real estate is recorded by someone other than the debtor, the Secured Party should have first priority interest in the fixtures as against someone with that subsequently recorded interest in the real estate. UCC § 9–334(e)(1). The debtor must either have a recorded interest in the real estate or be in possession of the real estate.

If another person has a recorded interest in the real estate so that the Secured Party's fixture financing statement is not first filed, the Secured Party should obtain the consent to the Secured Party's interest in the fixture from the person with the previously recorded interest in the real estate. UCC § 9–334(f).

To obtain priority over other persons with security interests in the fixtures but without interests in the real estate, the Secured Party should have a first-filed financing statement before anyone else has filed or perfected as to the fixtures, including through using the proceeds perfection rules. UCC §§ 9–322(a), 9–315. This filing need not be a fixture financing statement but may be a regular financing statement filed in the central filing office designated by UCC § 9–301, 9–501. The fixture financing statement should count as a filing for purposes of the first to file or perfect rule of UCC § 9–322.

Question 3

If the contract between Larry and Darla is a "true lease," State Bank's security interest is subordinate to Larry's interest in the road grader. UCC § 2A–307. If the contract between Larry and Darla is a disguised security interest, then under the priority rule that a perfected security interest has priority over an unperfected security interest, State Bank's security interest in the road grader is superior to Larry's interest. UCC § 9–322(a).

Based upon these facts, this transaction may be a disguised security transaction based upon the factors in UCC § 1–203(b)(1). Darla has the obligation to make all the lease payments even if she returned the grader early and the term of the lease is 10 years compared to the usual economic life of road graders from 8 to 12 years. The question is whether there will be a meaningful residual interest in the grader to be returned to Larry. If it is determined that the road grader actually has an economic value beyond the 10 year lease term, then the question is one based upon the facts of the case and is hard to make a definitive conclusion on these facts. UCC § 1–203(a).

Question 4

State Bank had a properly perfected security interest in the SUV as inventory of the dealer, Autoworld. The security interest was attached in the SUV pursuant to the debtor authenticated security agreement with the adequate collateral description, the giving of value, and Autoworld having rights in the collateral. UCC § 9–203. Filing a financing statement against the cars was the proper method of perfection for goods covered by a certificate of title law while the item is inventory of a dealer. UCC § 9–311. The financing statement complied with UCC § 9–502 and was filed in the correct place. UCC § 9–501, 9–301. However, when the SUV was sold to Daniel Boone, Daniel Boone likely qualified as a buyer in ordinary course of business under UCC § 1–201(b)(9), and took free of that security interest. UCC § 9–320(a). Assume that Daniel did so qualify as a buyer in ordinary course of business.

Although First Bank took a security interest in Daniel's goods and a car qualifies as a good, under UCC § 9–108(e), this description is not adequate if the transaction between First Bank and Daniel is a consumer transaction and the car is a consumer good. Without an adequate description in the security agreement, First Bank would not have an attached security interest in the vehicle. The limitation on after acquired property clauses in the case of consumer goods does not apply, UCC § 9–204, as First Bank did give value within 10 days of Daniel acquiring rights in the SUV.

Assume that the transaction between First Bank and Daniel was not a consumer transaction because the loan was not primarily for family, personal or household use. UCC § 9–102(a)(26). In that case First Bank has an attached security interest in the SUV but has not properly perfected its interest. First Bank should have its security interest noted on the certificate of title. UCC § 9–311. Thus First Bank would have an attached but unperfected security interest in the SUV.

Assuming the transaction between First Bank and Daniel was not a consumer transaction, the SUV could still be consumer goods in the hands of Daniel. If the SUV was consumer goods in the hands of both Daniel and Ted, then Ted would take the SUV free of First Bank's security interest under UCC § 9–320(b) and comment 6. In addition, the rule of UCC § 9–317(b) may protect Ted if he gave value and took possession of the SUV without knowledge of First Bank's unperfected security interest.

Even if the transaction between Autoworld and Daniel is a consumer transaction and the SUV is consumer goods, Autoworld's retention of title is effective to create a security interest, UCC §§ 2–401, 1–201(b)(35), assuming the description of the SUV in the purchase agreement is more specific than a UCC collateral description term, UCC § 9–108(e). Autoworld properly perfected its security interest by obtaining notation of its interest on the certificate of title for the SUV. UCC § 9–311. That notation is sufficient to prevent Ted from taking the SUV free of Autoworld's security interest under either UCC § 9–317(b) or § 9–320(b).

Daniel has no interest in the SUV after its sale to Ted even though the sale was on credit. Daniel has not retained any property interest in the SUV to secure the obligation to pay the price.

Thus, assuming Daniel was a buyer in ordinary course of business from Autoworld, the likely priority of interests in the SUV is Autoworld first and Ted second.

Question 5

To analyze a complex factual scenario, first identify who has interests in each asset and the nature of those interests (security interest, agricultural lien, execution lien, etc.). Second, identify and apply the appropriate priority rules to resolve the relative priority between each entity that has an interest in the asset. For example, if there are three creditors, A, B, and C, there are three priority contests: A v. B, A v. C and B v. C. Third, construct a timeline of events for the purpose of applying any priority rules that depend upon timing. A focused and methodical approach is the only way to find through a complex scenario that has many different types of assets and creditors.

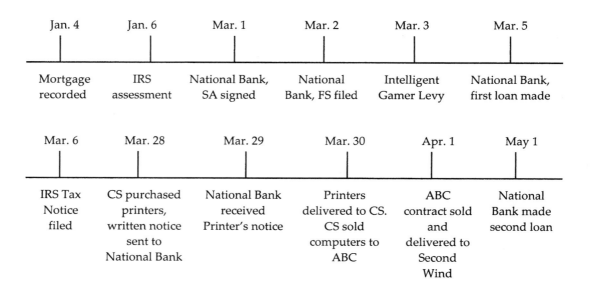

A. Type of collateral: Software, UCC § 9–102(a)(76).
1. *Software is not identifiable proceeds of other collateral.*

Execution lien. If under other state law, Intelligent Gamer can levy on software and has done so properly, Intelligent Gamer would likely have an execution lien on the software.

Tax lien. Assuming the software is property for purposes of the federal tax lien statute, the IRS has a tax lien on the software.

Security interest. National Bank has not taken a security interest in the software as original collateral because neither software nor general intangibles are listed as collateral in the security agreement, and this software does not fall within the definition of inventory (software is not a "good." UCC § 9–102(a) (definition of "inventory," "goods," "software," and "general intangibles").

Priority rule. Because National Bank has no interest in the software, the only priority contest is between the IRS and Intelligent Gamer. Under 26 U.S.C. § 6323(a), the execution lien would have priority because it was in existence prior to the filing of the IRS tax lien notice.

2. *Software is identifiable proceeds of other collateral.*

Security interest. The only way for National Bank to have an attached security interest in the software is if it was identifiable proceeds of other collateral in which National Bank had an attached security interest. UCC § 9–315(a). Assuming that factual connection can be made so the security interest has attached to the software, National Bank's security interest in the software would be perfected only if the software was not acquired with cash proceeds, and the security interest in the original collateral that generated the software as proceeds is properly perfected by the filing in Minnesota.[2] UCC § 9–315(d)(1). It those two criteria cannot be met, then National Bank's security interest in the software as identifiable proceeds would be attached but unperfected. This is the more likely scenario, because in the retail business, it is far more likely that proceeds of the inventory collateral would be in the form of cash proceeds and that proceeds of inventory sold would be used to buy more inventory.

Priority rules.

Execution lien v. tax lien. Even if the software is identifiable proceeds of other collateral, the priority rule that governs the execution lien vs. the tax lien would not change.

Execution lien v. security interest. To resolve the priority contest between the security interest and the execution lien, UCC § 9–317(a) provides that the security interest either has to be perfected before the levy (here it was not as value was advanced after the levy, UCC § 9–308), or the security agreement has to be entered into with an adequate collateral description and a filed financing statement has to "cover" the collateral. The security agreement is arguably adequate because proceeds are included even though they are not specifically described, UCC § 9–203(f), and the financing statement could arguably cover the software only if the rule of UCC § 9–315(d)(1) was met (see above discussion of the perfection point). If those two points are resolved in National Bank's favor, then its security interest in the software to secure first advance made on March 5 would have priority over the execution lien. As to the security interest securing the subsequent advance the security interest does not have priority over the execution lien. UCC § 9–323. If the two criteria of UCC § 9–315(d)(1) were not met, then National Bank's security interest is unperfected and does not meet the criteria of UCC § 9–317(a) and the execution lien would have priority over National Bank's attached but unperfected security interest.

---

[2]The filing in Minnesota is proper as that is where the debtor is located, UCC §§ 9–301, 9–307, and the name of the debtor, collateral indication, and secured party name on the financing statement all comply with UCC § 9–502, as to the collateral types listed. In addition, the Secretary of State's office is likely the proper place to file within Minnesota, UCC § 9–501.

Tax lien v. security interest. Under 26 U.S.C. § 6323(a), if National Bank's security interest was perfected in the software under UCC § 9–315(d)(1), then its security interest to secure the first advance made on March 5 would be senior to the tax lien. Even if the security interest in the software is perfected, National Bank's security interest to secure the second advance would be inferior to the tax lien, as it was not made within 45 days of the tax lien notice filing. If the security interest in the software is not perfected, then it will be subordinate to the tax lien.

Order of priority if security interest in software is perfected under UCC § 9–315(d)(1). Security interest (to secure $100,000 advance), execution lien, tax lien, security interest (to secure $5,000 advance)

Order of priority if security interest in software is attached but not perfected under UCC § 9–315(d)(1). Execution lien, tax lien, security interest.

B.   Collateral classification: Equipment, UCC § 9–102(a)(33).

Lien interests and security interests. National Bank has an attached and perfected security interest in the equipment. UCC § 9–203. The financing statement was properly filled out and filed in the right place. UCC §§ 9–301, 9–501, 9–502. For the same reason as in Part A, Intelligent Gamers has an execution lien on the equipment. The IRS has a tax lien on the equipment under 26 U.S.C. § 6321.

Priority of interests in the equipment.

Execution lien v. tax lien. Under 26 U.S.C. § 6323(a), the execution lien has priority over the tax lien because the execution lien was in existence prior to the filing of the IRS tax lien notice.

Security interest v. tax lien. National Bank's security interest that secures the $100,000 advance given before the filing of the tax lien notice is superior to the tax lien, and its security interest that secures the $5,000 advance is inferior to the tax lien. 26 U.S.C. § 6323(a), (d).

Security interest v. execution lien. National Bank's security interest that secures the $100,000 advance will be superior to the execution lien, and its security interest that secures the $5,000 advance is subordinate to the execution lien. UCC §§ 9–317, 9–323.

Order of priority. National Bank's security interest (securing the $100,000 advance), execution lien, tax lien, National Bank's security interest (securing the $5,000 advance).

C. Collateral classification: Equipment or inventory? It is unclear whether the printers are going to be for sale or lease (i.e. inventory) or whether they are going to be used in the business (equipment). UCC § 9–102(a)(33), (48).

Execution lien. Under most states' execution statutes, the execution lien does not attach to property that the debtor acquires after the levy. Thus, regardless of whether the property is inventory or equipment, Intelligent Gamer's execution lien does not attach to the printers.

Tax lien. The IRS' tax lien attaches to all property the debtor had an interest in at the time of assessment and to all property the debtor acquires thereafter. Thus the IRS has a tax lien in these printers, regardless of whether they are inventory or equipment.

Printer's Inc. title retention. Retention of title is treated as a security interest after delivery of the printers to buyer, UCC § 2–401, regardless of whether the printers are equipment or inventory. Thus Printer's Inc. has a purchase money security interest in the printers. UCC § 9–103. Printer's security interest is unperfected as it is not in possession of the printers, it did not file a financing statement, and its security interest does not qualify for automatic perfection. UCC § 9–310.

National Bank's security interest. National Bank has an attached security interest in the printers pursuant to the collateral description in the security agreement and the after-acquired property clause, regardless of whether the printers are equipment or inventory. National Bank's security interest is perfected due to its properly filed financing statement covering both inventory and equipment.

Priority if collateral is inventory.

National Bank's security interest v. Printer's security interest. National Bank's perfected security interest has priority over Printer's unperfected security interest. UCC § 9–322(a). Printer's security interest does not qualify for purchase money priority under UCC § 9–324(b).

National Bank's security interest v. tax lien. National Bank's security interest that secures the $100,000 advance is superior to the tax lien under 26 U.S.C. § 6323(c). National Bank's security interest to secured the $5,000 advance is subordinate to the tax lien.

Tax lien v. Printer's security interest. Under 26 U.S.C. § 6323(a), Printer's security interest is subordinate to the tax lien. The tax lien statute does not address purchase money security interests. Although there is some case law that may give priority to a purchase money security interest over a pre-existing tax lien, it is more likely that the unperfected subsequently arising security interest would be inferior to the tax lien.

Order of priority if collateral is inventory. First, National Bank's security interest to secure $100,000. Second, tax lien. Third, National Bank's security interest to secure the $5,000 advance. Fourth, Printer's security interest.

Priority if collateral is equipment.

National Bank's security interest v. Printer's security interest. National Bank's perfected security interest has priority over Printer's unperfected security interest. UCC § 9–322(a). Printer's security interest does not qualify for purchase money priority under UCC § 9–324(a).

National Bank's security interest v. tax lien. Under 26 U.S.C. § 6323(a), National Bank's security interest in the printers is subordinate to the tax lien. Because the collateral is equipment, 26 U.S.C. § 6323(c) does not apply.

Tax lien v. Printer's security interest. Under 26 U.S.C. § 6323(a), Printer's security interest is subordinate to the tax lien. The tax lien statute does not address purchase money security interests. Although there is some case law that may give priority to a purchase money security interest over a pre-existing tax lien, it is more likely that the unperfected subsequently arising security interest would be inferior to the tax lien.

Order of priority if collateral is equipment. First, tax lien. Second National Bank's security interest. Third, Printer's security interest.

D. Collateral classification: Equipment and fixtures, UCC § 9–102(a)(33), (41). The problem stipulates these items are fixtures under Iowa law, which would be the governing law on this issue (where the items are located). Minnesota law is not relevant to the classification of the items as fixtures. Fixtures and equipment are not mutually exclusive categories.

Real estate mortgage. If, under real estate law in Iowa, which governs the mortgage, the lien interest attaches to fixtures, then Real Estate Moguls has a lien interest in these items.

Execution lien. If, under Iowa law governing execution levies, the execution lien attaches to fixtures, then Intelligent Gamers has an execution lien on these items.

Tax lien. The IRS has a tax lien on these items pursuant to its assessment.

National Bank's security interest. National Bank's security interest is attached and perfected in equipment, which would include these fixtures. National Bank need not have filed a fixture financing statement in the real estate records in Iowa in order to perfect in these items as equipment. The properly filled out financing statement filed in Minnesota is a sufficient perfection step.

Priority rules.

National Bank's security interest v. Real Estate Moguls' mortgage. In order to National Bank's security interest to have priority over the mortgage interest, National Bank would have had to file a fixture financing statement in appropriate real estate records in Iowa, unless Computer Systems had a right to remove the fixtures as against Real Estate Moguls or Real Estate Moguls consented to the priority of National Bank's security interest. UCC § 9–334. Nothing in the facts indicates that is so, thus Real Estate Moguls' mortgage interest has priority over National Bank's security interest.

National Bank's security interest v. execution lien. Although National Bank's security interest was not perfected prior to the execution levy and thus does not qualify for priority under UCC § 9–334(d)(3), it qualifies for priority over the execution lien under the rule of UCC § 9–317(a) as to the $100,000 advance, but not as to the $5,000 advance. UCC § 9–323.

Real estate mortgage v. execution lien. This priority contest would be governed by Iowa real property law. Assuming a "first in time" principle applied, the mortgage interest has priority over the execution lien.

National Bank's security interest v. tax lien. National Bank's security interest that secures the $100,000 advance has priority over the tax lien, 26 U.S.C. § 6323(a). The security interest that secures the $5,000 advance does not have priority over the tax lien. 26 U.S.C. § 6323(d).

Tax lien v. Real Estate Moguls' mortgage. Real Estate Moguls' mortgage has priority over the tax lien under 26 U.S.C. § 6323(a).

Execution lien v. tax lien. Under 26 U.S.C. § 6323(a), the execution lien has priority over the tax lien.

Order of priority. First, Real Estate Moguls' mortgage. Second, National Bank's security interest that secures the $100,000 advance. Third, execution lien. Fourth, tax lien. Fifth, National Bank's security interest that secures the $5,000 advance.

E. Collateral classification: Deposit account, UCC § 9–102(a)(29).

Security interest. National Bank has an attached security interest in the account through two methods. First, National Bank has an interest in the deposit account as original collateral due to the collateral description in the security agreement. UCC § 9–203. Second, to the extent the deposit account is identifiable proceeds of sales of collateral, such as inventory, National Bank has an automatically attached security interest in such proceeds. UCC § 9–315(a). National Bank has not achieved control of the deposit account, UCC § 9–104, and thus the only way in which it is perfected in the deposit account is through automatic perfection of a security interest in identifiable cash proceeds. UCC § 9–315. Whether the deposit account is in fact "identifiable" cash proceeds would depend factually tracing the proceeds of other collateral into the account.

Tax lien. The tax lien attached to the deposit account upon assessment and to all amounts deposited in the account subsequently.

Execution lien and mortgage. Intelligent Gamers has not served its execution levy on the bank and the real estate mortgage only attaches to real property interests. Thus neither entity has an interest in the deposit account.

Priority rule. As of March 6, National Bank's security interest in funds on deposit at that time would have priority over the tax lien. 26 U.S.C. § 6323(a). As to amounts deposited in the account subsequently to the filing of the tax lien (assuming those amounts are proceeds of inventory) National Bank's security interest does not qualify for priority over the tax lien as the amounts were not "in existence" at that time. National Bank cannot take advantage of either 26 U.S.C. § 6323(b)(1) (deposit accounts are probably not "securities" as defined in the tax lien statute) nor 26 U.S.C. § 6323(c) (deposit accounts are not covered by this exception) to obtain priority in those subsequently deposited amounts. If the $2,000 remaining in the account is presumed to be remaining from the March 6 amount of $10,000 under a rule like the lowest intermediate balance rule, then National Bank has an argument that its security interest in that $2,000 has priority over the tax lien. If either a different tracing presumption is applied or the account was totally depleted (down to $0) and then replenished, the tax lien would have priority.

F. Under the analysis in part E above, only National Bank and IRS have interests in the checking account, and hence are the only two possible creditors with interests in the funds transferred from the account. Even if National Bank has an attached and perfected security interest in the deposit account as proceeds of other collateral, the utility company will take the funds transfer free of that security interest. UCC § 9–332. Whether the utility company can take the funds transfer free of the tax lien depends upon application of 26 U.S.C. § 6323(b), a "purchaser" of a "security" without knowledge or notice of the tax lien. The funds transfer may be considered "money" (one of the asset types within the definition of "security" in 26 U.S.C. § 6323(h)) under the tax lien statute.

G. Collateral classification: Chattel paper, UCC § 9–102(a)(11).

Security interests. National Bank has an attached and perfected security interest in chattel paper under its security agreement and properly filed financing statement. Second Wind's purchase of the chattel paper is deemed to create a security interest in the chattel paper, as long as the transaction is not excluded from Article 9 under UCC § 9–109(d). Assuming the transaction is not excluded from the scope of Article 9, Second Wind's possession of the contract is perfection of its security interest. UCC § 9–313.

Tax lien. The tax lien attached to the chattel paper as soon as the contract was enforceable against ABC Industries.

Execution lien. Under applicable state statutes, the execution lien generally does not automatically attach to after-acquired property. If the computers were in the store at the time of the levy and thus subject to the execution lien, the applicable state statutes may or may not provide for attachment of the execution lien to the proceeds of property subject to the execution lien. Unless that unique set of facts is true, Intelligent Gamers has no interest in this chattel paper.

Priority rules.

National Bank's security interest v. Second Wind's security interest. If the chattel paper did not indicate it had been assigned to anyone else, and Second Wind paid new value, took possession of the chattel paper in the ordinary course of its business, and without knowledge that the purchase violated the rights of the secured party, Second Wind will have priority in the chattel paper under UCC § 9–330.

National Bank's security interest v. tax lien. Under 26 U.S.C. 6323(c), National Bank's security interest would have priority over the tax lien.

Second Wind's security interest v. tax lien. Second Wind's security interest does not qualify for priority under 26 U.S.C. § 6323(c) because its security agreement (the purchase contract) does not predate the tax lien notice filing. Second Wind would only be able to take advantage of 26 U.S.C. § 6323(b) if the chattel paper qualified as a "security" as defined in 26 U.S.C. § 6323(h), a dubious proposition. Thus the tax lien would have priority over Second Wind's security interest.

Order of priority. A circular priority is created by application of these priority rules. Second Wind has priority over National Bank, National Bank has priority over the tax lien, and the tax lien has priority over Second Wind.

H. Collateral classification: Inventory, UCC § 9–102(a)(48), assuming the computers were held for sale or lease, and not excess equipment sold as part of the periodic turnover of equipment.

National Bank's security interest. As previously discussed, National Bank has a properly attached and perfected security interest in inventory. If ABC qualified as a buyer in ordinary course of business, UCC § 1–201(b)(9), ABC took the computers free of this security interest.

Tax lien. Even if the tax lien attached to the computers prior to their sale to ABC, ABC may qualify as a purchaser who will take the computers free of the tax lien as long as it meets the criteria of 26 U.S.C. § 6323(b)(3).

Execution lien. Assuming the computers were in the store on the date of the execution levy, and thus the execution lien attached, whether ABC takes the computers free of the execution lien will be determined by Iowa's law governing execution liens. Generally, a purchaser would take subject to the execution lien.

Second Wind's security interest. As the buyer of the chattel paper, Second Wind succeeds to Computer Associates' status as a secured party, with a security interest in the computers granted by ABC. Second Wind's security interest is not perfected as there is no filed financing statement as to the computers, nor does Second Wind have possession of the computers.

Priority rule. Assuming that National Bank's security interest and the tax lien are no longer attached to the computers, the priority contest is between Second Wind's security interest and the execution lien. When Computer Associates sold the computers to ABC, those computers were already subject to the execution lien. ABC's rights are subject to the execution lien, and under UCC § 9–203, ABC can only grant a security interest in property to the extent of its rights in that property, or the power to grant greater rights than it has. Under these facts, ABC does not have the right to grant greater rights than it has, and thus Second Wind's security interest is subordinate to the pre-existing execution lien.

I. Collateral classification: Accounts, UCC § 9–102(a)(2).

National Bank's security interest. National Bank's security interest is attached and perfected in accounts, whenever they arose, given the security agreement and the properly filed financing statement.

Tax lien. The tax lien has a tax lien in all the accounts that were in existence at the time of assessment and that arose thereafter.

Execution lien. Under most states' execution process, in order to levy on obligations owed to the debtor, notices must be given to the persons who owe the obligations. Assuming that those notices were not given in this case, there is no execution lien on the accounts.

Priority rule. To determine the priority as between the tax lien and National Bank's security interest in the accounts under 26 U.S.C. § 6323(a) and (c), three different groups of accounts must be considered: accounts in existence on March 6, when the notice of tax lien was filed; accounts arising between March 6 and 45 days thereafter; accounts arising after 45 days after the tax lien filing. As to the first group of accounts, National Bank's security interest has priority, 26 U.S.C. § 6323(a). As to the second group of accounts, National Bank's security interest has priority but only to secure the $100,000 advance, not the $5,000 advance. As to the third group of accounts, the tax lien has priority over National Bank's security interest.

J. Collateral classification: Investment property, and securities entitlement, UCC §§ 9–102(a)(49), 8–102.

Security interests. National Bank has an attached and properly perfected security interest in investment property, including these securities entitlements, based upon its security agreement and properly filed financing statement. Churn has a security interest in the securities entitlements based upon its brokerage agreement with Computer Systems and its interest is automatically perfected by control. UCC §§ 9–314, 9–106, 8–106.

Tax lien. The tax lien attached to these securities entitlements upon assessment.

Execution lien. Under most states' law, to execute on obligations owed to a debtor, service must be made on the person who owes the obligation, here Churn, the securities intermediary. Assuming such notice was not given, there is no execution lien on this asset.

Priority rules.

National Bank's security interest v. Churn's security interest. Churn's security interest has priority over National Bank's security interest. UCC § 9–328.

National Bank's security interest v. tax lien. National Bank's security interest has priority over the tax lien as to the $100,000 advance. 26 U.S.C. § 6323(a). The tax lien has priority over the security interest that secures the $5,000 advance.

Churn's security interest v. tax lien. Churn's security interest has priority over the tax lien. 26 U.S.C. § 6323(a).

Order of priority. First, Churn's security interest. Second, National Bank's security interest to secure the $100,000 advance. Third, the tax lien. Fourth, National Bank's security interest that secures the $5,000 advance.

Chapter VI

Question 1

Default. The first thing to verify is that there is actually a default under the terms of the security agreement or other lending documents and that there is not an argument that First Bank waived the default or is estopped from asserting a default.

Ability to enforce even though security interest is unperfected. The fact that First Bank's security interest is unperfected does not affect its enforcement options, although if there were competing creditors with liens in the assets, it may affect how much First Bank is actually able to realize through its enforcement actions.

Security interest in flowers and green plants and amounts owed to debtor. The second thing to verify is that First Bank has an attached security interest in the two types of items listed. First Bank has an attached security interest in inventory and equipment, including after-acquired collateral of that description to secure all obligations owed to First Bank, including after-incurred obligations. The flowers and green plants are likely inventory, if the term in the security agreement is interpreted to mean the same as the definition in UCC § 9–102 and the items are held for sale by the debtor. For First Bank to have a security interest in the amounts owed to the debtor by the debtor's customers, the question will be whether First Bank can demonstrate that the amounts owed are identifiable proceeds of inventory or equipment so that its security interest automatically attached to those obligations. UCC §§ 9–315, 9–203. Assuming that First Bank can make that factual showing, First Bank would have a security interest in those amounts owed to the debtor.

Enforcement against the flowers and green plants. To enforce its security interest against the plants and flowers, First Bank will need to obtain possession of them either by obtaining a court order that requires the debtor to allow First Bank possession of the items or by repossessing those items without a court order and without a breach of the peace. UCC § 9–609. Upon possession of the collateral, First Bank has the obligation to take reasonable care of the collateral. UCC § 9–207.

Once First Bank has possession of the items, the two basic obligations of First Bank to conduct a commercially reasonable disposition of the items and to do so after any required notices before the disposition. UCC § 9–610. A commercially reasonable disposition depends upon all the relevant facts and should be calculated to bring the best possible price. UCC § 9–610, 9–627.

Because these items may be considered perishable, First Bank may be excused from sending the required notices. UCC § 9–611(d). If First Bank is not excused from sending the notices, it must send a notice of disposition at least ten days before the disposition, UCC § 9–612, to the debtor, any secondary obligor, any person with an interest in collateral that has requested notice prior to the date the secured party sends the notices, and to any person that has filed a financing statement against the debtor in the correct place covering the collateral. UCC § 9–611. The content of the notice must comply with UCC § 9–613.

Once the collateral is disposed of, the secured party must apply the proceeds in accordance with the requirements of UCC § 9–615.

Enforcement against the obligations owed to debtor. First Bank should notify the persons that owe the obligations to the debtor that the payments should be made to First Bank. UCC § 9–607. First Bank should respond promptly to any requests to verify the amounts owed and the assignment so as to preserve its right to get payments as allowed by UCC § 9–406. Once First Bank collects the payments, First Bank must apply the payments to the obligation that Evergreen owes to First Bank in accord with UCC § 9–608. If First Bank has a right of recourse against the debtor or secondary obligor based upon uncollected obligations, First Bank must proceed in its collection activity in a commercially reasonable manner. UCC § 9–607(c).

First Bank could also use the disposition process set forth in UCC § 9–610 to sell the accounts to a buyer. In that case, First Bank must comply with the notice and commercial reasonableness requirements set forth in UCC § 9–610 through § 9–613 and apply the proceeds in accord with UCC § 9–615.

Question 2

A. As in Question 1, first verify that there is indeed a default that has not been waived or that the secured party is not estopped from asserting. Second, obtain possession of the collateral without a breach of the peace or pursuant to a court order. Third, send the required notices within a reasonable time before the disposition and hold a commercially reasonable disposition of the collateral. Because this appears to be consumer goods in a consumer-goods transaction, the secured party is not able to take advantage of the safe harbor time period in UCC § 9–612 and the secured party must send the more extensive notice specified in UCC § 9–614. If the collateral is consumer goods, the secured party need not send notice to anyone other than the debtor and any secondary obligors. UCC § 9–611(c)(3).

B. Perfection of a security interest is not required to engage in enforcement of the security interest. Failure to perfect a security interest, however, may result in the attached but unperfected security interest being subordinate to another perfected security interest in the collateral. UCC §§ 9–322, 9–317, 9–320(b). If there is an interest in the car that is superior to the unperfected security interest, that may affect the ability of the secured party to obtain value from the asset. For example, if Jamie has transferred the car to another consumer and that transfer results in the transferee taking the car free of the unperfected security interest, First Bank will be unable to obtain possession of the car from the transferee. UCC §§ 9–320(b), 9–317. On the other hand, if Jamie has not transferred her interest in the car or granted any other liens in the car, the lack of perfection will not affect First Bank's enforcement effort. Thus a full evaluation of the secured party's priority position is important to the effectiveness of the enforcement effort.

C. The secured party may not obtain a waiver of the debtor's rights or the secured party's obligations regarding retention of collateral in satisfaction of the debt. UCC § 9–602(10). The secured party may obtain after default a wavier of the secured party's obligation to conduct a disposition of consumer goods where the debtor has paid 60 percent of the principal amount. UCC § 9–624(b). The secured party must comply with the process outlined in UCC § 9–620 and § 9–621 to retain collateral that is consumer goods in full satisfaction of the debt. That in effect requires an agreement with the debtor to do so that is entered into after the default, UCC § 9–620, after sending the appropriate notices to that effect, UCC § 9–621, and receiving no timely objection to the retention.

Chapter VII

1. Secured party's liability is for either actual damages or for elimination of the deficiency pursuant to the rebuttable presumption rule. UCC § 9–625. The secured party's additional liability for a penalty of 10% of the loan amount or purchase price of the goods and a return of the interest charges only applies if the collateral is consumer goods.

2. The secured party's liability is for actual damages for the harm caused by the breach of the peace. UCC § 9–625(a). Although the comments to UCC § 9–627 indicate that the elimination of a deficiency judgment should not be an alternative consequence, it is difficult to get that result out of the language of that section.

3. The secured party has no liability for failing to perfect except for taking the risk that the priority rules will result in subordination of the security interest to another's interest in the collateral.

4. In addition to actual damages as provided in UCC § 9–625(b), the secured party is liable for a $500 penalty for failure to file a termination statement or provide one when it should have done so. UCC § 9–625(e).

5. In addition to actual damages as provided in UCC § 9–625(b), the secured party is liable for a $500 penalty only if the secured party's failure is part of a pattern, or practice of noncompliance.

Appendix B

Practice Exam

Idaho's Secretary of State's office is the designated central filing office under Idaho's UCC § 9–501. Washington's Department of Licensing is the designated central filing office under Washington's UCC § 9–501. Both Washington and Idaho allow a nonconsensual possessory lien to be asserted by a person who has furnished repairs to personal property.

Ace Hardware Inc. is an Idaho corporation with its headquarters in Spokane, Washington. Ace Hardware has two retail stores, one in Post Falls, Idaho, and one in Spokane, Washington. Ace is in the business of selling hardware, home maintenance supplies, yard care equipment and other items normally found in a hardware store.

Ace's president negotiated a lending agreement with National Bank for a $200,000 line of credit and on September 2, 2013, signed an agreement that granted National Bank a security interest in:

"all inventory and equipment now owned or hereafter acquired to secure all obligations that debtor now or hereafter owes to National Bank."

That same day, National Bank filed a financing statement in the Idaho Secretary of State's office. The financing statement named "Ace Hardware, Inc." as the debtor, "inventory and equipment" as the collateral, and National Bank as the secured party. After filing the financing statement electronically and receiving confirmation of the filing, that same day National Bank allowed Ace to draw $100,000 on the line of credit with National Bank. Ace used the funds to pay employees, sales taxes, employee taxes, and rent on its office space in Spokane.

On November 1, 2017, Hammer Supply Inc. sold tools to Ace with a purchase price of $50,000. Ace borrowed the entire purchase price from State Bank, signing a security agreement granting State Bank a security interest in "tools" to secure the purchase price. That same day, State Bank filed a financing statement in the Washington Department of Licensing office naming "Ace Hardware, Inc." as the debtor, "tools" as the collateral, and State Bank as the secured party. Also on November 1, 2017, State Bank sent a notice to National Bank that it was supplying tools on credit to Ace Hardware and that State Bank had a security interest in the tools. National Bank received that notice on November 4, 2017. Ace paid Hammer Supply with the funds from State Bank and Hammer Supply delivered the tools to the Spokane store on November 7, 2017.

On November 15, 2017, Ace sold $30,000 worth of the tools that Hammer Supply had delivered to the Spokane store to Best Construction Inc. Best paid $5,000 of the purchase price with a check and signed a promissory note promising to pay $25,000 plus interest to Ace by January 30, 2018. Ace took possession of the promissory note.

Ace deposited the check issued by Best to a checking account owned by Ace Hardware at State Bank on November 17, 2017. Ace delivered the tools to Best on November 18, 2017. The agreement between Ace and State Bank provided that State Bank had "a security interest in all deposits to secure any obligations Ace owed to State Bank." After the deposit of the $5,000 Best check, the balance in the State Bank checking account was $20,000.

On December 1, 2017, Ace sold a riding lawnmower to Michael Ebert for cash. Michael Ebert was planning to start a lawn service business in March 2018 and bought the lawnmower for use in that business when it went on sale during the winter season. Ebert borrowed most of the purchase price from Financial Company and signed a security agreement with Financial Company granting a security interest in the lawnmower to secure payment of the loan. Financial Company did not file a financing statement. Ebert in fact used the lawnmower for the lawn service business in the summer of 2018, but he did not make enough money and so shut down the business in September 2018. Ebert thereafter used the lawnmower to mow his own yard.

On December 15, 2017, Ace paid off all amounts it owed to National Bank and on December 30, 2017 drew $50,000 on its line of credit.

On January 2, 2018, Ace purchased new cash registers for use in Ace's two retail locations, from Grassley Associates. Grassley Associates is a sole proprietorship run by William Grassley, who is in the business of supplying equipment to retail stores. Grassley lives in Idaho, and has his office and all his items held for sale in a warehouse in Spokane, Washington. Ace put $10,000 down and signed an agreement granting Grassley a security interest in the cash registers to secure Ace's obligation to pay the remaining price, which was $30,000.

Grassley is financed by Continental Bank. That financing arrangement was entered into on July 1, 2013 when Grassley signed a security agreement granting a security interest in all of its inventory then owned or thereafter acquired to Continental Bank to secure all present and future debts owed to Continental Bank. On July 1, 2013, Continental Bank filed a financing statement against William Grassley as the debtor in the Idaho Secretary of State's office, identifying the collateral as "inventory," Continental Bank as the secured party, and "William Grassley" as the debtor. William Grassley is the name on Grassley's current Idaho driver's license.

On January 5, 2018, Grassley sold the contract with Ace to Jasper Enterprises, Inc. for $15,000 and delivered the contract to Jasper. Jasper notified Ace to make all payments to Jasper. Jasper Enterprises is in the business of buying payment obligations.

On February 2, 2018, one of Ebert's creditors (Rever's Inc.) levied on the lawn mower in execution of a judgment obtained against Ebert. The judgment was for $8,000.

On March 1, 2018, Ace decided it did not need all of the cash registers it had purchased and traded five of them to Breaker Industrial, Inc. in exchange for Breaker's services in fixing the furnace in the Post Falls store. Breaker Industrial is incorporated in Wyoming.

On March 1, 2018, Ace paid Jasper $10,000 by issuing a check drawn on the checking account at State Bank.

On March 15, 2018, Breaker sold the five cash registers on Ebay to Silly Toys, Inc. for $3,000, which Silly paid by a certified check drawn on its bank. Breaker deposited the check to its bank account held by Western Trust Bank and delivered possession of the cash registers to Silly Toys at its headquarters in California. Silly Toys is incorporated in California.

On May 1, 2018, Ace sold some of the tools that it had purchased from Hammer Supply to Welding Co., a Washington corporation, for $10,000. Welding Co. agreed to pay for the tools in 90 days with interest accruing at 1% per month.

On May 15, 2018, Ace sold the promissory note issued by Best Construction and Welding Co.'s obligation to pay for the tools to Factoring, Inc. Factoring, Inc. did not take possession of the note nor file any financing statement against Ace. Factoring, Inc. bought these two obligations in the ordinary course of its business.

On June 1, 2018, Continental Bank filed a continuation statement in the Idaho Secretary of State's office referencing its previous filing against Grassley.

On July 1, 2018, one of the cash registers used in the Spokane store broke and Ace took the cash register to Gadgets Repair, Inc. repair shop in Post Falls, Idaho, for servicing. Gadgets expended $750 in labor and material to fix the cash register. Gadgets has possession of the cash register.

On August 1, 2018, Ace borrowed an additional $5,000 from State Bank.

On September 30, 2018, Ace drew $25,000 on its line of credit with National Bank.

On November 5, 2018, Zenia Justin had the sheriff levy on all of Ace's inventory and equipment located at the Spokane store in execution of a judgment against Ace arising out of a slip and fall at the Spokane store. The amount of the judgment is $100,000. The estimated value of the inventory and equipment in the Spokane store at the time of the levy was $90,000.

Between November 18, 2017 and November 30, 2018, the checking account at State Bank had the following activity:

Date	Credits to account	Debits from account	Balance after debit or credit
Dec. 1, 2017	2,000 (sale of lawnmower)		22,000
Jan. 2, 2018		10,000 (cash register purchase)	12,000
Mar. 1, 2018		10,000 (payment to Jasper)	2,000
May 1, 2018	8,000 (tax refund)		10,000

On November 30, 2018, Ace owed the following amounts:
National Bank—$75,000; State Bank—$55,000; Jasper—$20,000; Gadgets—$750; and Justin—$100,000.

On November 30, 2018, Grassley owed Continental Bank was $50,000.

On November 30, 2018, Ebert owed Financial Company $3,000, and owed Rever's $8,000.

On November 30, 2018, Best owed on $25,000 on its promissory note and Welding Co. owed $10,000 on its contract.

It is December 1, 2018. Determine the priority of interests in the following items:
A. Tools sold by Hammer Supply to Ace and located in Ace's store in Spokane.
B. Tools sold by Hammer Supply to Ace and in hands of Best Construction.
C. Tools sold by Hammer Supply to Ace and in hands of Welding Co.
D. Promissory note issued by Best and in Ace's possession.
E. Checking account at State Bank.
F. Riding lawnmower in Ebert's possession.

G. Contract Ebert signed with Financial Company.
H. Cash registers purchased from Grassley in Ace's possession at Spokane store.
I. Cash registers purchased from Grassley in Ace's possession at Post Falls store.
J. Cash registers purchased from Grassley in Silly Toy's possession.
K. Cash register purchased from Grassley in Gadget's possession.
L. Contract between Grassley and Ace.
M. Contract between Ace and Welding Co.
N. Inventory and equipment in Ace's store in Post Falls (excluding items in I above).

Outline of issues for exam

The following discussion touches on the issues and rules used to resolve the priority contests in each asset. No attempt has been made to follow the usual IRAC (issues, rule, analysis, conclusion) format that is typically used on law school essay exams.

For each asset, identify who has interests in the asset and the nature of that interest. Once all the interests in that asset are identified, select and apply the appropriate priority rule.

A. *Tools sold by Hammer Supply to Ace and located in Ace's store in Spokane.*

Collateral classification: Inventory. UCC § 9–102(a)(48).

National Bank's security interest. Under UCC § 9–203, and pursuant to the security agreement, National Bank's security interest attached to all inventory then owned or thereafter acquired to secure the loan then outstanding and all future advances ($50,000 on Dec. 30, 2017 and $25,000 on Sept. 30, 2018). The fact that the loan was paid off for a period of 15 days (Dec. 15, 2017 to Dec. 30, 2017) does not affect the ability of National Bank to attach its security interest to secure those subsequent advances. National Bank's security interest in the tools attached when the debtor obtained rights in the tools, no later than November 7, 2107, when the tools were delivered to Ace. The security interest could have attached earlier, when the tools were identified to the contract between Ace and Hammer Supply. The security interest was perfected by the properly filed financing statement (correct debtor's name, secured party's name, collateral indication, and filing location). However, the effectiveness of that financing statement was not continued, and has thus lapsed, as of Sept. 3, 2018. UCC § 9–515. As of December

1, 2018, National Bank has an attached, but unperfected security interest in these tools.

State Bank's security interest. State Bank has an attached purchase money security interest pursuant to its security agreement ("tools" is a sufficient description, UCC § 9–108) by lending the value that was used to pay Hammer Supply for the tools. UCC §§ 9–103, 9–203. Even though State Bank timely and properly sent the notice to National Bank, attempting to obtain purchase money priority for its security interest under UCC § 9–324(b), State Bank filed its financing statement in the wrong location (Washington, instead of Idaho). Thus State Bank's security interest is attached, but unperfected.

Execution lien. Assuming under state law, that a lien arises upon levy of a writ of execution, Zenia Justin obtained a levy lien on the tools on Nov. 5, 2018.

National Bank's security interest v. State Bank's security interest. As of Sept. 1, 2018, National Bank's security interest in the tools was attached and perfected, and State Bank's security interest was attached but unperfected. Given the lapse of National Bank's financing statement as of Sept. 3, 2018, National Bank's security interest is deemed retroactively unperfected as against a purchaser of value, in this case State Bank. UCC § 9–515. Thus, the priority rule to apply on December 1, 2018 is UCC § 9–322(a)(3), when both interests are unperfected, first to attach has priority. However, in this case, both security interests would have attached at the same time, when Ace acquired rights in the tools. Article 9 does not state a priority rule for that circumstance, and the inference is that the two security interests would have co-equal priority.

National Bank's security interest v. execution lien. At the time the execution lien arose, National Bank's security interest was attached but unperfected, and there was no effective financing statement filed as to these tools. Under UCC § 9–317(a), the execution lien has priority over the security interest.

State Bank's security interest v. execution lien. At the time the execution lien arose, State Bank's security interest was attached but unperfected, and there was no effective financing statement filed as to these tools. Under UCC § 9–317(a), the execution lien has priority over the security interest.

Order of priority. Execution lien, supposedly co-equal priority for State Bank's and National Bank's conflicting attached, but unperfected security interests.

B. *Tools sold by Hammer Supply to Ace and in hands of Best Construction.*

Collateral classification in the hands of Ace: Inventory, UCC § 9–102(a)(44).

   Security interests. For the same reasons as stated in part A of the answer, at the time of the sale of the tools to Best Construction on Nov. 15, 2017, State Bank had an attached but unperfected security interest in the tools and National Bank had an attached and perfected security interest in the tools (financing statement had not yet lapsed).
   Buyer in ordinary course of business (BIOCOB). If Best Construction is a buyer in ordinary course of business, UCC § 1–201(b)(9), then Best Construction would take the tools free of both security interests under UCC § 9–320.
   Purchaser not a BIOCOB. If Best Construction is not a buyer in ordinary course of business, then it took the tools free of State Bank's security interest under UCC § 9–317(b) as long as Best Construction did not have knowledge of the security interest at the time it took delivery of the tools. If Best Construction is not a buyer in ordinary course of business, UCC § 9–317(b) does not protect it from National Bank's security interest until the effectiveness of National Bank's financing statement lapses. Because of that lapse, UCC § 9–515(c) provides that National Bank is deemed retroactively unperfected as to purchasers for value (Best Construction) and thus as of Sept. 3, 2018, Best Construction is deemed to have taken the goods free of National Bank's security interest, retroactively to the time of purchase (Nov. 15, 2017), as long Best Construction did not know of National Bank's security interest at that time.
   Priority. Because under either scenario (BIOCOB or nonBIOCOB), Best Construction takes the tools free of both security interests, there is no priority contest as to these tools. Best Construction has the only interest.

C. *Tools sold by Hammer Supply to Ace and in hands of Welding Co.*

Collateral classification in the hands of Ace: Inventory, UCC § 9–102(a)(44).

   Security interests. For the same reasons as stated in part A of the answer, at the time of the sale of the tools to Welding Co. on May 2, 1018, State Bank had an attached but unperfected security interest in the tools and National Bank had an attached and perfected security interest in the tools (financing statement had not yet lapsed).

Buyer in ordinary course of business (BIOCOB). If Welding Co. is a buyer in ordinary course of business, UCC § 1–201(b)(9), then it would take the tools free of both security interests under UCC § 9–320.

Purchaser not a BIOCOB. If Welding Co. is not a buyer in ordinary course of business, then it took the tools free of State Bank's security interest under UCC § 9–317(b) as long as it did not have knowledge of the security interest at the time it took delivery of the tools. If Welding Co. is not a buyer in ordinary course of business, UCC § 9–317(b) does not protect it from National Bank's security interest until the effectiveness of National Bank's financing statement lapses. Because of that lapse, UCC § 9–515(c) provides that National Bank is deemed retroactively unperfected as to purchasers for value (Welding Co.) and thus as of Sept. 3, 2018, Welding Co. is deemed to have taken the goods free of National Bank's security interest, retroactively to the time of purchase (May 2, 2018), as long Welding Co. did not know of National Bank's security interest at that time.

Priority. Because under either scenario (BIOCOB or nonBIOCOB), Welding Co. takes the tools free of both security interests, there is no priority contest as to these tools. Welding Co. has the only interest.

D. *Promissory note issued by Best and in Ace's possession.*

Collateral classification. Instrument and promissory note, UCC § 9–102(a)(47), (65).

National Bank's security interest. The promissory note is identifiable proceeds of National Bank's security interest in inventory. UCC § 9–315(a). At the time the promissory note was issued (Nov. 15, 2017), National Bank's security interest in the promissory note was perfected for 20 days, UCC § 9–315(c), and perfection continued in that note beyond the 20 days pursuant to UCC § 9–315(d)(1). However, once the effectiveness of the financing statement lapsed, that lapse is effective to unperfect National Bank's security interest as to the promissory note as to purchasers for value. UCC §§ 9–515(c), 9–315(e).

State Bank's security interest. The promissory note is identifiable proceeds of State Bank's security interest in the tools. UCC § 9–315(a). State Bank's security interest in the promissory note is unperfected because its security interest in the tools was unperfected, and State Bank has taken no sufficient perfection step as to the promissory note. UCC § 9–315(c), (d).

Factoring Co.'s interest. Factoring's purchase of the promissory note is likely a "security interest" in the note unless the transaction is excluded under UCC §

9–109(d)(5) or (7). If the sale to Factoring is within the scope of Article 9, UCC § 9–109(a), and thus Factoring has a deemed security interest in the promissory note that is automatically perfected, UCC § 9–309. If the transaction is excluded from the scope of Article 9, then Factoring's interest is an ownership interest that is not deemed a security interest.

National Bank's security interest v. Factoring's interest. If the sale to Factoring is excluded from the scope of Article 9 under UCC § 9–109(d), Factoring will not take the promissory note free of National Bank's security interests under UCC § 9–317(b) even if it purchased the promissory note without knowledge of the security interest because it did not take delivery of the promissory note. The note is still in Ace's possession. In that circumstance, Factoring owns the note subject to the National Bank's attached security interest. If the sale to Factoring is a deemed security interest and thus automatically perfected, Factoring's security interest has priority over National Bank's security interest because a perfected security interest has priority over unperfected security interests, UCC § 9–322(a).

State Bank's security interest v. Factoring's interest. The same analysis as above would apply to this priority contest.

National Bank's security interest v. State Bank's security interest. First to attach, UCC § 9–322(a), which was at the same time, when the note was issued. Thus they should have co-equal priority.

Order of priority. If the sale to Factoring is within scope of Article 9, Factoring's security interest first, then co-equal priority for State Bank and National Bank's security interests. If the sale to Factoring is not within the scope of Article 9, then first is co-equal priority for State Bank and National Bank's security interests, and then Factoring's ownership interest.

E. *Checking account at State Bank.*

Collateral classification: Deposit account, UCC § 9–102(a)(29).

National Bank's security interest. National Bank had a security interest in both the tools and the riding lawnmower as inventory. The $5,000 check from the sale of the tools and the $2,000 in cash from the lawnmower were identifiable proceeds of the inventory and deposited to the deposit account, which is also identifiable proceeds. All of these proceeds are "cash proceeds." UCC § 9–102(a)(9). The security interest was perfected in the original inventory and thus is perfected in the identifiable cash proceeds under UCC § 9–315(a)–(d). The lapse of the financing statement does not seem to affect that perfection. UCC § 9–315(e). Under the lowest intermediate balance rule, the amount of identifiable proceeds in the deposit account is $2,000. Thus, National Bank has a perfected security interest in $2,000 in the deposit account.

State Bank's security interest. Although State Bank has an unperfected security interest in $5,000 check that was deposited in the deposit account under a proceeds analysis, UCC § 9–315(a)–(d), it has a security interest in the deposit account's entire balance, $10,000, to secure the initial advance of $50,000, based upon its deposit agreement with Ace. That security interest is perfected by control. UCC § 9–104. That security interest does not secure the future advance of $5,000 because the deposit account security agreement did not contain a future advances clause.

Priority rule. Even though both National Bank and State Bank have perfected security interests in the deposit account, State Bank's perfection by control means that State Bank's security interest has priority in all of the funds in the deposit account. UCC § 9–327. As to $2,000 of the funds in the deposit account, National Bank's security interest has second priority. As to the remaining $8,000 in the deposit account, State Bank has the only security interest.

F. *Riding lawnmower in Ebert's possession.*

Collateral classification: Inventory in Ace's hands, UCC § 9–102(a)(44), and equipment in Ebert's hands, UCC § 9–102(a)(33).

National Bank's security interest. National Bank's security interest was attached and perfected in the lawnmower as inventory. If Ebert was a BIOCOB, then he took the lawnmower free of that security interest. UCC § 9–320.

If Ebert was not a BIOCOB, then he took the lawnmower subject to that perfected security interest. UCC §§ 9–315(a), 9–317(b). National Bank need not file a new financing statement against Ebert, as long as Ebert was located in the same state as Ace, Idaho. UCC § 9-507. If Ebert was located in another state, National Bank has one year from the sale or the period of effectiveness of its Idaho filing (whichever is shorter0 to file in the new state in order to remain perfected beyond that time period. UCC § 9–316(a). Because National Bank allowed its Idaho filing to lapse and it took no action in any state, as of September 3, 2018, National Bank's security interest, would be unperfected, and thus as to Ebert, under UCC § 9-317, be stripped off the lawnmower, if Ebert took delivery of the lawnmower without knowledge of National Bank's security interest.

Financial Company's security interest. Financial Company has an attached purchase money security interest in the lawnmower. Because Ebert purchased the lawnmower for business purposes, the lawnmower was not consumer goods at the time of the purchase. Thus Financial Company's security interest is not automatically perfected, UCC § 9–309, and without a filing or compliance with an applicable certificate of title law, Financial Company's security interest is unperfected. The subsequent use of the goods as consumer goods does not change that analysis.

Execution lien. Assuming under state law that a lien arises upon execution of a judgment, Rever's has an execution lien on the mower as of Feb. 2, 2018.

National Bank's security interest v. Financial Company's security interest. If Ebert was a BIOCOB, there is no priority contest. National Bank's security interest would be stripped off of the lawnmower. UCC § 9–320. Financial Company has the only security interest.

If Ebert was not a BIOCOB, then National Bank's perfected security interest initially had priority over Financial Company's unperfected security interest. UCC § 9–322(a). But, because of the lapse of the financing statement, and the retroactive "unperfection" of National Bank's security interest, Ebert would take free of the security interest under UCC § 9–317, and presumably, Financial Company's security interest would be co-extensive with Ebert's interest. Thus, Financial Company would have the only security interest.

National Bank's security interest v. execution lien. If Ebert was a BIOCOB, then there is no priority contest, as National Bank's security interest would be eliminated. UCC § 9–320.

If Ebert was not a BIOCOB, National Bank's security interest remained attached and perfected as of the time of the levy, Feb. 2, 2018, no matter what state Ebert was located in. National Bank's lapsed financing statement does not render National Bank's security interest retroactively unperfected as against the execution lien, because the lienholder is not a "purchaser." Thus, National Bank's security interest has priority over the execution lien. UCC § 9–317.

Financial Company's security interest v. execution lien. The execution lien has priority over Financial Company's unperfected security interest. UCC § 9–317.

Order of priority if Ebert was a BIOCOB. First execution lien, second Financial Company's security interest.

Order of priority if Ebert was not a BIOCOB. First, National Bank's security interest has priority over the execution lien. The execution lien has priority over Financial Company's security interest. Financial Company and Ebert have the lawnmower free of National Bank's security interest. This is a circular priority problem created by the deemed retroactive unperfection as to some but not all parties.

G. *Contract Ebert signed with Financial Company.*

Collateral classification: Chattel paper, UCC § 9–102(a)(11).

This contract is an asset of Financial Company, and no other entity other than Financial Company has an interest.

H. *Cash registers purchased from Grassley in Ace's possession at Spokane store.*

Collateral classification: Equipment in Ace's hands, UCC § 9–102(a)(33), inventory in Grassley's hands prior to sale to Ace, UCC § 9–102(a)(44). Although it is possible that the cash registers could be fixtures, because there is no real estate related claimant, such as a mortgagee, determining whether the cash registers are fixtures is not relevant to the analysis.

Continental Bank's security interest. Continental Bank had an attached and perfected security interest in Grassley's inventory, which included the cash registers, prior to their sale to Ace. Grassley is located at his residence in Idaho, UCC § 9–307, and the filing in that state of a properly filled out financing statement is sufficient to perfect the security interest. Continental Bank timely filed a continuation statement in Idaho against Grassley, thus maintaining continuous effectiveness of that Idaho filing.

If Ace is a BIOCOB, it takes the cash registers free of Continental Bank's security interest. UCC § 9–320.

If Ace is not a BIOCOB, it takes the cash registers subject to Continental Bank's perfected security interest. UCC §§ 9–315, 9–317(b). Continental Bank has one year from January 2, 2018 to file a financing statement in Washington, Ace's location, naming Ace as the debtor in order to continue perfection beyond that time period. UCC § 9–316(a).

Grassley's/Jasper's security interest. Grassley had an unperfected purchase money security interest in the cash registers which he sold to Jasper. Thus Jasper has an unperfected security interest in the cash registers.

National Bank's security interest. National Bank's security interest attached to the cash registers as after-acquired equipment pursuant to the after-acquired property clause in the security agreement to secure the entire obligation owed to National Bank (pursuant to future advances clauses). Given the lapse in National Bank's financing statement effectiveness, National Bank's security interest is unperfected, and deemed retroactively unperfected as of the time Ace purchased the cash registers as against all "purchasers for value," including secured parties. UCC § 9–515.

Execution lien. Assuming under state law, that a lien arises upon levy of a writ of execution, Zenia Justin obtained a levy lien on the cash registers on Nov. 5, 2018.

Priority if Ace is a BIOCOB. Continental Bank's security interest is stripped off. UCC § 9–320. First priority is Justin's execution lien, UCC § 9-317, as both Jasper's and National Bank's security interests were unperfected at the time of the levy. Second priority would be to Jasper and National Bank, as co-equal priority, under the first to attach rule of § 9–322, as the security interests would have attached when the debtor obtained rights in the collateral, given the purchase money security interest was granted to Grassley at the same time as the debtor acquired rights in the collateral. Jasper succeeds to whatever rights Grassley had under the contract.

Priority if Ace is not a BIOCOB. As of December 1, 2018, Continental Bank's security interest is still perfected and thus it would have priority over Justin's execution lien and both Jasper's and National Bank's unperfected security interests. UCC §§ 9–317, 9–322. Justin's execution lien would still have priority over both Jasper's and National Bank's unperfected security interests for the same reasons as given above.

I. *Cash registers purchased from Grassley in Ace's possession at Post Falls store.*

Collateral classification: Equipment in Ace's hands, UCC § 9–102(a)(33), inventory in Grassley's hands prior to sale to Ace, UCC § 9–102(a)(44). Although it is possible that the cash registers could be fixtures, because there is no real estate related claimant, such as a mortgagee, determining whether the cash registers are fixtures is not relevant to the analysis.

The analysis would be the same as in part H of the problem, except that there is no execution lien arising on the equipment in the Post Falls store.

J. *Cash registers purchased from Grassley in Silly Toy's possession.*

Collateral classification: Equipment in Ace's hands prior to transfer to Breaker Industrial, UCC § 9–102(a)(33), inventory in Grassley's hands prior to sale to Ace, UCC § 9–102(a)(44). Although it is possible that the cash registers could be fixtures, because there is no real estate related claimant, such as a mortgagee, determining whether the cash registers are fixtures is not relevant to the analysis.

Continental Bank's security interest. Continental Bank had an attached and perfected security interest in Grassley's inventory, which included the cash registers, prior to their sale to Ace. Grassley is located at his residence in Idaho, UCC § 9–307, and the filing in that state of a properly filled out financing statement is sufficient to perfect the security interest. Continental Bank timely filed a continuation statement in Idaho against Grassley, thus maintaining continuous effectiveness of that Idaho filing.

If Ace is a BIOCOB, it takes the cash registers free of Continental Bank's security interest. UCC § 9–320. Breakers would then also take the cash registers free of Continental Bank's interest as a matter of derivative rights, and so would Silly Toys.

If Ace is not a BIOCOB, it takes the cash registers subject to Continental Bank's perfected security interest. UCC §§ 9–315, 9–317(b). The BIOCOB rule of UCC § 9–320 does not protect Breakers as the Continental Bank's security interest was not created by Ace and Breakers does not qualify as BIOCOB. Continental Bank has one year from January 2, 2018 to file a financing statement in California, naming Silly Toys as the debtor in order to continue perfection beyond that time period. UCC § 9–316(a). As of December 1, 2018, Continental Bank's security interest would be perfected.

Grassley's/Jasper's security interest. Grassley had an unperfected purchase money security interest in the cash registers which he sold to Jasper. Thus Jasper has an unperfected security interest in the cash registers. Under UCC § 9–317(b), if Breakers did not have knowledge of the security interest on March 1, 2018, Breakers would take free of this security interest, and so would Silly Toys under the rule of derivative rights. If Breakers knew of the security interest, but Silly Toys did not know of the security interest as of March 15, 2018, Silly Toys would take free of this security interest, even if Breakers had not taken free.

National Bank's security interest. National Bank's security interest attached to the cash registers as after-acquired equipment pursuant to the after-acquired property clause in the security agreement to secure the entire obligation owed to

National Bank (pursuant to future advances clauses). Given the lapse in National Bank's financing statement effectiveness, National Bank's security interest is unperfected, and deemed retroactively unperfected as of the time Ace purchased the cash registers as against all "purchasers for value," including secured parties. UCC § 9–515. Under UCC § 9–317(b), if Breakers did not know of National Bank's security interest on March 1, 2018, it would take free of this unperfected security interest and so would Silly Toys, under a derivative rights concept. If Breakers knew of the security interest, but Silly Toys did not know of the security interest as of March 15, 2018, Silly Toys would take free of this security interest, even if Breakers had not taken free.

Likely order of priority if Ace is a BIOCOB. Silly Toys holds the cash registers free of all security interests as long as it did not know of either Grassley/Jasper's or National Bank's security interests at the time it took delivery of the cash registers.

Likely order of priority if Ace is not a BIOCOB. Silly Toys holds the cash registers subject to Continental Bank's perfected security interest (which could lapse as of January 1, 2019, if Continental Bank does not file against Silly Toys in California before then, and retroactively allow Silly Toys to take free as long as it did not know of Continental Bank's security interest as of the date Silly Toys took delivery of the cash registers). Silly Toys holds the cash registers free of Grassley/Jasper's and National Bank's security interests if it did not know of them at the time it took delivery of the cash registers.

K. *Cash register purchased from Grassley in Gadget's possession.*

The analysis is the same as part H of the problem, with the following differences. There is no execution lien, and Gadget's has a possessory lien which has priority over all security interests which may exist. UCC § 9–333.

Priority if Ace is a BIOCOB. Continental Bank's security interest is stripped off. UCC § 9–320. First priority is Gadget's lien, UCC § 9–333. Second priority would be to Jasper and National Bank, as co-equal priority, under the first to attach rule of § 9–322, as the security interests would have attached when the debtor obtained rights in the collateral, given the purchase money security interest was granted to Grassley at the same time as the debtor acquired rights in the collateral. Jasper succeeds to whatever rights Grassley had under the contract.

Priority if Ace is not a BIOCOB. First priority is Gadget's lien, UCC § 9–333. As of December 1, 2018, second priority is Continental Bank's perfected security interest. Third priority is co-equal priority for Jasper's and National Bank's unperfected security interests. UCC § 9–322.

L. *Contract between Grassley and Ace.*

Collateral classification: Chattel paper, UCC § 9–102(a)(11).

Continental Bank's security interest. The chattel paper is proceeds of inventory. Continental Bank's security interest attaches and is perfected under UCC § 9–315(a), (c) and (d)(1).

Jasper's interest. Jasper's purchase of the chattel paper is likely not excluded from Article 9 under UCC § 9–109(d) and thus is a deemed "security interest" within the scope of Article 9. Jasper's security interest is perfected by its possession of the contract. UCC § 9–313.

Priority. Under UCC § 9–330(a), Jasper's security interest likely qualifies for priority over Continental Bank's security interest. If not, then the first to file or perfect rule of § 9–322 would apply and Continental Bank's security interest would have priority.

M. *Contract between Ace and Welding Co.*

Collateral classification: Account, UCC § 9–102(a)(2).

National Bank's security interest. The account is identifiable proceeds of National Bank's security interest in inventory. UCC § 9–315(a). At the time the account was created (May 1, 2018), National Bank's security interest in the account was perfected for 20 days, UCC § 9–315(c), and perfection continued in the account beyond the 20 days pursuant to UCC § 9–315(d)(1). However, once the effectiveness of the financing statement lapsed, that lapse is effective to unperfect National Bank's security interest in the account as to purchasers for value. UCC §§ 9–515(c), 9–315(e).

State Bank's security interest. The account is identifiable proceeds of State Bank's security interest in the tools. UCC § 9–315(a). State Bank's security interest in the account is unperfected because its security interest in the tools was unperfected, and State Bank has taken no sufficient perfection step as to the account. UCC § 9–315(c), (d).

Factoring Co.'s interest. Factoring's purchase of the account is likely a "security interest" in the account unless the transaction is excluded under UCC § 9–109(d). If the sale to Factoring is within the scope of Article 9, UCC § 9–109(a), and thus Factoring has a deemed security interest in the account, Factoring has not perfected its interest. If the transaction is excluded from the scope of Article 9, then Factoring's interest is an ownership interest that is not deemed a security interest and perfection is not relevant.

Order of priority. If the sale to Factoring is within scope of Article 9, first priority would be co-equal priority for State Bank and National Bank's security interests based upon order of attachment, and then second level priority for Factoring, as its security interest attached last. UCC § 9–322. If the sale to Factoring is not within the scope of Article 9, first is co-equal priority for State Bank and National Bank's security interests, and then Factoring's ownership interest. UCC § 9–201.

N. *Inventory and equipment in Ace's store in Post Falls (excluding items in I above).*

The only entity with an interest in this property other than Ace is National Bank with an unperfected but attached security interest.

Appendix C

Table of Statutes

Other State Statutes